ASCENT®

CENTER FOR TECHNICAL KNOWLEDGE

3DEXPERIENCE CATIA 2022x
Generative Drafting (ANSI-ASME)

Learning Guide

1st Edition

ASCENT - Center for Technical Knowledge®
3DEXPERIENCE CATIA 2022x
Generative Drafting (ANSI-ASME)
1st Edition

Prepared and produced by:

ASCENT Center for Technical Knowledge
630 Peter Jefferson Parkway, Suite 175
Charlottesville, VA 22911

866-527-2368
www.ASCENTed.com

Lead Contributor: Mark Potrzebowski

ASCENT - Center for Technical Knowledge (a division of Rand Worldwide Inc.) is a leading developer of professional learning materials and knowledge products for engineering software applications. ASCENT specializes in designing targeted content that facilitates application-based learning with hands-on software experience. For over 25 years, ASCENT has helped users become more productive through tailored custom learning solutions.

We welcome any comments you may have regarding this guide, or any of our products. To contact us please email: feedback@ASCENTed.com.

AS-3DE22-GDR1-SG // RS-3DE22-GDR1-SG

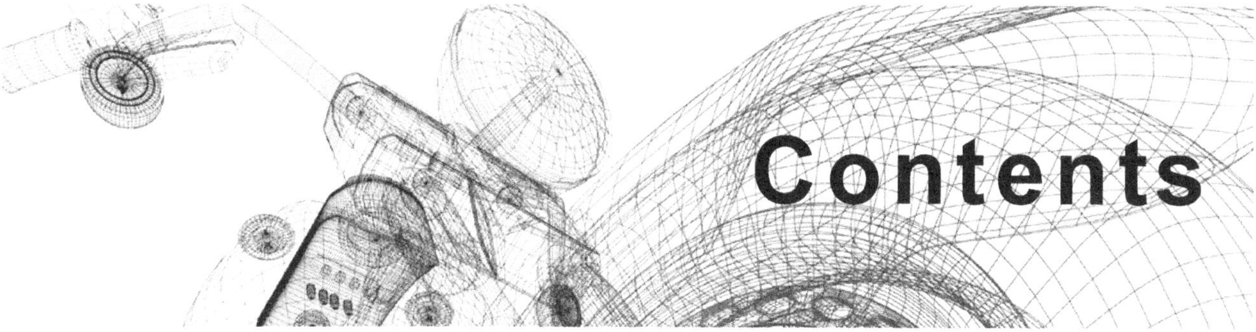

Contents

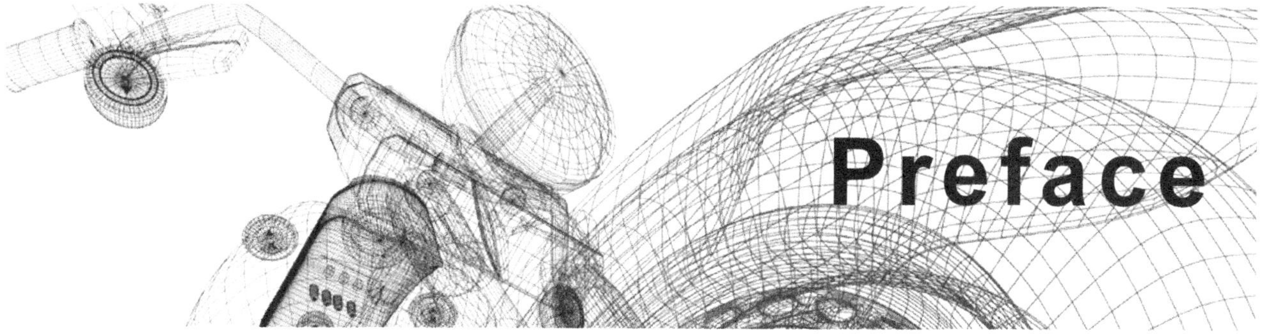

Preface

The *3DEXPERIENCE CATIA 2022x: Generative Drafting (ANSI-ASME)* learning guide enables you to use the generative capabilities of CATIA to create an ANSI-ASME drawing from a 3D solid part. This guide is appropriate for new 3DEXPERIENCE users.

Topics Covered

- Start a generative drawing
- Define the main views
- Define section views and cuts
- Define secondary views: detail, clipping, broken, breakout, auxiliary, isometric and unfolded views
- Edit a view and sheet properties
- Add sheets to a drawing
- Reposition views
- Modify section, detail, and auxiliary profiles
- Modify section, detail, and auxiliary graphical definitions
- Modify section hatching representations
- Create generative dimensions and tolerances
- Generate assembly drawings
- Create annotations and drawing tables
- Create balloons
- Check links to a solid 3D part and update a drawing
- Add a title block
- Print the drawing
- Set drafting options

Prerequisites

- Access to the 3DEXPERIENCE CATIA 2022x version of the software, to ensure compatibility with this guide. Future software updates that are released by Dassault Systèmes may include changes that are not reflected in this guide. The practices and files included with this guide might not be compatible with prior versions (e.g., 3DEXPERIENCE CATIA 2021x).
- Completion of the *3DEXPERIENCE CATIA 2022x: Introduction to Modeling* or *3DEXPERIENCE CATIA 2022x: Introduction for Non-Designers* course is recommended.

Note on Software Setup

This guide assumes a standard installation of the software using the default preferences during installation. Lectures and practices use the standard software templates and default options for the Content Libraries.

Lead Contributor: Mark Potrzebowski

Mark Potrzebowski has been a trainer and curriculum developer in the PLM industry for over 14 years, with experience on multiple CAD systems, including Pro/ENGINEER, Creo Parametric, Inventor, and CATIA. Trained in Instructional Design, Mark uses his skills to develop instructor-led and web-based training products. Before joining ASCENT, Mark worked as a Technical Trainer with a focus on CATIA, Creo, and PLM systems. Mark holds a Bachelors degree in Computer Graphics Technology from Purdue University, West Lafayette, Indiana.

Mark has been the Lead Contributor for *3DEXPERIENCE CATIA: Generative Drafting* since 2023.

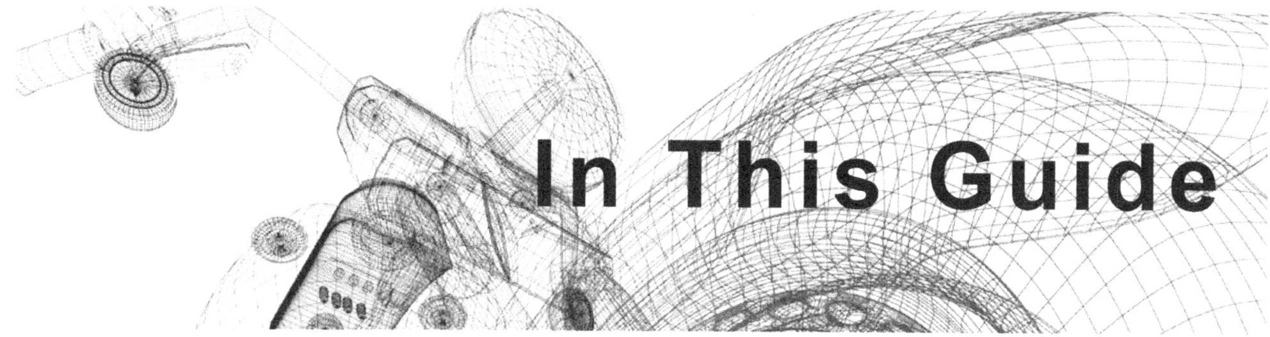

In This Guide

The following highlights the key features of this guide.

Feature	Description
Practice Files	The Practice Files page includes a link to the practice files and instructions on how to download and install them. The practice files are required to complete the practices in this guide.
Chapters	A chapter consists of the following: Learning Objectives, Instructional Content, and Practices. • **Learning Objectives** define the skills you can acquire by learning the content provided in the chapter. • **Instructional Content**, which begins right after Learning Objectives, refers to the descriptive and procedural information related to various topics. Each main topic introduces a product feature, discusses various aspects of that feature, and provides step-by-step procedures on how to use that feature. Where relevant, examples, figures, helpful hints, and notes are provided. • **Practice** for a topic follows the instructional content. Practices enable you to use the software to perform a hands-on review of a topic. It is required that you download the practice files (using the link found on the Practice Files page) prior to starting the first practice.
Appendices	Appendices provide additional information to the main course content. It could be in the form of instructional content, practices, tables, projects, or skills assessment.

Practice Files

To download the practice files for this guide, use the following steps:

1. Type the URL ***exactly as shown below*** into the address bar of your Internet browser to access the Course File Download page.

   Note: If you are using the ebook, you do not have to type the URL. Instead, you can access the page simply by clicking the URL below.

   https://www.ascented.com/getfile/id/ficusPF

2. On the Course File Download page, click the **DOWNLOAD NOW** button, as shown below, to download the .ZIP file that contains the practice files.

3. Once the download is complete, unzip the file and extract its contents.

   The recommended practice files folder location is:
   C:\3D EXPERIENCE CATIA Generative Drafting Practice Files

   Note: It is recommended that you do not change the location of the practice files folder. Doing so may cause errors when completing the practices.

Stay Informed!

To receive information about upcoming events, promotional offers, and complimentary webcasts, visit:

www.ASCENTed.com/updates

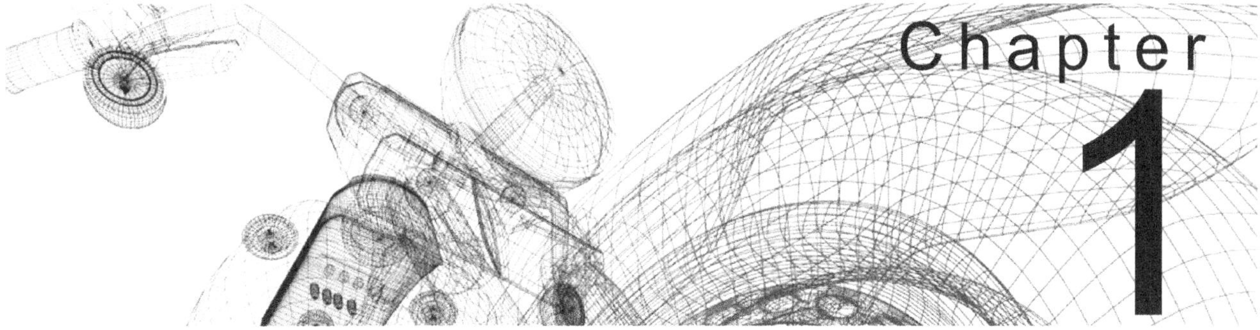

Generative Drafting App

The Generative Drafting app is used to create 2D drawings from 3D models that are created in the Part Design and Assembly Design apps. This chapter introduces the Generative Drafting interface and outlines the process that can be used to create simple and complex drawings.

Learning Objectives in This Chapter

- Understand the Generative Drafting process.
- Learn how to create a drawing.
- Recognize elements of the Generative Drafting user interface.
- Use the various view types.
- Create Section Views/Cuts.
- Create a manual view.
- Use the View Creation wizard.
- Add additional sheets to a drawing.
- Understand file associations.

1.1 Generative Drafting Process

To complete a production drawing, several steps must be performed as shown in Figure 1–1.

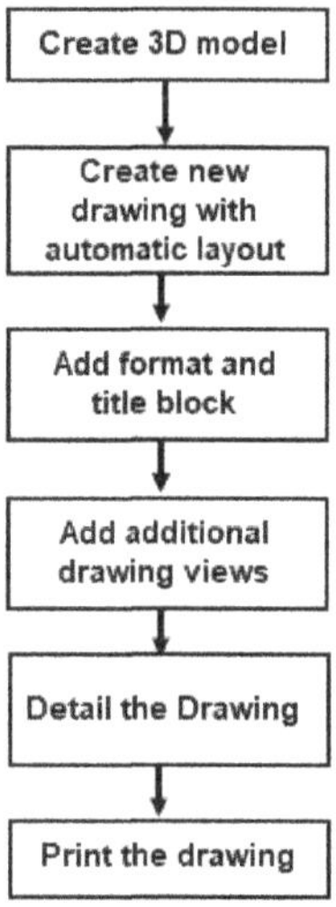

Figure 1–1

The creation of the 3D model is covered in the *Introduction to Modeling*, *Advanced Part Design*, and *Advanced Assembly Design & Management* courses. This course assumes that you are either familiar with the creation of 3D geometry or are not responsible for its creation.

In the Generative Drafting app, the geometry of each view is linked to the 3D model. This permits changes to the 3D model to drive the drawing and ensures that you are always working with the latest version of the 3D geometry.

With the 3D geometry in session, you are ready to move to the next step of creating a new drawing.

1.2 Create a Drawing

You can access the Generative Drafting app by searching for and opening an existing drawing or creating a new drawing.

General Steps

Use the following steps to create a new drawing:

1. Open the 3D model.
2. Modify parameters of the drawing.

Step 1 - Open the 3D model.

You should always create the 3D model before beginning any 2D work when working in the Generative Drafting environment. The part or assembly model should be open in CATIA, as shown in Figure 1–2, in preparation for drawing creation.

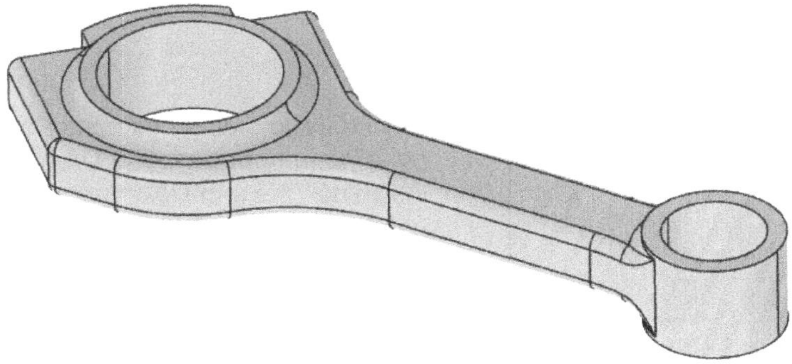

Figure 1–2

Step 2 - Modify parameters of the drawing.

Enter the Drafting app by selecting **the Outer Ring of the compass>My Apps>Drafting** with the model active. The Drawing dialog box opens as shown in Figure 1–3. A drawing can also be created by selecting (Add)>**Drawing**.

A new drawing can also be created by right-clicking on the top node of the specification tree and selecting ***Insert>Drawing****.*

However, this method does not permit you to select an automatic layout in the Drawing Information tab.

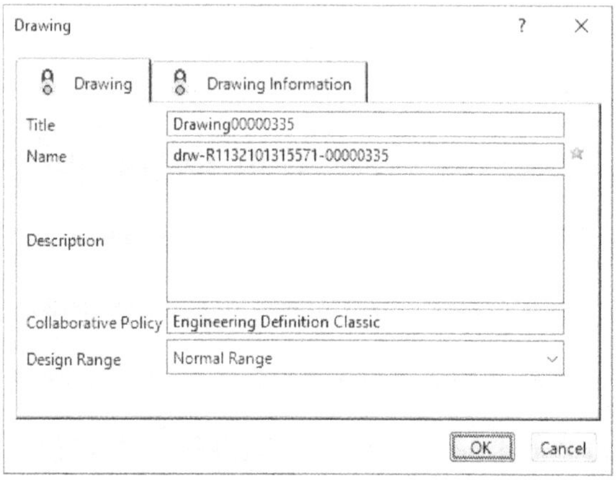

Figure 1–3

The Drawing dialog box consists of two tabs: *Drawing* and *Drawing Information*. The *Drawing* tab has a variety of text fields including *Title* and *Description* that can be customized as needed. The *Drawing Information* tab controls settings specific to how the drawing will look when created. An example of *Drawing Information* is shown in Figure 1–4.

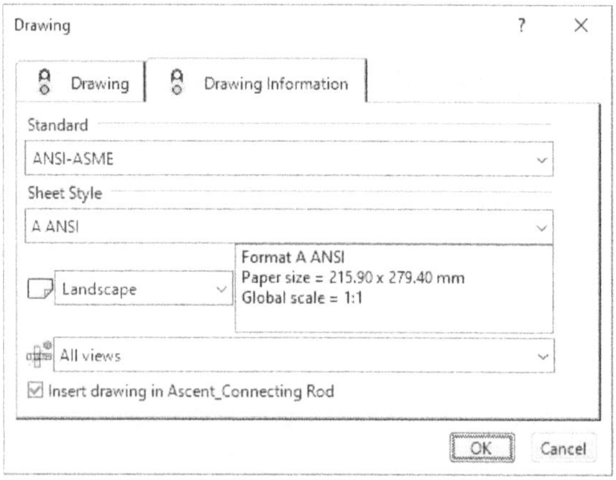

Figure 1–4

The *Drawing Information* options will need to be filled out, and are described as follows:

Option	Description
Standard	Select the drawing standard to use: ANSI-ASME, ISO, or JIS.
Sheet Style	Based on the Standard selected, the Sheet Style will allow you to select the size of the paper used in the drawing.
Orientation	Landscape, Portrait
Automatic Layout	Standard views automatically created in the drawing.
 (Empty Sheet)	No views are added to the drawing. The new drawing consists of an empty sheet.
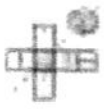 (All Views)	Seven views are automatically added to the drawing: Front, Back, Top, Bottom, Right, Left, and Isometric.
 (Front, Bottom, and Right)	Three views are automatically added to the drawing: Front, Bottom, and Right.
 (Front, Top, and Left)	Three views are automatically added to the drawing: Front, Top, and Left.
Insert drawing in...	Places a reference to the drawing at the bottom of the specification tree of the associated model.

Once you are ready to create the drawing, select on the surface of the model that you want to display as the front view, then click **OK** in the Drawing dialog box. The drawing displays as shown in Figure 1–5. The active view displays with a red border.

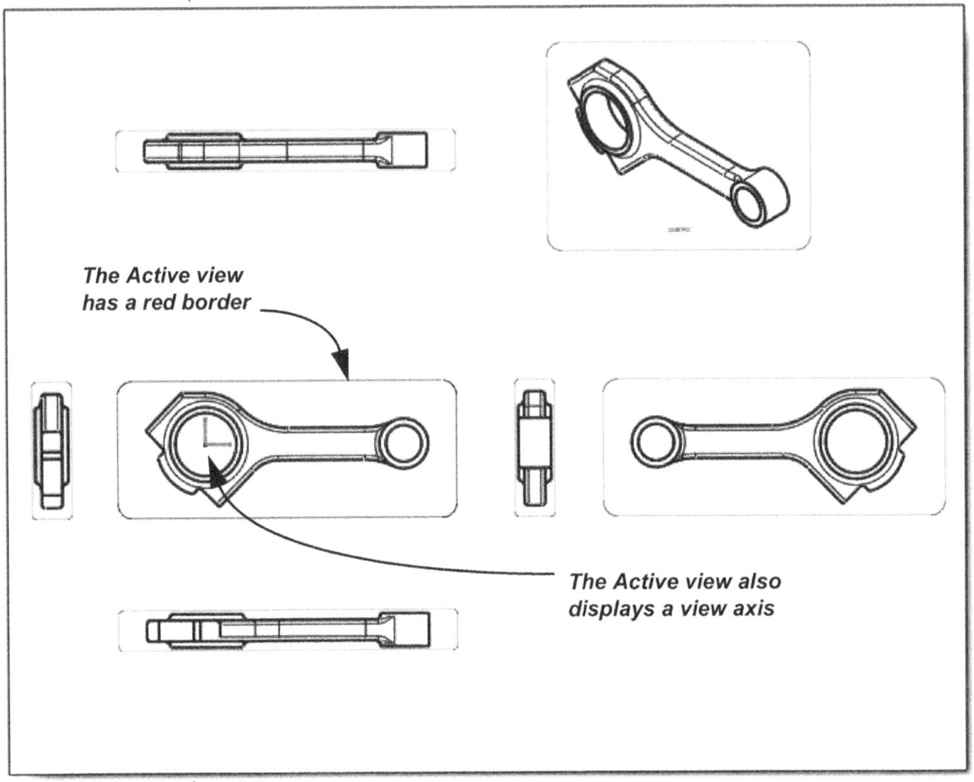

Figure 1–5

1.3 User Interface

The user interface of the Generative Drafting app displays as shown in Figure 1–6.

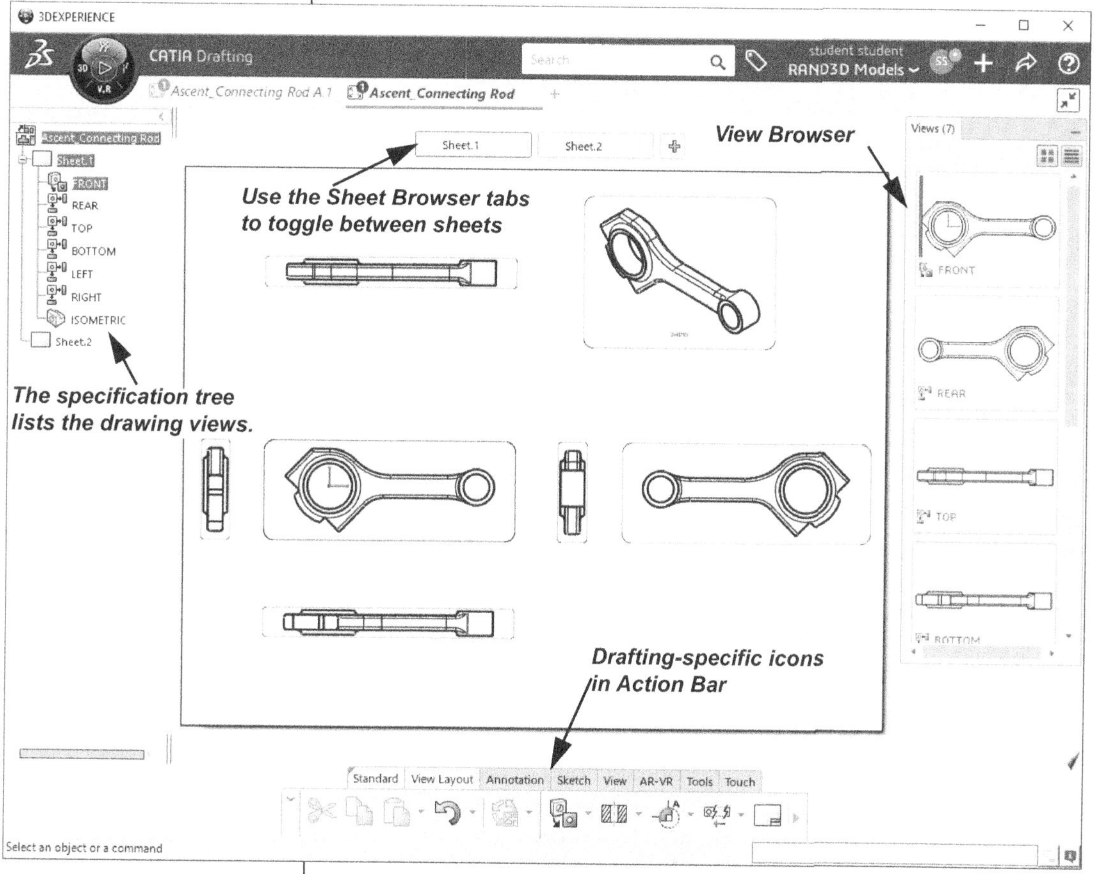

Figure 1–6

Active View

All actions are performed in the Active view. For example, the view geometry is projected from the Active view when a Projection view is created.

The Active view is highlighted in the specification tree and also indicated by the color of its view border, as shown in Figure 1–7. The Active view has a red border, while all other views have a blue border. To set the Active view, double-click on the view border or the view name in the specification tree.

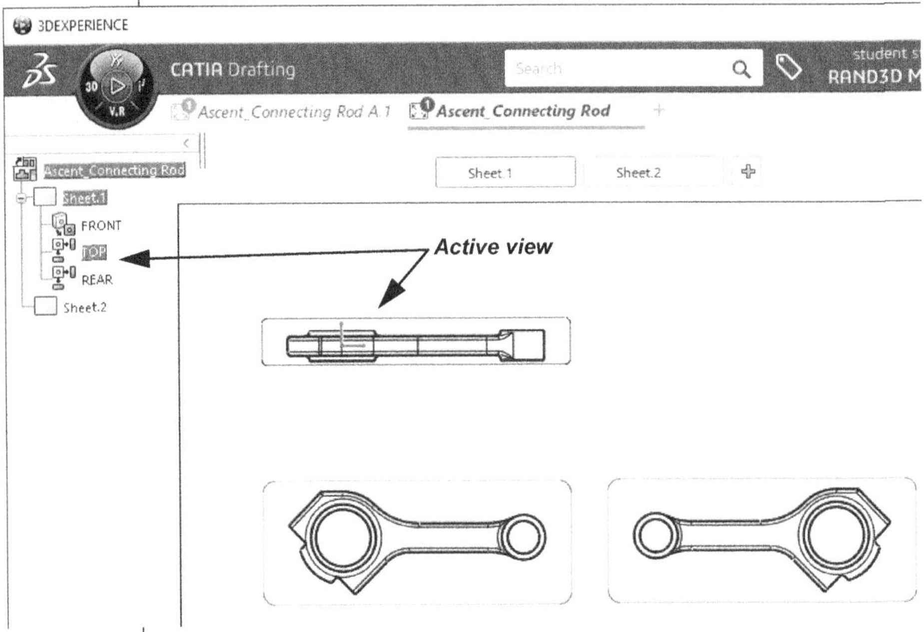

Figure 1–7

Action Bar

The Generative Drafting app has an Action Bar with a variety of different sections to help organize the Drafting specific and general use icons. While all of the sections have their purpose, two sections are unique to the drafting app: View Layout and Annotation, as shown in Figure 1–8. These sections focus on the ability to create views, dimension features, and add annotations, and will be a main focus of the this training material.

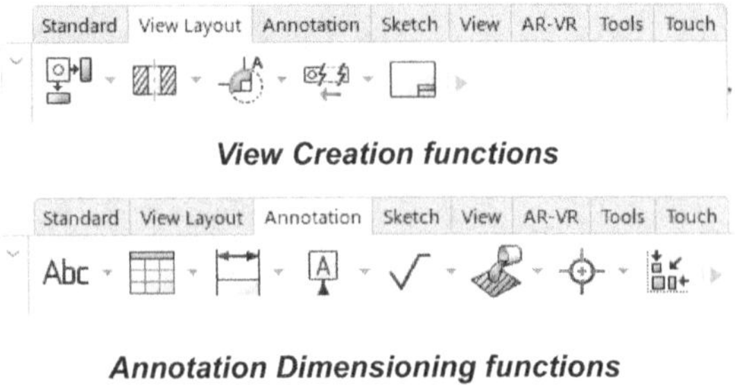

Figure 1–8

Below is a list of most of the sections found in the Action Bar in the Drafting app. The *Features Provided* category is not meant to be all inclusive, but is meant to give a basic understand of the tools that are found in that section.

Section	Features Provided
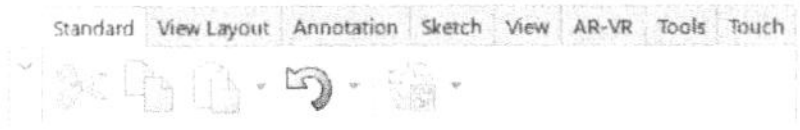	Standard tools including Cut, Copy, Past, Undo, and Update current sheet.
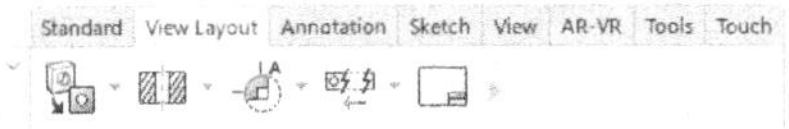	Create front, projection, isometric, section, detail, clipping, and broken view types. Open the View Wizard.
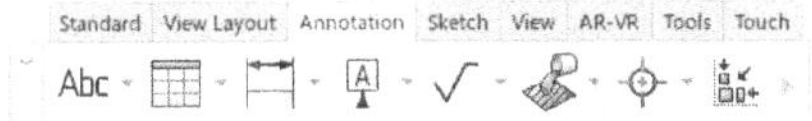	Insert text, symbols, tables, dimensions, and datum features.
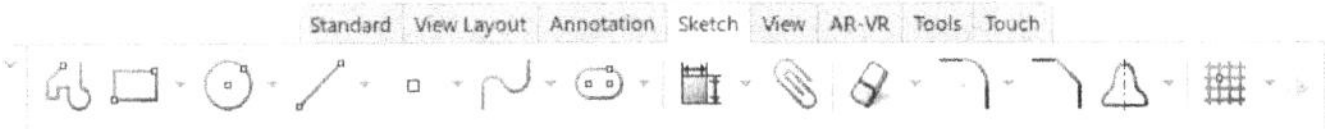	Create sketch-based objects in a drawing view. Tools include Profile, Rectangle, Circle, Line, Quick Trim, etc.
	Controls the current display of drawing elements, including View Browser, Template Browser, Sheet Browser, Grid, Constraints, Frames, and Elements' Analysis.
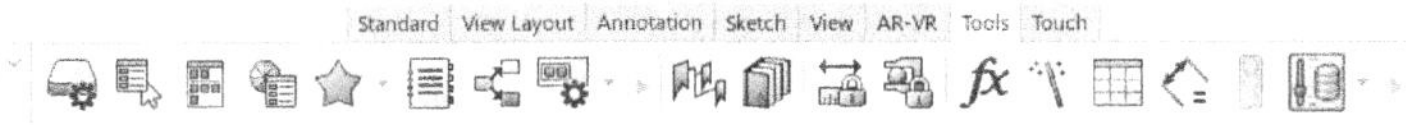	Generic tools that aid in model creation and are applicable to most apps. Commands include Action Pad, BI Essentials, Catalog Browser, Links and Relations, and Formula.

Widget Layout

The geometry of a drawing is always driven from the 3D geometry of the model. You need to switch between the drawing and model window/tabs frequently to locate views and build your drawing. The feature that controls how the windows/tabs work in CATIA are referred to as widgets.

By default, when a drawing, part, or assembly is open/created, the widget (window) displays in its own tab. CAD objects can then be toggled by selecting on the tabs at the top of the screen, as shown in Figure 1–9. Because of this, it is easy to think that widgets and tabs are the same thing. For many users, this is perfectly acceptable and no further customization is needed; however, depending on how many objects you want open in the same session, further customization maybe desired.

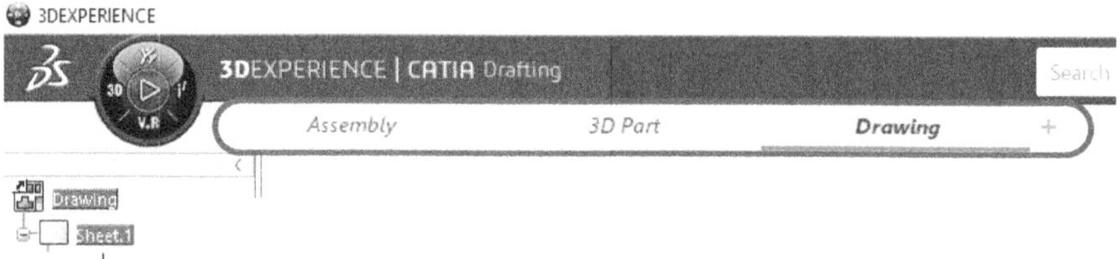

Figure 1–9

For example, multiple widgets can display in the same tab. This grants more interface customizations that allow for multiple widgets (windows) to display at the same time. Toggling from one widget to the other could become unnecessary.

To customize settings related to widgets, right-click on one of the tab names. A drop-down list will appear, the length of which is determined based on your settings and what currently displays in the tab, as shown in Figure 1–10.

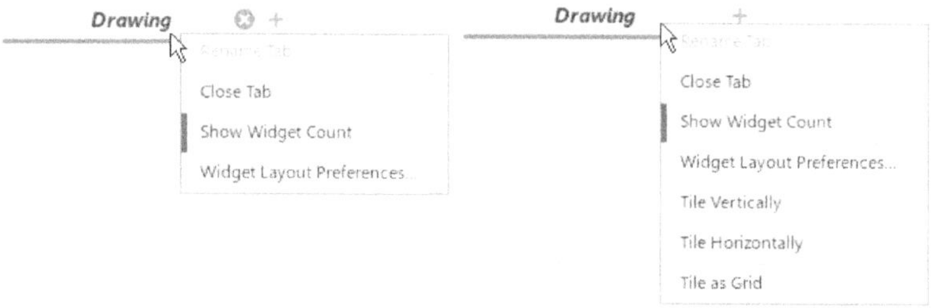

Figure 1–10

Select **Widget Layout Preferences** to open the preferences window to the *Widget Layout* settings. Figure 1–11 shows what settings can be customized and how tabs work.

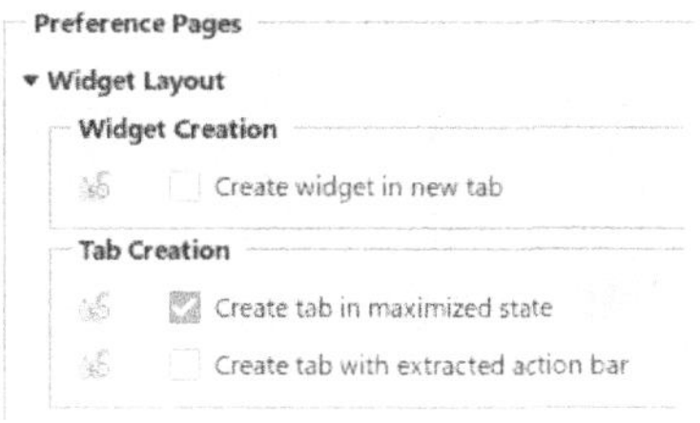

Figure 1–11

Option	Description
Create widget in new tab	When selected, one widget displays per tab. When turned off, multiple widgets can display in the same tab.
Create tab in maximized state	When new tabs are created, the widget fills the entire work area.
Create tab with extracted Action Bar	The Action Bar automatically displays at the bottom of each new tab created.

When multiple widgets are in the same tab, the tile options become available in the right-click menu, as shown previously in Figure 1–10. These right-click options include:

Option	Description
Rename Tab	When multiple widgets are in a tab, this allows for the tab to be renamed something other than the CAD object's name.
Show Widget Count	 Displays the number of widgets in the tab next to the tab name.
Widget Layout Preferences...	Opens the preferences window directly to Widget Layout settings.
Tile Vertically	Aligns all of the widgets side by side from left to right of the screen.
Tile Horizontally	Stacks all of the widgets from top to bottom of the screen.
Tile as Grid	Displays all of the widgets in the active tab.

For example, lets take a look at Tile horizontally. To do this, right-click on the tab and select **Tile Horizontally** to horizontally align your widgets. The drawing and model widgets display as shown in Figure 1–12. Maximize the drawing widget to switch back to a full view of the drawing.

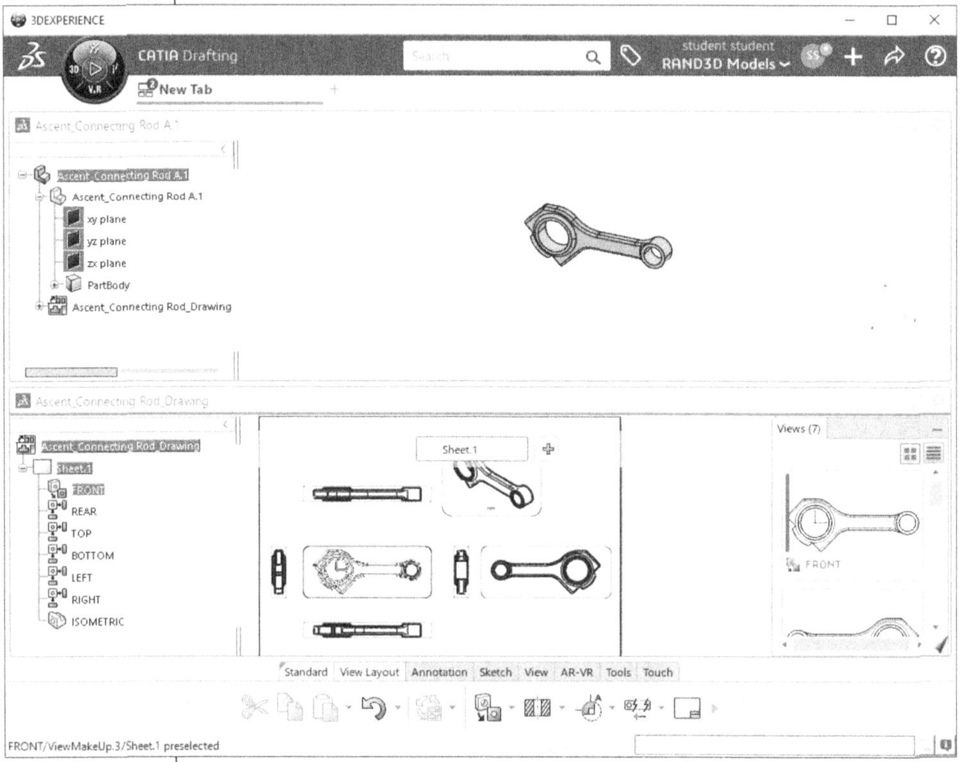

Figure 1–12

If multiple widgets are in the same tab and a widget has been maximized, the other widgets are obscured from view. You can switch between “hidden” widgets by hovering the cursor over the tab the widget is associated with. All of the widgets will display as a thumbnail version, as shown in Figure 1–13. Select the desired one. It will now be maximized, displaying the widget.

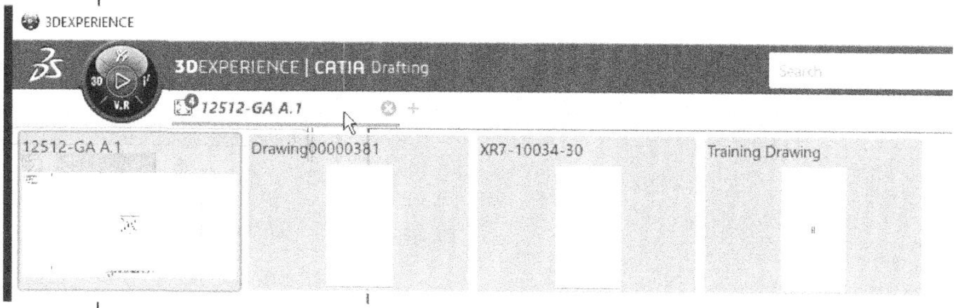

Figure 1–13

1.4 View Types

The View Layout section of the Action Bar (shown in Figure 1–14) enables you to create a variety of different types of drawing views. This is the standard look of the View Layout section, but many more commands can be found in flyouts and/or the secondary area of the section.

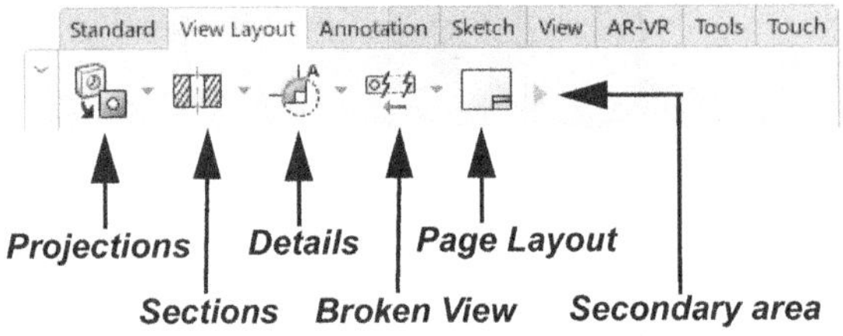

Figure 1–14

Projections

Use the Projections flyout to create a view of the model based on its projection from a parent view. The types of views that can be created using the Projections flyout are shown in Figure 1–15.

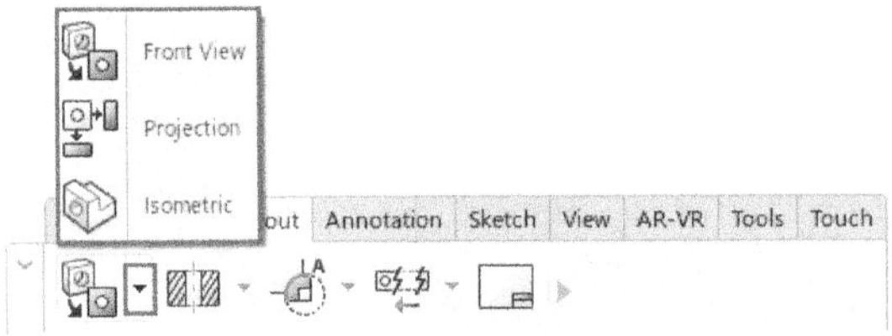

Figure 1–15

Front View

The Front view is also known as the main view, as shown in Figure 1–16. It is the parent to any related projection, auxiliary, and detail views that reference it.

Figure 1–16

Unfolded View

The Unfolded view displays the flat pattern of a sheet metal model. The drawing view automatically displays the bend axes and bend limits of the sheet metal part, as shown in Figure 1–17.

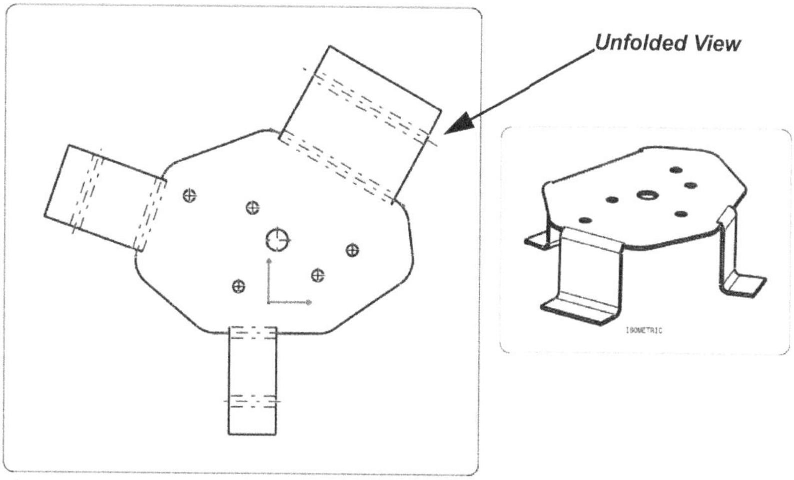

Figure 1–17

View from 3D

The View from 3D view displays a saved view from a model that was generated using the 3D Tolerancing & Annotation app. CATIA creates a view based on the selected annotation plane. All geometric dimensions and tolerances added to the annotation plane automatically display in the new view.

Projection View

The Projection view projects a view from the active view. This creates views, such as top, right, left, and bottom. It is placed by selecting a location on the screen. The system applies the correct view name based on its position to the Front view. A Projection view maintains the same scale value as its parent view, as shown in Figure 1–18.

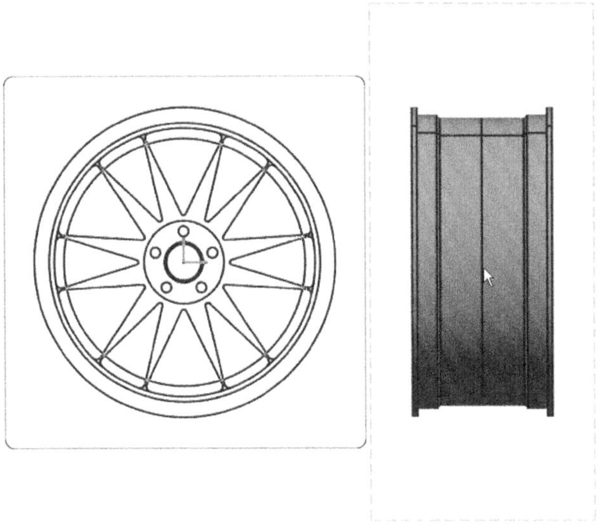

Figure 1–18

Auxiliary View

An Auxiliary view projects a view normal to a reference plane, edge, or axis of the active view, as shown in Figure 1–19. Auxiliary views can be created by referencing a reference plane, edge, or axis from the active view.

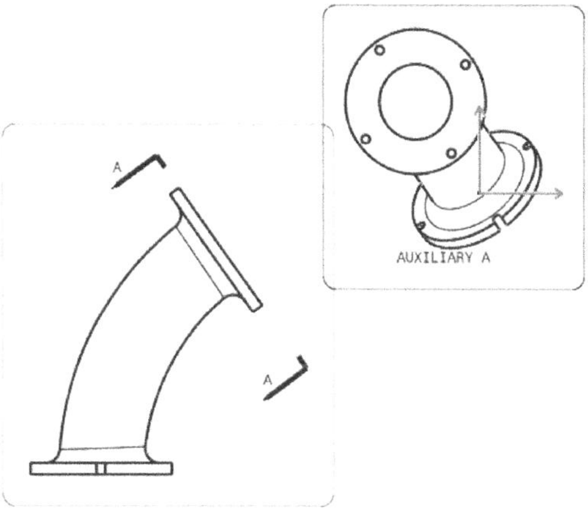

Figure 1–19

Isometric View

An Isometric view is used as a reference view, as shown in Figure 1–20, and is typically set at a smaller scale. CATIA creates the view based on the current model orientation when the reference face is selected from the 3D model.

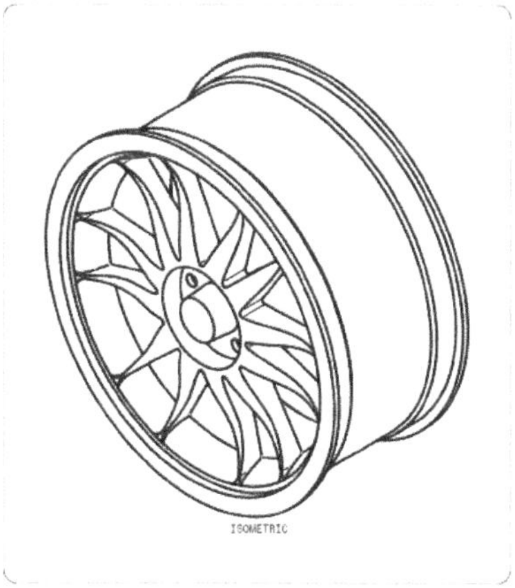

Figure 1–20

Sections

Once a view of the model is created using Projections, you can begin to create new views to display specific sections of the model. Section views must be created as separate views. An existing view cannot be modified to become a section view.

Use the icons in the Sections flyout to create section views, as shown in Figure 1–21.

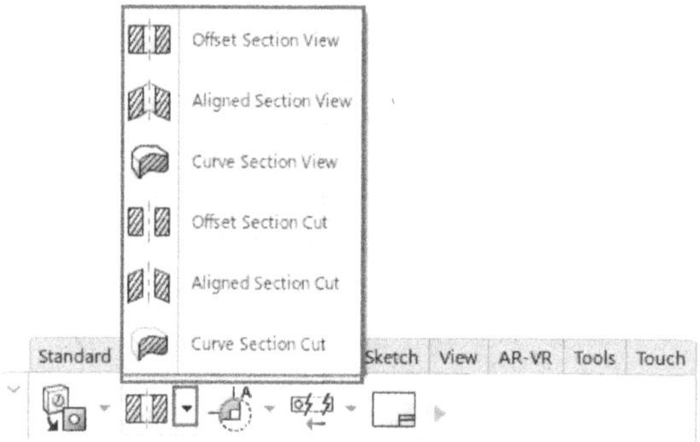

Figure 1–21

Offset Section View

The Offset section view creates a section and displays all of the edges that are behind the cutting plane. You can create this view as planar (as shown in Figure 1–22) or as a sketched cutting plane (as shown in Figure 1–23).

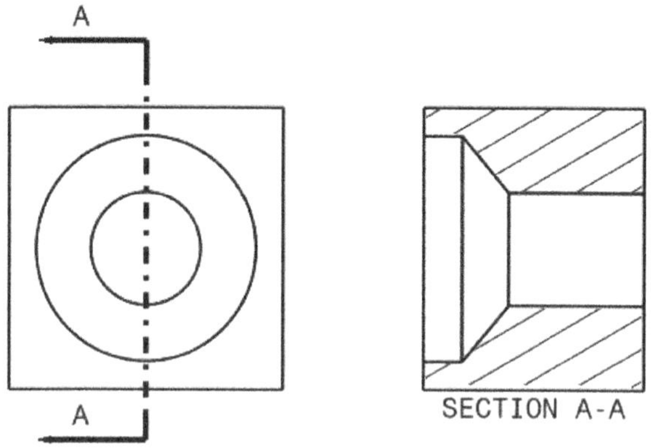

Figure 1–22

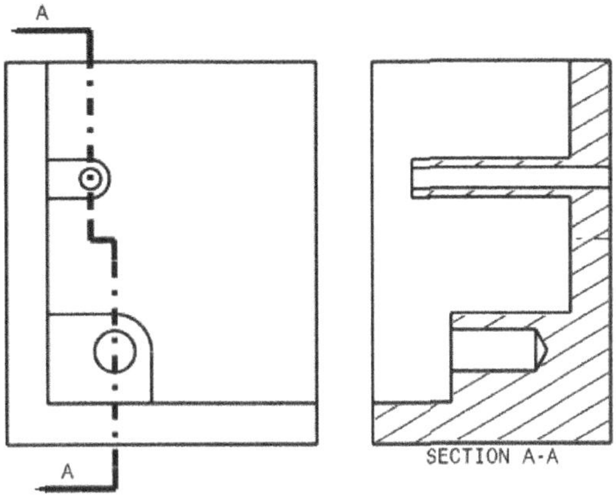

Figure 1–23

Aligned Section View

The Aligned Section view unfolds the view until it is parallel to the screen, as shown in Figure 1–24.

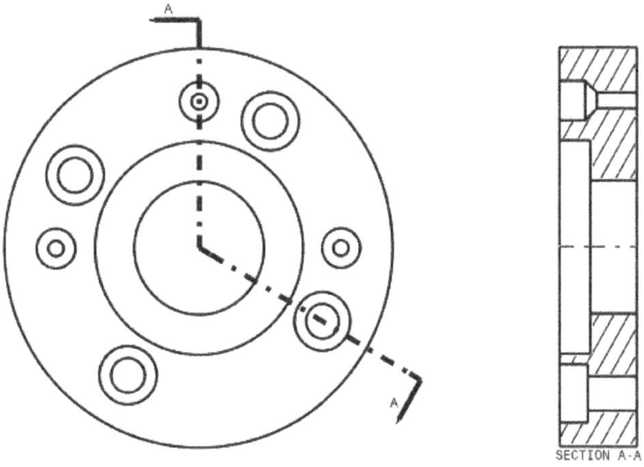

Figure 1–24

Offset Section Cut View

The Offset Section Cut view creates a section that only displays the material in the cutting plane, as shown in Figure 1–25. Edges behind the cutting plane are hidden.

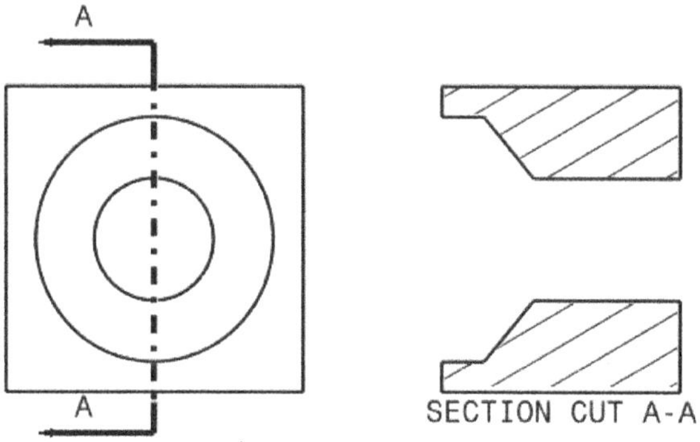

Figure 1–25

Aligned Section Cut View

The Aligned Section Cut view unfolds the view until it is parallel to the screen but only displays material that is in the cutting plane. Edges behind the cutting plane are hidden, as shown in Figure 1–26.

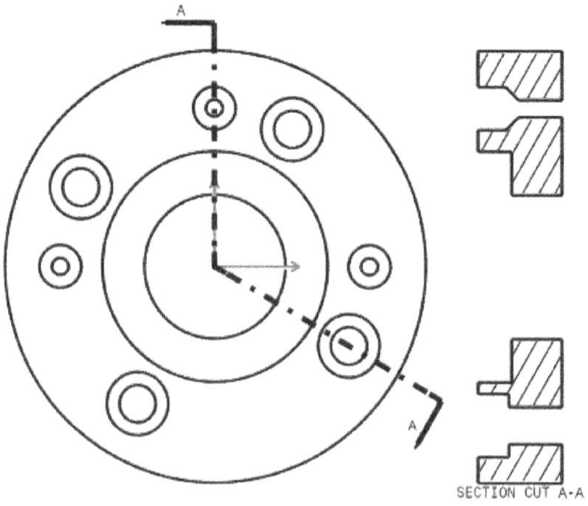

Figure 1–26

Curve Section View / Curve Section Cut

The Curve Section View and Curve Section Cut view both create a section with the use of a 3D spline. The only difference between the two is whether the edges behind the cutting plane are hidden or not. Examples of both are shown in Figure 1–27.

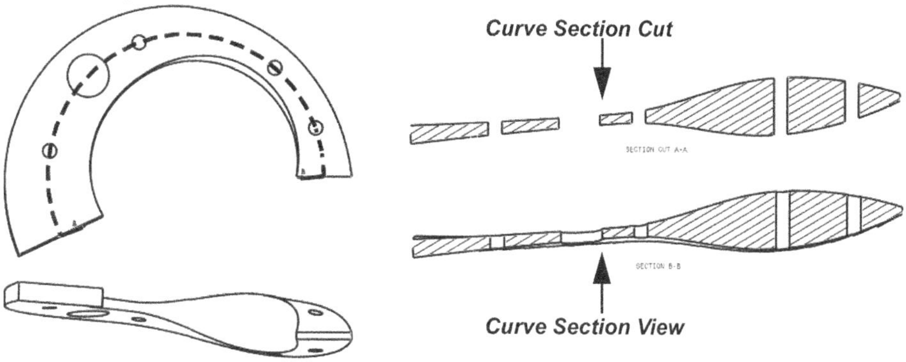

Figure 1–27

Details

The Detail view creates a scaled view that focuses on a specific area of an existing view. The Detail view is created by defining a boundary on an existing view that encloses the geometry to be represented and selecting a location in which to place the view. The system automatically assigns a label identifying the scale value and view name of the Detail view. The orientation of this view corresponds to its parent view. The types of views that can be created using the Action Bar are shown in Figure 1–28.

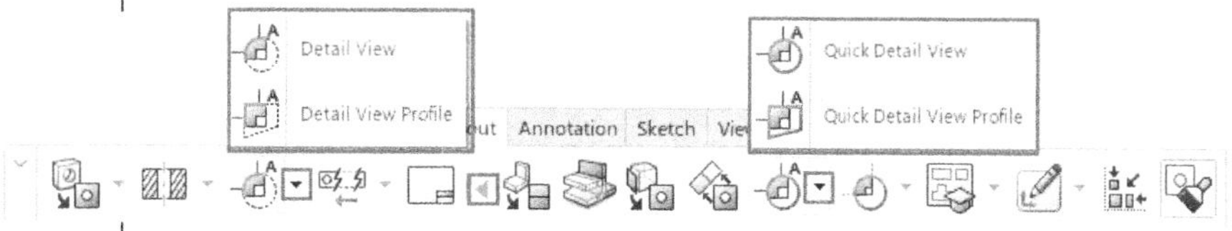

Figure 1–28

Detail View

Define the boundary of the Detail view by sketching a circle in the parent view. The view is generated by calculating a boolean cut from the 3D model geometry. An example of a Detail view is shown in Figure 1–29.

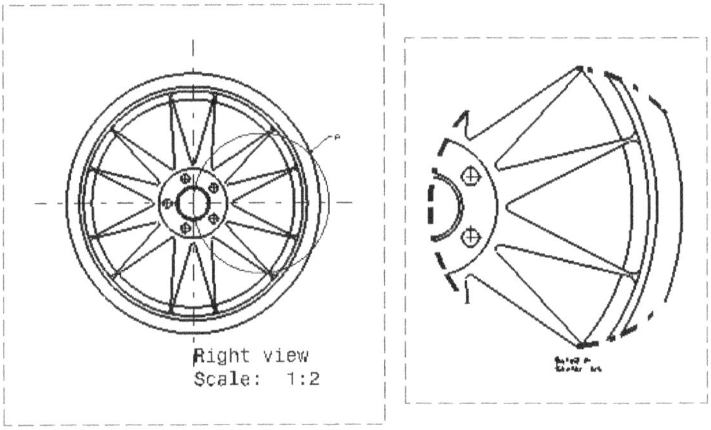

Figure 1–29

Detail View Profile

Define the boundary of the Detail view profile by sketching a closed chain of lines in the parent view. This enables the view to remove any unwanted geometry from the parent view by sketching around it. An example of a Detail view profile is shown in Figure 1–30.

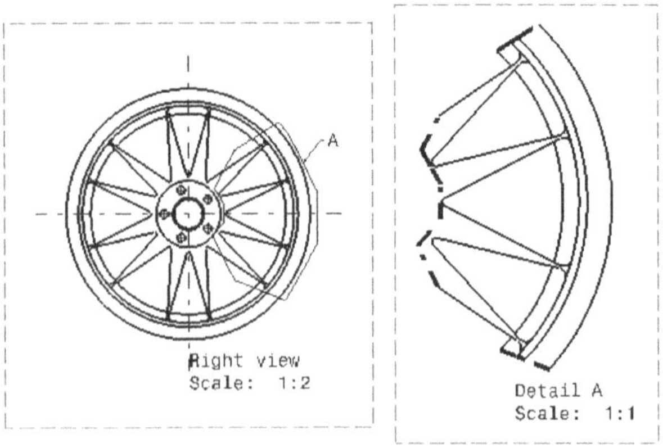

Figure 1–30

Quick Detail View /Quick Detail View Profile

These views are identical to the Detail View and Detail View Profile except that the view is generated from the 2D geometry of the parent view rather than the 3D model. This enables a view that is still associative to the 3D model to be generated quickly. The display properties of the view are different. For example, the line display of the view cannot be altered.

Clipping View

A Clipping view simplifies an existing view. It displays a focused area by removing the geometry outside the circle or profile boundary. You must sketch the boundary in the active view. The types of views that can be created using the View Layout section of the Action Bar are shown in Figure 1–31.

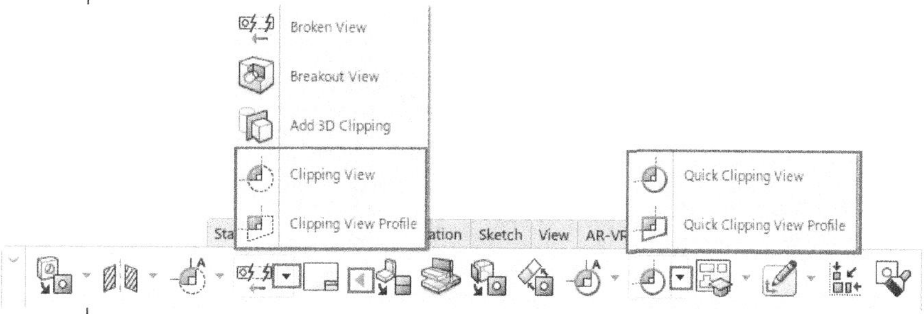

Figure 1–31

A Clipping view is different from a Detail view in that a new view is not created. The Clipping view modifies an existing view by removing geometry from the view.

Similar to a Detail view, a Clipping view defines the view boundary using a sketched circle, while the Clipping View Profile defines the view boundary using a closed chain of lines. Figure 1–32 shows a Front Projection view that has been clipped using a circular boundary.

A Clipping view can be restored to a regular view by right-clicking on the view and selecting **** object>View Definition>Unclip****, where * is the view name.*

Figure 1–32

Break Views

The Break view flyout enables you to remove view geometry from within a sketched area on an existing view. The types of view breaks that can be created using the Break view flyout display in Figure 1–33.

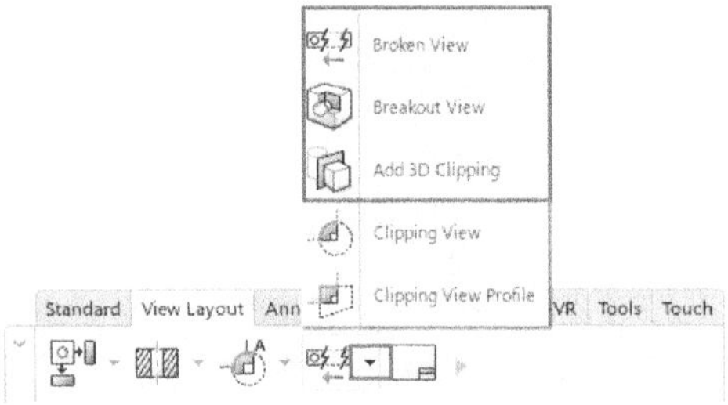

Figure 1–33

Broken View

A Broken view removes the view geometry between two break lines and only displays the important features of a model, as shown in Figure 1–34.

*A Broken view can be restored to a regular view by right-clicking on the view and selecting *** view object>View Definition>Unbreak**, where * is the view name.*

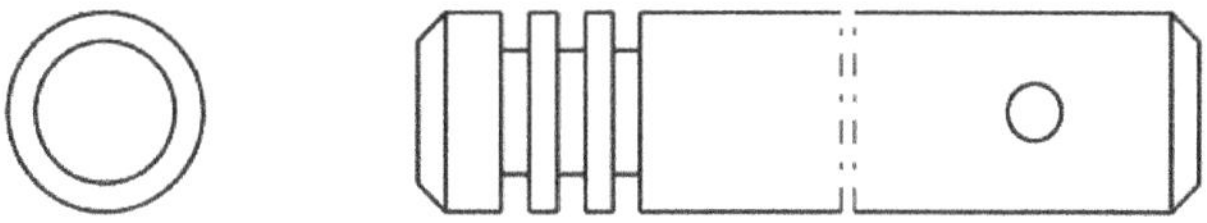

Figure 1–34

Breakout

The Breakout view displays a section in a sketched area. The system automatically adds the rough edges to your sketched area, as shown in Figure 1–35.

*A Breakout view can be restored to a regular view by right-clicking on the view and selecting *** view object>View Definition>Remove Breakout**, where * is the view name.*

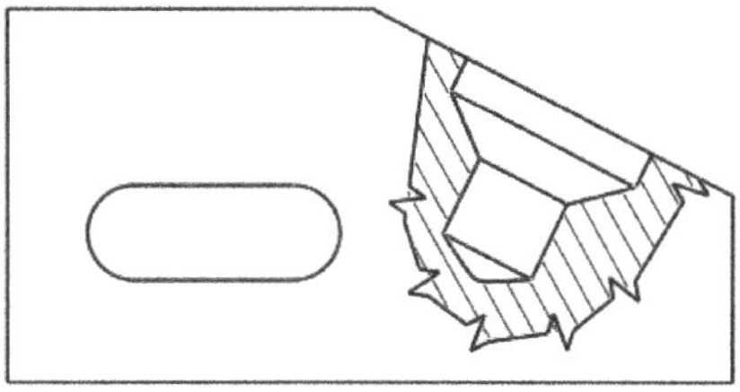

Figure 1–35

1.5 Section Views/Cuts

The three methods used to create section views are as follows:

- Create a Section View/Cut
- Create a Profile in 3D
- Use Planes

Create a Section View/Cut

The Section view/cut method involves sketching the section profile on the parent drawing view.

How To: Create a Section View

1. Activate the parent view and click (Offset Section View).
2. Define the starting point of the profile.
3. Create the profile. While creating your profile, you can snap to existing geometry in the view. For example, to place a section through the center of a hole, select its edge, as shown in Figure 1–36.

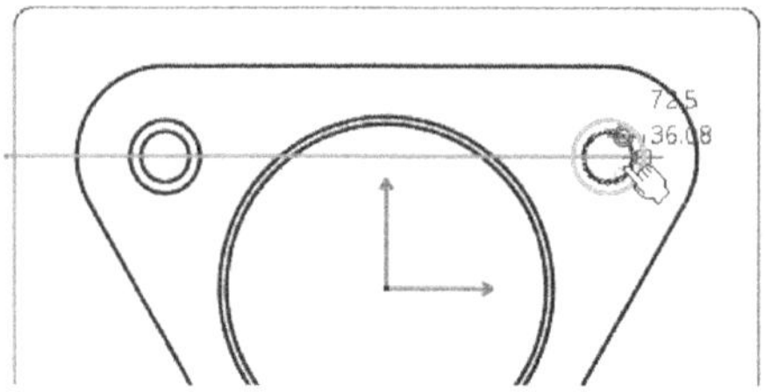

Figure 1–36

Additionally, you can use the Tools Palette toolbar. You can specify four types of constraints, as shown in Figure 1–37.

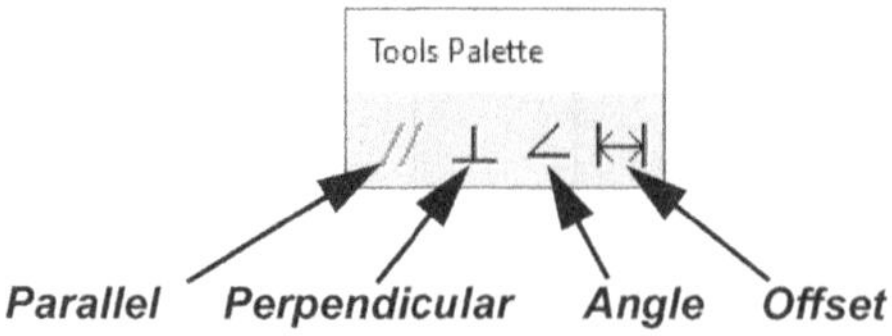

Figure 1–37

For example, to keep the profile perpendicular to one of the edges of the model, click ⊥ (Perpendicular). Then select the edge in the view, as shown in Figure 1–38.

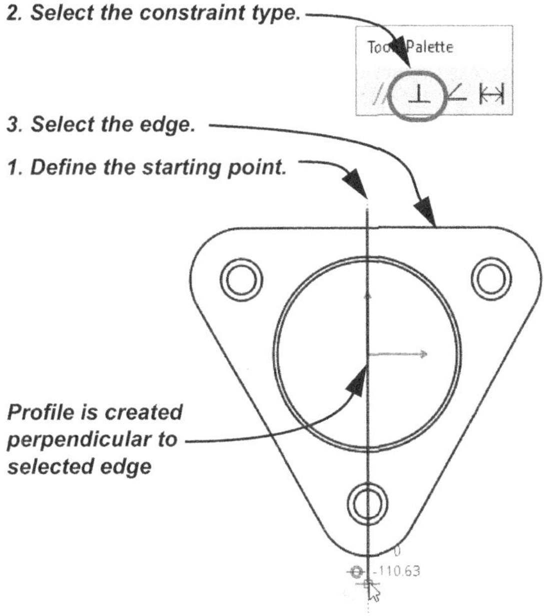

Figure 1–38

4. To finish the profile creation, double-click at the end of your profile. Then place the view in an appropriate location on the drawing.

Create a Profile in 3D

Positioned sketches are considered a best practice. They ensure more robust models with predictable results.

How To: Create a Section View/Cut Using the Profile in 3D Method

1. Create a sketch in the 3D part.
2. Draw the approximate shape of the required cutting line in Sketcher.

3. Constrain the profile to the geometry through which the section must cut, as shown in Figure 1–39.

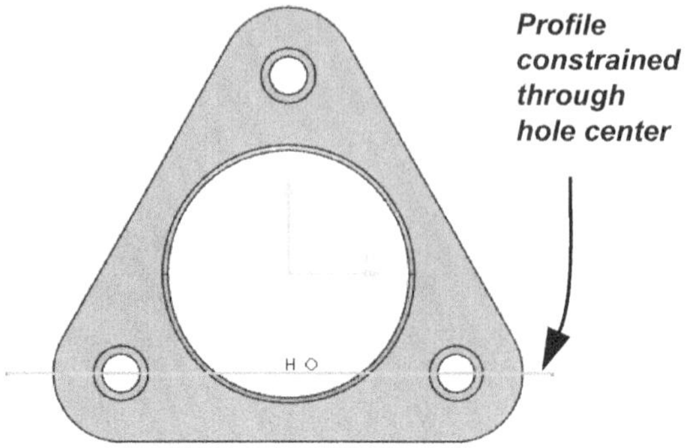

Figure 1–39

4. Exit the sketch.
5. Activate the drawing.
6. Ensure that the parent view for the section is activated.

You can only select 3D profiles that are appropriate for the type of view selected.

7. In the Action Bar, click the appropriate icon. For example, click (Offset Section View) to create an offset section view.
8. Activate the 3D model and select the sketch.
9. Activate the drawing and select a location for the view. The section profile is now linked to the 3D geometry and changes if the cutting sketch is changed.

Use Planes

Reference planes can also be selected from the 3D model to define a section view. When this is done, the position of the reference plane determines the cut location on the part. Modifications to the reference plane update in the section view.

To use a plane to define a section cut, select the appropriate icon in the Action Bar. Activate the 3D model and select the reference plane in the model or specification tree.

1.6 Create a Manual View

The creation of drawing views is the first step in creating a drawing. View creation takes a 2D view from the 3D model and displays it on the drawing. You can use the following two methods of view creation when using the Generative Drafting app: manual view creation or View Wizard.

Drawing views can be created once a 3D model has been opened and a new drawing document has been created.

General Steps

Use the following general steps to manually create drawing views:

1. Create a Front view.
2. Orient the view.
3. Create additional views.

Step 1 - Create a Front view.

Click  (Front View) to create a front view.

Step 2 - Orient the view.

Activate the 3D model window and select a planar reference, as shown in Figure 1–40. A preview of the drawing view displays in the bottom right corner of the window.

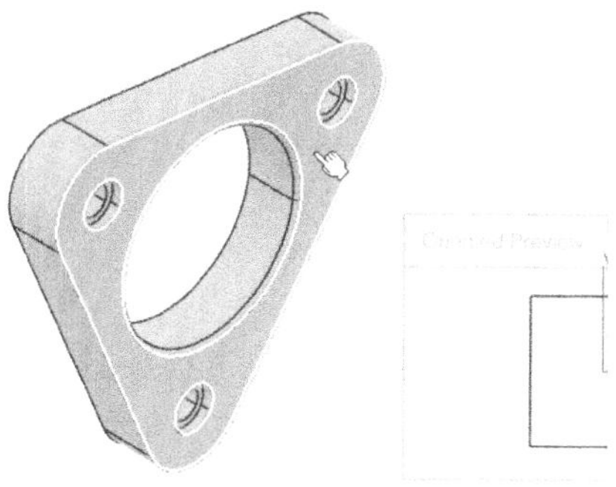

Figure 1–40

The view orientation compass enables you to rotate and flip the front view until the required orientation has been achieved, as shown in Figure 1–41.

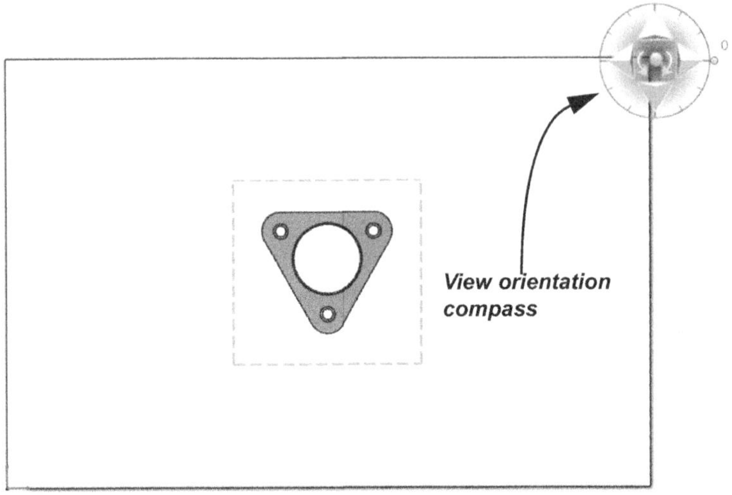

Figure 1–41

The view compass functionality is shown in Figure 1–42.

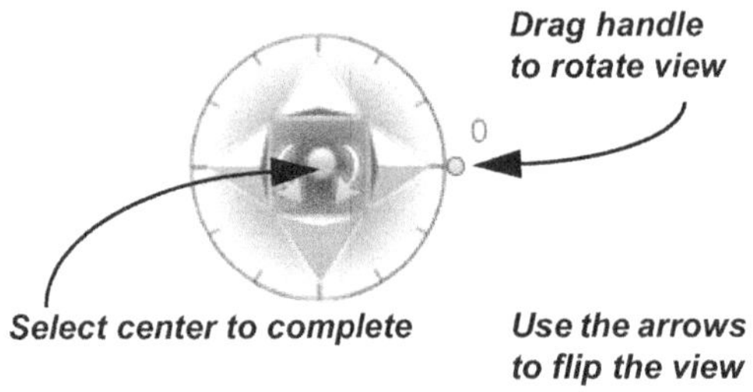

Figure 1–42

Use the shortcut menu to change the compass properties, as shown in Figure 1–43 (right-click on the green rotate handle).

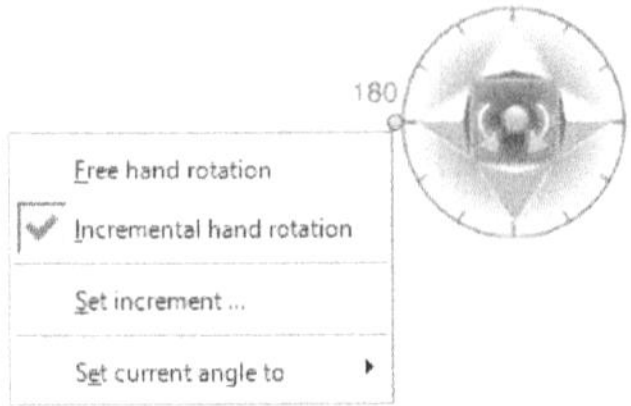

Figure 1–43

Orient the view using the compass. When you reach the required view orientation, select the center of the compass or select anywhere on the drawing sheet to complete the view definition. The completed view definition displays as shown in Figure 1–44.

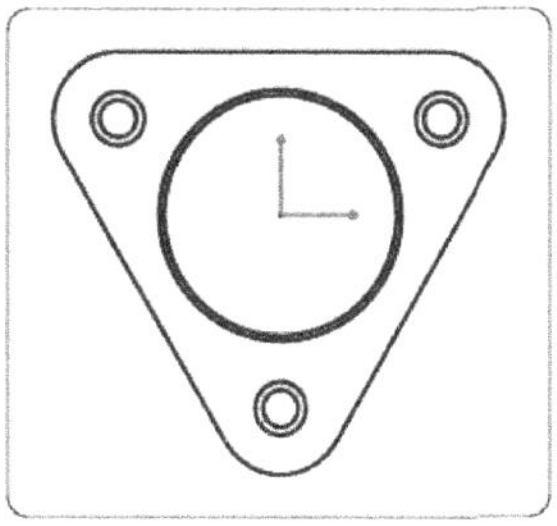

Figure 1–44

Step 3 - Create additional views.

Use the View Layout section to create additional views as required. The View Layout section is shown in Figure 1–45.

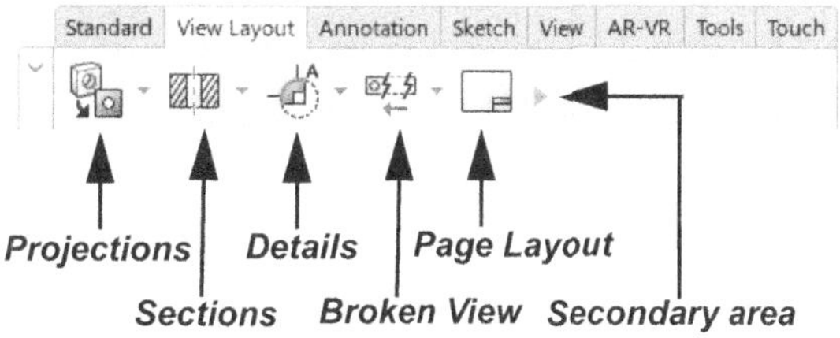

Figure 1–45

1.7 View Wizard

The Wizard command can be used to quickly customize the view layout.

To access the **Wizard** command, ensure that the 3D model is open in a CATIA window and click  (Wizard) from the expanded View Layout section. The View Wizard dialog box opens as shown in Figure 1–46.

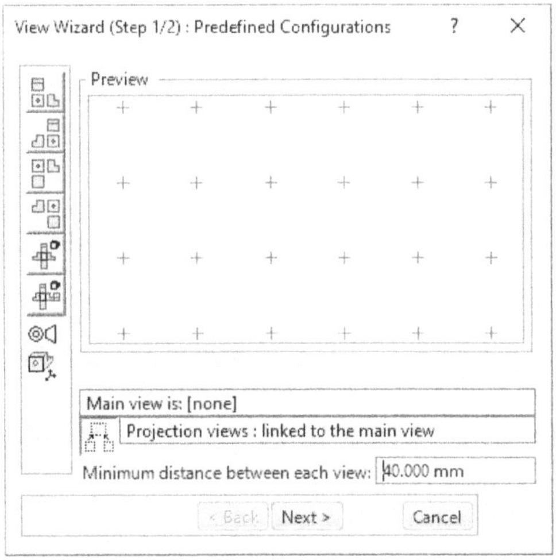

Figure 1–46

General Steps

Use the following steps to customize the view layout using the View Wizard:

1. Select a predefined configuration.
2. Arrange the configuration.
3. Orient the drawing views.
4. Generate the views.

Step 1 - Select a predefined configuration.

Select the required view layout from the icons on the left side of the dialog box. Drag the layout to a location on the sheet, as shown in Figure 1–47.

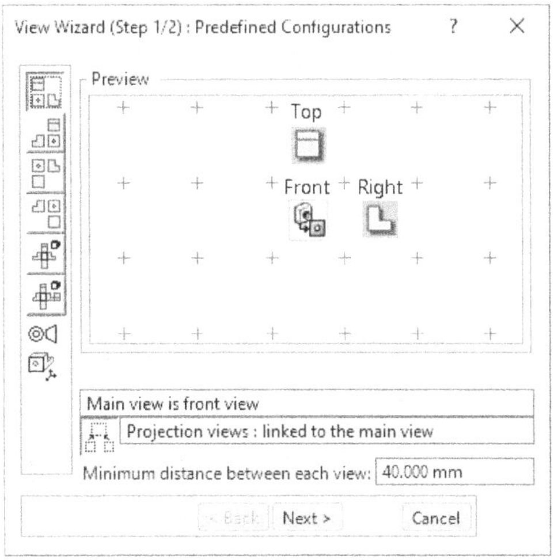

Figure 1–47

Toggle  (Views Link) to unlink the views, if required. Keeping a link with projection views is recommended. It ensures that any linked views are moved to the new location if the parent view is moved. Click **Next** to proceed to the next step.

Step 2 - Arrange the configuration.

Select the icons on the left side of the dialog box to add additional views to the drawing, as shown in Figure 1–48.

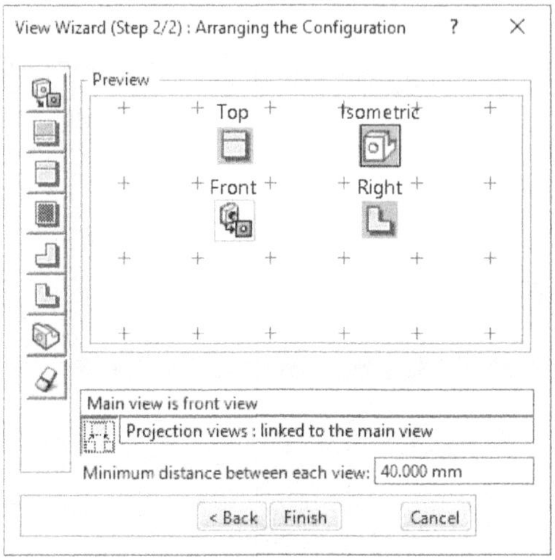

Figure 1–48

Delete unwanted views by right-clicking on a view and selecting **Delete**, as shown in Figure 1–49.

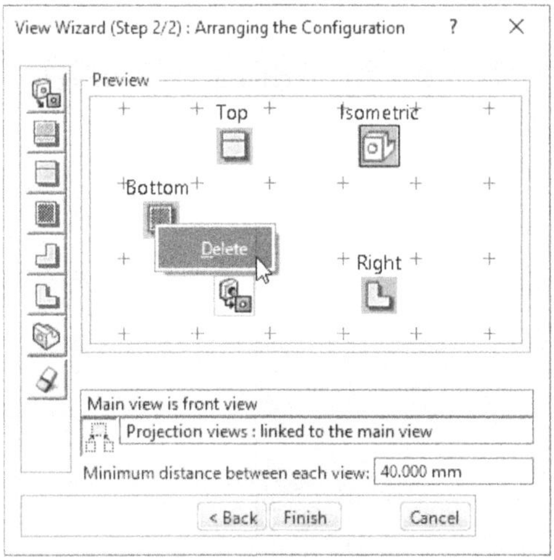

Figure 1–49

Enter the minimum distance between views in the field at the bottom of the dialog box. Note that the main view is specified as the front view in the View Wizard dialog box. Click **Finish** to complete the operation.

Step 3 - Orient the drawing views.

With the model already open in a second widget, activate the model widget and/or tab and select a surface on the model to determine the orientation of the Front view, as shown in Figure 1–50.

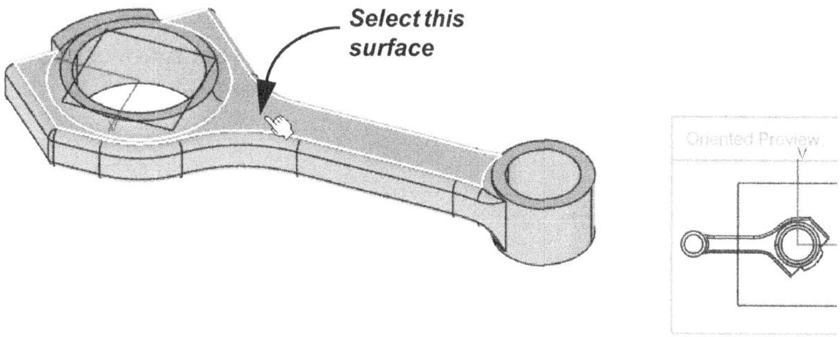

Figure 1–50

Step 4 - Generate the views.

Reorient the views as required using the compass, as shown in Figure 1–51.

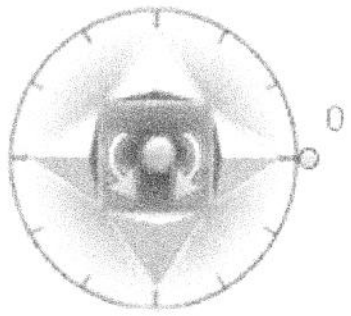

Figure 1–51

Generate the views by selecting anywhere on the sheet.

1.8 Adding an Additional Sheet

A drawing can contain more than one sheet. The sheets display in the specification tree and along the top of the drawing window as tabs. To switch between sheets, either double-click on the sheet in the tree or select the tab.

Use one of the following methods to add a new sheet:

If the sheet tabs or (Create a new sheet) does not display, ensure (Sheet Browser) is toggled on. This is found in the View section of the Action Bar.

- Click (Create a new sheet) at the top of the drawing within the Sheet Browser, as shown in Figure 1–52.

Figure 1–52

- In the specification tree, right-click on the drawing name or on the sheet name and select **New Sheet.**

Sheet Properties

To display the sheet properties, right-click on the sheet name in the specification tree and select **Properties**. The Properties dialog box opens as shown in Figure 1–53.

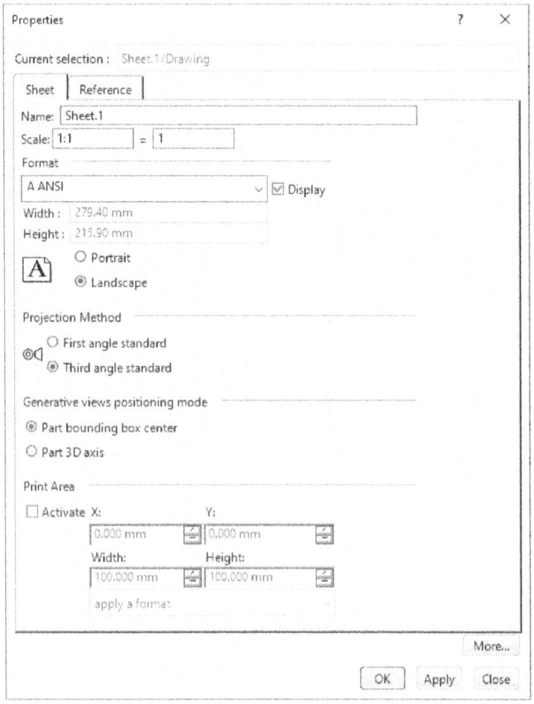

Figure 1–53

The following sheet properties can be modified:

- Sheet name and scale
- Sheet size and orientation
- Projection method (first or third angle)
- View positioning in the frame (geometric center or part axis)
- Print area

Reordering Sheets

Views can also be reordered in the specification tree using the same technique.

How To: Reorder Sheets

1. In the specification tree, right-click on the sheet name and select * **object>Reorder**, as shown in Figure 1–54.

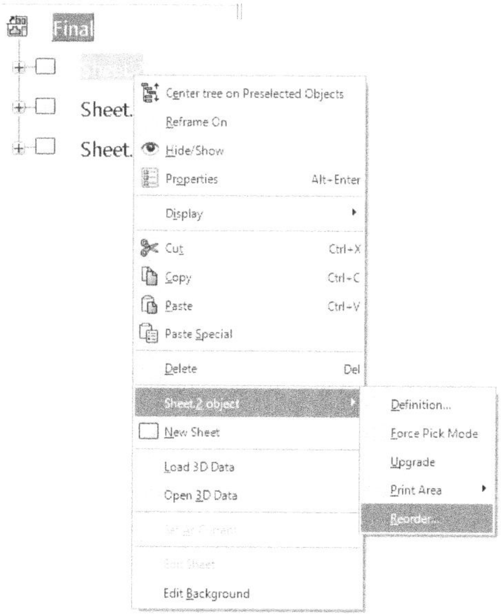

Figure 1–54

2. When you move the cursor over the sheets in the specification tree, the cursor changes to indicate where the selected sheet is going to be placed in the tree. By default, the selected sheet is placed below the target sheet, as shown in Figure 1–55.

Press and hold <Ctrl> to place the selected sheets above the target sheet. The cursor changes to 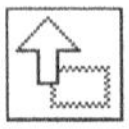.

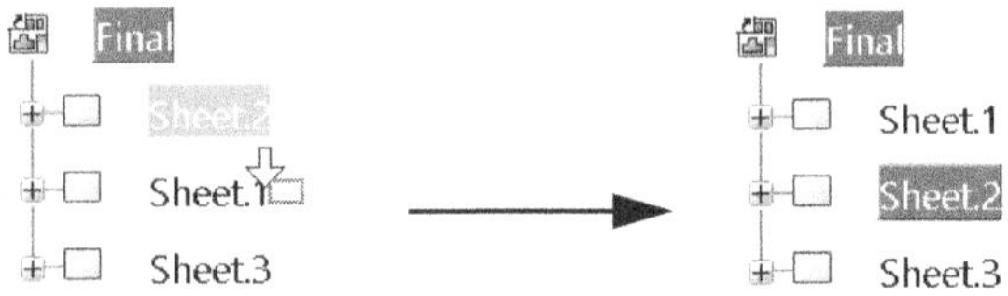

Before ***After***

Figure 1–55

Limitations

Reordering has the following limitations:

- Sheets and views cannot be reordered at the same time.
- Sheets can only be reordered under their parent drawing.
- Views can only be reordered under their parent sheet.
- Detail sheets can only be placed after regular sheets.

1.9 File Associations

Since the views of a drawing depend on the 3D model geometry, a link is established between the model and drawing when drawing views are created. CATIA must be able to load the 3D geometry from the associated 3D Part or Physical Product object for the drawing views to update.

In general, with 3DEXPERIENCE, both the 3D Model and the Drawing are managed by the software. Links are created between the two objects when views are created, and when the drawing is saved so is the 3D Model. However, in the situation that a problem occurs, it is important to understand how to re-establish a broken link to drawing views.

Restoring Links

The specification tree displays with a broken link icon when a drawing is opened without its linked document, as shown in Figure 1–56. The symbols indicate that the links to the referenced document are broken.

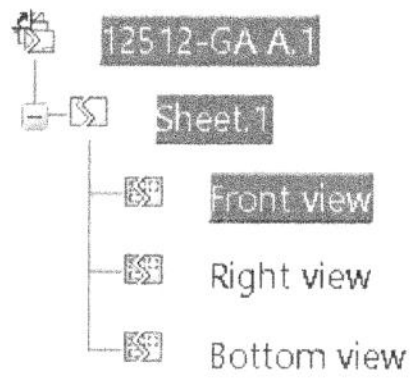

Figure 1–56

At this point, the views of the drawing display and you can modify the properties of the views. However, you cannot add new views or add detail to existing views until the link to the model has been re-established.

You can restore the link to a broken view as long as the original file can be found. From the specification tree, right-click on the name of the broken view, then select * **object>Modify Links**. This will open a Link Modification window, as shown in Figure 1–57.

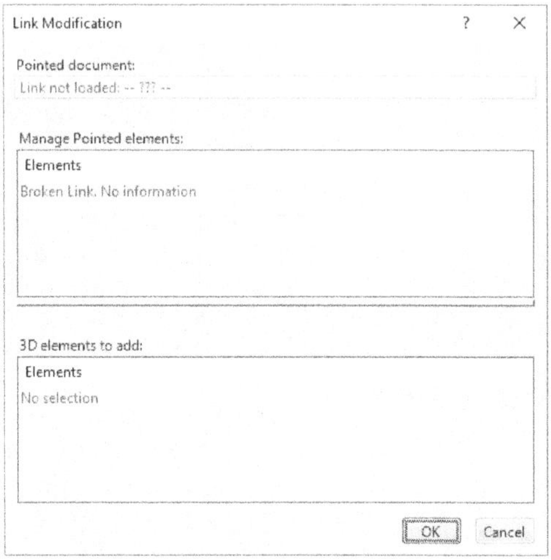

Figure 1–57

With the Link Modification window open, locate, open, and select the body of the original model. The selected PartBody will be added, as shown in Figure 1–58.

Figure 1–58

Select the ✚ icon to the right of the PartBody to add it to the *Managed Pointed elements* list, then select **OK** to re-establish the link to the broken view.

Practice 1a

Create a Part Drawing

Practice Objectives

- Create a part drawing.
- Create Front, Projection, Detail, and Isometric views.
- Modify page properties and drawing options.

In this practice, you will create a part drawing for **ExhaustFlange.3dxml**.

Task 1 - Import and open a part.

1. In the Top Bar, click (Add)>**Import**.
2. In the Import dialog box, click (Open).
3. Browse to the practice files folder, select **ExhaustFlange.3dxml**, and click **Open**.
4. Ensure the settings in the Import dialog box match those shown in Figure 1–59.
   - For the *Duplication string*, replace **###_** with your initials to differentiate the model from others.

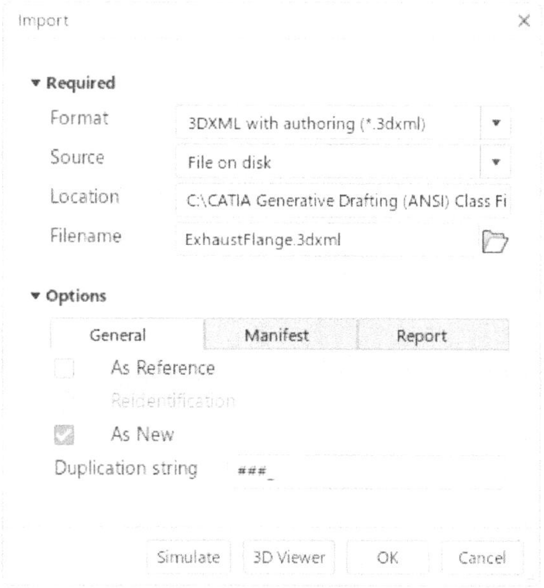

Figure 1–59

5. Click **OK**.

6. The Import Progression window opens momentarily, as shown in Figure 1–60.

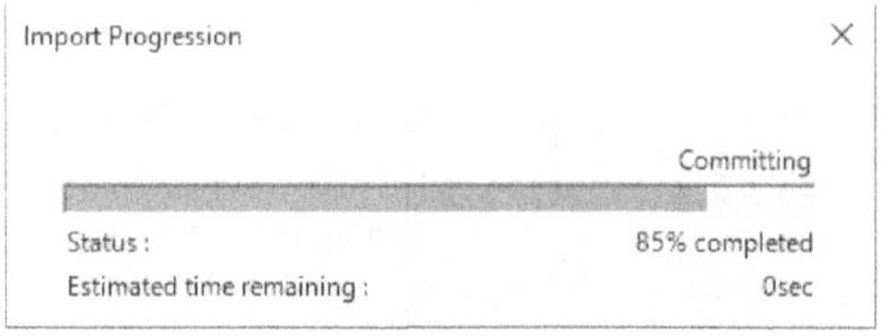

Figure 1–60

7. When the import is finished, the Operation report dialog box appears showing the import was successful, as shown in Figure 1–61.

Figure 1–61

8. Click **OK** in the Operation report dialog box.

9. In the specification tree, right-click on **ExhaustFlange** and select **Open**.

10. The part displays as shown in Figure 1–62.

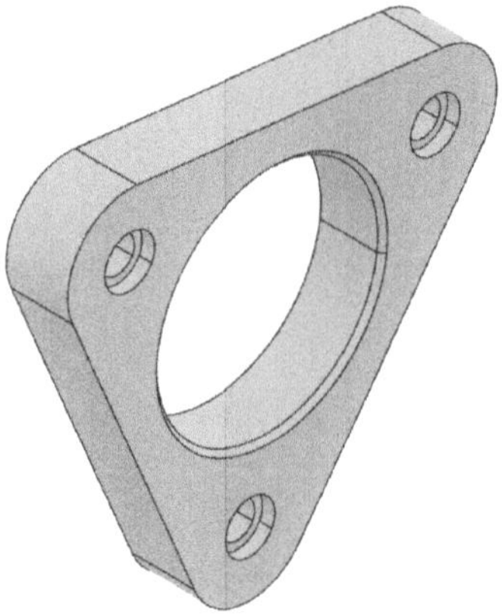

Figure 1–62

Task 2 - Create a drawing.

1. Double-click on the top level in the tree to activate it. It should turn blue.

2. Right-click on the top level and select **Insert>Drawing**, as shown in Figure 1–63.

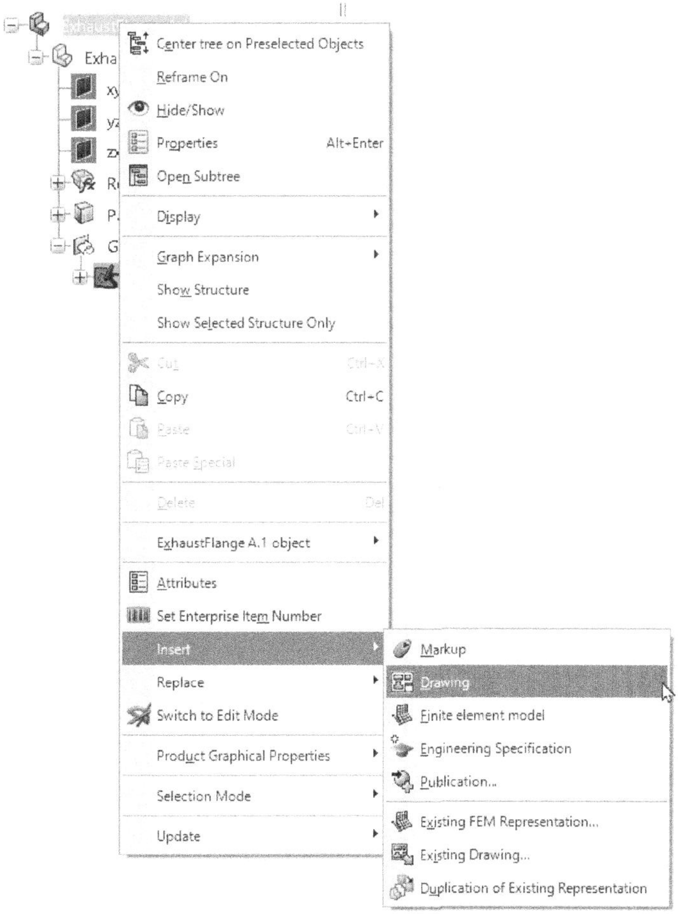

Figure 1–63

3. The Drawing window appears. In the *Title* field, enter **###_ExhaustFlange** but replace ### with your initials, as shown in Figure 1–64.

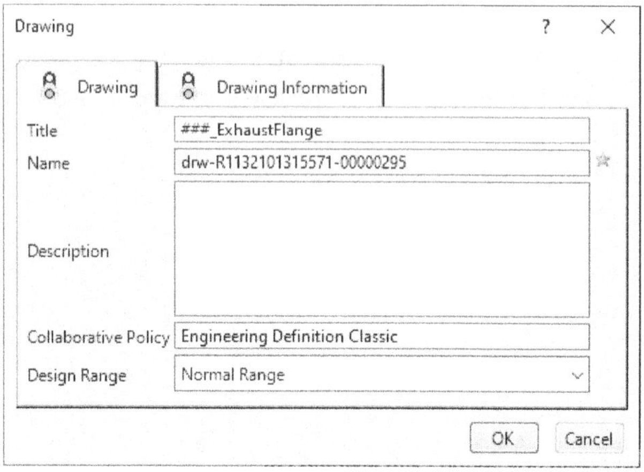

Figure 1–64

4. Click the *Drawing Information* tab and select **ANSI-ASME** for the *Standard* and **C ANSI** for the *Sheet Style*, as shown in Figure 1–65.

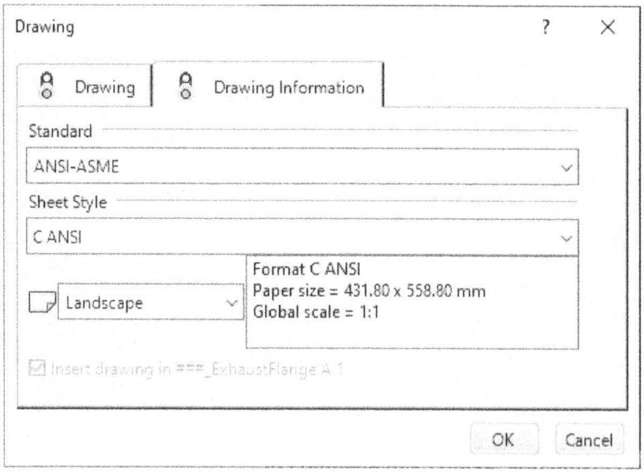

Figure 1–65

5. Click **OK** to complete the drawing creation.

6. Right-click on the drawing in the tree and select * **object> Open in New App**, as shown in Figure 1–66.

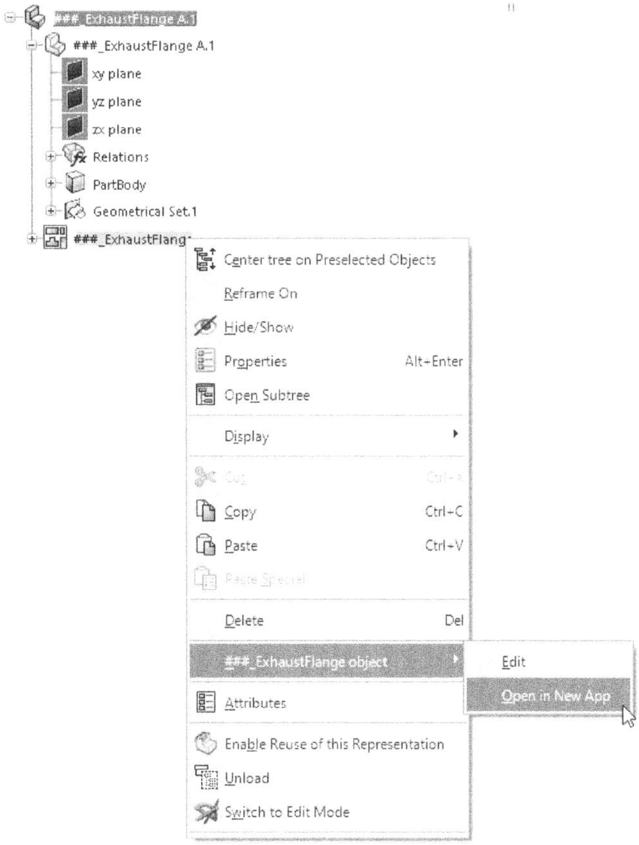

Figure 1–66

The **###_ExhaustFlange** drawing will open in a new tab. This will be an empty sheet for now.

Task 3 - Create a Front view.

1. In the View Layout section of the Action Bar, select  (Front View).

Note the preview in the bottom right corner of the display.

2. Select a planar surface to orient the view by selecting the *###_ExhaustFlange A.1* tab to bring up the part model and then selecting the surface shown in Figure 1–67.

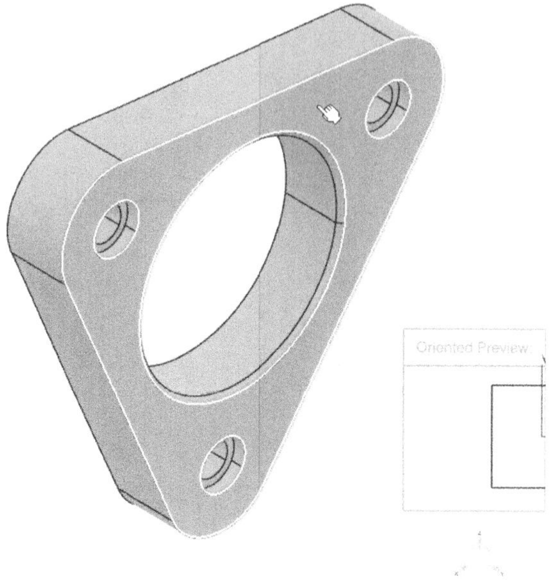

Figure 1–67

The drawing window becomes active, and the view preview and the compass display, as shown in Figure 1–68.

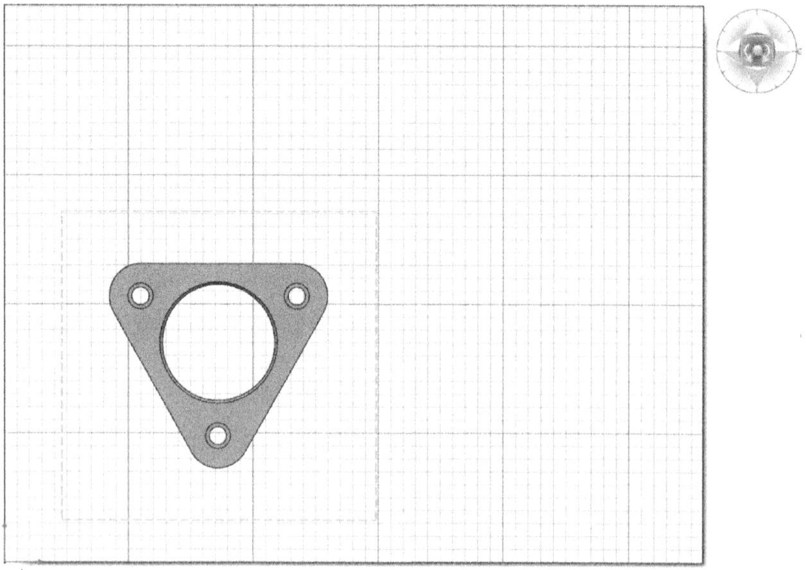

Figure 1–68

3. Select anywhere in the display to complete the creation of the Front view, as shown in Figure 1–69.

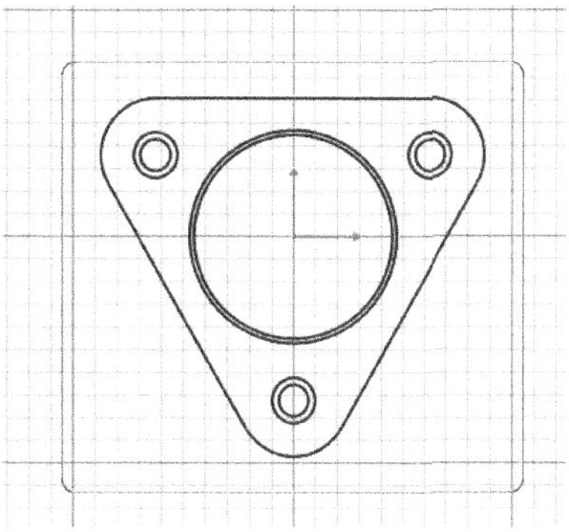

Figure 1–69

Task 4 - Modify properties of a view.

1. In the specification tree, right-click on the **Front view** and select **Properties**, as shown in Figure 1–70. The Properties dialog box opens.

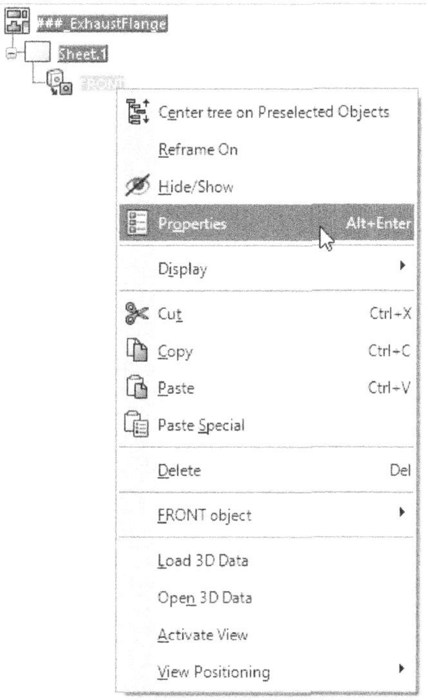

Figure 1–70

2. Select the *View* tab. For the *Scale* value, enter **1:2**, as shown in Figure 1–71.

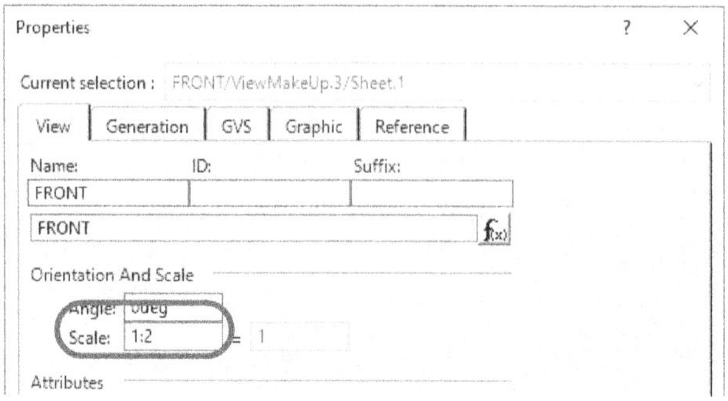

Figure 1–71

3. Click **OK** to complete the change. The view updates with the new scale value.

4. Move the view to the location shown in Figure 1–72 by selecting the view frame and dragging it to the new location.

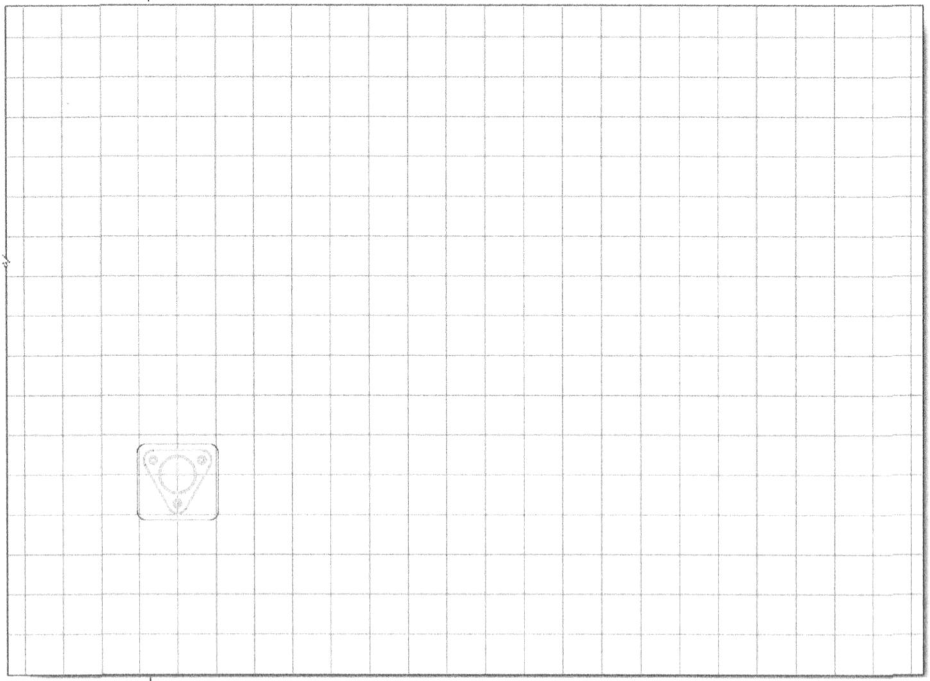

Figure 1–72

Task 5 - Modify the sheet size.

1. At the top of the drawing, right-click on **Sheet.1** (this is called the Sheet Browser) and select **Properties**, as shown in Figure 1–73. The Properties dialog box opens.

If the Sheet Browser is not showing, select  *(Sheet Browser) from the View section of the Action Bar.*

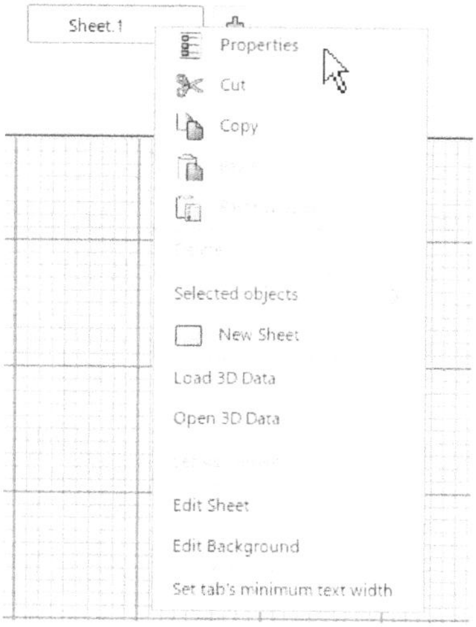

Figure 1–73

2. In the Format drop-down list, select **B-ANSI**, as shown in Figure 1–74.

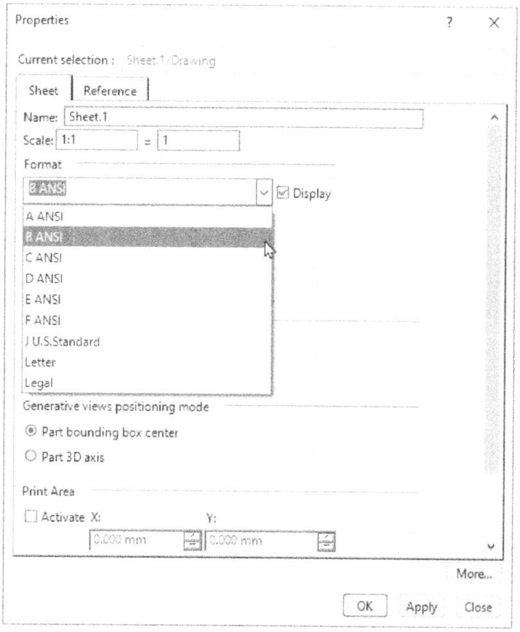

Figure 1–74

3. Click **OK**. The sheet size updates as shown in Figure 1–75.

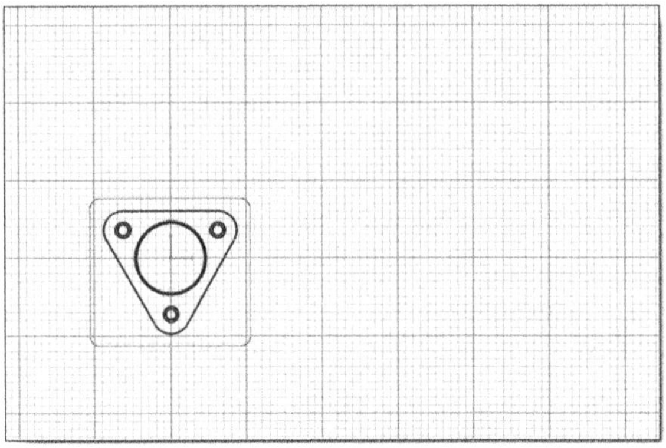

Figure 1–75

Task 6 - Change grid display.

1. In the *View* tab, select  (Display Grid), as shown in Figure 1–76, to turn off the display of the drawing grid.

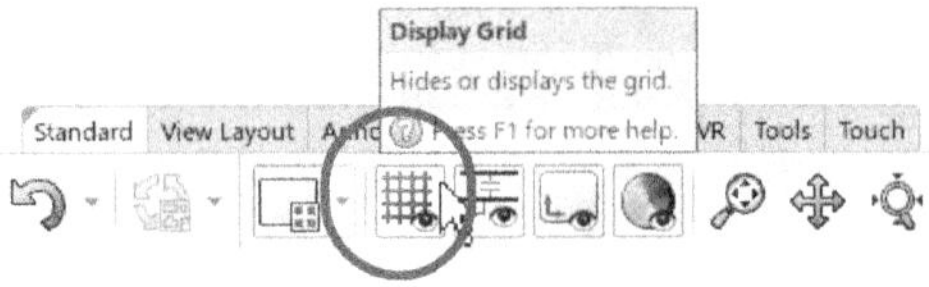

Figure 1–76

Task 7 - Create a section view.

Section views can only be created from the active view. Ensure that the view you are cutting has a red border.

1. Zoom in on the Front view, as shown in Figure 1–78. In the *View Layout* tab, select  (Offset Section View), as shown in Figure 1–77.

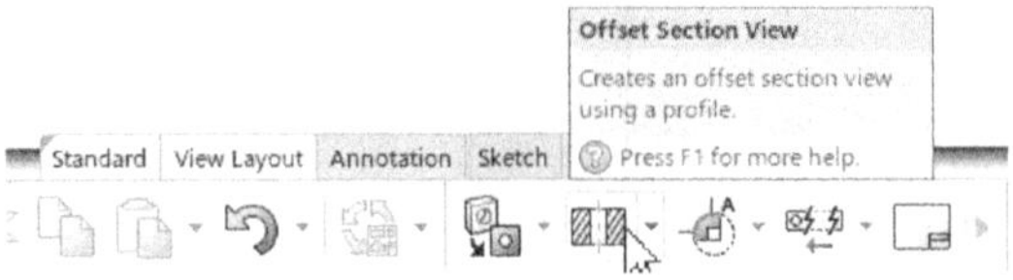

Figure 1–77

2. Position the cursor so that a witness line displays at the center of the hole, as shown in Figure 1–78. Select the location with the left mouse button.

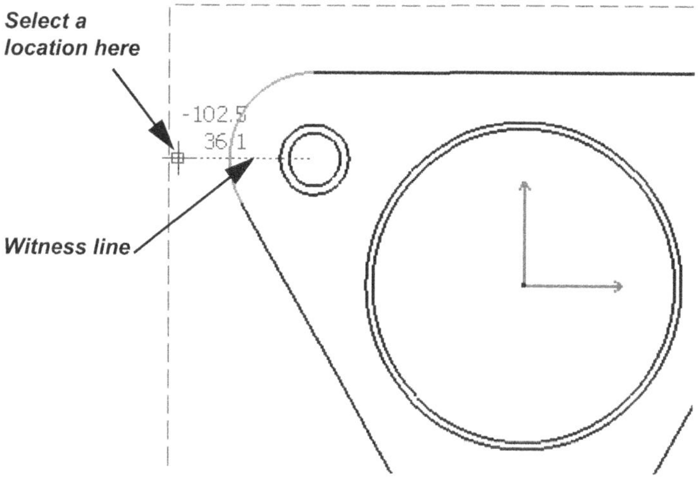

Figure 1–78

3. Move the cursor to the right of the view, as shown in Figure 1–79. Ensure that the line is blue (this indicates that the line is horizontal). Double-click on the end point of the line to finish defining the location of the cross-section.

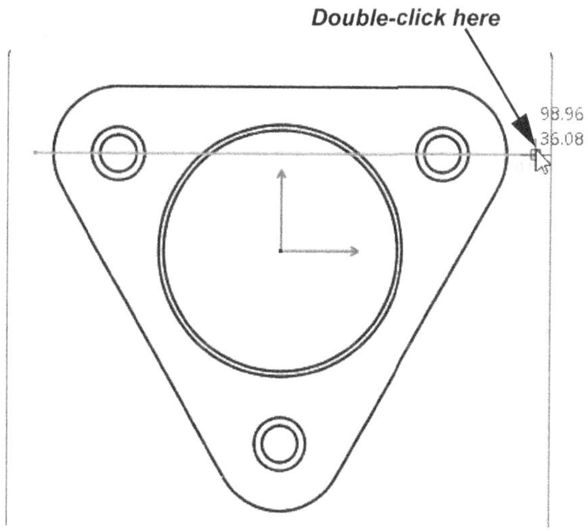

Figure 1–79

4. Place the cursor above the Front view, as shown in Figure 1–80, and click to place the view.

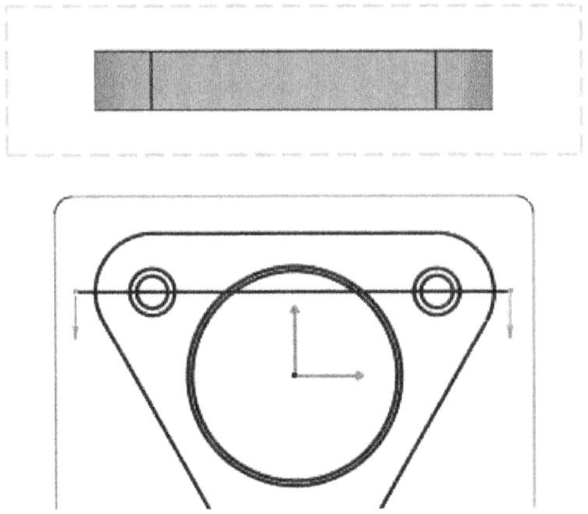

Figure 1–80

The section view displays as shown in Figure 1–81.

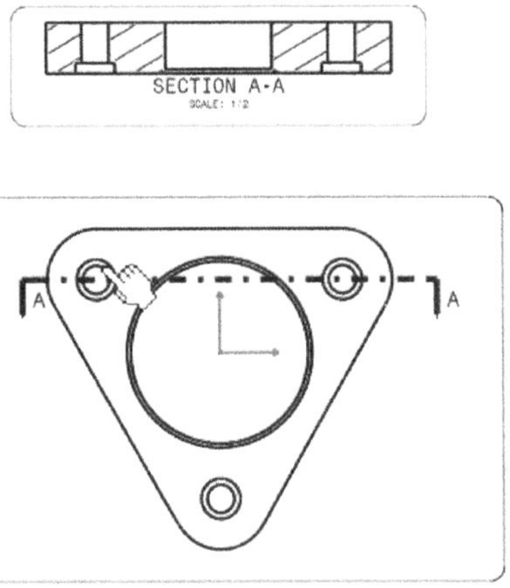

Figure 1–81

Task 8 - Create a projection view.

1. In the View Layout section of the Action Bar, select the flyout arrow next to  (Front View), then select  (Projection), as shown in Figure 1–82.

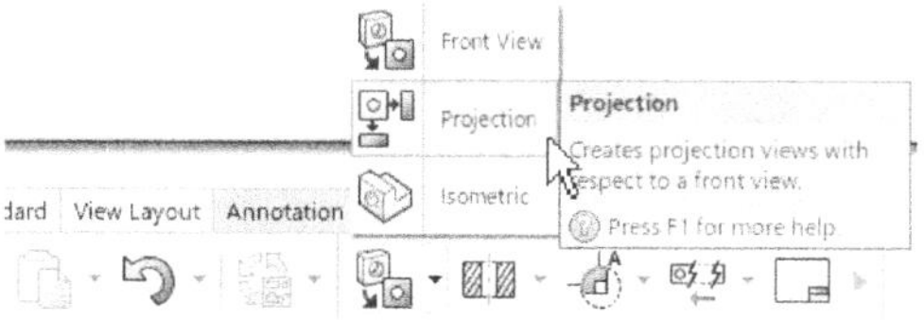

Figure 1–82

2. Place the projection view, as shown in Figure 1–83.

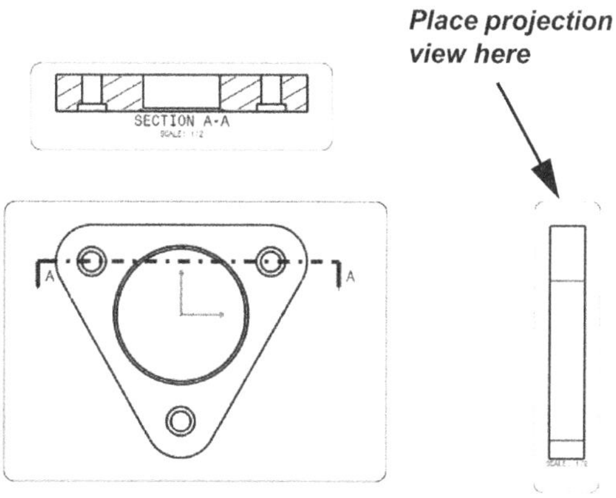

Figure 1–83

Task 9 - Activate and modify a view.

1. Double-click on the view frame of the projection view created in Task 8 to activate the view. The view frame of an active view displays in red.

2. Right-click on the newly created projection view and select **Properties**, as shown in Figure 1–84.

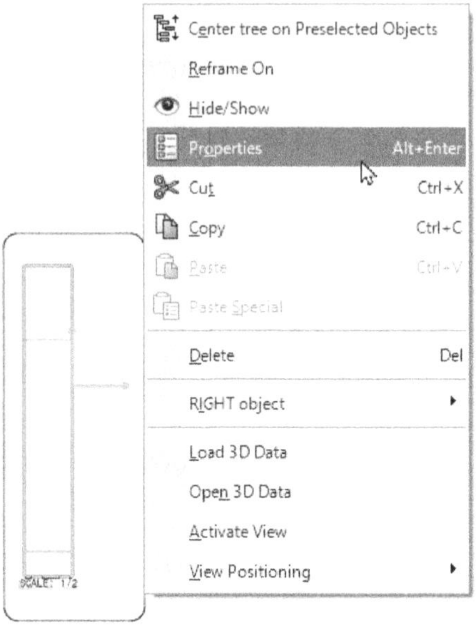

Figure 1–84

3. In the *Generation* tab, select **Hidden Lines**, as shown in Figure 1–85.

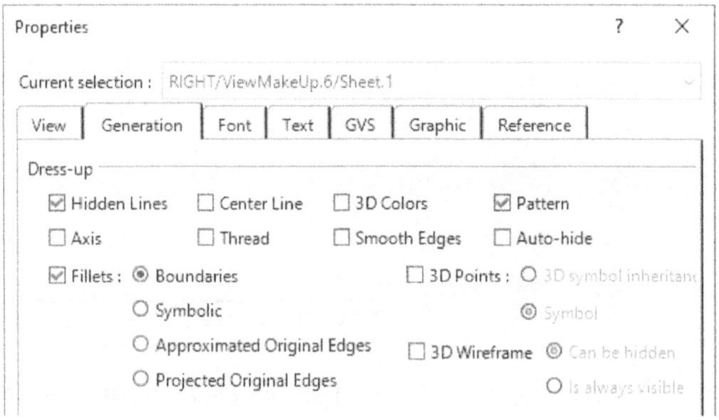

Figure 1–85

4. Click **OK**. The projection view displays as shown in Figure 1–86.

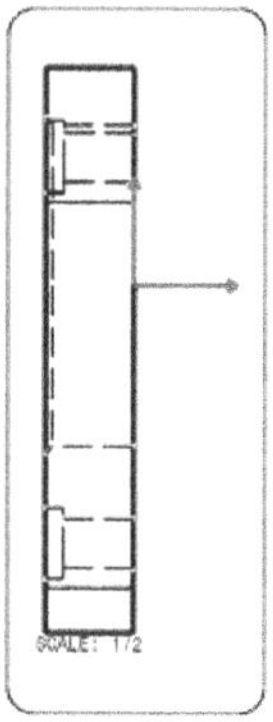

Figure 1–86

Task 10 - Create a detail view.

1. In the View Layout section of the Action Bar, click (Detail View).

2. Select a location on the section view, as shown in Figure 1–87.

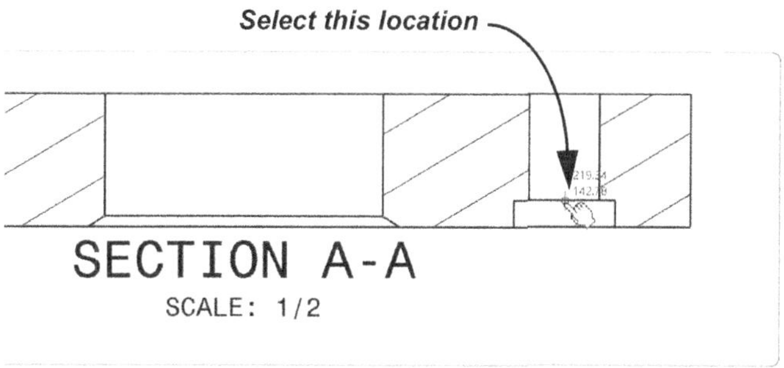

Figure 1–87

3. Draw the circle callout with the cursor, as shown in Figure 1–88, and click the left mouse button.

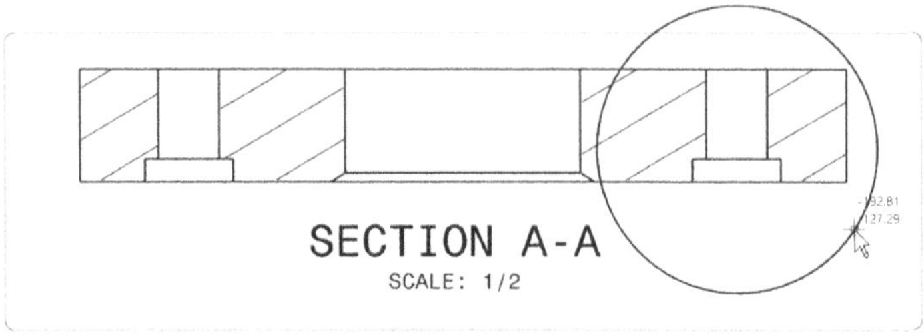

Figure 1–88

4. An error message box opens, as shown in Figure 1–89, indicating that a detail view definition does not intersect with the active view. Click **OK** to close the dialog box.

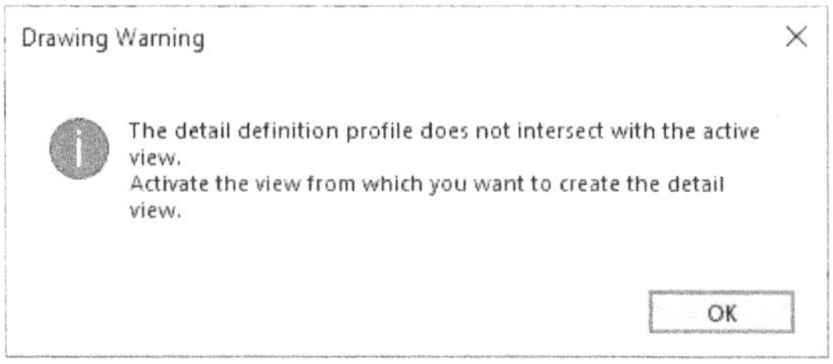

Figure 1–89

5. Click (Detail View) to deactivate it.

The radius for the detail callout can be entered in the Tools Palette

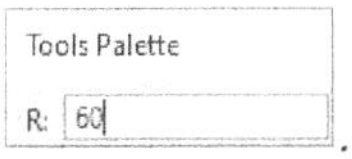

6. Activate by double-clicking the section view and create the detail view shown in Figure 1–90.

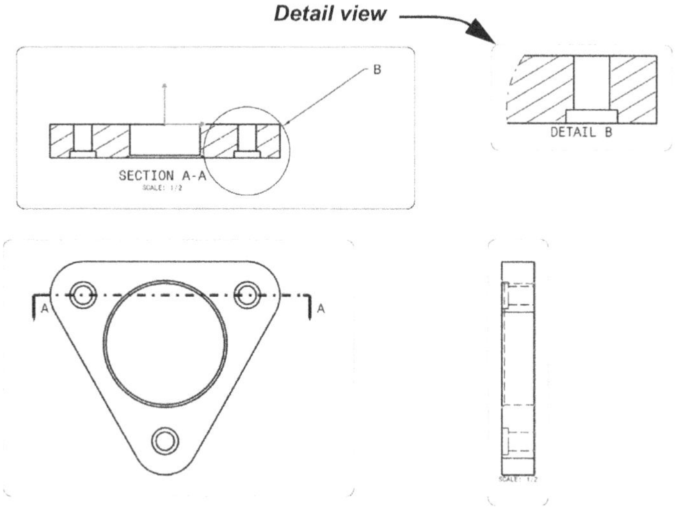

Figure 1–90

Task 11 - Create an isometric view.

1. In the View Layout section of the Action Bar, select the flyout arrow next to  (Front View), then select  (Isometric), as shown in Figure 1–91.

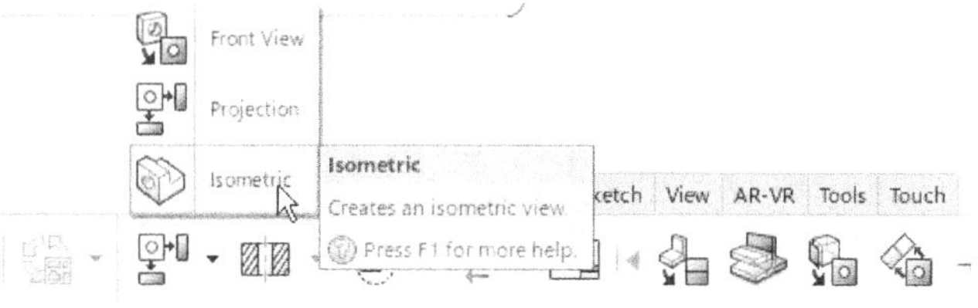

Figure 1–91

2. Select the *###_ExhaustFlange A.1* tab to display the model.

3. Select the part, as shown in Figure 1–92.

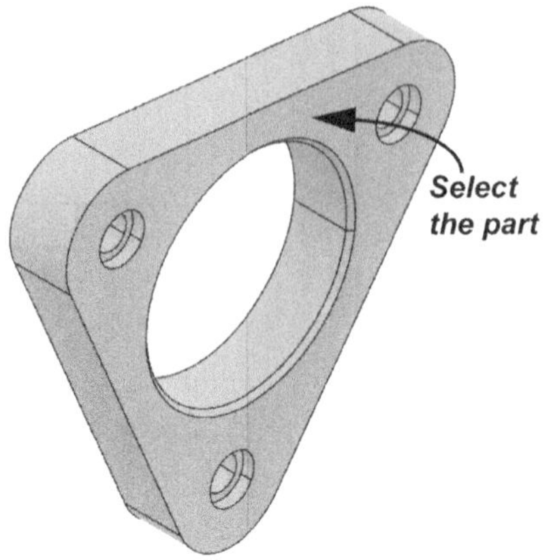

Figure 1–92

When creating an Isometric view, you select the part to orient it rather than a planar surface. The drawing view displays the result of the current orientation of the model and is not necessarily a true isometric orientation.

4. Place the isometric view in the location shown in Figure 1–93.

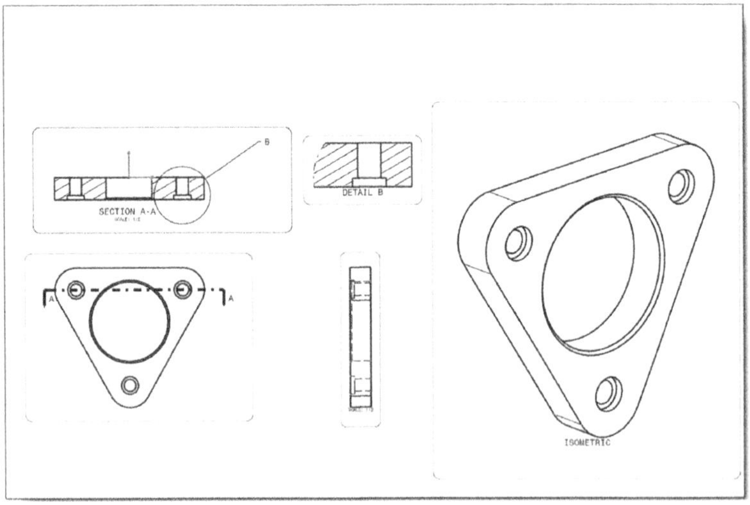

Figure 1–93

5. Rescale the Isometric view to **1:3** and move it to the location shown in Figure 1–94.

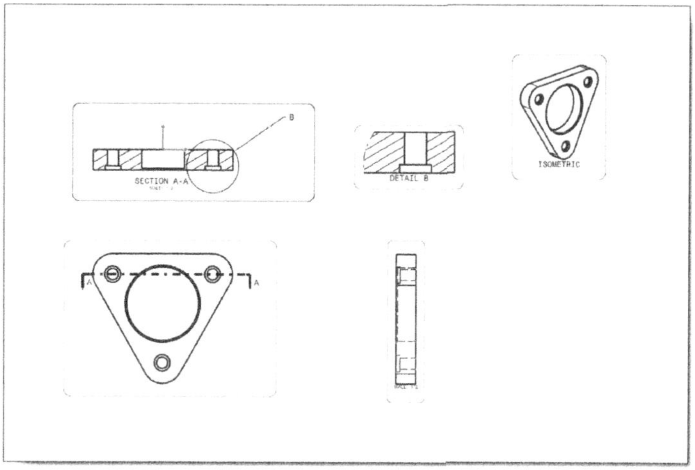

Figure 1–94

6. Move the Names and Scale notes for each view so that they display as shown in Figure 1–95. Relocate the Detail view to the bottom right corner of the page.

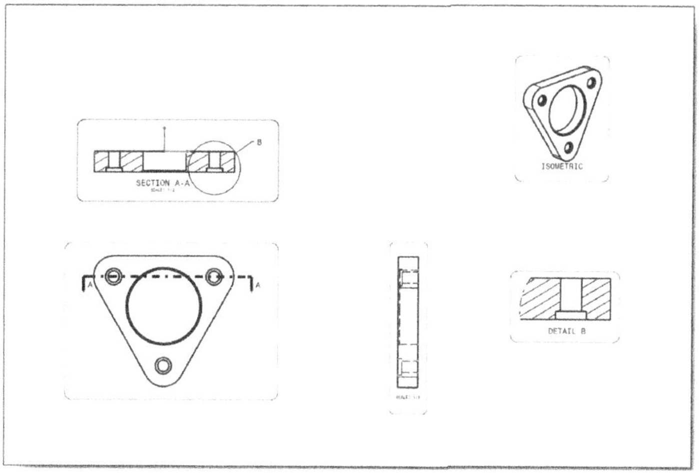

Figure 1–95

7. Open the Properties dialog box for the Isometric view and enter **Reference View** in the *Prefix* field, as shown in Figure 1–96.

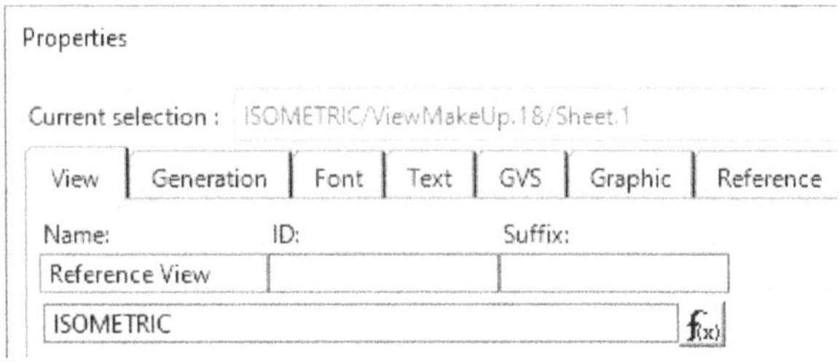

Figure 1–96

8. Click  (Share)>**Save** to save the drawing.
9. Close all tabs.

Practice 1b Create a Sectional View

Practice Objectives

- Create a cross-section view.
- Create a cross-section view from 3D.

In this practice, you will create a sectional view in a drawing and on the model.

Task 1 - Import and open the drawing.

1. In the Top Bar, click (Add)>**Import**.
2. In the Import dialog box, click (Open).
3. Browse to the practice files folder, select **Bracket.3dxml**, and click **Open**.
4. Ensure the settings in the Import dialog box match those shown in Figure 1–97.
   - For the *Duplication string*, replace **###_** with your initials to differentiate the model from others.

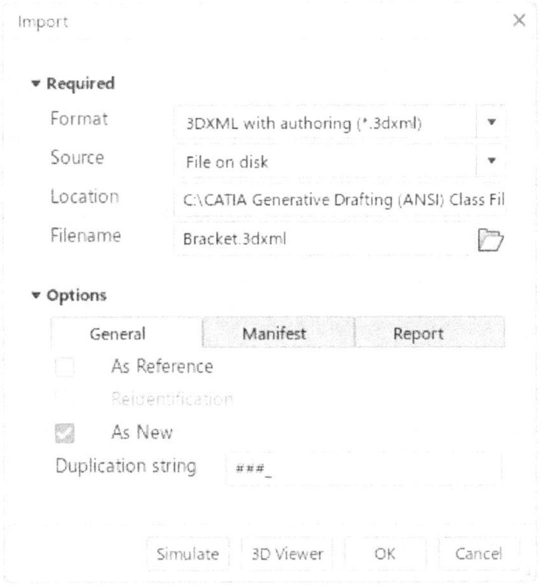

Figure 1–97

5. Click **OK**.

6. The Import Progression window opens momentarily, as shown in Figure 1–98.

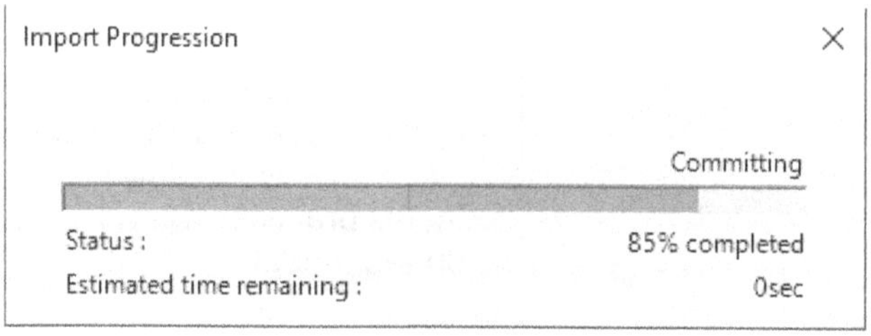

Figure 1–98

7. When the import is finished, the Operation report dialog box appears showing the import was successful, as shown in Figure 1–99.

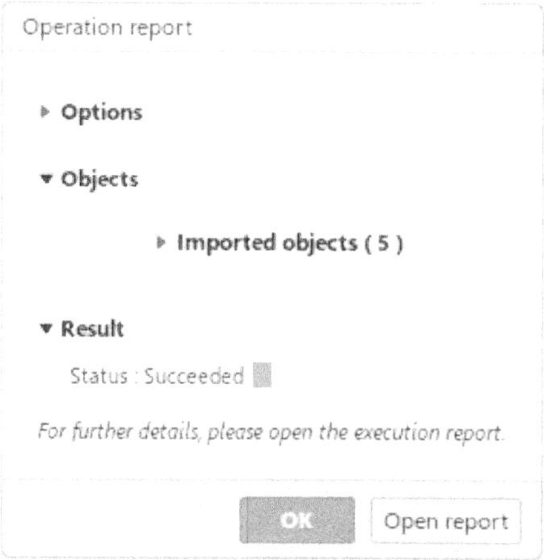

Figure 1–99

8. Click **OK** in the Operation report dialog box.
9. In the specification tree, right-click **###_Bracket** and select **Open**.

10. The part displays as shown in Figure 1–100.

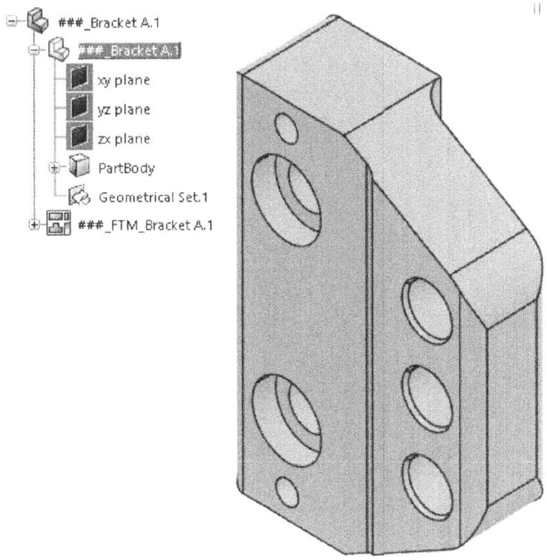

Figure 1–100

11. Right-click on **###_FTM Bracket A.1** in the tree and select **###_FTM_Bracket A.1 object>Open in New App**, as shown in Figure 1–101.

Figure 1–101

12. The drawing displays as shown in Figure 1–102.

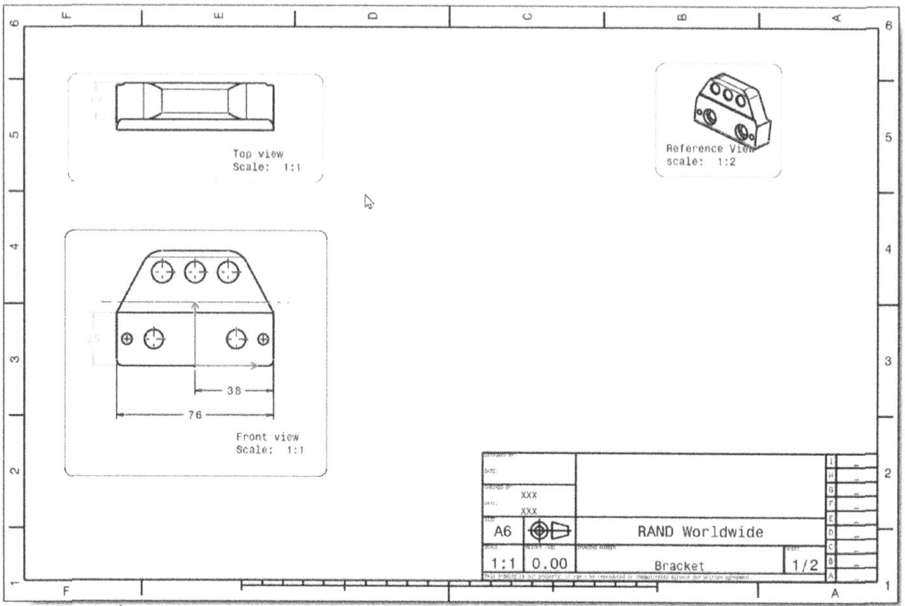

Figure 1–102

Task 2 - Create a cross-section view.

1. If necessary, double-click on the Front view to make it active. It will turn red.

2. Click (Offset Section View) from the View Layout section of the Action Bar.

3. Sketch the cross-section profile shown in Figure 1–103. Ensure that the section intersects the two holes at their centers. Double-click on the sketch to complete it.

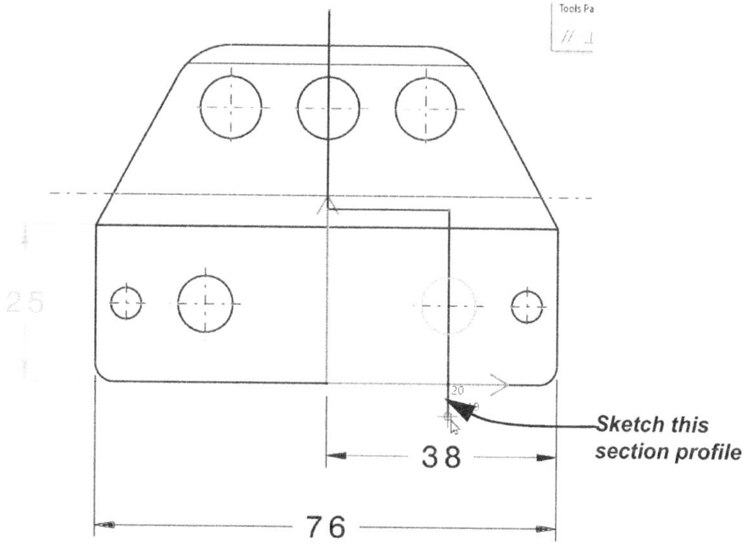

Figure 1–103

4. Move the cursor to the right of the Front view. Position the section preview and click to place the view on the drawing.

Task 3 - Modify the part.

1. Select the ###_*Bracket A.1* tab that has the 3D Part model. The model displays as shown in Figure 1–104.

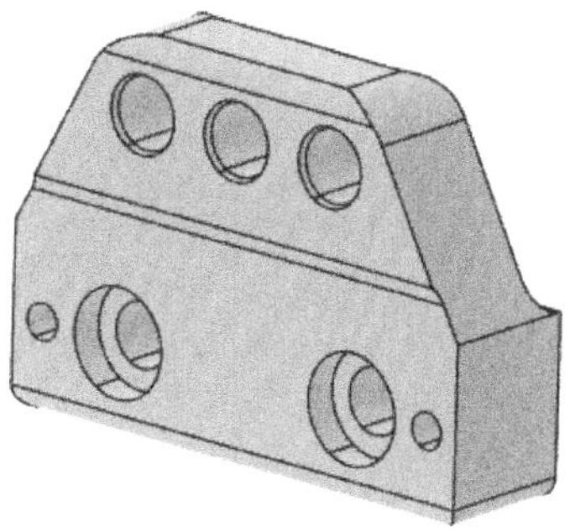

Figure 1–104

2. In the specification tree, locate and double-click on the **Pad.1** feature.

3. Double-click on the **38mm** dimension. For the *new dimension value*, enter **44mm** and click **OK**.

The standard Windows shortcut keys, <Ctrl>+<Tab>, can also be used to toggle display tabs.

4. Select the *###_FTM_Bracket A.1* tab to switch to the drawing view.

5. Update the drawing by clicking (Update current sheet). The drawing views update to display the modified part geometry.

6. Note that Section view A-A, created in Task 2, no longer intersects the counterbored holes at their centers, as originally intended. This type of cross-section profile sketch is not constrained to the geometry of the model.

Task 4 - Create a sketch in the 3D model.

1. Switch back to the 3D part model tab.

2. Click (Positioned Sketch) from the Model section of the Action Bar to start the creation of a positioned sketch.

3. Select the icon, as shown in Figure 1–105. This will allow for changes to be made to the *Support Type* field.

Figure 1–105

4. Select the surface shown in Figure 1–106.

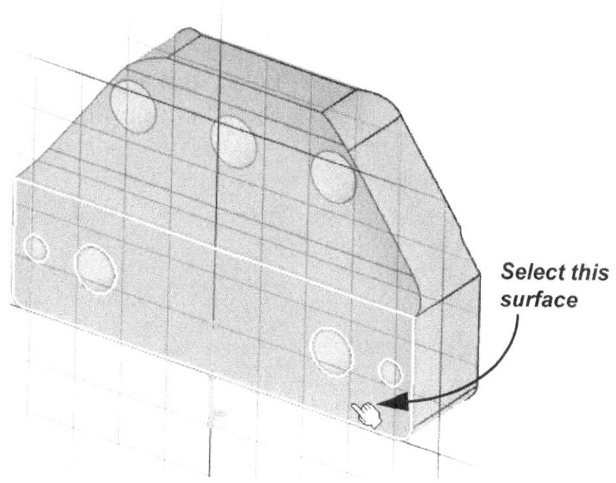

Figure 1–106

5. Select **Swap** first and then select **Reverse V**, as shown in Figure 1–107. Ensure to select these in that order because the order will affect the result. The V Arrow should be pointing up, and the H Arrow should be pointing to the right.

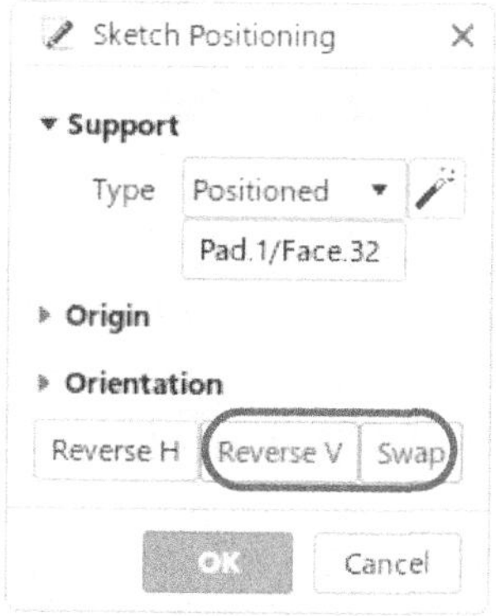

Figure 1–107

6. Click **OK** to close the dialog box and enter the Sketcher app.

7. Sketch the cross-section profile shown in Figure 1–108. Constrain the left vertical line of sketch to the vertical axis, and the right vertical line to the center of the hole. This can be done by selecting the vertical line and the inside surface of the hole (which automatically selects the implicit axis of the hole), and applying a coincidence constraint. Exit the Sketcher app when the sketch is complete.

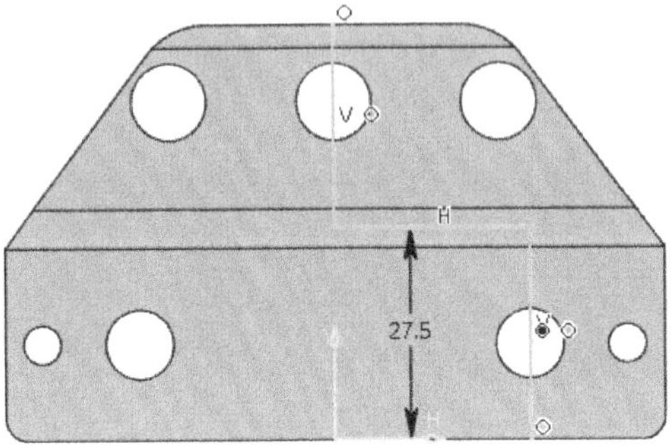

Figure 1–108

8. In the specification tree, locate and double-click on the **Pad.1** feature. Revert the *44mm dimension* to **38mm**.

Task 5 - Create a 3D-linked section view.

1. Select the drawing tab and update the drawing.
2. Delete the **Section A-A** view.
3. In the View Layout section of the Action Bar, click (Offset Section View) to create a new section view.
4. Without sketching any cross-section lines, switch to the part tab and select the newly created sketch feature.
5. The display automatically reverts to the drawing tab. Move the cursor to the right of the Front view. Position and place the section view.
6. Switch to the part tab and change the *38mm Pad.1* dimension to **44mm**.
7. Activate the drawing tab and update the drawing. Note the positioning of the cross-section profile. The intent of the drawing has been captured using a positioned sketch.
8. Save and close all of the files.

Practice 1c

Create a Part Drawing

Practice Objectives

- Create a projection view.
- Create a broken view.
- Create a clipping plane.
- Modify view properties.

In this practice, you will create a drawing that includes multiple view types.

Task 1 - Import the CAD model.

1. In the Top Bar, click (Add)>**Import**.
2. In the Import dialog box, click (Open).
3. Browse to the practice files folder, select **SteeringColum.3dxml**, and click **Open**.
4. Ensure the settings in the Import dialog box match those shown in Figure 1–109.
   - For the *Duplication string*, replace **###_** with your initials to differentiate the model from others.

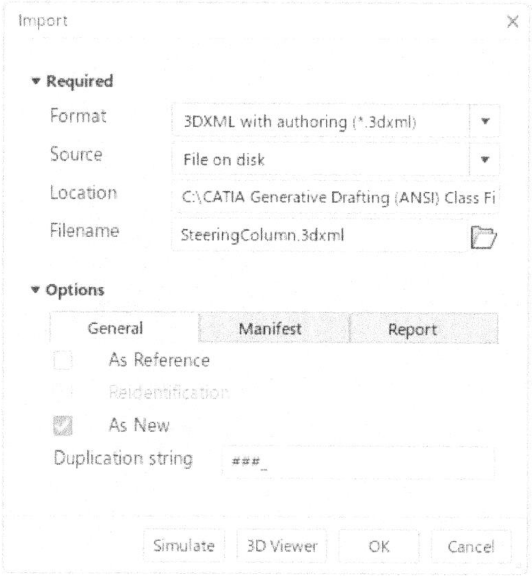

Figure 1–109

5. Click **OK**.

6. The Import Progression window opens momentarily, as shown in Figure 1–110.

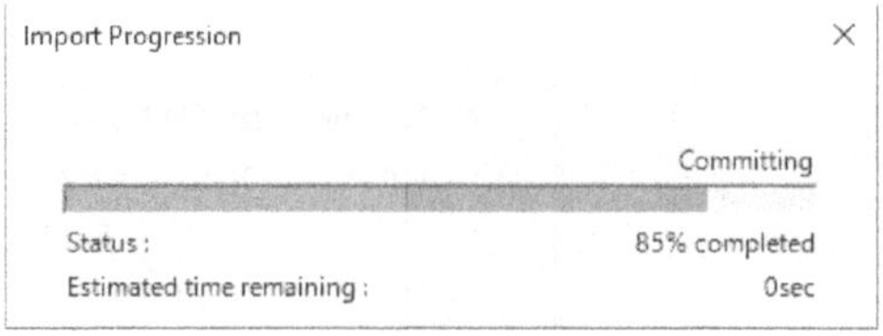

Figure 1–110

7. When the import is finished, the Operation report dialog box appears showing the import was successful, as shown in Figure 1–111.

Figure 1–111

8. Click **OK** in the Operation report dialog box.

9. In the specification tree, right-click **###_Column** and select **Open**.

10. The part displays as shown in Figure 1–112.

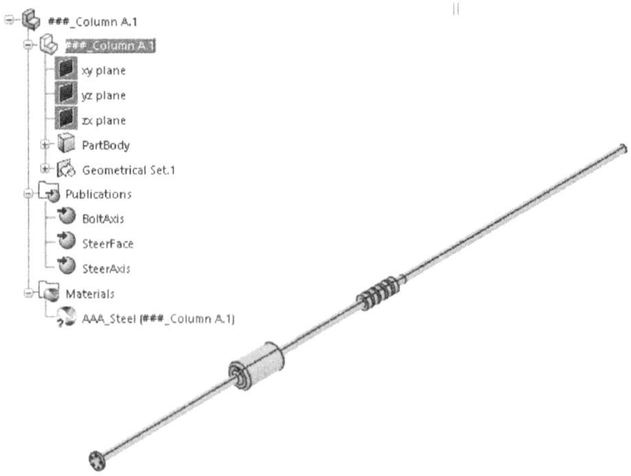

Figure 1–112

Task 2 - Create the drawing.

1. Activate the top level of the tree by double-clicking on **###_Column A.1** so that it turns blue.
2. Right-click on the top level and select **Insert>Drawing.** The drawing creation window appears.
3. For the *Title,* enter **###_SteeringColumn** but replace ### with your initials.
4. Select the *Drawing Information* tab, and select **ANSI-ASME** for the *Standard* and **C ANSI** for the *Sheet Style*, as shown in Figure 1–113.

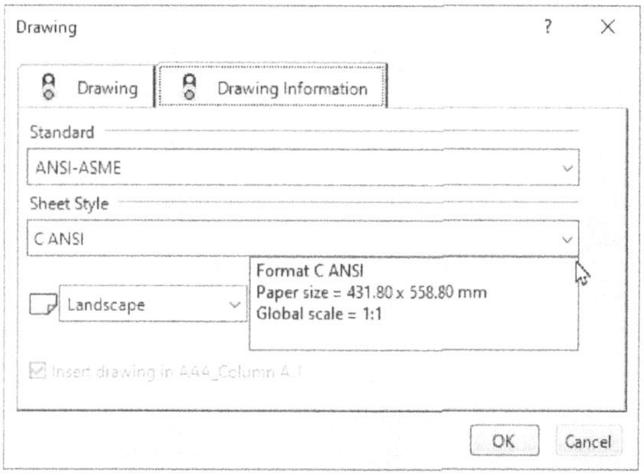

Figure 1–113

5. Select **OK** to complete the drawing creation.
6. Right-click on the new drawing in the tree and select **###_SteeringColumn object>Open in New App**. An empty sheet displays.

Task 3 - Create a Front view.

1. In the View Layout section of the Action Bar, click  (Front View).

2. Activate the *###_SteeringColumn* part tab by selecting it. Orient the part and select the surface shown in Figure 1–114.

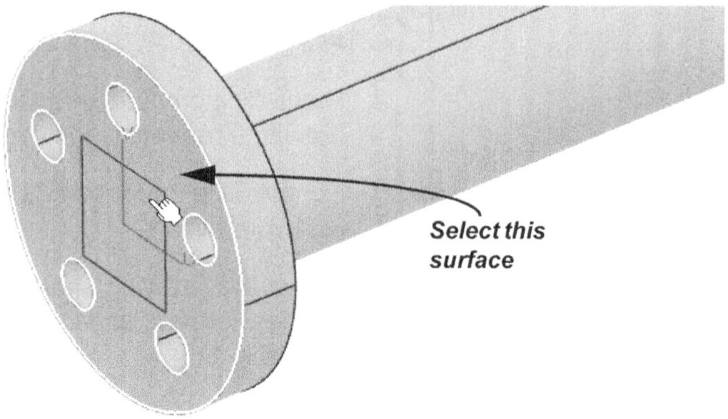

Figure 1–114

3. Select the **EAST** arrow in the compass to obtain the correct orientation, as shown in Figure 1–115.

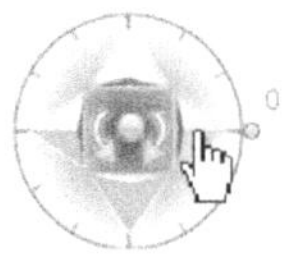

Figure 1–115

4. The view should be oriented as shown in Figure 1–116. Select anywhere on the sheet to complete the view.

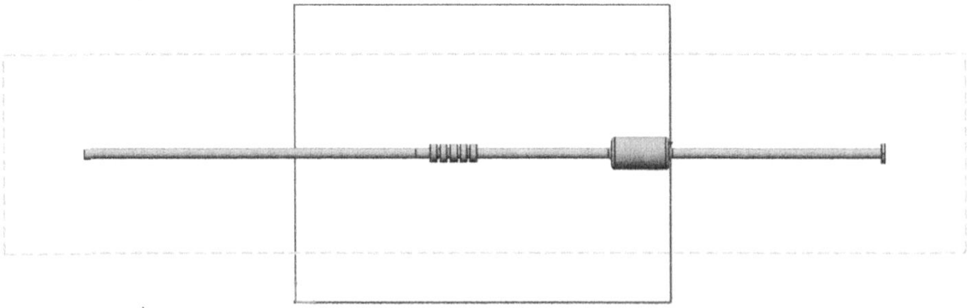

Figure 1–116

Task 4 - Create a broken view.

1. From the View Layout section of the Action Bar, click (Broken View).

2. To specify the first breaking line, select the **Front view** at the position shown in Figure 1–117.

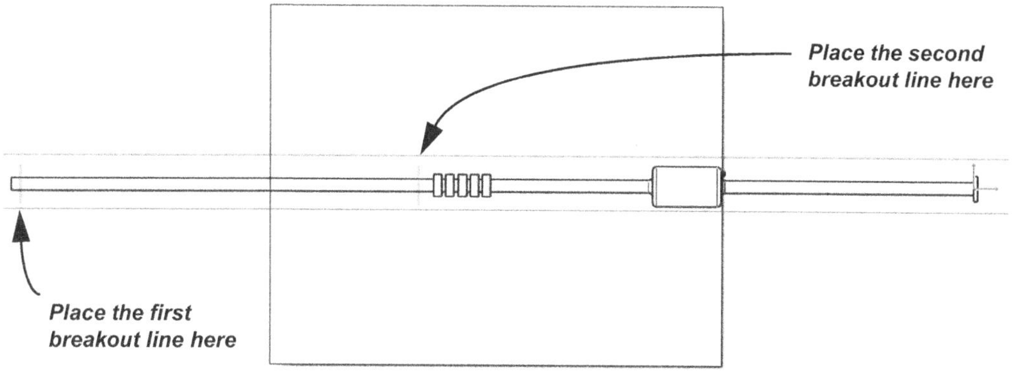

Figure 1–117

3. A dashed green line perpendicular to the column shaft displays. Select the dashed line so that it becomes solid. It defines the orientation of the breakout lines, which can be horizontal or vertical.

4. Select the position of the second vertical breakout line, as shown in Figure 1–117.

5. Select on the sheet to complete the view. The broken front view displays as shown in Figure 1–118.

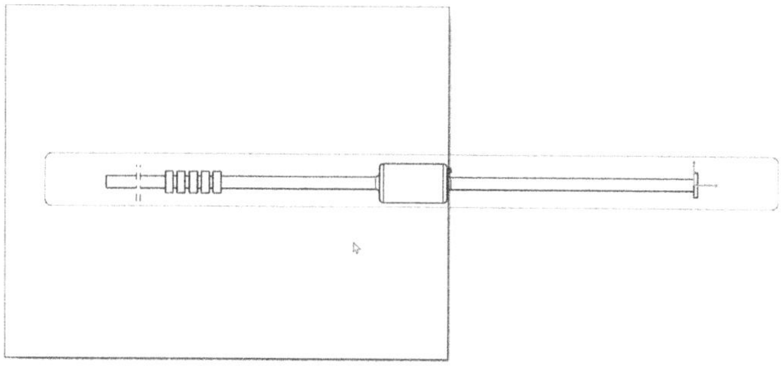

Figure 1–118

6. Create a second broken view on the right side of the column shaft, as shown in Figure 1–119. Note that a dotted line does not display during the placement of the first breakout line because the orientation of the breakout has already been defined for this view.

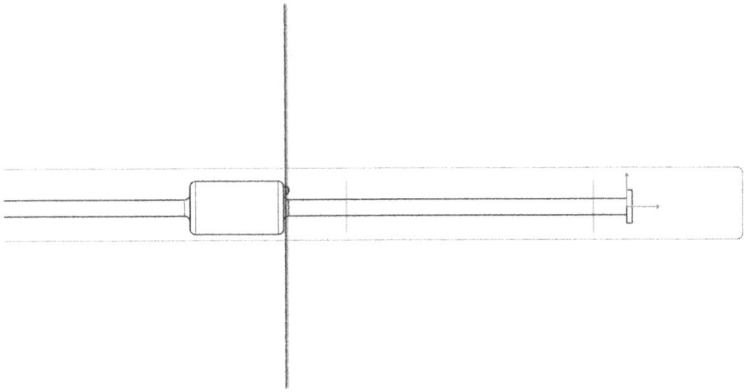

Figure 1–119

7. Click and drag the view to the location shown in Figure 1–120.

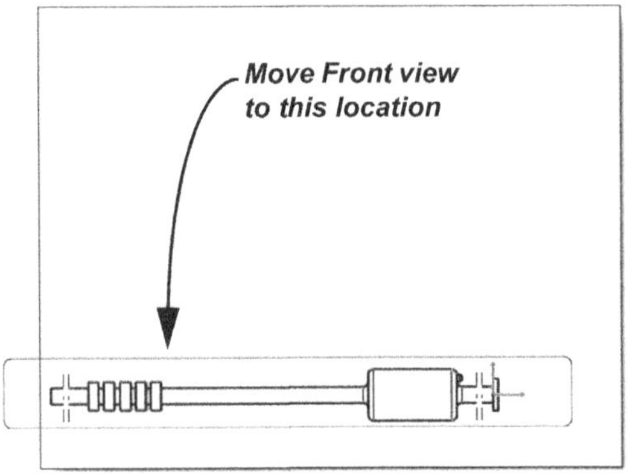

Figure 1–120

Task 5 - Create a projection view.

1. In the View Layout section of the Action Bar, click  (Projection View). Place the projection view at the location shown in Figure 1–121.

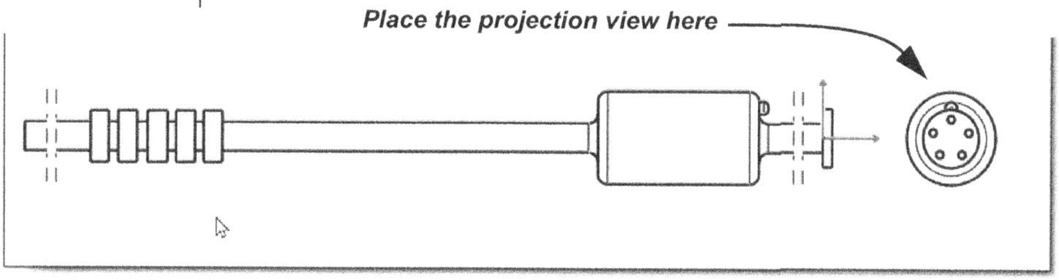

Figure 1–121

Task 6 - Create an isometric view.

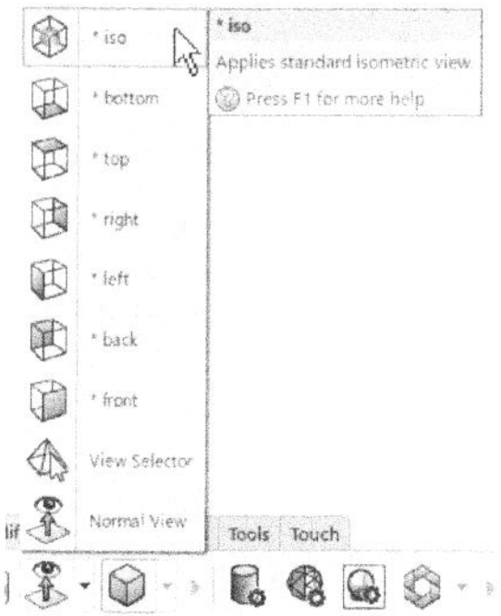

1. In the View Layout section of the Action Bar, click  (Isometric).
2. Activate the ###_ *SteeringColumn* part tab.
3. From the View section of the Action Bar, select  (Isometric) and select the part, as shown in Figure 1–122.

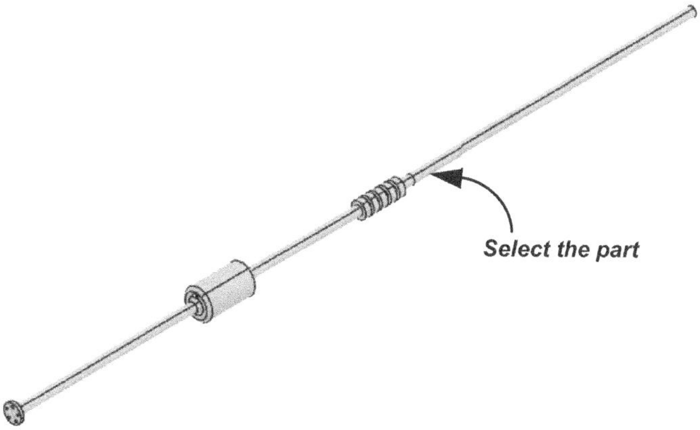

Figure 1–122

4. Place the isometric view. Rescale the *view* to **1:4** and move it to the location shown in Figure 1–123.

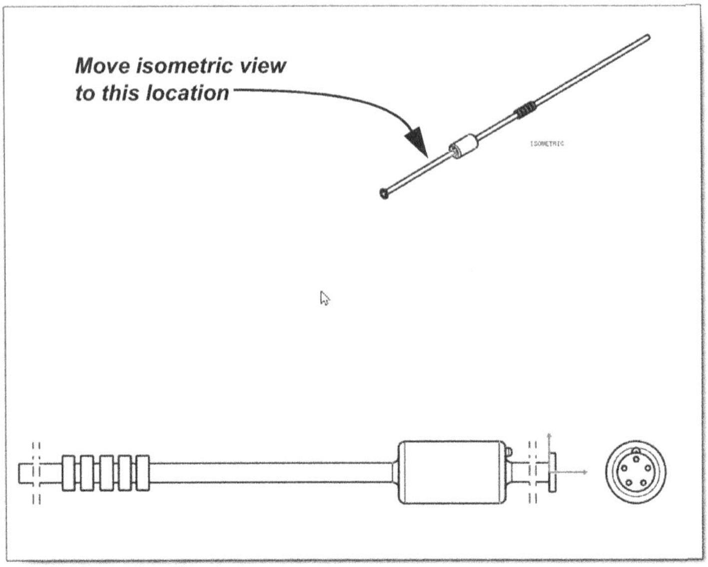

Figure 1–123

Task 7 - Create a Clipping view.

1. Create a new isometric view anywhere on the sheet. Do not rescale it.

2. Ensure that the new isometric view is active.

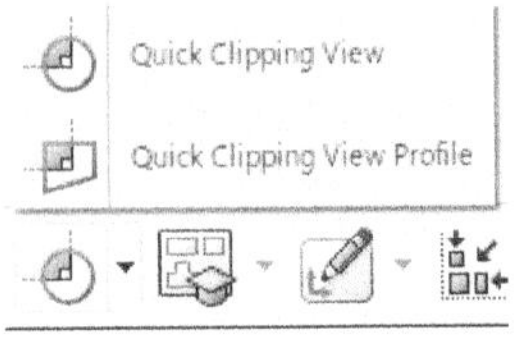

3. Expand the Secondary area of the View Layout section of the Action Bar. You can now click  (Quick Clipping View). Zoom in on the newly created isometric view and define the center of the clipping circle, as shown in Figure 1–124.

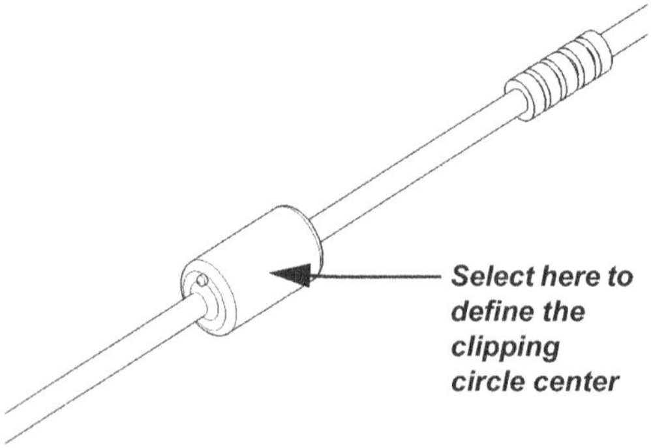

Figure 1–124

4. Expand the clipping circle so that it extends past the steering column spindle. Left-click on the circle to complete the view.

5. Move the clipped view to the location shown in Figure 1–125.

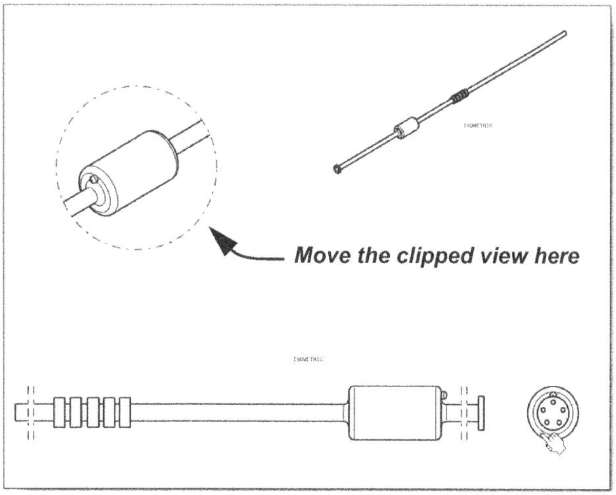

Figure 1–125

Task 8 - Display hidden lines in the clipped isometric view.

1. In the specification tree, right-click on the second **Isometric view** and select **Properties**. In the *Generation* tab, in the *Dress-up* area, select **Hidden Lines** to enable it, as shown in Figure 1–126.

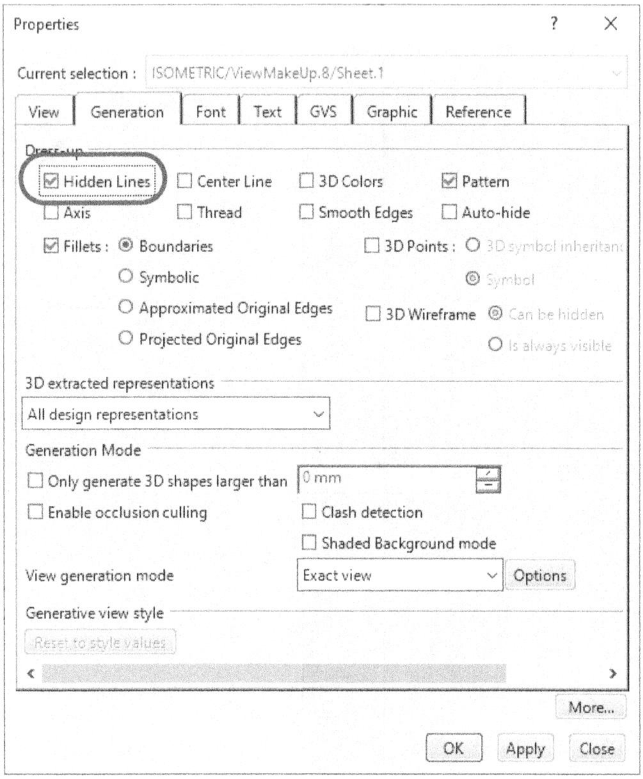

Figure 1–126

2. Click **OK** to close the Properties dialog box. The completed drawing displays as shown in Figure 1–127.

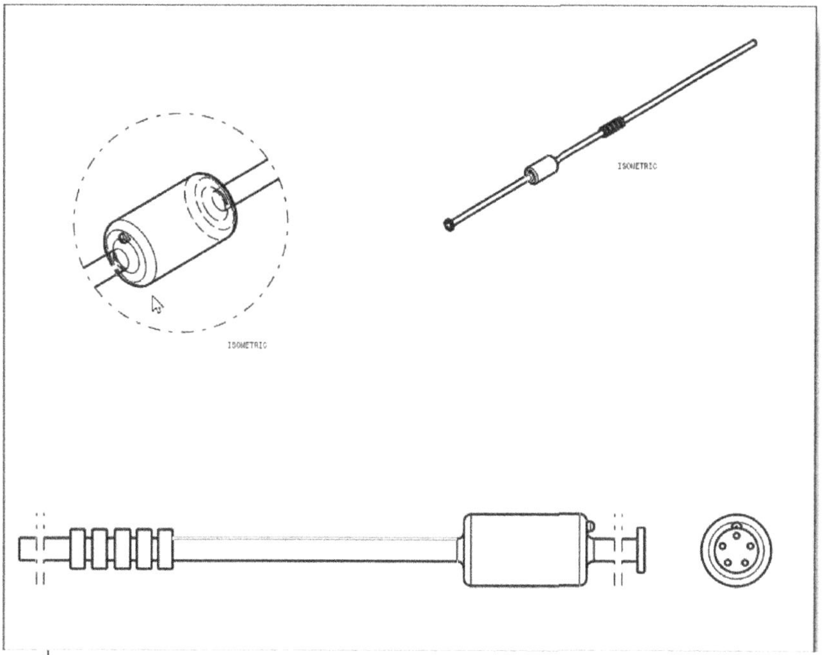

Figure 1–127

3. Save the drawing and close all of the tabs.

Practice 1d Create a Product Drawing

Practice Objectives

- Create a product drawing.
- Create drawing views using the View Wizard.
- Create an auxiliary view.

In this practice, you create a product drawing for **ExhaustManifold.3dxml**.

Task 1 - Import and open the assembly.

1. In the Top Bar, click (Add)>**Import**.
2. In the Import dialog box, click (Open).
3. Browse to the practice files folder, select **ExhaustManifold.3dxml**, and click **Open**.
4. Ensure the settings in the Import dialog box match those shown in Figure 1–128.
    - For the *Duplication string*, replace **###_** with your initials to differentiate the model from others.

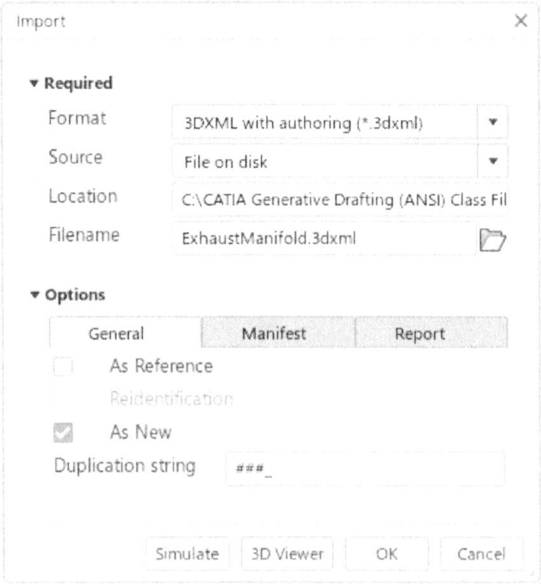

Figure 1–128

5. Click **OK**.
6. When the Operation report dialog box appears showing the import was successful, click **OK**.
7. In the specification tree, right-click **###_ExhaustFlange** and select **Open**.
8. The assembly displays as shown in Figure 1–129.

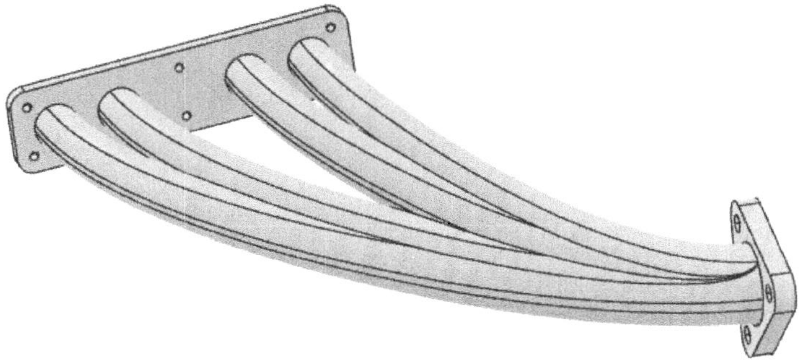

Figure 1–129

Task 2 - Create a new drawing.

1. Create a new drawing file with *Title* set to **###_Exhaust Flange_Drawing** but replace ### with your initals.
2. Under the *Drawing Information* tab, use **ANSI-ASME** as the *Standard* and **E ANSI** as the *Sheet Style*, then select **OK**.
3. Right-click on the newly created sheet (###_ExhaustFlange_Drawing) in the tree and select **###_ExhaustFlange_Drawing object>Open in New App**.

Task 3 - Set the global scale value.

1. In the specification tree, right-click on **Sheet.1** and select **Properties**.

2. Enter a *Scale* value of **1:3**. This controls the default scale for any new view that is added to the sheet. The Properties dialog box opens as shown in Figure 1–130.

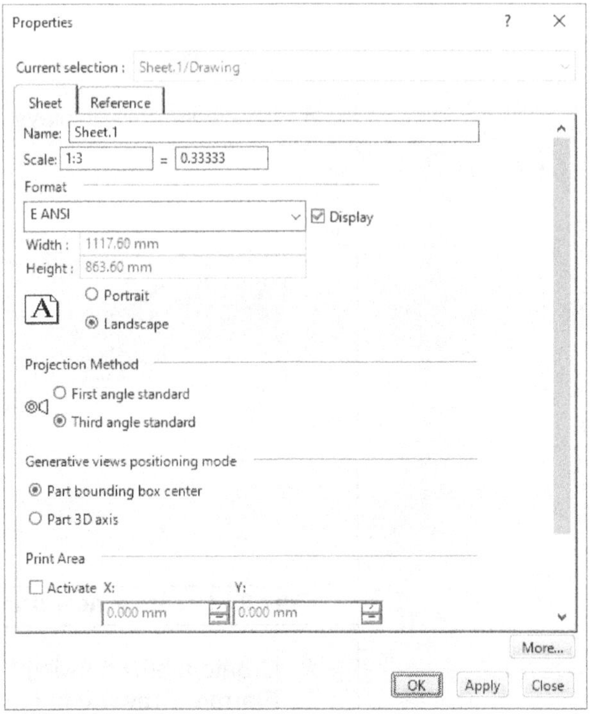

Figure 1–130

3. Click **OK**.

Task 4 - Use the View Wizard to create a drafting view layout.

1. Click  (Wizard) from the expanded View Layout section of the Action Bar. The View Wizard dialog box opens, enabling you to predefine the configuration of the layout.

2. In the *Minimum distance between each view* field, enter **195**, as shown in Figure 1–131.

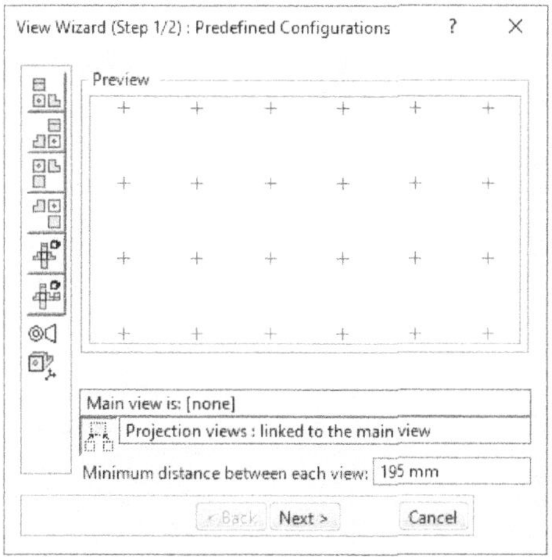

Figure 1–131

3. In the View Wizard dialog box, click the icon. The layout displays in the View Wizard Preview, as shown in Figure 1–132.

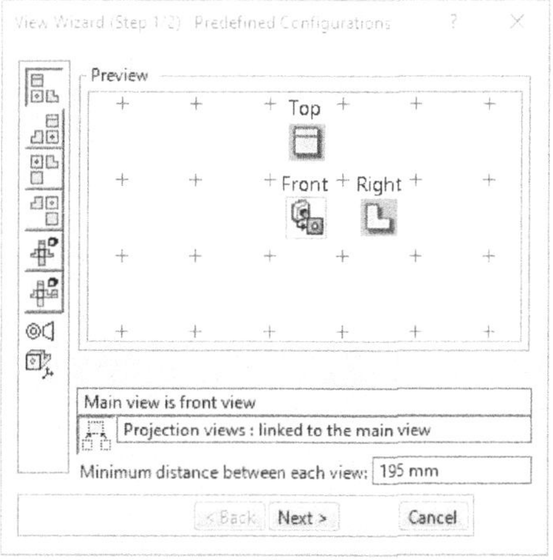

Figure 1–132

4. Click **Next**.

5. Click  to add an isometric view to the layout. Position the isometric view as shown in Figure 1–133.

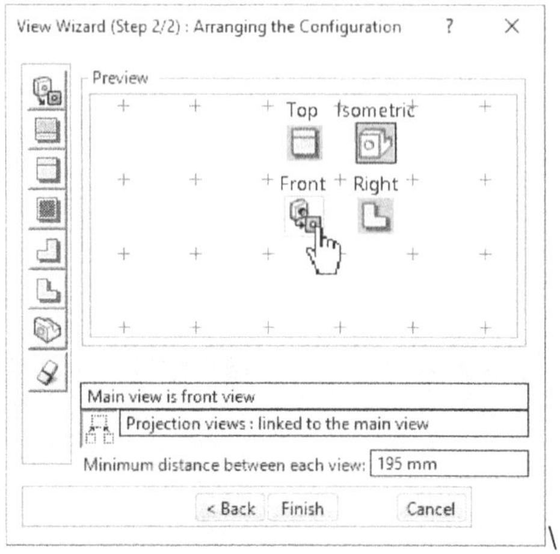

Figure 1–133

6. Click **Finish**.

7. Activate the assembly model tab by selecting on *###_ExhaustManifold* tab with the 3D Model shown in it. Rotate the assembly model and select the surface shown in Figure 1–134.

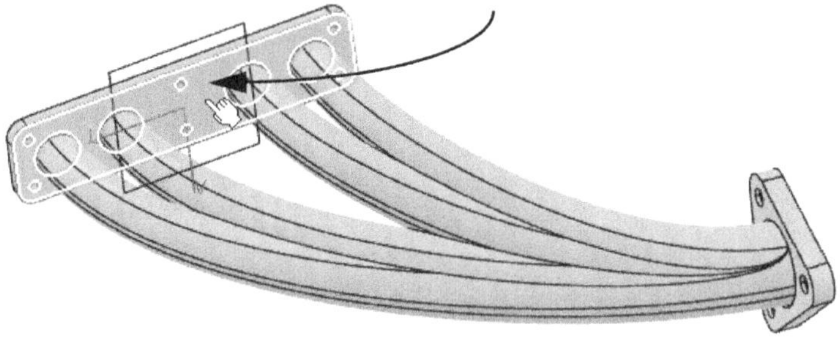

Figure 1–134

8. Accept the views by selecting anywhere in the display. The drawing updates as shown in Figure 1–135.

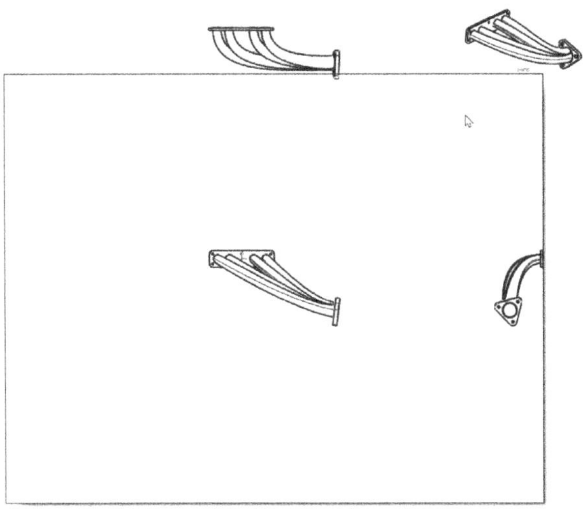

Figure 1–135

9. Move the Front view to the location shown in Figure 1–136. Note that all other views move relative to the Front view.

If the views cannot be moved because the frames around the views cannot be seen, toggle  (Display Frame) in the View section of the Action Bar.

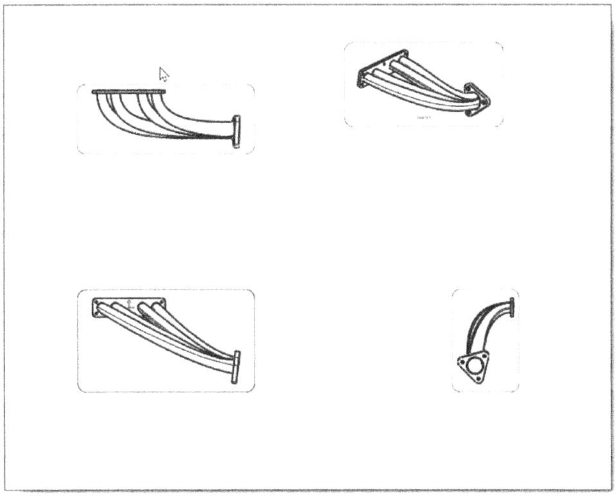

Figure 1–136

10. In the Properties dialog box of **Sheet.1**, change the *Scale* to **1:2**. All of the views update to reflect this change, as shown in Figure 1–137.

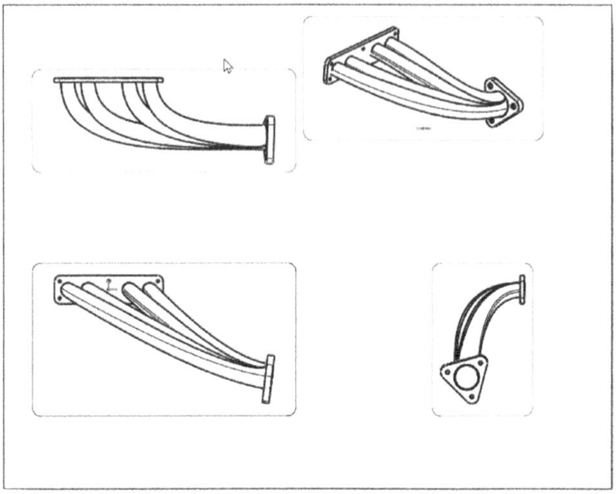

Figure 1–137

11. Modify the *Scale* value of the isometric view to **1:4**, as shown in Figure 1–138.

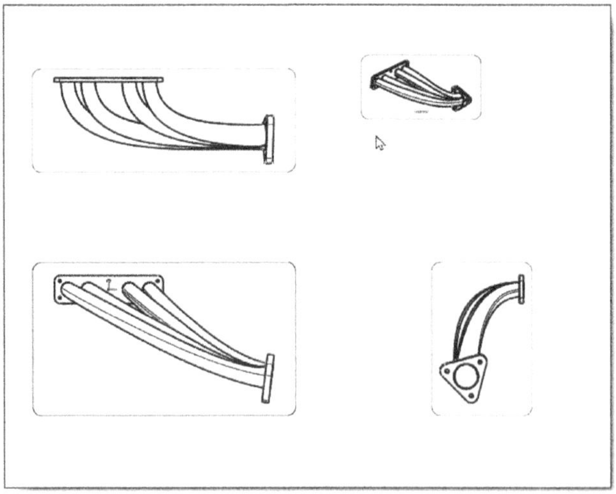

Figure 1–138

12. Move the Right view further to the right, as shown in Figure 1–139.

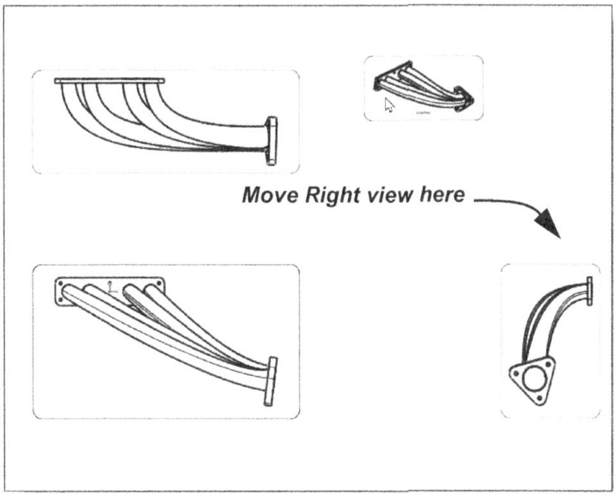

Figure 1–139

Task 5 - Create an auxiliary view of the exhaust flange.

1. Zoom in on the Front view, as shown in Figure 1–140.

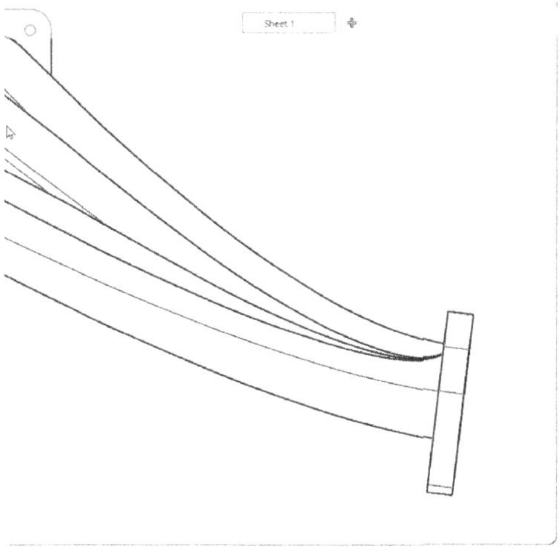

Figure 1–140

2. Ensure that the Front view is the active view.

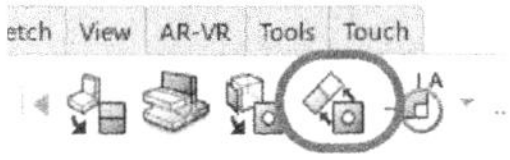

3. In the expanded area of the View Layout section of the Action Bar, click  (Auxiliary).

4. Select the edge of the Front view geometry, as shown in Figure 1–141.

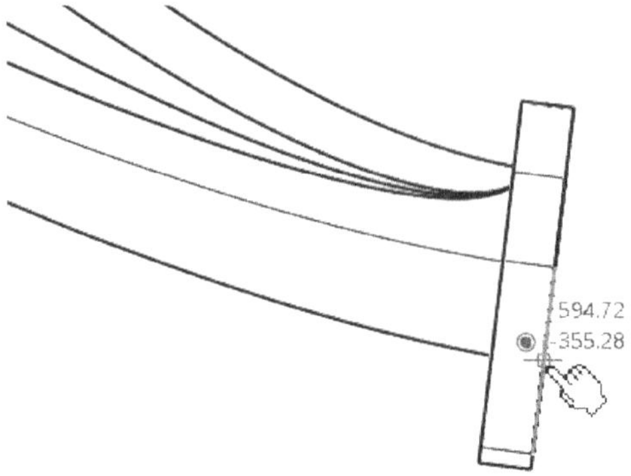

Figure 1–141

5. Select a location to the right of the Front view geometry, as shown in Figure 1–142.

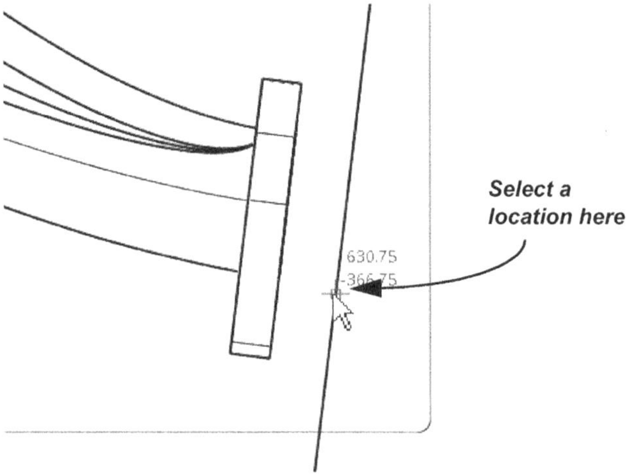

Figure 1–142

6. Move the cursor to the right of the Front view to locate the auxiliary view, as shown in Figure 1–143. Click to place the view.

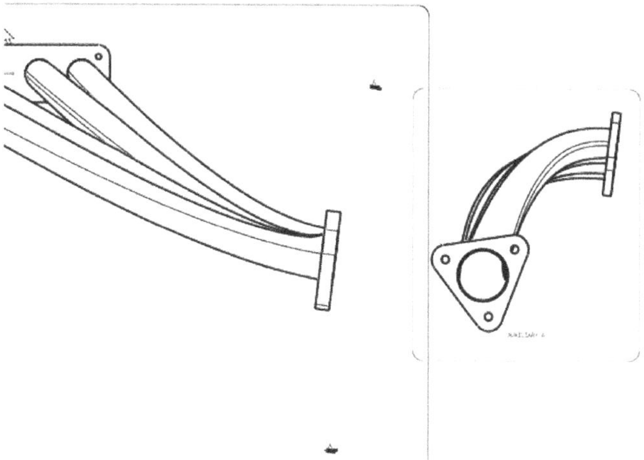

Figure 1–143

Task 6 - Modify the auxiliary view.

1. Double-click on the directional arrows of the auxiliary view, as shown in Figure 1–144. The system opens a context menu.

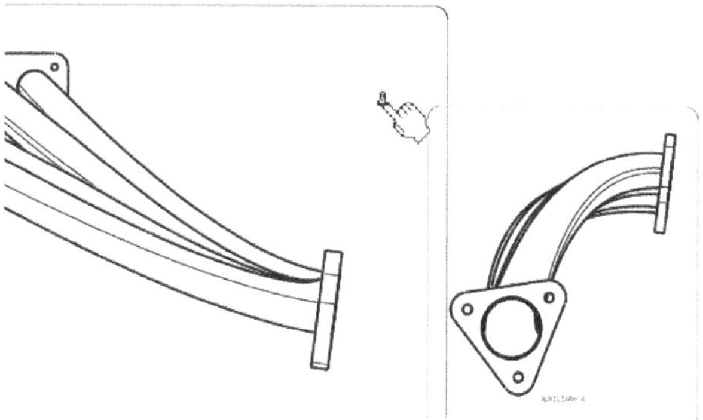

Figure 1–144

2. In the context menu, click (Reverse View Direction) to invert the arrows.

3. Click and hold the left mouse button to drag the lower vertex of the line to the location shown in Figure 1–145.

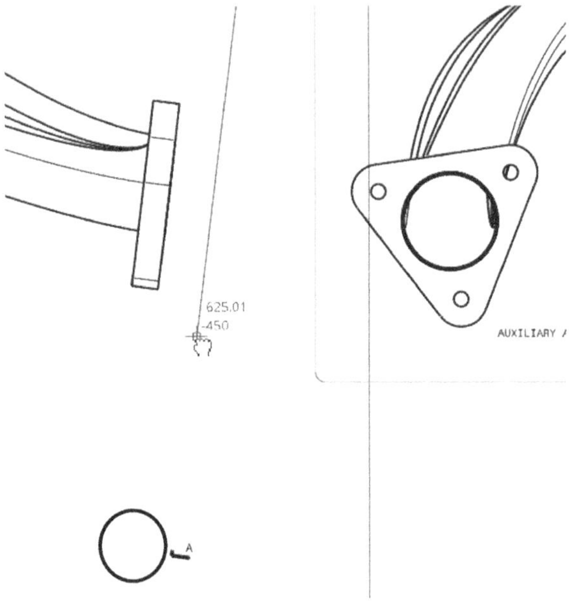

Figure 1–145

4. Move the other end of the line to the location shown in Figure 1–146.

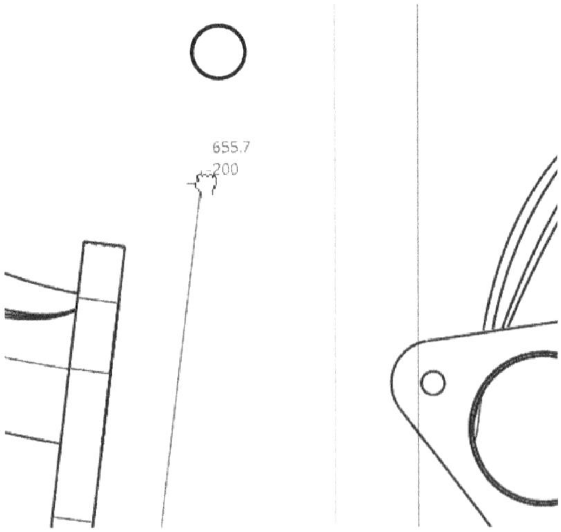

Figure 1–146

5. Click anywhere to complete the modification. The drawing displays as shown in Figure 1–147.

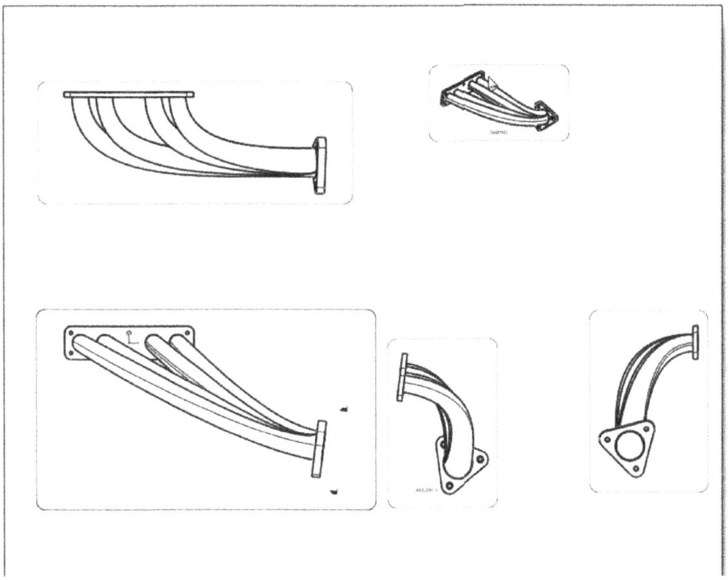

Figure 1–147

6. Move the auxiliary view to the right and the projection view to the left, as shown in Figure 1–148.

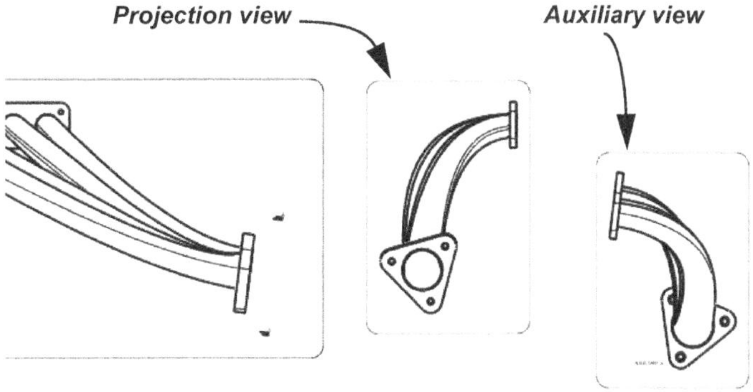

Figure 1–148

7. Save the drawing and close all tabs.

Practice 1e (Optional) Section and Cut Views

Practice Objectives

- Create a part drawing without instruction.
- Create a section cut with a 3D profile.

In this practice, you will create a part drawing using **TransitionTube.3dxml**.

1. Import and open **TransitionTube.3dxml**. The part displays as shown in Figure 1–149.

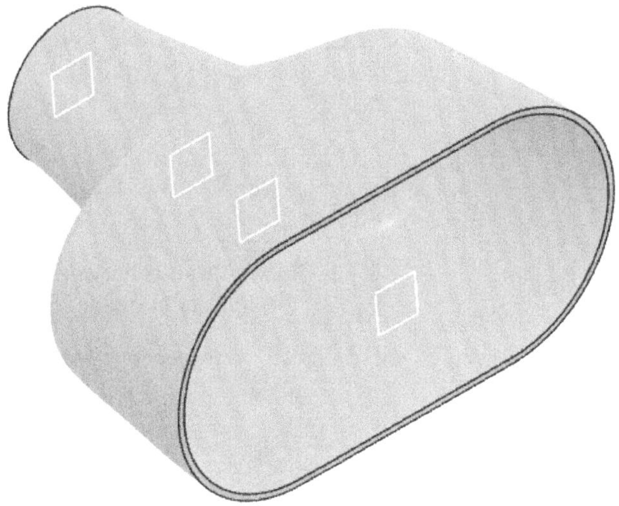

Figure 1–149

2. Create a new drawing file. Enter **ANSI-ASME** for the *Standard* and select **D ANSI** for the *Sheet Style.*

3. Open the newly created drawing in a new app.

4. Produce the views shown in Figure 1–150. The section cut views are aligned to the sections used to build the transition tube part. Build these sections in the 3D model to ensure that they are located correctly.

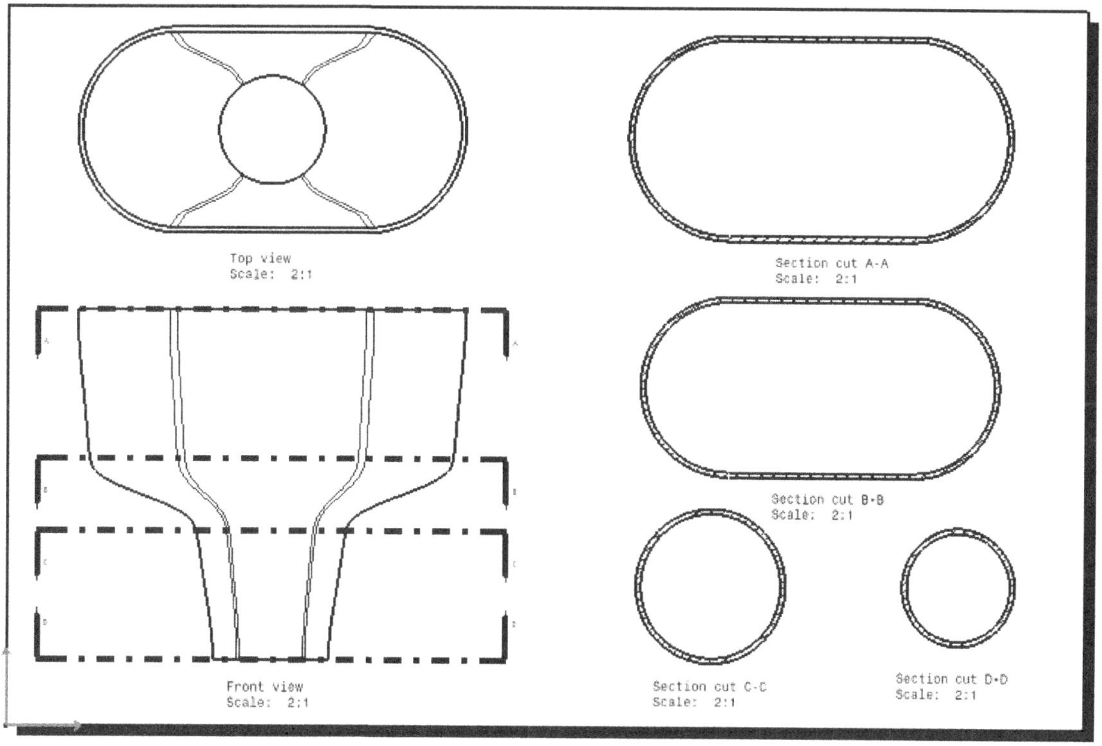

Figure 1–150

5. Save and close all of the tabs.

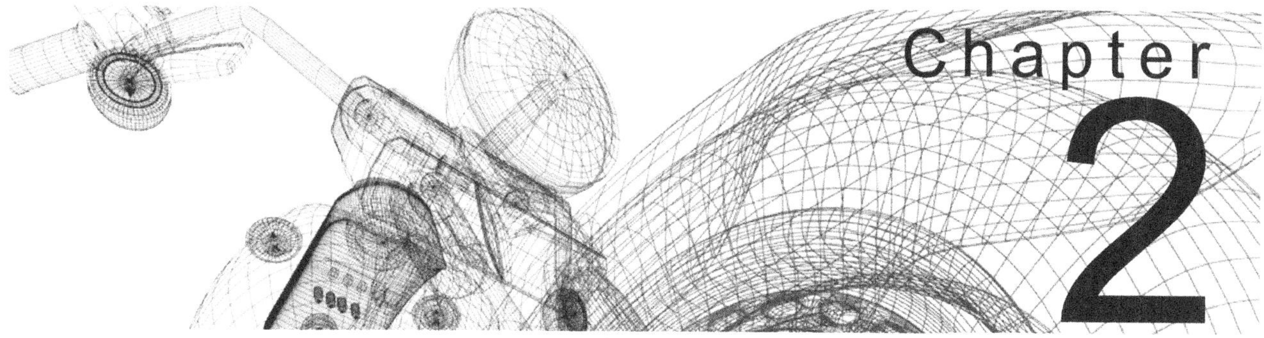

View Modification

This chapter focuses on the methods available for modifying drawing views.

Learning Objectives in This Chapter

- Understand how to manipulate and position views.
- Recognize and apply the various view properties.
- Recognize and apply the various section and detail view properties.
- Apply various hatching properties.
- Modify profiles.
- Understand the 3D View support.

2.1 View Manipulation

This section describes the following ways of manipulating a view:

- Delete
- Hide/Show
- Show Geometry in All Viewpoints

Delete View

To delete a view, right-click on the view in the display or specification tree and select **Delete**.

Hide/Show

You can hide a view to simplify the sheet. To hide a view, right-click on it in the display or specification tree and select **Hide/Show**.

Hidden views display in the hidden space. Click (Swap visible space) from the View section to toggle between visible and hidden space.

Show Geometry in All Viewpoints

If you are not sure how the geometry in a specific view relates to the 3D geometry of the part or product model, you can use the 3D model to assist you. By selecting (Show Geometry in All Viewpoints), a 3D view of the model displays in a sub-window. Any selected in the drawing geometry highlights in all views and in 3D sub-window to help you locate it. If the **Animate** option is activated, the model in the sub-window also orients according to the selected view.

An example is shown in Figure 2–1. This command is not part of the default Action Bar and will need to be added by using **Me>Preferences>Customize>Sections** and then adding it to the desired section.

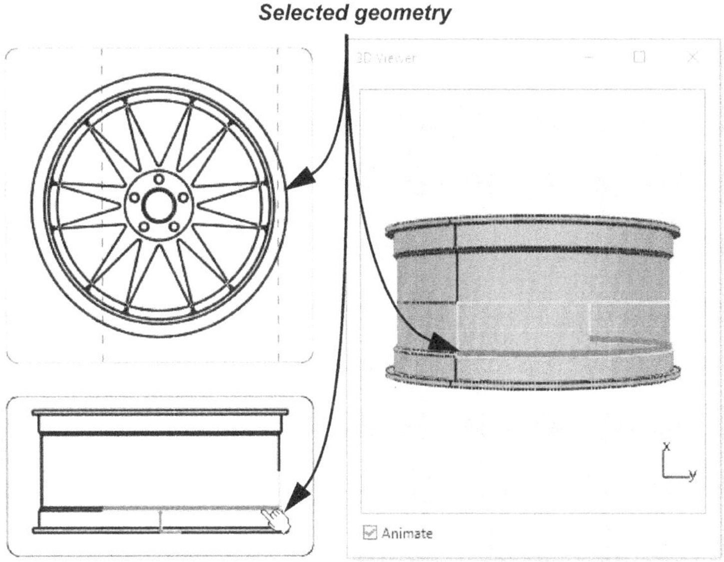

Figure 2–1

2.2 View Positioning

This section introduces view positioning commands that can be accessed from the shortcut menu, as shown in Figure 2–2, or by manipulating the view directly on the drawing.

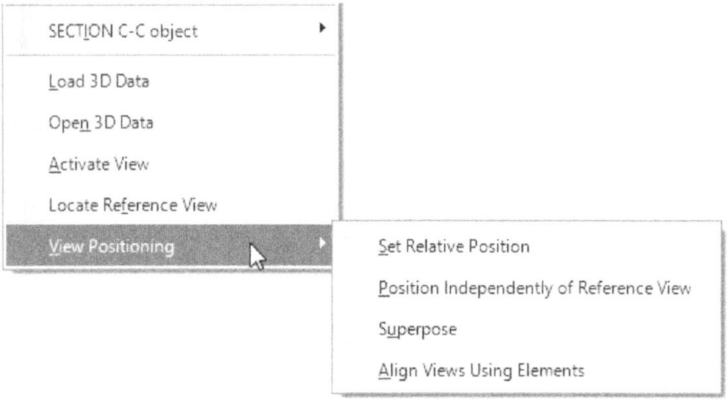

Figure 2–2

The following topics are covered:

- Moving Views
- Set Relative Position
- Superpose
- Align Views Using Elements

Moving Views

You can move a view in the same sheet or to another sheet. To move a view in the same sheet, select the colored line frame of the view and drag it to the required location.

If a parent view is moved, any child views are also moved because of the view alignment. To unalign a view, right-click on it in the specification tree and select **View Positioning>Position Independently of Reference View**. You can undo this operation by selecting **View Positioning>Position According to Reference View**.

You can use standard Windows shortcut keys: <Ctrl>+<X> (Cut) and <Ctrl>+<V> (Paste).

To move a view to another sheet, cut and paste it from the display or specification tree. You can press <Ctrl> to select multiple views. When pasting the views, select the required sheet in the specification tree. Once your views have been pasted, you can manipulate their location.

Set Relative Position

When the **View Positioning>Set Relative Position** option is selected, a positioning line and grid display on the model, as shown in Figure 2–3. The positioning line is anchored to the view at the center grid point.

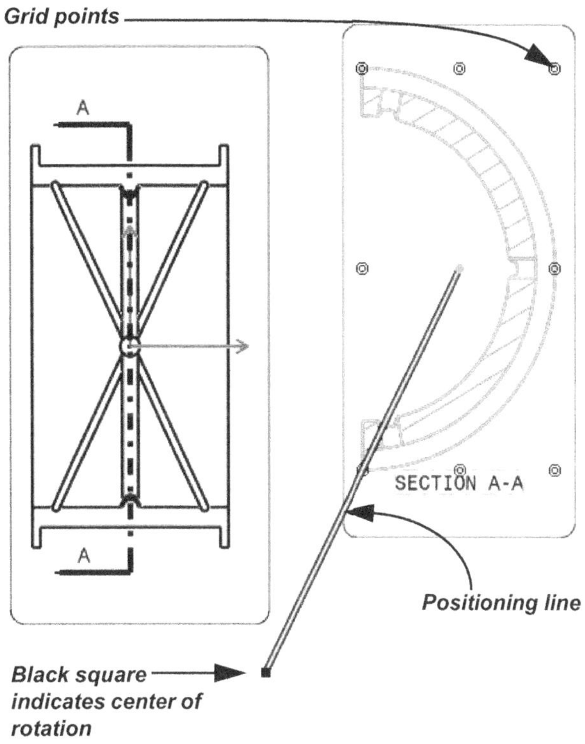

Figure 2–3

How To: Position Relative to Another View

1. Select the black square at the end of the positioning line. The square displays a blinking crosshair.
2. In the specification tree or the frame of another view in the drawing, select a view. The black square snaps to the origin of the selected view, enabling you to position relative to the selected view, as shown in Figure 2–4.

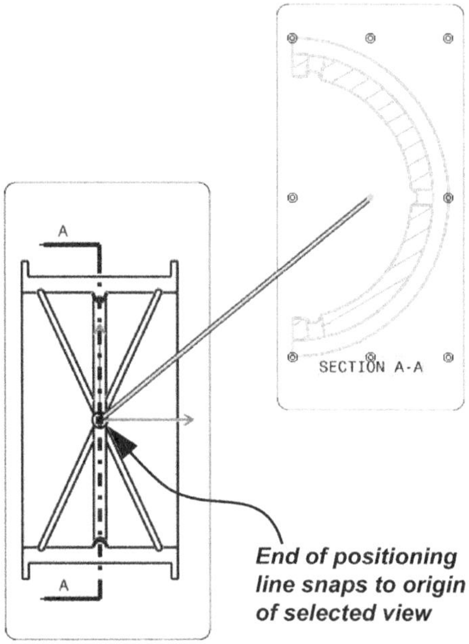

Figure 2–4

3. The view can now be repositioned in the following ways:
   - Select and drag the positioning line to translate the view along the positioning line.
   - Select and drag on the green dot to rotate the view about the black square.
   - Select a grid point to move the positioning line to a new anchor location on the view.

Note that when translating or rotating the view, coordinate information displays on the drawing, as shown in Figure 2–5.

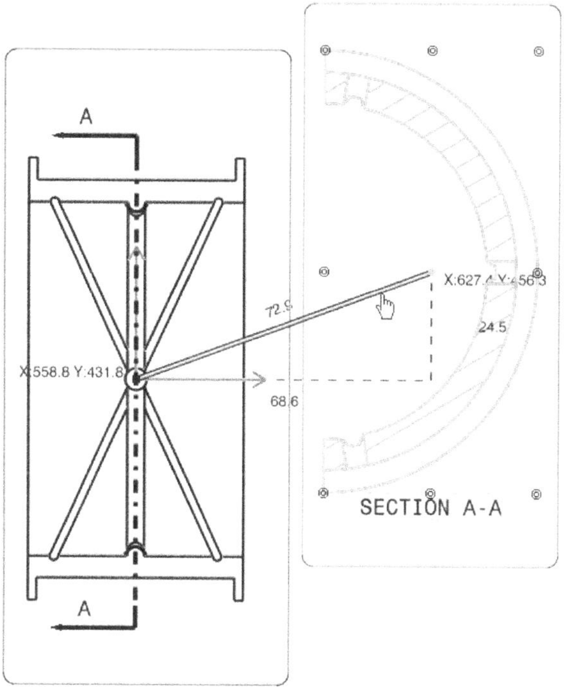

Figure 2–5

4. Once the view has been moved, select anywhere in the drawing background to complete the operation.

If the view is initially aligned to a parent view, the system automatically positions the view independent of the reference view during a **Set Relative Position** operation.

Superpose

Superpose is used to place a view directly on top of another view. The purpose of superposing is to display the various arrangements or the range of motion of an assembly.

To superpose a view, right-click on the border of the view to be moved and select **View Positioning>Superpose**. CATIA prompts you to select a view to use as a reference. The view selected first is placed on the center of the view referenced second. The Superposed view is not locked in place. You can still drag and change its location using the available view positioning techniques.

Align Views Using Elements

This operation aligns a view by referencing existing geometry between the two views. Right-click on the view border to be moved and select **View Positioning>Align Views Using Elements**, then select an edge or axis from each view. The system positions the first view so that the two selected elements are co-linear. An example is shown in Figure 2–6.

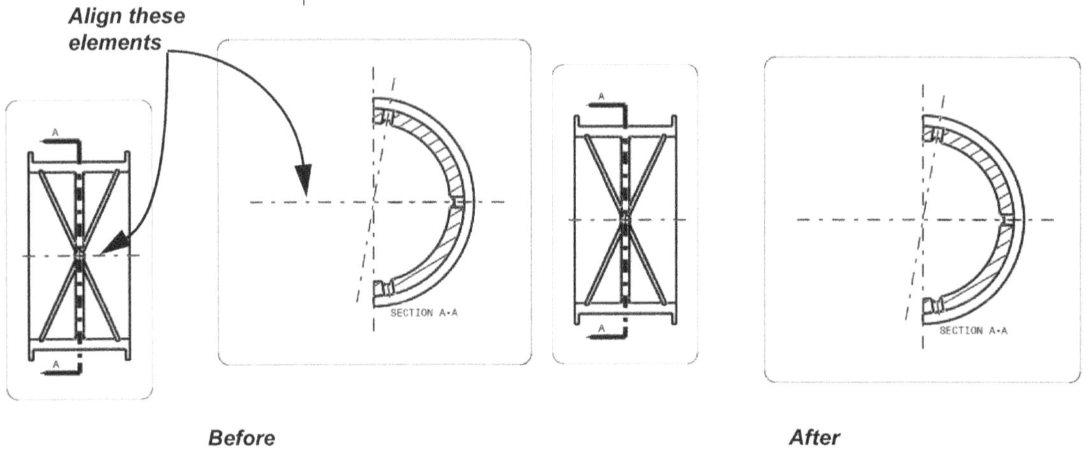

Figure 2–6

2.3 View Properties

View properties enable you to customize the display of all views except Quick views. To access view properties, right-click on the view and select **Properties**. The Properties dialog box opens as shown in Figure 2–7.

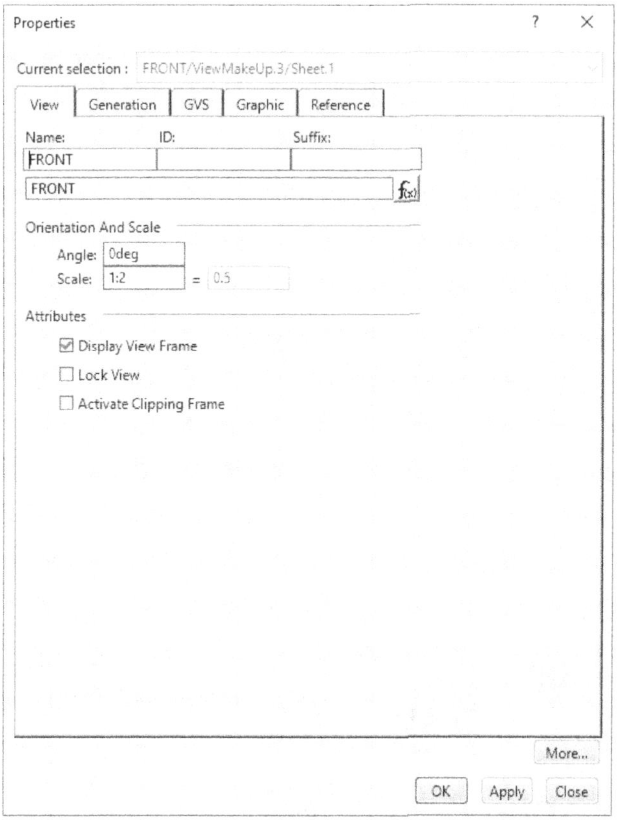

Figure 2–7

View Properties window settings are divided up into different tabs, including *View*, *Generation*, *GVS*, *Graphics*, and *Reference*. The following areas of the View Properties dialog box are covered:

- Attributes
- Scale and Orientation
- Dress-Up
- Name
- Generation Mode

Attributes

The options in the *Attributes* area are described as follows:

Option	Description
Display View Frame	By disabling this option, the colored view border lines no longer display. Once toggled off, the view cannot be moved or manipulated in the main window. It can still be accessed using the specification tree.
Lock View	When enabled, the properties for the view can no longer be modified, nor does the drawing update with 3D model changes.
Activate Clipping Frame	Displays a clipping box on the view, which can be resized and positioned to control the viewable area as shown below. 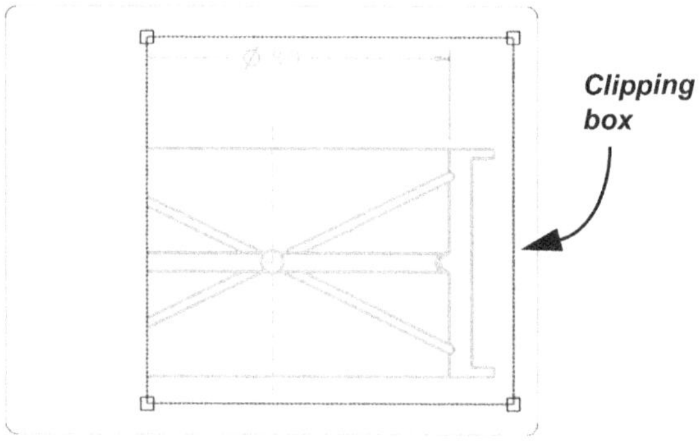

Orientation and Scale

These options control the scale and angle of the selected view. They can be applied to a child view independent of the parent.

Dress-Up

The *Dress-Up* area controls the display of dress-up elements on the view using the options described below:

Option	Description
Hidden Lines	Displays hidden lines on the view.
Center Line	Displays center lines on the view.
3D Colors	Displays the colors assigned to the 3D model in the drawing view.
Pattern	Controls if patterns are to be generated on the views during update.
Axis	Displays axes on the view.
Thread	Displays threads on the view.

Fillets	Controls the display of fillets using the four options shown below. Note that fillets that display with any option other than **Boundaries** do not inherit 3D colors, and do not produce associative dimensions. 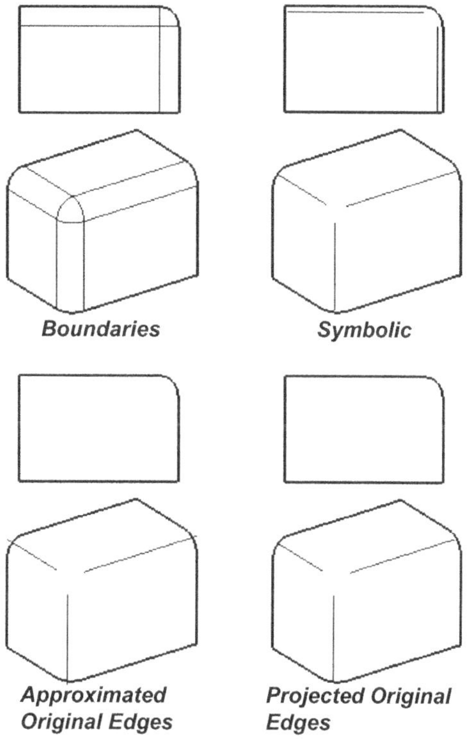
3D Points	Controls the display of reference point features present in the model. The system can reuse the point symbol assigned in the model by selecting the **3D symbol inheritance** option. To define a custom point display, select an option in the Symbol drop-down list.
3D Wireframe	Controls the display of sketches, wireframe, and surface elements present in the model. With the **Can be hidden** option enabled, the system applies hidden line removal to the elements if the **Hidden Line** option is enabled. If **Is Always visible** is selected, the visibility of the element is controlled by the 3D model.

Name

The name of the view is controlled using the *Prefix*, *ID*, and *Suffix* fields. The *Name Editor With Formula* field displays the values of *Name*, *ID*, and *Suffix* together (by default, as shown in Figure 2–8).

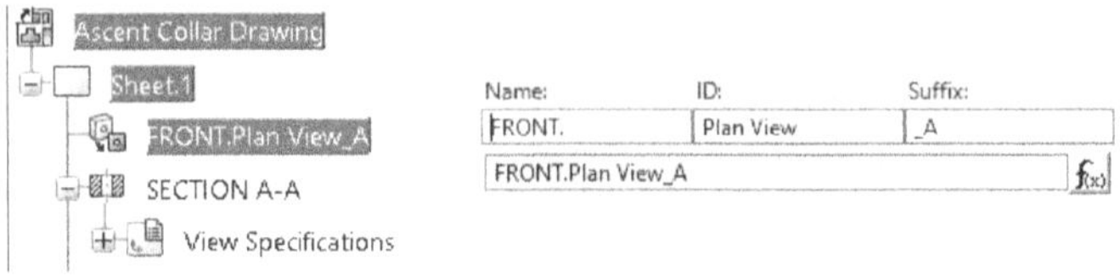

Figure 2–8

Click  to customize the formula.

Generation Mode

Options for the *Generation Mode* area in the View Properties dialog box are described as follows:

Option		Description
Only generate parts larger than		Specifies the lower limit for size of part that displays in assembly view. This is a good method of eliminating fasteners and other small geometry to improve update times for a view.
Enable occlusion culling		Applies to assemblies that have been opened in Visualization mode. When enabled, the system only loads components that can be seen in the resulting view. Improves update times for the view.
View generation mode		Controls the way CATIA generates view geometry. Selecting an option other than **Exact view** disables access to a variety of options in the View Properties dialog box.
	Exact view	Generates the view from the exact 3D model.
	CGR	Improves view generation time using a Computer Graphics Representation (CGR) to generate the view. This results in a faceted display of the external view geometry so that individual features cannot be selected. With this option, only the **Hidden Lines** and **3D Spec** dress-up options are available.

Approximate	Improves view generation time using an approximation method to generate the view. Clicking **Options** opens the Approximation mode dialog box, which enables you to control the *Level of Detail* (LOD) as shown below. The higher the LOD value, the more time required to generate the view. 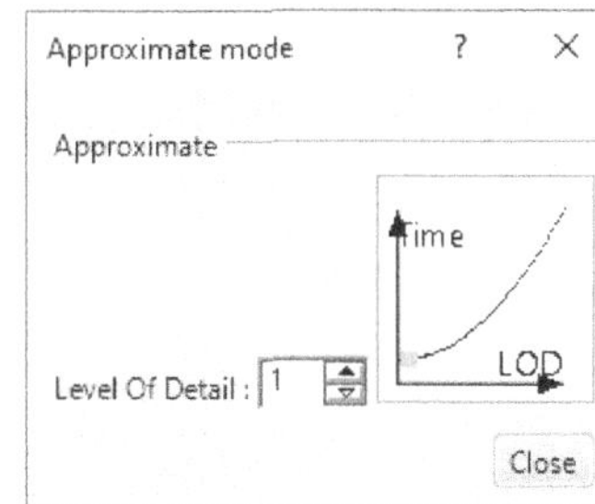 This mode is suited to large, complex assemblies and should not be used on simple part drawing views. With this option, only the **Hidden Lines**, **Pattern** and **Smooth Edges** dress-up options are available.
Raster	Converts the view to a raster image so that the resulting view is pixelated. Therefore, geometry cannot be selected for dimension creation. Clicking **Options** opens the Exact generation mode Options dialog box, which enables you to display the view using hidden line removal, shading, or shading with edges as shown below. You can also define the visualization and print quality of the view. 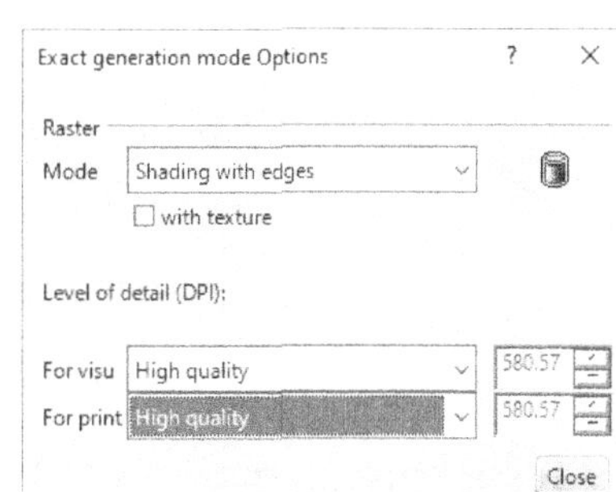 With this option, only the **Hidden Lines**, **3D Colors, Pattern**, and **3D SmoothEdges** dress-up options are available.

2.4 Section and Detail Properties

To modify the callouts for section and detail views, right-click on the arrows and select **Properties**. The Properties dialog box opens, as shown in Figure 2–9.

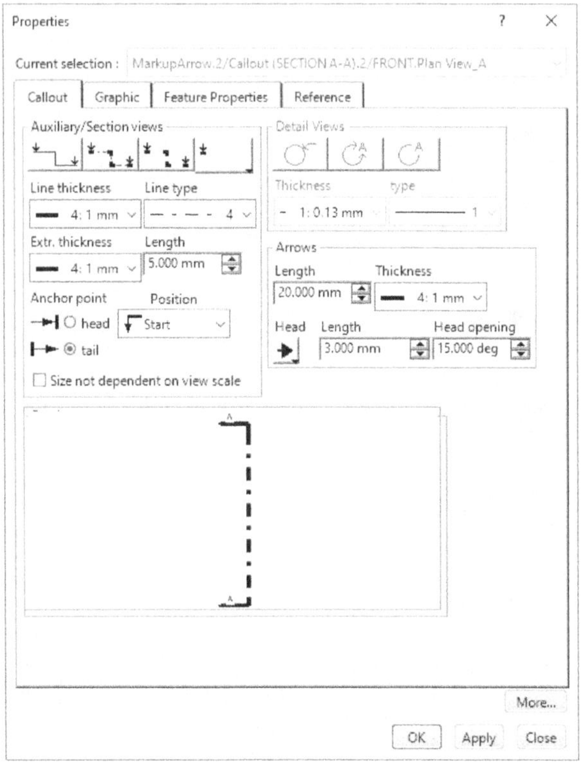

Figure 2–9

Depending on the type of callout selected, either the *Auxiliary/ Section views* or *Detail Views* fields are enabled. This dialog box enables you to customize the style and shape of the callout and to control how the font and text display.

Recreating the Callout

Callouts for section, detail, and auxiliary views can be recreated if they, or the view containing the callout, are deleted.

How To: Recreate a Callout

1. Right-click on the section, detail, or auxiliary view, and select *** object>Add Callout**, as shown in Figure 2–10.

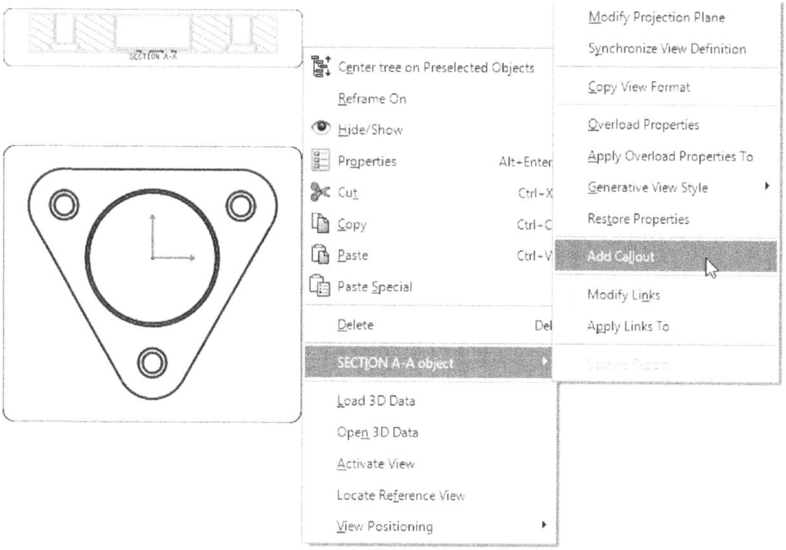

Figure 2–10

2. In the working area or specification tree, select the target view to add the callout, as shown in Figure 2–11.

If the target view that you want to add the callout is in a different sheet, the target view must be selected in the specification tree.

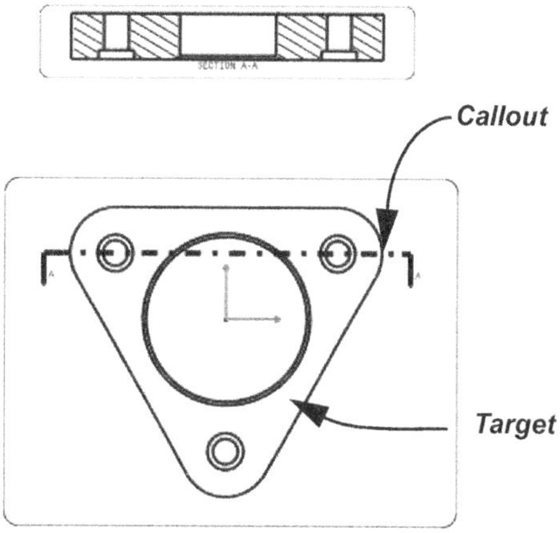

Figure 2–11

2.5 Hatching Properties

To modify section hatching, right-click on a hatch line in the section view and select **Properties**. The Properties dialog box opens as shown in Figure 2–12.

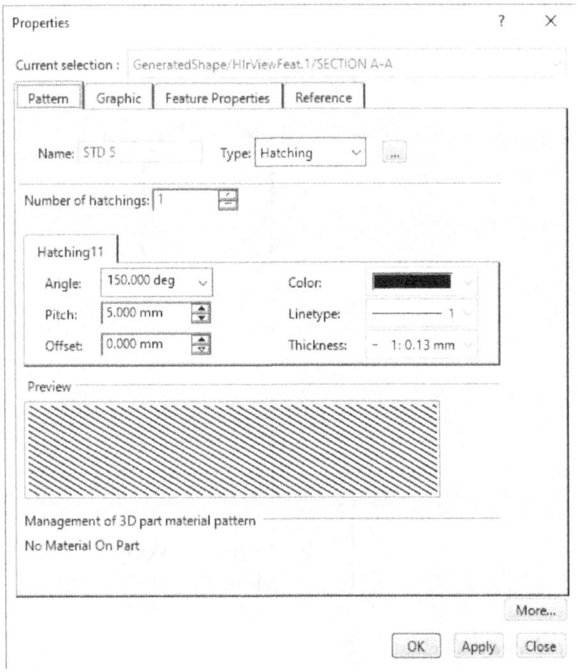

Figure 2–12

The *Pattern* tab enables you to modify the angle, pitch (spacing), offset, color, line type, and thickness of the hatching display.

2.6 Profile Modification

Section Profiles

Section profiles can be modified at any time by double-clicking on the section view profile in the parent view. This displays a context menu. You can invert, recreate, and move sections using the context menu, as shown in Figure 2–13. Selection in the background will cause the context menu to finish and hide.

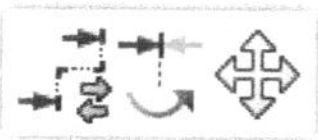

Figure 2–13

The icons are described as follows:

Option	Description
 (Replace Profile)	Replaces the current profile used to define the section. Once the icon is selected, sketch a new profile in the parent drawing view. The section view does not update until you exit the workspace.
 (Reverse View Direction)	Inverts the profile direction.
 (Pan)	Manipulation in two directions according to the call out.
 (Slide)	Manipulation in one direction according to the call out.

Detail Profiles

Detail profiles can be modified by double-clicking on the detail callout in the parent view. A context menu with just the **Replace Profile** command will display. Use  (Replace Profile) to draw a new detail profile then select in the background to finish. At any time while modifying, you can reposition the existing detail profile by dragging its handles to a new location on the view.

2.7 3D Support

When creating a model, 3D supports can be added to a 3D Part. The support creates a grid on the XY, YZ, and XZ planes of the active axis system. This grid can be used as a reference for the creation of geometry by selecting the vertices or edges of the grid. For example, a wireframe spline can be created by selecting grid locations, as shown in Figure 2–14.

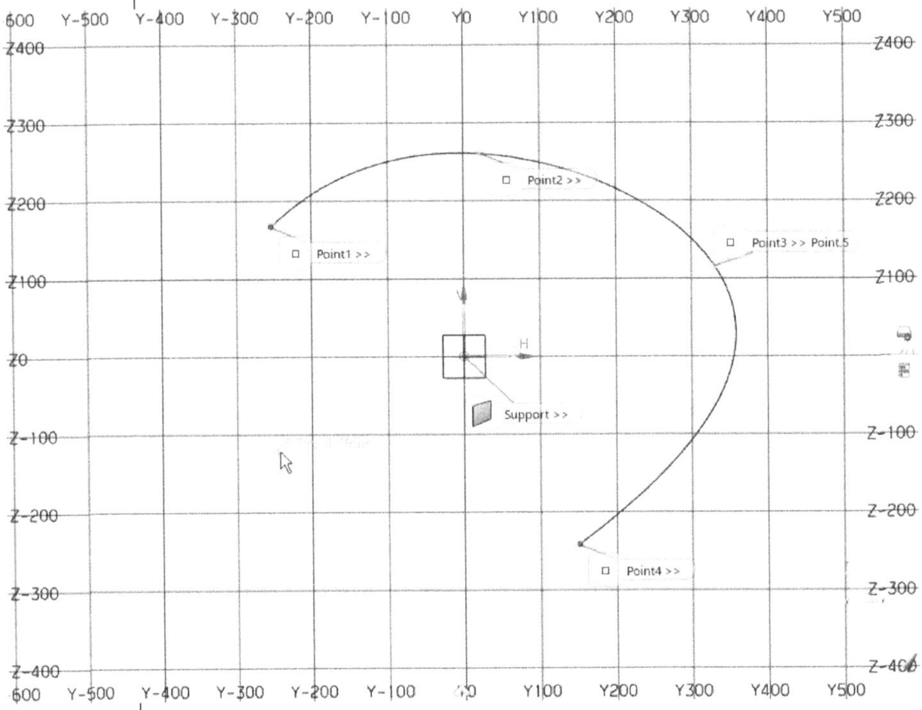

Figure 2–14

This 3D support can display when adding views to a drawing. By displaying the grid, the drawing can automatically convey positional information about the model, specifically for parts that were created using in-place modeling techniques.

For example, a support displays in the drawing view shown in Figure 2–15. From this drawing, the manufacturer can determine that the center of this part is located at the 400mm, 0mm location from the assembly axis system.

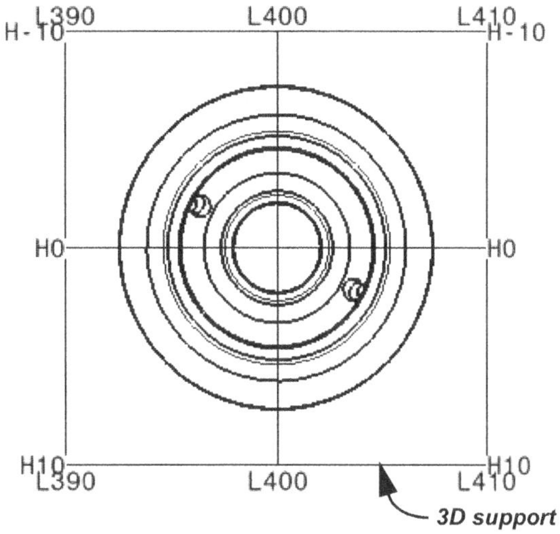

Figure 2–15

To display a 3D support in a drawing view, you must consult your CAD Administrator to have the following configurations set:

- Modify the *Generative Parameters* category in the drawing standards and set the **Me>Preferences>Standards> Standard>Generative Parameters>Default Generative Style>Generative Shape Design>Work On Support> Extraction** option to **Yes**.
- Clear the **Disable Generative View style definition on layout views** option, found by going to **Me>Preferences> App Preferences>3D Modeling>Mechanical Systems>2D Layout for 3D Design>Generative view style**.

Practice 2a View Manipulation

Practice Objectives

- Delete a view.
- Modify a view using Hide/Show.
- Relate a part to a drawing view.

Task 1 - Import and open the ExhaustFlange.

1. Import and open **ExhaustFlange_2A.3dxml** from the practice files folder. While importing, set the *Duplication string* to **###_** where ### represents your initials.

2. Right-click on the **###_ExhaustFlange_View_2A** drawing in the tree and select * **object>Open in New App**. The drawing displays as shown in Figure 2–16.

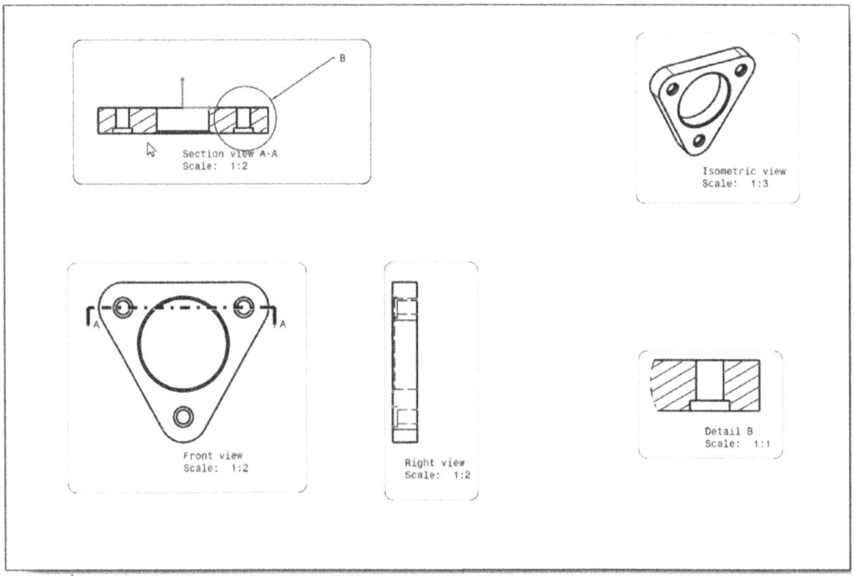

Figure 2–16

The view frame of an active view displays in red.

Task 2 - Delete a view.

1. Before performing modifications, always ensure that the view you intend to modify is set as the active view. In the specification tree, double-click on the **Right view** to make it active. When active, the view name displays in blue as shown in Figure 2–17.

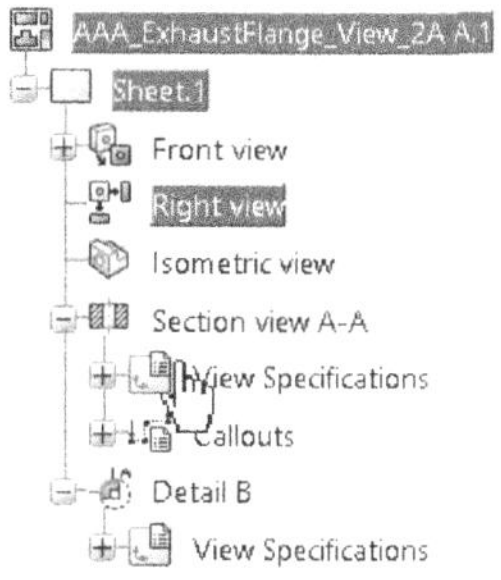

Figure 2–17

2. Right-click on the **Right view** and select **Delete**. The specification tree displays as shown in Figure 2–18.

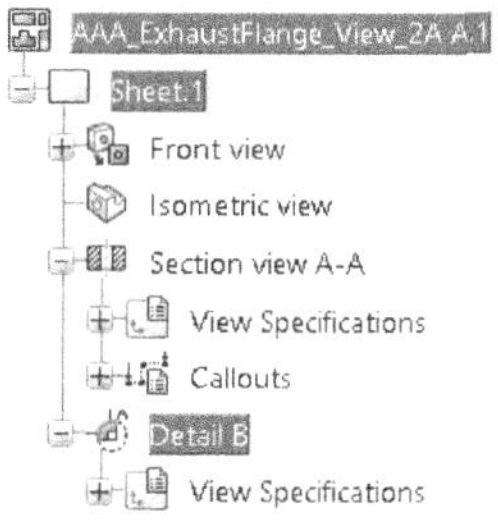

Figure 2–18

Note that the Right view has been removed from the drawing, as shown in Figure 2–19.

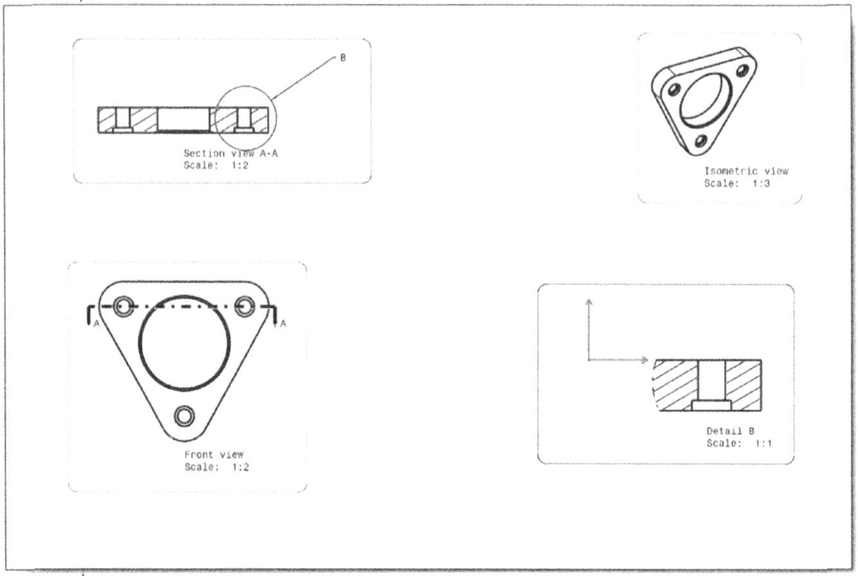

Figure 2–19

You can also use the Windows Undo shortcut (<Ctrl>+<Z>) to undo the operation.

3. From the Standard section of the Action Bar, select (Undo) to undo the deletion of the Right view.

Task 3 - Hide a view.

1. In the display window or specification tree, right-click on the **Right view** and select **Hide/Show**. The specification tree displays as shown in Figure 2–20.

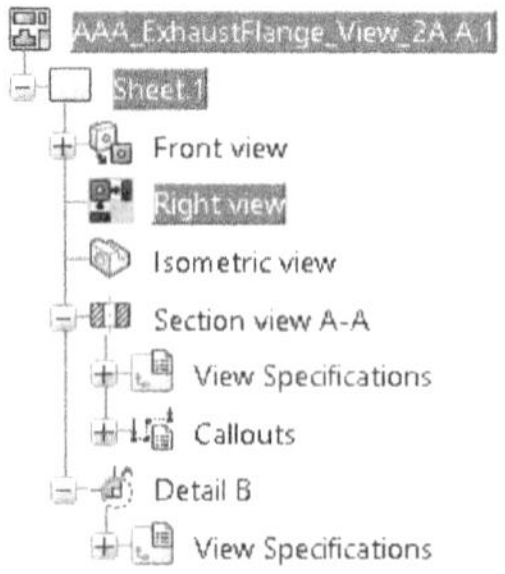

Figure 2–20

(Optional) The (Swap visible space) icon found in the lower right hand side of the screen can be selected as well.

2. In the View section of the Action Bar, click (Swap visible space). The Right view is located in the invisible display space and has not been permanently removed from the drawing.

Design Considerations

Use the **Hide/Show** and **Swap visible space** tools to simplify the drawing display when reorganizing a drawing. Since the system does not need to update the display of the hidden views, performance improvements can be obtained while working on the drawing in CATIA.

3. Click (Swap visible space) to return to the visible space.
4. In the specification tree, right-click on the **Right view** and select **Hide/Show**. The Right view displays in the drawing again.

Task 4 - Display a shaded view.

1. In the specification tree, right-click on **Isometric view** and select **Properties**.

2. In the *View* tab, change the *Scale* of the view to **1:2**, as shown in Figure 2–21.

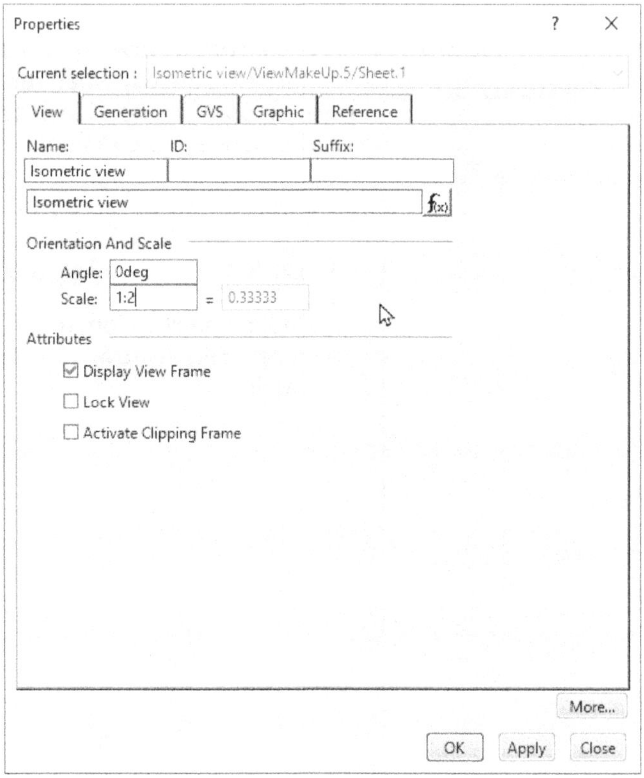

Figure 2–21

3. Activate the *Generation* tab. In the View generation mode drop-down list, select **Raster**, as shown in Figure 2–22.

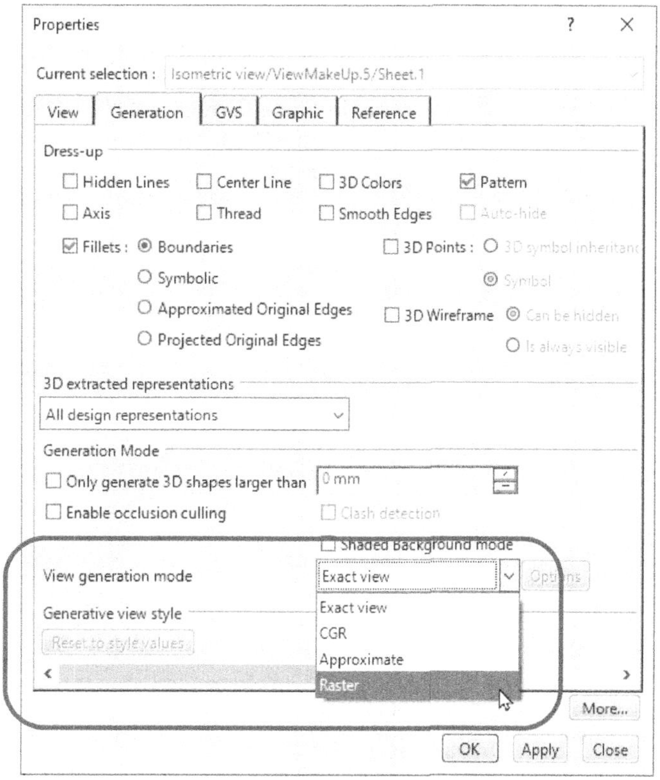

Figure 2–22

4. Click **Options**. The Exact generation mode Options dialog box opens as shown in Figure 2–23

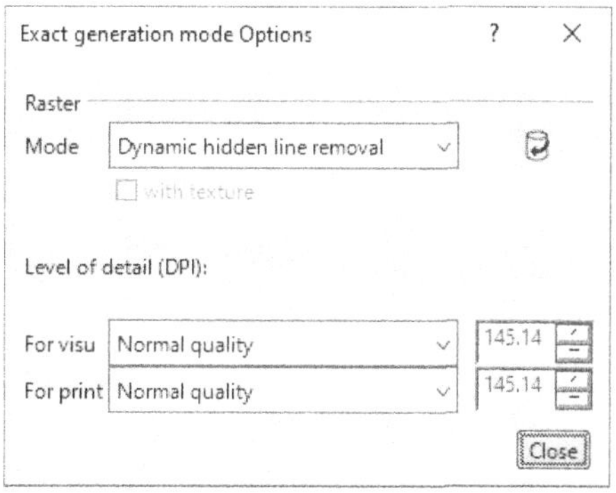

Figure 2–23

5. Make the following selections:

   - *Mode:* **Shading with edges**
   - *For visu*: **High quality**
   - *For print:* **High quality**

6. Click **Close** and click **OK** to apply the view property modifications. The reference view displays as shown in Figure 2–24.

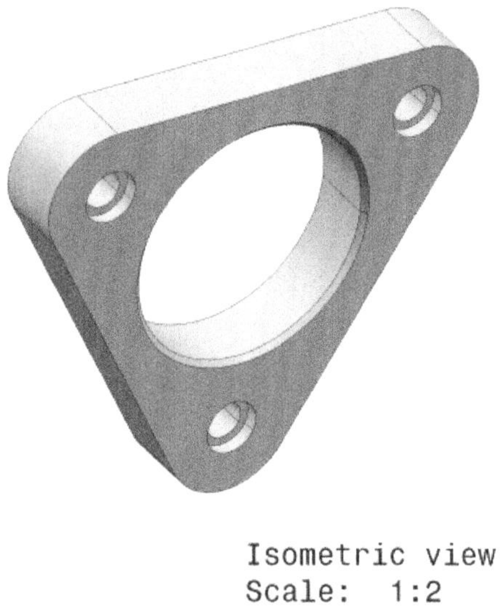

Figure 2–24

7. Save the drawing and close all of the tabs.

Practice 2b

View Manipulation II

Practice Objectives

- Move a view between sheets.
- Move a view in a sheet.
- Align views using elements.

Task 1 - Import and open Tire.

1. Import and open **Tire.3dxml** from the practice files folder. While importing, set the *Duplication string* to **###_** where ### represents your initials.

2. Right-click on the **###_Tire** drawing in the tree and select *** object>Open in New App**. The drawing displays as shown in Figure 2–25.

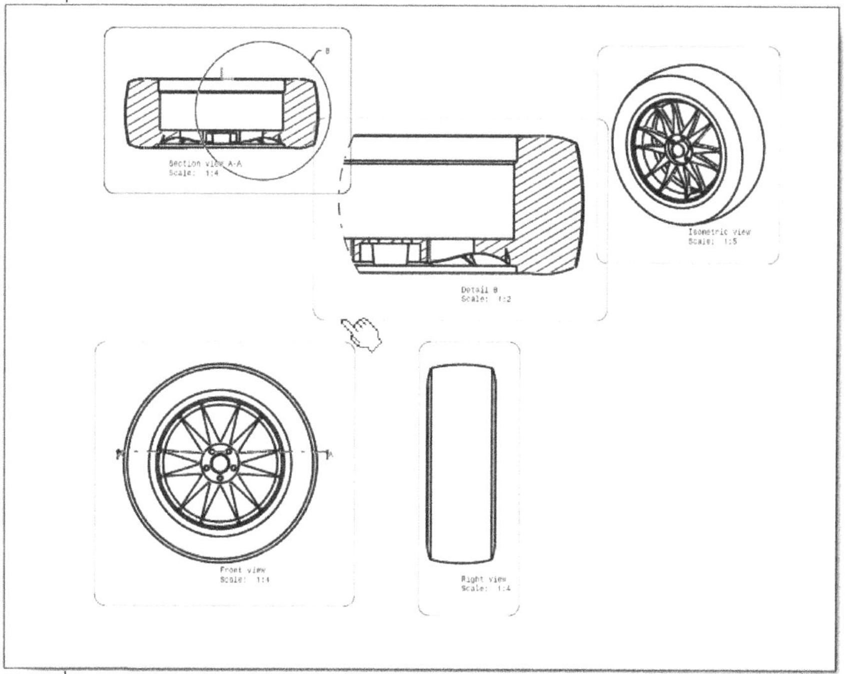

Figure 2–25

Task 2 - Insert a second sheet and insert the Isometric view.

If (Create a New Sheet) is not shown at the top center of the screen, toggle (Sheet Browser) on from the View section of the Action Bar.

The Windows shortcut keys, <Ctrl>+<X> (Cut) and <Ctrl>+<V> (Paste), can also be used.

1. At the top center of the screen, select (Create a New Sheet). A new sheet is added to the drawing.
2. Select the *Sheet.1* tab to toggle back to the first sheet of the drawing.
3. In the display or specification tree, double-click on the **Isometric view** to make it active.
4. Right-click on **Isometric view** in the tree and select **Cut**.
5. In the specification tree, right-click on **Sheet.2** and select **Paste**. The drawing displays as shown in Figure 2–26.

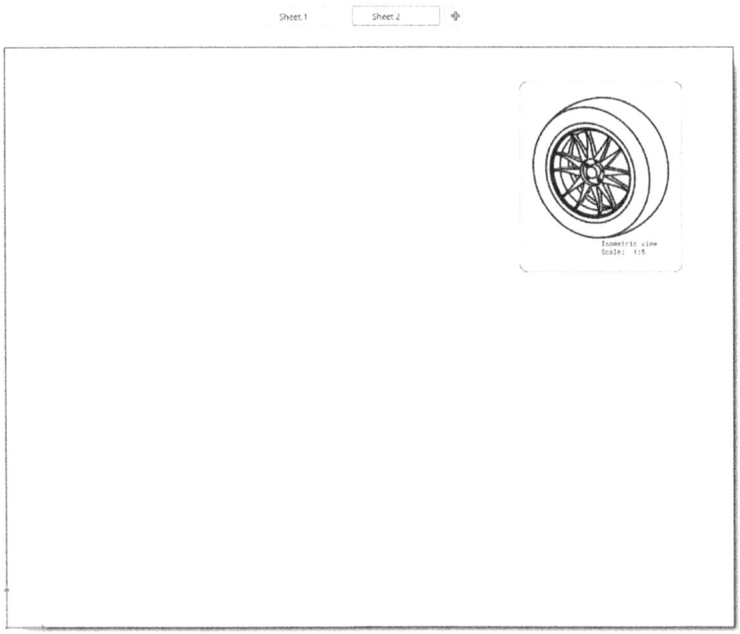

Figure 2–26

Task 3 - Move a view on the same sheet.

1. Activate **Sheet.1**.

2. Use the left mouse button to select the frame of the Front view and move the view to a new location on the same sheet. The child views are also moved due to a linked view alignment.

Task 4 - Move the Section view to a new location.

1. Select the frame of the Section view and drag it to a different location. The movement is vertically constrained.

2. In the specification tree, right-click on the **Section view** and select **View Positioning>Position Independently of Reference View**.

3. Drag the Section view again. The movement is no longer constrained to the Front view, as shown in Figure 2–27.

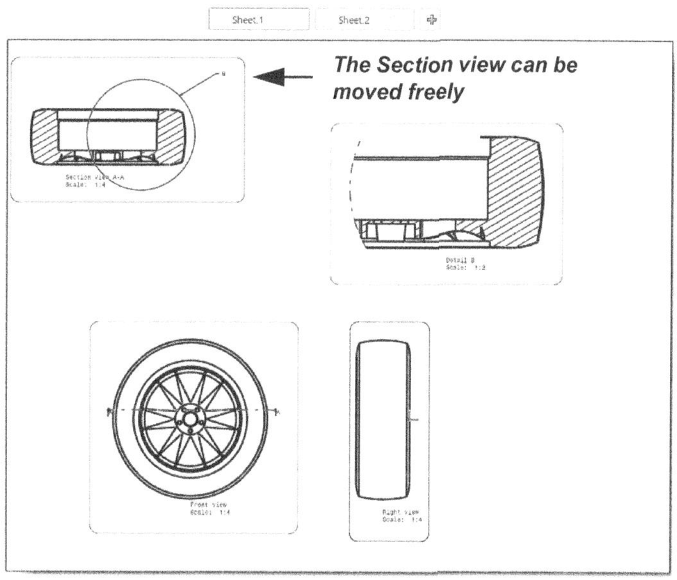

Figure 2–27

4. To realign the Section view with its default reference view, right-click on the view frame of the Section view and select **View Positioning>Position According to Reference View**. The Section view is once again vertically constrained to the Front view.

Task 5 - Align the Detail view with the Front view using elements.

Design Considerations

The **Align Views Using Elements** feature aligns the internal elements of separate views. This enables you to keep a drawing organized without creating referenced alignment constraints.

1. Right-click on the view frame around the Detail B view and select **View Positioning>Align Views Using Elements**.
2. Select the top edge of the Detail B view and the top edge of the Section view, as shown in Figure 2–28.

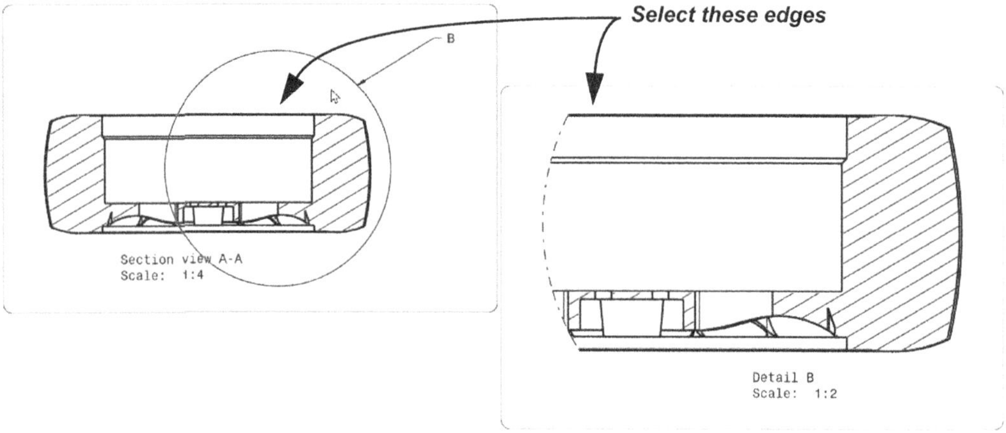

Figure 2–28

3. Select and move the **Detail B view**. Contrary to a reference alignment, the view is not constrained to the Section view.

Task 6 - Modify the hatching properties of Section view A-A.

1. Right-click on the hatching lines of Section view A-A and select **Properties**, as shown in Figure 2–29.

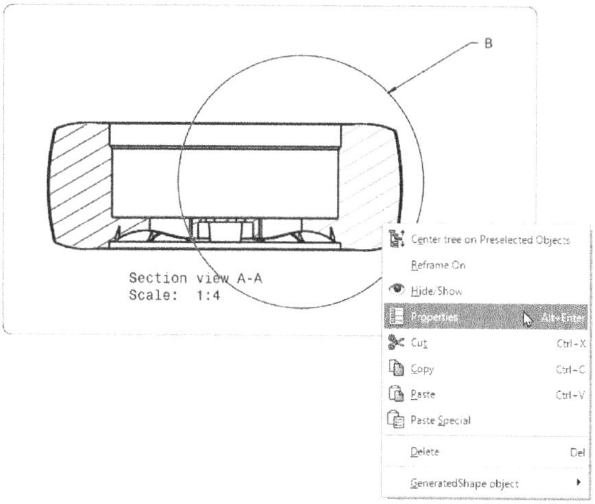

Figure 2–29

2. Select the *Pattern* tab, as shown in Figure 2–30.

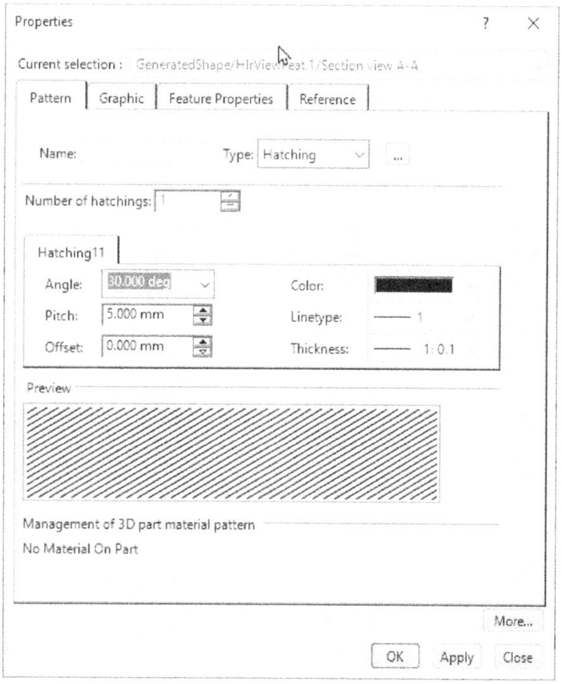

Figure 2–30

3. Make the following changes:
   - *Angle:* **60 deg**
   - *Pitch:* **2mm**
4. Click **Apply**. The view displays as shown in Figure 2–31. Keep the Properties dialog box open.

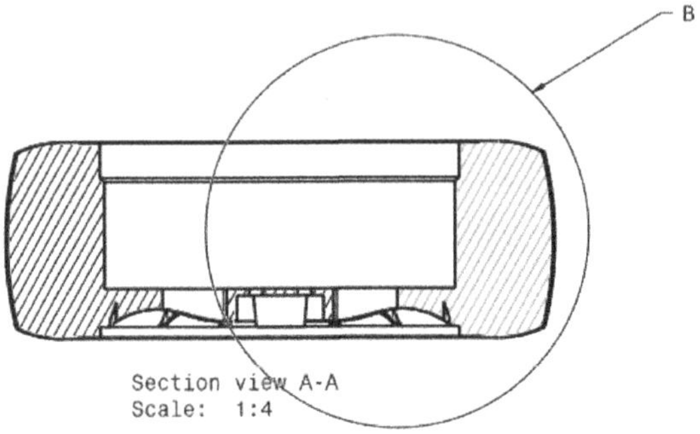

Figure 2–31

5. In the Type drop-down list, select **Coloring** as shown in Figure 2–32. This creates a filled section.

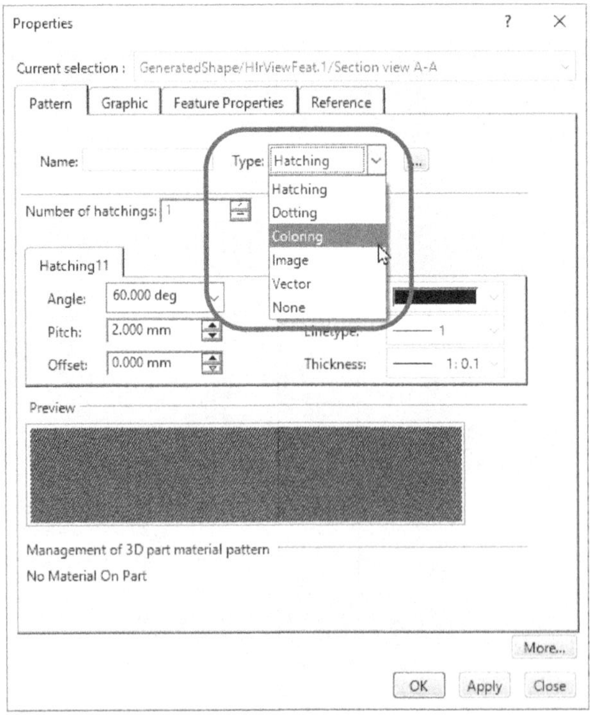

Figure 2–32

6. In the Color drop-down list, select **Black**.

7. Click **OK**. The drawing displays as shown in Figure 2–33.

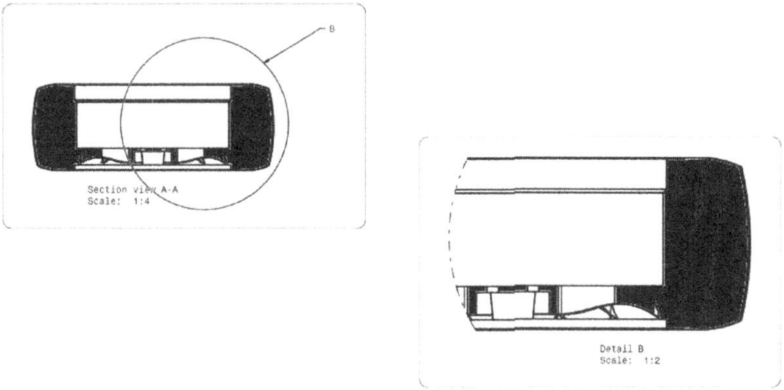

Figure 2–33

Design Considerations

Since the Detail B view was created from Section view A-A, both views display the modifications to the hatching properties.

Task 7 - Modify section profile properties.

1. Double-click on the section view profile in the Front view, as shown in Figure 2–34. The system displays a context menu.

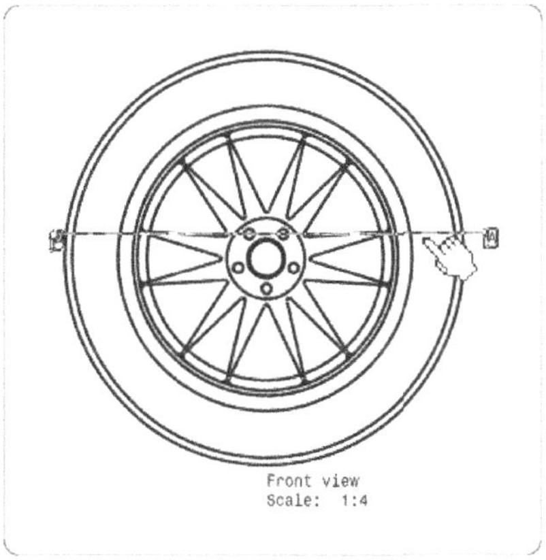

Figure 2–34

2. Click  (Replace profile). This tool enables you to draw a new profile to be used to define the section.

3. Sketch a horizontal section line that is coincident with the center of the tire, as shown in Figure 2–35. Do not forget to double-click when placing the end point of the line to complete the profile.

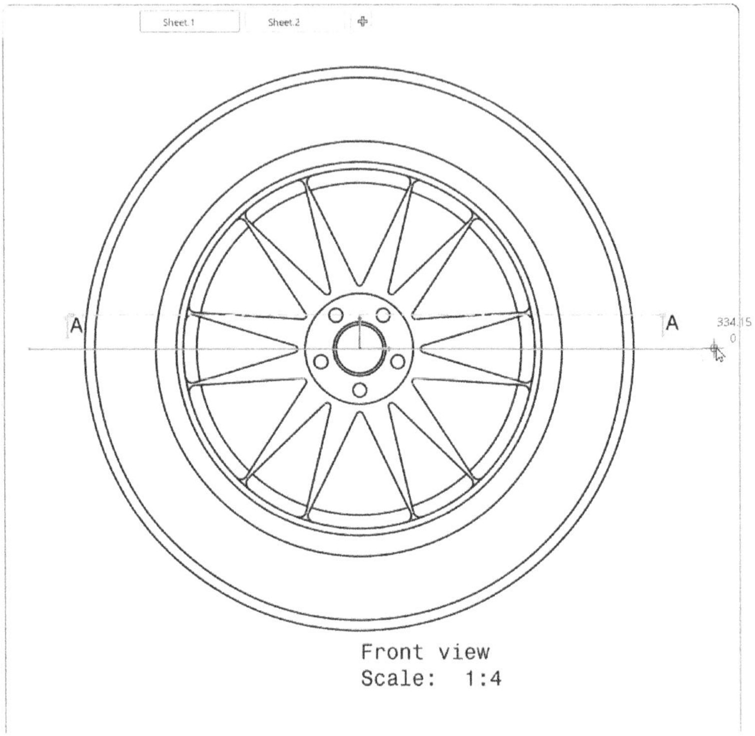

Figure 2–35

Once complete, the system replaces the old profile with the newly sketched one, as shown in Figure 2–36. The section view does not update until you have finished the section profile modification.

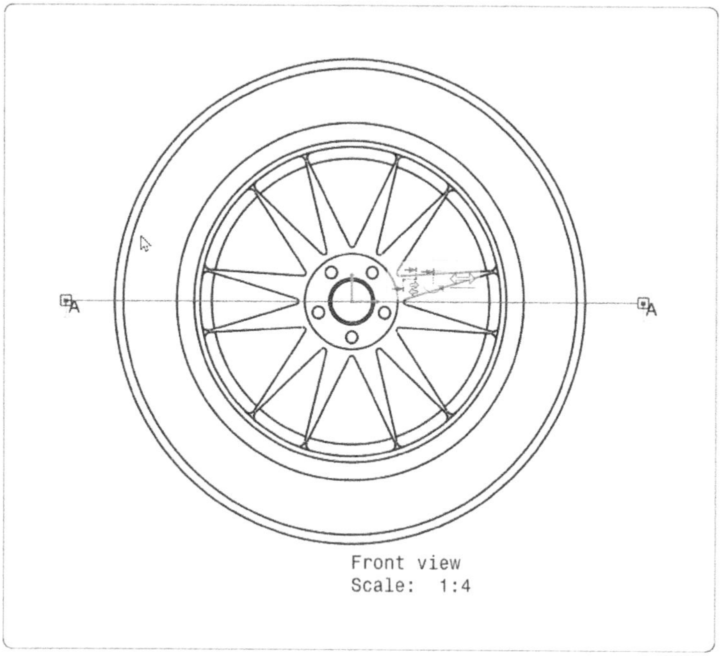

Figure 2–36

4. Click anywhere to complete the section profile modification. Section view A-A updates with the new profile.

Task 8 - Modify the section callout properties.

1. In the Front view, right-click on the section profile and select **Properties**. Select the *Callout* tab, and the Properties dialog box displays as shown in Figure 2–37.

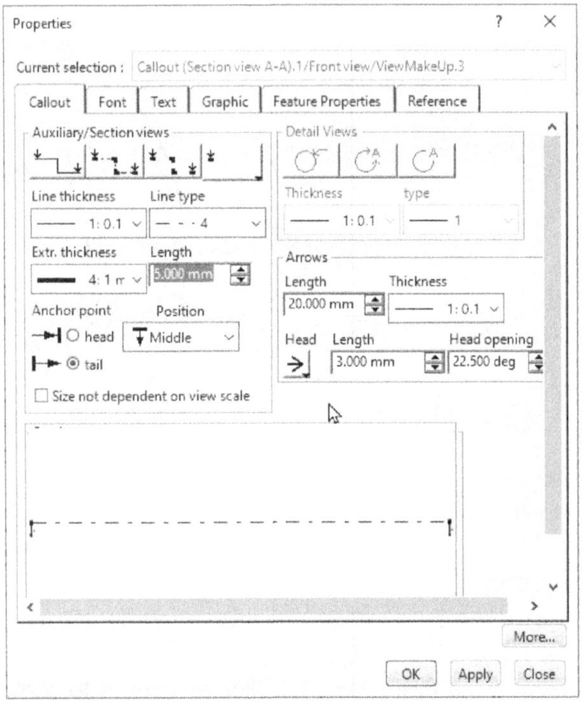

Figure 2–37

2. Click 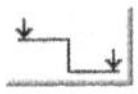 to define a solid callout line with a *thickness* of **1**.
3. Change the *Extr. thickness value* to **3: 0.7mm**.

4. Click **OK** to complete the operation. The Front view displays as shown in Figure 2–38.

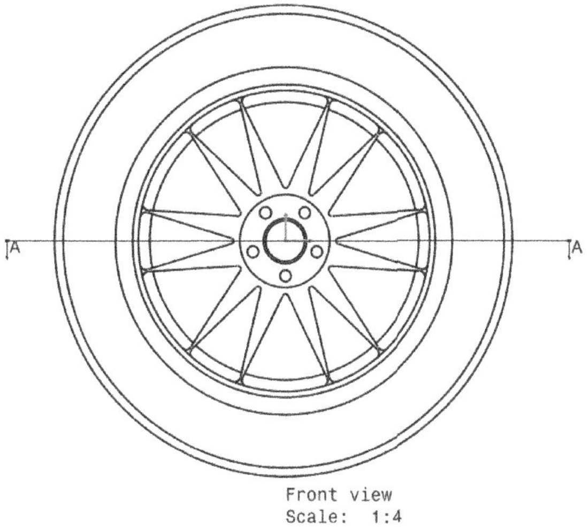

Figure 2–38

5. Save the drawing and close all of the tabs.

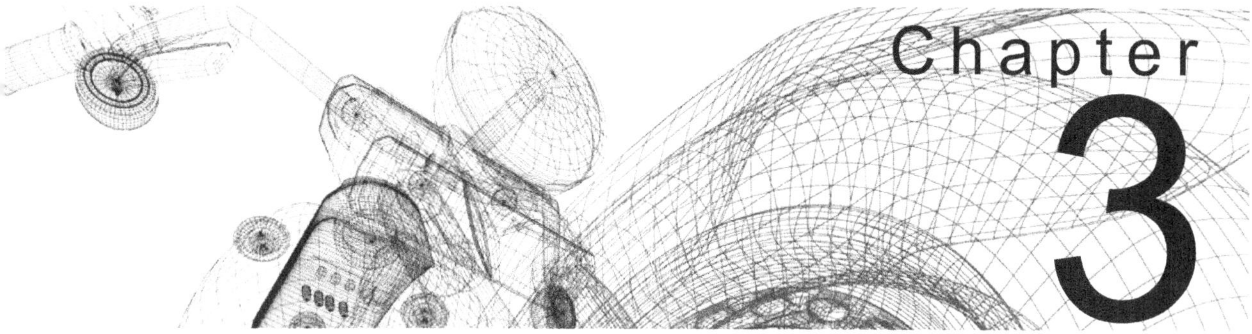

Chapter 3

Dimensioning

Detailing a drawing involves adding information from the model to the drawing so that all design information is effectively communicated. Detail items can include dimensions and notes.

Learning Objectives in This Chapter

- Add dimensions manually.
- Add dimensions automatically.
- Use One Step dimensioning.
- Apply Step by Step dimensioning.
- Recognize and apply dimension generation settings.
- Modify dimension properties.

3.1 Manual Dimensioning

The Drafting app provides the following two options to dimension a drawing:

- Manual dimensioning
- Automatic dimension generation

Use the Dimensions flyout shown in Figure 3–1 to manually create dimensions.

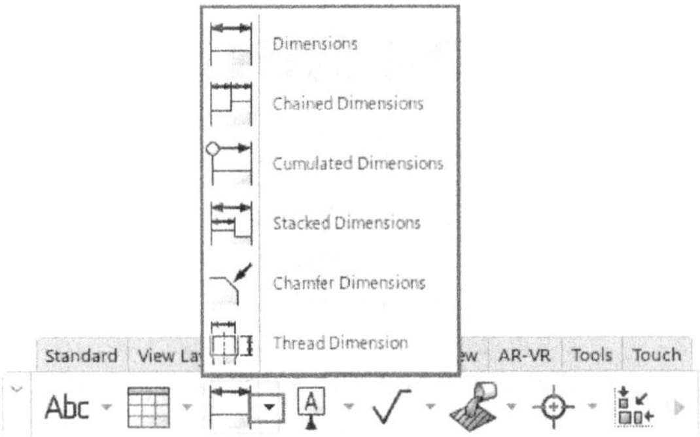

Figure 3–1

The dimension types are described as follows:

Dimension Type	Description
 **Dimensions**	Creates a length/distance, angle, radius, or diameter dimension from the selected references. The dimension type (length, distance, angle, etc.) is determined by the type and number of selected references. For example, selecting two parallel lines will result in a distance dimension, or selecting a circle will result in a diameter dimension. This default behavior can be over-ridden by the user through the contextual menu. Each dimension acts independently when moved, modified, or deleted.

 **Chained Dimensions**	Creates a chain of distance or angle dimensions by using the last selected reference to create the next dimension as shown below. The chain of dimensions is moved, modified, or deleted as a single element. To delete dimensions separately, select 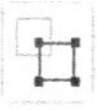 (Elements) from the context menu that appears when any of the chained dimensions are selected. 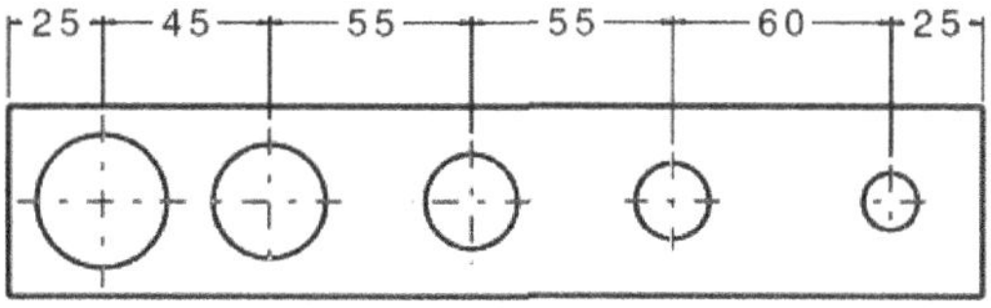
 **Cumulated Dimensions**	Creates a cumulated dimension. The first reference selected becomes the base dimension. All additional references are located with respect to the base as shown below. The cumulated dimensions are moved, modified, or deleted as a single element. To delete dimensions separately, select 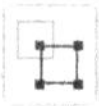 (Elements) from the context menu that appears when any of the cumulated dimensions are selected. 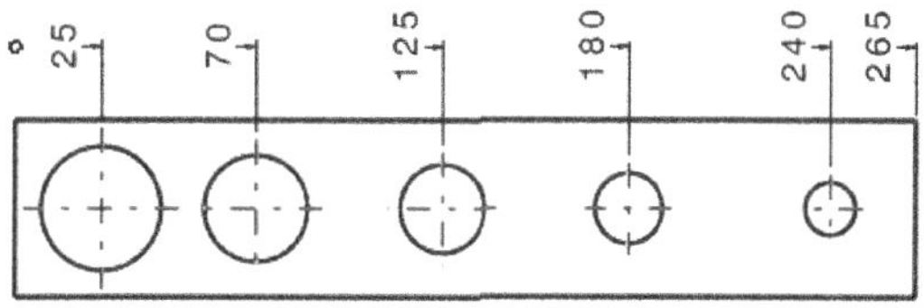
 **Stacked Dimensions**	Creates a stack of length dimensions using the first reference to create the next dimension as shown below. The stack of dimensions are moved, modified, or deleted as a single element. To delete dimensions separately, select 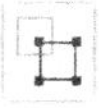 (Elements) from the context menu that appears when any of the stacked dimensions are selected. 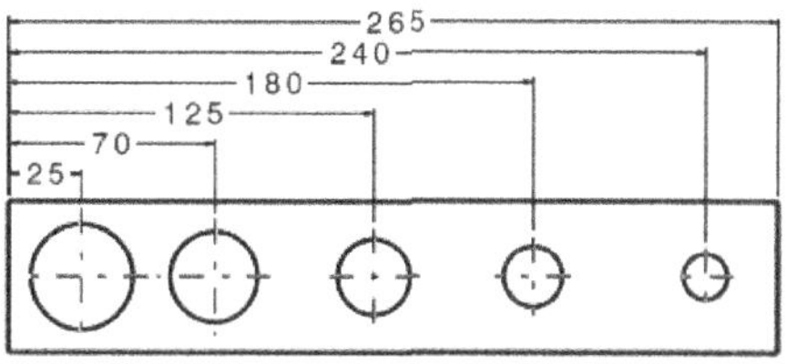

 **Length/ Distance Dimensions**	Dimensions the circumference of a circle, length of an arc, length of an edge, or distance between elements.
Angle Dimensions	Dimensions the angle between two linear elements.
Radius Dimensions	Dimensions the radius of an arc or circle.
Diameter Dimensions	Dimensions the diameter of an arc or circle.
 **Chamfer Dimensions**	Dimensions a Chamfer feature. The Tools Palette toolbar displays the dimension options, as shown below. 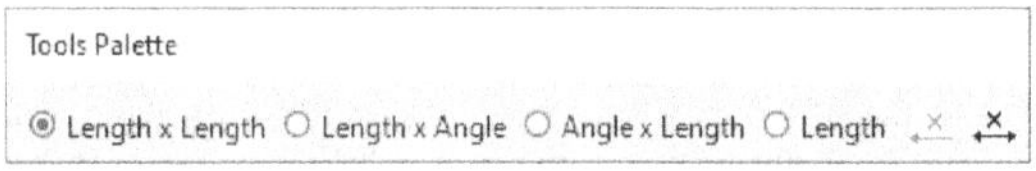 If the system detects the chamfer feature from the model, it displays three numbers representing the chamfer surface (1), first surface (2), and second surface (3) as shown below. The first surface is used to place the first length or angle. 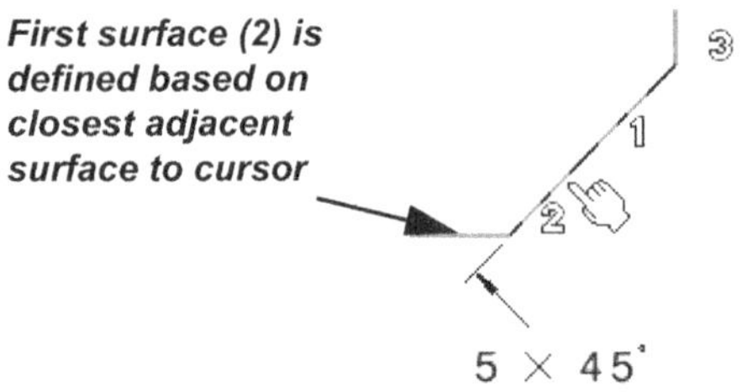
 **Thread Dimensions**	Displays thread parameters on the model of a selected thread surface as shown below. Thread surfaces are display by enabling the **Thread** option in the View Properties dialog box. 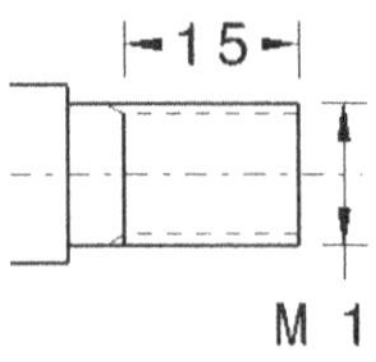

Coordinate Dimensions

Dimensions the horizontal and vertical coordinates of a selected vertex or point relative to the view origin as shown below.

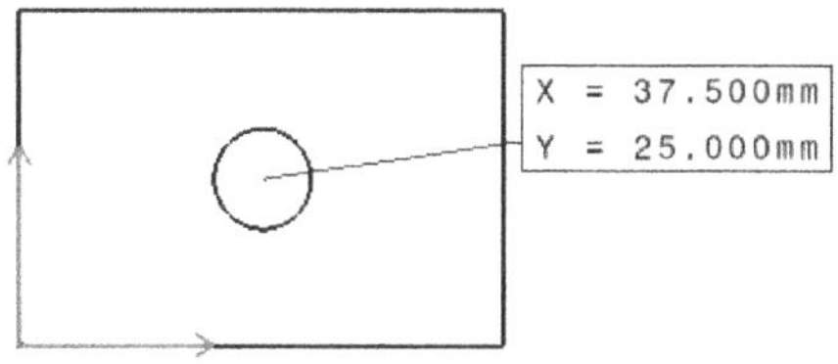

Hole Dimension Table

Creates a hole dimension table that displays the X- and Y-coordinates and diameters of all selected holes, relative to a user-defined origin as shown below. Select all holes using <Ctrl> before creating the hole dimension table.

The dimensions are created with the same unit, which is set in the CATIA options.

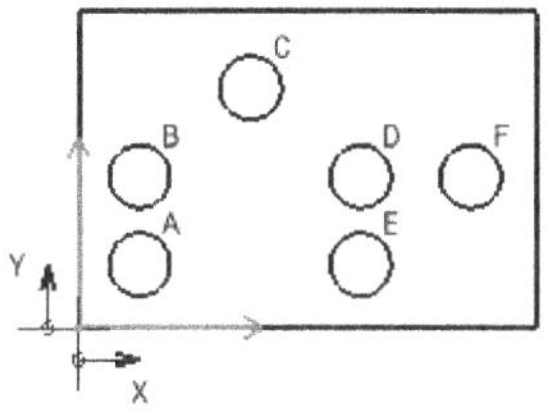

REF.	X	Y	Diameter
A	10	10	10
B	10	24	10
C	28	38	10
D	46	24	10
E	46	10	10
F	64	24	10

Coordinate Dimension Table

Creates a coordinate dimension table that displays the X-, Y-, and Z- (if applicable) coordinates for all selected points relative to a user-defined origin as shown below. Select all points using <Ctrl> before creating the coordinate dimension table.

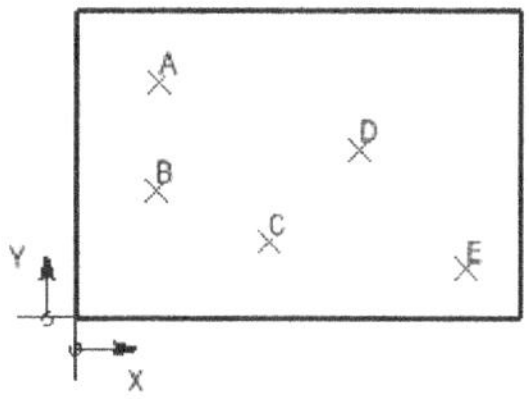

REF.	X	Y
A	13.8	38.48
B	13.24	20.86
C	32.14	12.37
D	47.64	27.58
E	65.59	7.94

3.2 Manually Create Dimensions

General Steps

Use the following general steps to manually create dimensions:

1. Set dimension creation options.
2. Select the appropriate dimensioning tool.
3. Select the appropriate elements of the view.
4. Manipulate dimensions, as required.

Step 1 - Set dimension creation options.

Select **Me>Preferences>App Preferences>3D Modeling>Mechanical Systems>Drafting >Dimension** section. The dimension creation options display as shown in Figure 3–2.

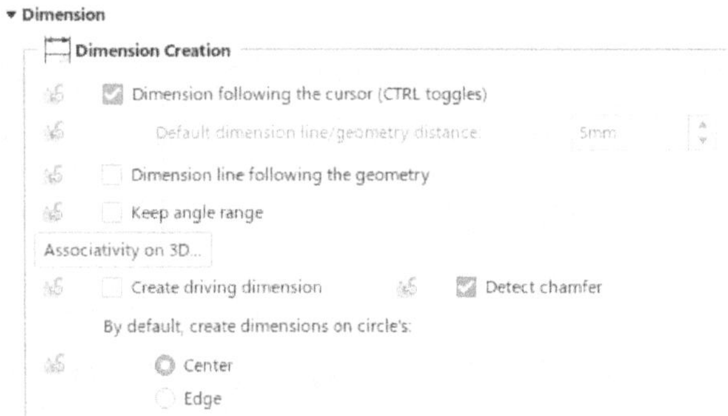

Figure 3–2

To take advantage of the full associativity of CATIA, click **Associativity in 3D** and select the **Never create non-associative dimensions** option in the Associativity on 3D section, as shown in Figure 3–3.

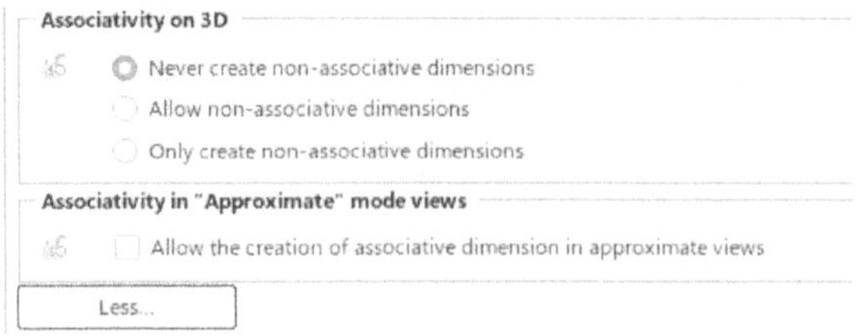

Figure 3–3

This option ensures that drawing dimensions update with changes to the referenced 3D geometry.

Step 2 - Select the appropriate dimensioning tool.

Select the appropriate dimensioning tool in the Annotation section of the Action Bar, as shown in Figure 3–4.

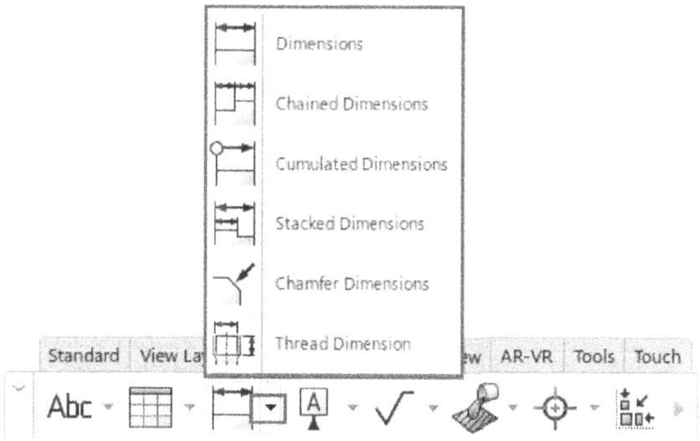

Figure 3–4

Step 3 - Select the appropriate elements of the view.

Select the appropriate elements that correspond to the type of dimensioning tool.

For example, to obtain a diameter dimension, select the **Diameter** tool in the Dimensions section of the Action Bar and select the hole to dimension. Click to place the dimension, as shown in Figure 3–5.

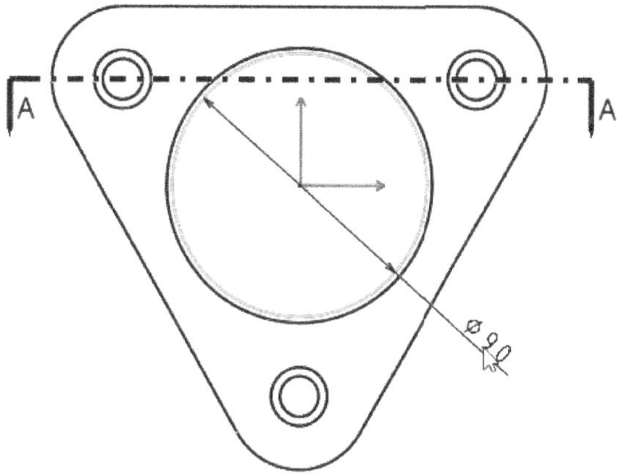

Figure 3–5

Tools Palette

The Tools Palette toolbar displays when you are placing a dimension, as shown in Figure 3–6. It enables you to select a forced dimension placement mode. These options ensure that the dimension is created correctly.

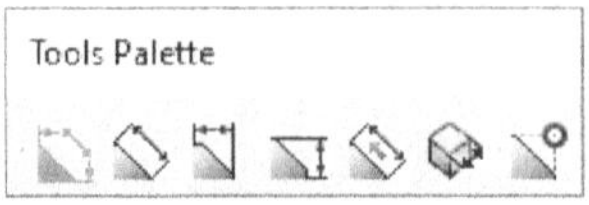

Figure 3–6

The options are described as follows:

Force Mode	Description
	Projected dimension according to cursor position.
	Force dimension on element.
	Force horizontal dimension.
	Force vertical dimension.
	Force dimension along a direction.
	True length dimension.
	Detect an intersection point.

Step 4 - Manipulate dimensions, as required.

Moving Dimensions

You can move dimensions once they have been created using the following methods (shown in Figure 3–7):

- Click and drag on a handle to move both witness lines.
- Click and drag on a dimension to move it left, right, up, or down.
- Click on an arrow head to flip it.

Hold <Ctrl> while dragging the handle to only move one extension line.

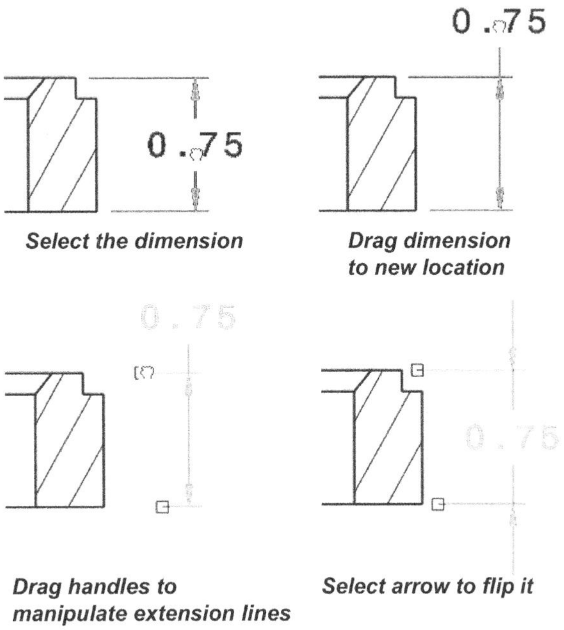

Figure 3–7

Object Properties

Dimension Properties and Numerical Properties

You can modify the tolerance format and value of a dimension using the Object Properties window. The Object Properties window enables you to modify the units and the number of decimal places of a dimension by changing the Dimension and Numerical Properties. The Object Properties window with *Dimension* and *Numerical* is shown in Figure 3–8.

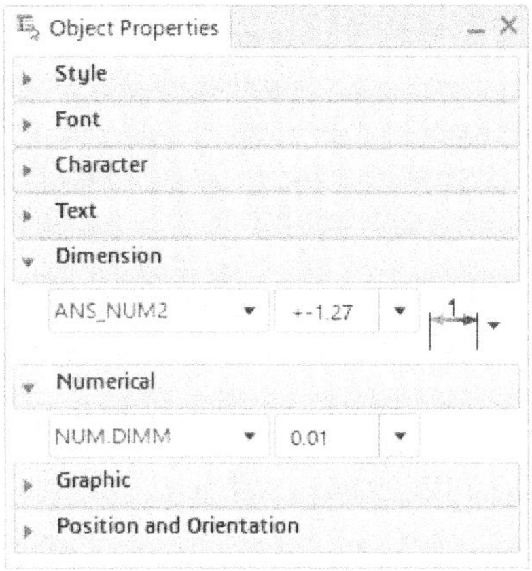

Figure 3–8

The Object Properties window can be toggled on/off by going to the Tools section of the Action Bar and selecting the (Object Properties) icon.

Properties Dialog Box

You can modify dimension properties using the Properties dialog box. To change dimension properties using the dialog box, right-click on the dimension and select **Properties**. The Properties dialog box contains various options (categorized under tabs) that you can use to change the properties of the selected dimension, as shown in Figure 3–9.

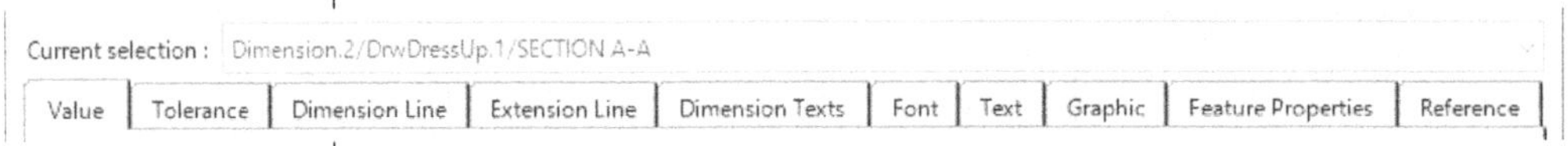

Figure 3–9

The following tabs are described:

- Value
- Tolerance
- Dimension Line
- Extension Line
- Dimension Texts

Value Tab

The *Value* tab enables you to orient a dimension, enter an offset value, enable dual dimensioning, and change the format of the value, as shown in Figure 3–10 and Figure 3–11.

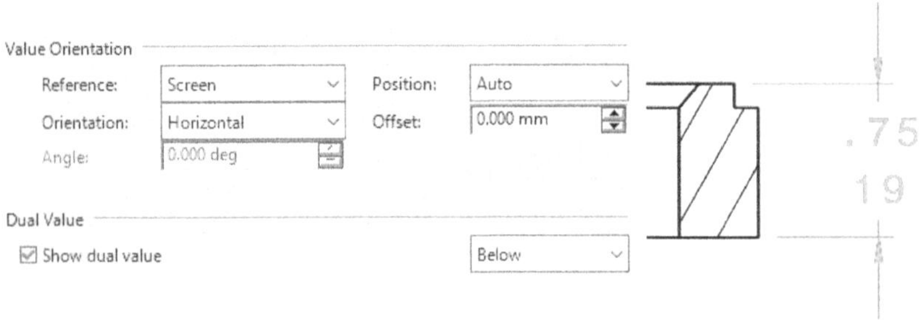

Figure 3–10

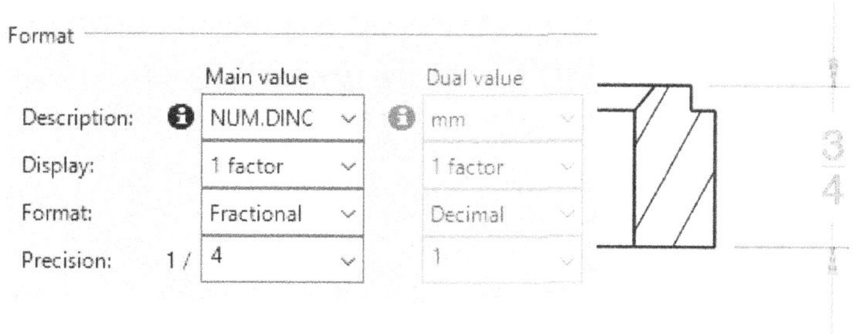

Figure 3–11

Tolerance Tab

The *Tolerance* tab enables you to enter tolerance values and apply the values to a dimension, as shown in Figure 3–12.

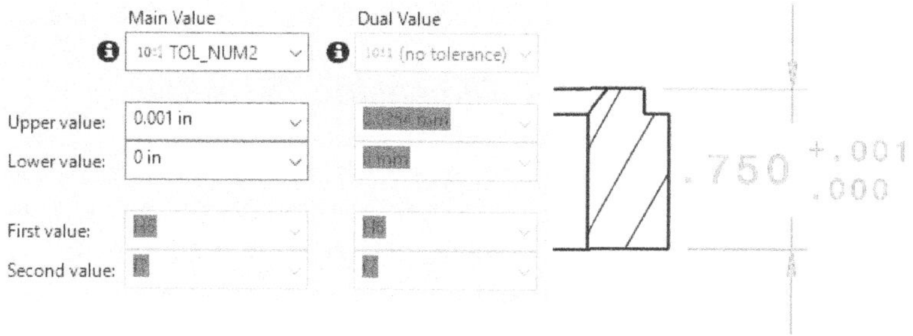

Figure 3–12

Dimension Line Tab

The *Dimension Line* tab enables you to modify the color, line thickness, and arrow shape of a dimension, as shown in Figure 3–13.

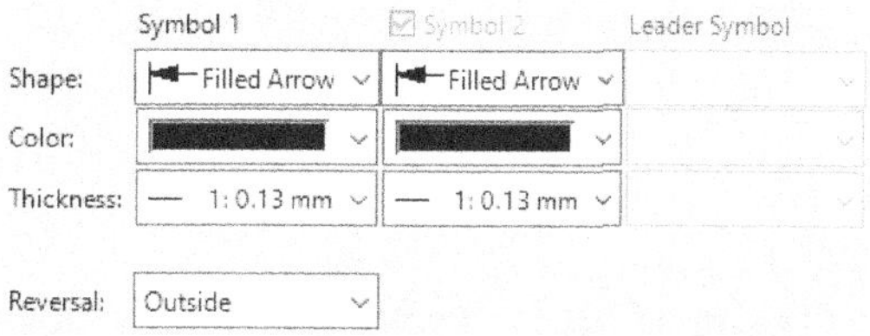

Figure 3–13

Extension Line Tab

The *Extension Line* tab enables you to define a funnel for a dimension, as shown in Figure 3–14.

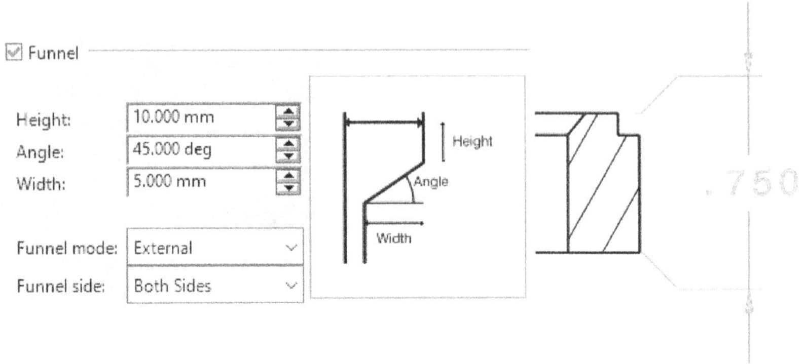

Figure 3–14

Dimension Texts Tab

The *Dimension Texts* tab enables you to add text to dimensions. You can add text above, below, before, or after a dimension value, as shown in Figure 3–15.

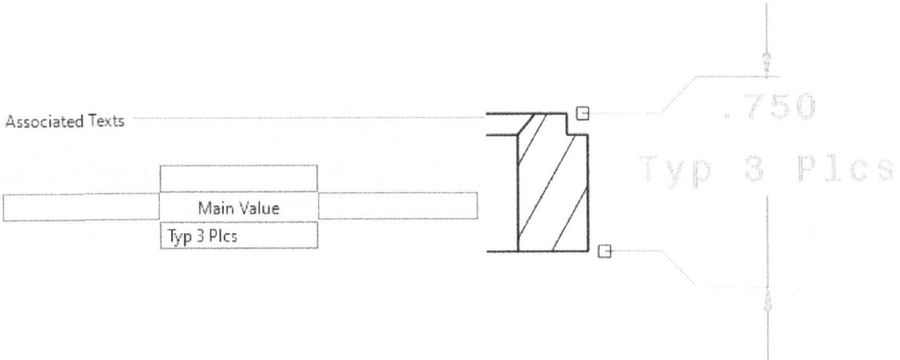

Figure 3–15

Transfer Dimensions Between Views

How To: Transfer Dimensions Between Views

1. Right-click on the dimension and select **Cut**.
2. Activate the view to which you want to transfer the dimension, right-click, and select **Paste**.

3.3 Automatic Dimensions

You can use one of the following methods to automatically create dimensions on your drawing:

- One Step Dimensioning
- Step by Step Dimension Generation

The One Step dimension generation method enables you to place all dimensions onto the drawing at the same time. You can reposition these dimensions after placement.

The Step by Step dimension generation method enables you to step through the creation of each dimension, as shown in Figure 3–16.

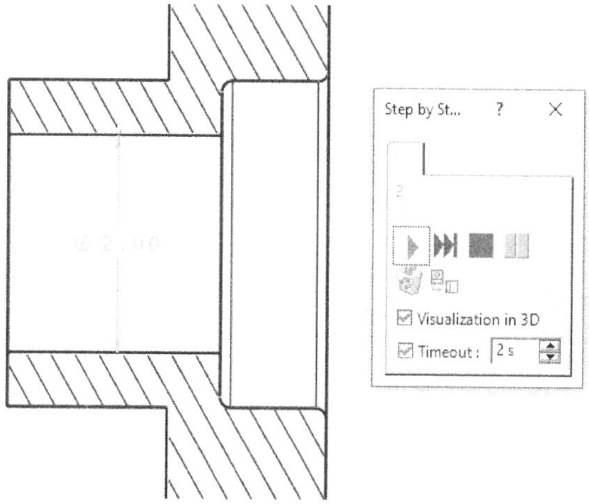

Figure 3–16

3.4 One Step Dimensioning

General Steps

Use the following general steps to create dimensions in one step:

1. Add **Generate Dimensions** command to the Action Bar.
2. Select the view to be dimensioned.
3. Start the creation of dimensions.
4. Reposition the dimensions.

Step 1 - Add Generate Dimensions command to the Action Bar.

By default, the **Generate Dimensions** command is not found in the Action Bar. It will need to be added before it can be used to create dimensions in views. To add it to the Action Bar, select **Me>Preferences>Customize>Sections** and then place the (Generate Dimensions) command onto a section by using **Add Commands...**.

If the Action Pad does not display, it can be toggled on by selecting (Action Pad) from the Tools section of the Action Bar.

Note: An alternative option would be to add the command to the Action Pad instead. The path for this would be **Me> Preferences>Customize>Action Pad**, then select **Add Commands.**

Step 2 - Select the view to be dimensioned.

Select the view to be dimensioned from the sheet or specification tree. The view does not need to be active.

CATIA dimensions all views on the current sheet if you do not select a view to be dimensioned.

Step 3 - Start the creation of dimensions.

Click (Generate Dimensions) from the customized Action Bar. All possible dimensions display for the view, as shown in Figure 3–17. All views are dimensioned appropriately if you did not select a view.

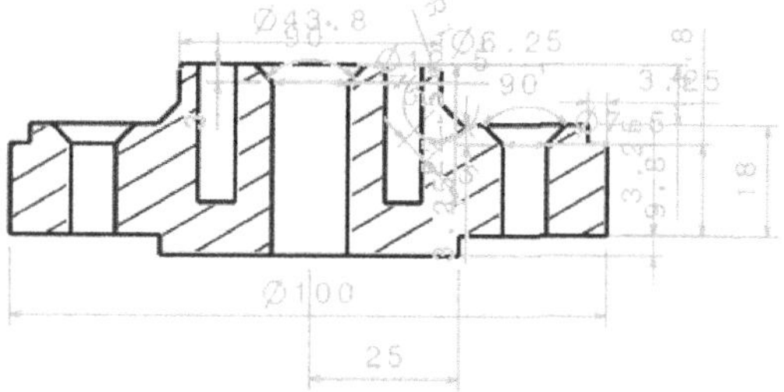

Figure 3–17

Step 4 - Reposition the dimensions.

Activate the view containing the dimensions and select (Dimension Positioning) to automatically reposition all linear dimensions, as shown in Figure 3–18. Radial dimension positions are not affected and must be manually repositioned.

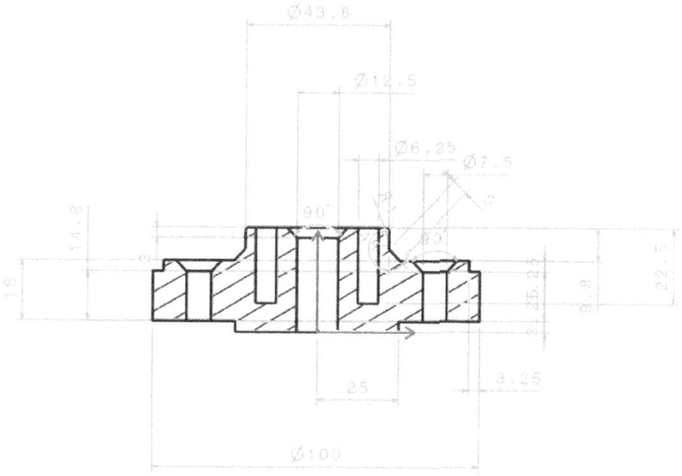

Figure 3–18

Note: By default, the **Dimension Positioning** command is not found in the Action Bar. It will need to be added before it can be used to align dimensions in views. To add it to the Action Bar, select **Me>Preferences>Customize>Sections** and then place the (Dimension Positioning) command onto a section by using **Add Commands...**.

If the Action Pad does not display, it can be toggled on by selecting (Action Pad) from the Tools section of the Action Bar.

An alternative option would be to add the command to the Action Pad instead. The path for this would be **Me>Preferences>Customize>Action Pad**, then select **Add Commands.**

3.5 Step by Step Dimensioning

General Steps

Use the following general steps to create dimensions step by step:

1. Add **Generative Dimensions Step by Step** command to the Action Bar.
2. Start the creation of dimensions.
3. Enter a timeout value.
4. Generate dimensions.
5. Remove or transfer dimensions.
6. Reposition dimensions.

Step 1 - Add Generative Dimensions Step by Step command to the Action Bar.

By default, the Generate Dimensions Step by Step command is not found in the Action Bar. It will need to be added before it can be used to create dimensions in views. To add it to the Action Bar, select **Me>Preferences>Customize>Sections** and then place the (Generate Dimensions Step by Step) command onto a section by using **Add Commands...**.

If the Action Pad does not display, it can be toggled on by selecting (Action Pad) from the Tools section of the Action Bar.

Note: An alternative option would be to add the command to the Action Pad instead. The path for this would be **Me> Preferences>Customize>Action Pad**. Then select **Add Commands.**

Step 2 - Start the creation of dimensions.

Select the view before beginning the options if you only want to dimension one view.

Click (Generate Dimensions Step by Step) from the customized Action Bar to start the creation of dimensions.

Step 3 - Enter a timeout value.

Enter a timeout value in seconds or clear the **Timeout** option to proceed manually, as shown in Figure 3–19.

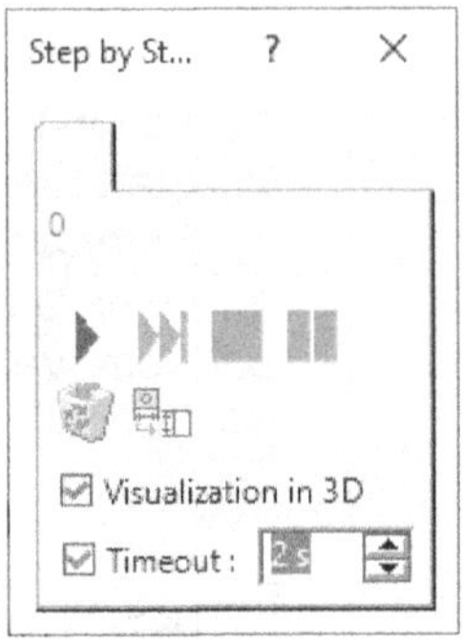

Figure 3–19

Step 4 - Generate dimensions.

Click (Next Dimension Generation) to begin generating dimensions. The first dimension displays on an appropriate view. The system pauses the length of time entered in the *Timeout* field and creates the next dimension.

Step 5 - Remove or transfer dimensions.

Click (Pause in Dimension Generation) to pause the dimension generation. When dimension generation has been paused, (Not Generated) and (Transferred) become available:

- Click (Not Generated) to remove a dimension that is not required.
- Click (Transferred) to switch from the current view to a different view by selecting the different view.

Step 6 - Reposition dimensions.

Manually reposition the dimensions or activate the view and then select (Dimension Positioning) to automatically reposition all of the linear dimensions. Radial dimension positions are not affected and must be repositioned manually.

Note: By default, the **Dimension Positioning** command is not found in the Action Bar. It will need to be added before it can be used to align dimensions in views. To add it to the Action Bar, select **Me>Preferences>Customize>Sections** and then place the (Dimension Positioning) command onto a section by using **Add Commands...**.

If the Action Pad does not display, it can be toggled on by selecting (Action Pad) from the Tools section of the Action Bar.

An alternative option would be to add the command to the Action Pad instead. The path for this would be **Me> Preferences>Customize>Action Pad**, then select **Add Commands.**

3.6 Dimension Generation Settings

You can modify dimension settings to generate dimensions on your drawing more effectively. Select **Me>Preferences>App Preferences> 3D Modeling>Mechanical Systems> Drafting> Generation** section to change the default dimension generation settings. When the Options dialog box opens, select the *Generation* tab.

The *Dimension generation* area is shown in Figure 3–20 and the options are described in the table below.

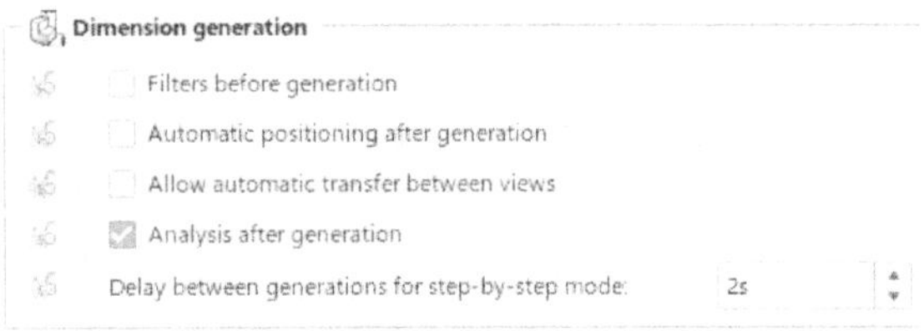

Figure 3–20

Option	Description
Filters before generation	Opens the Dimension Generation Filters dialog box, as shown below. 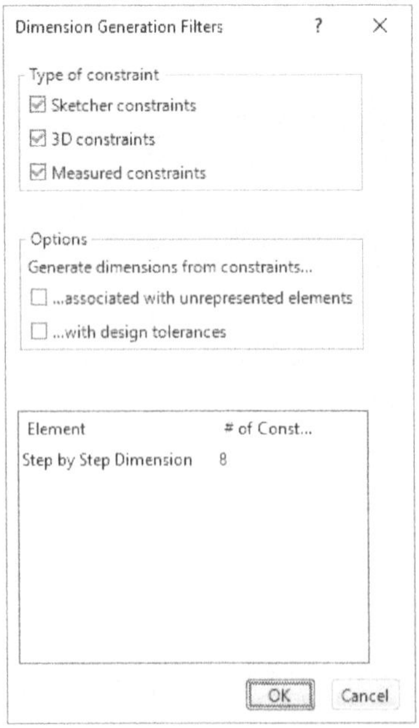

Automatic positioning after generation	Automatically cleans the display of dimensions after One Step dimension generation.
Allow automatic transfer between views	Enables transfer of dimensions between views using (Transferred).
Analysis after generation	Automatically opens the Generated Dimension Analysis dialog box after the dimension generation, which displays the number of constraints in the 3D model and the number of dimensions generated on the drawing. The dialog box also enables visual review of the 3D constraints and corresponding dimensions.

3.7 Modifying Dimension Properties

The standard Windows shortcut keys <Alt>+<Enter> can also be used to access Properties.

Automatically generated dimensions might contain lines and text that are difficult to read and interpret. Furthermore, they might not fulfill corporate standards in tolerancing and graphical representations. Dimension properties can be manually modified to improve drawing readability and to customize dimension tolerances and graphics.

To display dimension properties, right-click on the dimension and select **Properties**. If changing multiple dimensions is desired, start by pressing <Ctrl> first. The Properties dialog box opens as shown in Figure 3–21. It covers the following tabs: *Value*, *Tolerance*, *Dimension Line*, *Extension Line*, *Dimension Texts*, *Font*, and *Text*.

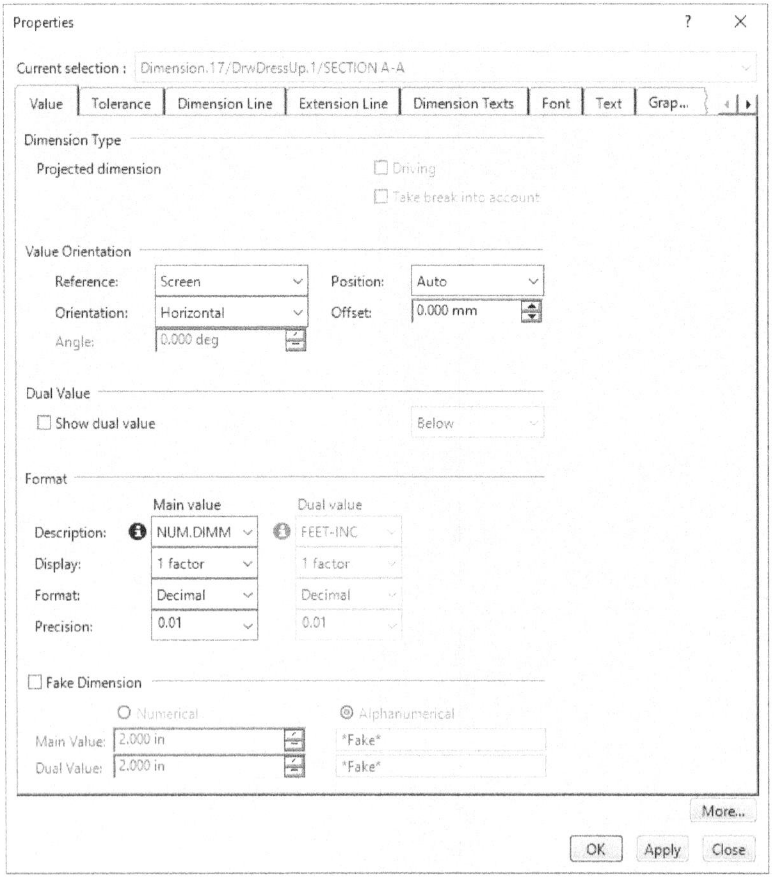

Figure 3–21

Value Tab

Projected Dimension

The **Driving** option controls the associativity of dimensions that have been added to geometry that is not imported from the 3D model but rather sketched in the Drafting app using tools such as Line, Circle, Profile, etc. When activated, this option enables you to modify the dimension values that drive the sketched geometry. Dimensions with the **Driving** option enabled display in blue in the drawing display. Double-click on the value to modify it in the Dimension Value dialog box, as shown in Figure 3–22.

*The **Drive geometry** option can also be selected in the Dimension Value dialog box.*

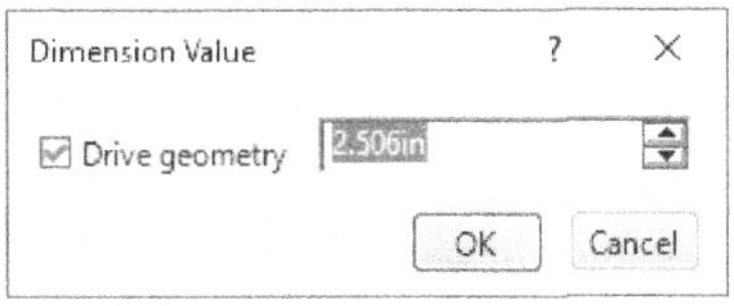

Figure 3–22

Value Orientation

The dimension value can be oriented horizontally, vertically, or at a fixed angle by changing the **Orientation** type. It can also be offset from the dimension line by an **Offset** distance. The value can be placed in or outside the extension lines by modifying **Position**. The dimension shown in Figure 3–23 is oriented at a fixed angle of 45 degrees and is offset from the dimension line (center) by 4.5mm.

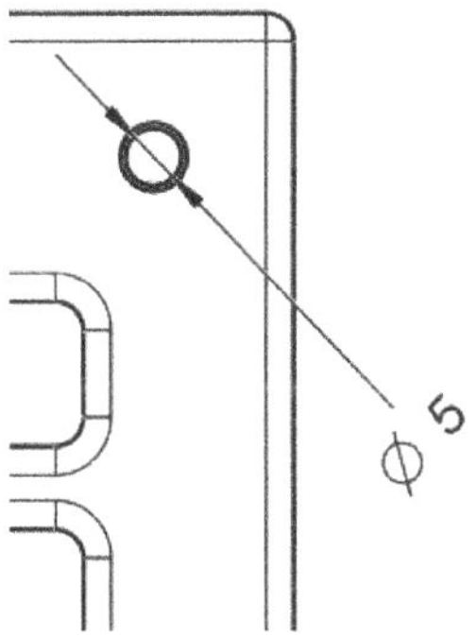

Figure 3–23

Dual Value

Selecting the **Show dual value** option inserts a second dimensional value below, beside, or as a fraction of the first dimensional value. The format options enable you to specify the units, precision, and display format for both the first and dual value dimensions.

A dual value in inches, with a decimal format with one-thousandth precision, and located below the first dimension value, is shown in Figure 3–24.

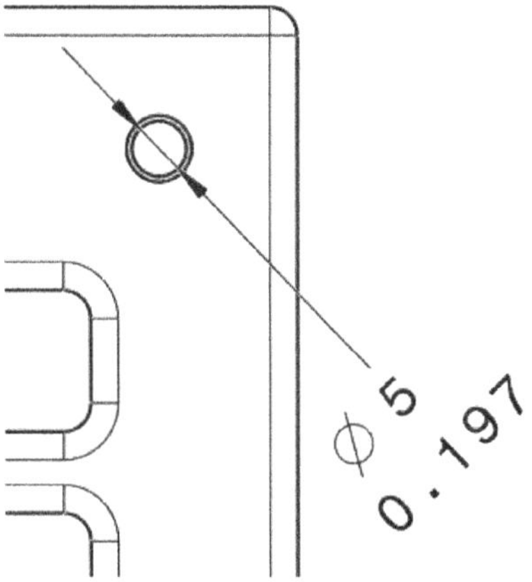

Figure 3–24

Fake Dimension

True dimension values can be replaced with user-defined numerical or alphanumeric values. Dimensions containing fake values display in brown on the drawing display.

Fake dimensions are useful when dimensioning a part that includes a design table. A symbolic dimension can be applied using a fake dimension. This symbol can then be related to a table on the drawing that defines the possible sizes in the design table, as shown in Figure 3–25.

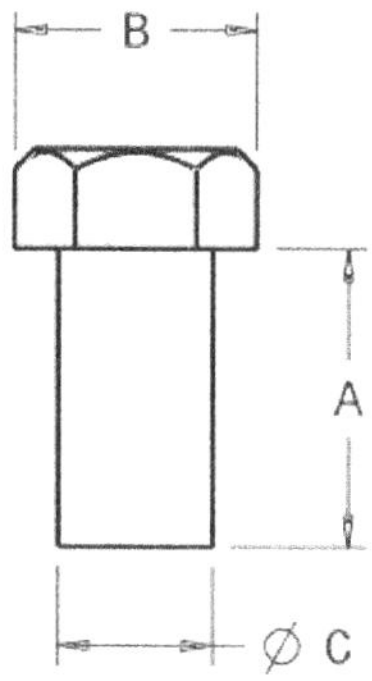

PartNumber	A	B	C
Bolt01	30	12.5	7.5
Bolt02	30	12.5	8
Bolt03	30	12.5	8.5
Bolt04	40	15	9
Bolt05	40	15	9.5
Bolt06	40	15	10

Figure 3–25

Tolerance Tab

Tolerance values can be created for the main and dual value dimensions separately. To create a tolerance, select the type in the drop-down list, and enter the upper and lower limits in the *Upper Value* and *Lower Value* fields. The tolerance value displays as shown in Figure 3–26.

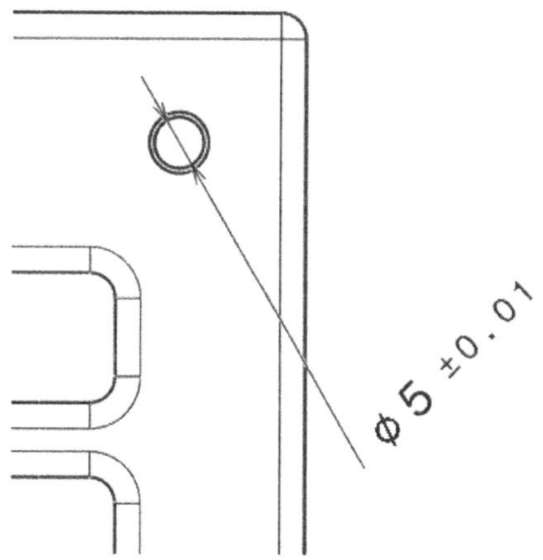

Figure 3–26

Dimension Line Tab

Change the dimension line graphics and symbol types. Select either the regular, two part, or leader-type line type in the Representations drop-down list, and customize the line and symbol thickness and color. The Reversal drop-down list switches the orientation of the dimension lines from inside to outside the extension lines.

The dimension line representation has been changed to **Two Parts** and *thickened* to **2** in Figure 3–27.

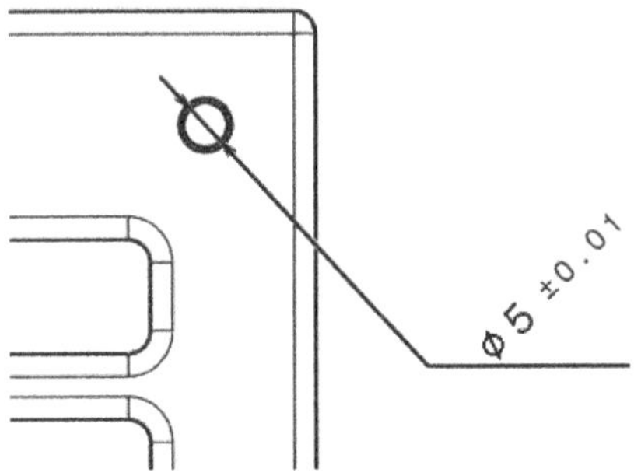

Figure 3–27

Extension Line Tab

Change the color and thickness of the extension lines, or disable them altogether by clearing the **Display extension line** option. By default, extension lines are perpendicular to the dimensioned edge. Skew the lines by entering a **Slant** angle.

Extremities

Overrun specifies the distance that an extension line extends past the dimension line. The **Blanking** option enables the extension line to be offset from the dimensioned face.

Funnel

Specify the height, width, and angle of an extension line funnel. **Funnel side** specifies which extension line to funnel, and **Funnel mode** switches between an external and internal funnel.

A slant angle of 5 degrees and a top funnel have been applied to the dimension shown in Figure 3–28.

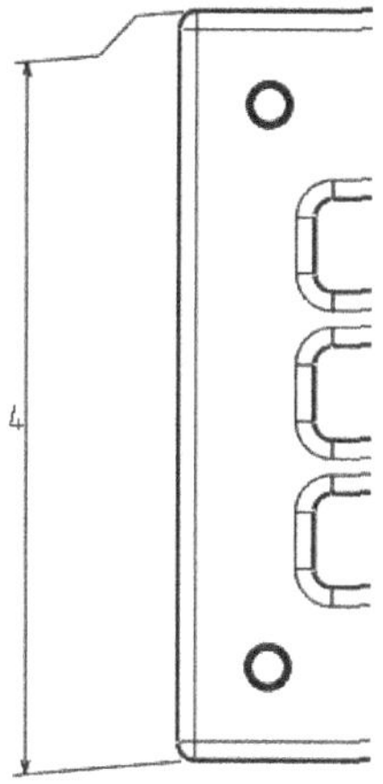

Figure 3–28

Dimension Texts Tab

Dimension texts are used to annotate dimensions. **Main value** represents the main dimension value text. The orientation of the text fields in this tab indicate the orientation of the text in the drawing view. You can also enter **Prefix - Suffix** and **Associated Texts**, which can contain symbols.

The **Typ** annotation has been added as a suffix in the *Associated Texts* field on the dimension shown in Figure 3–29.

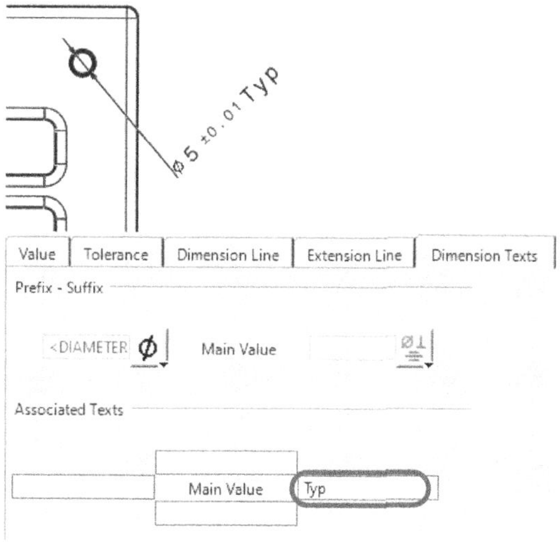

Figure 3–29

Font Tab

Customize dimension font style, size, and character ratio/ spacing.

Text Tab

Create text frames and set text positioning, as shown in Figure 3–30.

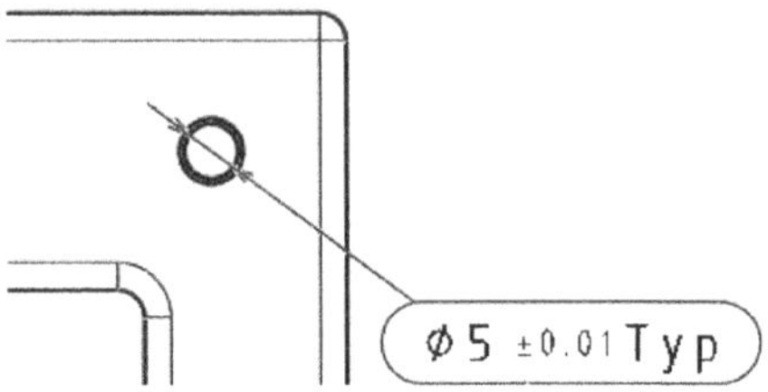

Figure 3–30

Practice 3a

Annotate a Drawing

Practice Objectives

- Create and manipulate dimensions.
- Create tolerances.

In this practice, you will continue developing the **ExhaustFlange** drawing by adding dimensions and other annotations. The annotated Front view is shown in Figure 3–31.

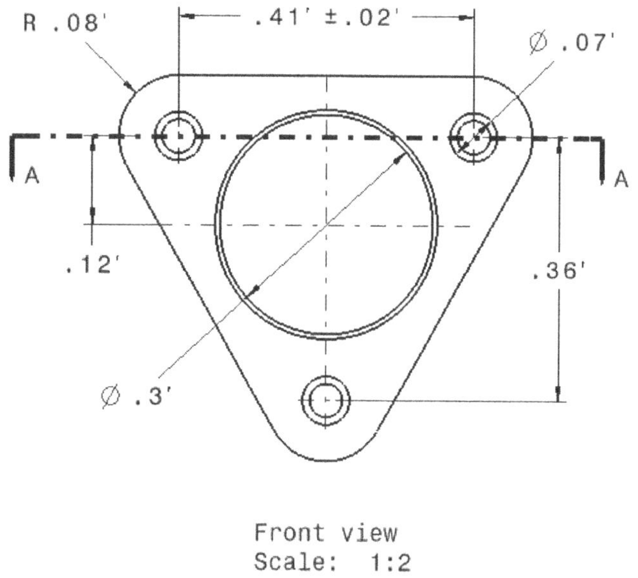

Figure 3–31

Task 1 - Import and open the ExhaustFlange.

1. Import and open **ExhaustFlange_3A.3dxml** from the practice files folder. While importing, set the *Duplication string* to **###_** where ### represents your initials.

2. Right-click on the **###_ExhaustFlange_Dims_3A** drawing in the tree and select *** object>Open in New App**. The drawing displays as shown in Figure 3–32.

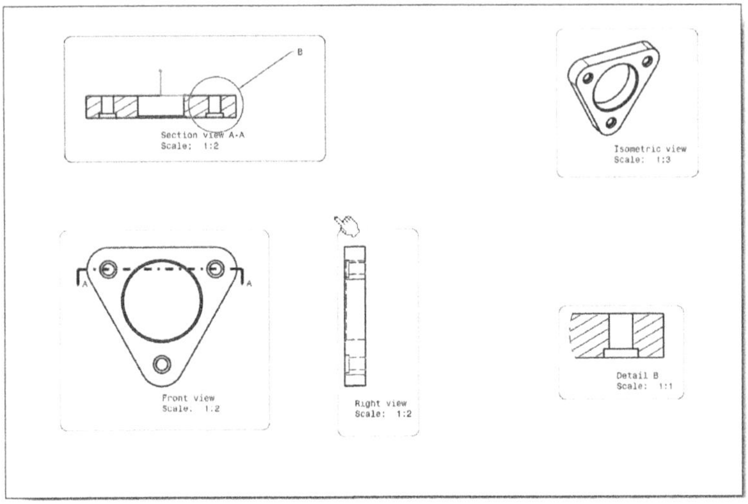

Figure 3–32

Task 2 - Show the Axis and Center Lines of a view.

1. Activate the **Front view**.
2. In the specification tree, select the **Front view**.
3. In the specification tree, hold <Shift> and select the **Detail B** view. All of the views in between should be highlighted, as shown in Figure 3–33.

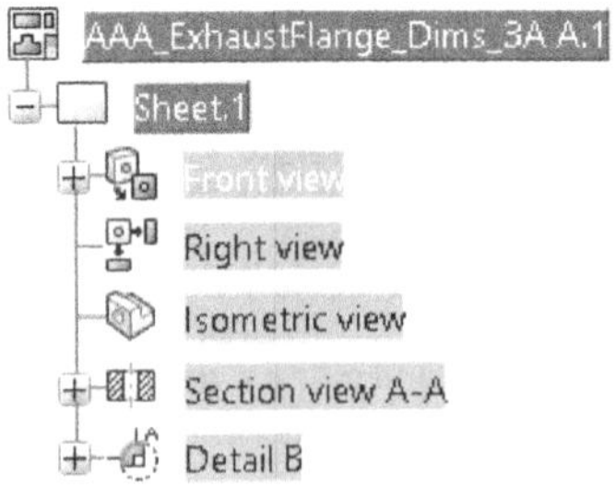

Figure 3–33

4. With all of the views highlighted, hold <Ctrl> and select **Isometric view**. This will drop it from the selection group, as shown in Figure 3–34.

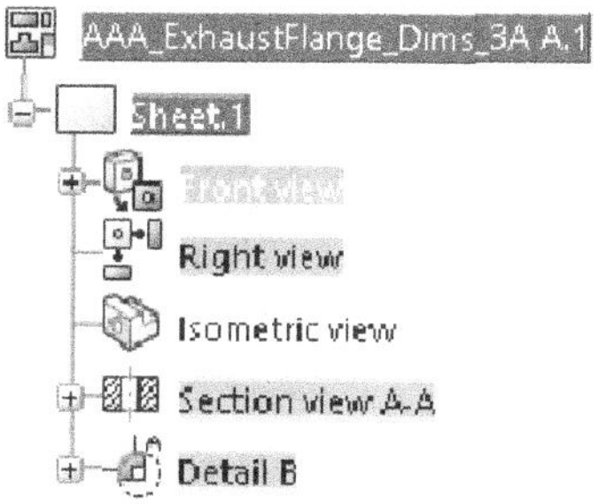

Figure 3–34

5. In the specification tree, right-click on any selected view and select **Properties**. The Properties dialog box opens.

6. In the Properties dialog box, in the *Generation* tab, select the **Axis** and **Center Line** options, as shown in Figure 3–35. Apply the changes and note the result.

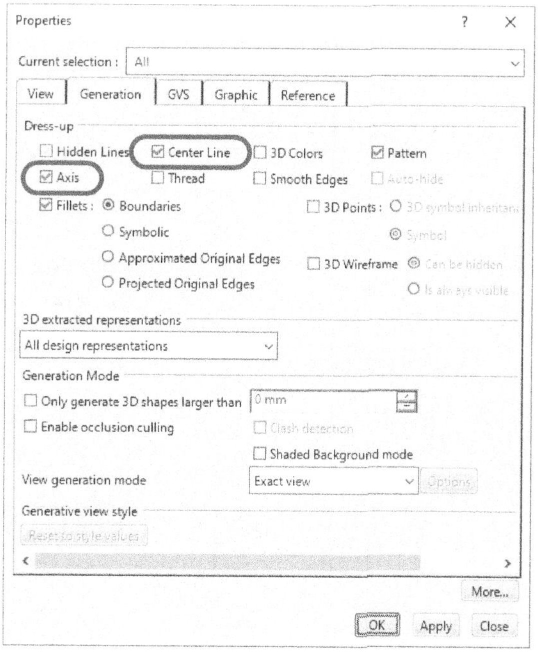

Figure 3–35

7. Click **OK**.

Task 3 - Add dimensions to the drawing.

1. Ensure that the Front view is active.
2. Zoom in on the Front view. In the Annotation section of the Action Bar, click (Dimensions).
3. Select the hole on the left side for the first dimension reference, as shown in Figure 3–36. The system creates a diameter dimension.

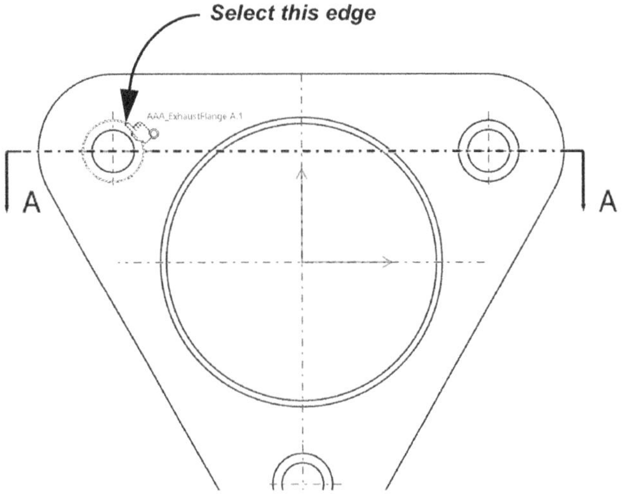

Figure 3–36

4. Select the hole on the right side for the second dimension reference, as shown in Figure 3–37. A length dimension displays between the two references.

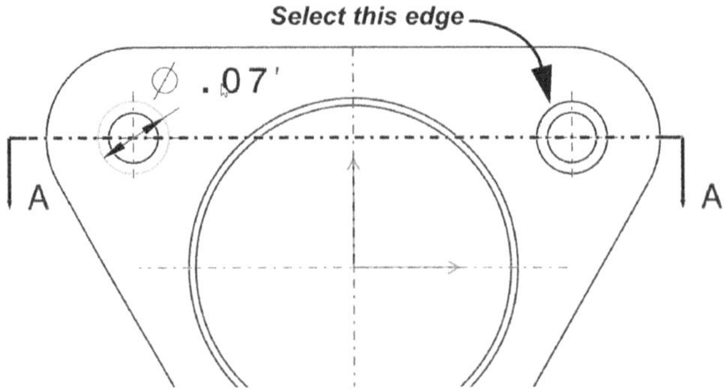

Figure 3–37

5. Drag the dimension line to the position shown in Figure 3–38 and place the dimension by clicking the left mouse button.

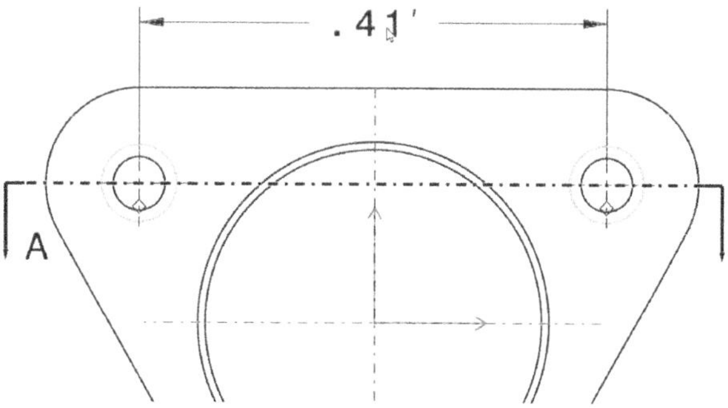

Figure 3–38

Task 4 - Create a dimension.

1. Double-click  (Dimensions) from the Annotation section of the Action Bar to create the dimensions shown in Figure 3–39.

Use the Force dimension placement mode options in the Tools Palette toolbar to force the dimension to be vertical, as required.

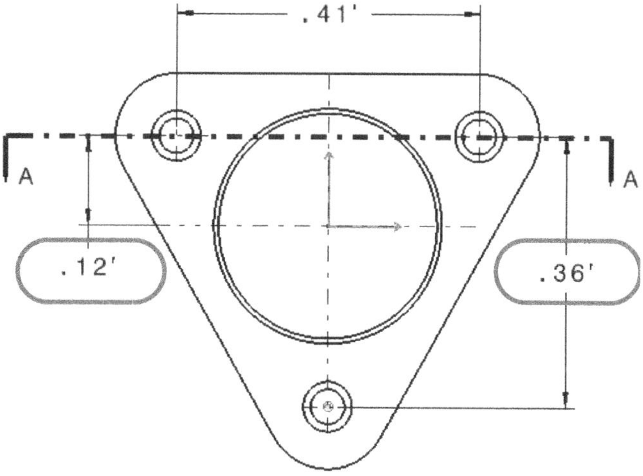

Figure 3–39

2. Create the two diameter dimensions shown in Figure 3–40.

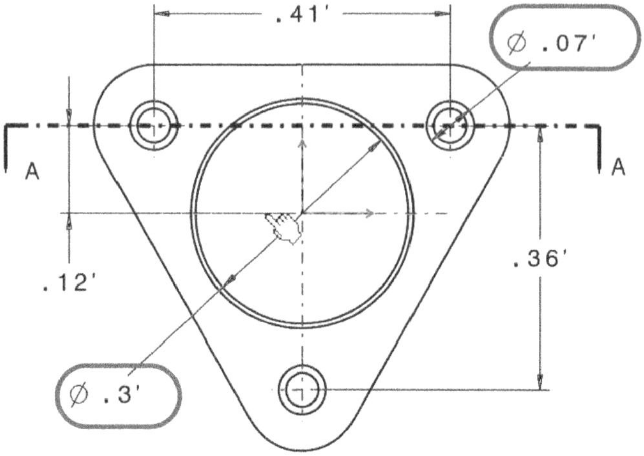

Figure 3–40

3. Use (Dimensions) to create the R.08' dimension shown in Figure 3–41. Select the arc shown in Figure 3–41 and right-click on **Radius Center** to create the dimension.

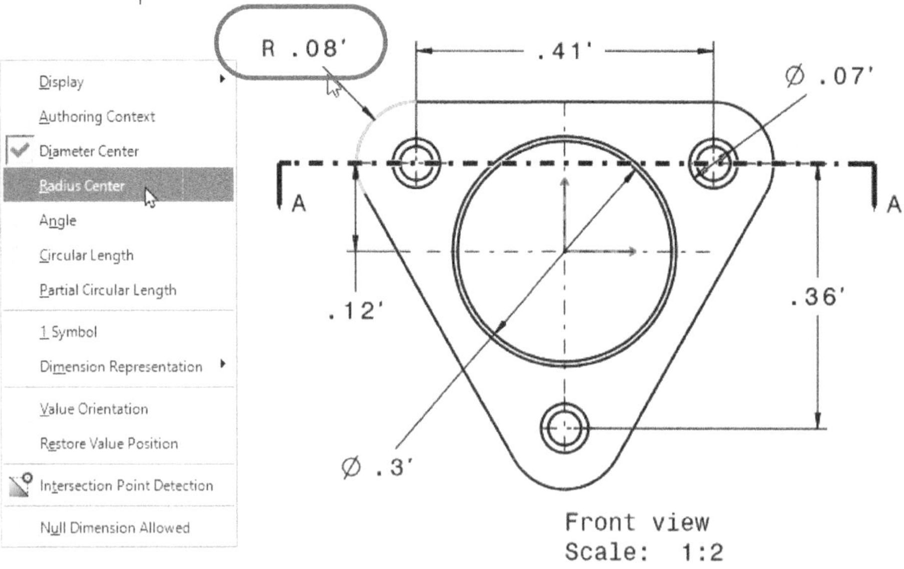

Figure 3–41

4. Create the dimensions shown in Figure 3–42.

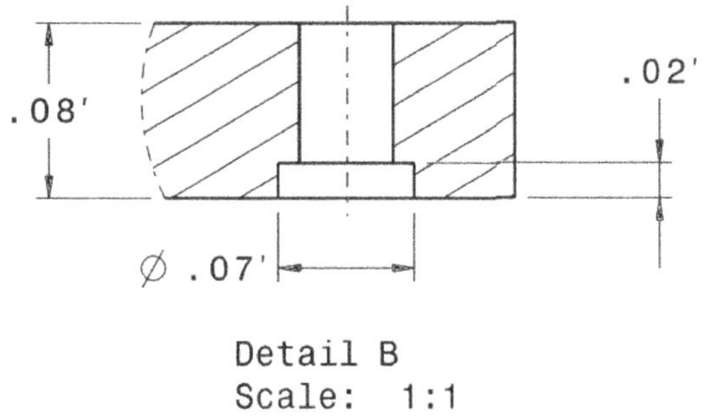

Figure 3–42

Task 5 - Manipulate dimensions.

1. Select the **.08' dimension** from Detail B. Right-click and select **Cut**, as shown in Figure 3–43.

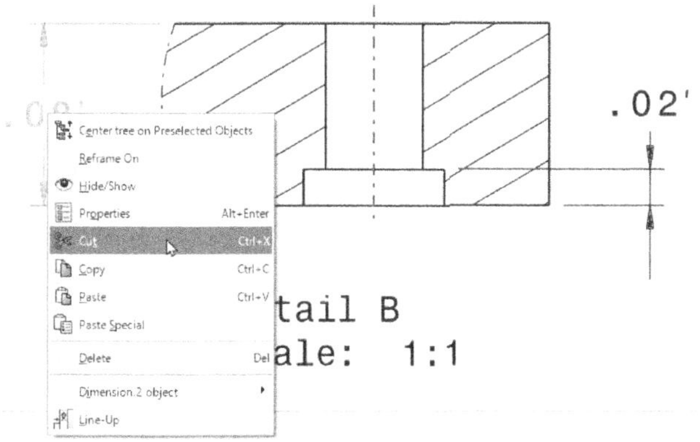

Figure 3–43

2. In the View section of the Action Bar, click  (Fit All In) to display the complete drawing.

3. In the specification tree, right-click on **Section view A-A** and select **Paste**, as shown in Figure 3–44.

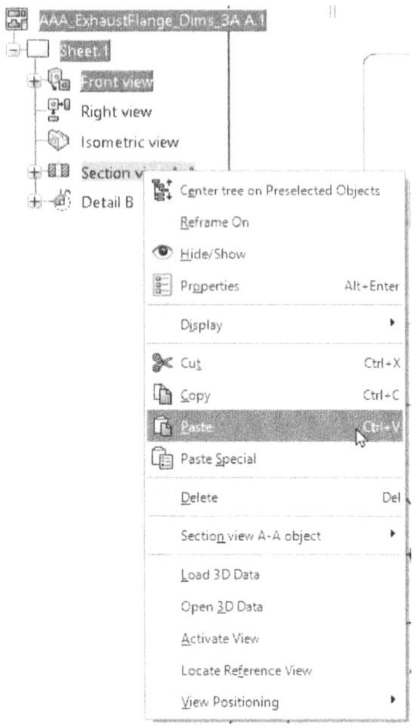

Figure 3–44

4. Move the .08' dimension to the position shown in Figure 3–45.

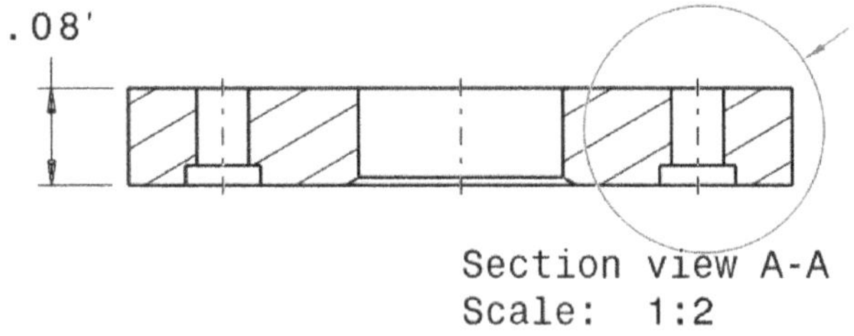

Figure 3–45

Task 6 - Add tolerance to a dimension.

1. Right-click on the **.41'** dimension and select **Properties**.

2. In the Properties dialog box, select the *Tolerance* tab and set the tolerance to **ANS_NUMS** for the *Main Value*, as shown in Figure 3–46.

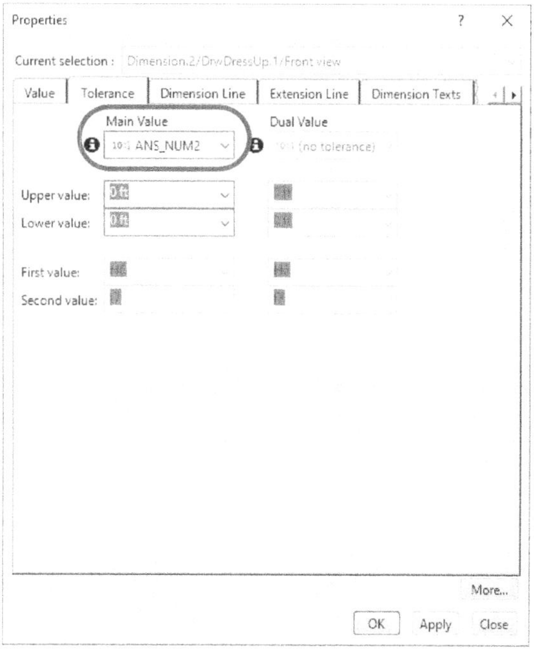

Figure 3–46

3. Select **Apply**. The .41' dimension updates, as shown in Figure 3–47.

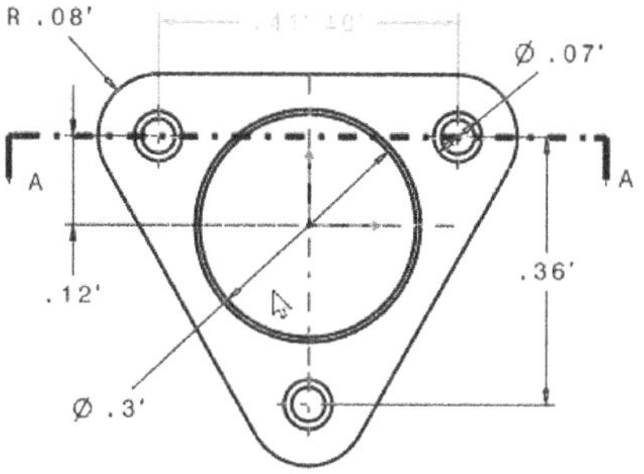

Figure 3–47

4. Set the *Upper value* to **0.2 ft** and *Lower value* to **-0.2 ft**, as shown in Figure 3–48.

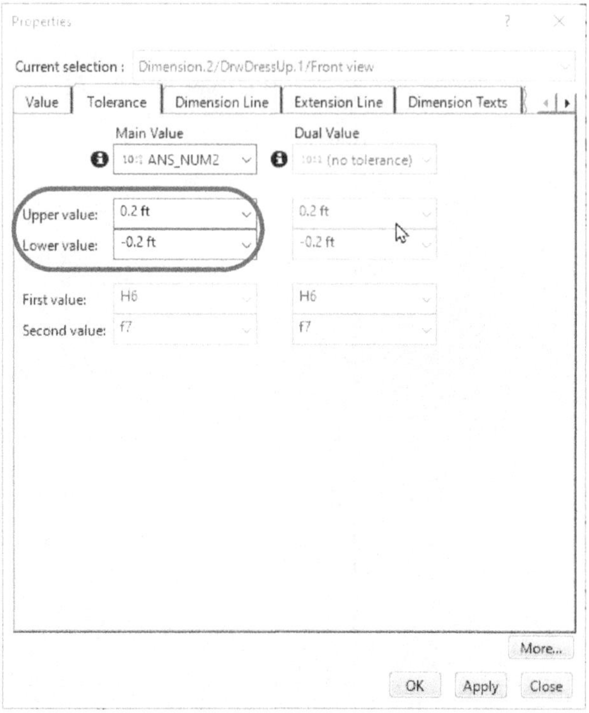

Figure 3–48

5. Click **Apply**. The .41' dimension updates, as shown in Figure 3–49.

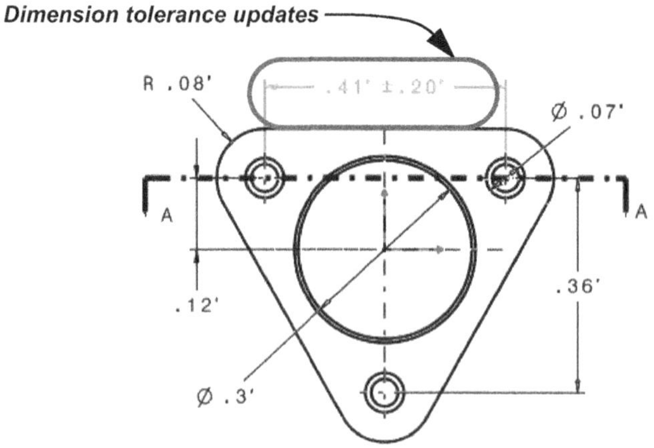

Figure 3–49

6. Zoom in on the Detail view and select the **.02'** dimension, as shown in Figure 3–50.

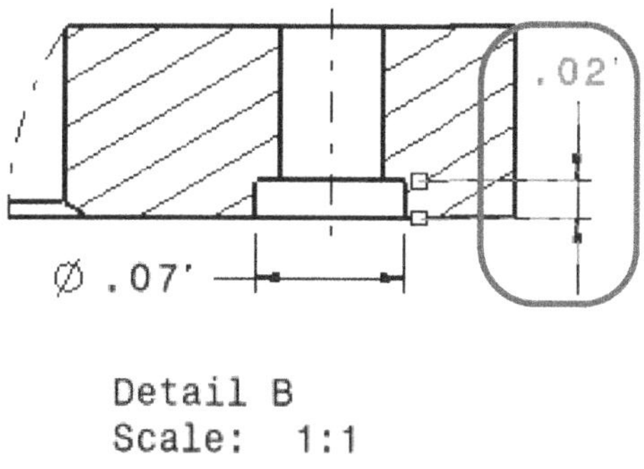

Figure 3–50

7. Right-click on the **.02'** dimension and select **Properties**.

8. Select the *Tolerance* tab and set the following values, as shown in Figure 3–51:

- *Main Value:* **ANS_NUM2**
- *Upper value:* **0.008**
- *Lower value:* **-0.004**

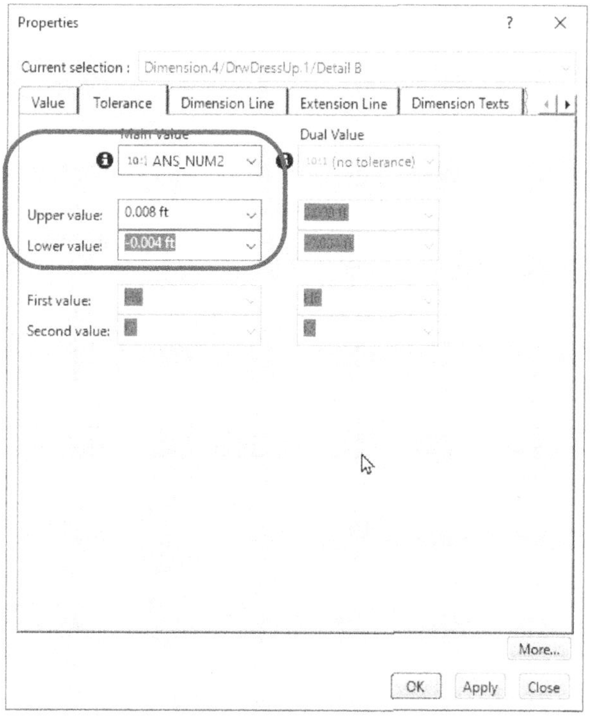

Figure 3–51

9. Click **OK**. The drawing displays as shown in Figure 3–52.

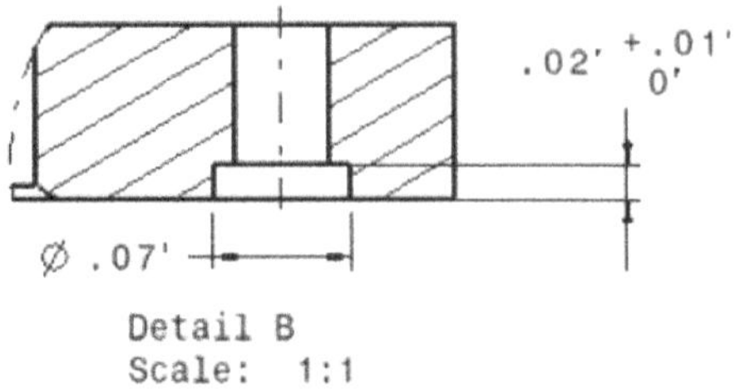

Figure 3–52

Note that the tolerance reads 0'. This is because the dimension precision is currently set to 0.01. In the next steps, you will increase the precision so that the tolerance can be seen.

10. Open the Properties dialog box for the .02' dimension and select the *Value* tab. Set the following values, as shown in Figure 3–53:

Setting the display to 2 factors will show the dimension values in inches instead of feet.

- *Display:* **2 factors**
- *Precision:* **0.001**

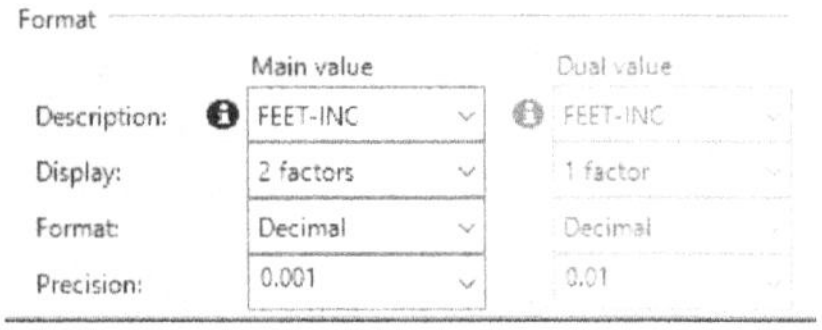

Figure 3–53

11. Click **OK**. The drawing updates as shown in Figure 3–54. Note that the dimensions have changed to inches.

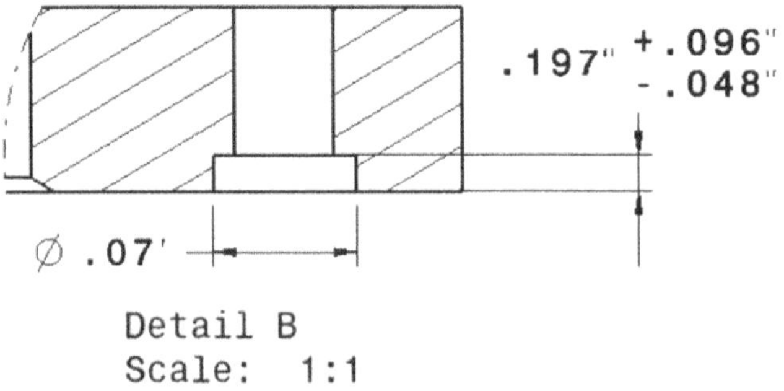

Figure 3–54

Task 7 - Create a chamfer dimension.

1. Zoom in on the Right view, as shown in Figure 3–55.

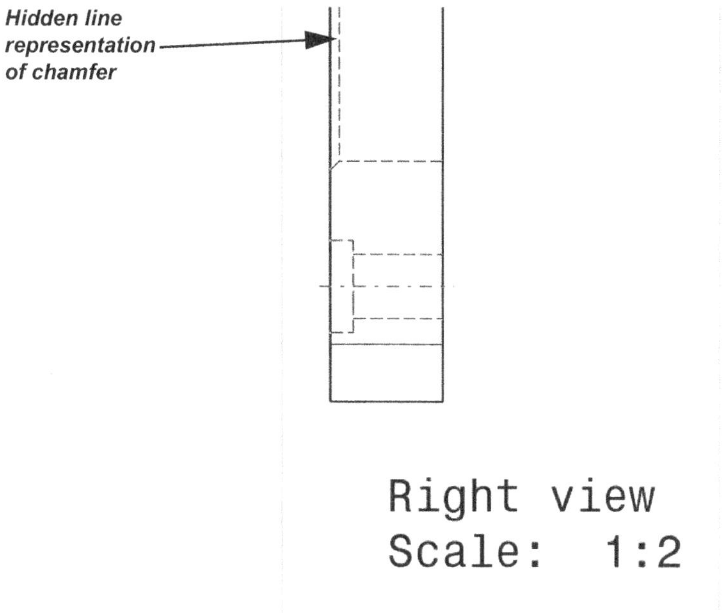

Figure 3–55

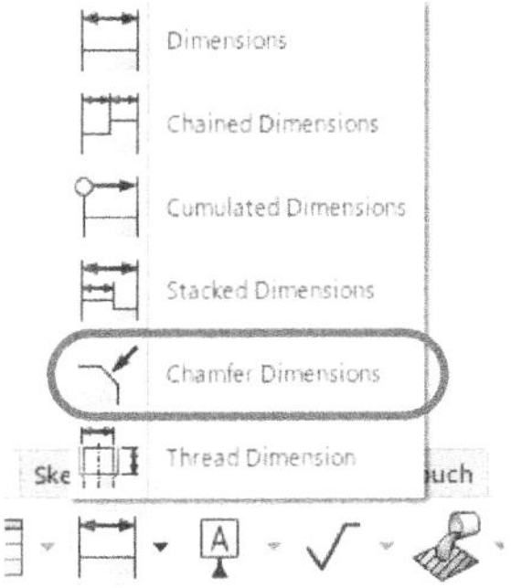

2. From the (Dimension) flyout in the Annotation section of the Action Bar, click (Chamfer Dimensions). The Tools Palette toolbar displays with the options for controlling the chamfer dimension, as shown in Figure 3–56.

Figure 3–56

3. Select the **Length x Angle** option and select the three references shown in Figure 3–57.

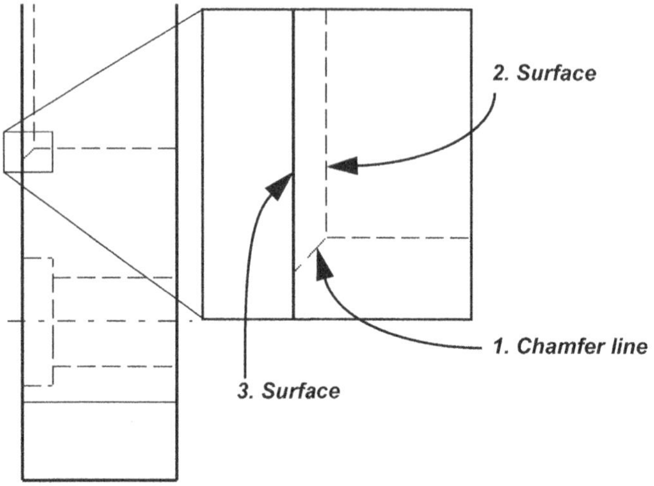

Figure 3–57

4. Place the chamfer dimension. The drawing displays as shown in Figure 3–58.

*If the dimension does not look like the one in Figure 3–58, right-click and select **Length x Angle** before placing the dimension.*

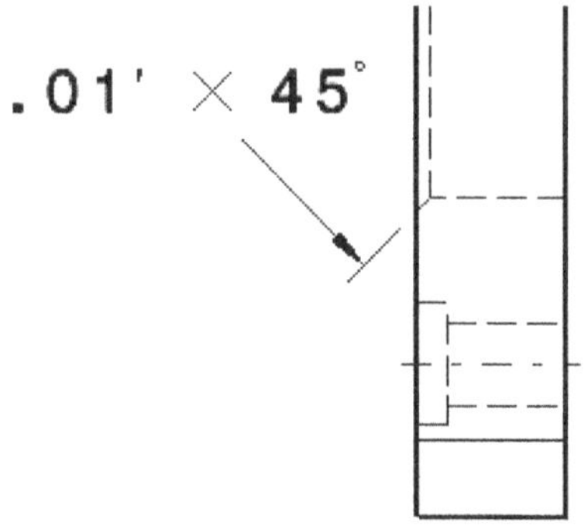

Figure 3–58

Task 8 - Create a thread dimension.

In this task, you will add a thread dimension to the drawing. The thread dimension can only be shown by selecting the representation of a thread surface. You must enable thread display in the drawing view.

1. In the specification tree, press and hold <Ctrl>, select **Section view A-A** and **Detail B**, then right-click and select **Properties**.

2. Enable the **Thread** option, as shown in Figure 3–59.

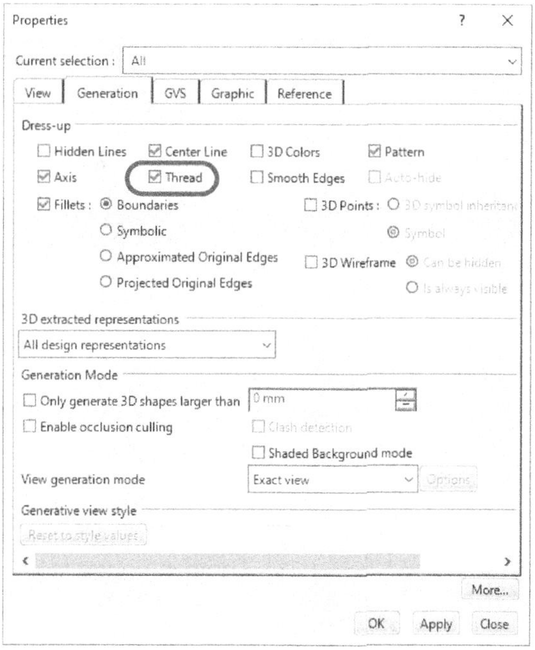

Figure 3–59

The updated drawing view displays as shown in Figure 3–60.

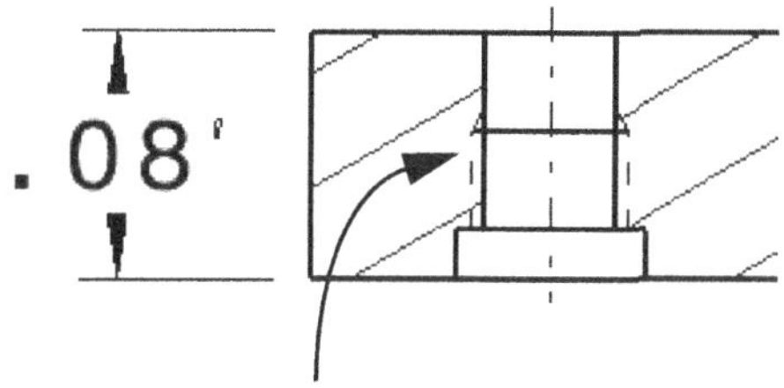

Thread representation

Figure 3–60

3. Zoom in on Section view A-A. From the Annotation section in the Action Bar, click (Thread Dimension) and select the thread representation.

4. Arrange the dimensions so that the drawing displays as shown in Figure 3–61.

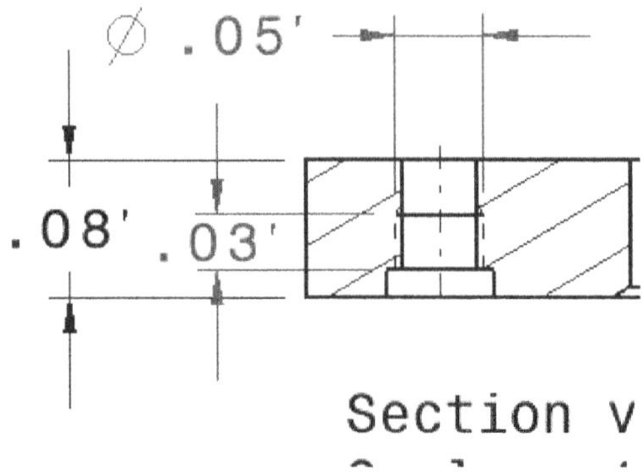

Figure 3–61

Task 9 - Create a true length dimension.

1. Zoom in on the Isometric view.

2. Click  (Length/Distance Dimensions) to create a Length/ Distance dimension between the two holes shown in Figure 3–62.

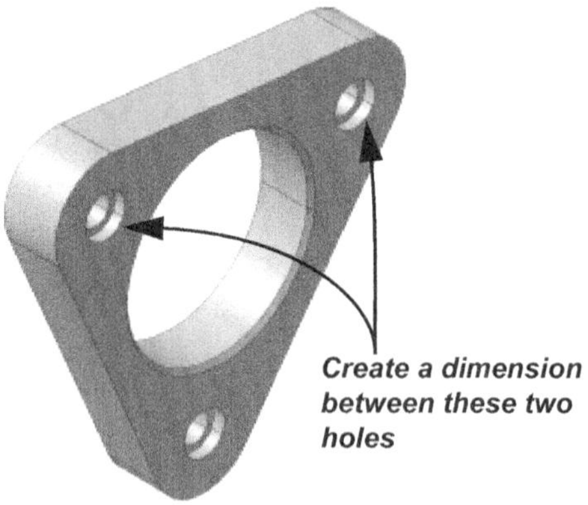

Figure 3–62

Note that you cannot create the dimension because the view generation mode is currently set to **Raster**. To create the dimension, the view generation mode must first be changed to **Exact view**.

3. Press <Esc> to cancel the dimension creation.
4. In the specification tree, right-click on **Isometric view** and select **Properties**.
5. In the *Generation* tab, in the View generation mode drop-down list, select **Exact view**.
6. Click **OK**.
7. Create a dimension between the two holes shown in Figure 3–63.

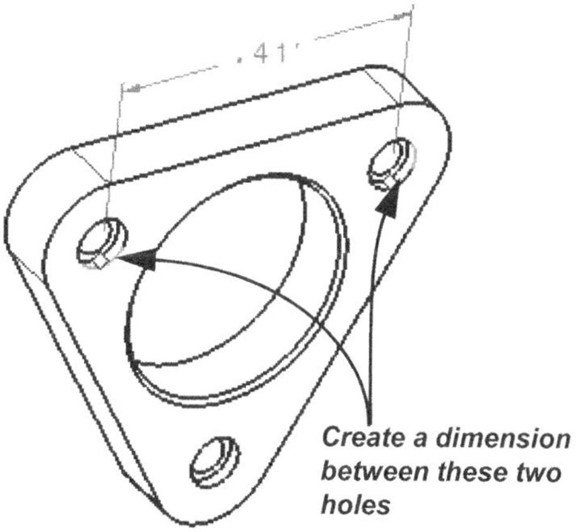

Figure 3–63

Design Considerations

When dimensioning an isometric view, the system automatically switches the dimension representation to **True Length Dimension**, as indicated by the highlighted icon in the Tools Palette toolbar, as shown in Figure 3–64.

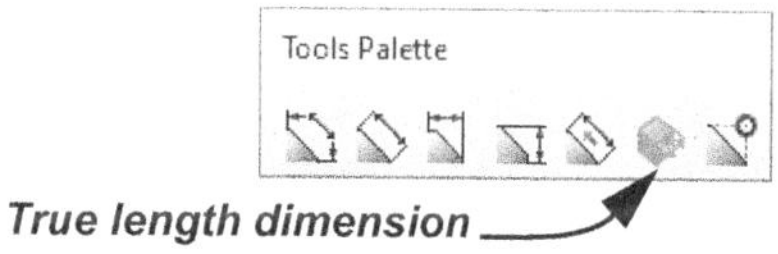

Figure 3–64

8. Place the dimension on the drawing. The extension lines of the dimension are not exactly vertical. To change this orientation, you will use the Dimension Properties dialog box.

9. Right-click on the **.41'** dimension and select **Properties**. Select the *Extension Line* tab, as shown in Figure 3–65.

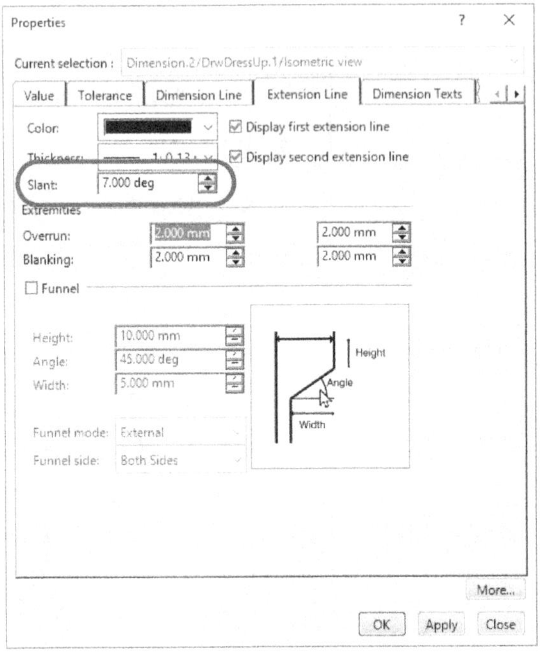

Figure 3–65

Note: A negative angle may need to be entered. Use ***-7deg*** *if needed to get vertical extension lines.*

10. Enter **7deg** for the *Slant value*, as shown above in Figure 3–65, and click **OK**. The drawing displays as shown in Figure 3–66.

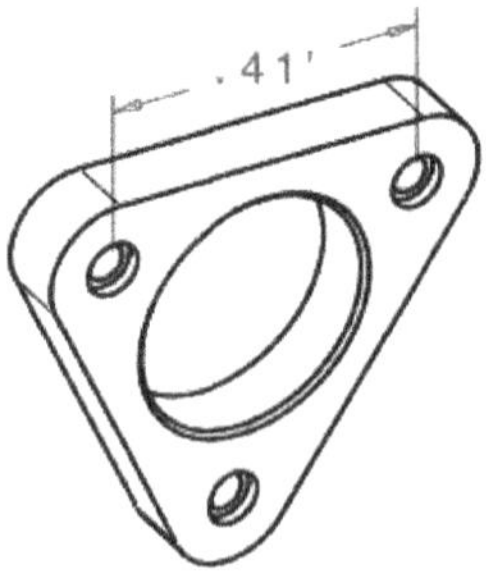

Figure 3–66

Task 10 - Create a drawing sheet and add a view.

1. Select (Create a New Sheet) at the top of the drawing next to *Sheet.1* to add **Sheet.2**.

2. Create a Front view on **Sheet.2**. Select the surface from the 3D model shown in Figure 3–67.

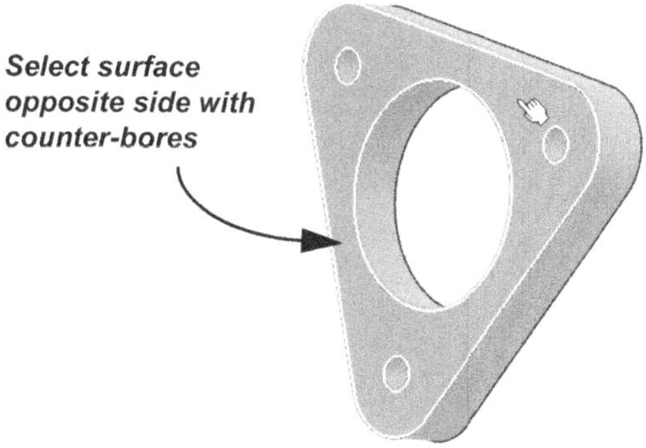

Figure 3–67

3. Click anywhere on **Sheet.2** to place the Front view.

4. Change the *scale* of the view to **1:2**. The Front view displays as shown in Figure 3–68.

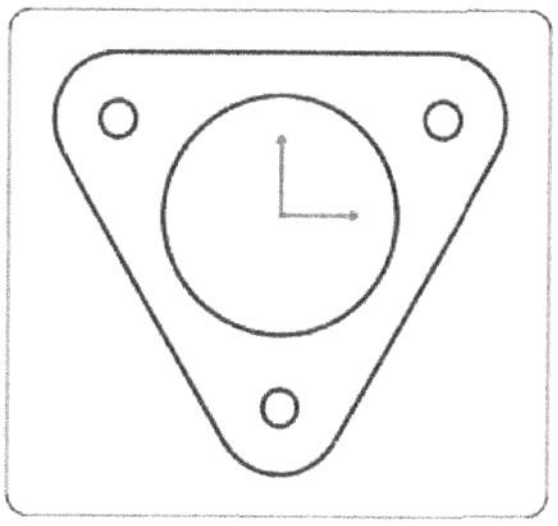

Figure 3–68

Task 11 - Create a hole table.

Design Considerations

The units defined in the Options dialog box affect the creation of the hole dimension table. To create a hole dimension table in inches, the default unit system must be also be in inches.

1. Select **Me>Preferences>Common Preferences> Parameters, Measures, and Units>Units.**

2. In the list, select **Length**. Change the *Units* to **Inch**, as shown in Figure 3–69.

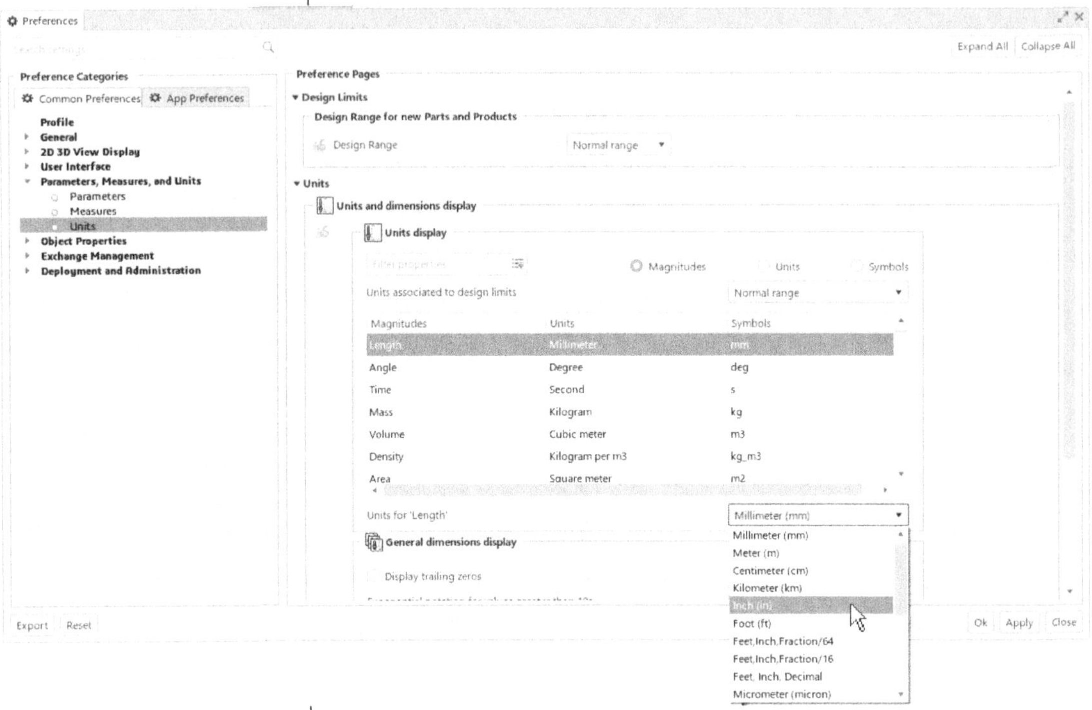

Figure 3–69

3. Click **OK**.

4. Hold <Ctrl> and select the three holes shown in Figure 3–70.

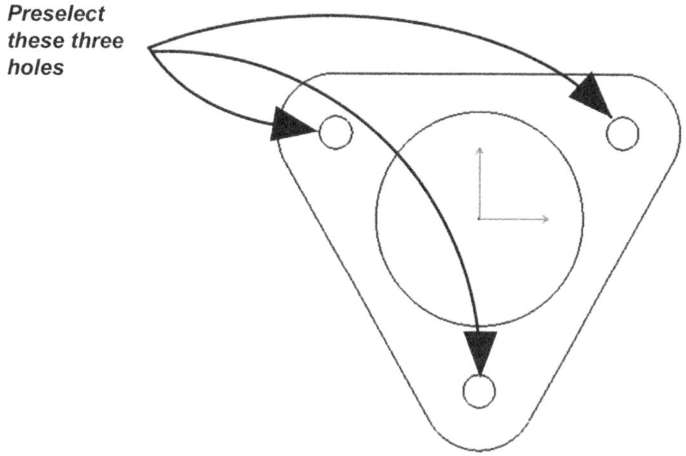

Figure 3–70

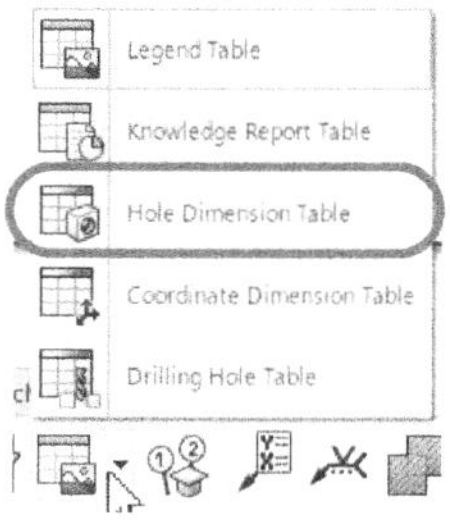

5. In the expanded area of the Annotation section of the Action Bar, click  (Hole Dimension Table). The Axis System and Table Parameters dialog box opens, as shown in Figure 3–71.

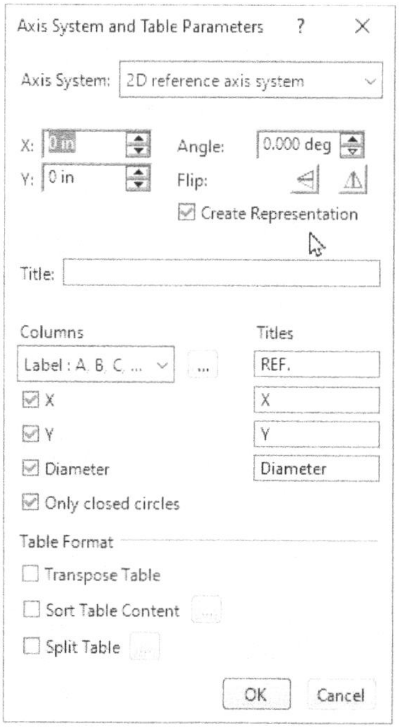

Figure 3–71

6. Click **OK** to accept all of the default values.

7. Drag the hole table to a location, as shown in Figure 3–72. Click to finalize the creation of the hole table.

Holes are labeled in the order in which they are selected.

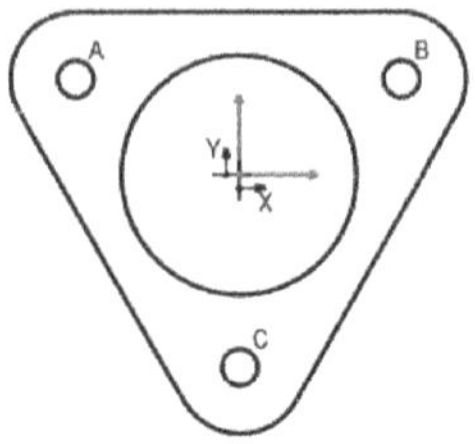

REF.	X	Y	Diameter
A	-2.46	1.42	0.54
B	2.46	1.42	0.54
C	0	-2.84	0.54

Figure 3–72

8. Select **Me>Preferences>Common Preferences>Parameters, Measures, and Units>Units**. Reset the *Length unit* to **Millimeter**.

9. Save the drawing and close all of the tabs.

Practice 3b Linear Dimensioning

Practice Objectives

- Create length/distance dimensions.
- Create chained dimensions.
- Create stacked dimensions.
- Create cumulated dimensions.

This practice is intended to demonstrate the differences between the four linear dimensions tools in the Drafting app. The drawing created in this practice is not intended to be fully detailed. It is only used to demonstrate the chained, cumulated, and stacked dimension tools.

The completed drawing is shown in Figure 3–73.

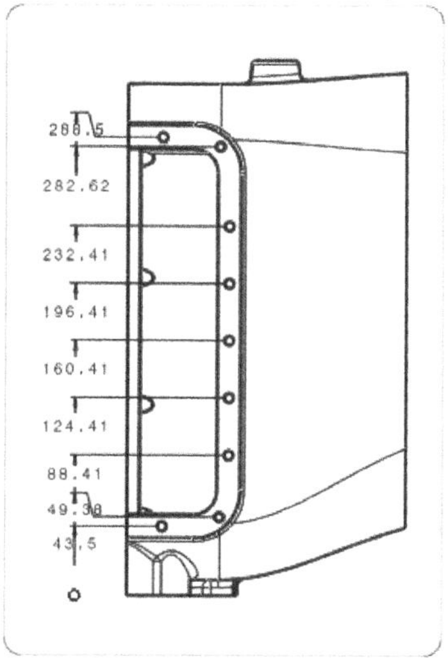

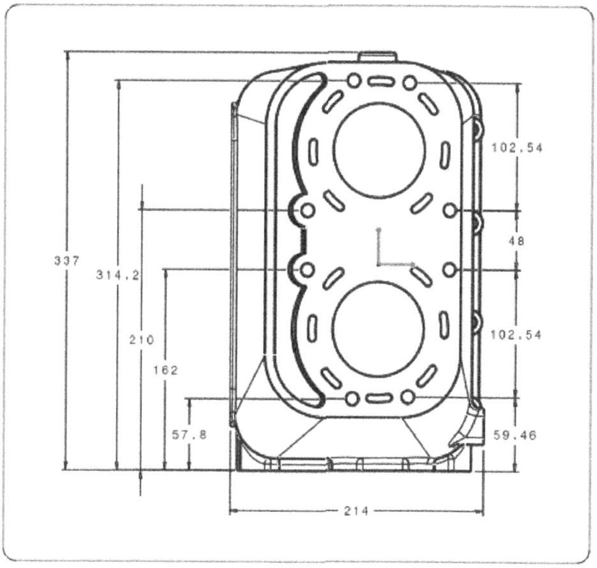

Figure 3–73

Task 1 - Import and open LinearDimensioning.

1. Import **LinearDimensioning.3dxml** from the practice files folder. While importing, set the *Duplication string* to **###_** where ### represents your initials.
2. Right-click on **###_1703** and select **Open.**
3. Right-click on the **###_LinearDimensioning** drawing in the tree and select *** object>Open in New App**. The drawing displays as shown in Figure 3–74.

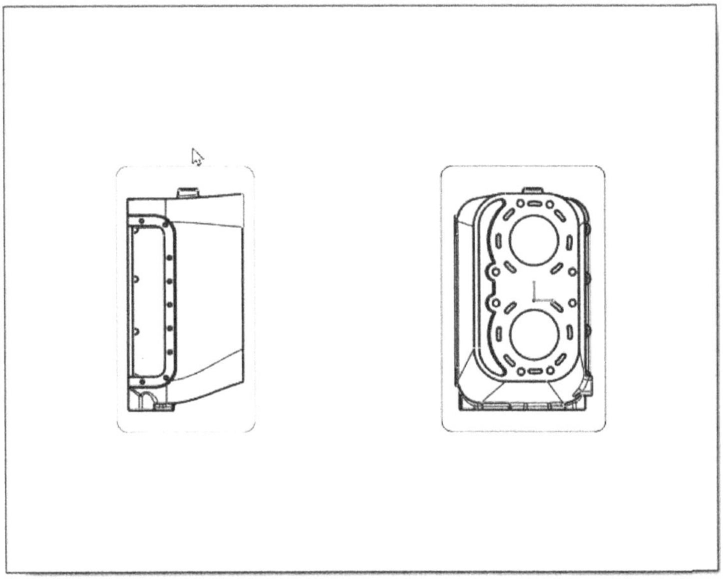

Figure 3–74

Task 2 - Create a length dimension.

In this task, you will create an overall height and width dimension for the view on the right side of the drawing.

1. Zoom in on the Front view, activate it, and select

    (Dimensions).

2. Create the two dimensions shown in Figure 3–75.

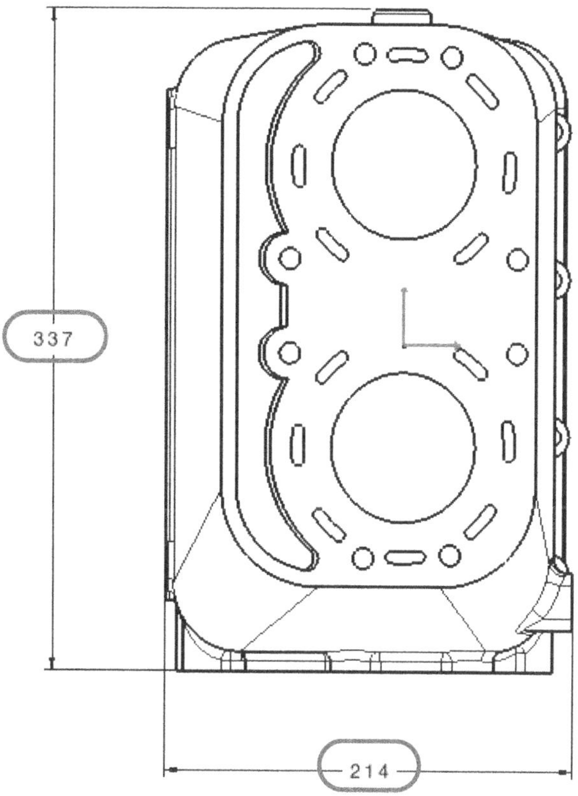

Figure 3–75

Design Considerations

The **Dimensions** icon is used to create a variety of independent dimensions. Each dimension can be modified, moved, and deleted independent of the rest.

Task 3 - Create a chained dimension.

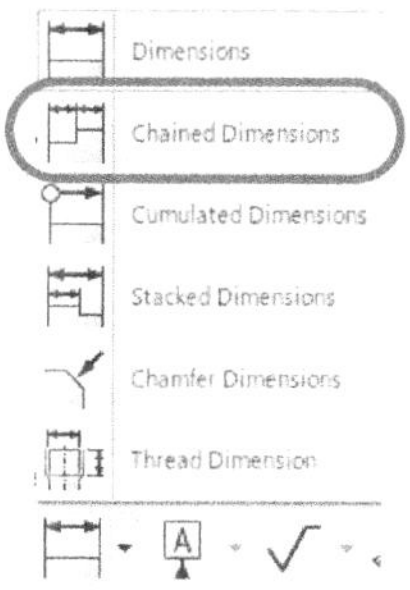

1. Expand the flyout next to  (Dimensions), then click  (Chained Dimensions).

2. In the Tools Palette toolbar, click  (Force Vertical Dimension).

3. Begin the chain by selecting the bottom edge of the Front view, as shown in Figure 3–76.

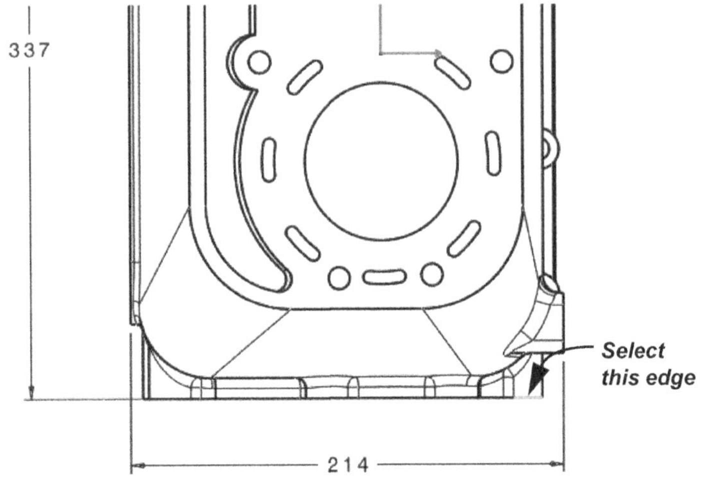

Figure 3–76

4. Select the hole shown in Figure 3–77.

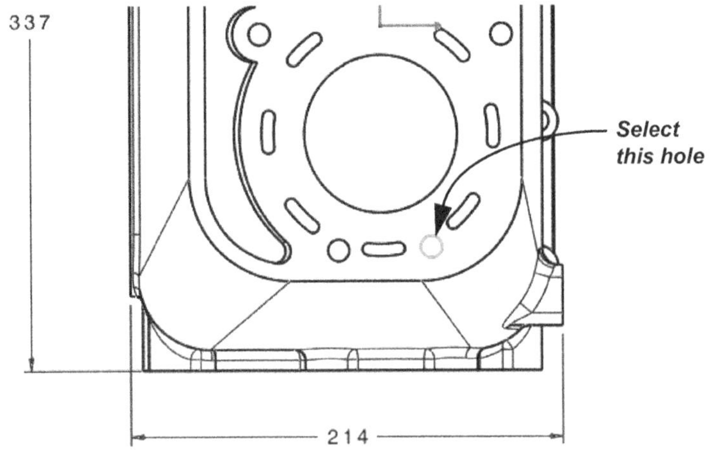

Figure 3–77

A length dimension displays between the two selected entities, as shown in Figure 3–78. Do not place the dimension.

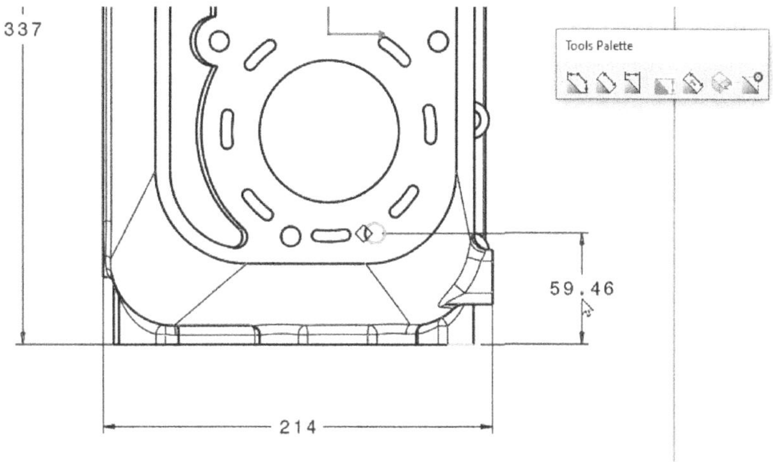

Figure 3–78

5. Continue to select the three holes, as shown in Figure 3–79. A chain of dimensions is created.

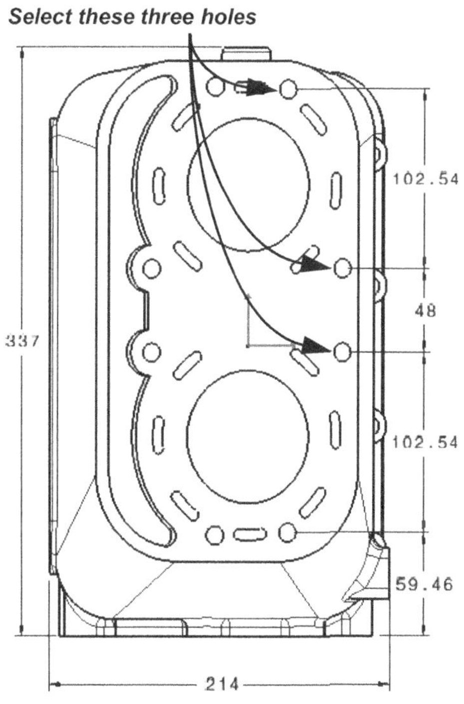

Figure 3–79

6. To complete the creation of the dimension chain, select a placement location on the drawing.

7. Select and drag any of the dimensions. Since the dimensions were created as a chain, all four dimensions move together.

Design Considerations

A dimension chain is a quick method of developing a series of connected dimensions. It minimizes the number of references selected.

Task 4 - Create a stacked dimension.

To compare the results of chained and stacked dimensions, you will create a similar set of dimensions on the left side of the Front view.

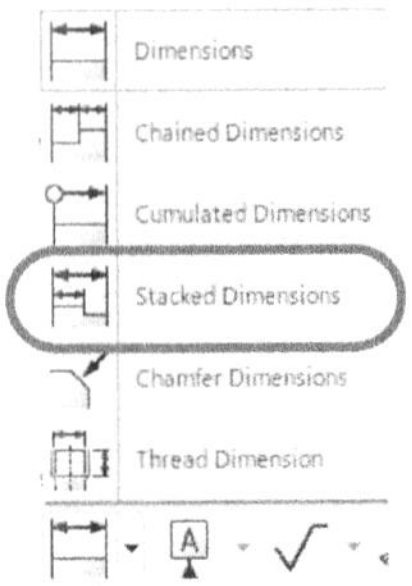

To lock the orientation of the dimensions, hold <Ctrl>.

1. Expand the flyout next to  (Dimensions), then click  (Stacked Dimensions).
2. Select the edge and the holes as shown in Figure 3–80.

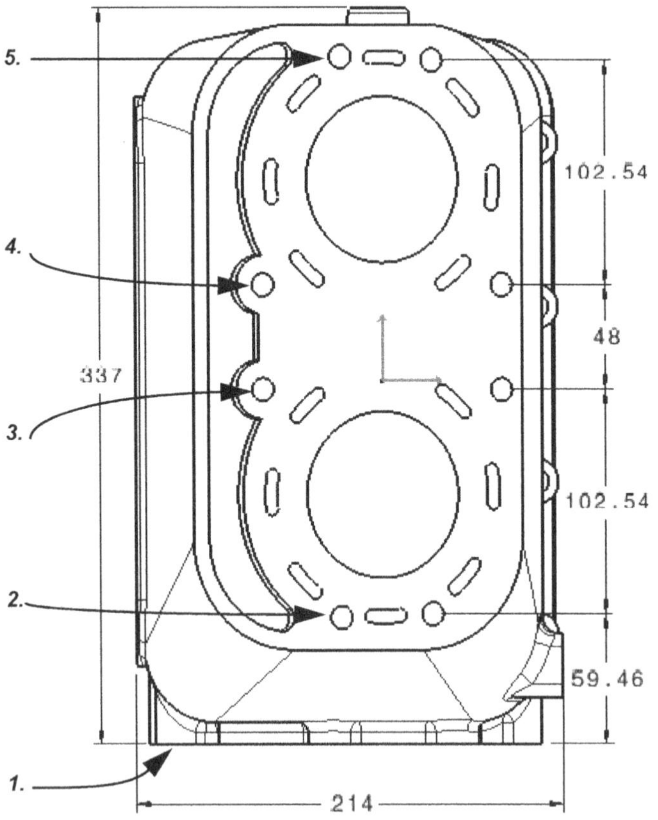

Figure 3–80

3. As you place the dimension, note that the order of dimensions automatically adjusts, depending on the side of the selected features on which the dimension is placed.

4. Place the dimension. You will need to adjust the position of the 337 dimension, as shown in Figure 3–81.

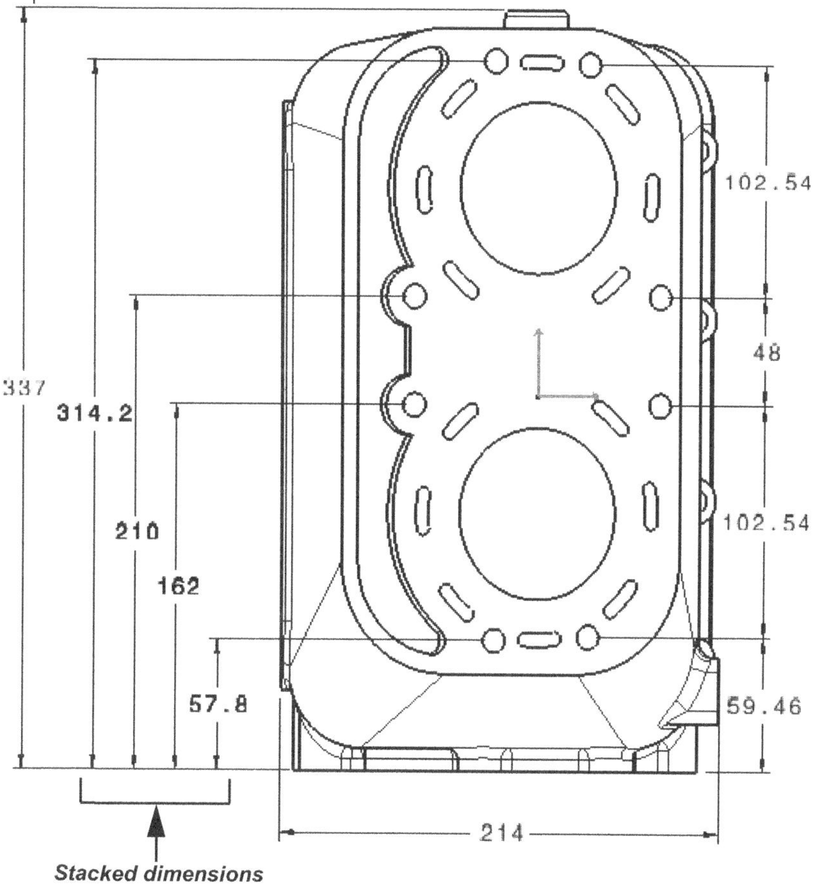

Figure 3–81

Design Considerations

Stacked dimensions behave in the same way as chained dimensions. By default, all of the stacked dimensions are grouped together and selecting any one dimension will select them all. To change this, select any of the dimensions created and a context menu will appear. (Group) is the icon shown by default and keeps them acting as one unit. Toggle the **Group** icon to (Elements) instead. This will enable you to select and/or delete the dimensions independently of the group.

Unlike chained dimensions, stacked dimensions share a common baseline, defined by the first selection.

Task 5 - Create a cumulated dimension.

In this task, you will create a cumulated dimension to dimension the hole positions in the Left view. A cumulated dimension is similar to a stacked dimension, because it uses the baseline defined by the first selection. The difference lies in the way the dimensions are represented.

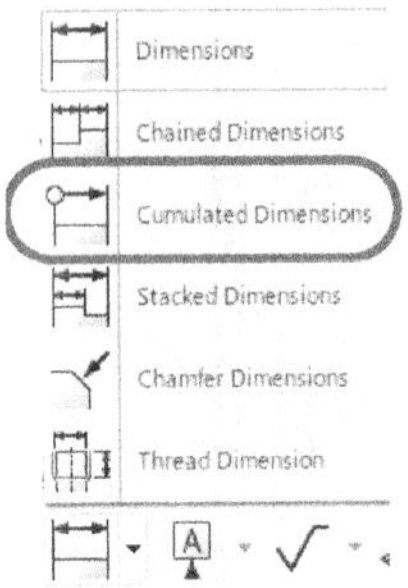

1. Activate the **Left view**.
2. From the Annotation section of the Action Bar, click  (Cumulated Dimensions).
3. Select the bottom edge of the Left view and select the hole to create the dimension shown in Figure 3–82. Do not place the dimension.

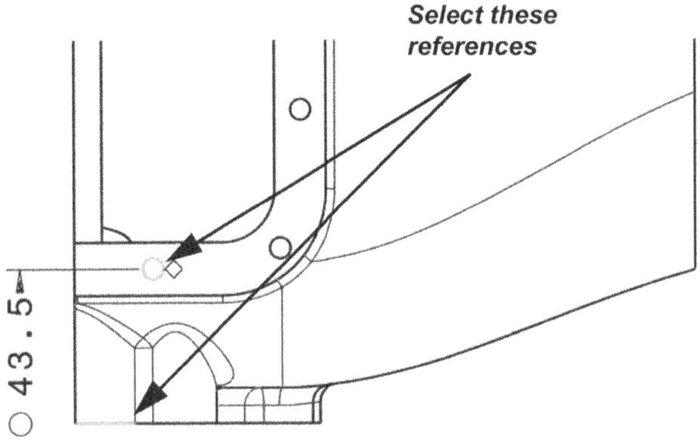

Figure 3–82

Design Considerations

Note the default orientation of the dimension. To dimension all of the holes on the bottom mounting surface, the orientation should be rotated 90 degrees. This is done using the **Value Orientation** option.

4. Before placing the dimension, right-click on it and select **Value Orientation**.
5. In the Orientation drop-down list, select **Perpendicular** and click **OK**. The system displays the dimension horizontally.

6. Continue to select the remaining eight holes to create the dimensions shown in Figure 3–83.

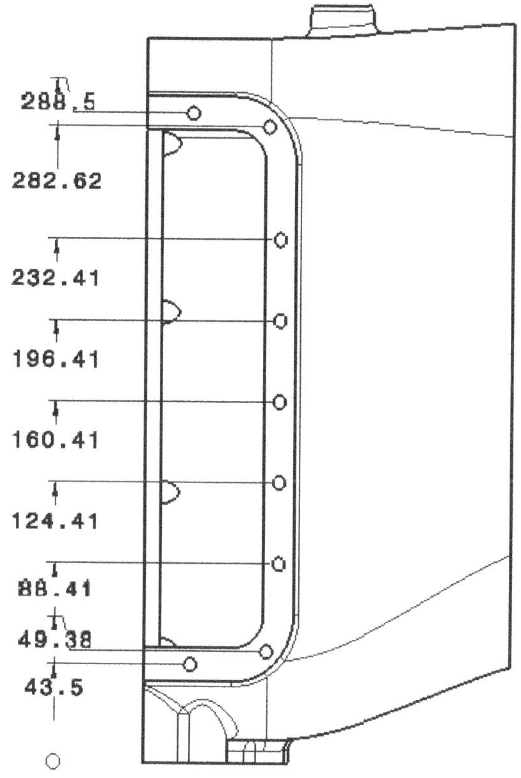

Figure 3–83

7. Save all of the tabs and close all of the windows.

Design Considerations

The units of a dimension can be changed after it has been created using the options in the *Numerical* section of the Object Properties window. Note that changing the default units of dimensions must be done by a CAD Administrator from the Drawing Standards.

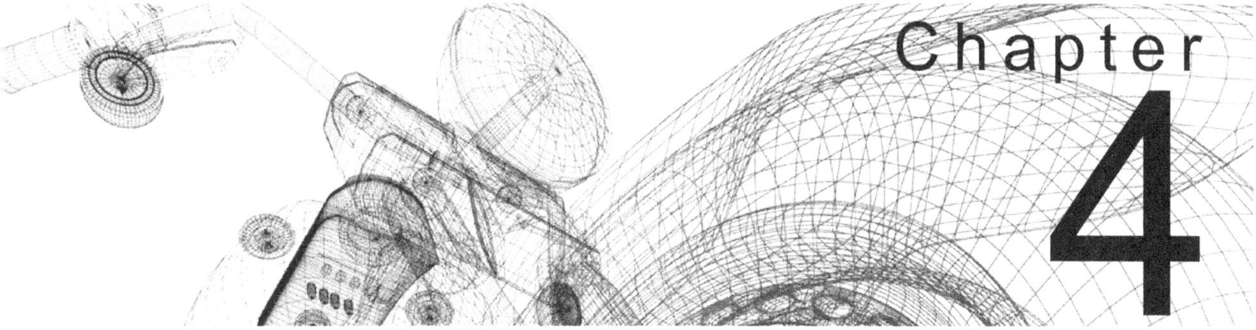

Geometric Tolerancing

Geometric tolerancing is used to display manufacturing and assembly tolerances in the drawing.

Learning Objectives in This Chapter

- Review Geometric Tolerancing terminology.
- Create Geometric Tolerances.

4.1 Geometric Tolerancing Terminology

In many cases, the manufacturing process inherently controls the accuracy of machined parts. If there is doubt about the adequacy of the manufacturing control or if a particular form must be held within closer limits to meet functional or interchangeability requirements, a geometrical tolerance must be specified.

Geometrical tolerances control the position of features or the form, orientation, or location of surfaces. Geometrical tolerances are created using the Datum Feature flyout, as shown in Figure 4–1.

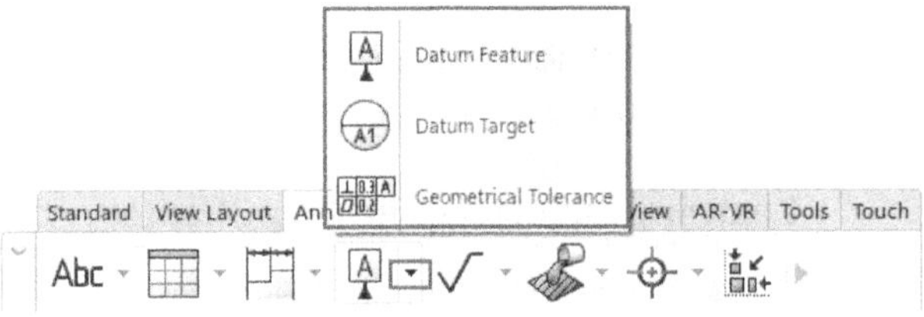

Figure 4–1

Figure 4–2 shows an example of a geometrical tolerance control frame.

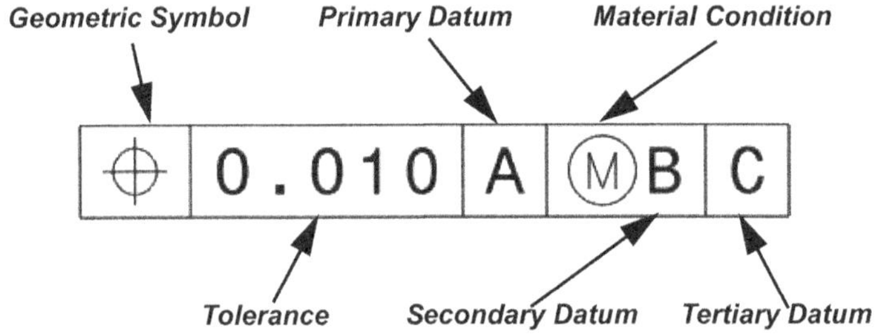

Figure 4–2

Definition of Terms

The datum, material condition, and supplementary symbols are as follows:

Symbol	Description	Symbol	Description
	Datum Feature		Tangent Plane

Ø	Diameter	(ST)	Statical Tolerance
°	Degree	Ⓤ	Unequally
Ⓔ	Envelope	Ⓒ	Minimax Feature
Ⓕ	Free State	Ⓖ	Least Squares Feature
Ⓛ	Least Material Condition	Ⓝ	Minimum Circumscribed Feature
Ⓜ	Maximum Material Condition	Ⓣ	Tangent Feature
Ⓟ	Projected Tolerance Zone	Ⓧ	Maximum Inscribed Feature
Ⓢ	Regardless of Feature Size	Δ	Dynamic Profile

The geometric characteristic symbols used to define geometric tolerances are as follows:

Symbol	Description	Symbol	Description
—	Straightness	⊥	Perpendicularity
⏥	Flatness	//	Parallelism
○	Circularity	⌖	Position
⌭	Cylindricity	◎	Concentricity
⌒	Line Profile	⌯	Symmetry
⌓	Surface Profile	↗	Circular Runout
∠	Angularity	⌰	Total Runout

4.2 Create Geometric Tolerances

General Steps

Use the following general steps to create geometric tolerances:

1. Create datum features.
2. Create geometric tolerances.

Step 1 - Create datum features.

How To: Create a Datum Feature

1. In the Annotation section of the Action Bar, click (Datum Feature).
2. Select elements from the view to locate the datum features, as shown in Figure 4–3.

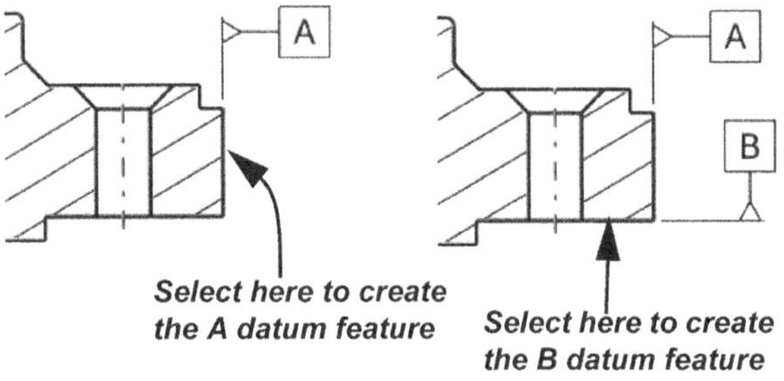

Figure 4–3

3. Drag the datum tag to the required location.
4. Enter the datum identifier in the immersive dialog box, as shown in Figure 4–4. The system automatically enters the next sequential letter. Click .

Figure 4–4

Step 2 - Create geometric tolerances.

How To: Create a Geometric Tolerance

1. Click  (Geometrical Tolerance) in the Annotation section of the Action Bar.
2. Select a dimension or feature to place the control frame.
3. In the Geometrical Tolerance dialog box, enter the required information as shown in Figure 4–5. Additional frames can be added using the icons in the *Add Tolerance* area.

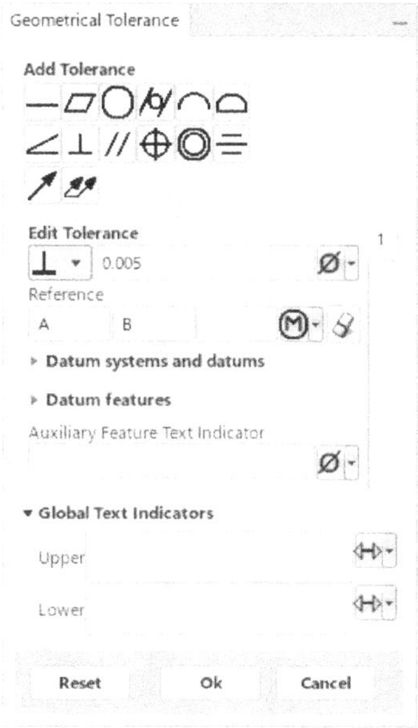

Figure 4–5

4. Drag the control frame to the required location. The geometrical tolerance control frame displays as shown in Figure 4–6.

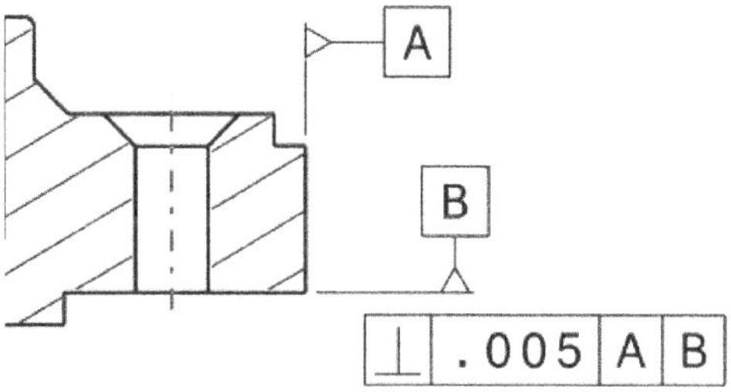

Figure 4–6

Practice 4a Geometric Tolerances I

Practice Objectives

- Create geometric tolerances.
- Modify geometric tolerances.

In this practice, you will create and modify geometry tolerances for the drawing of **Arm.3dxml**. Once complete, the drawing displays as shown in Figure 4–7.

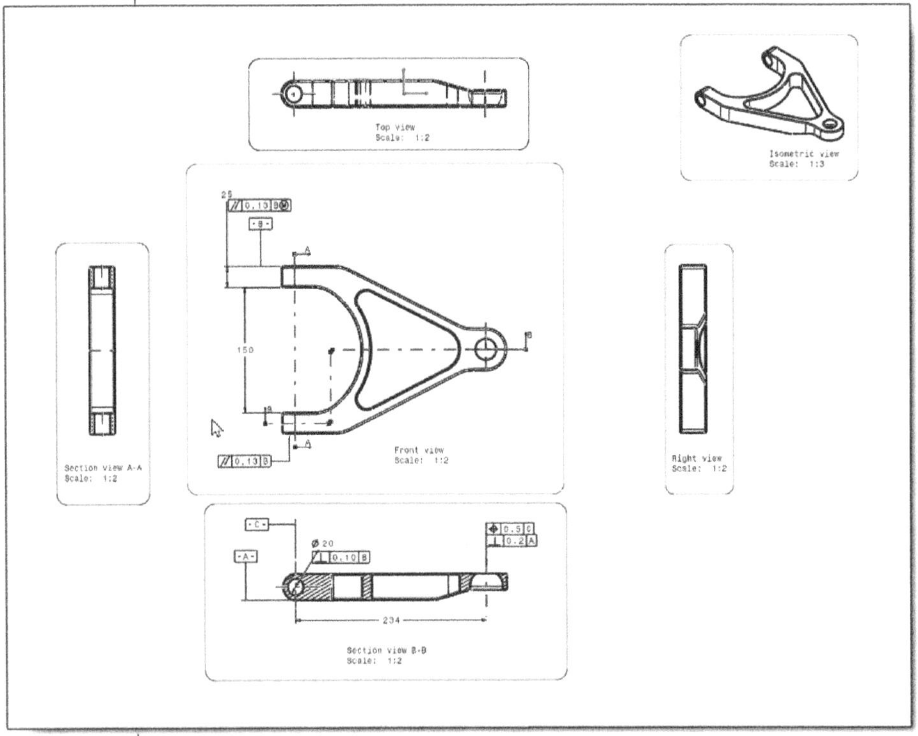

Figure 4–7

Task 1 - Import and open a drawing.

1. Import and open **Arm.3dxml** from the practice files folder. While importing, set the *Duplication string* to **###_** where ### represents your initials.

2. Right-click on the **###_Arm** drawing in the tree and select *** object>Open in New App**. The drawing displays as shown in Figure 4–8.

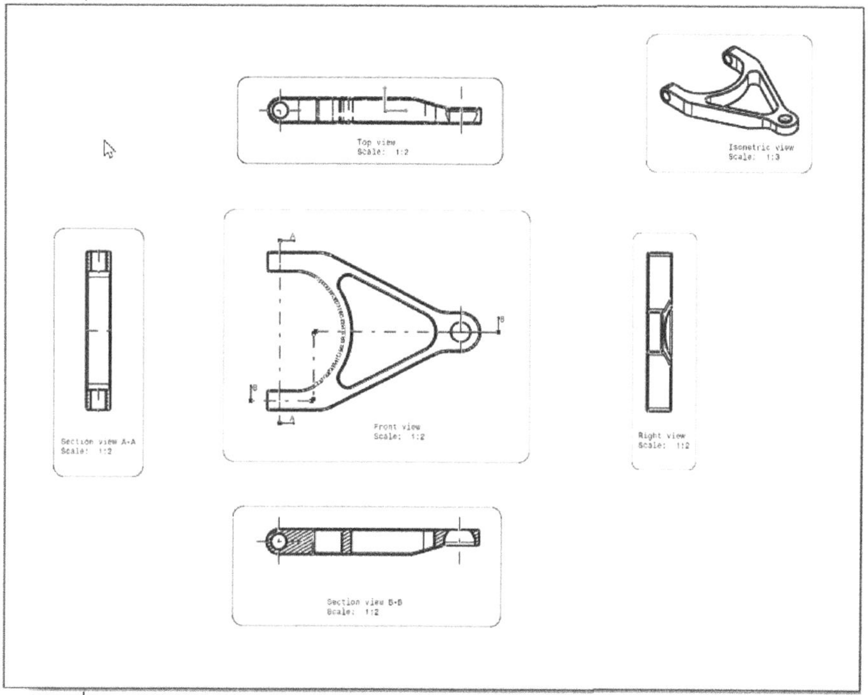

Figure 4–8

Task 2 - Use links to confirm associated part file.

1. From the Tools section of the Action Bar, select (Links and Relations). The Edit Links and Relations dialog box opens, as shown in Figure 4–9.

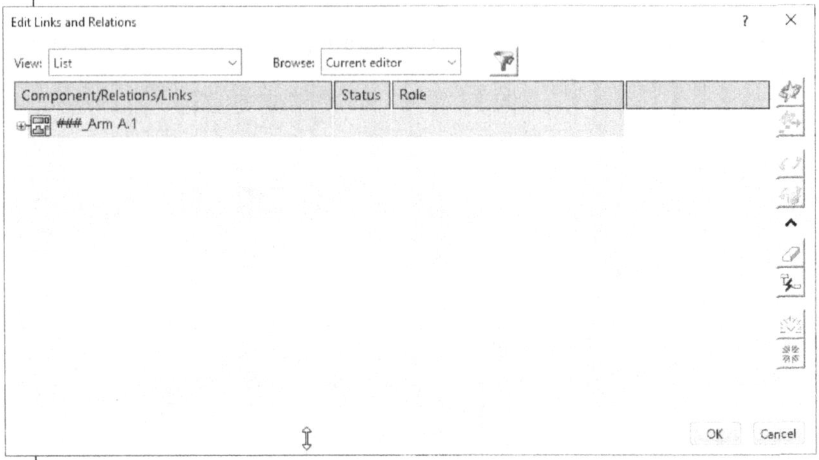

Figure 4–9

2. Select the icon to the left of the **###_Arm. A.1** drawing to expand its links, as shown in Figure 4–10.This shows the current links and any status issues to the current drawing.

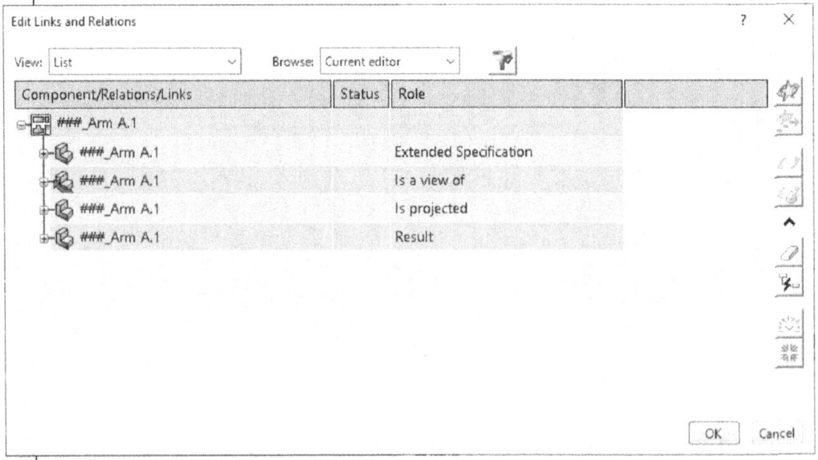

Figure 4–10

3. Select **OK** to close the dialog box.

Task 3 - Create dimensions.

1. In the Standard section of the Action Bar, click

    (Update) if required.

2. Create the **150** dimension in the Front view, as shown in Figure 4–11.

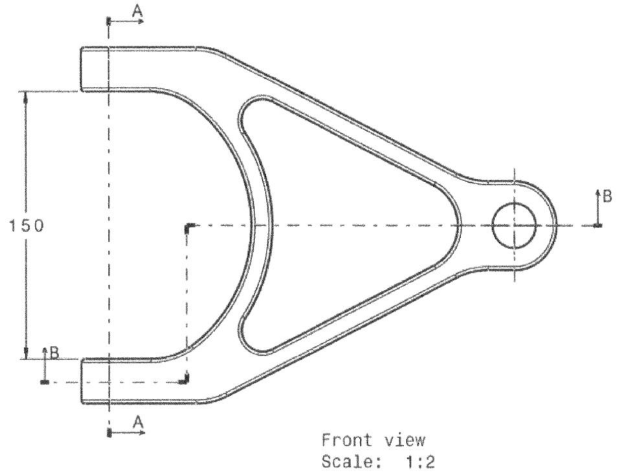

Figure 4–11

3. Create the two dimensions in the Section view B-B, as shown in Figure 4–12.

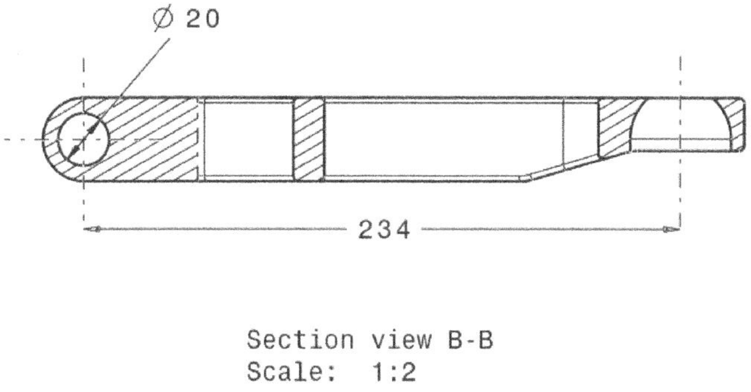

Figure 4–12

Note: When creating the **234** dimension, it may appear as **468**. When creating a dimension and an axis line is used as a reference, CATIA defaults to a revolved size which is why the value is doubled. To fix this, right-click while placing the dimension and disable **Half Dimension**, as shown in Figure 4–13.

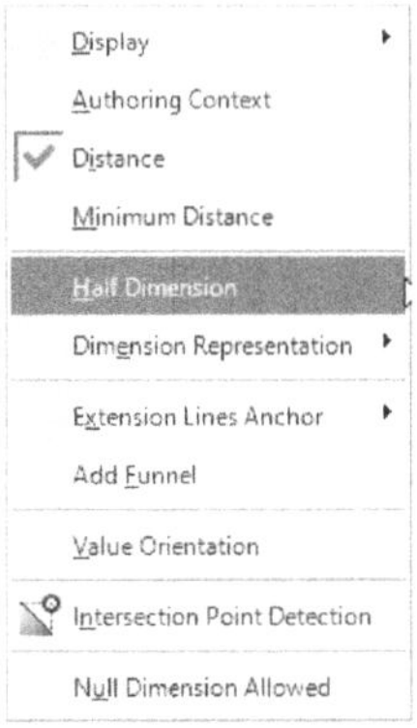

Figure 4–13

Task 4 - Create a datum.

1. In the Annotation section of the Action Bar, click (Datum Feature).
2. Select the bottom edge of the geometry in Section view B-B and place the datum feature, as shown in Figure 4–14.

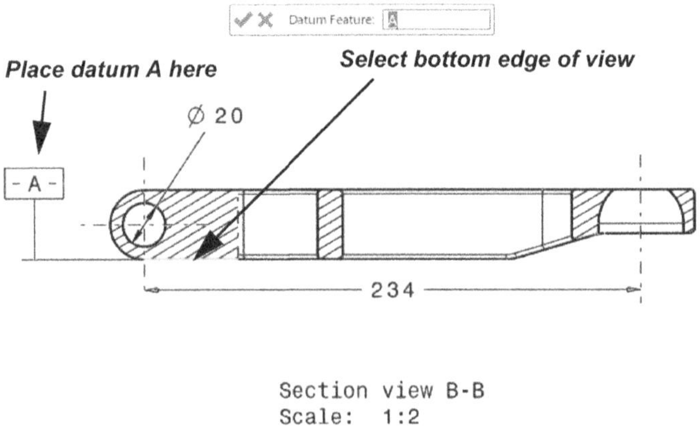

Figure 4–14

3. At the top of the screen, ensure the datum label is **A**, as shown in Figure 4–14, then click (OK) to complete the datum feature.
4. Create datum feature **B**, as shown in Figure 4–15.

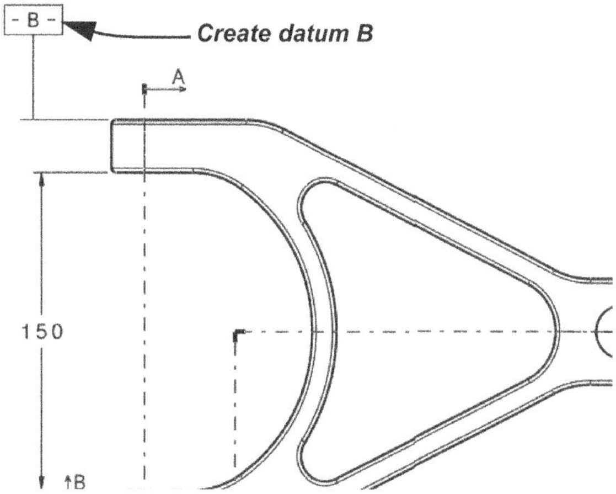

Figure 4–15

Task 5 - Create a geometrical tolerance.

1. In the Annotation section of the Action Bar, click (Geometrical Tolerance).
2. Select the diameter dimension, as shown in Figure 4–16.

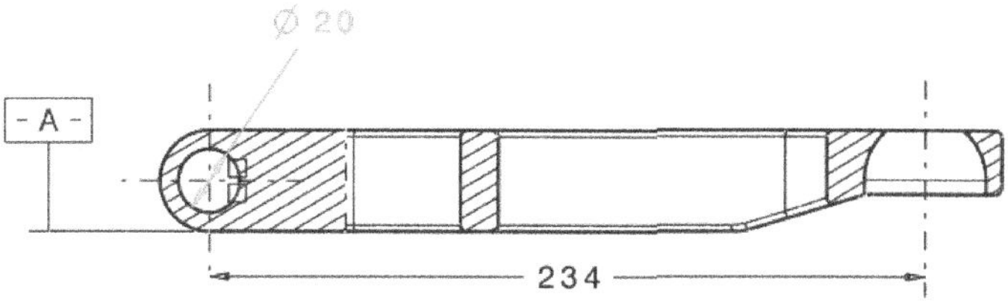

Figure 4–16

3. In the *Edit Tolerance* area, select the ⊥ (perpendicularity) symbol, and enter **0.10** to define the geometrical tolerance.
4. The *Reference* area should clear when the *Tolerance* area was changed in the previous step. However if needed, clear the *Reference* area by clicking (Erase).

5. Expand the *Datum features* area and click on **B**, as shown in Figure 4–17.

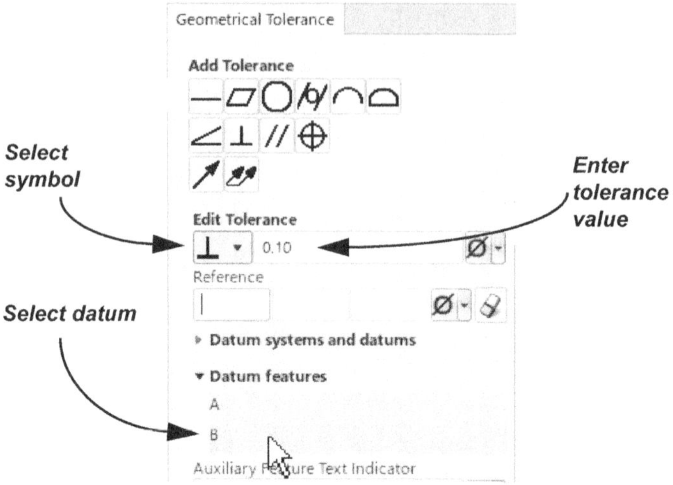

Figure 4–17

Note the datum B should now be listed under *Reference*, as shown in Figure 4–18.

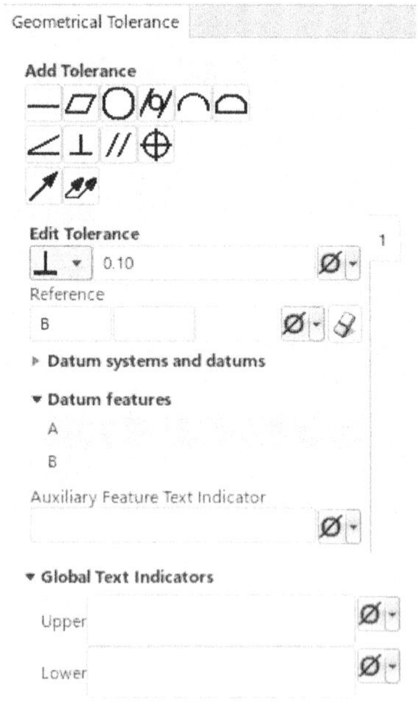

Figure 4–18

6. Click **OK** to complete the feature. The Section view displays as shown in Figure 4–19.

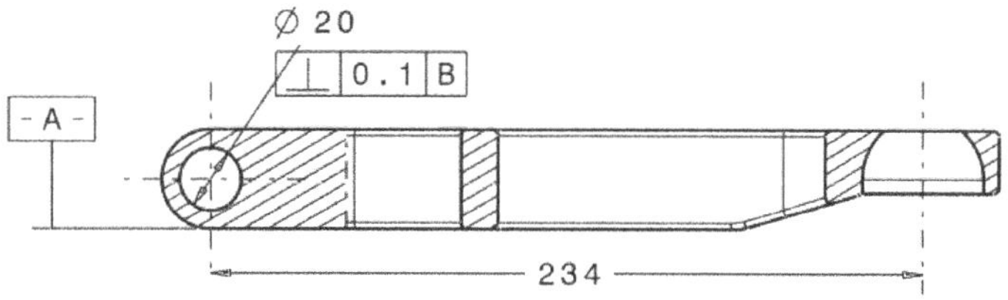

Figure 4–19

7. Create the **25 dimension** in the Front view, as shown in Figure 4–20.

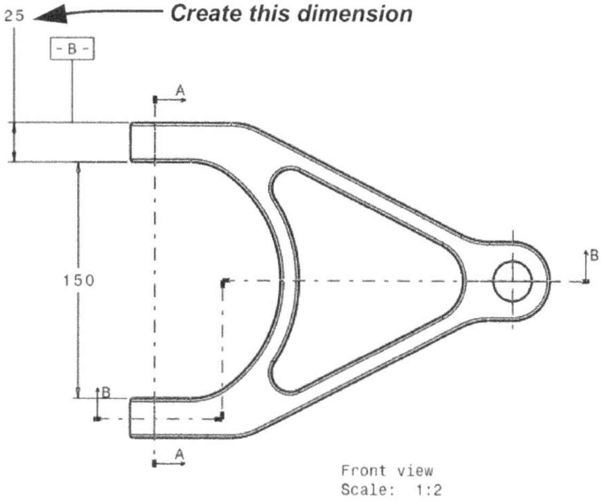

Figure 4–20

8. Create the geometrical tolerance shown in Figure 4–21.

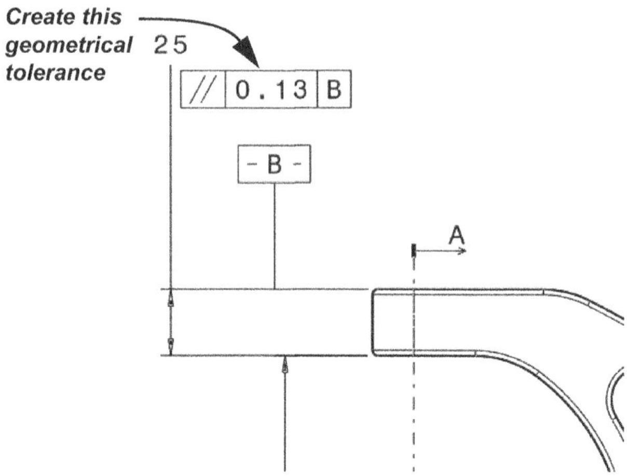

Figure 4–21

9. Create a geometrical tolerance to control the surface shown in Figure 4–22.

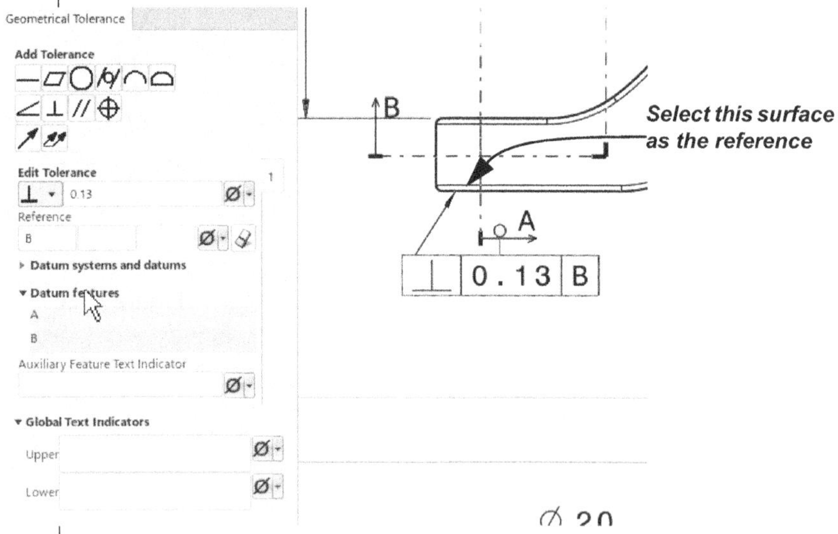

Figure 4–22

10. Click **OK**. The feature displays with handles.

11. Select the circle handle (not the middle of the circle) and drag it to the position shown in Figure 4–23.

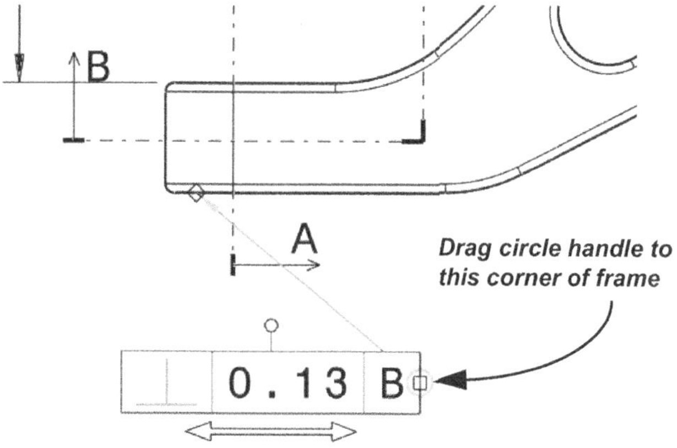

Figure 4–23

12. Use the double-headed arrow to move the geometrical tolerance frame to the location shown in Figure 4–24.

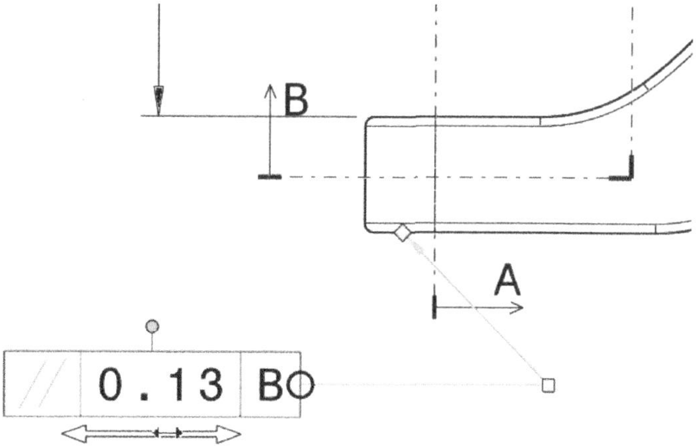

Figure 4–24

13. Select the handle to move the line, as shown in Figure 4–25.

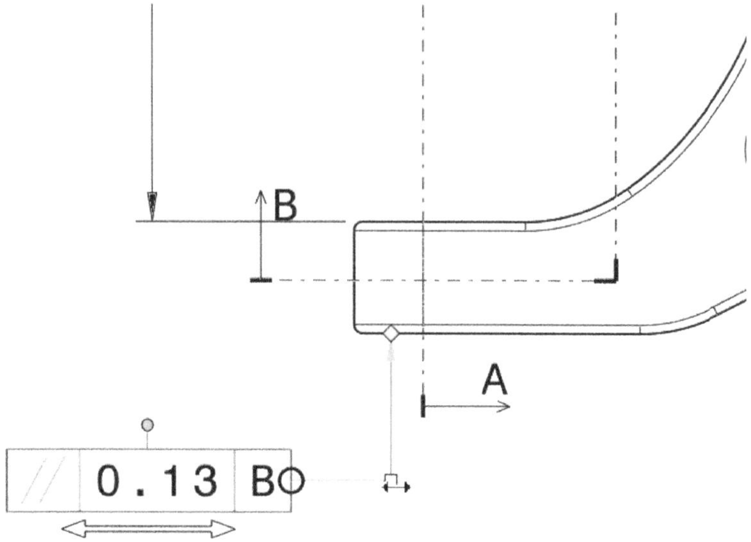

Figure 4–25

14. Select anywhere on the sheet to complete the placement, as shown in Figure 4–26.

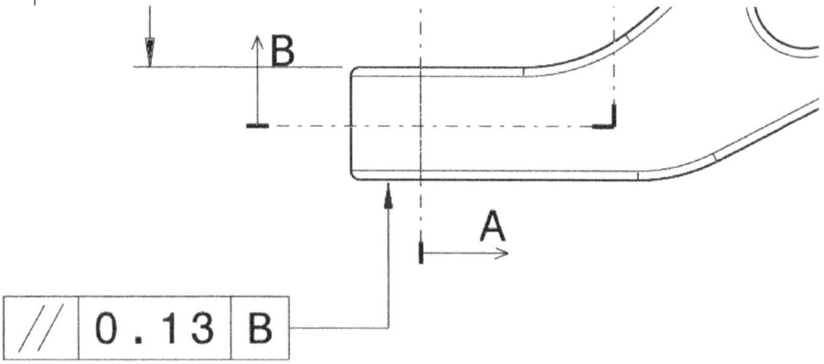

Figure 4–26

15. Save the drawing.

Task 6 - Modify a geometrical tolerance.

1. Double-click on the geometrical tolerance created for the 25 value of the Front view. The Geometrical Tolerance dialog box opens.

2. In the *Reference* field, click to the right of letter **B**. In the Symbol selection drop-down list, select the (Maximum Material condition) symbol, as shown in Figure 4–27.

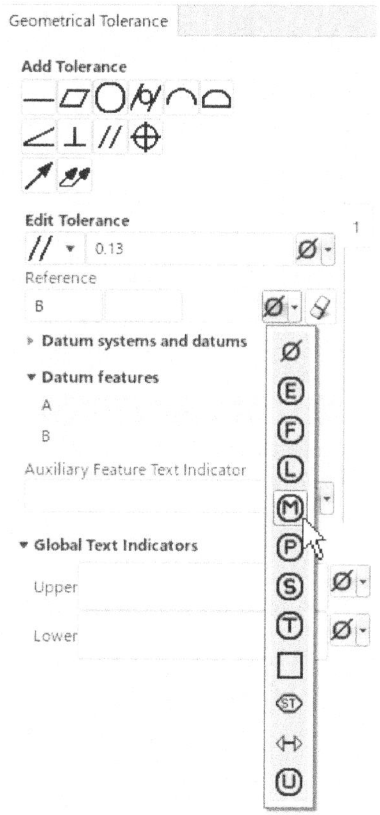

Figure 4–27

3. Click **OK** to complete the modification. The geometrical tolerance displays as shown in Figure 4–28.

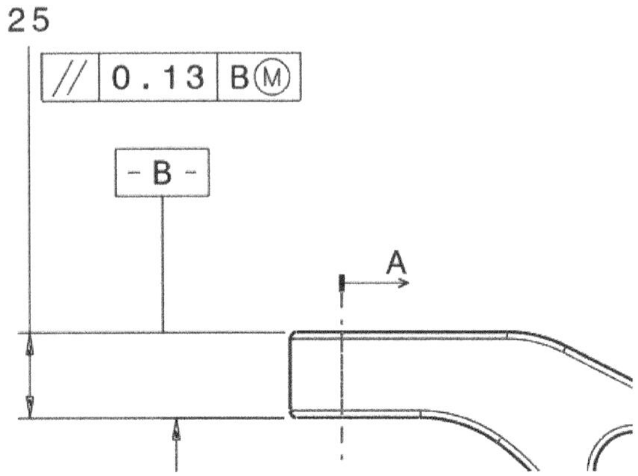

Figure 4–28

Task 7 - Create a datum feature.

1. Create the **C** datum on the axis of the hole in Section view B-B, as shown in Figure 4–29.

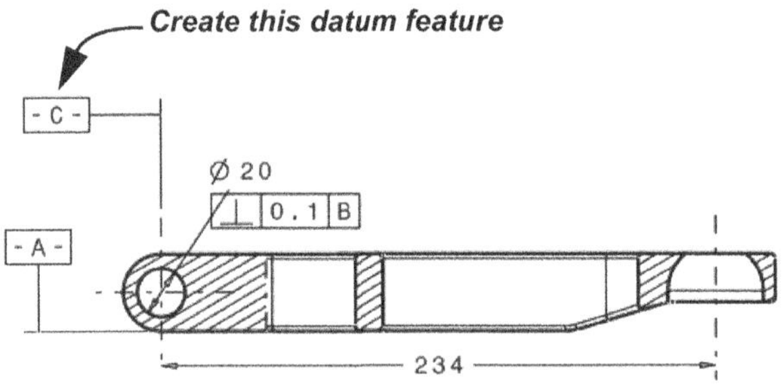

Figure 4–29

2. Create the geometrical tolerance frame defining the position of the feature, as shown in Figure 4–30. In the Geometrical Tolerance dialog box, in the *Add Tolerances* area, click ⊥ (Perpendicularity) to enter information in the second line.

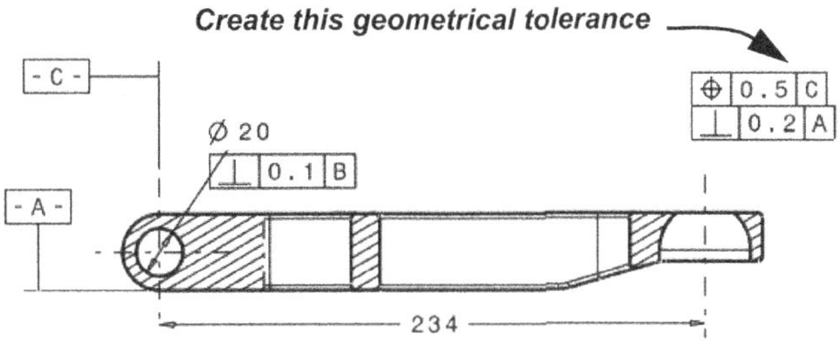

Figure 4–30

The drawing displays as shown in Figure 4–31.

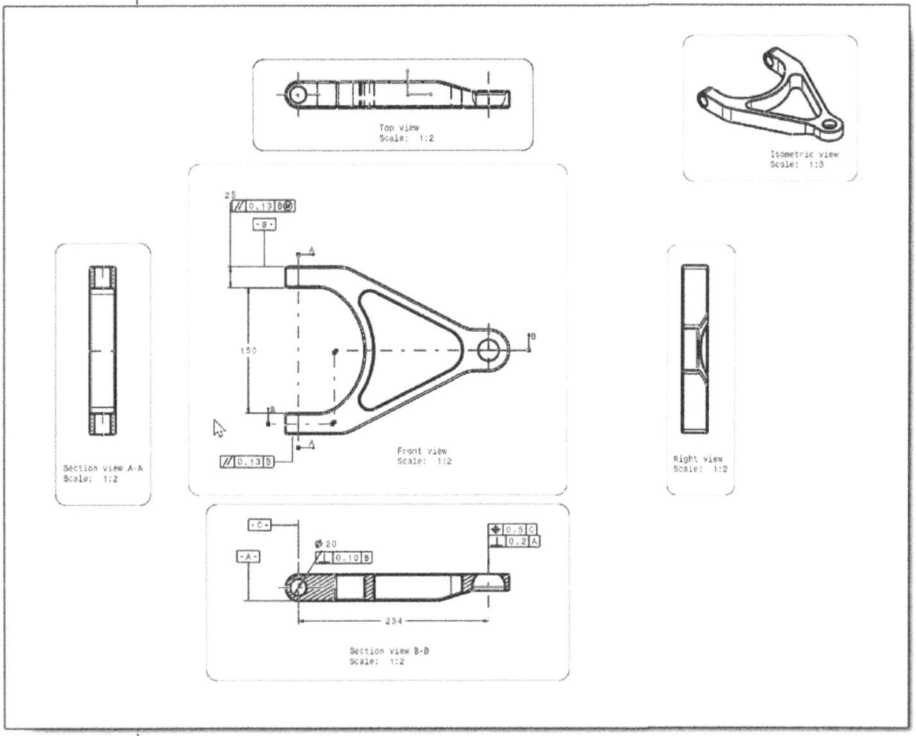

Figure 4–31

3. Save the drawing and close all of the tabs.

Practice 4b Geometric Tolerances II

Practice Objectives

- Create dimensions with tolerances.
- Create geometric tolerances.

This practice can be completed at any time during the course, as time permits.

Task 1 - Import and open files.

1. Import and open **Cover.3dxml** from the practice files folder. While importing, set the *Duplication string* to **###_** where ### represents your initials.
2. Right-click on the **###_Cover** drawing in the tree and select *** object>Open in New App**.
3. Complete the Front view and a Section view, as shown in Figure 4–32. Refer to Figure 4–33 and Figure 4–34 for details.

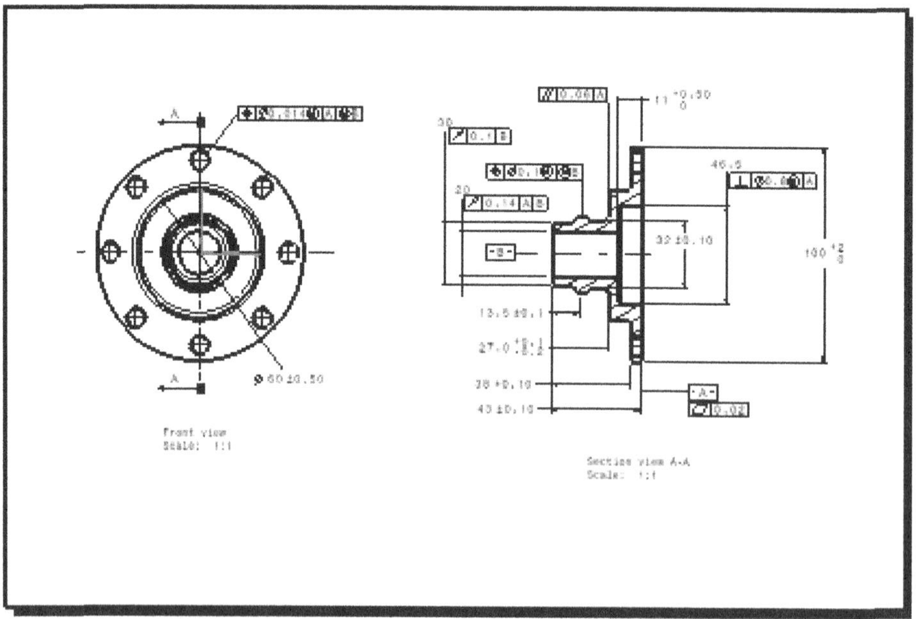

Figure 4–32

4. Create dimensions and geometrical tolerances, as shown in Figure 4–33 and Figure 4–34. The Tolerance format used is **ANS_NUM2**.

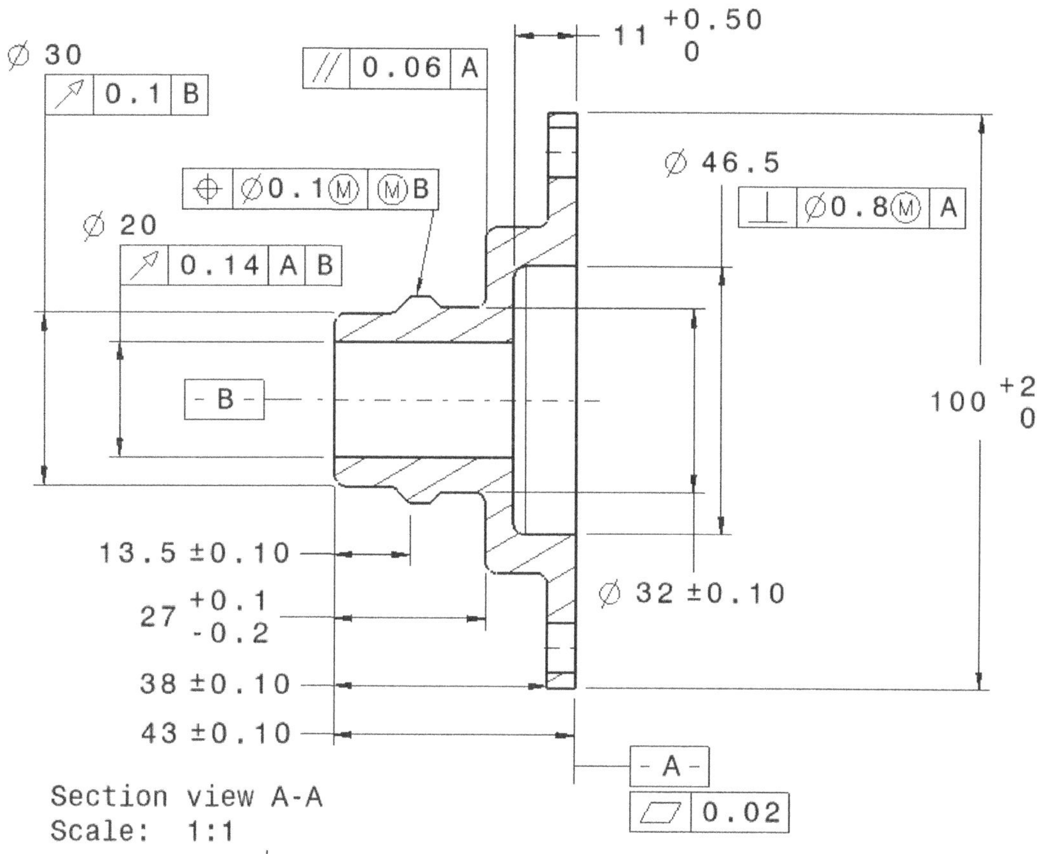

Figure 4–33

Design Considerations

To change the orientation of a Geometric Tolerance, access its Properties dialog box and change the **Orientation** in the *Text* tab.

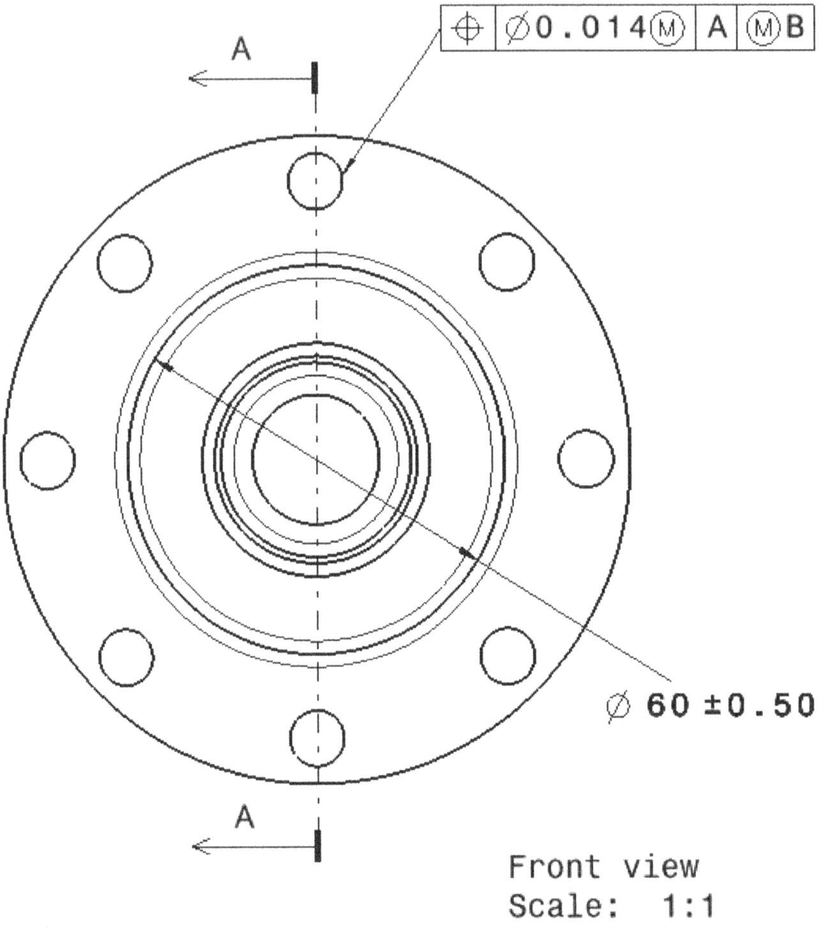

Figure 4–34

5. Save the tabs and close all windows.

Design Considerations

The units of a dimension can be changed after it has been created using the options in the *Numerical* area of the Object Properties window. Note that changing the default units of dimensions must be done by a CAD Administrator from the Drawing Standards file.

Practice 4c Geometric Tolerances III

Practice Objectives

- Create dimensions with tolerances.
- Create geometric tolerances.

This practice can be completed at any time during the course, as time permits.

Task 1 - Open a part file.

1. Import and open **Spindle.3dxml** from the practice files folder. While importing, set the *Duplication string* to **###_** where ### represents your initials.
2. Create a drawing with the *Title* of **###_Spindle** using **C ANSI** for the *Sheet Style* and **Empty Sheet** for the *format.*
3. Create the Front view, Section view, and Isometric view, as shown in Figure 4–35.

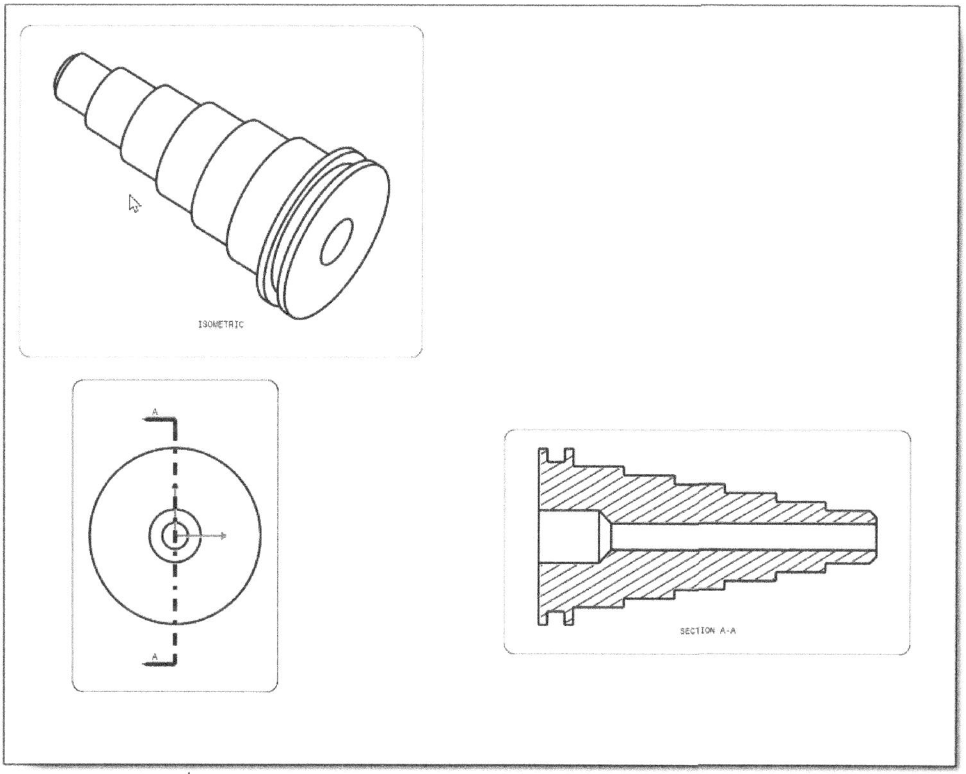

Figure 4–35

4. Create datum features and geometrical tolerances on the Section view, as shown in Figure 4–36.

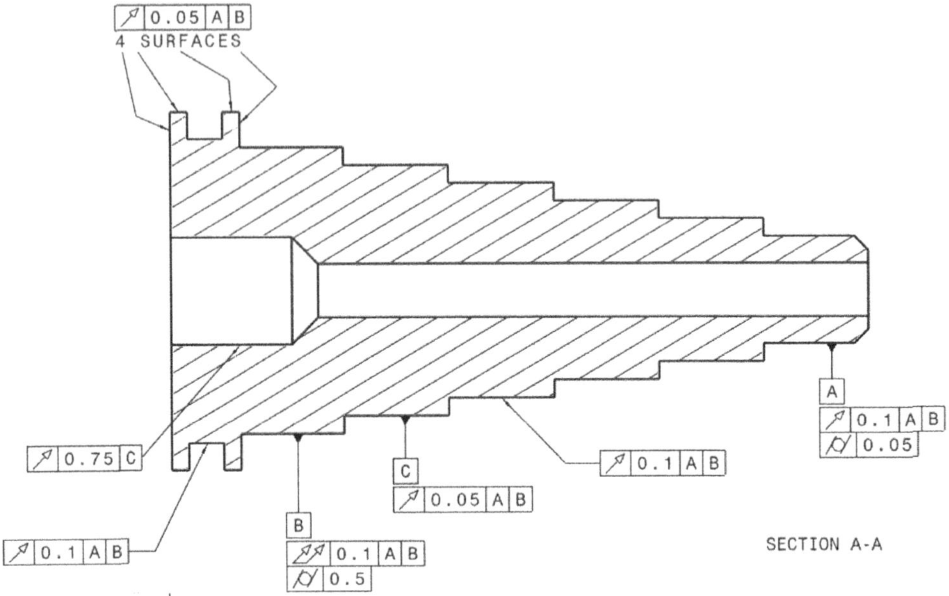

Figure 4–36

To add the additional leader lines for the top circular runout, right click on the geometrical tolerance and select **Add Leader**, as shown in Figure 4–37.

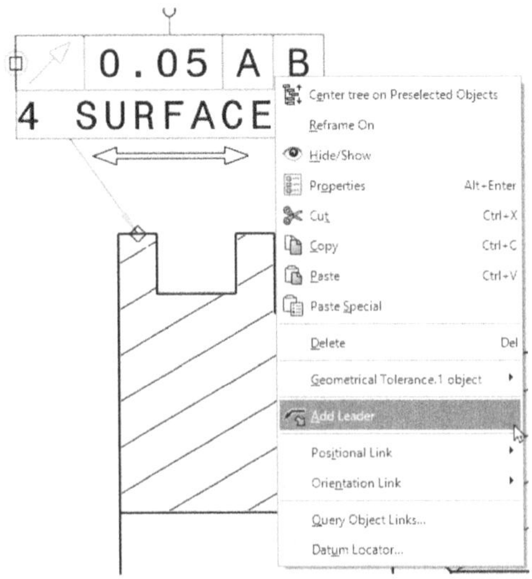

Figure 4–37

Adjust the leader line connecting point by left-clicking and dragging on the circles, as shown in Figure 4–38.

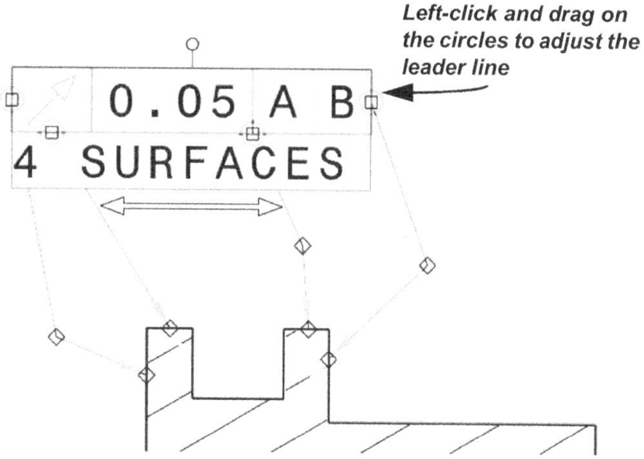

Figure 4–38

Design Considerations

To add a break to a leader (such as the four surface circular runout tolerance), right-click on the yellow square of the leader and select **Add a Breakpoint**.

5. Save the drawing and close all of the tabs.

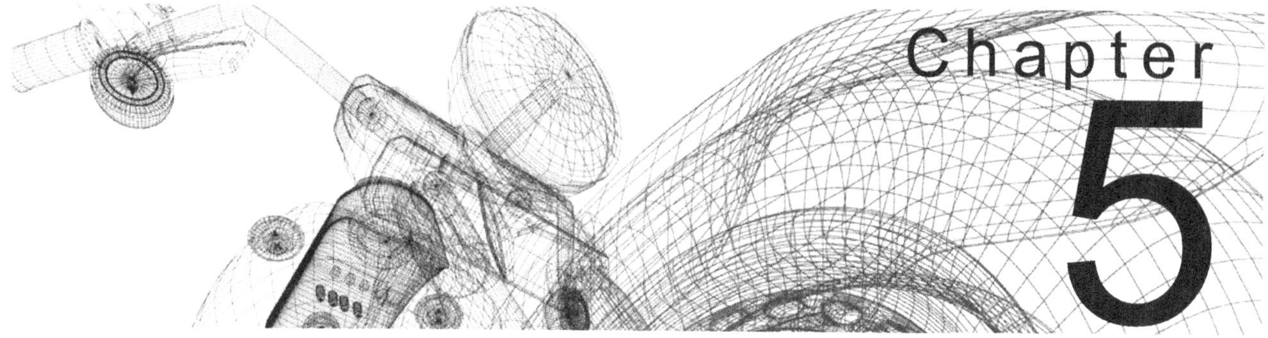

Detailing

Detailing a drawing involves adding information to the drawing so that all of the design information is effectively communicated. A fully detailed drawing should communicate enough information to manufacture the part. Detail items include, but are not limited to, notes, tables, and symbols.

Learning Objectives in This Chapter

- Understand annotation creation.
- Create text annotations with and without leaders.
- Edit text with leaders.
- Understand how to organize annotations by alignment.
- Create symbols such as surface texture and weld.
- Annotate dress-up elements.
- Learn how to create tables.
- Understand and apply attribute links and dimension and annotation settings.

5.1 Annotation Creation

Text is used to communicate information that cannot be communicated through views or dimensions. You can create two types of text in CATIA generative drafting:

- Free Text
- Associative Text

Free text is added to the background or to the active view when working in Working Views mode. By default, text displays in a horizontal orientation, as shown in Figure 5–1.

Break All Sharp Edges

Figure 5–1

Hold <Alt> when selecting a location in which to place vertically oriented text, as shown in Figure 5–2.

Break All Sharp Edges

Figure 5–2

Text associated with a dimension follows any changes to the position of the dimension. Text can be associated with existing dimensions by pressing <Shift> or using the shortcut menu.

To associate text with a dimension, hold <Shift> and select the dimension to which associativity is required when placing the text.

5.2 Create Text Annotations

General Steps

Use the following general steps to create text:

1. Double-click the view to which to add text.
2. Activate the **Text** tool.
3. Select a location for the text.
4. Enter text.
5. Complete the creation of text.

Step 1 - Double-click the view to which to add text.

Activate the view in which you want to add text or right-click on the sheet name in the specification tree and select **Edit Background** to add text to the background. Text added to the background is not associated to any view. Generally, you use this mode to fill in information in the title block and revision columns.

Step 2 - Activate the Text tool.

Click Abc (Text) in the Annotation section of the Action Bar.

Step 3 - Select a location for the text.

Select a location for the text. The view frame expands to include the text if it is being placed in a view.

Step 4 - Enter text.

The Text Editor dialog box opens once a location for the text has been selected. Enter the text in the Text Editor, as shown in Figure 5–3. To add another line of text to a note, press <Shift>+<Enter>.

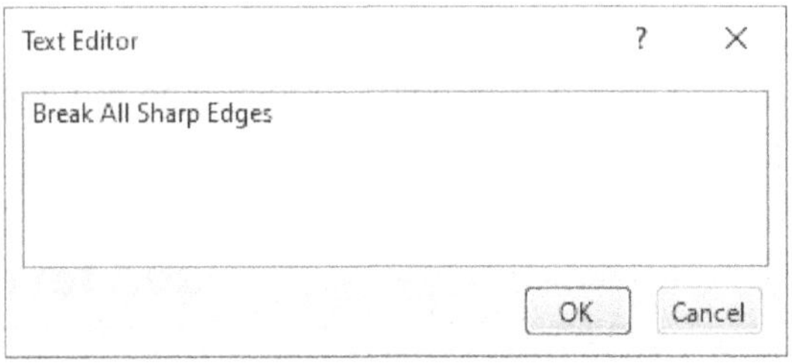

Figure 5–3

Step 5 - Complete the creation of text.

When the required text has been entered, click **OK** and select anywhere in the display to complete the creation of text.

Linking Existing Text

If the text already exists and you require associativity to a dimension, do the following:

1. Move the text to an appropriate location with respect to the dimension to which it is going to be associated.
2. Right-click on the text and select **Positional Link>Create**.
3. Select the dimension to which you want to link the text.

5.3 Create Text with Leader

Text that is added to a drawing can also be attached to a drawing view or other geometry using a leader. An example of text with a leader is shown in Figure 5–4.

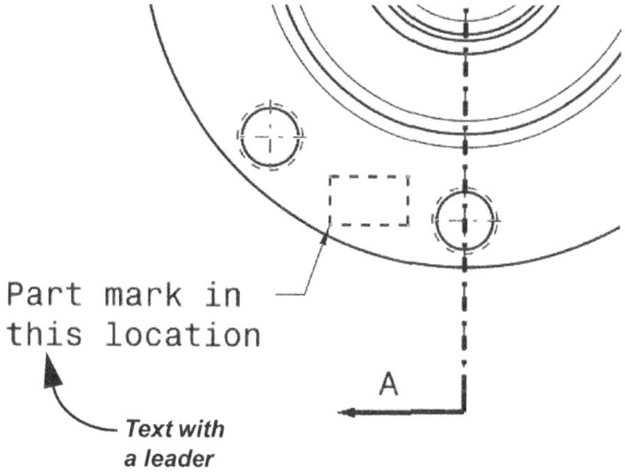

Figure 5–4

General Steps

Use the following general steps to create text with a leader:

1. Activate the **Text with Leader** tool.
2. Select an attachment reference for the leader.
3. Select a location for the text.
4. Enter the text.
5. Complete the creation of text.

Step 1 - Activate the Text with Leader tool.

Click  (Text with Leader) in the Annotation section of the Action Bar.

Step 2 - Select an attachment reference for the leader.

Select an element in the active view to which to attach the leader, as shown in Figure 5–5.

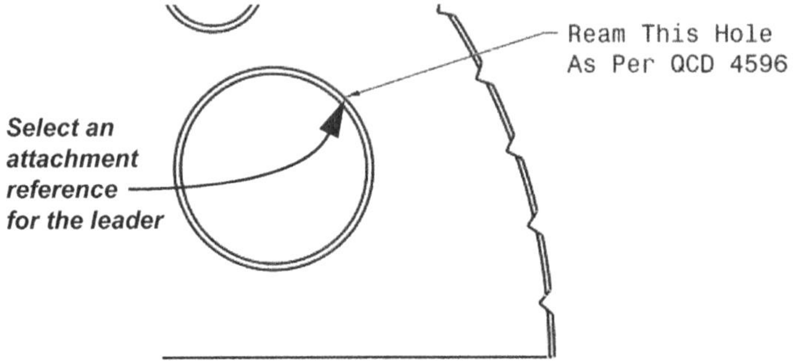

Figure 5–5

Step 3 - Select a location for the text.

Select a location for the text. The view frame expands to include the text.

Step 4 - Enter text.

The Text Editor dialog box opens once a location for the text has been selected. Enter text in the Text Editor, as shown in Figure 5–6.

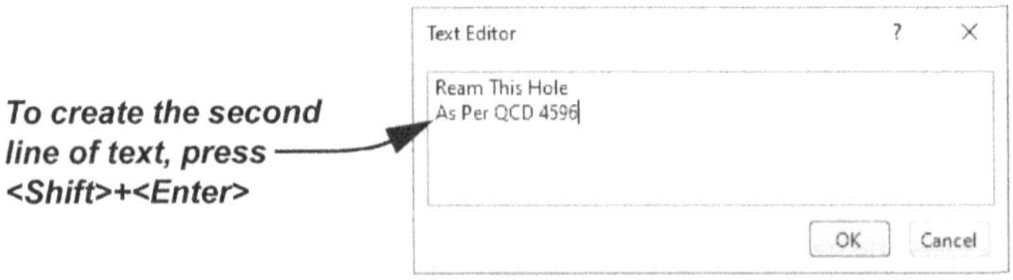

Figure 5–6

Step 5 - Complete the creation of text.

When the required text has been entered, click **OK** and select anywhere in the display to complete the creation of text.

5.4 Edit Text with Leader

Use the following methods to edit the properties of text with a leader.

Handling Annotation Leaders

Select the yellow box on the leader and right-click to display the handling options, as shown in Figure 5–7 and Figure 5–8.

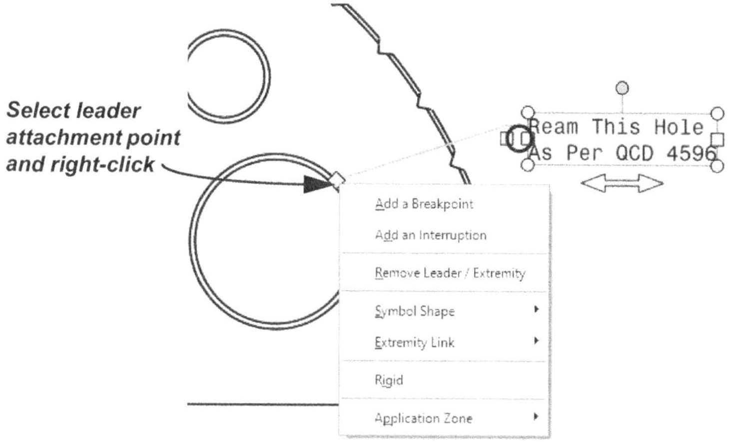

Figure 5–7

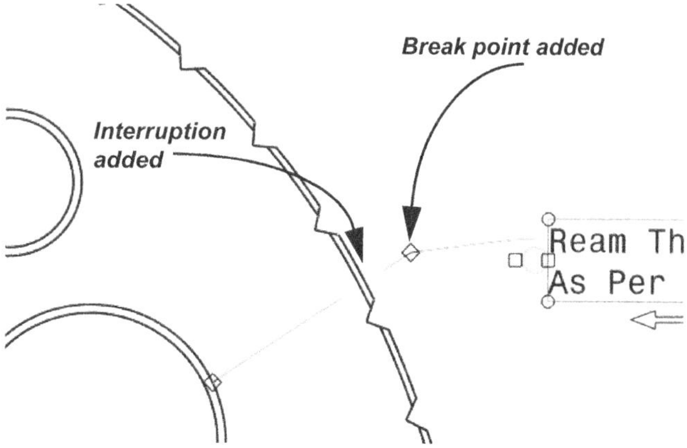

Figure 5–8

You can change the Attachment Symbol Shape, as shown in Figure 5–9.

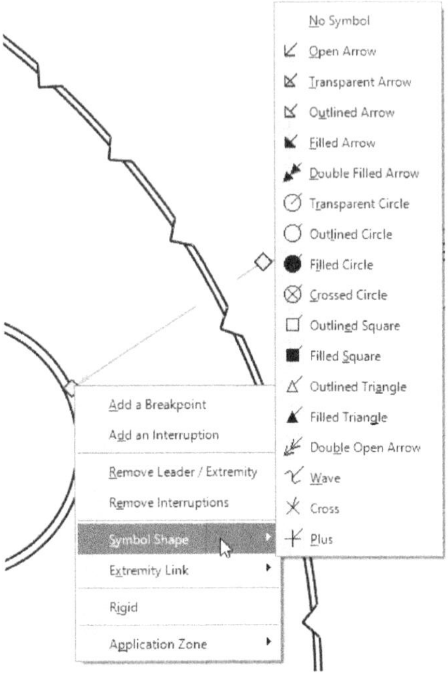

Figure 5–9

Adding Frames

The Object Properties window can be turned on by selecting (Object Properties) from the Tools section of the Action Bar.

How To: Add a Frame to a Dimension or Text

1. Select the dimension or text.
2. In the *Text* area of the Object Properties window, click (Frame).

3. In the flyout menu, select the required frame as shown in Figure 5–10.

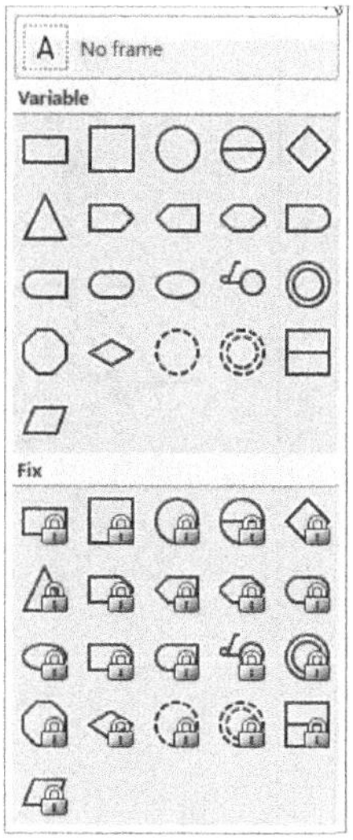

Figure 5–10

A basic dimension is shown in Figure 5–11, indicated by a rectangular frame.

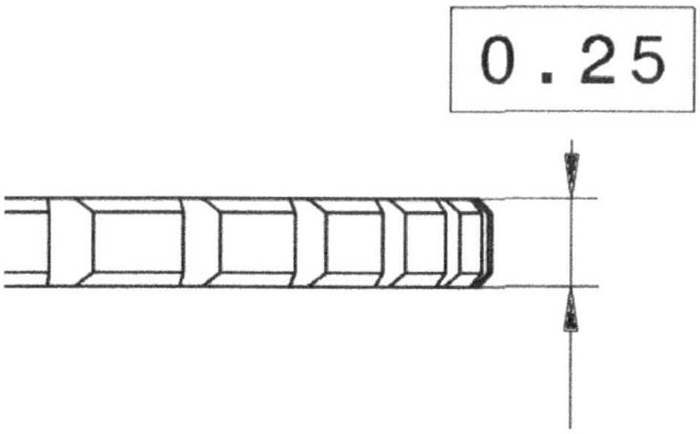

Figure 5–11

Copy Object Graphical Format

The graphical format can be copied from a dimension or text to one or multiple dimensions or text.

How To: Copy the Graphical Format of an Annotation

1. Select one or more annotations to change.
2. In the *Graphic* area of the Object Properties window, click  (Copy Object Format).

3. Select the annotation from which to copy the format, as shown in Figure 5–12.

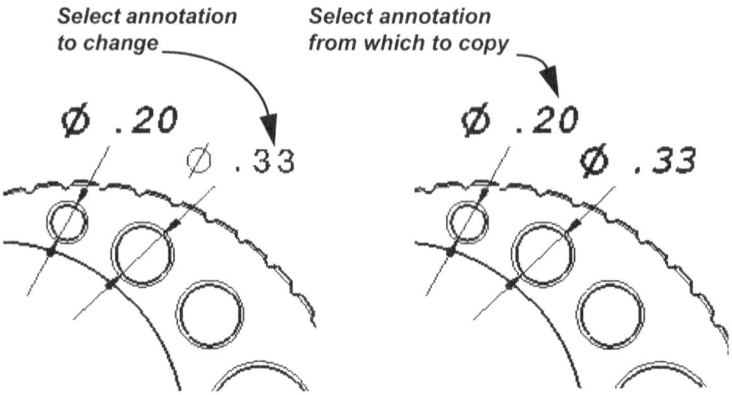

Figure 5–12

5.5 Organizing Annotations - Align Text

You can align and space dimensions and annotation elements (e.g., text) to organize the appearance of drawings.

General Steps

Use the following general steps to align text in your drawing:

1. Select annotation elements.
2. Activate element positioning.
3. Specify alignment conditions.
4. Complete the positioning.

Step 1 - Select annotation elements.

Select the annotation elements by holding <Ctrl>. Selected elements are shown in Figure 5–13.

All selected elements must be from the same view.

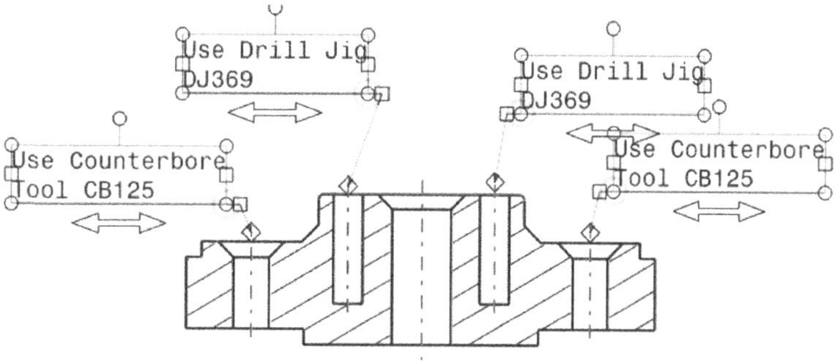

Figure 5–13

Step 2 - Activate element positioning.

Select (Element Positioning) from the Annotation section of the Action Bar. The Positioning dialog box opens as shown in Figure 5–14.

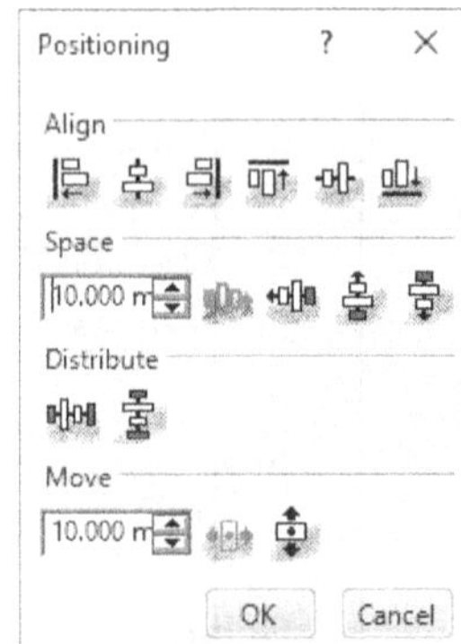

Figure 5–14

Step 3 - Specify alignment conditions.

Specify the alignment and spacing as required. The text elements shown in Figure 5–15 have been aligned by clicking (Align to Top) in the *Align* area in the Positioning dialog box.

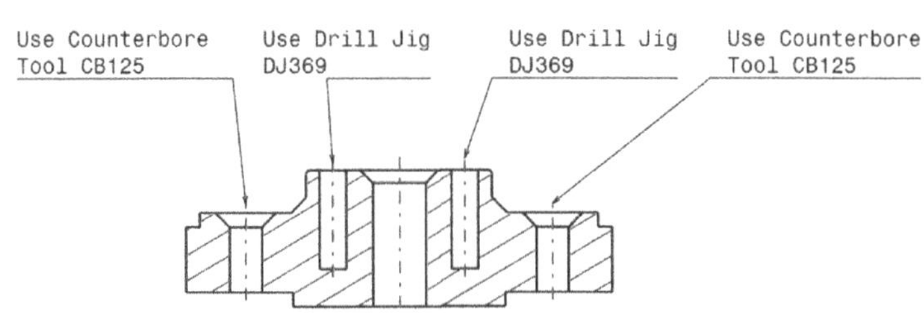

Figure 5–15

Step 4 - Complete the positioning.

Complete the element positioning by selecting **OK** in the Positioning dialog box and selecting the display.

5.6 Organizing Annotations - Align Dimensions

You can align and space dimensions and annotation elements (e.g., text) to organize the appearance of drawings.

General Steps

Use the following general steps to align dimensions in your drawing:

1. Select the dimensions to be aligned.
2. Activate the **Line-Up** tool.
3. Select a reference element.
4. Specify alignment conditions.
5. Complete the positioning.

Step 1 - Select the dimensions to be aligned..

Select the dimensions to be aligned. Press <Ctrl> while selecting the dimensions to highlight multiple entities at the same time. Selected dimensions are shown in Figure 5–16.

All selected elements must be from the same view.

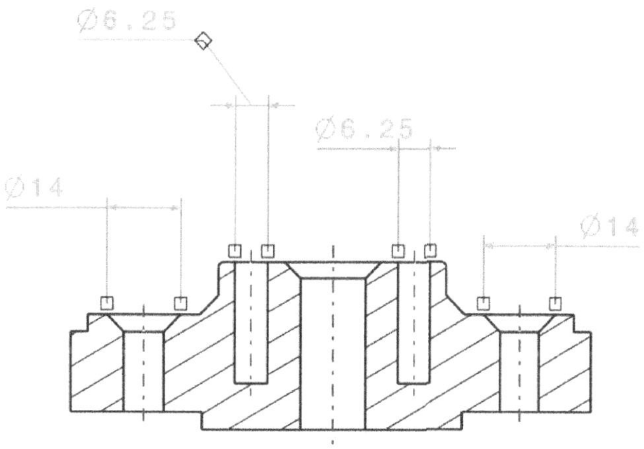

Figure 5–16

Step 2 - Activate the Line-Up tool.

Right-click on one of the selected dimensions and select

 (Line-Up) to align the dimensions.

Step 3 - Select a reference element.

Select a reference element relative to which all other dimensions are going to be aligned. The reference element can be a dimension or an element in the view. In the example shown in Figure 5–17, a dimension has been selected as the reference element.

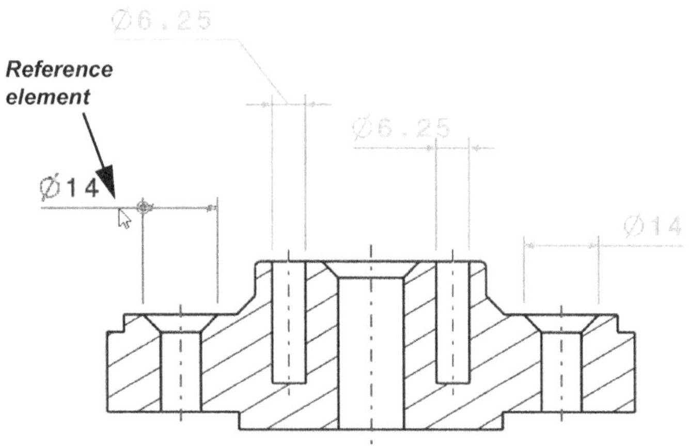

Figure 5–17

Step 4 - Specify alignment conditions.

The Line Up dialog box opens once a reference element has been selected. Enter the required line-up conditions, as shown in Figure 5–18.

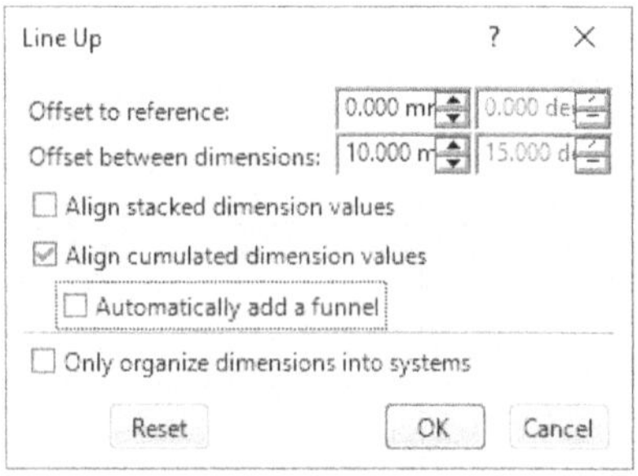

Figure 5–18

Step 5 - Complete the positioning.

Complete the dimension positioning by clicking **OK** in the Line Up dialog box and selecting in the display area. Dimensions that have been aligned relative to the selected reference display as shown in Figure 5–19.

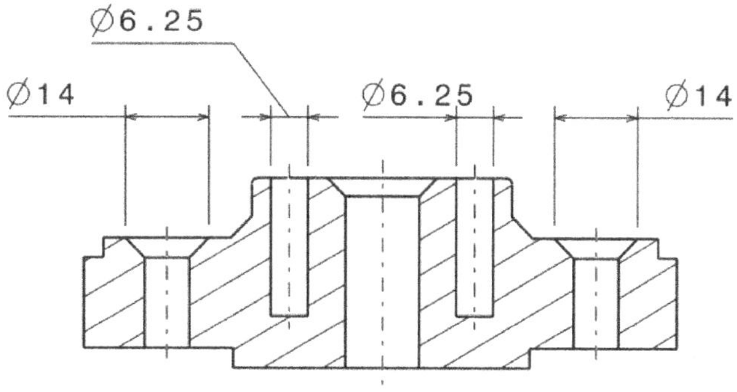

Figure 5–19

5.7 Create Surface Texture Symbols

Surface texture symbols are used to communicate the surface finish texture of a drawing view. The **Surface Texture** tool can be found in the Annotation section of the Action Bar, as shown in Figure 5–20.

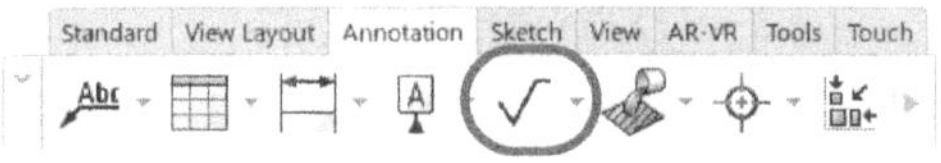

Figure 5–20

General Steps

Use the following general steps to create a surface texture symbol:

1. Activate the **Surface Texture** tool.
2. Select the geometry representing a surface.
3. Specify symbol properties.
4. Complete the symbol creation.

Step 1 - Activate the Surface Texture tool.

Click √ (Surface Texture) in the Annotation section of the Action Bar.

Step 2 - Select the geometry representing a surface.

Select the geometry representing the machined surface for which you want to specify a surface texture value, as shown in Figure 5–21.

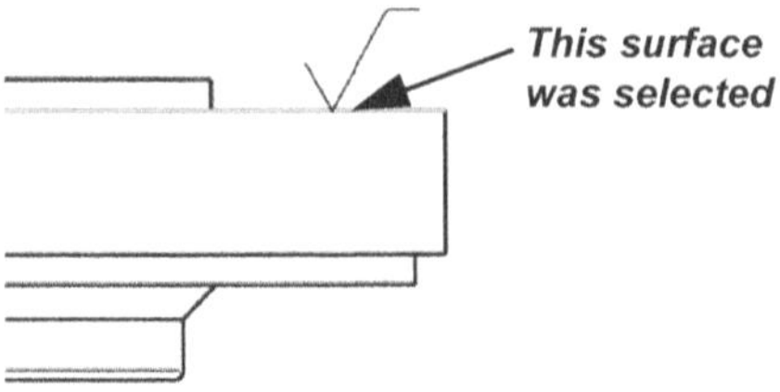

Figure 5–21

Step 3 - Specify symbol properties.

The Surface Texture dialog box opens once a reference has been selected. Specify surface texture symbol properties by entering text and using the flyout arrows to specify surface texture symbology, as shown in Figure 5–22.

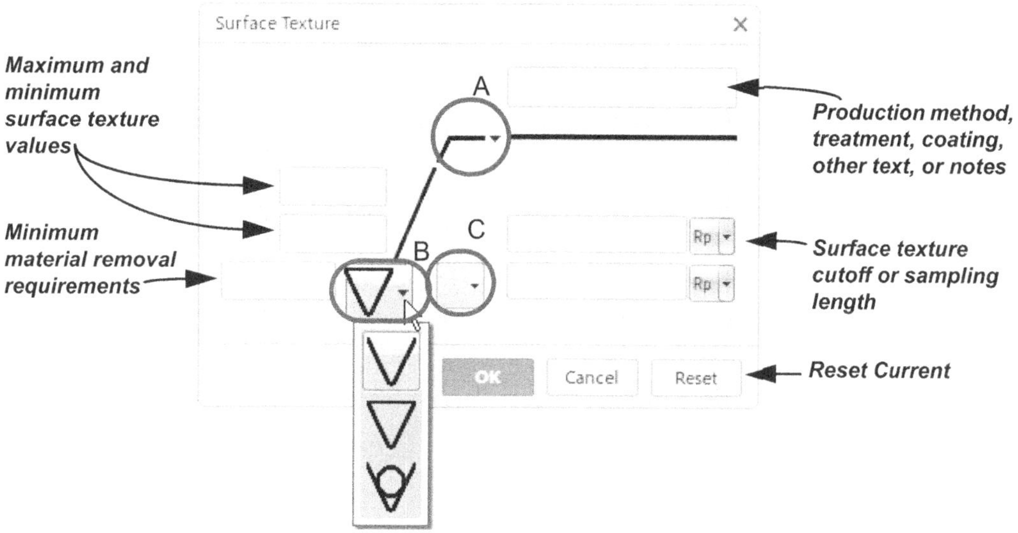

A	B	C
Contact Surface Texture	Surface Texture Type	Direction of Lay
	Any manufacturing process permitted	= ***Approximately parallel***
	Removal of Material Required	⊥ ***Approximately perpendicular***
	Removal of Material not permitted	X ***Angular in both directions***
		M ***Multidirectional***
		C ***Approximately circular***
		R ***Approximately radial***
		P ***Particulate, non-directional***

Figure 5–22

Step 4 - Complete the symbol creation.

Click **OK** in the Surface Texture dialog box to complete the creation of the symbol. A completed surface texture symbol is shown in Figure 5–23.

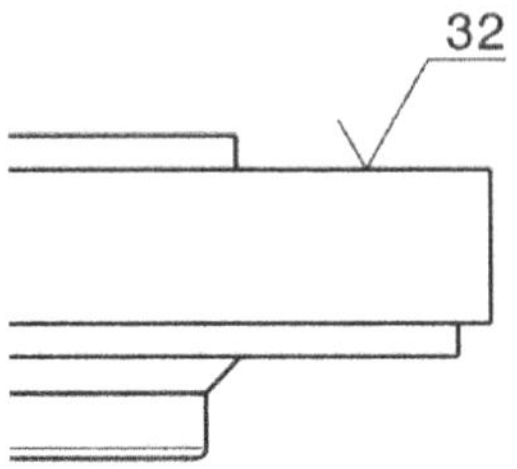

Figure 5–23

5.8 Create Weld Symbols

Two types of weld symbols can be created in a drawing view. The first, **Welding Symbol**, can be found in the Annotation section of the Action Bar, as shown in Figure 5–24.The second, **Weld**, would need to be added to the Action Bar via Customize Mode.

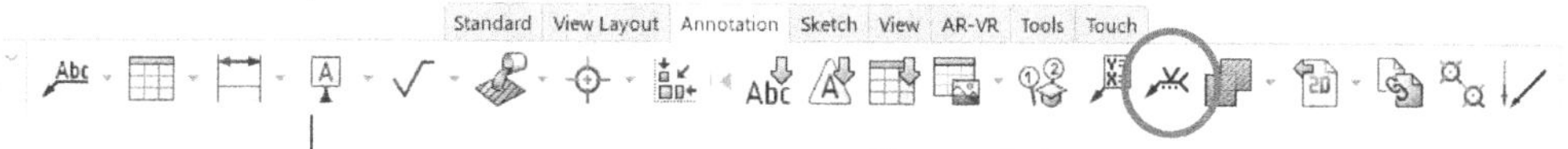

Figure 5–24

General Steps

Use the following general steps to create a welding symbol:

1. Activate the **Welding Symbol** tool.
2. Select a reference.
3. Select a location.
4. Specify weld symbol properties.
5. Complete the weld symbol.

Step 1 - Activate the Welding Symbol tool.

Click  (Welding Symbol) in the expanded area of the Annotation section of the Action Bar.

Step 2 - Select a reference.

Select geometry to define the location of the arrow of the welding symbol, as shown in Figure 5–25.

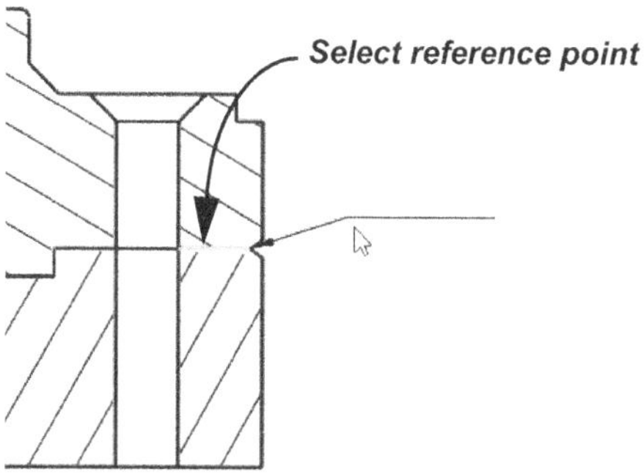

Figure 5–25

Step 3 - Select a location.

Select a location for the welding symbol, as shown in Figure 5–26.

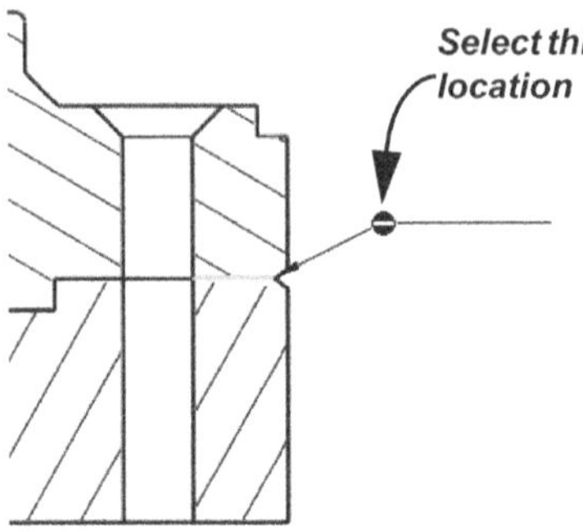

Figure 5–26

Step 4 - Specify weld symbol properties.

The Welding Symbol dialog box opens once a location for the welding symbol has been selected. Specify welding symbol properties as required by entering values and text and using the flyout menus to define symbol geometry. The dialog box is shown in Figure 5–27.

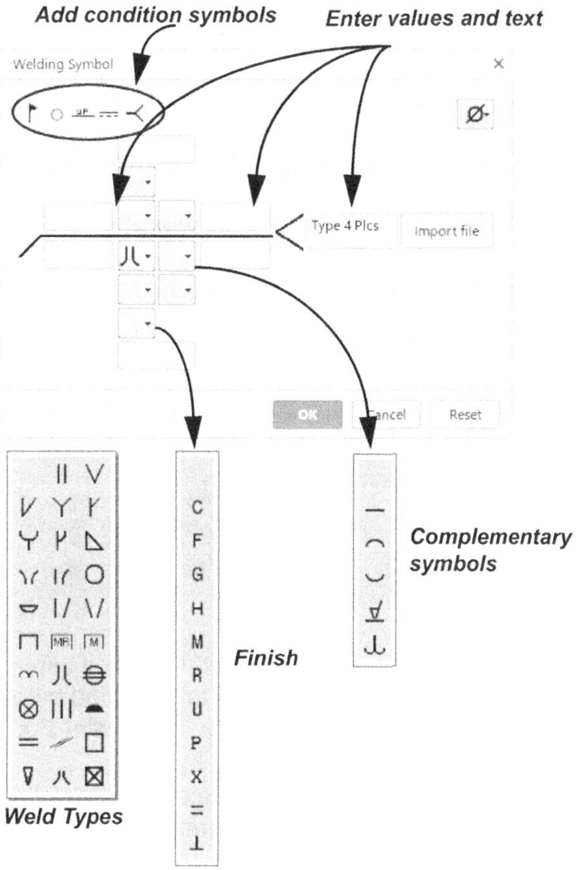

Figure 5–27

Step 5 - Complete the weld symbol.

Click **OK** in the Welding Symbol dialog box to complete the creation of the welding symbol. The completed welding symbol displays as shown in Figure 5–28.

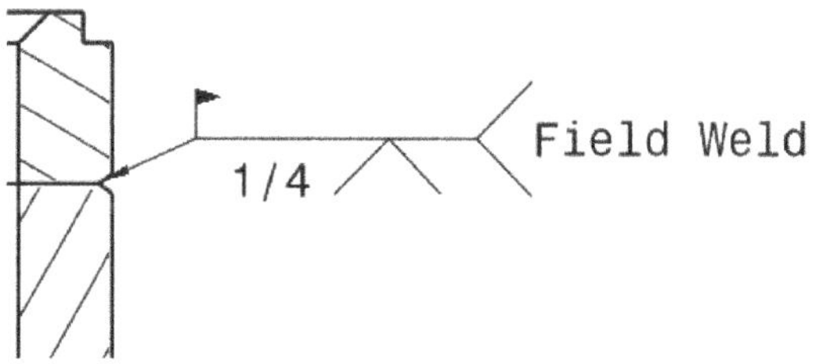

Figure 5–28

Weld Creation

Click (Weld) to create a graphical representation of a weld. Select the appropriate references and specify the thickness and bead type, as shown in Figure 5–29.

Select references to place the weld

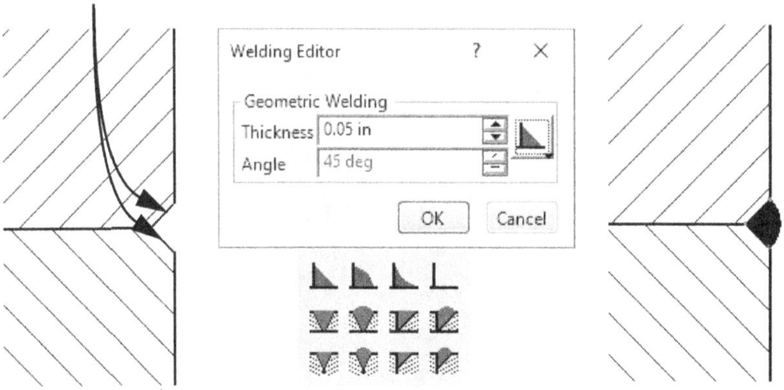

Figure 5–29

By default, the **Weld** command is not found in the Action Bar. It will need to be added before it can be used. To add it to the Action Bar, select **Me>Preferences>Customize>Sections** and then place the (Weld) command onto a section by using **Add Commands...**.

If the Action Pad does not display, it can be toggled on by selecting (Action Pad) from the Tools section of the Action Bar.

Note: An alternative option would be to add the command to the Action Pad instead. The path for this would be **Me> Preferences>Customize>Action Pad**, then select **Add Commands.**

5.9 Dress-Up Elements

You can create threads, axis, and center lines while generating the view, provided those options have been set in the Properties dialog box, as shown in Figure 5–30.

Figure 5–30

If the features have not been generated with the view, have been deleted, or if you only want to display one or two features of a single type, you can create dress-up features from the Annotation section of the Action Bar, as shown in Figure 5–31.

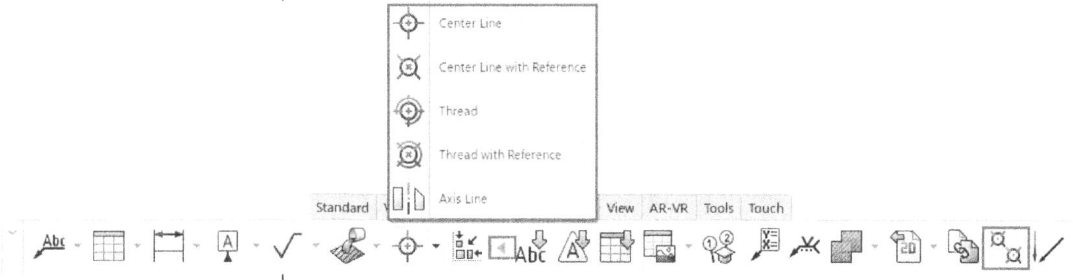

Figure 5–31

Center Line

Click (Center Line) to create a center line without a reference or (Center Line with Reference) to create a center line with a reference. The no-reference center line creates a center line that is oriented horizontally and vertically. The reference center line enables you to select a reference to define the orientation of the center line. Note that a center line with a reference cannot be created on an ellipse. The two types of center lines are shown in Figure 5–32.

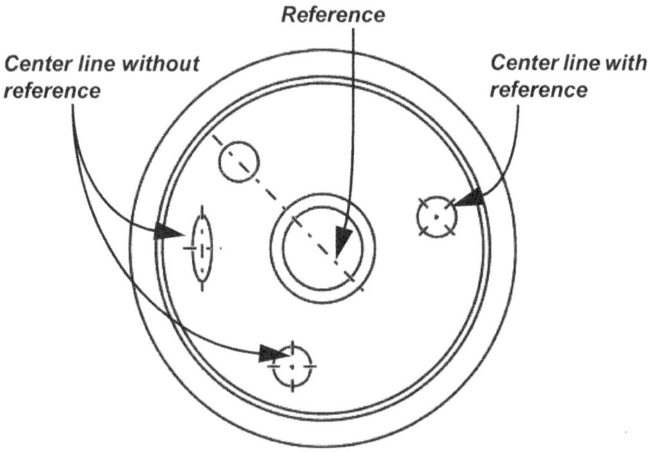

Figure 5–32

Thread

Click (Thread) to create a thread without a reference or (Thread with Reference) to create a thread with a reference. The no-reference thread is created with a center line that is oriented horizontally and vertically. The reference thread enables you to select an object to determine the orientation of the thread center line. The two types of threads are shown in Figure 5–33.

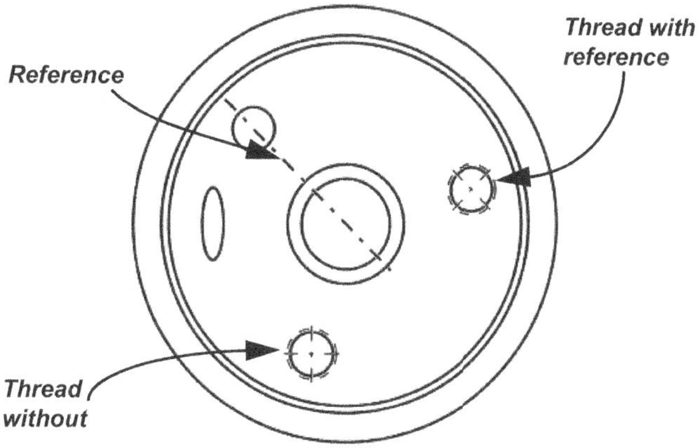

Figure 5–33

Axis Line

Click  (Axis Line) to create an axis line. If you are working with a section that has been cut through a hole in the part, you only need to select this icon and a reference line to create an axis, as shown in Figure 5–34.

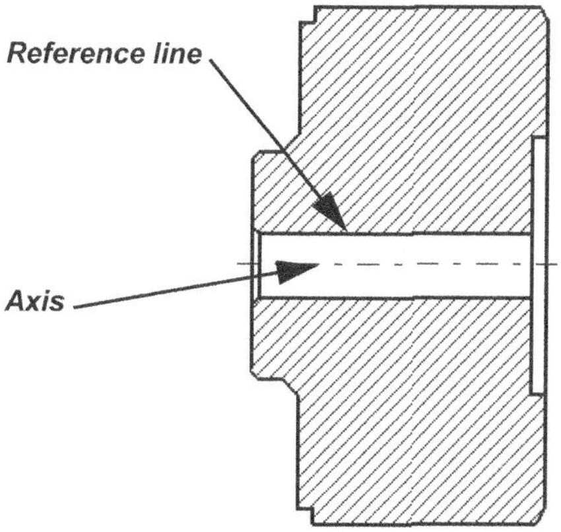

Figure 5–34

If you want to add an axis line between two lines anywhere in a view, click (Axis Line) and select the two lines between which you want to locate the axis line, as shown in Figure 5–35.

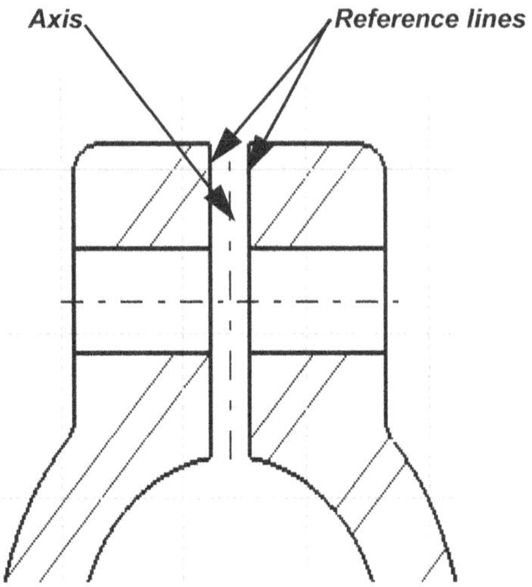

Figure 5–35

Axis Line and Center Line

Click (Axis line and Center line) and select two holes. The resulting axis and center line are shown in Figure 5–36.

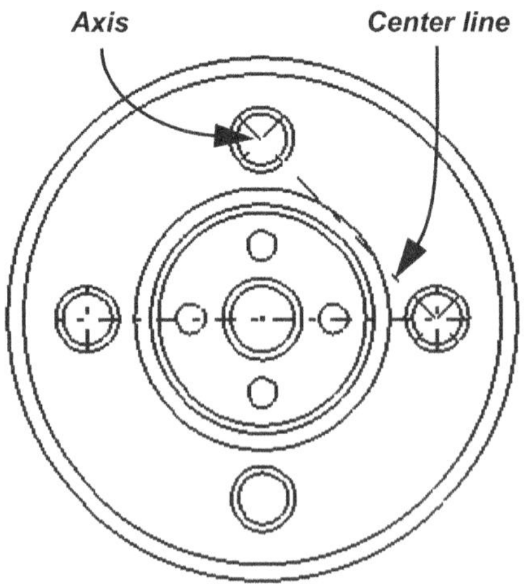

Figure 5–36

Area Fill

Click  (Area Fill) to fill a selected area or profile with hatching or a solid color. A filled area is shown in Figure 5–37.

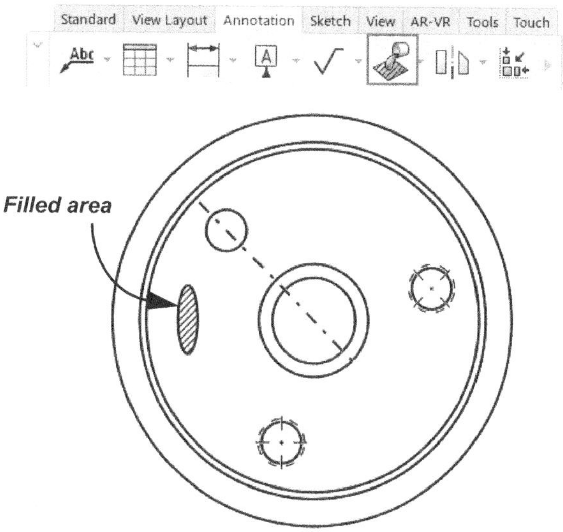

Figure 5–37

5.10 Create Tables

Using tables in a drawing is an effective method of conveying information. The Drafting app provides a method for creating a table from scratch by defining the number of rows and columns.

General Steps

Use the following general steps to create a table:

1. Activate the view or background.
2. Select the **Table** tool.
3. Select a location.
4. Specify the number of rows and columns.
5. Enter the required data.
6. Complete the table.
7. Modify the table, as required.

Step 1 - Activate the view or background.

You can add a table to the active view or background. Double-click on the appropriate view to activate a view or right-click on the sheet name in the tree and select **Edit Background** to activate the background.

Step 2 - Select the Table tool.

Click (Table) in the Annotation section of the Action Bar.

Step 3 - Select a location.

Select a location on the drawing sheet to place the table. The table displays as shown in Figure 5–38.

Figure 5–38

Once the table location is placed, moving the cursor will determine the direction the table will go. Moving the cursor up, down, left, or right will create different arrangements of the table. An example of moving the cursor to the down and to the right is shown in Figure 5–39.

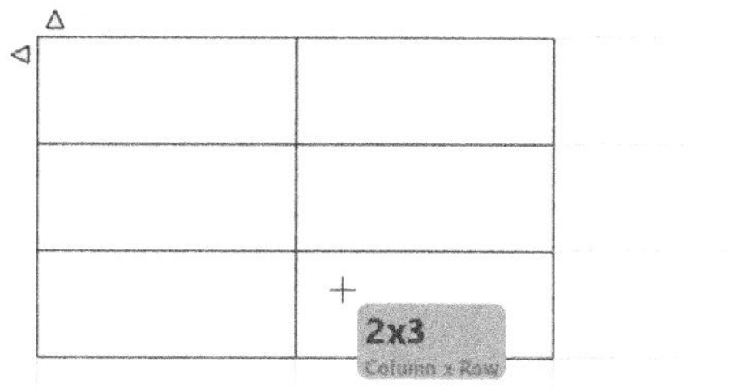

Figure 5–39

If the incorrect direction was used, the table can be flipped by selecting the Δ icons in the corner of the table.

Step 4 - Specify the number of rows and columns.

Now that the location and direction of the table has been defined, you will need to define the number of rows and columns to be used in the table. After moving the cursor in the previous step, you will notice a pop-up window that shows how many columns and rows are to be created. Moving the cursor farther from the original table location point will increase these numbers, as shown in Figure 5–40. Simply left-click once the desired table size is shown.

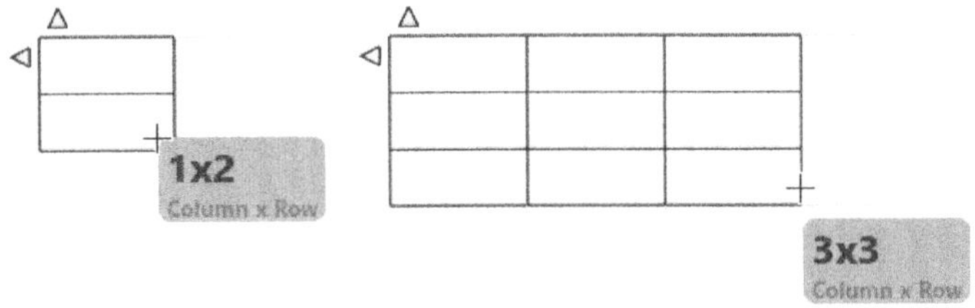

Figure 5–40

An alternative to using the cursor to define the table size is to type the number of columns and rows into the pop-up window that appears at the top of the screen, as shown in Figure 5–41. This will appear when the table direction is defined. Simply enter a number in the (Columns) and (Rows) fields, then select when finished.

Figure 5–41

Step 5 - Enter the required data.

Double-click on the table. Rows and columns display on the screen, and the outside border displays as shown in Figure 5–42.

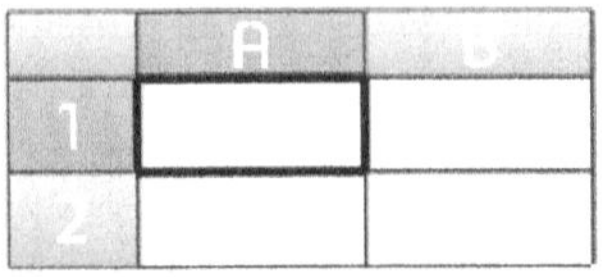

Figure 5–42

Double-click on a cell to add text, as shown in Figure 5–43.

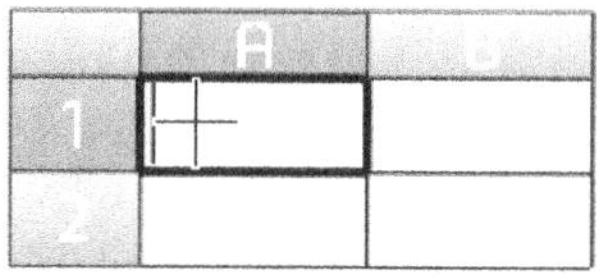

Figure 5–43

Enter the required text in the Text Editor, as shown in Figure 5–44.

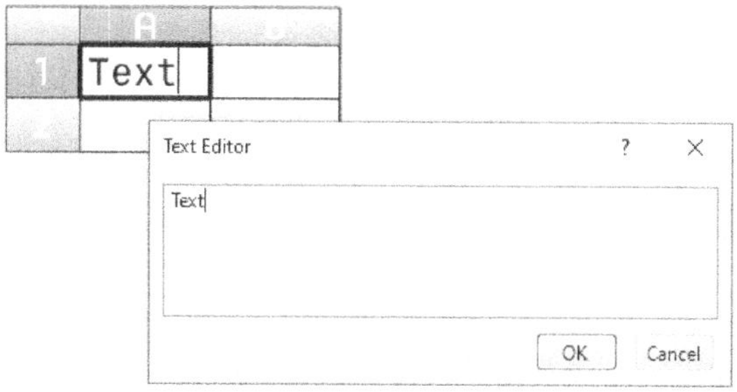

Figure 5–44

Click **OK**.

Step 6 - Complete the table.

Select anywhere on the drawing sheet to deactivate the table. The table with text displays as shown in Figure 5–45.

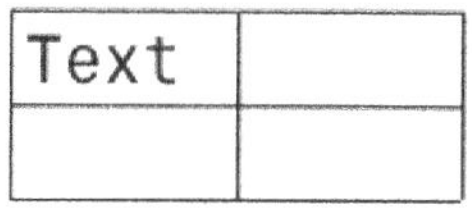

Figure 5–45

Step 7 - Modify the table, as required.

You might need to make changes to the table once it has been completed. Double-click on the table to make it active. Drag the handles in the border, as shown in Figure 5–46, to modify the column and/or row size.

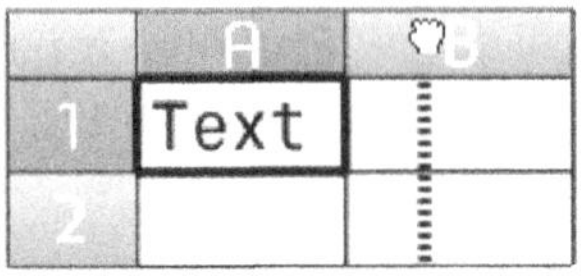

Figure 5–46

Right-click on the border to display the options for changing the table attributes. For example, the shortcut menu displays (shown on the right in Figure 5–47) when the cursor displays (shown on the left in Figure 5–47). This menu enables you to manipulate the selected row. Depending on where the cursor is located on the border, the shortcut menu displays different options that enable you to insert, delete, clear, or resize the rows and columns.

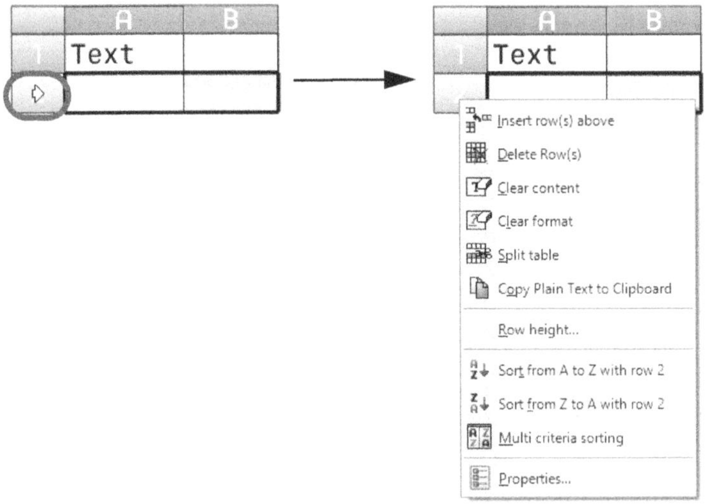

Figure 5–47

Create Table from CSV

If you want to insert existing data from an Excel spreadsheet, the .XLSX file must be saved as a .CSV file format.

How To: Insert a Table from CSV

1. In the Annotation section of the Action Bar, click (Insert from File).
2. Browse to the required .CSV file.
3. Select a location on the drawing sheet in which to place the table.

   Figure 5–48 shows an example of an inserted table from CSV. This functionality can be used to display design table information on a drawing.

PartNumber	Width (mm)	Radius (mm)
B121463	20	22.5
B121464	20	23
B121465	20	23.5
B121466	20	24
B121467	20	24.5
B121468	20	25
B121469	20	25.5
B121470	20	26

Figure 5–48

Note: Insert From File can also be used to insert file formats .CGM, .DWG, .DXF, .GL2, .PS, .SVG, and .IG2.

5.11 Attribute Links

Attribute links enable table and annotation text to be linked to model parameter values. Inserting an attribute link in place of static text increases drawing effectiveness and flexibility. When a pointed parameter value changes, linked text automatically updates with the drawing as shown in Figure 5–49.

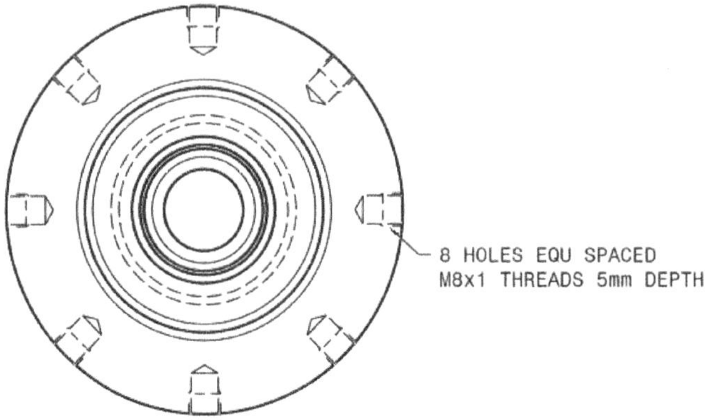

Figure 5–49

Creating an Attribute Link

To create an attribute link, open the Text Editor dialog box by double-clicking on the text box in the drawing display. In the Text Editor, highlight the text to be replaced. Right-click on the highlighted text (or specify a new insertion point by left-clicking with the cursor) in the display area and select **Insert Attribute Link**, as shown in Figure 5–50.

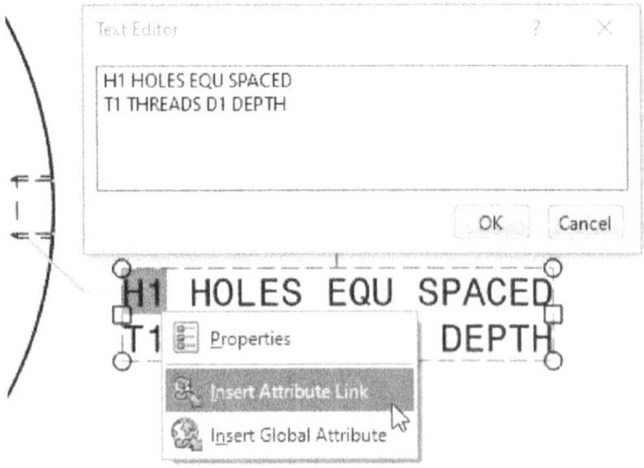

Figure 5–50

The Insert Attribute Link dialog box will appear, as shown in Figure 5–51. This dialog box allows for the selection of the objects that you want to link to. This selection can be from the tree, from the work area, from the drawing, or from search results.

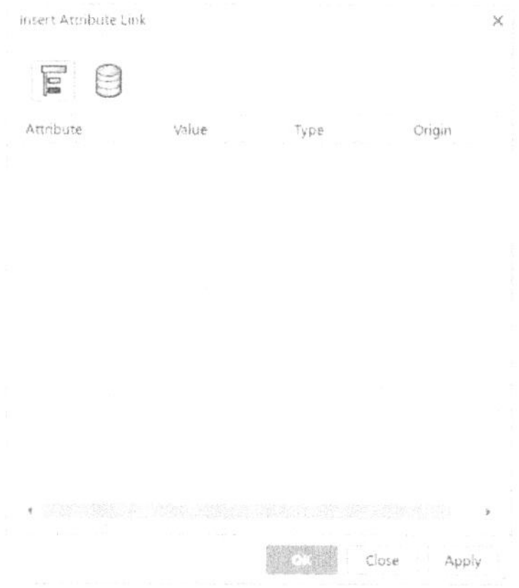

Figure 5–51

Activate the 3D Part or Physical Product widget and select the parameter or feature to which to link (in this case the specification tree). Selecting a parameter automatically completes the attribute link.

If a feature has been selected, the Insert Attribute Link dialog box updates as shown in Figure 5–52. The names and values of the parameters associated with the feature are listed in the Attribute list.

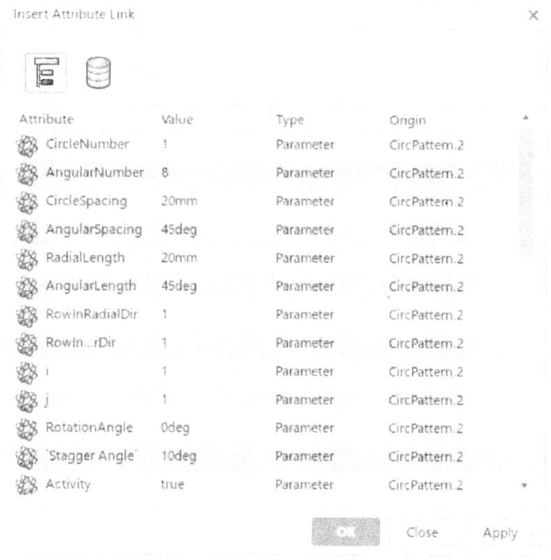

Figure 5–52

Select the parameter in the *Attribute* list and click **OK**. The Text Editor dialog box updates as shown in Figure 5–53.

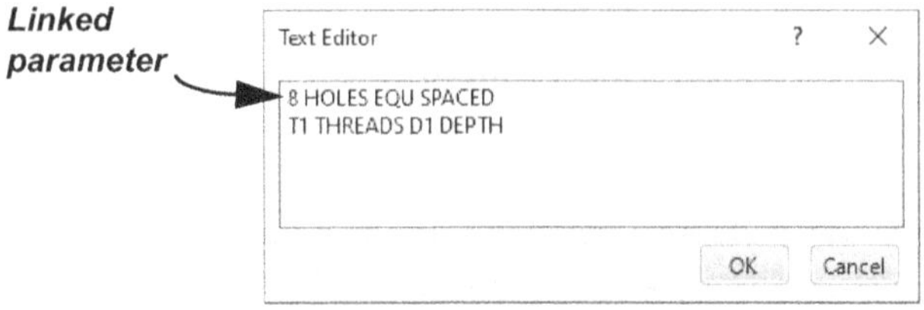

Figure 5–53

Managing Attribute Links

To view properties and synchronize individual attribute links, select  (Links and Relations) from the Tools section of the Action Bar. Attribute links are found under the *Text parameter* Role in the Edit Links and Relations dialog box, as shown in Figure 5–54. These links can be isolated from the Edit Links and Relations dialog box.

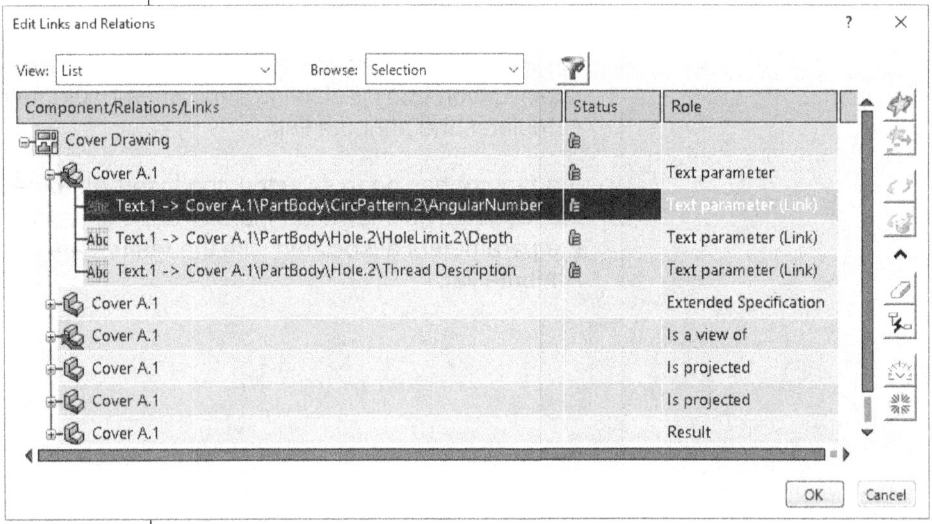

Figure 5–54

Part parameter modifications are included in the update of the drawing, as shown Figure 5–55.

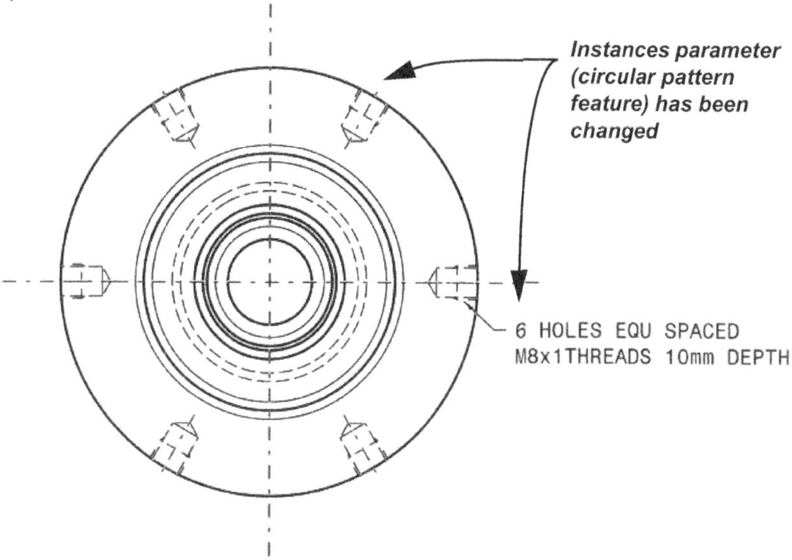

Figure 5–55

5.12 Dimension and Annotation Settings

Various options can be set to control how dimension generation and annotations are created.

Geometry and Dimension Generation

To change options, select **Me>Preferences>App Preferences>3D Modeling/Mechanical Systems/Drafting** and expand the *View* section. The options are shown in Figure 5–56.

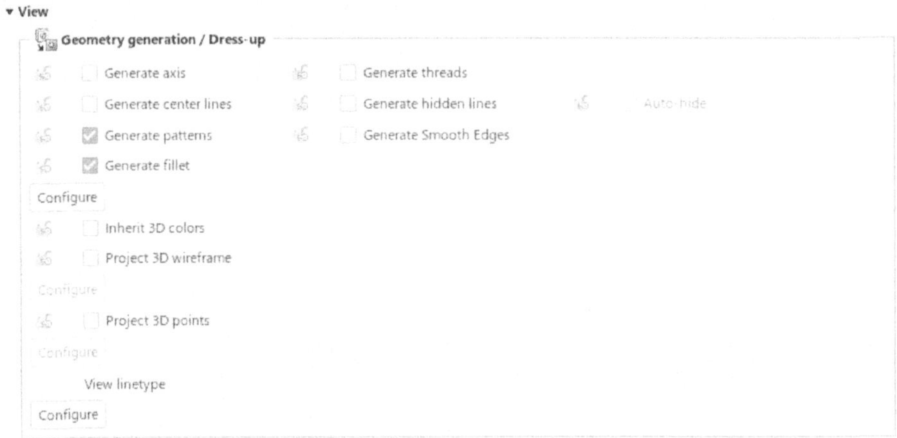

Figure 5–56

The options are described as follows:

- **Geometry Generation/Dress up:** Enables you to generate axes, threads, center lines, hidden lines, and fillets in the drawing. When generating fillets, you can click **Configure** and select the required type of representation for the fillets.
- **Inherit 3D colors:** Enables you to generate the colors of the 3D part.
- **Project 3D wireframe** or **Project 3D points:** Enable you to project wireframe elements or points from the 3D part. You can click **Configure** and specify options for the selection of wireframe or point elements.
- **View linetype:** You can set the line types that you want to use for the section, detail, broken, and breakout views. Click **Configure** next to the View linetype.

Additional options are available in the *Generation* section, as shown in Figure 5–57.

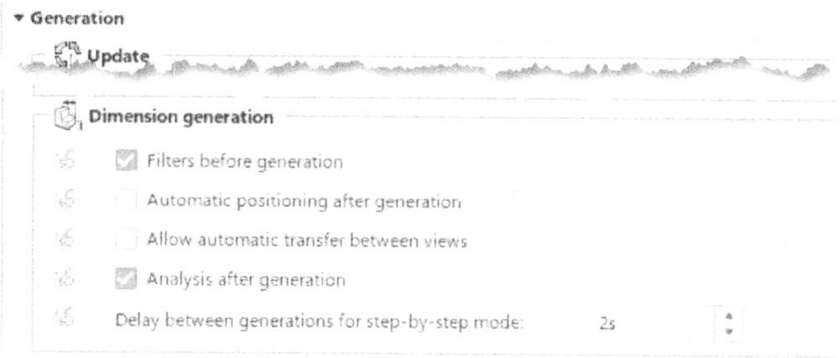

Figure 5–57

Dimension Generation settings enable you to perform the following tasks:

- Apply filters to select which dimensions to change.
- Automatically position the created dimensions.
- Automatically transfer dimensions between views.
- Display the Dimension Analysis box after dimension creation.
- Set the time delay between the creation of dimensions using step by step mode.

Dimension Creation Settings

Expand the *Dimension* section. The options are shown in Figure 5–58.

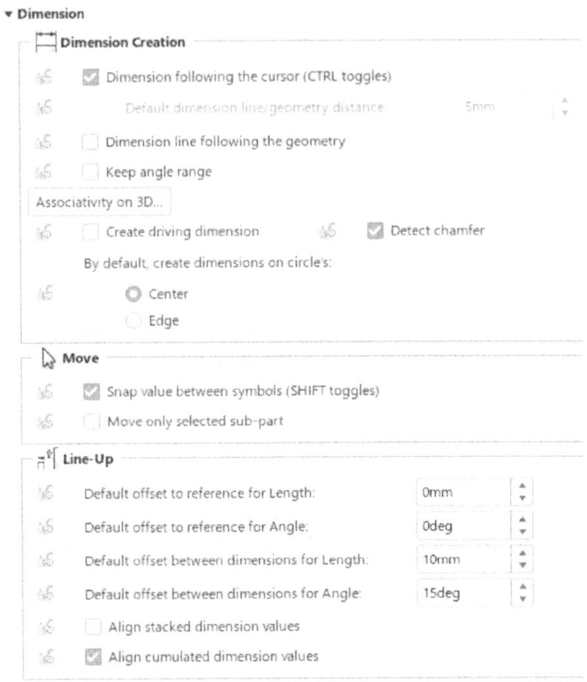

Figure 5–58

The options are described as follows:

- **Dimension following the cursor:** Enables you to have the dimension line follow the cursor as you create a dimension. If you hold <Ctrl> while creating a dimension, this option is toggled off temporarily.
- **Dimension line following the geometry:** The dimension line maintains a defined distance from the geometry, when the geometry is moving.
- **Keep angle range:** Maintains the value of an angle dimension between 0-90, 90-180, or 180-360 degrees.
- Clicking **Associativity on 3D** enables you to create non-associative dimensions.
- **Create driving dimension:** Enables you to create dimensions that drive (change) the geometry.
- **Detect chamfer:** Detects chamfers, enabling chamfer dimensions to be created with a single click.

- **Center** and **Edge:** Enable you to dimension to the center or edge of a circle.

- The options in the *Move* area enable you to toggle the **Snapping** function on or off, configure how you want the snap to occur, and specify whether you want to move only the selected sub-part (text, line, etc.).

- The options in the *Line-Up* area enable you to align stacked and cumulated dimensions, and automatically add funnels to dimensions. You can specify the distance to offset the dimensions when this option is selected.

Handles Settings

Expand the *Handles* section. The options are shown in Figure 5–59.

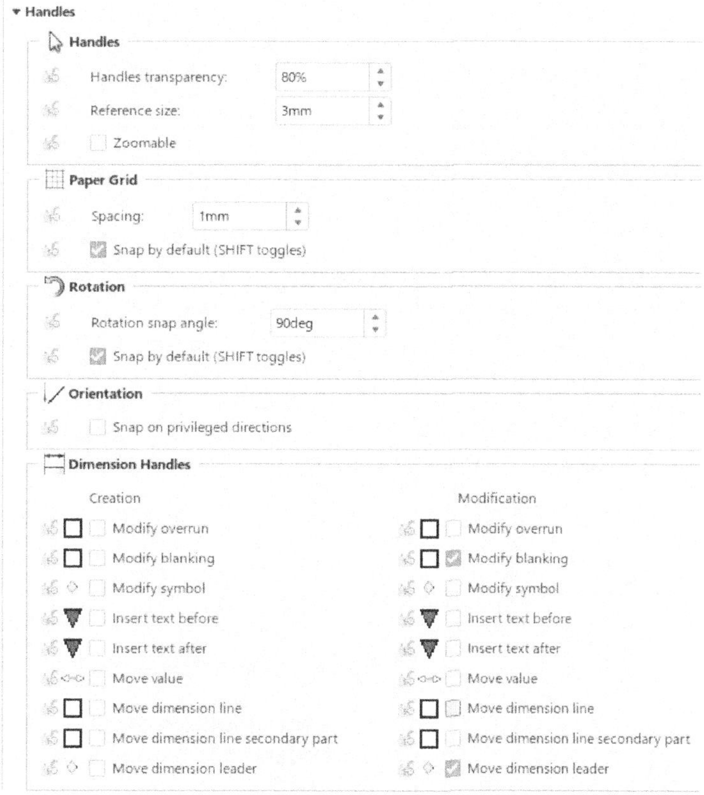

Figure 5–59

The options are described as follows:

- The options in the *Handles* area enable you to set the size and transparency of the dimensions and determine whether or not they can be zoomed.

- The options in the *Dimension Handles* area enable you to modify the overrun and blanking of dimensions. The overrun specifies the distance that the extension line passes the dimension line, and blanking is the amount of space from the selected object and the start of the extension line. You can add symbols (that are selectable) to add text before and after the dimension number, and add manipulator arrows that make it easier to move the dimensions.

Annotation Settings

Expand the *Annotation and Dress-Up* section. The options are shown in Figure 5–60.

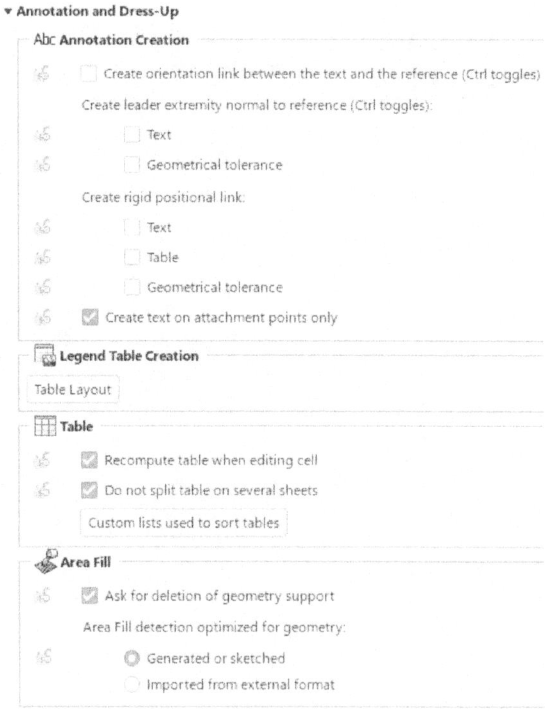

Figure 5–60

Some of the options are described as follows:

- **Annotation Creation:** Enables you to snap text, text with leader, and Geometric Tolerances.
- **Table**: Enables you to control updating and splitting of tables in the drawing.
- **Area Fill**: Controls how Area fill detects geometry.

Practice 5a

Annotate a Drawing II

Practice Objectives

- Create annotations.
- Create symbols.

In this practice, you will add the following annotations to a drawing:

- Text
- Sketched geometry
- Geometric tolerances
- Dress-up features
- Surface symbols

The completed drawing is shown in Figure 5–61.

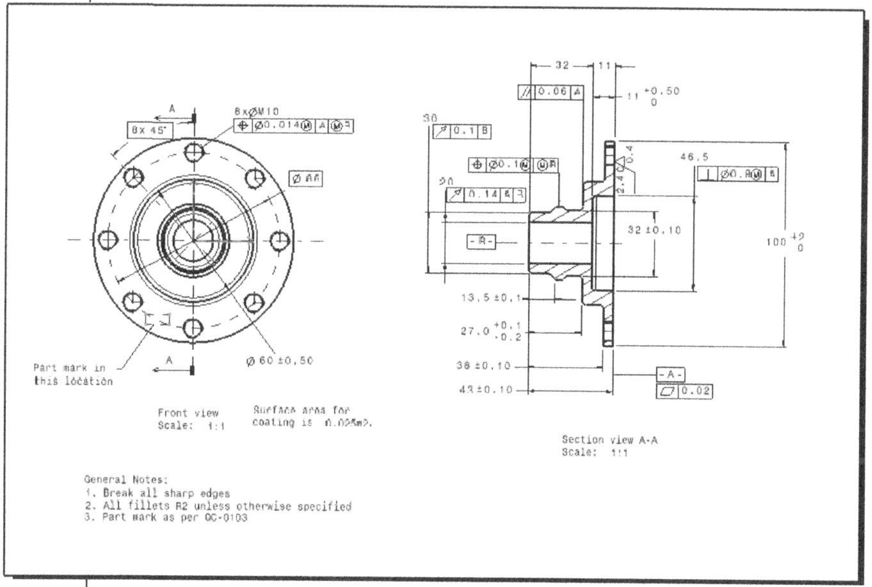

Figure 5–61

Task 1 - Import and open a drawing.

1. Import and open **Adapter_5A.3dxml** from the practice files folder. While importing, set the *Duplication string* to **###_** where ### represents your initials.

2. Right-click on the **###_Adapter_5A** drawing in the tree and select * **object>Open in New App**. The drawing displays as shown in Figure 5–62.

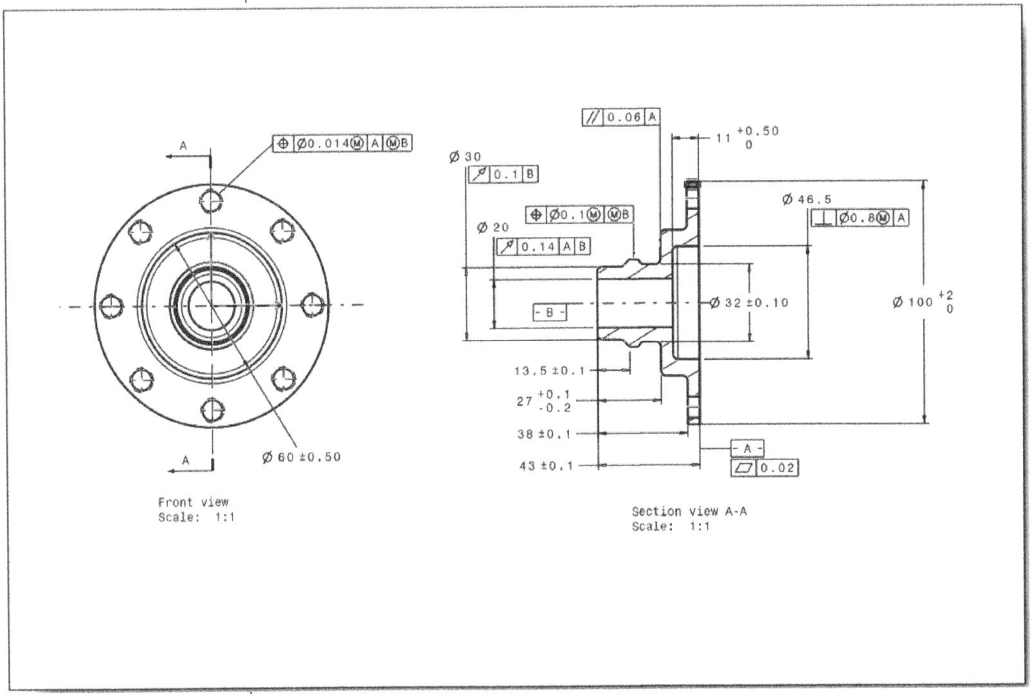

Figure 5–62

3. Right-click on **Sheet.1** in the tree and select **Edit Background**, as shown in Figure 5–63, to activate Background mode.

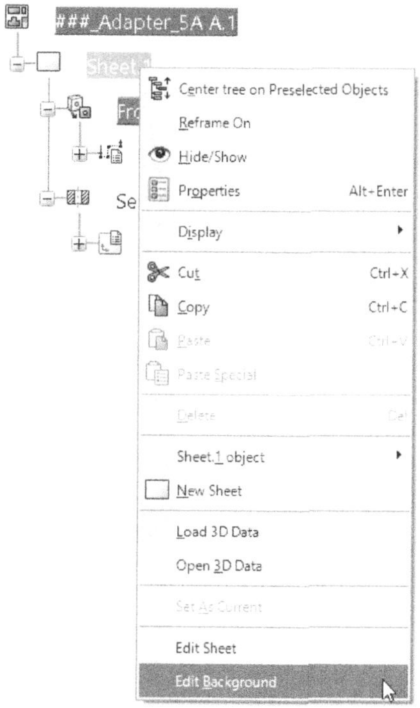

Figure 5–63

Task 2 - Create text.

1. In the Annotation section of the Action Bar, click Abc (Text).

2. Select the location shown in Figure 5–64.

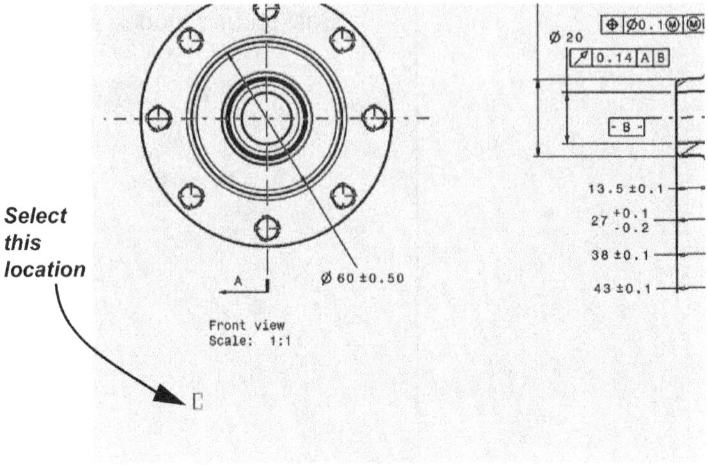

Figure 5–64

3. Enter the following text in the Text Editor, as shown in Figure 5–65. To add another line of text to the note, press <Shift>+<Enter>.

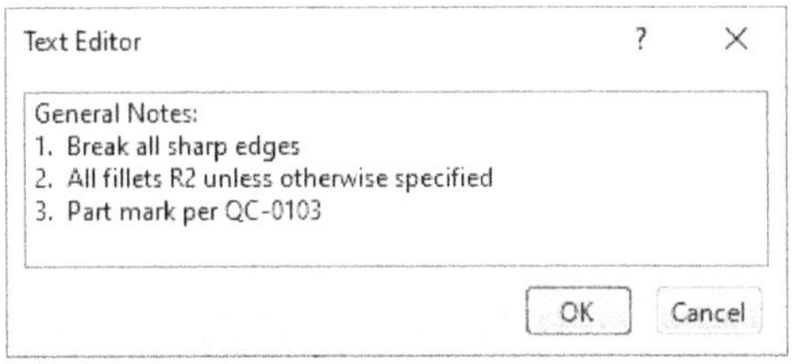

Figure 5–65

4. Click **OK**.

5. Position the text as shown in Figure 5–66.

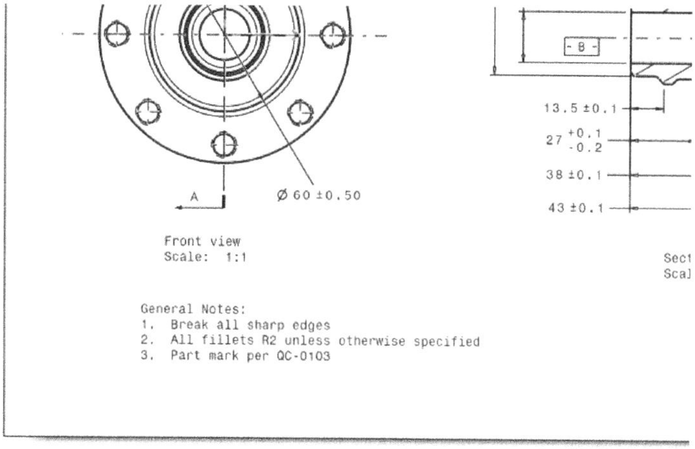

Figure 5–66

6. Right-click on **Sheet.1** in the tree and select **Edit Sheet** to activate Working views mode.

Task 3 - Create sketched geometry.

1. Ensure that the Front view is active. If the view frames are hidden, the view can be activated by double-clicking it in the specification tree.

2. In the Sketch section, click  (Rectangle) to sketch a rectangle.

3. Sketch the rectangle in the location shown in Figure 5–67.

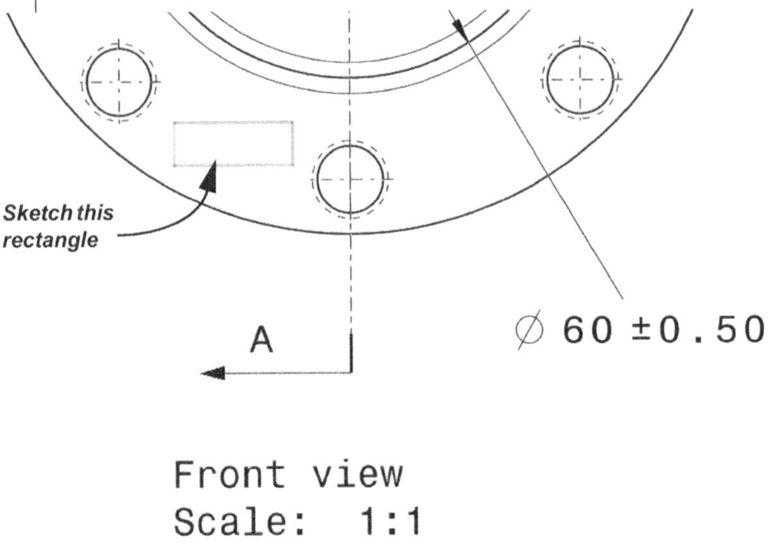

Figure 5–67

4. With the rectangle lines still selected, right-click on one of the lines of the rectangle and select **Properties**.

5. In the *Graphic* tab, set the *Linetype* to **2** and the *Thickness* to **1**, as shown in Figure 5–68.

Figure 5–68

The rectangle displays as shown in Figure 5–69.

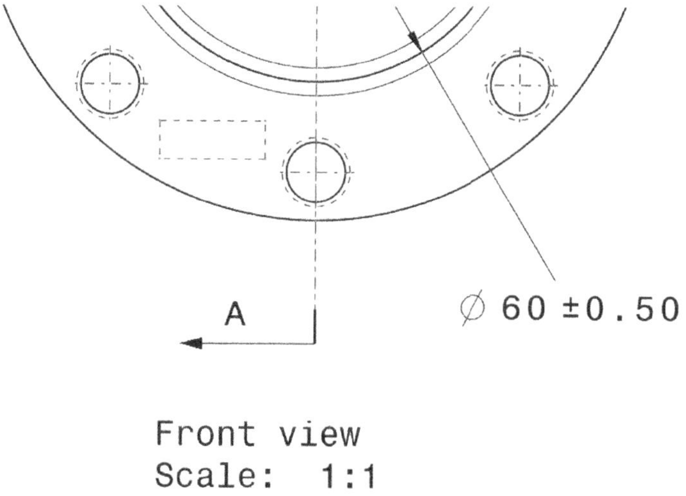

Figure 5–69

6. In the Annotation section of the Action Bar, click (Text with Leader) to create text with a leader, and select the rectangle you just created.
7. Enter the text shown in Figure 5–70. Position the text as required.

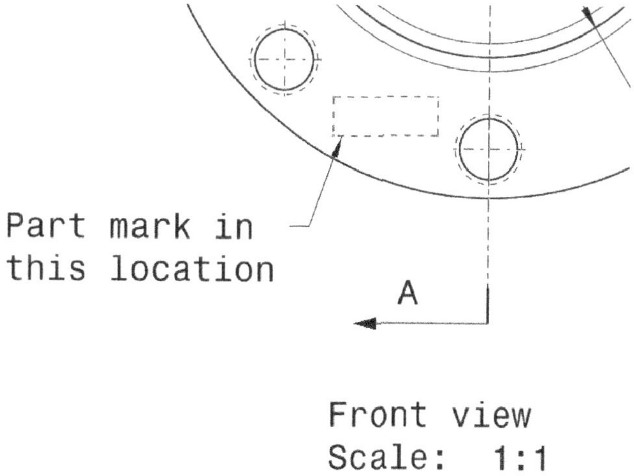

Figure 5–70

8. In the Sketch section of the Action Bar, click  (Circle) and snap the center of the circle to the center of the view. Drag the circle out and snap it to one of the holes, as shown in Figure 5–71.

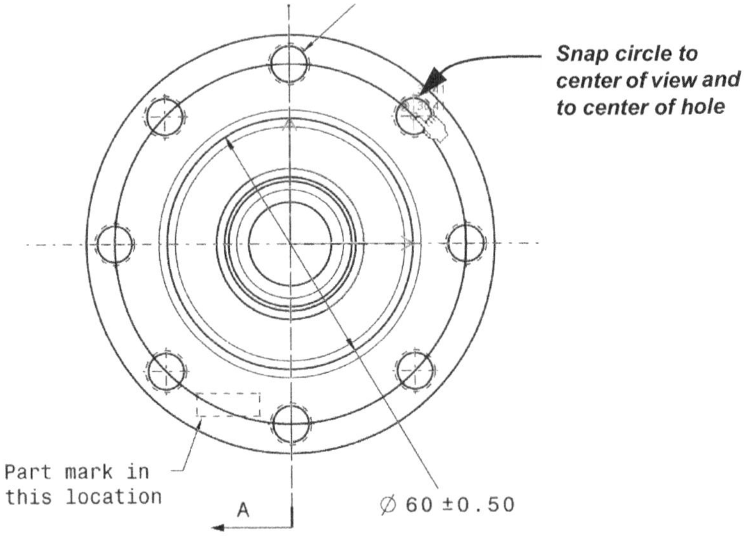

Figure 5–71

9. Change the sketched circle properties to the following:
   - *Linetype* to **2**
   - *Thickness* to **1**

10. Create a dimension on the sketched circle, as shown in Figure 5–72.

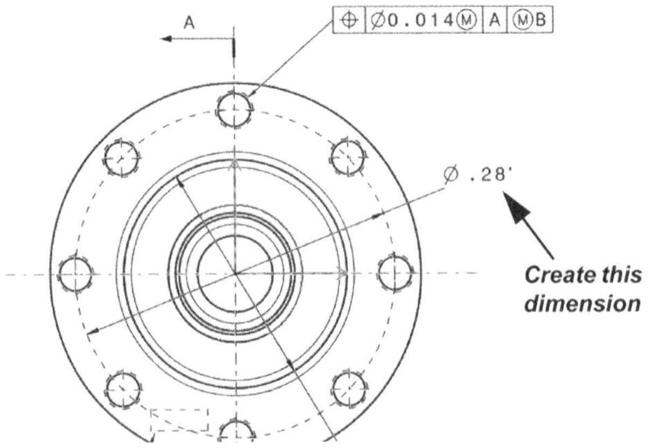

Figure 5–72

If needed, the Object Properties window can be toggled on by selecting  *(Object Properties) from the Tools section of the Action Bar.*

11. With the **.28**’ dimension selected, change the dimension to **mm** in the *Numerical* section of the Object Properties window. The dimension will update to 86.

12. With the **86** dimension still selected, in the *Text* section of the Object Properties window, expand  and click  (Rectangle). The value now displays as a basic dimension, as shown in Figure 5–73.

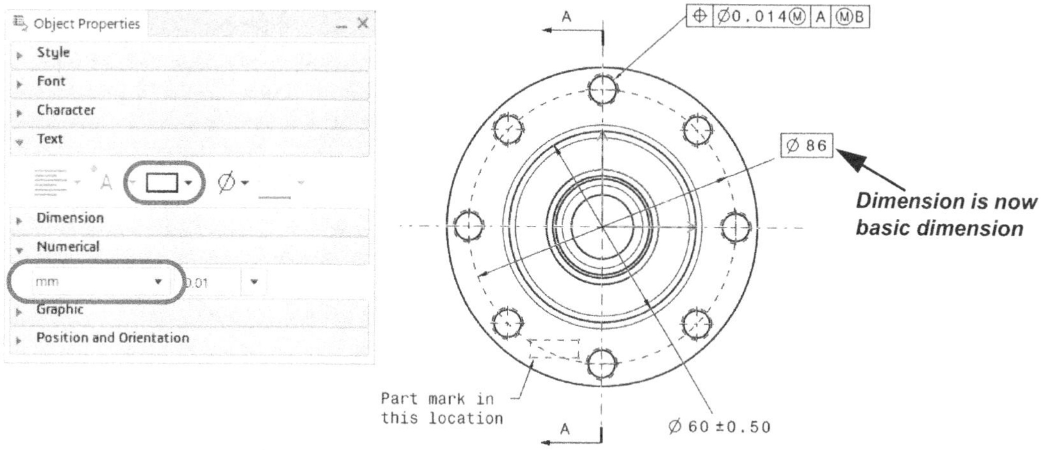

Figure 5–73

Task 4 - Add text to a geometrical tolerance.

1. Double-click on the geometrical tolerance of the hole, as shown in Figure 5–74.

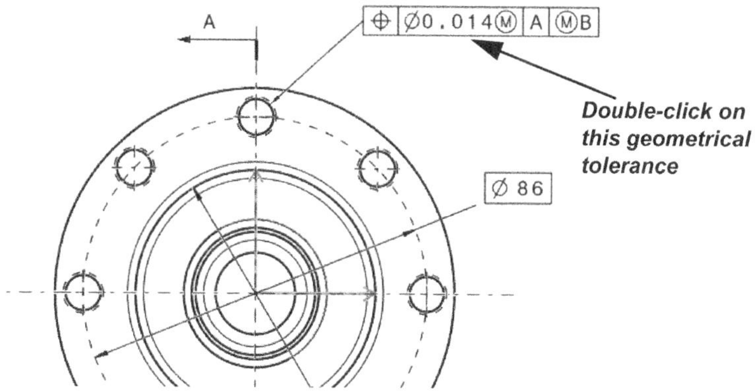

Figure 5–74

2. The Geometrical Tolerance dialog box opens. Enter **8x M10** in the *Upper* field, as shown in Figure 5–75.

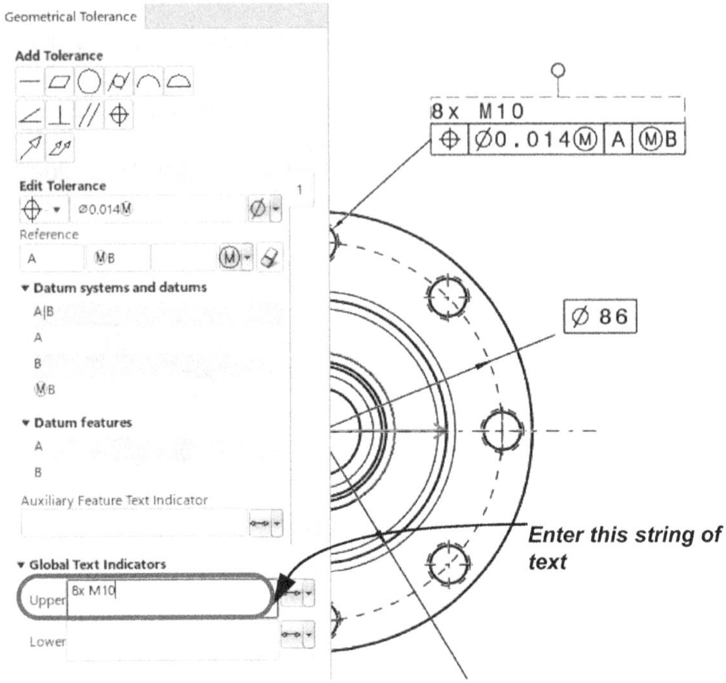

Figure 5–75

Task 5 - Create a dress-up feature.

1. In the expanded Annotation section of the Action Bar, click (Axis line and Center line).
2. Select the inner-most circle of the view, as shown in Figure 5–76.

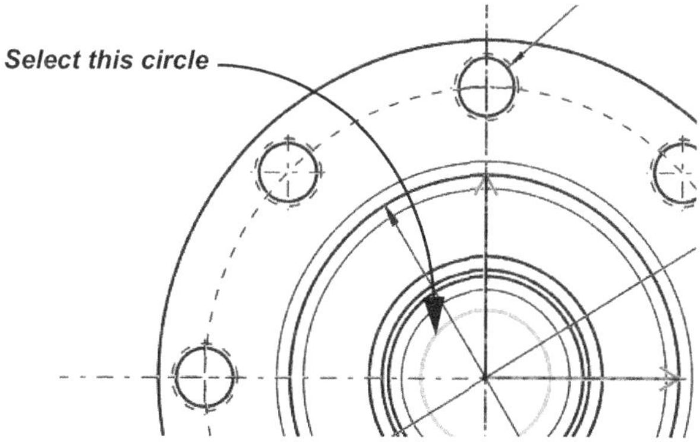

Figure 5–76

3. Select the hole shown in Figure 5–77.

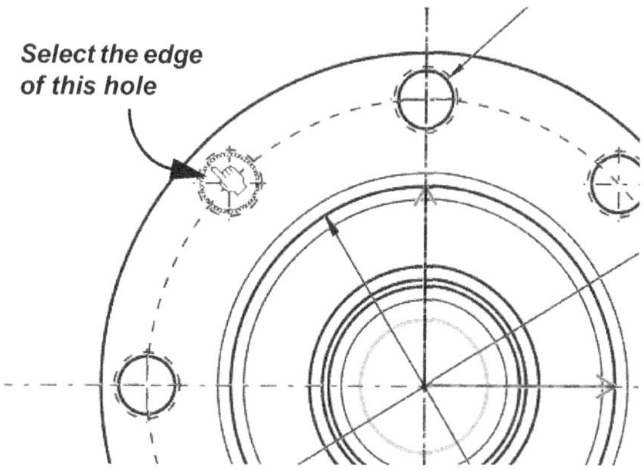

Figure 5–77

The axis displays as shown in Figure 5–78.

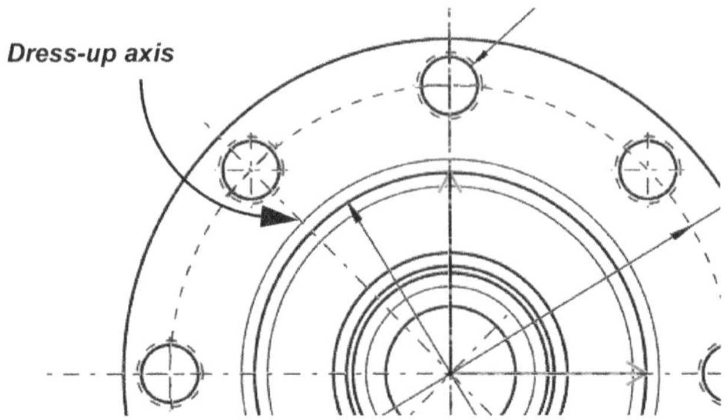

Figure 5–78

4. Create an angled basic dimension using the previously created axis, as shown in Figure 5–79.

*If the angle that displays is 90 degrees, disable the **Half Dimension** option in the shortcut menu while creating the dimension. The menu is not available once the dimension has been placed.*

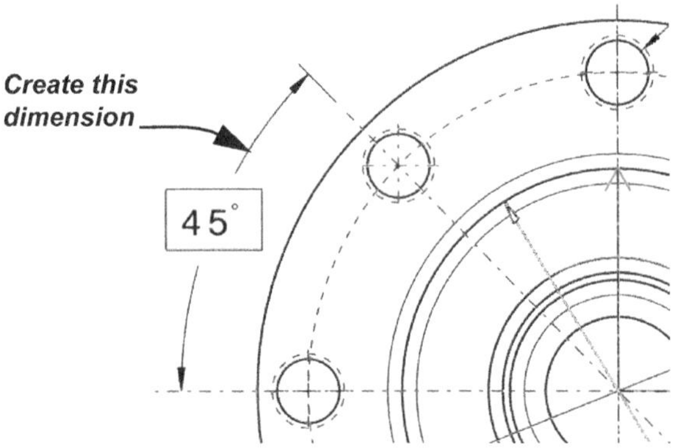

Figure 5–79

5. Select the angled basic dimension that you just created and press <Alt>+<Enter> to edit the properties of the dimension.

6. In the *Dimension Texts* tab, add a *prefix* of **8x**, as shown in Figure 5–80.

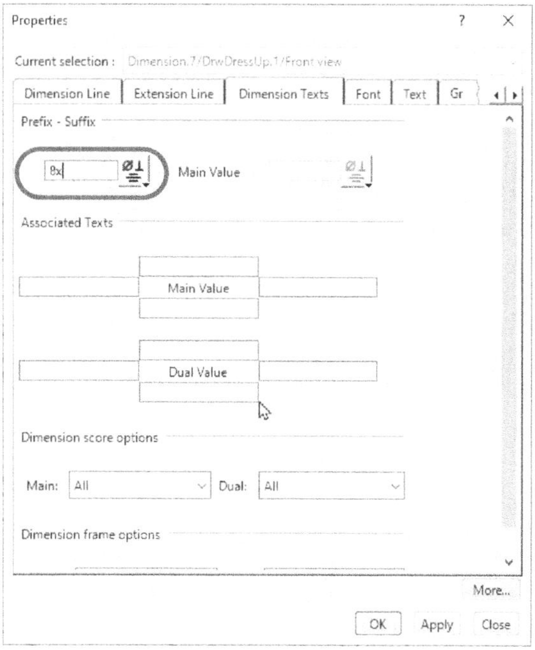

Figure 5–80

The dimension displays as shown in Figure 5–81.

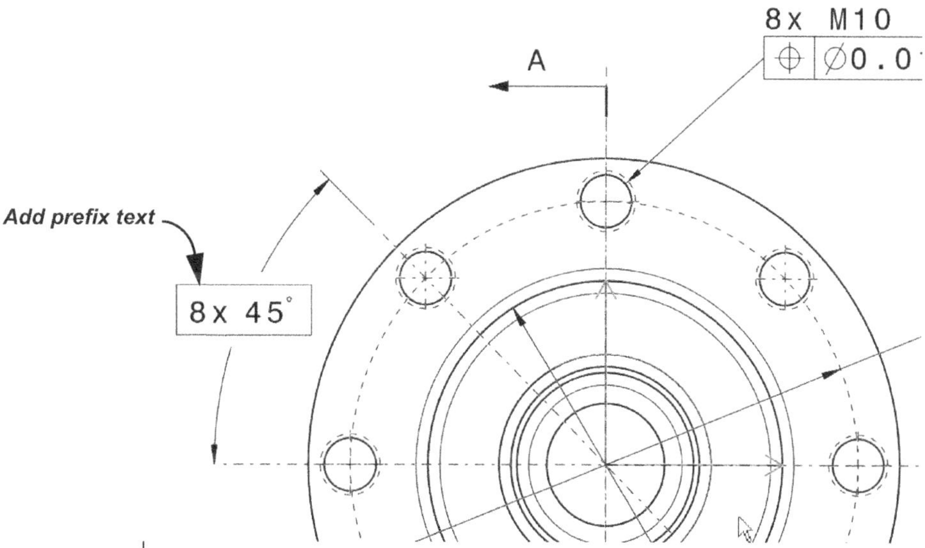

Figure 5–81

Task 6 - Create an attribute link.

1. Click Abc (Text). Place a new text box beneath the Front view, as shown in Figure 5–82.

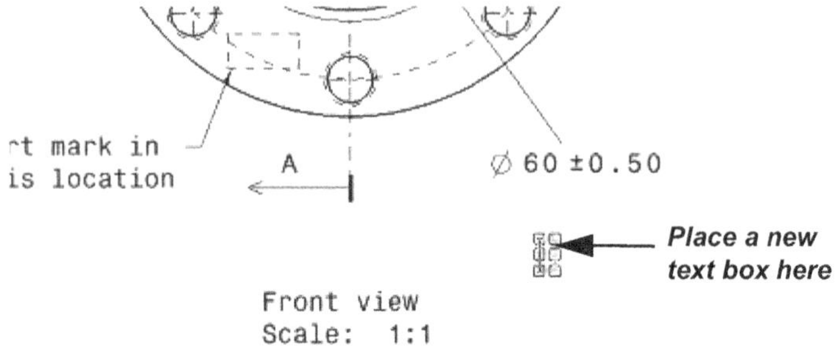

Figure 5–82

2. In the Text Editor dialog box, enter the text shown in Figure 5–83.

Figure 5–83

3. In the Text Editor dialog box, highlight the **xxx** text. Right-click on the highlighted text in the drawing view and select **Insert Attribute Link**, as shown above in Figure 5–83.

4. Activate the **###_Adapter_5A** part window. In the specification tree, under the **GeometricalSet.1> InertiaVolume.2** node, select the **Area** parameter. The Insert Attribute Link dialog box opens as shown in Figure 5–84.

*If the value does not display as shown in Figure 5–84, select **Me>Preferences> Common Preferences> Parameters, Measures, and Units>Units** and select Area in the Units associated to design limits list. Change the value for the Decimal place for read/write numbers to **3**.*

Figure 5–84

5. In the *Attribute* list, select the **###_Adapter_5A A.1\GeometricSet.1\InteriaVolume2\Area** parameter, as shown in Figure 5–85.

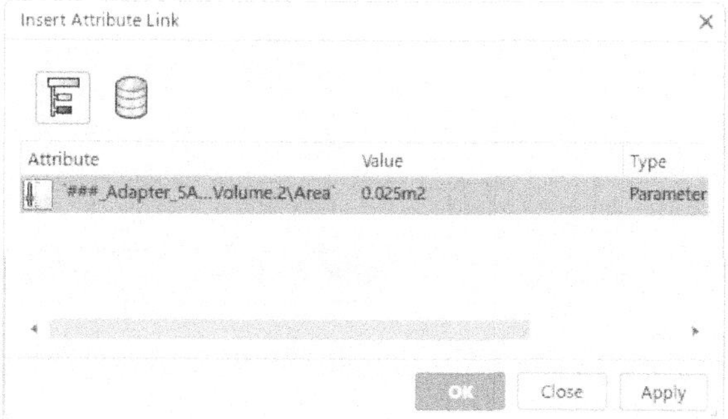

Figure 5–85

6. In the Insert Attribute Link and Text Editor dialog boxes, click **OK**. The completed text box and attribute link display as shown in Figure 5–86.

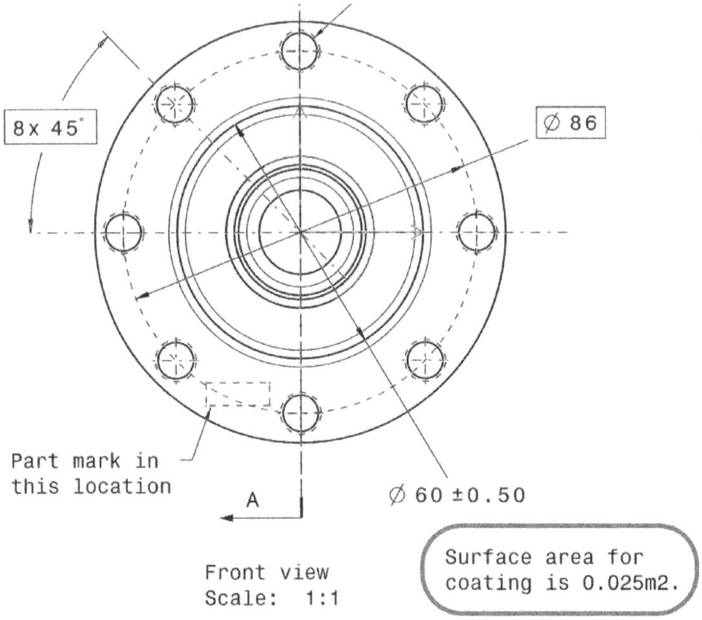

Figure 5–86

Task 7 - Create a surface texture symbol.

1. In the Annotation section of the Action Bar, click ✓ (Surface Texture).

2. Select a location at which to place the symbol, as shown in Figure 5–87.

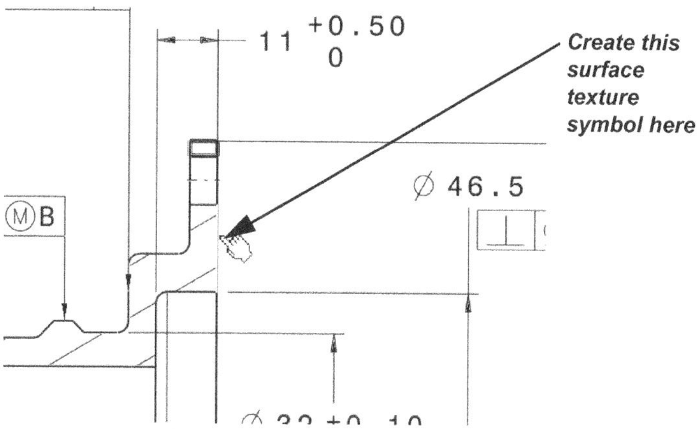

Figure 5–87

3. Define the surface texture symbol, as shown in Figure 5–88.

   You might need to click (Invert) to change the side of the entity on which the surface texture symbol is created.

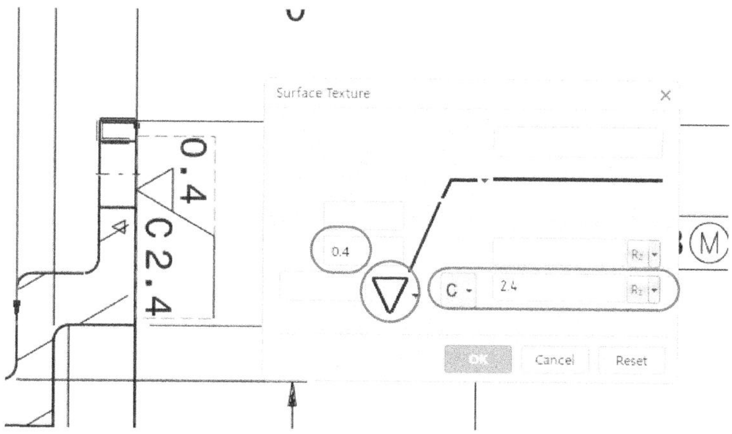

Figure 5–88

4. Save the drawing and close all of the tabs.

Practice 5b Create a Table

Practice Objective

- Create a table from CSV.

In this practice, you will modify a drawing to display design table data for a part model. A drawing has already been started and is shown in Figure 5–89.

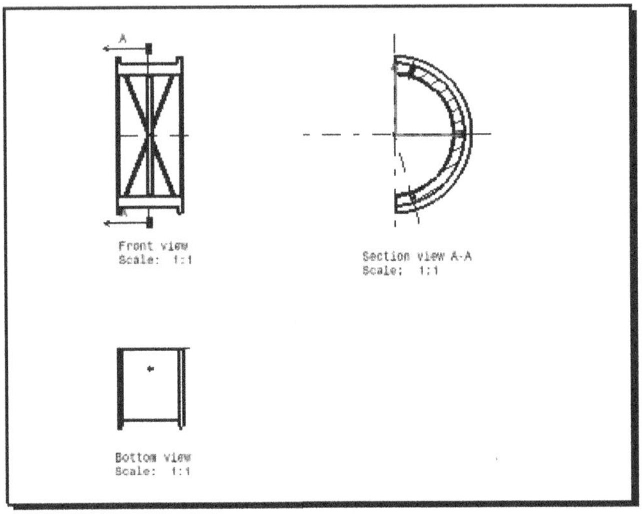

Figure 5–89

The Excel spreadsheet containing the design table data has been modified to use a .CSV extension (file name **B121463_Bushing.csv**). This is required to read the table data into the drawing. The table data is shown in Figure 5–90.

	A	B	C
1	PartNumber	Width (mm)	Radius (mm)
2	B121463	20	22.5
3	B121464	20	23
4	B121465	20	23.5
5	B121466	20	24
6	B121467	20	24.5
7	B121468	20	25
8	B121469	25	25.5
9	B121470	25	26
10			

Figure 5–90

The table refers to two model parameters: **Width** and **Radius**. Fake dimensions are used to display these parameters on the drawing to link the table data to the drawing geometry. The completed drawing is shown in Figure 5–91.

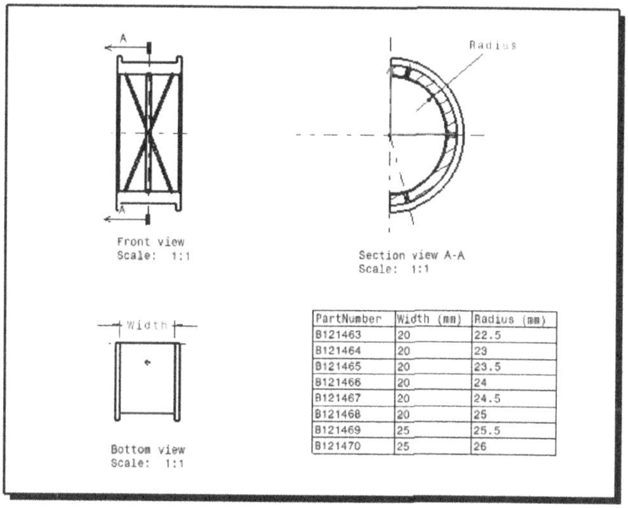

PartNumber	Width (mm)	Radius (mm)
B121463	20	22.5
B121464	20	23
B121465	20	23.5
B121466	20	24
B121467	20	24.5
B121468	20	25
B121469	25	25.5
B121470	25	26

Figure 5–91

Task 1 - Import and open a drawing.

1. Import and open **B121463_Bushing.3dxml** from the practice files folder. While importing, set the *Duplication string* to **###_** where ### represents your initials.

2. Right-click on the **###_B121463_Bushing** drawing in the tree and select * **object>Open in New App**. The drawing displays as shown in Figure 5–92.

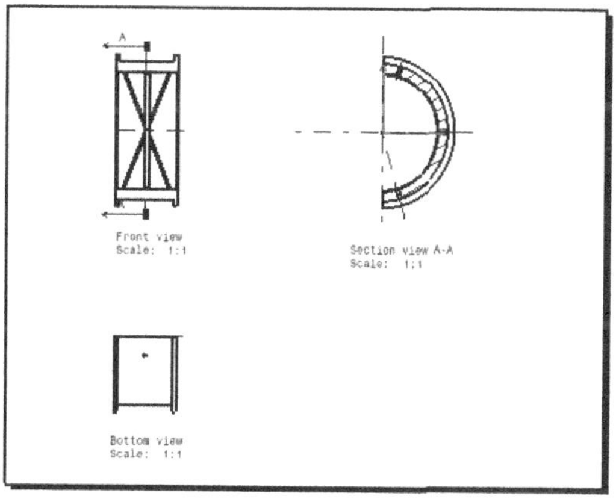

Figure 5–92

Task 2 - Create a dimension.

1. Zoom in on the Section view and create a radius dimension for the inside of the bushing, as shown in Figure 5–93.

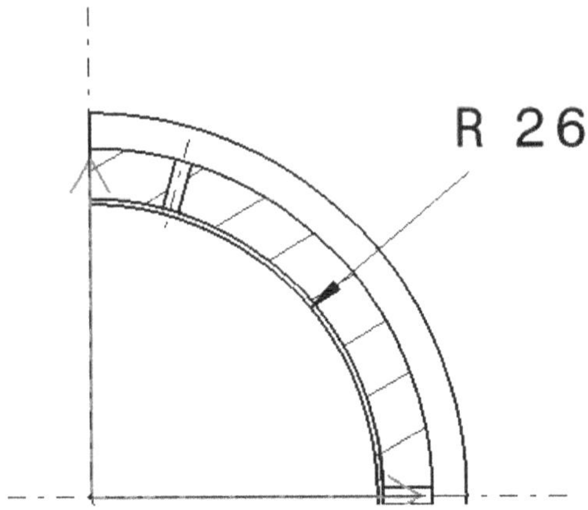

Figure 5–93

You can also select the arrow to reverse its direction.

2. Right-click on the dimension and select **Properties**.

3. Select the *Dimension Line* tab and change the *Thickness* to **2**, as shown in Figure 5–94. Change the **Reversal** option to **Outside**.

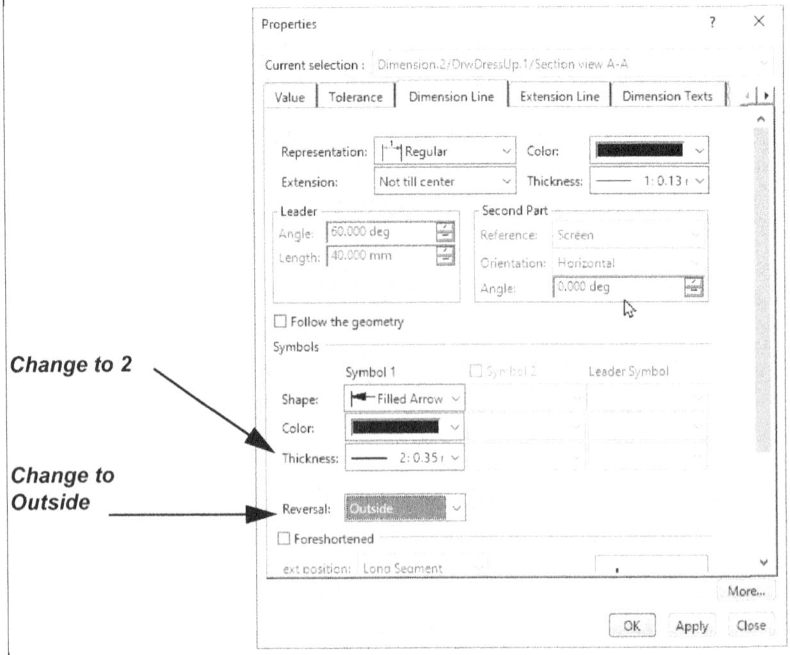

Figure 5–94

4. Click **OK**. The radius dimension displays as shown in Figure 5–95.

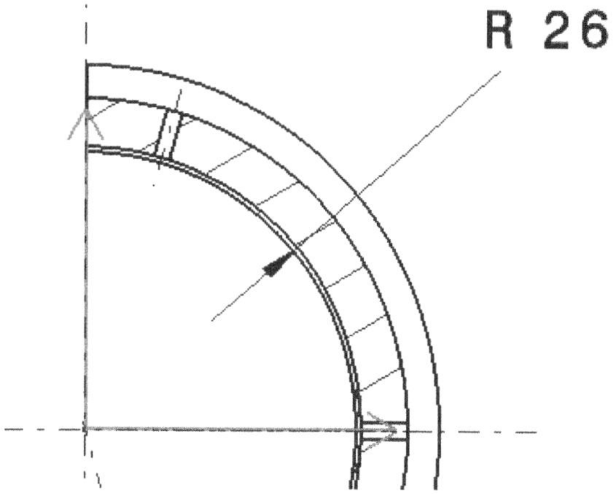

Figure 5–95

5. Zoom in on the Bottom view and create the 25 dimension shown in Figure 5–96.

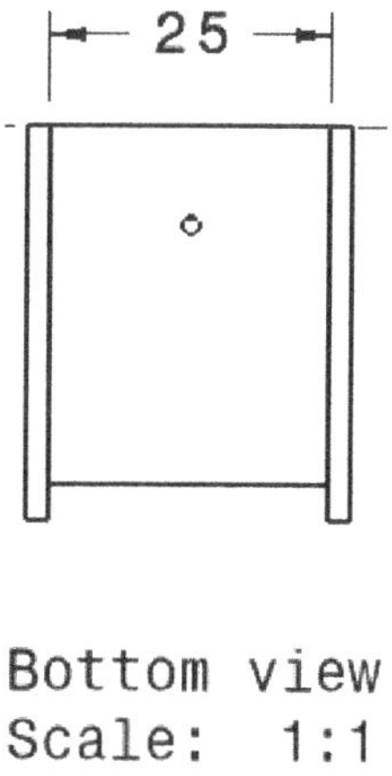

Figure 5–96

Task 3 - Create a fake dimension.

1. Open the Properties dialog box for the 25 dimension and select the *Value* tab.

2. Select the **Fake Dimension** option. In the *Main Value* field, under the **Alphanumerical** option, enter **Width** as shown in Figure 5–97.

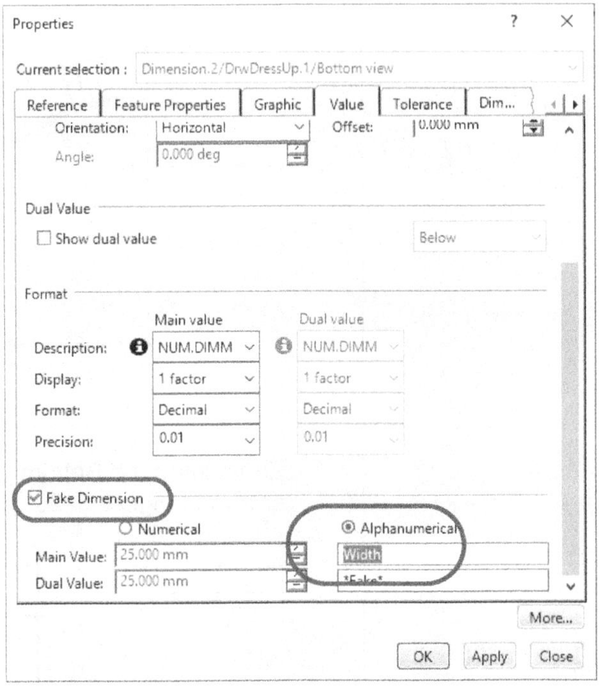

Figure 5–97

The fake dimension displays as shown in Figure 5–98.

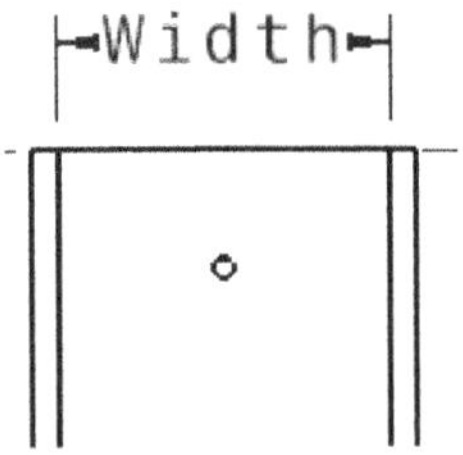

Figure 5–98

3. Open the Properties dialog box for the Width dimension. Select the *Dimension Line* tab and set the **Reversal** option to **Outside**, as shown in Figure 5–99.

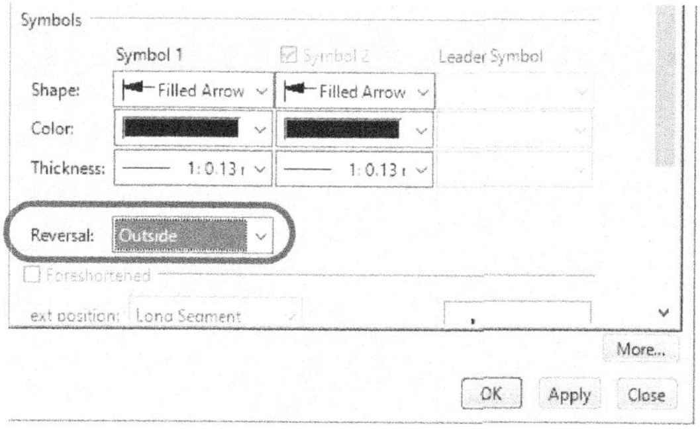

Figure 5–99

4. Click **OK**. The fake dimension displays as shown in Figure 5–100.

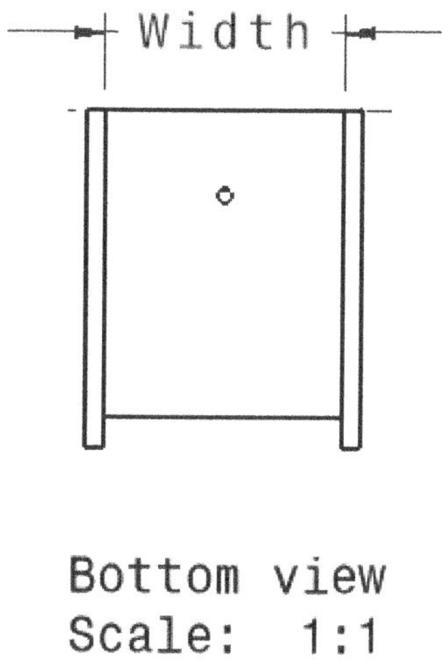

Figure 5–100

5. Create a fake dimension for the R26 value. You need to use the *Dimension Texts* tab to remove the R prefix. The view displays as shown in Figure 5–101.

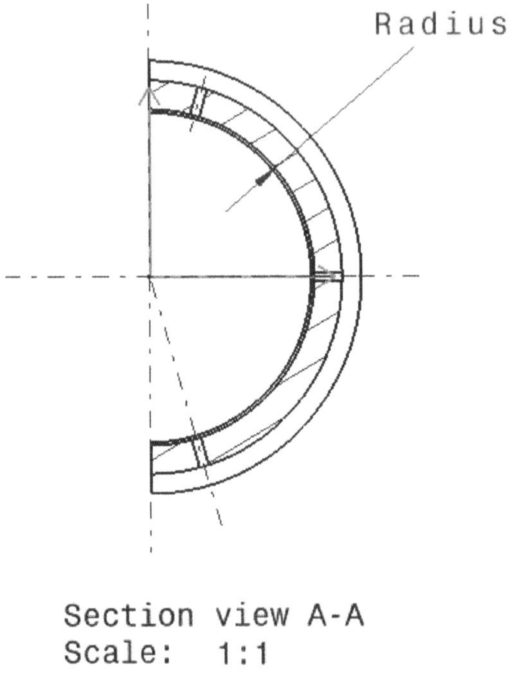

Figure 5–101

Task 4 - Create a dimension table from a .CSV file.

1. Activate the background by right-clicking on **Sheet.1** in the tree and selecting **Edit Background**.
2. In the expanded Annotation section of the Action Bar, click  (Insert from File).
3. Change the file type filter to **csv (*.csv)**, then select **B121463_Bushing.csv**.

To ensure that the table does not split on several sheets, select ***Me>Preferences>App Preferences>3D Modeling>Mechanical Systems>Drafting****, expand the Annotation and Dress-Up section, and toggle on the* ***Do not split table on several sheets*** *checkbox.*

4. Select a location for the table, as shown in Figure 5–102. If you select a location too close to the edge of the sheet, the system creates a second sheet and continues the table on the second sheet.

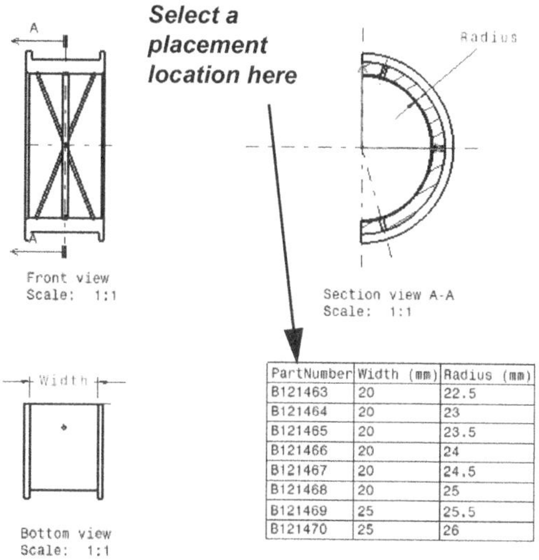

PartNumber	Width (mm)	Radius (mm)
B121463	20	22.5
B121464	20	23
B121465	20	23.5
B121466	20	24
B121467	20	24.5
B121468	20	25
B121469	25	25.5
B121470	25	26

Figure 5–102

Task 5 - Add an attribute link to the drawing.

In this task, you will display the value of a part model parameter in the drawing. This value is associative to the part and therefore updates when modified in the model. The parameter value is added to the table. The string parameter is named **MasterPart** and the value is the title of the part model.

1. Double-click on the table to edit it.

2. Right-click on the blue cell with the number 1 and select **Insert row(s) above**, as shown in Figure 5–103.

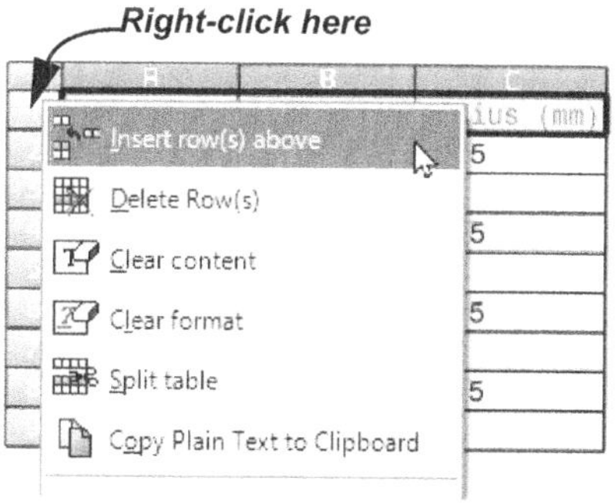

Figure 5–103

3. Starting in cell A-1, hold down the left mouse button and drag over cells B-1 and C-1 to select the top row of the table. Right-click and select **Merge**. The table displays as shown in Figure 5–104.

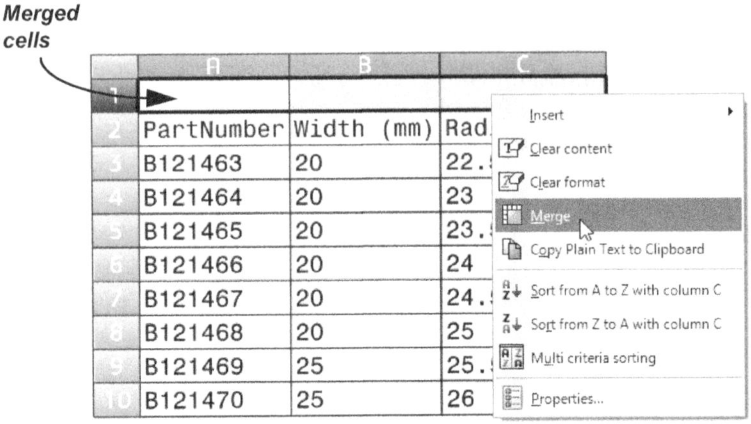

Figure 5–104

4. Double-click on the new merged cell to open the Text Editor dialog box.

5. Right-click in the merged cell in the table and select **Insert>Insert Attribute Link**, as shown in Figure 5–105. This operation cannot be performed in the Text Editor dialog box.

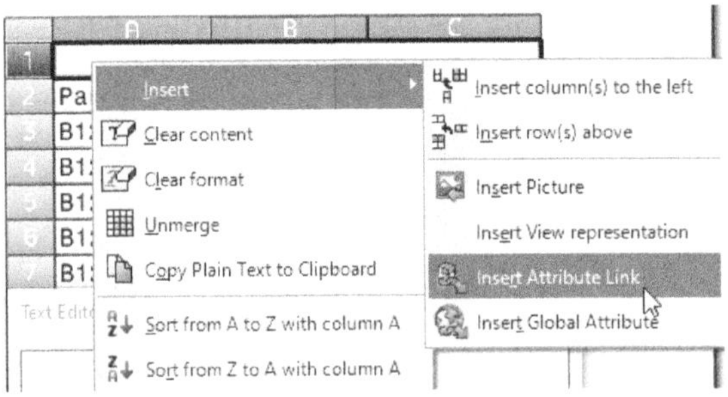

Figure 5–105

6. Activate the tab with the ###_B121463_Bushing part model.

7. In the specification tree in the part model window, select **###_B121463_Bushing**. This opens the Insert Attribute Link dialog box, as shown in Figure 5–106.

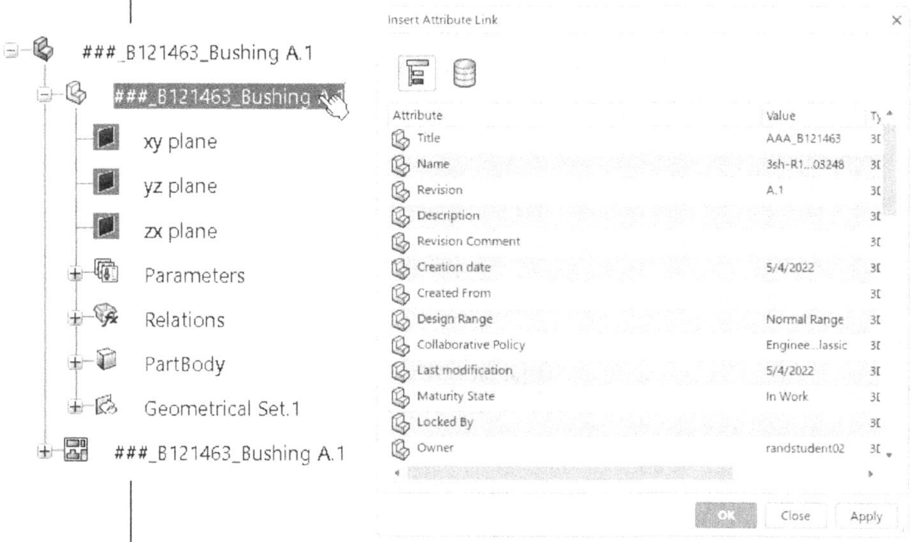

Figure 5–106

8. Scroll to the bottom of the *Attribute* list and select the **MasterPart** parameter, as shown in Figure 5–107.

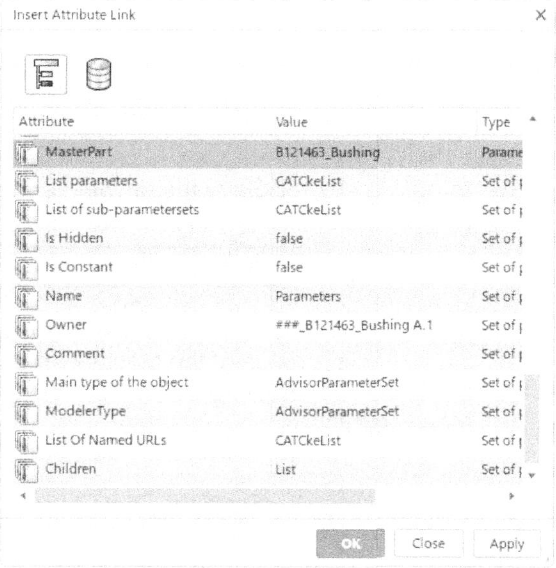

Figure 5–107

9. Click **OK**. The system places the value of the selected parameter into the Text Editor, as shown in Figure 5–108.

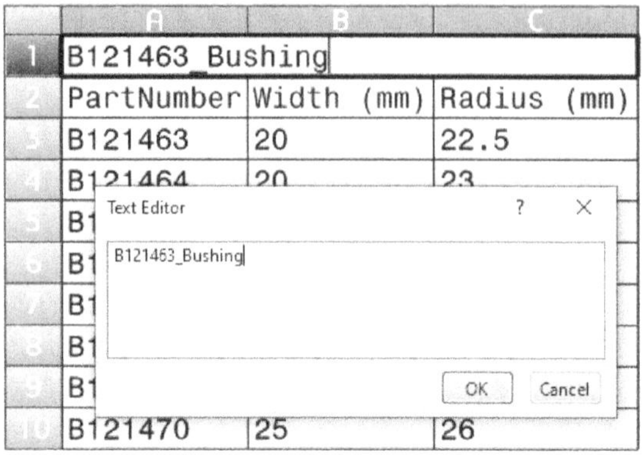

Figure 5–108

10. Click **OK** in the Text Editor and clear the table selection. The table displays as shown in Figure 5–109.

B121463_Bushing		
PartNumber	Width (mm)	Radius (mm)
B121463	20	22.5
B121464	20	23
B121465	20	23.5
B121466	20	24
B121467	20	24.5
B121468	20	25
B121469	25	25.5
B121470	25	26

Figure 5–109

11. Save the drawing and close the tab.

Task 6 - (Optional) Modify the parameter.

Complete this task if time permits. In this task, you will modify the value of the MasterPart parameter and update the change in the drawing.

1. Activate the part model widget.
2. From the Tools section of the Action Bar, select (Formula). The Formulas dialog box opens.

3. In the Filter Type drop-down list, select **User parameters**, as shown in Figure 5–110. The system displays the **MasterPart** parameter.

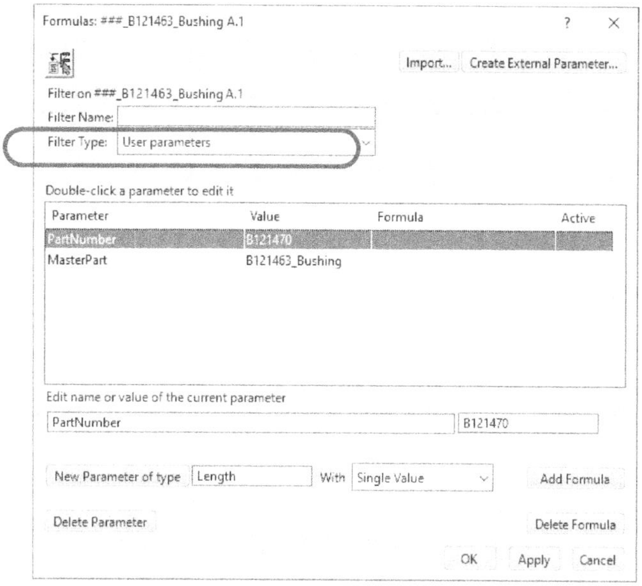

Figure 5–110

4. In the list, select **MasterPart**. The system places the parameter and value in the fields as shown in Figure 5–111.

Figure 5–111

5. Modify the value of *MasterPart* to **B121463_Bushing_Sizes** and press <Enter> to register the change.

6. Click **OK** to complete the operation.

7. Activate the tab with the **###_B121463_Bushing** drawing.

8. To update the drawing, you must force an update. This is done by entering **c:force update** in the *Power Input* field in the bottom right corner of the CATIA window, as shown in Figure 5–112.

*If the Power Input Field does not display, right-click on the screen and select **Display> Status Bar.***

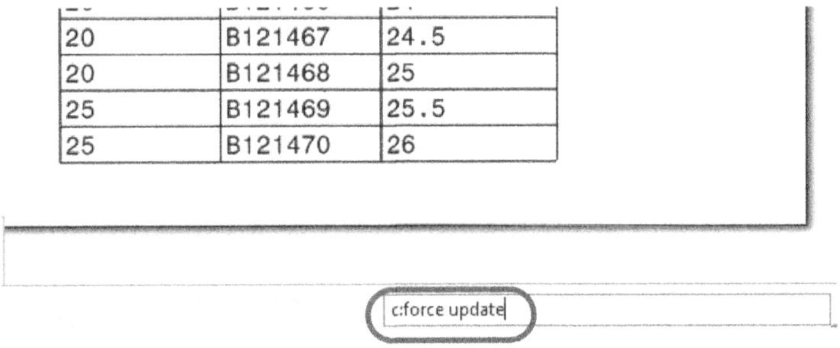

Figure 5–112

Once the drawing has updated, the table displays as shown in Figure 5–113.

B121463_Bushing_Sizes		
PartNumber	Width (mm)	Radius (mm)
B121463	20	22.5
B121464	20	23
B121465	20	23.5
B121466	20	24
B121467	20	24.5
B121468	20	25
B121469	25	25.5
B121470	25	26

Figure 5–113

9. Save all of the files and close all of the tabs.

Practice 5c Add Weld Symbols

Practice Objective

- Create weld symbols.

In this practice, you will practice the weld symbol functionality by creating two weld symbols on the **ExhaustManifold** assembly.

Task 1 - Import and open an assembly drawing.

1. Import and open **ExhaustManifold_5C.3dxml** from the practice files folder. While importing, set the *Duplication string* to **###_** where ### represents your initials.
2. Right-click on the **###_ExhaustManifold_Detail_5C** drawing in the tree and select * **object>Open in New App**. The drawing displays as shown in Figure 5–114.

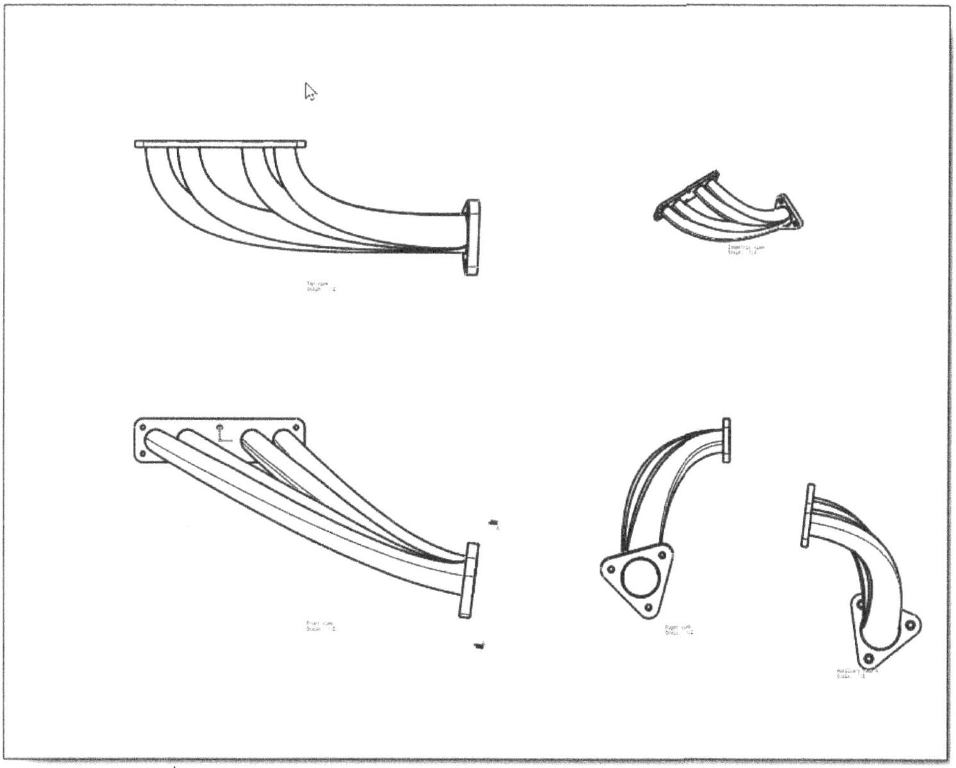

Figure 5–114

Task 2 - Create a detail view.

1. Create a detail view of the Front view, as shown in Figure 5–115.

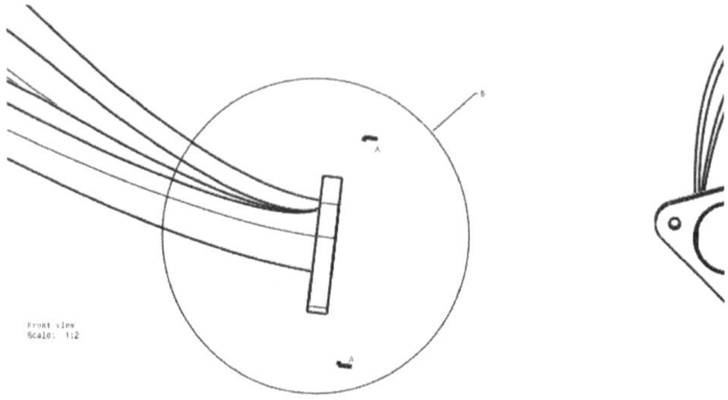

Figure 5–115

2. Place the detailed view as shown in Figure 5–116.

The display view frames have been turned off for all other views, for clarity.

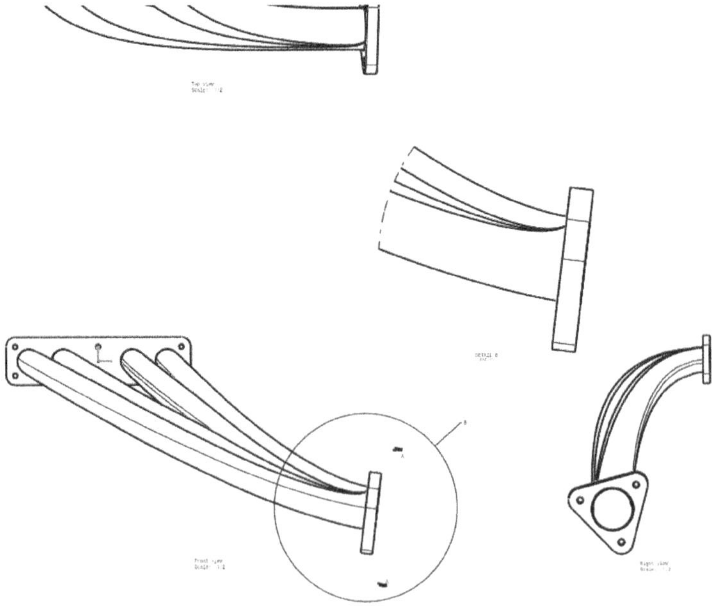

Figure 5–116

Task 3 - Create a new drawing sheet.

1. Create a new drawing sheet using the (Create a New Sheet) icon.
2. Cut and paste the detail view from *Sheet.1* to **Sheet.2**. The detail view displays on **Sheet.2**, as shown in Figure 5–117. Change the *Scale* of the detail view to **2:1**.

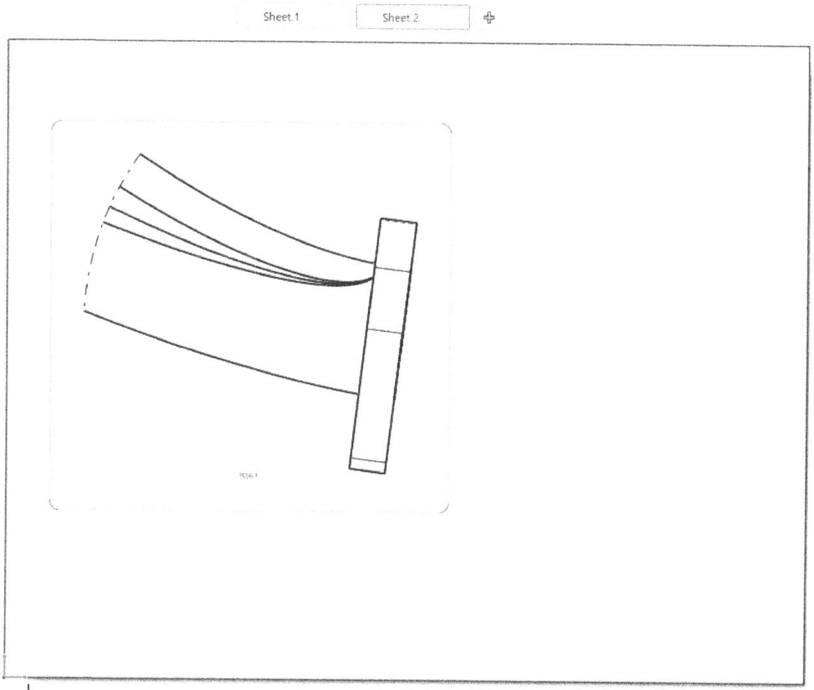

Figure 5–117

Task 4 - Create a weld symbol.

1. In the expanded Annotation section of the Action Bar, click (Welding Symbol) and select the two references, as shown in Figure 5–118.

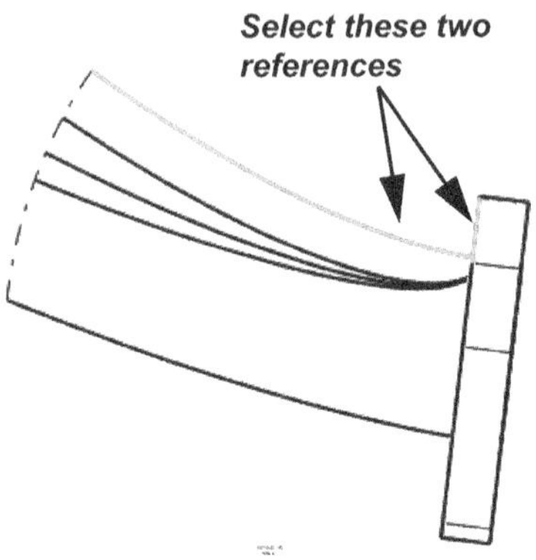

Figure 5–118

2. Select a location at which to place the weld symbol, as shown in Figure 5–119.

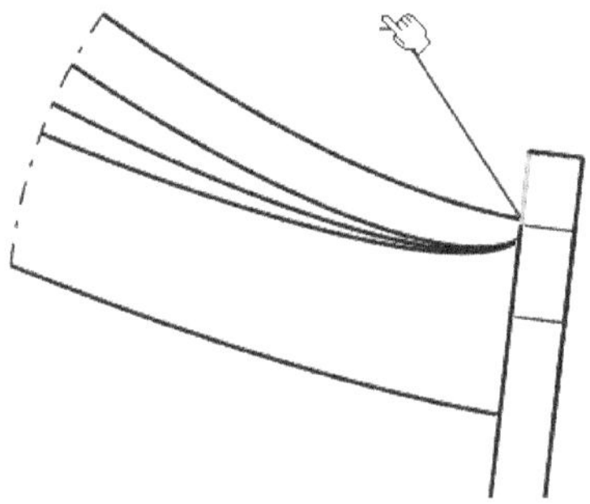

Figure 5–119

3. Specify the information for the weld symbol, as shown in Figure 5–120.

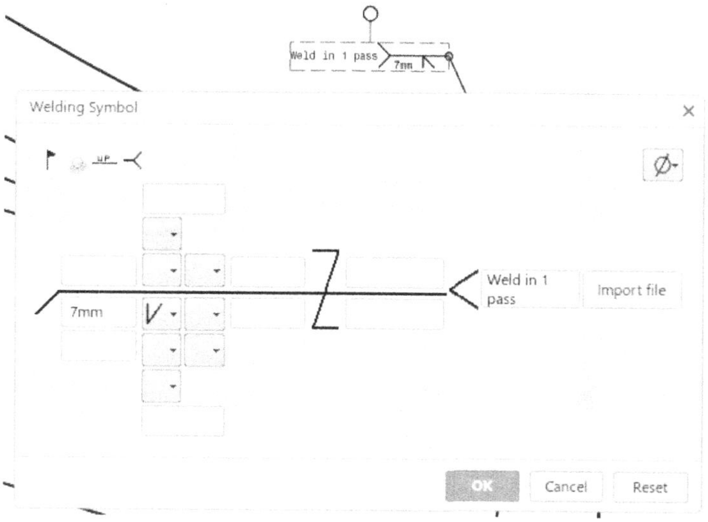

Figure 5–120

4. Click **OK** to complete the creation of the weld symbol. The weld symbol displays as shown in Figure 5–121.

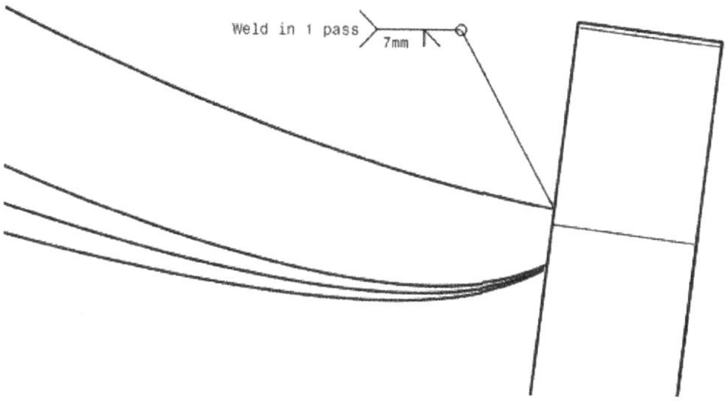

Figure 5–121

5. Copy and paste the Top view from *Sheet.1* to **Sheet.2**. Position the view as shown in Figure 5–122.

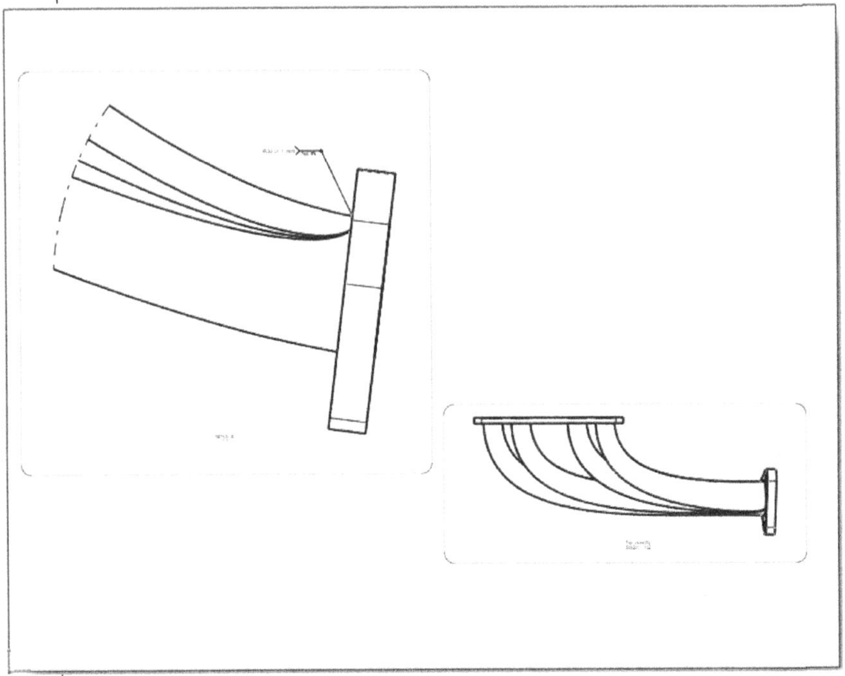

Figure 5–122

6. Click (Welding Symbol) to create a weld symbol and select the references shown in Figure 5–123.

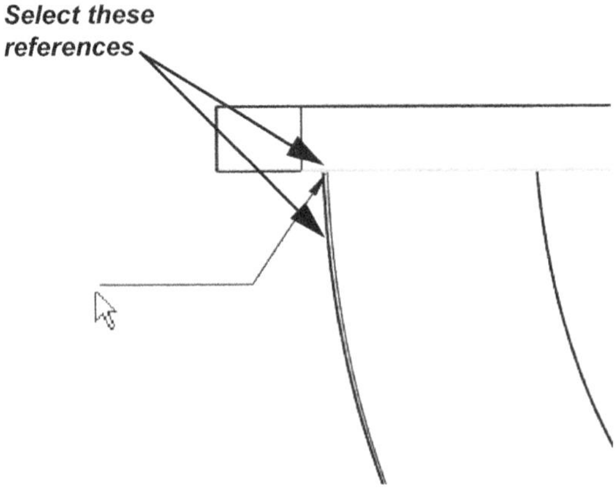

Figure 5–123

7. Define the weld symbol, as shown in Figure 5–124.

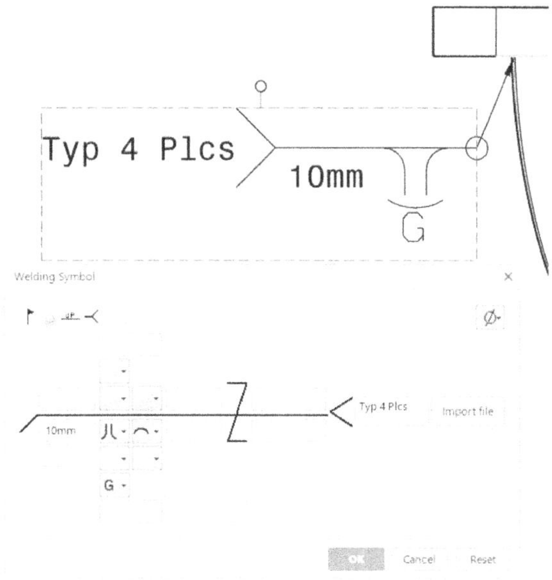

Figure 5–124

8. Click **OK** to complete the weld symbol definition.
9. You can change the attachment point for the leader by selecting the weld symbol to make it active and moving the yellow handle, as shown in Figure 5–125.

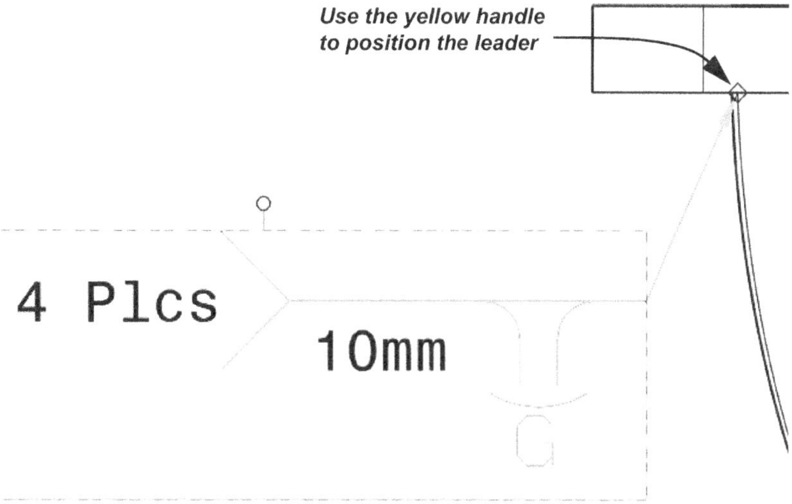

Figure 5–125

10. Save the drawing and close all of the tabs.

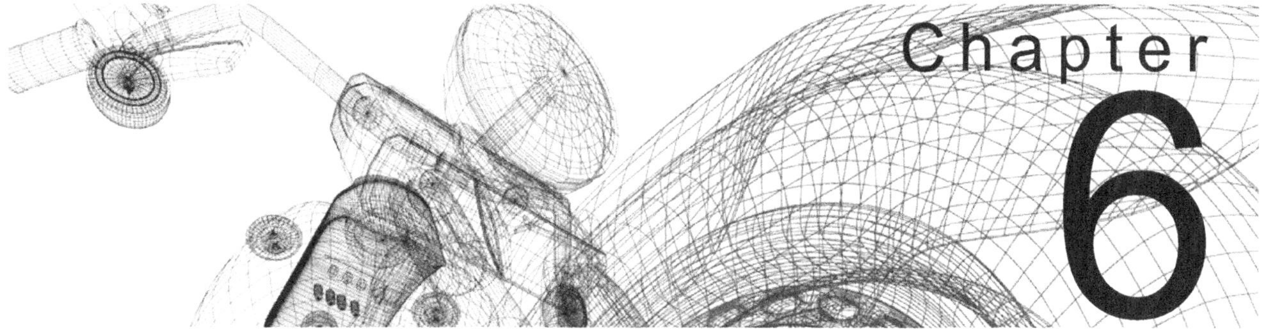

2D Components

2D components consist of sketched elements, text, leaders, and other geometry created in the Drafting app. These 2D components can be instantiated from a drawing or catalog. This chapter also introduces sketching functionality in the Drafting app that can be used to add geometry to imported drawing views.

Learning Objectives in This Chapter

- Create 2D sketches in drawings.
- Analyze sketches.
- Create 2D components.
- Instantiate a 2D Component.
- Instantiate components from catalogs.
- Modify an instantiated 2D component.

6.1 2D Sketching

2D draft entities are used to manually add geometry and detail to a drawing. You can create points, closed profiles, and open profiles independent of the view geometry. The sketched 2D draft entities can also be constrained. The process for creating and modifying 2D draft entities is similar to the Sketch app. 2D draft entities can be used to do the following:

- Create 2D components
- Create symbols
- Create formats and title blocks
- Update and maintain legacy data of drawings imported from other CAD systems

Tools for creating 2D draft entities can be found in the Sketch section of the Action Bar, as shown in Figure 6–1.

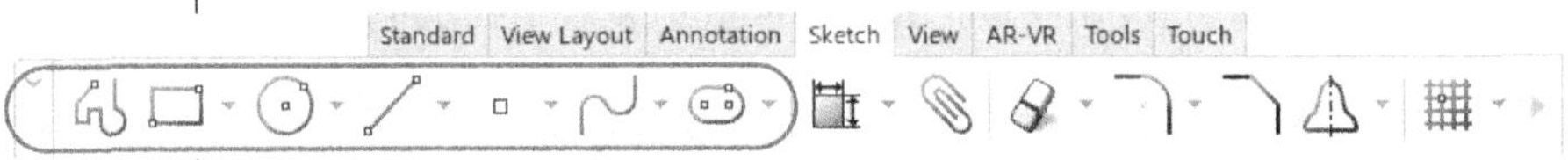

Figure 6–1

Draft entities can be manipulated using the tools, as shown in Figure 6–2.

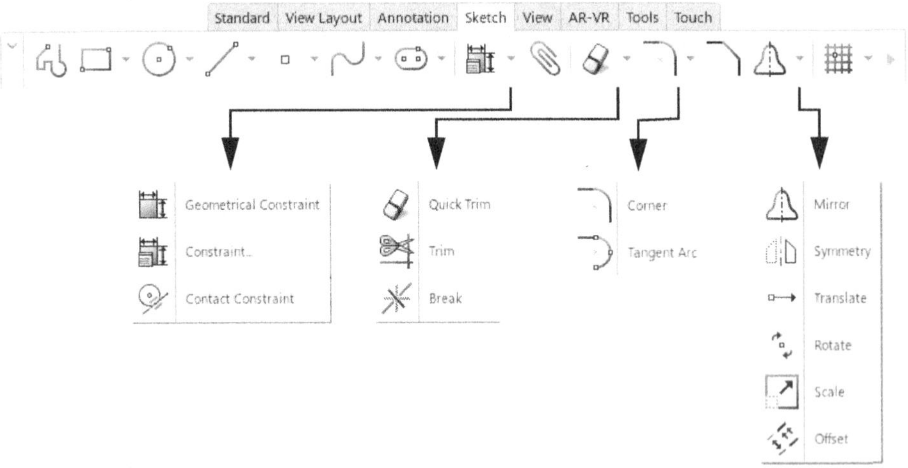

Figure 6–2

General Steps

Use the following general steps to sketch 2D drafting entities:

1. Activate a view.
2. Sketch the 2D entities.
3. Modify the properties of the 2D entities.
4. Constrain the 2D entities.

Step 1 - Activate a view.

The drawing view shown in Figure 6–3 is a legacy drawing. It was created by importing a DXF file into CATIA's Drafting app. Since no 3D model is associated with the view, modifications must be sketched directly on the drawing (such as the addition of a hole).

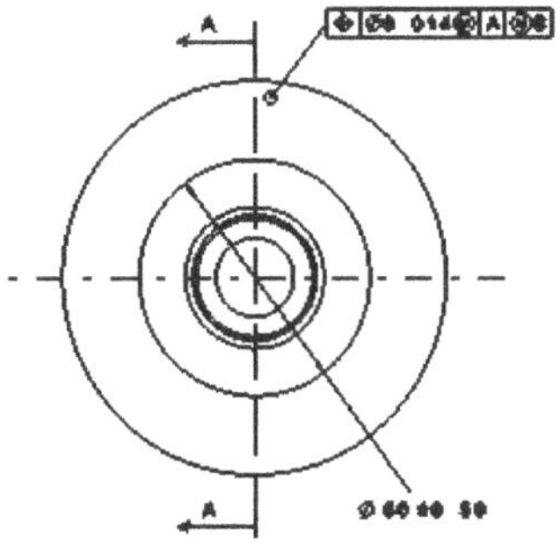

Figure 6–3

Activate the drawing view onto which the 2D sketched elements are going to be added by double-clicking on either the view's border or its name in the specification tree.

Step 2 - Sketch the 2D entities.

Using the tools available in the Sketch section of the Action Bar, sketch new geometry. Two circles have been sketched in the example shown in Figure 6–4. The first circle represents a hole that is going to be cut in the resulting part. The second circle is going to be used to locate the radial distance of the hole from the center of the part.

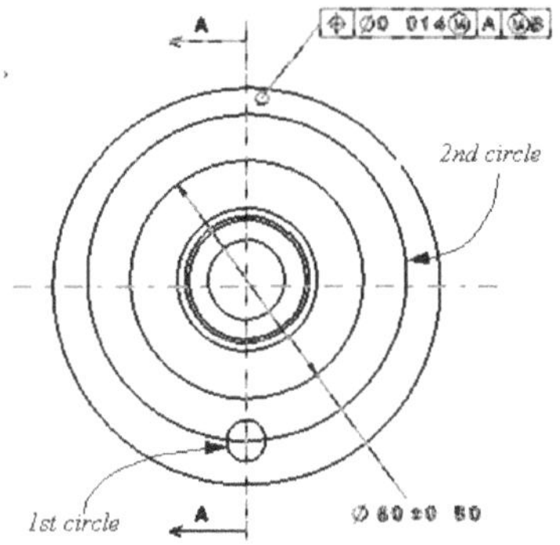

Figure 6–4

The current placement of the two holes is approximate and not important. Constraints are going to be used to position and constrain the sketched geometry.

Step 3 - Modify the properties of the 2D entities.

To modify the style or color of the 2D geometry, right-click on it and select **Properties**. The Properties dialog box provides options for controlling the color and linestyle of the selected geometry, as shown in Figure 6–5.

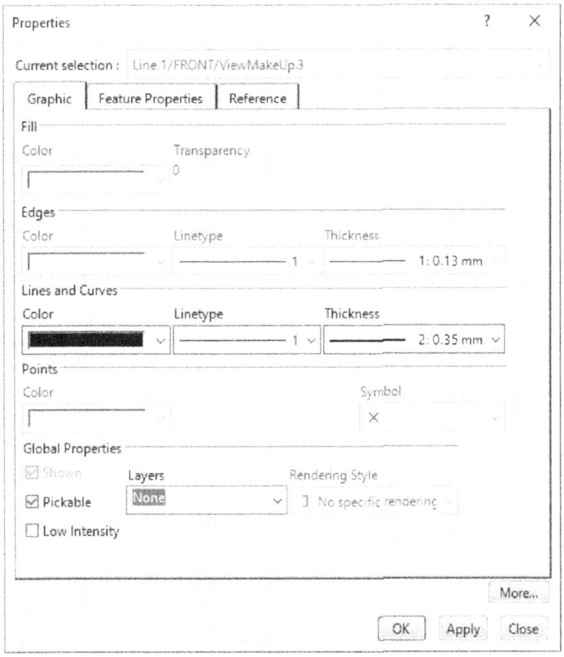

Figure 6–5

These options can also be accessed in the *Graphic* section of the Object Properties window, as shown in Figure 6–6.

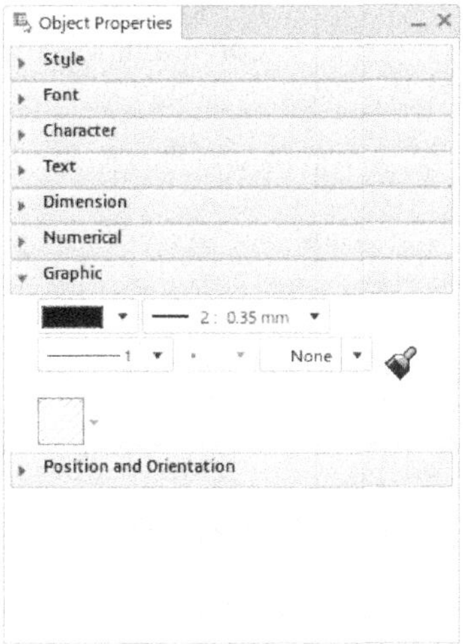

Figure 6–6

For example, the color and line font of the diameter circle can be assigned the appearance of a construction element, as shown in Figure 6–7.

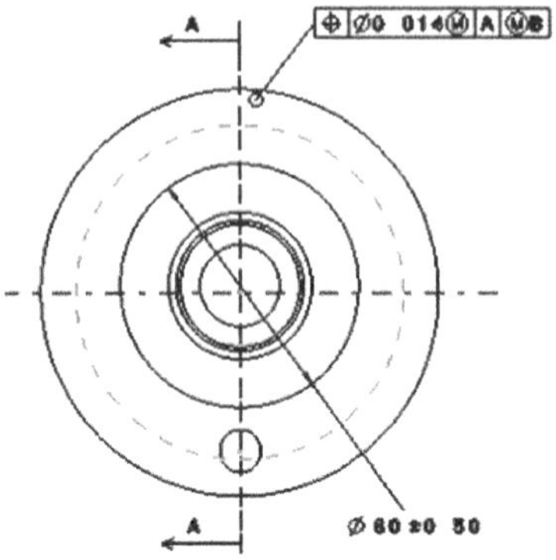

Figure 6–7

Step 4 - Constrain the 2D entities.

To create a constraint, select the entities to constrain and click (Constraints with Dialog Box) in the Sketch section of the Action Bar. The Constraint Definition dialog box opens as shown in Figure 6–8. Constraining 2D draft entities is identical to constraining sketched entities in the Sketcher app.

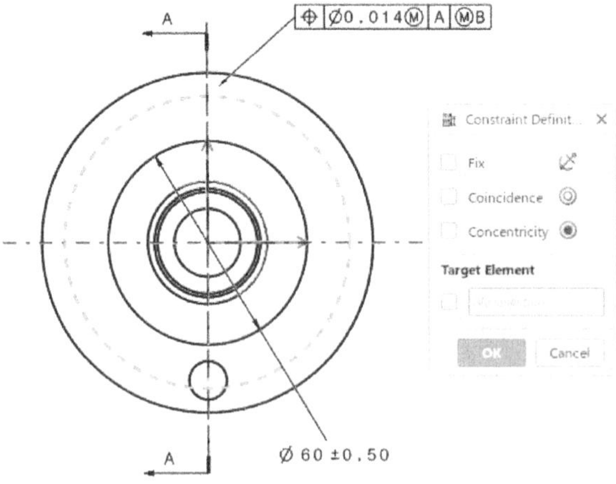

Figure 6–8

The constraints placed on 2D draft entities can be hidden/shown by clicking (Show Constraints) in the View section of the Action Bar.

6.2 Sketch Analysis

After the 2D draft entities have been created and constrained, you can analyze them by clicking  (Sketch Analysis). The Sketch Analysis dialog box opens as shown in Figure 6–9.

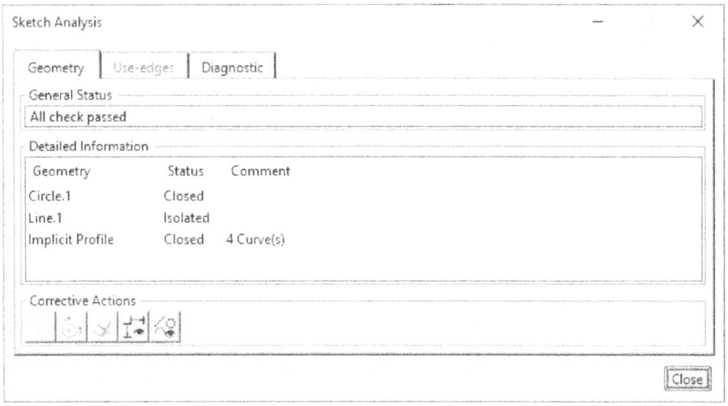

Figure 6–9

Geometry Tab

The *Geometry* tab is used to analyze individual elements in the active view. It displays the general status of the elements being analyzed. The different values available in the *Status* column are described as follows:

Status	Description
Opened	A collection of 2D entities that form an open loop. Open loops can occur when the start and end points of a loop appear to be touching, but actually have a gap between them.
Closed	A collection of 2D entities that form a closed loop.
Isolated	A single 2D entity that is not touching or connected to any other 2D geometry.

The *Geometry* tab also displays detailed information about each selected element type and general comments, as shown in Figure 6–10.

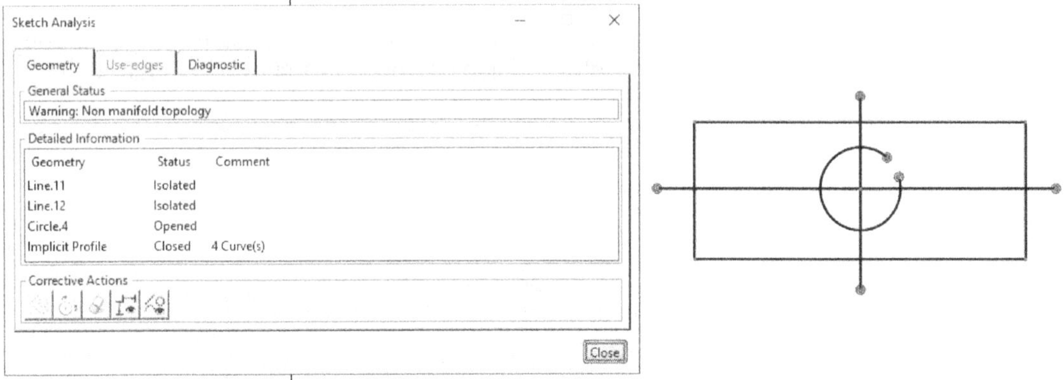

Figure 6–10

The entities shown in Figure 6–10 have several problems. The detailed information indicates that the circle is not closed (which is not the design intent), and that two line entities in the profile should be construction lines. The icons in the *Corrective Actions* area in the dialog box enable you to correct problems. These icons are described as follows:

Icon	Description
	Changes the selected entity to a construction entity.
	Closes the selected circle.
	Deletes the selected entity.
	Toggles the display of constraints on and off in the view and in the *Diagnostic* tab in the Sketch Analysis dialog box.
	Toggles the display of construction geometry on and off in the view and in the *Diagnostic* tab in the Sketch Analysis dialog box.

The icons in the *Corrective Actions* area correct the problem, as shown in Figure 6–11. Line.5 and Line.6 were converted to construction entities using . **Circle.1** was closed using .

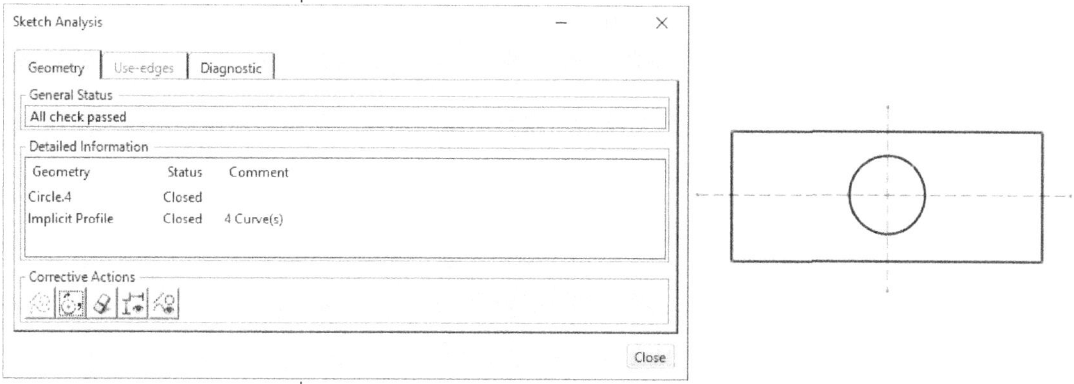

Figure 6–11

Diagnostic Tab

The *Diagnostic* tab gives a detailed summary of each 2D entity in the active view and its solving status. A 2D entity can have one of the following three status values:

- **Under-Constrained:** Additional dimensions or constraints must be applied to the entity.
- **Over-Constrained:** Too many dimensions or constraints have been applied to the element.
- **ISO-Constrained:** The entity is fully constrained.

The *Detailed Information* area lists all of the 2D entities in the active view, their current constraint status, and the type of entity (e.g., geometry, constraint, construction geometry, etc.), as shown in Figure 6–12.

Use-edges *is not available in the Drafting app.*

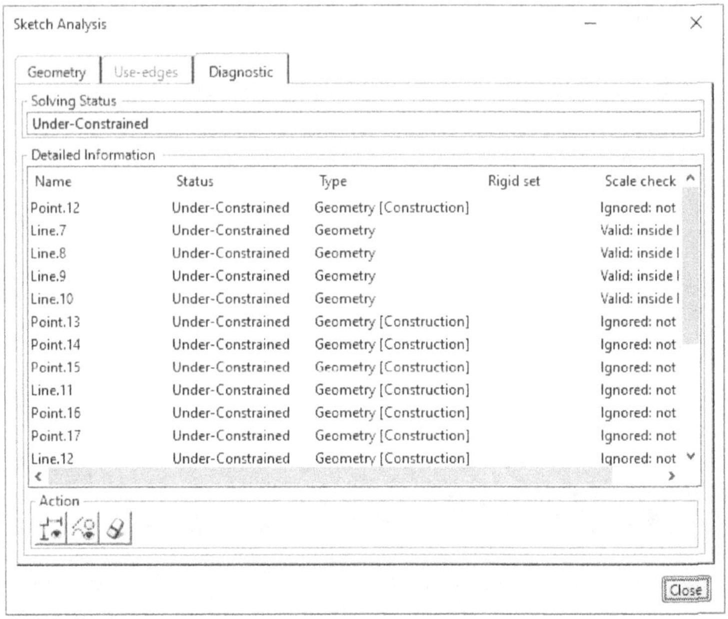

Figure 6–12

Sketch Solving Status

The Sketch Solving Status dialog box is used to determine the constraint status of the 2D entities in the active view. 2D entities can be under-constrained, over-constrained, or fully constrained (ISO-constrained). If the section is over- or under-constrained, the system highlights the affected entities on the sketch.

By default, Sketch Solving Status is not found on the Action Bar but can be added using **Me>Preferences>Customize> Sections>Add commands.** Once added, click  (Sketch Solving Status) to open the Sketch Solving Status dialog box, as shown in Figure 6–13.

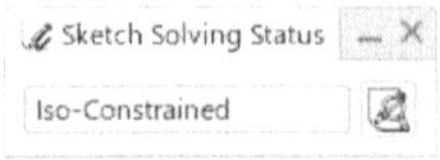

Figure 6–13

You can launch the **Sketch Analysis** tool from the Sketch Solving Status dialog box by clicking  (Sketch Analysis).

6.3 Creating 2D Components

2D components are 2D geometry and annotations that can be reused in drawings. You can instantiate a 2D component in the same drawing or in other drawings. You can also add the components to a catalog to further control standardized 2D components.

General Steps

Use the following general steps to create a 2D component:

1. Create a detail sheet.
2. Create the 2D component.
3. Save the drawing.

Step 1 - Create a detail sheet.

2D components are created on detail sheets that house the 2D components to be instantiated. You can create as many detail sheets as required. They can be added to an existing drawing or instantiated as a new drawing.

After creating or opening a drawing object, right-click on the drawing title at the top of the specification tree, then select (New Detail Sheet) to create a detail sheet. The system adds a new sheet, as shown in Figure 6–14.

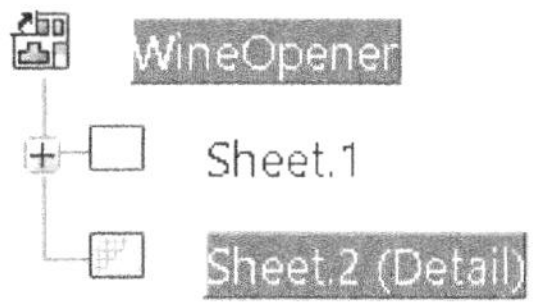

Figure 6–14

Step 2 - Create the 2D component.

To create 2D components on a single detail sheet, click (2D Component) from the Template section of the Action Bar, and select a location at which to place 2D component.

The 2D components will look and act like standard views that you have been using in a default drawing. When you have multiple 2D components, the active 2D components is denoted by a red border. To activate a different 2D component, double-click on its border or name in the specification tree. Geometry and text will only be created in the active 2D component.

Create the 2D component in the view by sketching 2D draft entities found in the Annotation and Sketch sections of the Action Bar. A 2D component with a sketched profile and text is shown in Figure 6–15.

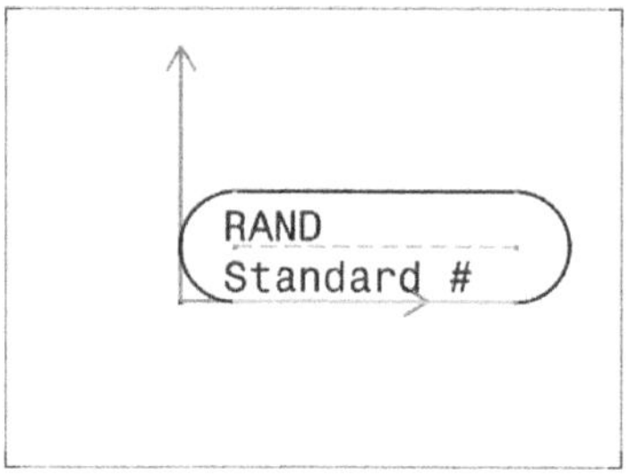

Figure 6–15

Modifiable Text

By default, text created in a 2D component cannot be modified inside the destination document. Once instantiated, text links to the original detail view and only updates if changes are made in the original 2D component. If you want the text in your 2D component to be editable once instantiated, use the **Modifiable Text** option.

Attribute links can also be added to the text.

To create modifiable text, right-click on the original text and select **Modifiable in instance**. The Text Editor dialog box then opens when you double-click on the component instantiated in the destination drawing.

Step 3 - Save the drawing.

Once you are satisfied with the 2D component, save the drawing.

6.4 Instantiating a 2D Component

Once you have created a 2D component, you can insert it as many times as required in the same (or an external) drawing.

General Steps

Use the following general steps to instantiate a 2D component:

1. Start the instantiation process.
2. Place the instance.

Step 1 - Start the instantiation process.

How To: Start the Instantiation Process

1. Activate the view into which you want to instantiate the 2D component.
2. Click  (Instantiate 2D component) from the Sketch section of the Action Bar.
3. Activate the detail sheet containing the 2D component to be inserted.
4. Select the 2D component in the detail sheet or specification tree.

Step 2 - Place the instance.

Once the 2D component has been selected, CATIA returns to the active view to place the instance. The Tools Palette toolbar displays. Use the Position tools, as shown in Figure 6–16, to orient the component.

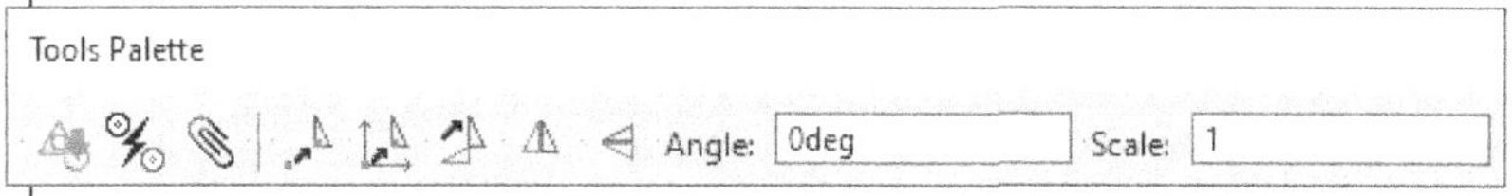

Figure 6–16

The positioning tools are described as follows:

Icon	Description
	Changes the origin of the component. Click the icon and select a new point to act as the origin of the component.
	Changes the position of the component. Click the icon. A Horizontal and Vertical option appears. Type in values or click the cursor in the new location. The component is moved away from the origin by that distance.
	Changes the angle of the component. Click the icon. An angle vector displays. Use the mouse to change the angle. Left-click to confirm the new angle.
	Mirrors the component about the horizontal axis.
	Mirrors the component about the vertical axis.

Scale and angle values can be changed using the Tools Palette toolbar. After these modifications have been made, click to finalize the 2D component's placement in the drawing view.

Place Instance in Another Drawing

You can also instantiate a 2D component created in a different drawing using the **Copy** and **Paste** tools.

How To: Copy a 2D Component from a Different Drawing

1. Activate the detail view containing the 2D component to be copied. Select the geometry and annotations inside the detail view, as shown in Figure 6–17.

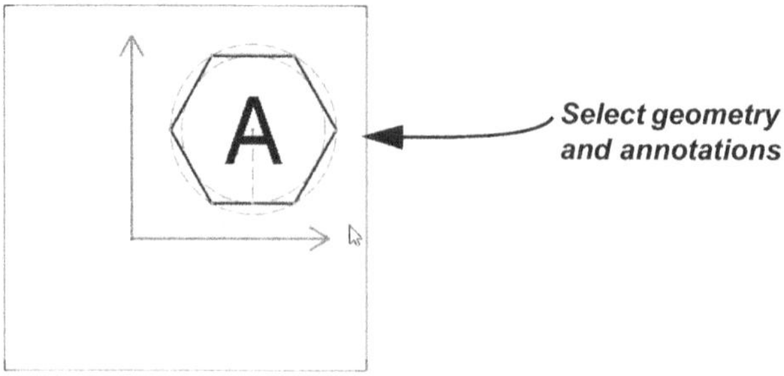

Figure 6–17

2. Select (Copy).
3. Activate the target drawing.
4. Select (Paste). The instantiated 2D component can now be moved in the drawing view.

6.5 Instantiating from Catalogs

In the Drafting app, a catalog is a repository of 2D components. Catalogs enable the grouping of similar components, searching, editing, and instantiation. Components that are commonly reused should be stored in a catalog.

Cataloged 2D components reference existing detail views. When instantiated into a drawing file, the cataloged 2D component is, by default, associative. However, the instantiated 2D component can be made non-associative.

Catalog Creation

To create a new catalog that contains all of the 2D components that have been created in the current drawing, select (New)>**Generate Catalog**. A Catalog window will appear. In the *Name* field, enter the name of the catalog, as shown in Figure 6–18, then select **OK**.

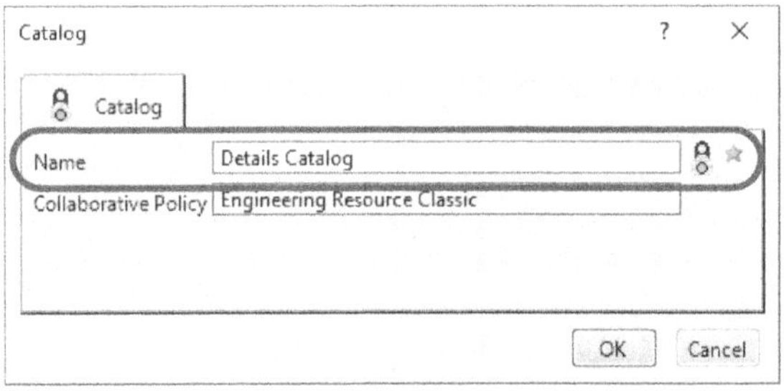

Figure 6–18

The name of the detail sheet becomes the name of the chapter when saved as a catalog. A chapter is a group of 2D components inside the catalog. For example, the catalog shown in Figure 6–19 was created from a drawing that contained two detail sheets named **Balloon Symbols** and **Datum Target**. Standard drawing sheets are not saved into the catalog.

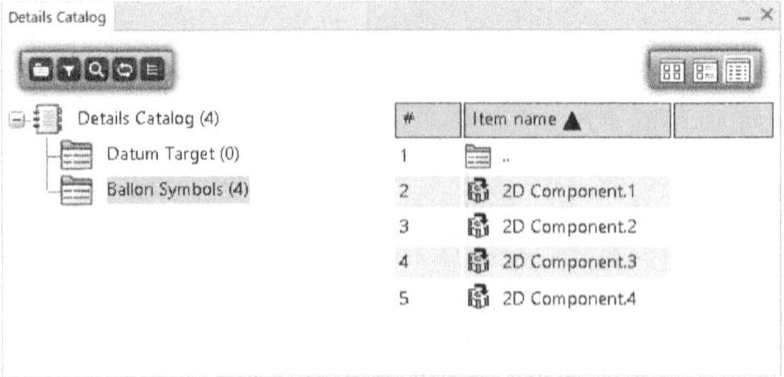

Figure 6–19

Instantiate from a Catalog

How To: Instantiate a 2D Component from a Catalog

1. Open the drawing into which the 2D component is going to be instantiated.
2. Activate the view in which the 2D component is going to be placed.
3. Click  (Catalog Browser) from the Tools section of the Action Bar. The Catalog Browser opens.
4. In the Catalog Browser dialog box, click  (Open a catalog) and search for the catalog from which you want to instantiate. The contents of the catalog display, as shown in Figure 6–20.

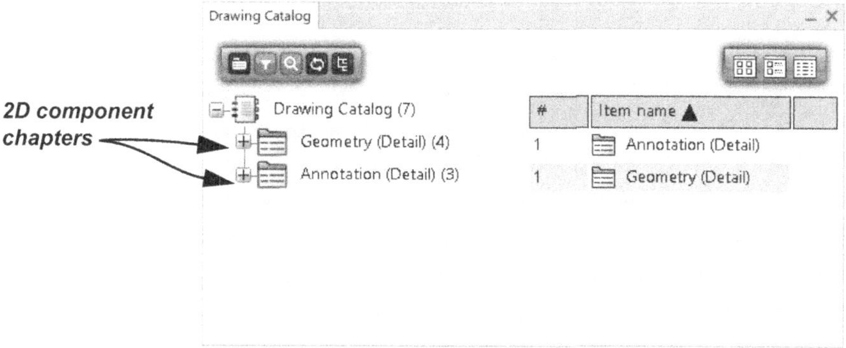

Figure 6–20

Note: If this is not the first time a catalog has been loaded, a Choose a Catalog or Chapter window will appear, as shown in Figure 6–21.

Figure 6–21

Selecting the drop-down arrow will allow you to pick from previously loaded catalogs. Selecting the **More...** button will allow for searching of unloaded catalogs.

5. Select on the chapter to display a list of 2D components grouped in it, as shown in Figure 6–22.

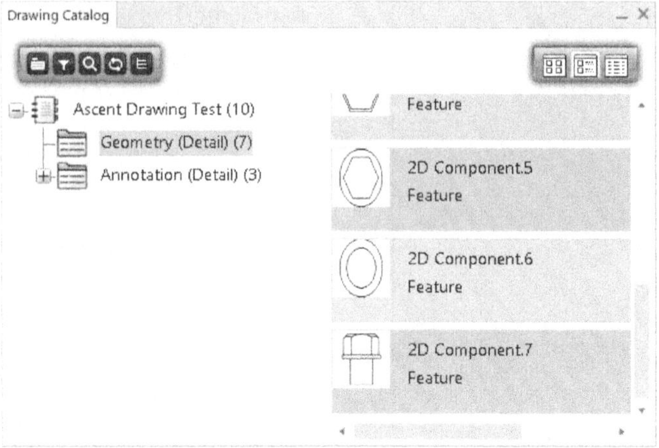

Figure 6–22

6. Double-click on the 2D component in the list to instantiate it in the active drawing view.
7. Use the Position and Tools Palette toolbars to scale, rotate, and modify the orientation of the 2D component.
8. Select a location in the view to place the 2D component. The Catalog Browser remains open until you click × (Close).

Links

When a 2D component is instantiated into a drawing, it is linked to the drawing from which it was instantiated. This link requires that the source drawing file be loaded into CATIA to be updated.

To display the links for a drawing, select (Links and Relations) from the Tools section of the Action Bar. The Edit Links and Relations dialog box lists the links for the drawing, as shown in Figure 6–23.

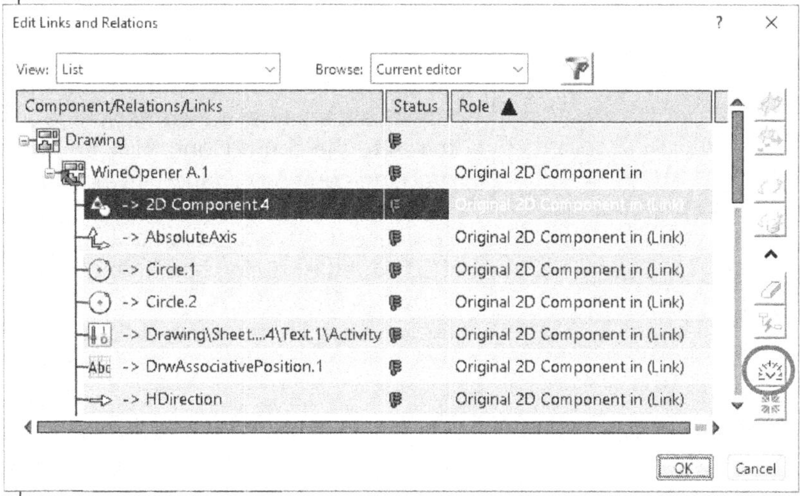

Figure 6–23

The *Status* column reports whether or not an element is (Synchronized) or (Not Synchronized). If an element is not synchronized, it uses the display of the linked element from the last synchronization.

When modifications are made to the pointed document, the instantiated 2D component can be updated through sychronization. To synchronize an element with its pointed document, select the element from the list and click (Synchronize), as shown above in Figure 6–23. The 2D component then reflects any updates that were made to the source document.

6.6 Modifying an Instantiated 2D Component

Placement

Once a component has been placed, you can modify its location and scale in the display window or use the Properties dialog box.

To modify a 2D component on the screen, select the component. Handles display at the corner of the 2D component. Drag them to resize the component. Click anywhere on the component and drag the cursor to change its location.

To define the exact placement and scale of the component, open the Properties dialog box. In the *2D Component Instance* tab, as shown in Figure 6–24, you can change the position (relative to the view origin), angle, and scale of the component.

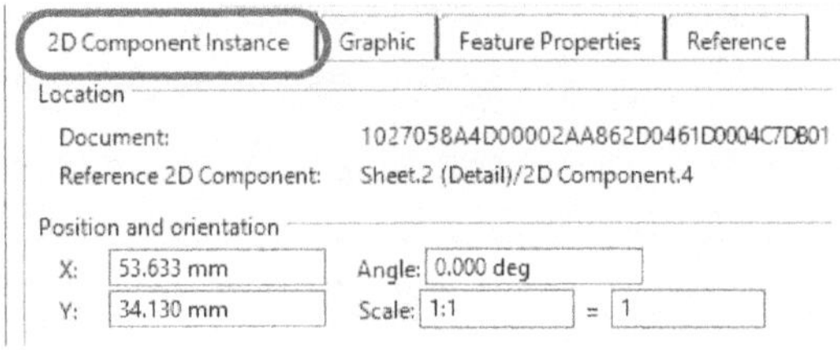

Figure 6–24

Explode the Component

Components instantiated from a catalog reference the original detail sheet used to make the 2D component. Exploding a 2D component makes it non-associative. This breaks the link between the instantiated 2D component and the source. To explode a 2D component, right-click on it and select *** object>Explode 2D Component**.

Exposing a 2D Component

Exposing a 2D component removes the link to the pointed document by copying the original 2D component into a detail sheet in the current drawing. This is an ideal method of removing the external links from a drawing, while still being able to update changes to a multi-instantiated 2D component from a single location.

For example, the datum target shown in Figure 6–25 was instantiated from a catalog. This 2D component is linked to the drawing file in which the original sketched geometry was created.

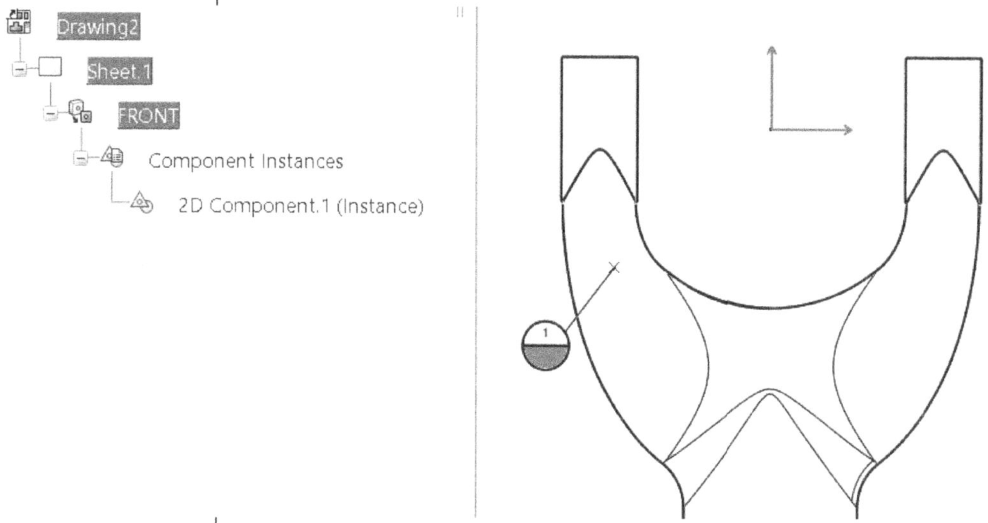

Figure 6–25

Expose the 2D component to break the link between the two drawings. The 2D component is copied into a new detail sheet that is automatically created in the drawing, as shown in Figure 6–26.

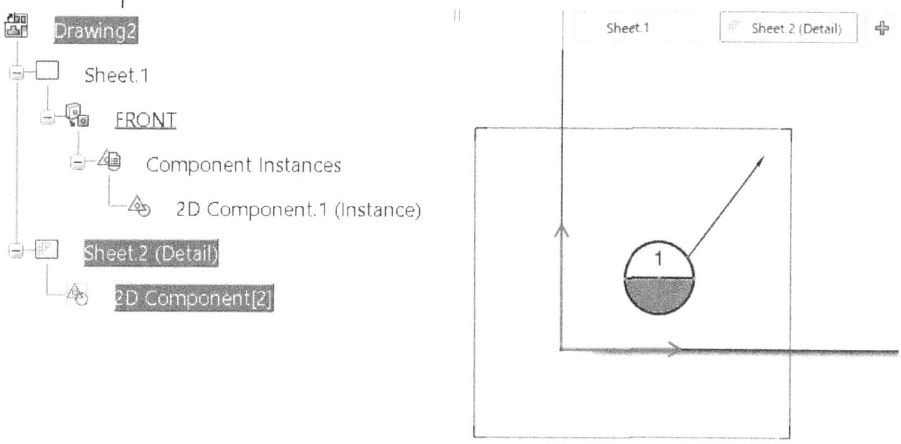

Figure 6–26

How To: Expose an Instantiated 2D Component

1. Right-click on the 2D component and select *** object>Expose 2D Component.** The Expose 2D Component Instance dialog box opens, as shown in Figure 6–27.

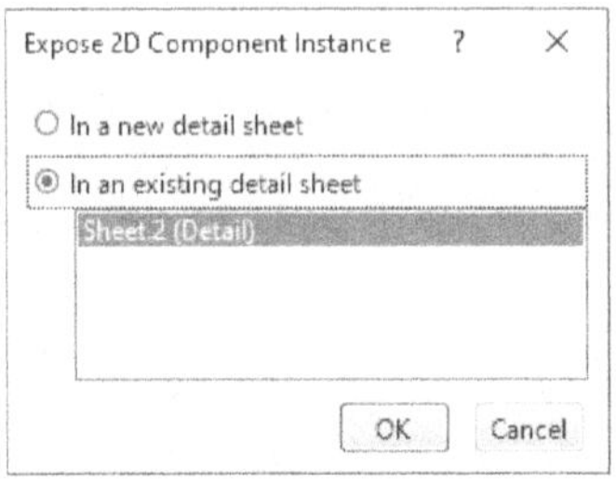

Figure 6–27

2. Select an option in the dialog box:
   - **In a new detail sheet:** Adds the exposed component to a new detail sheet
   - **In an existing detail sheet:** Adds the exposed component to the detail sheet selected from the list. If no detail sheet exists in the current drawing, this option is not available.

Replacing

How To: Replace a 2D Component

1. If required, instantiate the replacing 2D component into the drawing.
2. Right-click on the 2D component to be replaced and select *** object>Replace Reference**.
3. Select the replacing 2D component.

   2D components that have been pasted from a different drawing cannot be exploded, exposed, or replaced. They also cannot be scaled, rotated, or translated using the Properties dialog box.

Practice 6a Creating 2D Components

Practice Objectives

- Create 2D components.
- Reuse a 2D component in the same drawing.

In this practice, you will create 2D components consisting of sketched geometry and annotations. The 2D components will be added to a new detail sheet in the drawing. They will then be instantiated into a drawing view. The completed drawing view displays as shown in Figure 6–28.

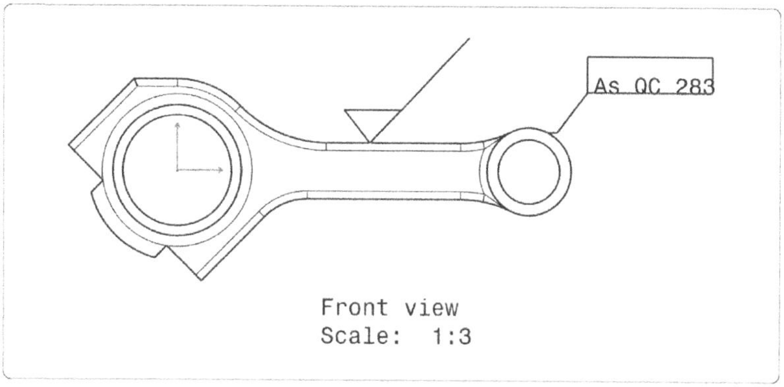

Figure 6–28

Task 1 - Import and open a drawing file.

1. Import and open **ConnectingRod.3dxml** from the practice files folder. While importing, set the *Duplication string* to **###_** where ### represents your initials.

2. Right-click on the **###_ConnectingRod** drawing in the tree and select *** object>Open in New App**. The drawing displays as shown in Figure 6–29.

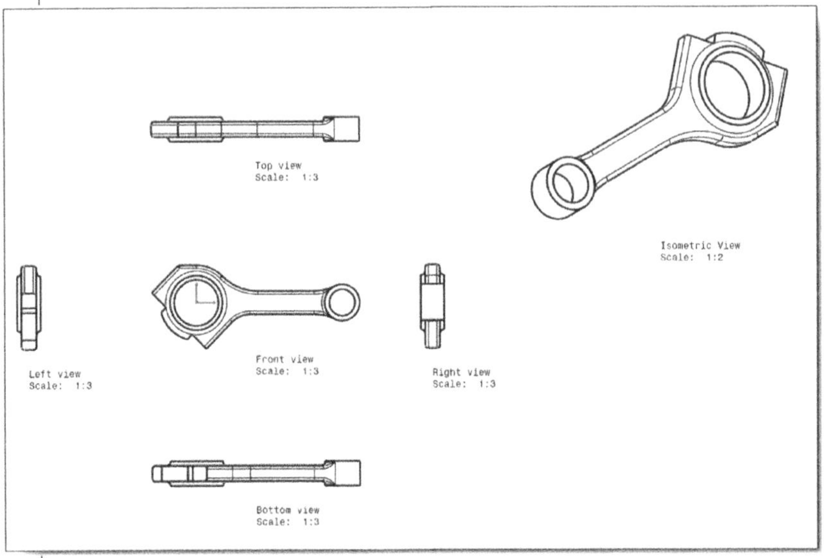

Figure 6–29

Task 2 - Create a new detail sheet.

1. Right-click on the top level of the tree and select **New Detail Sheet**. The newly created detail sheet displays.

2. From the Template section of the Action Bar, click  (2D Component), then click in the lower left corner of the sheet. This will create a blank 2D component, as shown in Figure 6–30.

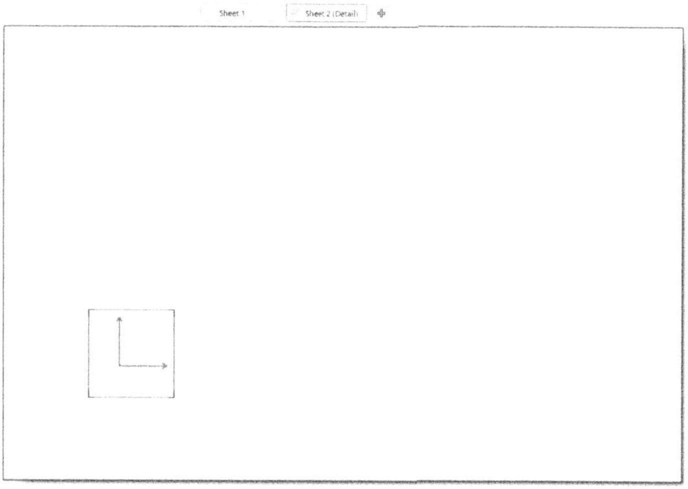

Figure 6–30

Task 3 - Create a 2D component inside the new view.

1. In the Sketch section of the Action Bar, use (Line) to create the 2D sketch (three lines), as shown in Figure 6–31. 2D geometry and annotations are created in the active view.

The view frame of an active view displays in red.

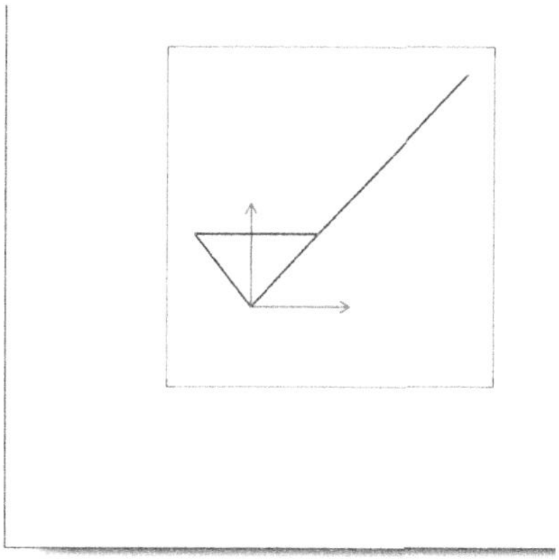

Figure 6–31

Task 4 - Create another 2D component.

In this task, you will create another 2D component. This component will consist of geometry and text. It will represent a quality control symbol.

1. In the Template section of the Action Bar, click (2D Component).
2. Click to place the new 2D component anywhere on the detail sheet. The new 2D component is not active.
3. Double-click on the border of the view you just created to make it active.
4. Using (Rectangle) and (Line) from the Sketch section of the Action Bar, create the shape shown in Figure 6–32.

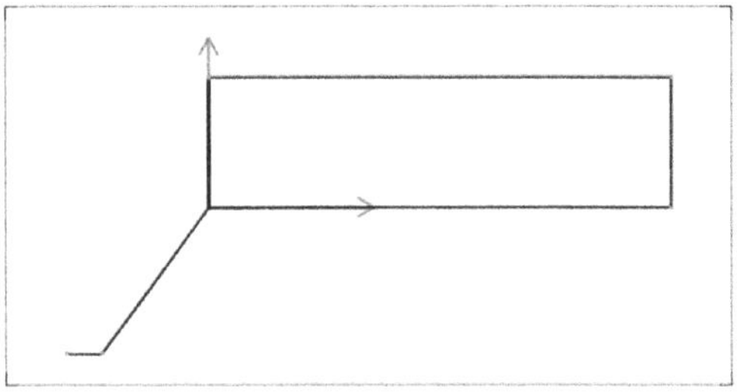

Figure 6–32

5. In the Annotations section of the Action Bar, click (Text).
6. Click in the active view to define where to place the text.
7. The Text Editor dialog box opens. Enter the text shown in Figure 6–33. Click **OK** when you are finished.

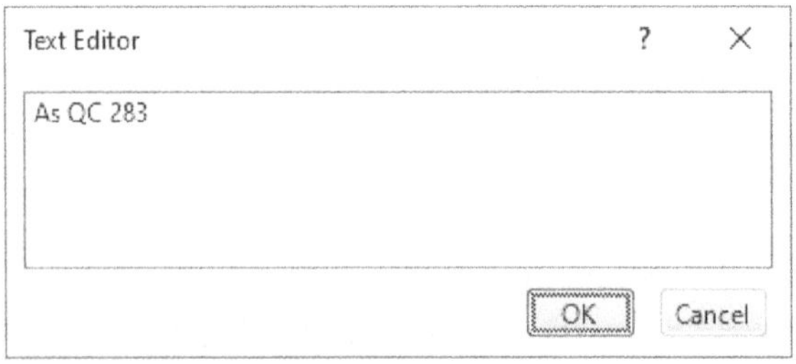

Figure 6–33

The completed 2D component displays as shown in Figure 6–34.

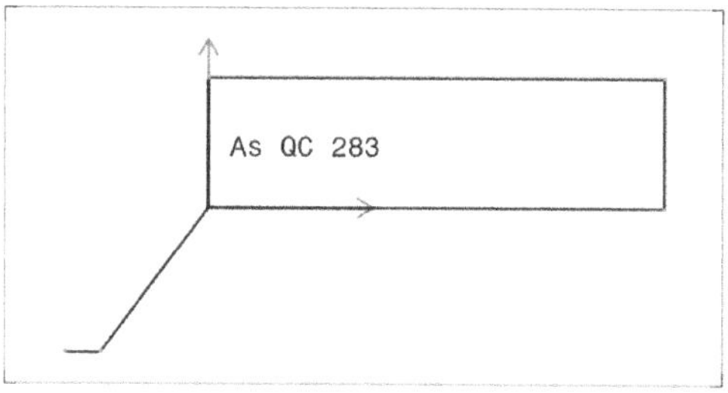

Figure 6–34

8. Right-click on the text and select **Modifiable in instance**. This enables you to modify the text in the instance.

Task 5 - Create a 2D component instance in the drawing.

In this task, you will instantiate 2D components. Instantiated 2D components are always placed in the active view.

1. Double-click on the **Front view** in *Sheet.1* to make it active.
2. In the expanded Sketch section of the Action Bar, click  (Instantiate 2D component).
3. In the specification tree, select **2D component.1**.

Design Considerations

The 2D component will follow the cursor inside the Front view. The position, scaling, and angle can be changed using the Position and the Tools Palette toolbars.

4. Click to place the 2D component in the view. Position it as shown in Figure 6–35.

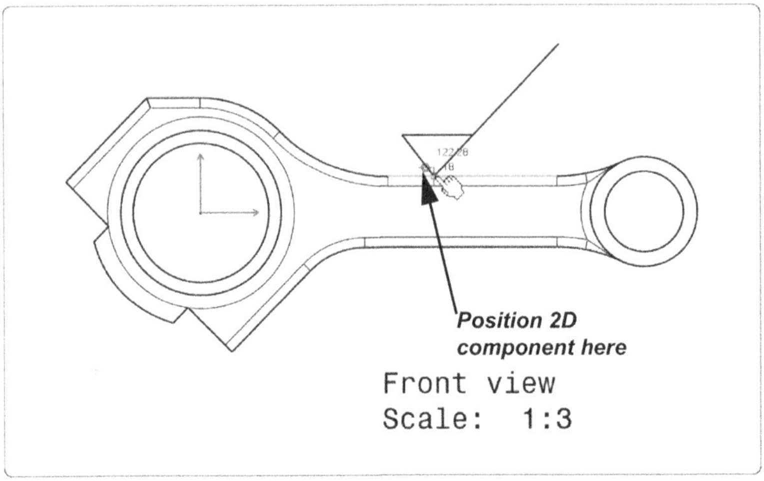

Figure 6–35

5. Click anywhere in the background of the drawing to complete the action.

Design Considerations

Consider the scale of the views and the scale of the 2D component required to obtain predictable results. The size of the sketched elements in the 2D component will be scaled by the view in which it is placed.

6. Instantiate **2D component.2** in the Front view, as shown in Figure 6–36.

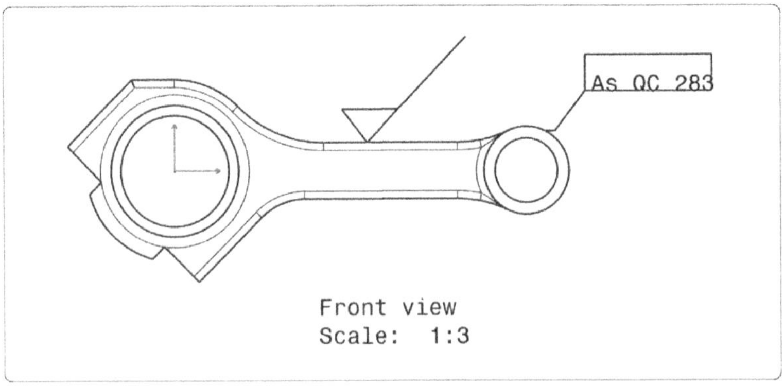

Figure 6–36

Task 6 - Apply a scale to the 2D component text.

Design Considerations

The 2D component is scaled according to the scale of the front view. However, the text size will always remain identical to the size defined on the detail sheet. Text can be adjusted using the *Text* section of the Object Properties window.

Alternatively, you can apply a scale to the text in the detail sheet. When you apply a scale, the text is scaled according to the scale of the view in which it is placed.

1. Activate **Sheet.2 (Detail)**.
2. Right-click on the text in the 2D Component.2 view and select **Properties**.
3. Select the *Text* tab.
4. Enable the **Apply Scale** option and close the dialog box.
5. Activate **Sheet.1.** Similar to the geometry in the 2D component, the text is now scaled according to the Front view.
6. Save and close the drawing.

Practice 6b

Reusing 2D Components from a Catalog

Practice Objectives

- Create a 2D component.
- Add a 2D component to a catalog.
- Insert a 2D component from a catalog.

In this practice, you will continue working with 2D components. A catalog will be created consisting of 2D components. Instead of sketching the 2D component, you will copy and paste from a DXF file. The created catalog will then be used to instantiate 2D components into a drawing.

Task 1 - Create a new drawing.

1. Select (New)>**Drawing.**
2. Give the drawing the *Title* of **###_2D_Components_6B** where ### represents your initials.
3. In the *Drawing Information* tab, set the *Standard* to **ANSI-ASME** and the *Sheet Style* to **B ANSI**, then select **OK**.

Task 2 - Create a new detail sheet.

1. Right-click on the top level of the tree and select **New Detail Sheet**.
2. In the Template section of the Action Bar, select (2D Component). Place the 2D component in the center of the detail sheet.

Task 3 - Create a 2D component.

In this task, you will copy and paste geometry from a DXF file into the newly created detail sheet.

1. Select (New)>**Import**. In the Format drop-down list, select **DXF2D(*.dxf)** and choose **2DComponent.dxf** for the *File name*. The imported drawing displays as shown in Figure 6–37.

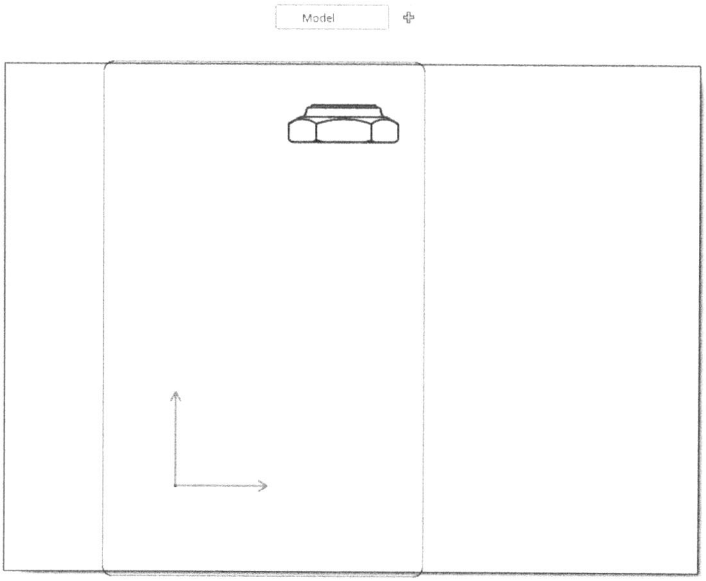

Figure 6–37

2. Select the geometry from the view in the imported drawing by dragging a box around it. Do not select the view in the specification tree.

3. In the Standard section of the Action Bar, select (Copy).

4. Activate the empty drawing widget and ensure that Sheet.2 (Detail) is active.

5. In the Standard section of the Action Bar, select (Paste). The geometry from the DXF file pastes into the view on the detail sheet.

6. Drag a box to select all of the geometry (nut). Click to drag the geometry to the origin of the view, as shown in Figure 6–38.

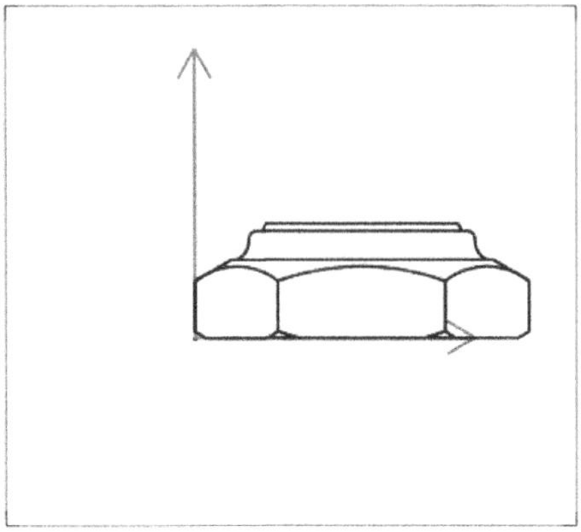

Figure 6–38

Task 4 - Create more 2D components.

1. In the Template section of the Action Bar, select (2D Component).
2. Place the 2D component to the right of the current view on the detail sheet, as shown in Figure 6–39.

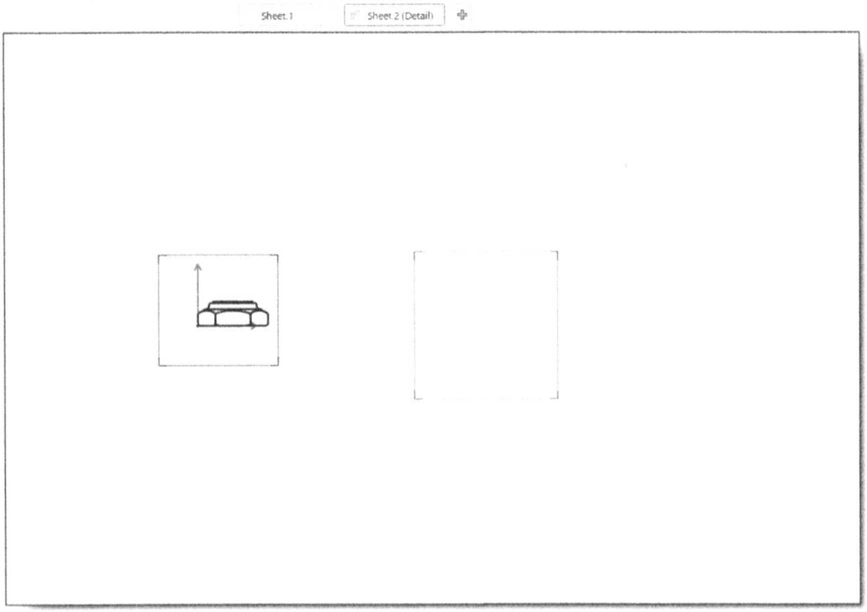

Figure 6–39

3. Double-click on the newly placed view to make it active.
4. Sketch a circle in the active view, as shown in Figure 6–40.

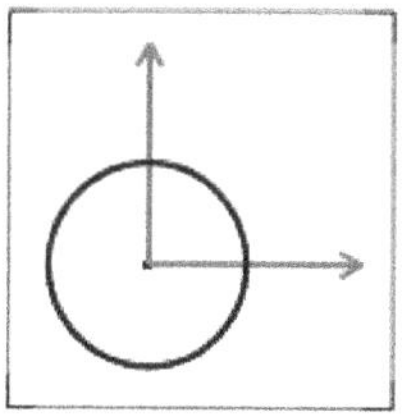

Figure 6–40

5. In the Annotation section of the Action Bar, select (Area Fill). The Tools Palette toolbar opens.
6. Ensure that (Automatic Detection) is highlighted.
7. Click inside the circle to indicate where to apply the fill. The drawing displays as shown in Figure 6–41.

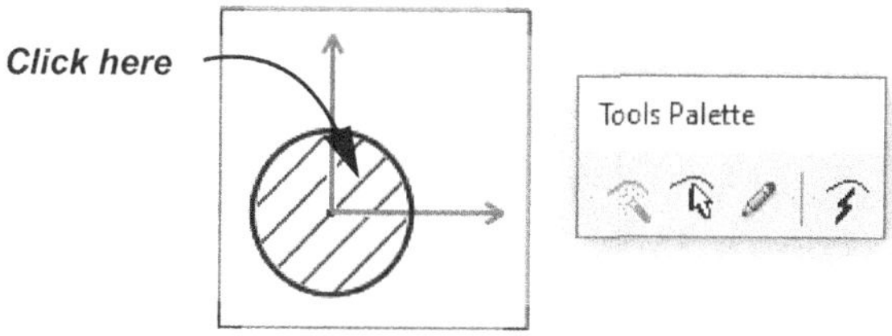

Figure 6–41

8. Click directly on the cross-hatching, not the circle.
9. Right-click and select **Properties.** You will change the properties of the fill added to the inside of the circle.
10. Select the *Pattern* tab.

11. In the Type drop-down list, select **Coloring**. Change the fill *Color* to **black**, as shown in Figure 6–42.

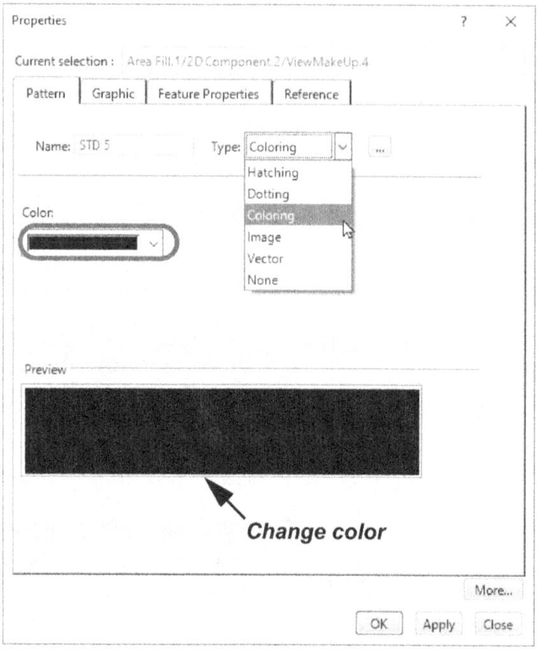

Figure 6–42

12. Click **OK** when you have finished adjusting the Fill properties. The model displays as shown in Figure 6–43.

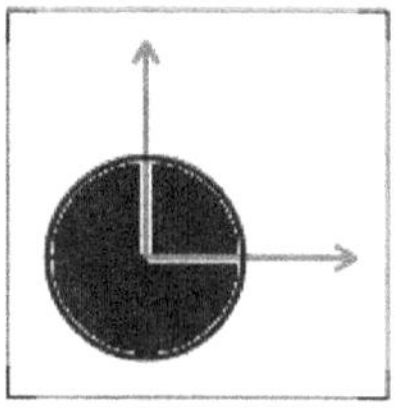

Figure 6–43

13. In the Annotation section of the Action Bar, click Abc (Text).

14. Click in the view to place the text. The Text Editor dialog box opens.

15. Enter the text shown in Figure 6–44.

To add the second line of text, press <Shift>+<Enter>

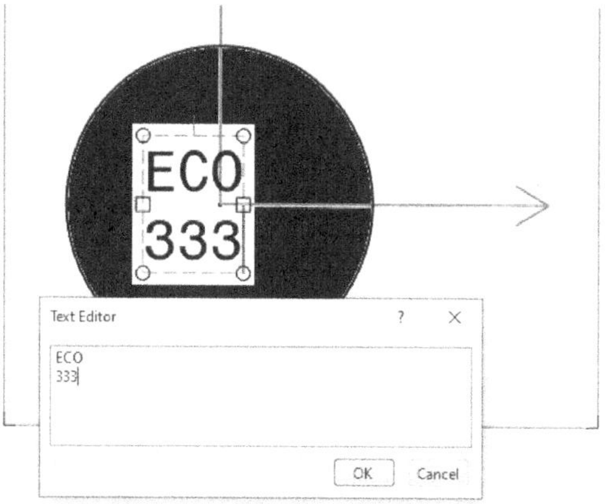

Figure 6–44

16. Click **OK** when you have finished. The 2D component displays as shown in Figure 6–45.

To position an element freely on the drawing, press <Shift> while dragging the element.

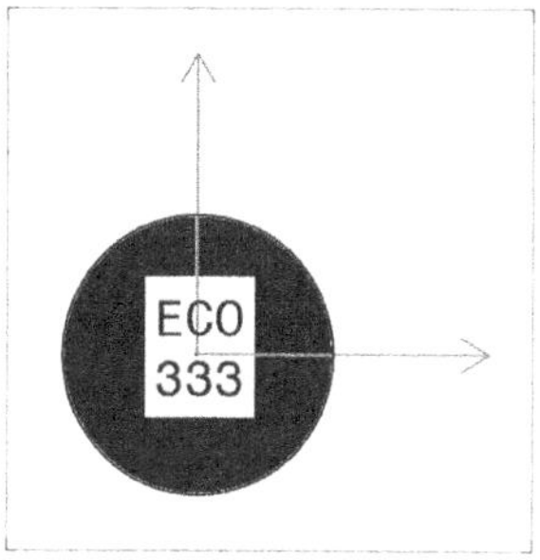

Figure 6–45

17. Right-click on the text and select **Modifiable in Instance**. This will enable you to edit the text when the 2D component is instantiated into another drawing. If this option is not set, the text cannot be changed upon instantiation.

Task 5 - Save the 2D components to a catalog.

In this task, you will save the drawing files as a catalog. Before this can be done, the drawing must be saved.

1. Save the **###_2D_Components_6B** drawing.

2. Select  (New)**>Generate Catalog** to create a catalog.

3. In the Catalog dialog box, enter **###_2DComp** for the *Name*, as shown in Figure 6–46, where ### represents your initials.

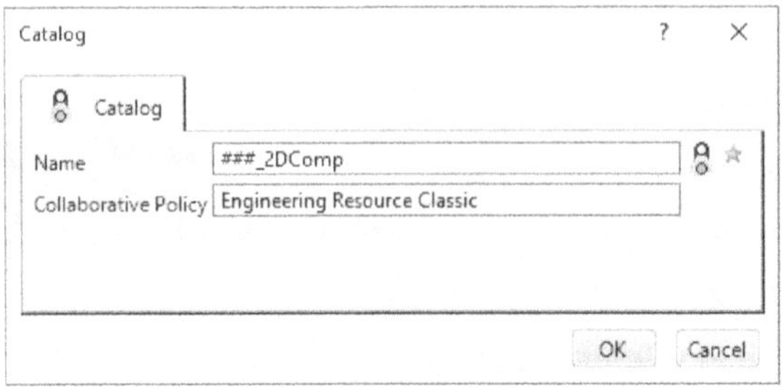

Figure 6–46

4. Select **OK** to complete and save the catalog.

5. Close all tabs.

Task 6 - Import and open a drawing.

1. Import and open **Adapter_Comp_6B.3dxml** from the practice files folder. While importing, set the *Duplication string* to **###_** where ### represents your initials.

2. Right-click on the **###_Adapter_Comp_6B** drawing in the tree and select *** object>Open in New App**. The drawing displays as shown in Figure 6–47.

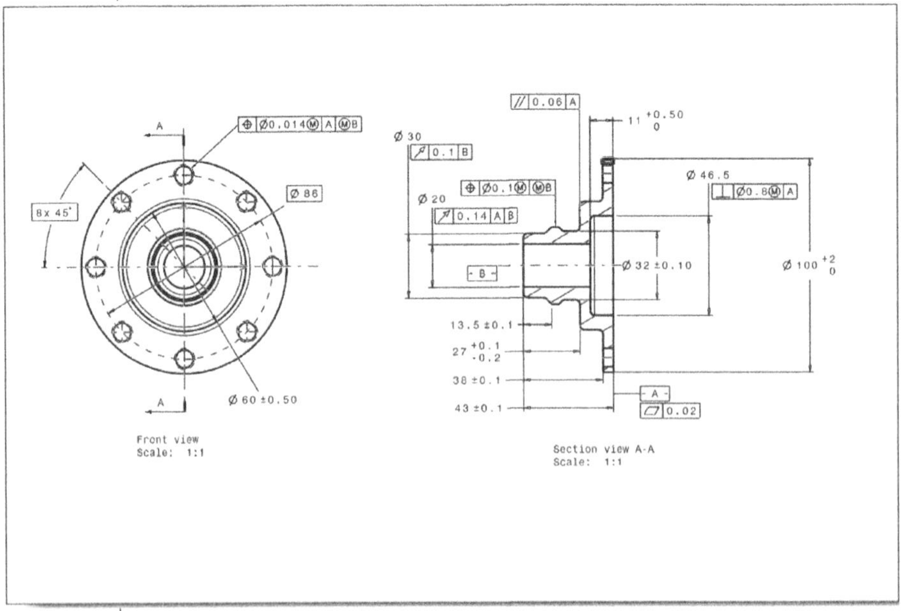

Figure 6–47

Task 7 - Import and open a drawing.

1. In the *Search* field at the top of the window, enter **###_2DComp** and press **Enter**.

2. In the Search results for ###_2DComp drop-down list, select **Explore**, as shown in Figure 6–48.

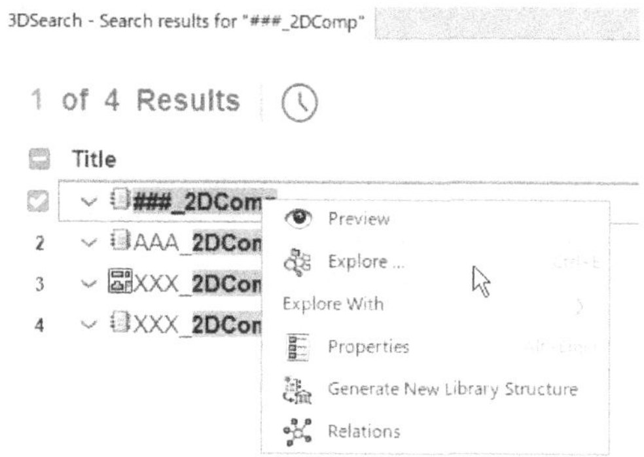

Figure 6–48

3. The ###_2DComp catalog opens in the Catalog app, as shown in Figure 6–49.

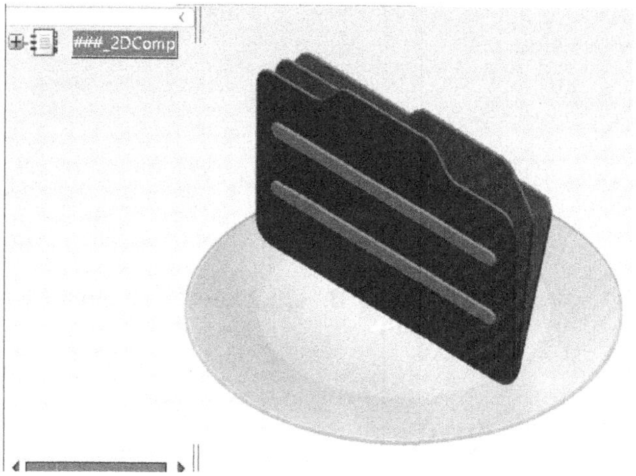

Figure 6–49

Task 8 - Instantiate a 2D component from a catalog.

1. Activate the widget with the **###_Adapter_Comp_6B** drawing and ensure the Front view is active by double-clicking on it in the specification tree.This step is required because the 2D component will instantiate into the active view.

2. In the Tools section of the Action Bar, select (Catalog Browser). In the Catalog Browser dialog box, click (Open a Catalog).

3. In the Choose a Catalog or Chapter dialog box, select **More**.

4. Activate the tab with the ###_2DComp Catalog app.

5. Click **###_2DComp** from the top of the specification tree. The Catalog Browser should appear, as shown in Figure 6–50.

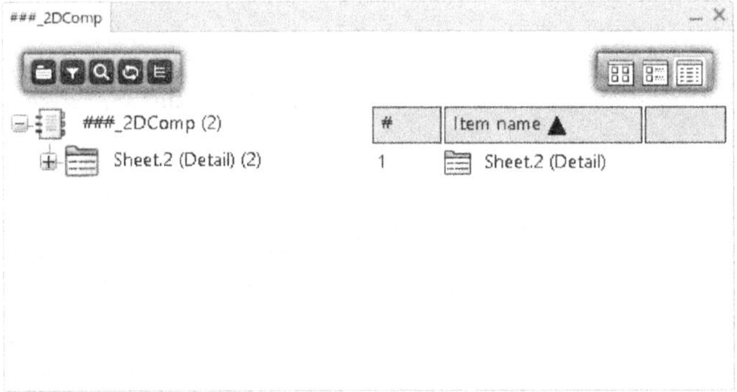

Figure 6–50

6. Double-click on **Sheet.2 (Detail)**, as shown in Figure 6–51.

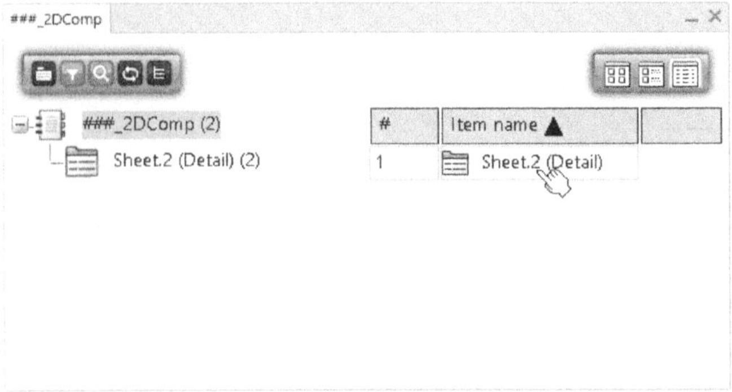

Figure 6–51

7. Double-click on **2D Component.2**, as shown in Figure 6–51.

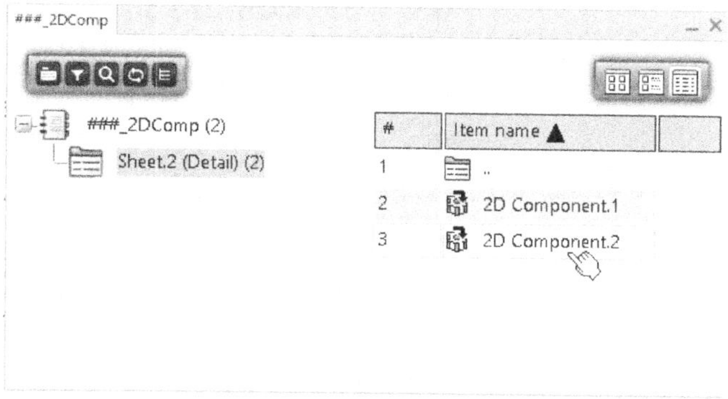

Figure 6–52

8. Place the 2D Component.2 in the upper-left of the drawing, as shown in Figure 6–53.

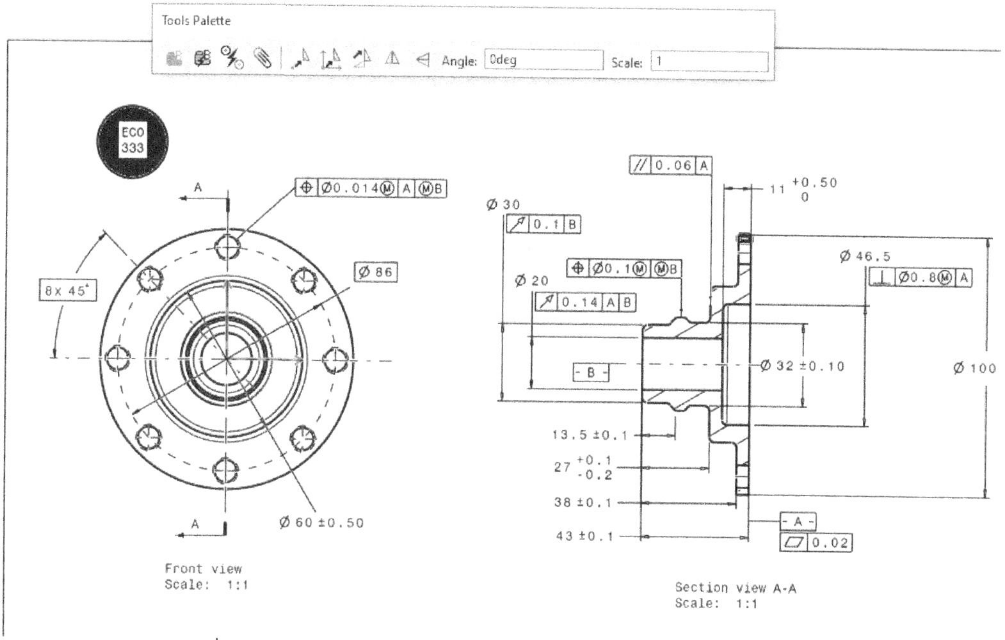

Figure 6–53

9. Click anywhere in the background to complete the instantiation and close the Catalog Browser.

Task 9 - Modify the instantiated 2D component.

1. Click the newly instantiated 2D component, then double-click on the text in it.

2. In the Text Editor, change *333* to **123**.
3. Click **OK**. The drawing displays as shown in Figure 6–54.

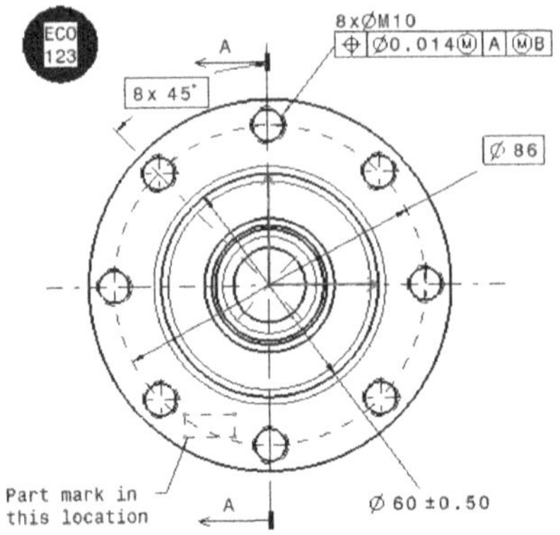

Figure 6–54

Task 10 - Investigate the model links.

In this task, you will review the links that have been created when instantiating the 2D component.

1. In the Tools section of the Action Bar, select (Links and Relations). The Edit Links and Relations dialog box opens as shown in Figure 6–55.

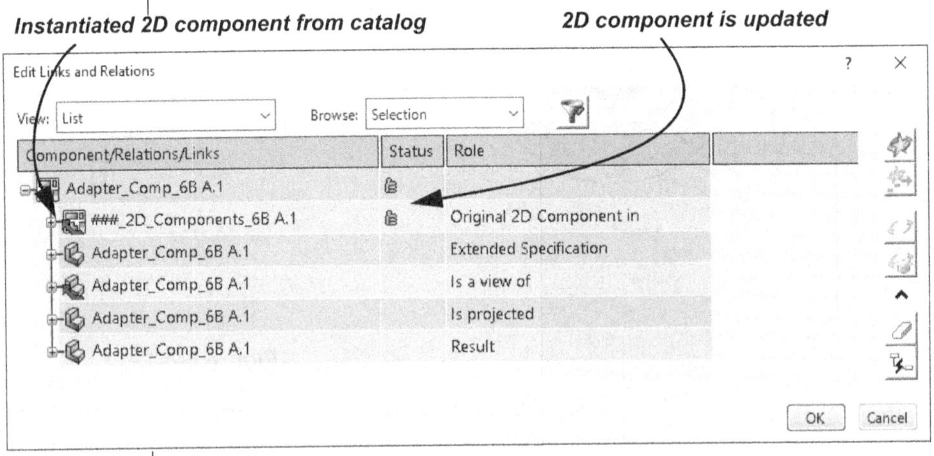

Figure 6–55

Design Considerations

The instantiated 2D component (**2D component.2**) references **###_2D_Component_6B A.1**. The 2D component was originally created in this document. The 2D component is now up to date.

2. Click **OK** to exit the Edit Links and Relations dialog box.

Task 11 - Expose a 2D component.

In this task, you will break the link between the instantiated 2D component and the drawing in which it was created. This is done by exposing the 2D component.

1. Right-click on the instantiated 2D component and select **2D component.x (Instance) object>Expose 2D component.** The Expose 2D Component dialog box opens as shown in Figure 6–56.

*Since there is no existing detail sheet in the drawing, only the **In a new detail sheet** option is available.*

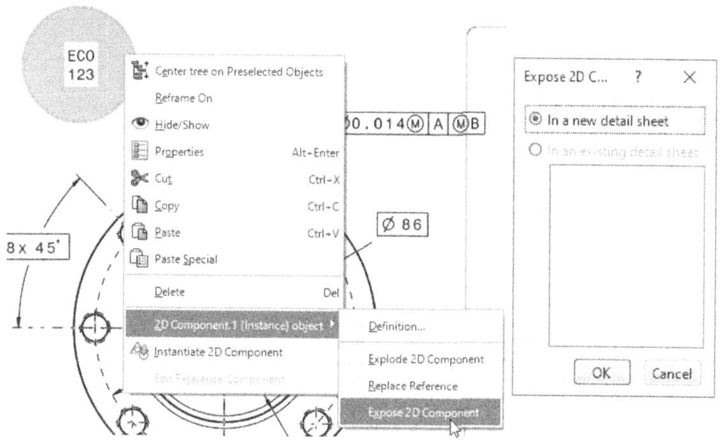

Figure 6–56

2. Click **OK**. Note the changes after the 2D component is exposed. The model and specification tree are shown in Figure 6–57.

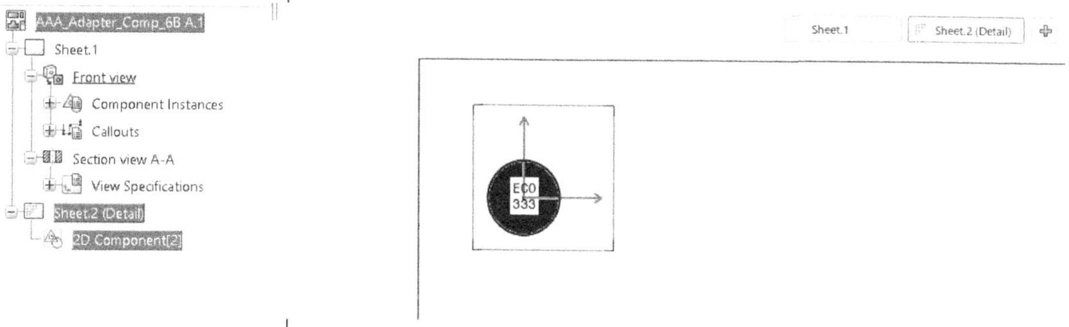

Figure 6–57

3. Activate **Sheet.1**.

4. In the Tools section of the Action Bar, select (Links and Relations). Notice the ###_2D_Components_6B A.1 is no longer linked to the document, as shown in Figure 6–58. The 2D component no longer references **2DComp.CATDrawing**. It now points to the newly created detail sheet.

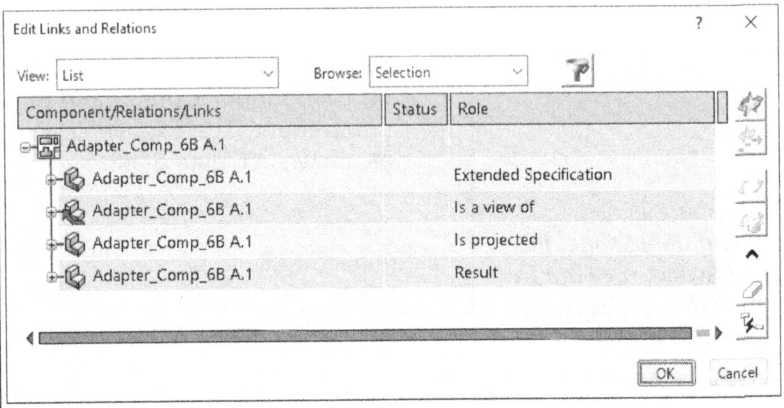

Figure 6–58

5. Click **OK** in the Edit Links and Relations dialog box.

Task 12 - Insert a second 2D component.

In this task, you will instantiate the quality control symbol a second time in the same drawing.

1. Activate **Section view A-A**.

2. In the expanded Sketch section of the Action Bar, click (Instantiate 2D component). On the detail sheet in the specification tree, select the 2D component.

3. Place the symbol in the location shown in Figure 6–59.

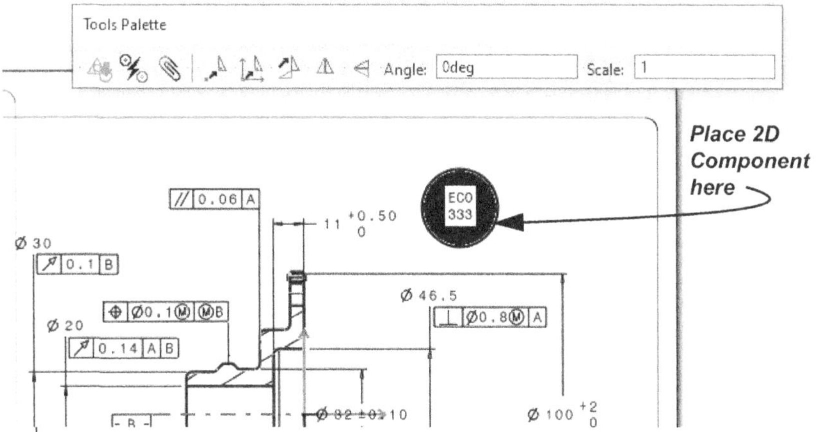

Figure 6–59

4. Modify the text in the symbol to read **ECO 124**.

Task 13 - Modify the 2D component.

Modifying the 2D component must be done using the detail sheet.

1. Activate **Sheet.2 (Detail)**.
2. Change the color of the fill from *black* to **red**. This can be done by double-clicking on the fill and selecting a new color in the Properties dialog box.

3. Activate **Sheet.1**. The instantiated 2D components have updated associatively with the changes to the detail sheet, as shown in Figure 6–60.

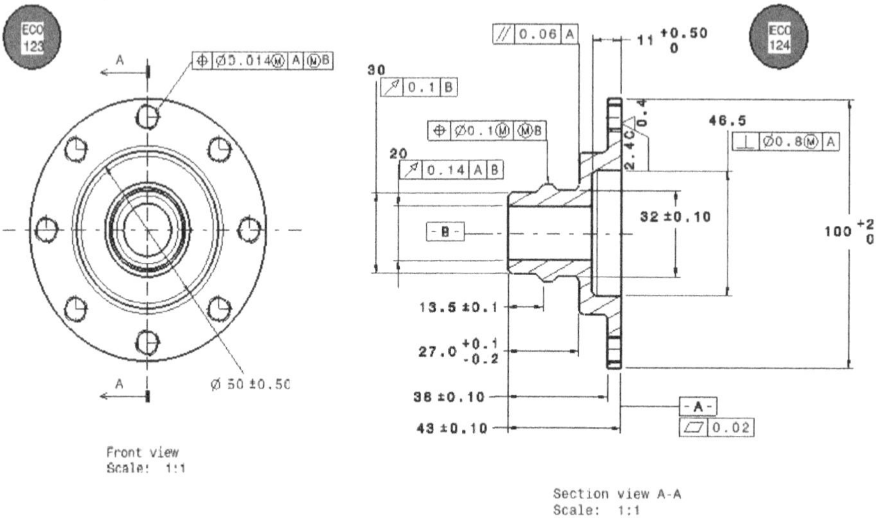

Figure 6–60

4. Save the drawing.

Task 14 - (Optional) Replace a 2D component.

In this task, you will add a new 2D component to the detail sheet and replace one of the symbols added to **Sheet.1**.

1. Activate **Sheet.2 (Detail)** and add a new 2D Component from the Template section of the Action Bar.

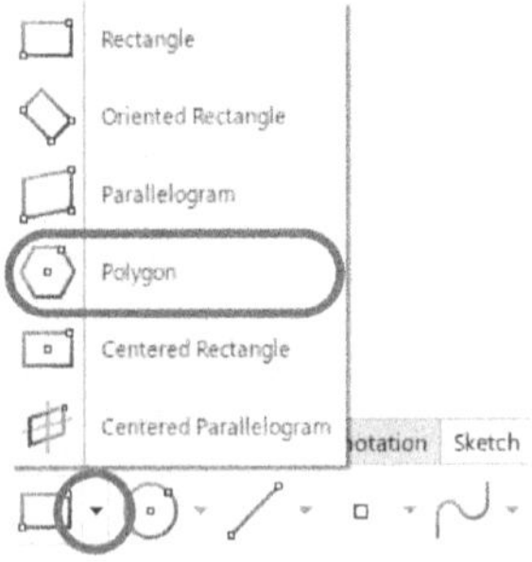

2. Activate the newly created 2D Component and create the geometry shown in Figure 6–61. Ensure that the text is modifiable in the instance.

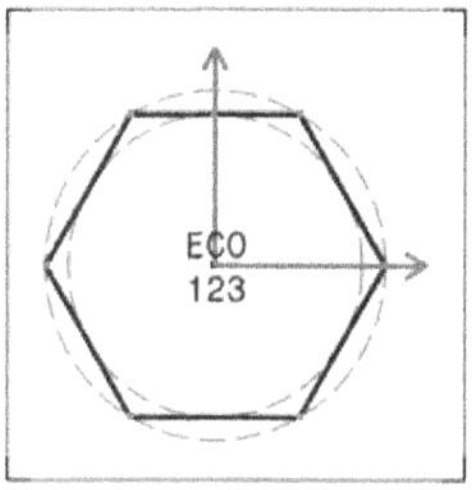

Figure 6–61

Hide the two construction circles before filling the hexagon.

3. In the Annotation section of the Action Bar, select  (Area Fill) and click anywhere inside the hexagon. The system will apply a default hatch to the view, as shown in Figure 6–62.

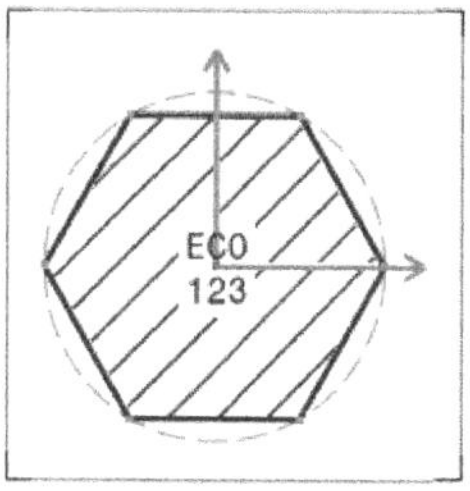

Figure 6–62

4. Modify the hatching properties to use a *Coloring* type of **Black**. The completed 2D component displays as shown in Figure 6–63.

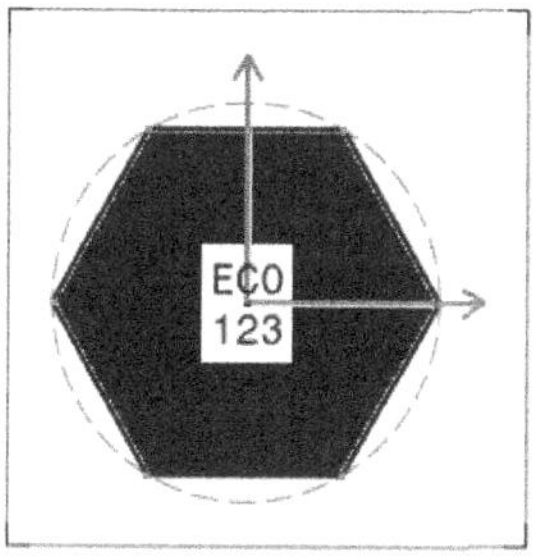

Figure 6–63

5. Activate **Sheet.1.**

6. Right-click on one of the instantiated 2D components and select **2D Component.# (Instance) object>Replace Reference**, as shown in Figure 6–64.

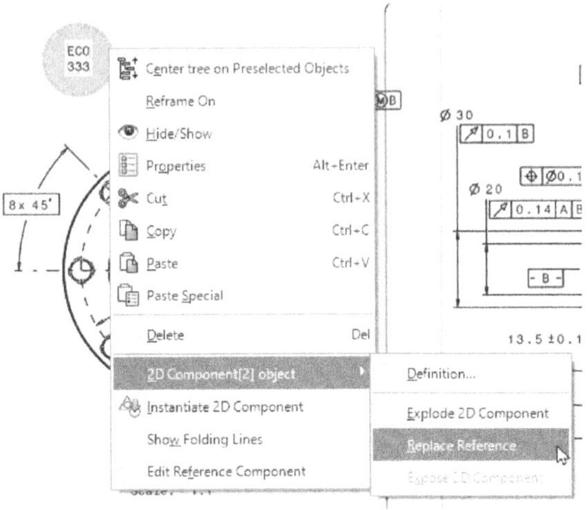

Figure 6–64

7. In the specification tree, select the new 2D component. The system will replace the circular symbol with the new hexagonal one, as shown in Figure 6–65.

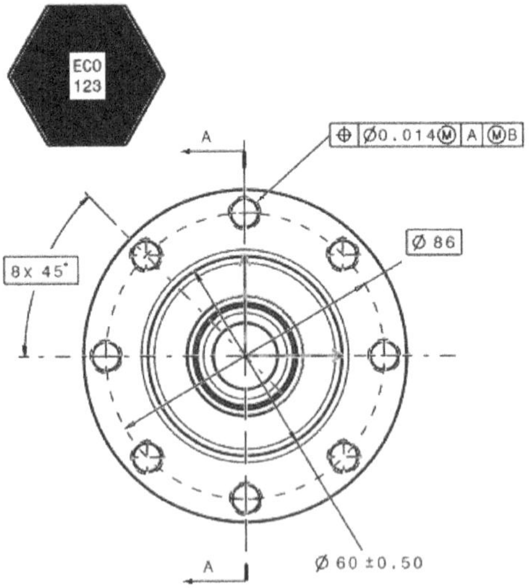

Figure 6–65

8. Save the drawing and close all of the tabs.

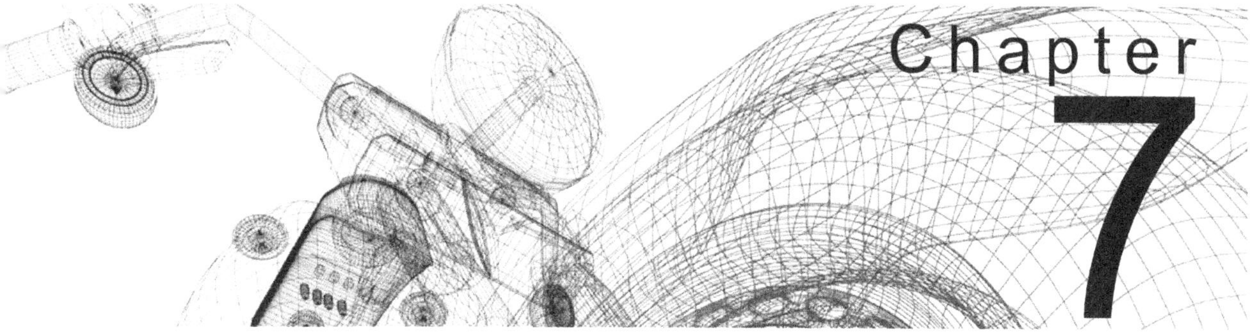

Product Drawings

Most assembly drawings use the same techniques and functionality to create views, notes, and dimensions. This chapter focuses on functionality specific to assembly drawing creation.

Learning Objectives in This Chapter

- Generate a Bill of Materials.
- Display balloons on a drawing.
- Create slides to simplify the display of the assembly.
- Create a view from a slide.
- Use overload properties.
- Use Modify Links to permit components to be excluded from an assembly drawing view for illustrative purposes.
- Recognize and apply various view generation modes.

7.1 Generate Bill of Materials

The Bill of Materials (BOM) report can display on the assembly drawing to report the component names and the quantities used in the assembly.

In the drawing, the BOM format can be customized to display a variety of parameters and model information. The drawing report reflects the customization performed in the drawing file.

General Steps

Use the following general steps to display the BOM report:

1. Select BOM icon.
2. Choose BOM style.
3. When applicable, pick which product.
4. Place the BOM.
5. Customization of the BOM.

Step 1 - Select BOM icon.

Select the  (Bill of Material) icon found in the Annotation section of the Action Bar. This command is found by expanding the arrow next to **Table**, as shown in Figure 7–1.

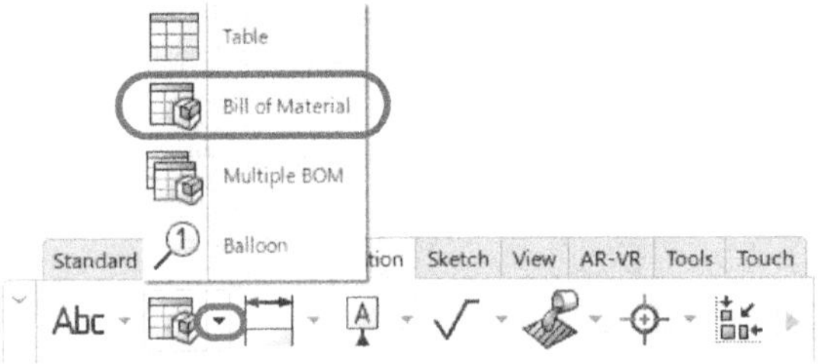

Figure 7–1

Step 2 - Choose BOM style.

The Bill of Material Creation window will appear, as shown in Figure 7–2. In this window, the user is able to select the BOM *Style* type. This determines what the starting format of the BOM will be. Without administration customization of the *3DEXPERIENCE* environment, the only style available to the user will be called **Default**.

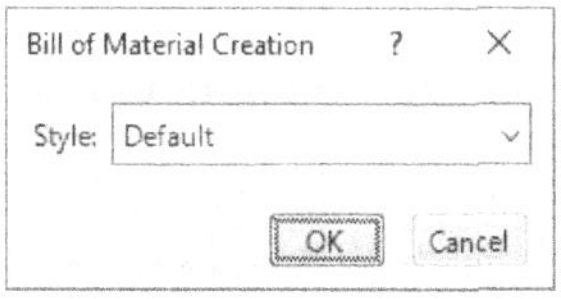

Figure 7–2

Select **OK** once a style is chosen.

Note: Someone with Admin privileges would be needed to customize the Standards file **(Me>Preferences>Standards> Drafting>ANSI-ASME>Styles>Bill of Material Format)** to be able to create more custom styles to choose from.

Step 3 - When applicable, pick which product.

If the drawing has two or more views using two different products, the BOM that you want to generate needs to be defined. This is done by either selecting the product from the specification tree in the product widget or selecting the view in the drawing of the product you want a BOM of, as shown in Figure 7–3.

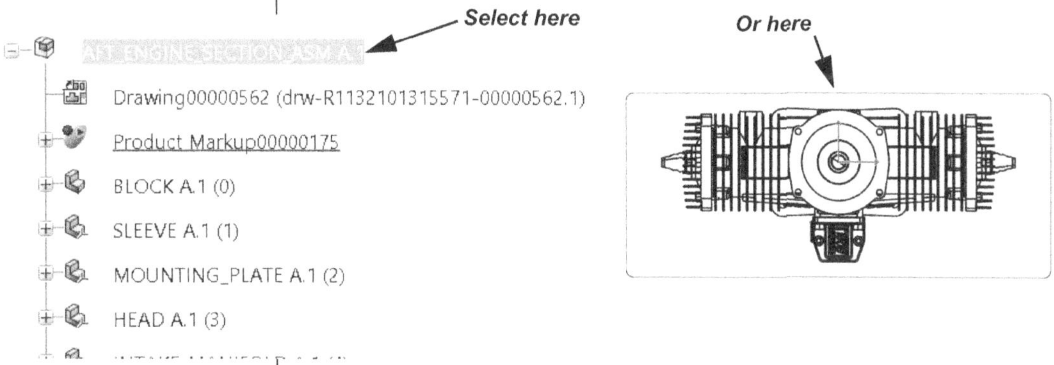

Figure 7–3

If there is only one product being used to create all views, then this step can be ignored and the BOM will default to the only product linked to the drawing.

Step 4 - Place the BOM.

Select the location on the drawing where the BOM will be placed. The location of the cursor will locate the upper left corner of the Bill of Materials, as shown in Figure 7–4. This can take a few moments to load.

Item Number	Quantity	Title	Description	Material	Weight
1	1	1741	-	Steel	-
2	1	1652	-	Steel	-
3	4	20c	-	Steel	-
4	72	20-3-R	-	Steel	-
5	1	1742	-	Steel	-
6	4	658923	-	Steel	-

Figure 7–4

Not only is the table placed on the sheet, but a BOM.# is placed in the specification tree under a **Reports** node.

Step 5 - Customization of the BOM.

The *Style* chosen in Step 2 defines the default format of the table. However, the table can be customized after it has been placed. To customize an existing table, right-click on the table in the drawing or in the specification tree and select **Properties**.

There are two tabs specific to a Bill of Materials that will help customize the look on a drawing. The two tabs are *BOM Format* and *Report Properties*.

BOM Format

The *BOM Format* tab allows for customizing the look of the properties that display in the Bill of Materials. For example, the header can be move from top to bottom, or item numbering can be switched from **Integer** (1, 2, 3) to **Letters** (A, B, C). An example of *BOM Format* is shown in Figure 7–5.

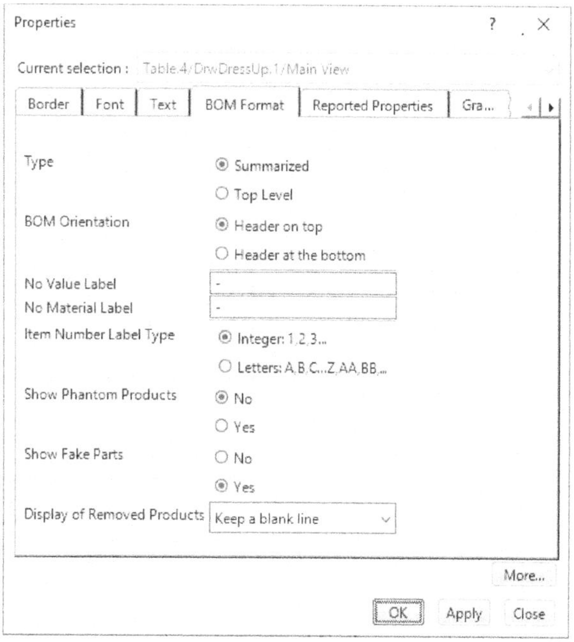

Figure 7–5

Report Properties

The *Report Properties* tab allows for the addition and subtraction of properties that display in the BOM. To customize these properties, select on a line item. The options to customize are listed on the right. An example of the *Report Properties* tab is shown in Figure 7–6.

Action	Description
(New)	Creates a new line item in the *List of Properties* and another column in the Bill of Materials.
(Delete)	Deletes the selected line item from the *List of Properties* and removes the column from the Bill of Materials.
(Move Up)	Moves the selected line item up in the *List of Properties* and adjusts the *BOM* column to the left.
(Move Down)	Moves the selected line item down in the *List of Properties* and adjusts the *BOM* column to the right.

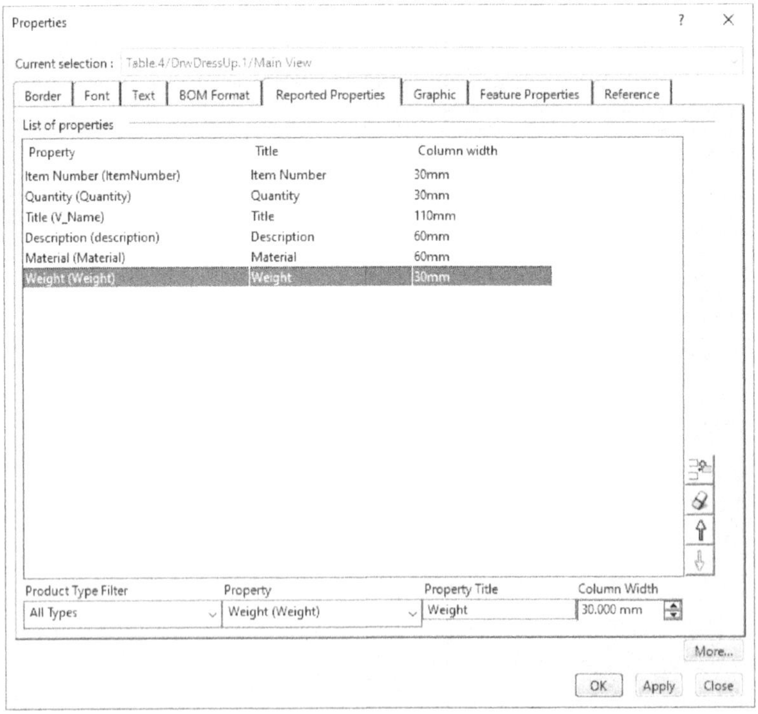

Figure 7–6

7.2 Display Balloons on a Drawing

Balloons provide a correlation between the geometry of a drawing view and the Bill of Materials report. The item number for each component displays in a balloon with a leader pointing to the component geometry in the active drawing view. Assembly components can be located in a view or on a Bill of Materials report using the index number.

General Steps

Use the following general steps to display the balloons on a drawing:

1. Generate a BOM.
2. Select the **Automation Balloons Generation** tool.
3. Define Automatic Ballooning Options.
4. Adjust balloons as needed.

Step 1 - Generate a BOM.

A BOM is used as reference when using the **Automatic Balloon Generation** tool. While not required, it is recommend to create a BOM before using **Automatic Balloon Generation**. This is so the balloons can reference the same Item Number (or other properties) as the BOM does. An example of this is shown in Figure 7–7. Follow the steps described in the previous section to create the Bill of Materials.

Item No.	Quantity	Name
1	1	prd-R1132101315571-00003334
2	1	prd-R1132101315571-00003335
3	3	prd-R1132101315571-00003336
4	1	prd-R1132101315571-00003337
5	1	prd-R1132101315571-00003338
6	1	prd-R1132101315571-00003339
7	1	prd-R1132101315571-00003340
8	1	prd-R1132101315571-00003341
9	1	prd-R1132101315571-00003342
10	1	prd-R1132101315571-00003343

Figure 7–7

Step 2 - Select the Automatic Balloon Generation tool.

Activate the drawing view to which the balloons are going to be attached. Click (Automatic Balloons Generation) in the expanded area of the Annotation section of the Action Bar. The Automatic Ballooning Options window appears, as shown in Figure 7–8.

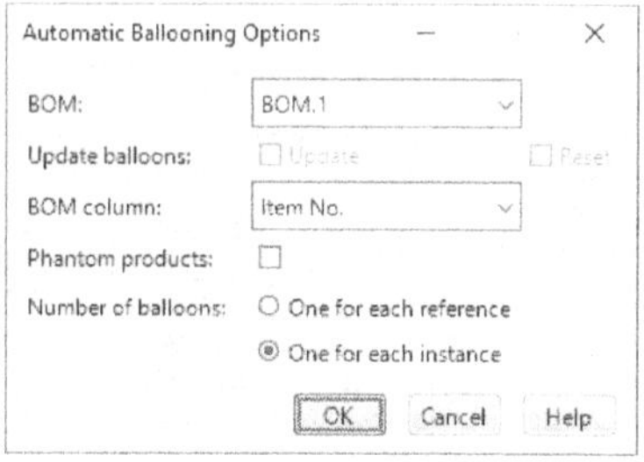

Figure 7–8

Step 3 - Define Automatic Ballooning Options.

In the Automatic Ballooning Options window, you can customize the settings below as needed.

Options	Description
BOM	Select the BOM that you want to associate the balloons to. This allows those BOM properties to displays in the balloons.
Update Balloons	**Update**: Updates existing balloons if changes have been made. **Reset**: Deletes existing balloons and creates new ones.
BOM column	Allows for the selection of different properties to display in the Balloons. (Item No., Quantity, Name)
Phantom Products	Checkbox to include Phantom products in the incremental numbers of the BOM. By default, they are ignored.
Number of balloons	One for each reference: Only one balloon displays if the same part is referenced more than once. One for each instance: One balloon for every instance of the same part.

Select **OK** when finished. The balloons are added to the active view in a random arrangement, as shown in Figure 7–9.

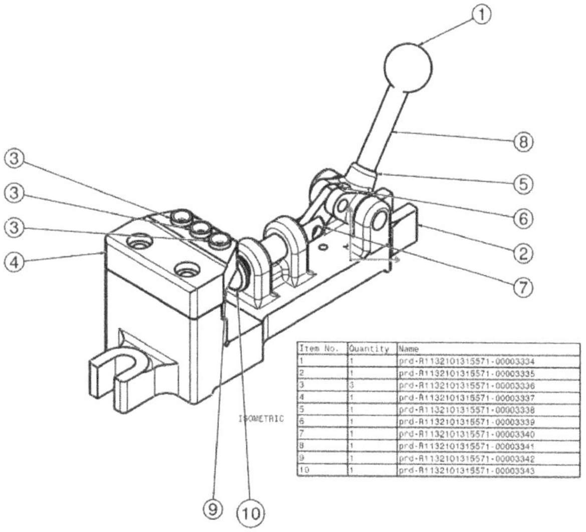

Figure 7–9

Step 4 - Adjust balloons as needed.

Rearrange the balloons and customize the font and size as required. An example is shown in Figure 7–10.

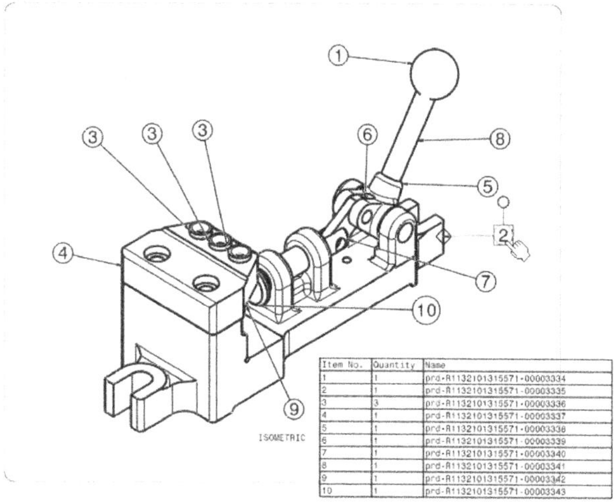

Figure 7–10

Draft Balloons

Balloons can also be created individually in a drawing instead of being generated from the product.

How To: Create a Balloon

1. In the Annotation section of the Action Bar, click (Balloon).
2. Select a component from any view to attach and identify the balloon.
3. Select the location the balloon graphic should be located.
4. Enter a number for the balloon in the top center pop-up window, as shown in Figure 7–11. If a BOM has already been generated for the product, the system defaults to the assigned instance number for the component. A unique number can also be entered. However, try to avoid using numbering that does not correlate to the BOM report.

Figure 7–11

5. Select the background or icon to confirm and complete the balloon.

Draft balloons display and behave identically to generated balloons. However, since the balloon number must be entered manually for a draft balloon, they are less likely to correspond to the number convention that was applied to the product and displayed in the BOM.

7.3 Slides

Product drawings differ from part drawings in that they need to display manufacturing and assembly information for multiple parts that are included in the product. Due to the complexity of product models, visualizing specific details of the assembly becomes difficult. Slides can be used to simplify the display of the assembly in a product drawing and reduce the system requirements required to manipulate and update the drawing.

Slides enable a designer to store the display settings of components in an assembly. Slides can be used in the following ways:

- Hide/Show components to simplify the display.
- Explode the assembly to visualize all components in the assembly in a single view.
- Use viewpoints to display critical orientations of the model.
- Capture sections of components in the assembly.
- Display annotations and images along with the assembly.

You can use slides to configure the display of the model in the product drawing. When a slide is applied to the model and a drawing view is created, the state of the model in the slide is used to generate the drawing view geometry.

Slides in a product model can be found in the **Product Markup** node in the specification tree, as shown in Figure 7–12.

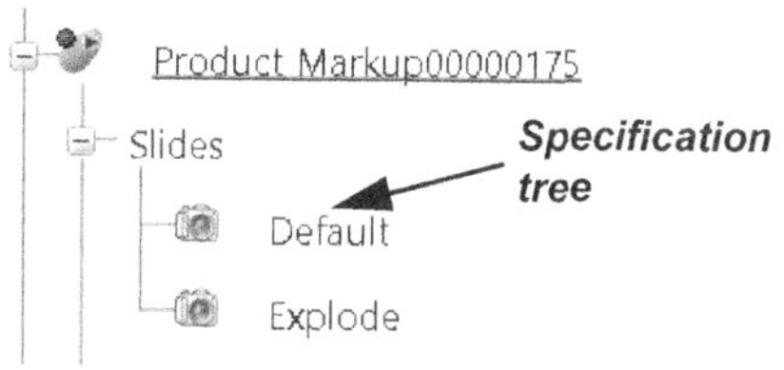

Figure 7–12

Product Markup

The advantage of creating a Product Markup is the slides will be maintained in the main product file. No external links are created to generate the slides. If someone wants to edit the slide, they will need to open the original product to do so.

How To: Create a Slide in a Product Markup

1. Right-click on the top of the product tree and select **Insert>Markup**.
2. Fill out the Product Markup, as shown in Figure 7–13, and select **OK**.

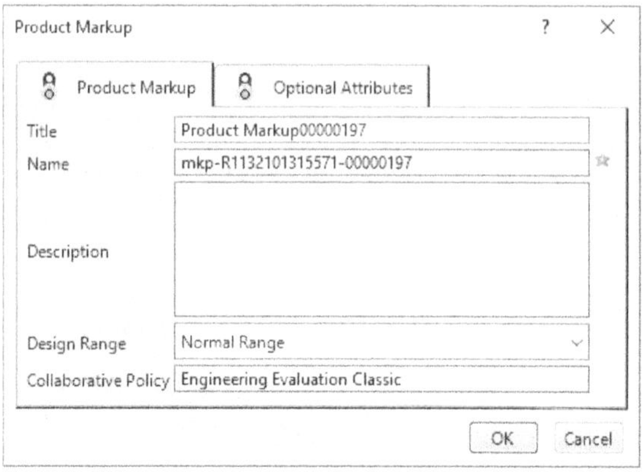

Figure 7–13

3. With the Product Markup active, switch to the Design Review app, as shown in Figure 7–14.

Figure 7–14

4. Customize the orientation, positions, and display attributes of the assembly components as desired.

5. In the Review section of the Action Bar, select  (Slide) to capture this display of the product, as shown in Figure 7–15. Rename the slides as needed by adjusting their properties.

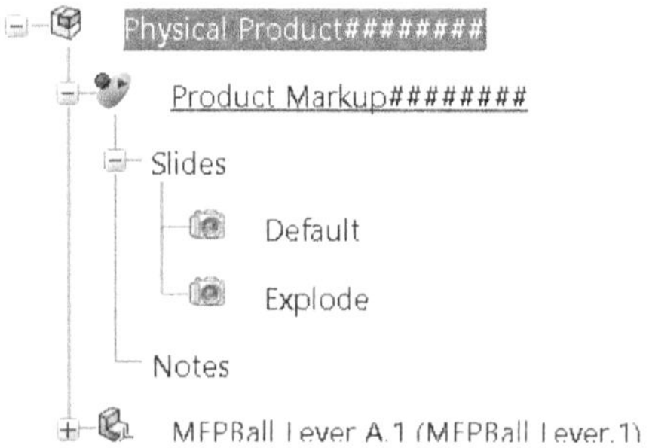

Figure 7–15

7.4 Create a View from a Slide

General Steps

Use the following general steps to create a view of an assembly slide in your drawing:

1. Create a new drawing view.
2. Select a slide from the assembly.
3. Select a reference from the assembly.

Step 1 - Create a new drawing view.

Click  (Front View) or  (Isometric View) to create a new drawing view.

Step 2 - Select a slide from the assembly.

Activate the assembly window. Select the required slide from the **Markup** node in the specification tree, as shown in Figure 7–16.

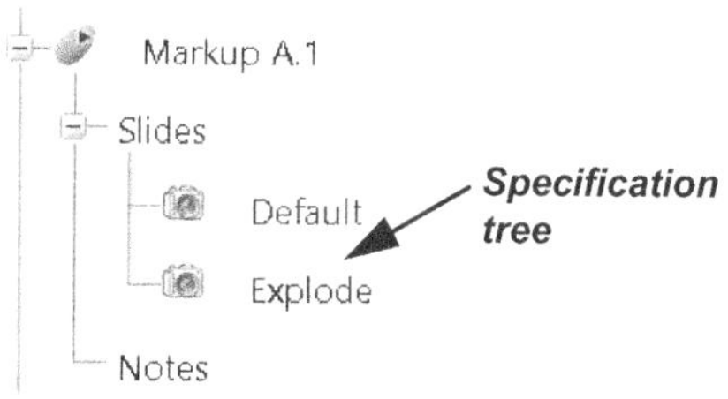

Figure 7–16

Step 3 - Select a reference from the assembly.

Select a reference from the model. The reference has to be a planar face or surface for a Front view, or any model surface for the Isometric view. The view of the selected slide displays in the drawing, as shown in Figure 7–17.

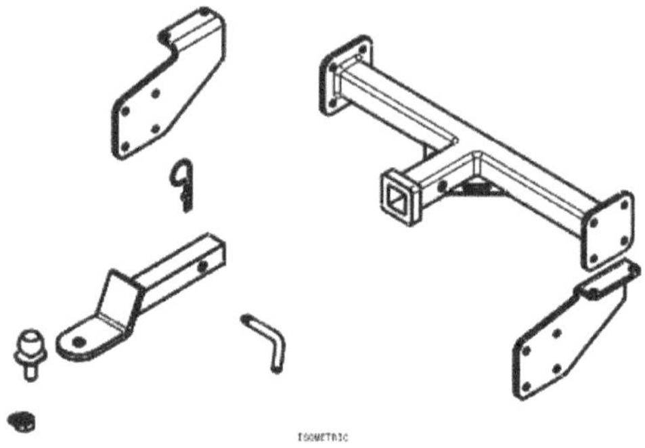

Figure 7–17

7.5 Use Overload Properties

Overload Properties enables you to change the graphics properties of the components that display in a selected drawing view.

General Steps

Use the following general steps to configure an assembly view using overload properties:

1. Activate the **Overload Properties** tool.
2. Select the components to manipulate.
3. Edit the properties of the selected components.

Step 1 - Activate the Overload Properties tool.

Right-click on the view in the specification tree and select * **object>Overload Properties**, as shown in Figure 7–18.

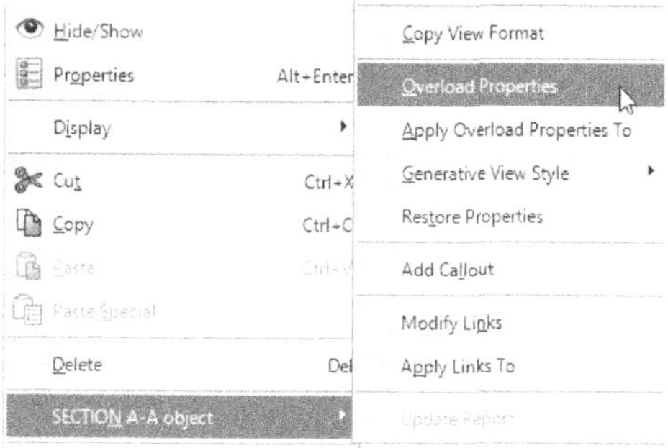

Figure 7–18

The Overload Properties dialog box opens, as shown in Figure 7–19.

Figure 7–19

Step 2 - Select the components to manipulate.

Select the parts of the assembly that you want to control in the view. The part numbers of the selected components are listed in the Overload Properties dialog box, as shown in Figure 7–20.

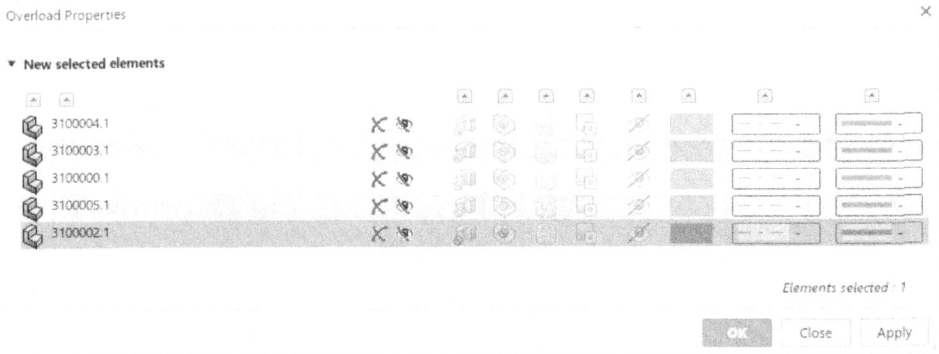

Figure 7–20

Step 3 - Edit the properties of the selected components.

After selecting one or more of the parts, their properties can be customized in the Overload Properties dialog box, as shown in Figure 7–21.

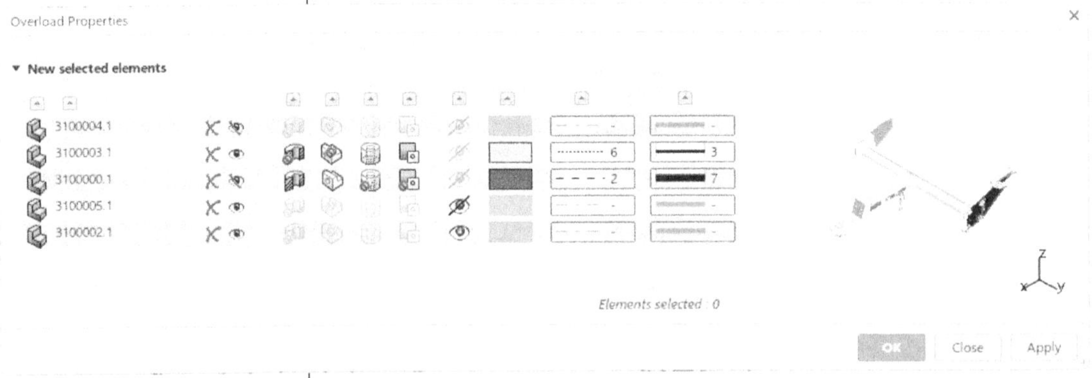

Figure 7–21

You can change the following properties for selected components:

Options	Description
	Remove element from the list.
	Click to preview/remove the element from the 3D Preview.
	Click to Activate/Force/Reset the Cut and Uncut Property.
	Toggle on/off/reset to control the part from being used in a projected view. When toggled off, the details of other parts can be seen in areas that would have been obscured from view.
	Toggle on/off/reset to control whether hidden lines of the selected part will display.
	Sets the selected part as the background. This helps to visually display other parts that are behind the selected part in the view while still showing the selected part.
	Toggle to turn on/off/reset the display of the part in the view.
	Click to modify the color.
	Click to modify the line type.
	Click to modify the line thinness.

Figure 7–22 shows a partial cross-section view.

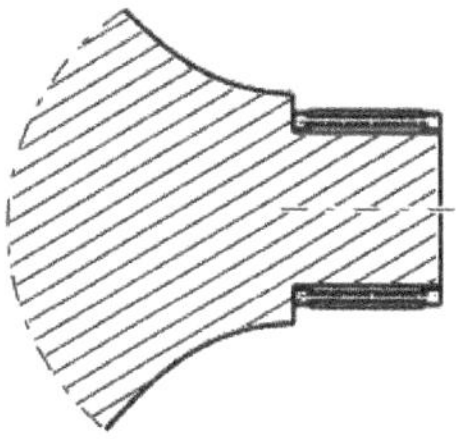

Figure 7–22

Figure 7–23 shows the same view with the **Uncut Property** option activated for the indicated part.

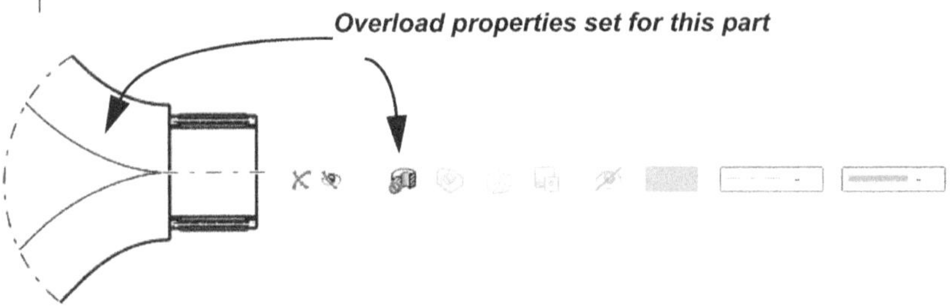

Figure 7–23

Figure 7–24 shows the same view with the **No Show** option selected for the same component.

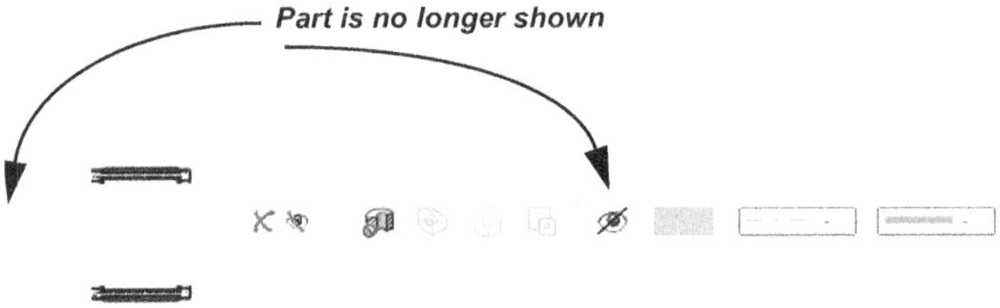

Figure 7–24

7.6 Modify Links

The **Modify Links** option permits components to be excluded from an assembly drawing view for illustrative purposes. Drawing views created from an assembly automatically display all of the parts in the product. By breaking the link between the part and drawing view, the part is no longer represented in the product drawing view.

General Steps

Use the following general steps to modify the components shown in a product drawing view:

1. Open the Links Modification dialog box.
2. Select the components to display in the product model.
3. Add the selected components.
4. Update the drawing view to display the link modifications.

Step 1 - Open the Links Modification dialog box.

A drawing view is shown in Figure 7–25 with all of the parts on display. This view is linked to every component of the product.

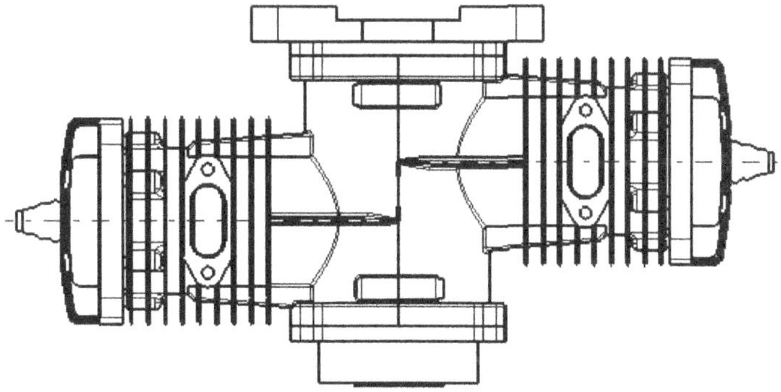

Figure 7–25

To remove parts from the view, you will need both the drawing and the product widgets open in the session. Depending on your settings, these widgets can either be tiled or toggled between while modifying links. Right-click on the product drawing view and select *** object>Modify Links**, as shown in Figure 7–26.

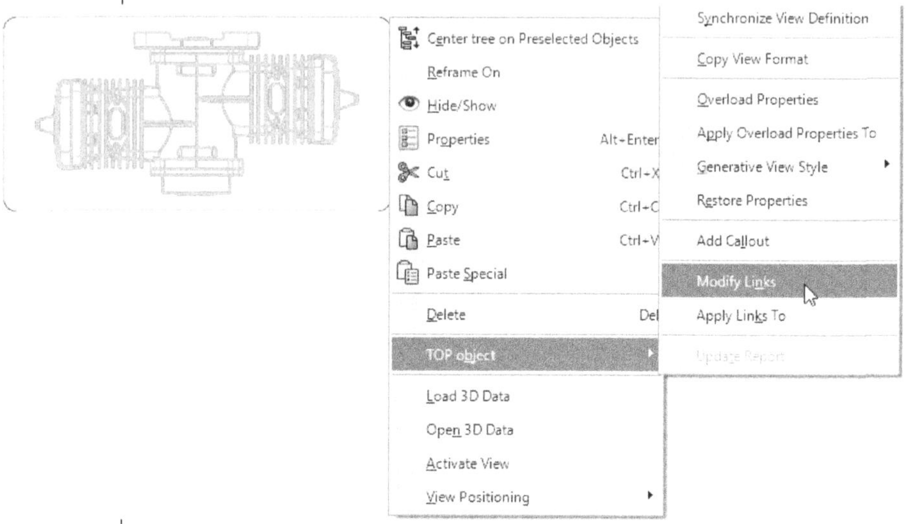

Figure 7–26

The Links Modification dialog box opens, as shown in Figure 7–27. Note that the pointed document is the assembly product file. The *Manage Pointed elements* field indicates that the drawing is linked to the whole assembly.

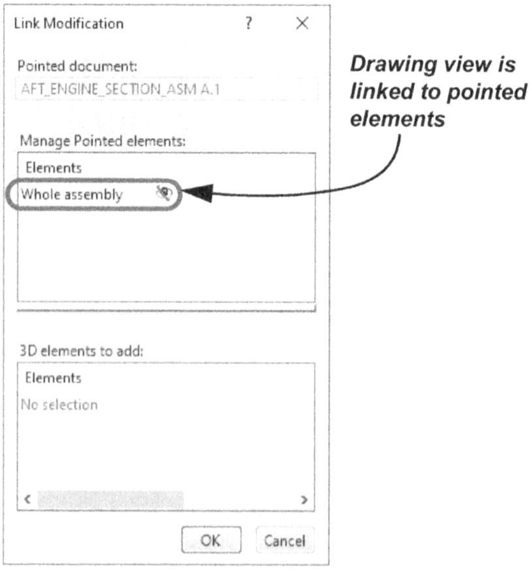

Figure 7–27

Step 2 - Select the components to display in the product model.

With the Links Modification dialog box open, activate the product window. In the specification tree, select the components to display in the drawing view. Multiple components can be selected by pressing <Ctrl>.

When you have finished selecting components, activate the drawing window. The components selected in the product window are listed in the *3D elements to add* area in the Link Modification dialog box, as shown in Figure 7–28.

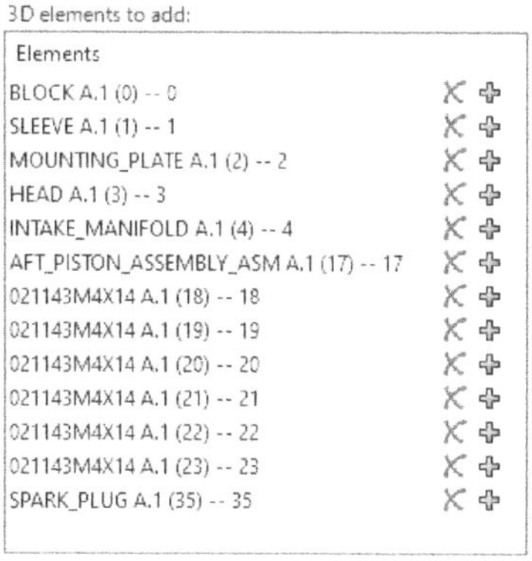

Figure 7–28

Step 3 - Add the selected components.

Click (Add) for each of the elements in the Links Modification dialog box that you want to display in the view. The dialog box updates, as shown in Figure 7–29. The preview window displays the newly added pointed elements if (Preview) has been toggled on for each element.

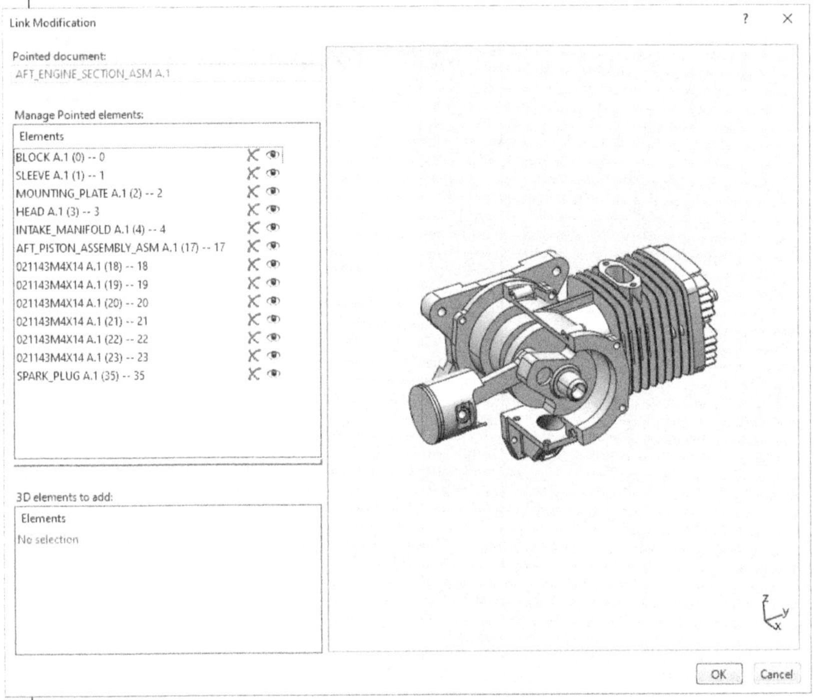

Figure 7–29

Click **OK** to complete the link modification.

Step 4 - Update the drawing view to display the link modifications.

Update the drawing view by clicking [icon]. The view updates to display the modified links, as shown in Figure 7–30.

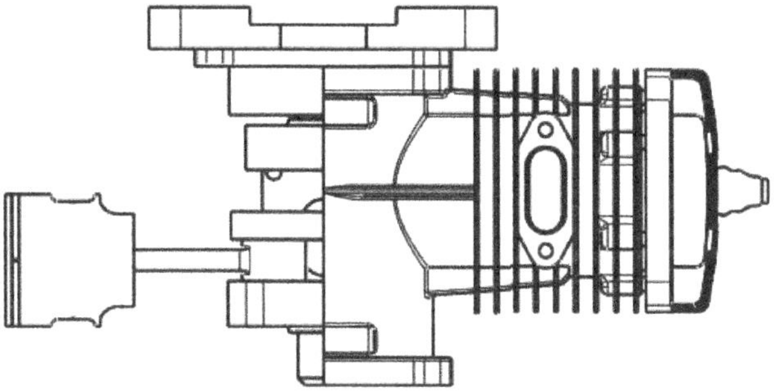

Figure 7–30

The drawing view is now only linked to the specified components rather than to the entire assembly.

7.7 View Generation Modes

CGR

You can use a CGR representation to enhance the performance of CATIA when updating the display of model geometry in drawing views. A CGR (CATIA Graphical Representation) file loads faster than a standard Physical Product because it is tessellated data. Therefore, only the external appearance of the model is used and displays. It is the same concept that is used when exploring a model to keep the file sizes small and make the model load and move faster on the screen.

You can replace the view geometry with a CGR representation using one of two methods:

View Setting

Open the Properties dialog box for the selected view and select the *Generation* tab. Select **CGR** in the View generation mode drop-down list (at the bottom of the dialog box), as shown in Figure 7–31.

Figure 7–31

Global Setting

Select **Me>Preferences>App Preferences>3D Modeling>Mechanical Systems>Drafting>View>View generation** and select **CGR** in the View generation mode drop-down list, as shown in Figure 7–32. All of the created views display using a CGR representation.

Figure 7–32

Additionally, a size filter can be established by entering a minimum part size in the field next to the **Only generate parts larger than** option. In this example, all models that are smaller than 1mm are removed from the drawing views.

Approximate

For large assemblies, the Approximate view generation mode is beneficial. It is similar to CGR mode in that it improves CATIA's performance. However, Approximate mode is able to further reduce memory usage at the expense of view detail and quality.

Approximate view generation mode has the following restrictions:

- You cannot create detail views.
- Dress-up features (threads, arrows, fill, and center lines) can be created.
- Auxiliary view profiles are non-associative.
- Annotations are non-associative.
- Not all radius/diameter dimensions can be created.

To change the View generation mode to **Approximate**, open the Properties dialog box for the selected view. In the *Generation* tab, scroll down to *Generation Mode*. Select **Approximate** in the drop-down list, as shown in Figure 7–33.

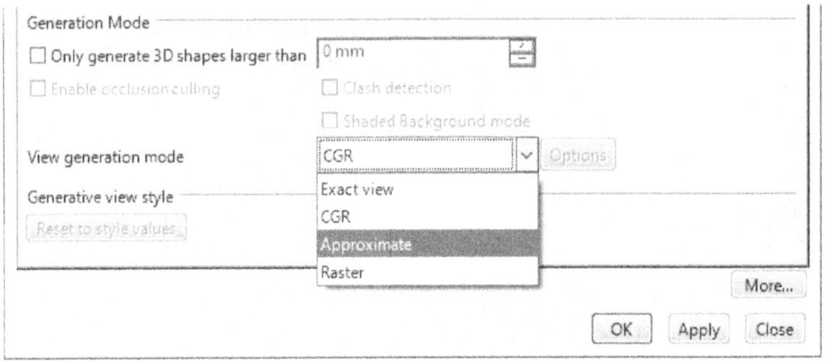

Figure 7–33

Practice 7a

BOM, Balloons, and CGR Views

Practice Objectives

- Generate a BOM and add it to the drawing.
- Use balloons to reference the BOM index.
- Create views from CGRs.

In this practice, you will generate a drawing with views, a Bill of Materials (BOM), and balloons. The completed drawing is shown in Figure 7–34.

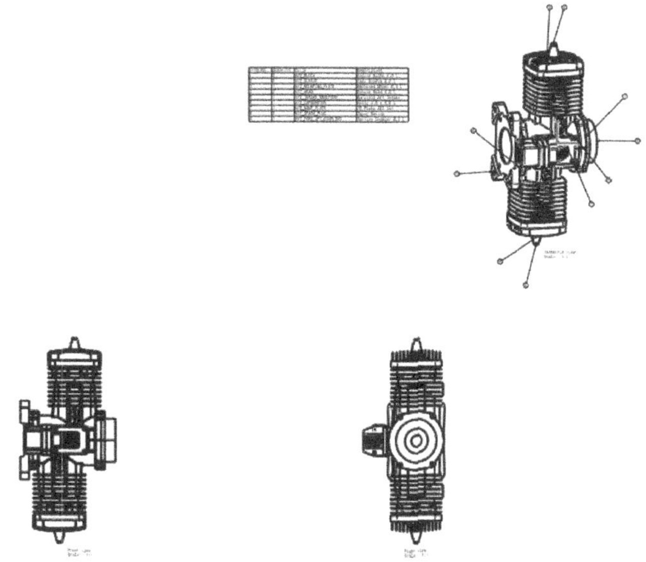

Figure 7–34

Task 1 - Import and open a drawing file.

1. Import and open **Engine_Aft_7A.3dxml** from the practice files folder. While importing, set the *Duplication string* to **###_** where ### represents your initials.

2. Right-click on the **###_Engine_Aft_7A** drawing in the tree and select * **object>Open in New App**.

Task 2 - Add the BOM report to the drawing.

1. If the option is available, select  (Update) from the Standard section of the Action Bar. If the views do not need to be updated, this option will not be available.

2. In the Annotation section, click  (Bill of Material).The Bill of Material Creation window will appear, as shown in Figure 7–35.

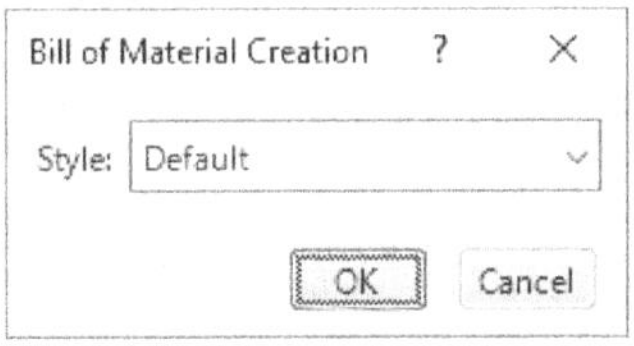

Figure 7–35

3. In the Bill of Material Creation window, select **OK**.

4. Click to place the BOM table, as shown in Figure 7–36. This might take a moment to load.

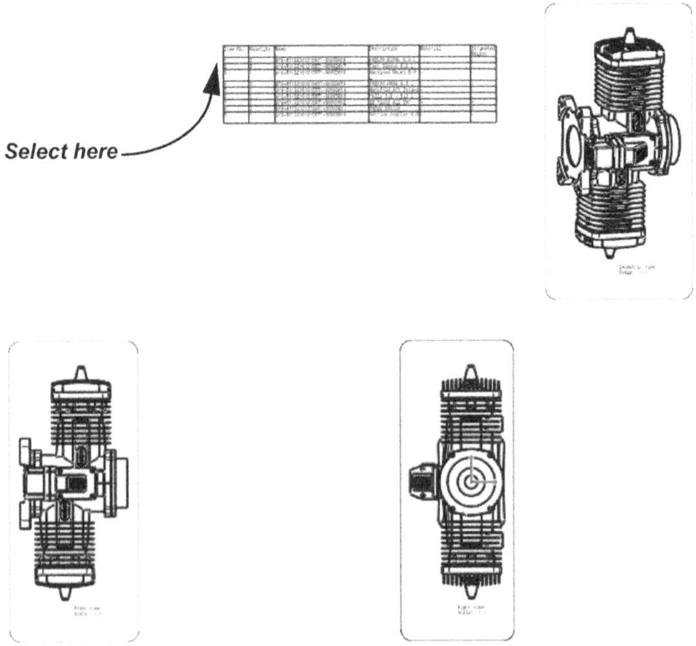

Figure 7–36

5. Right-click on the newly created table and click **Properties**.
6. Select the *Reported Properties* tab.
7. Click on the row with the **Name (PLM ExternalID)** found under the *Property* column, as shown in Figure 7–37.

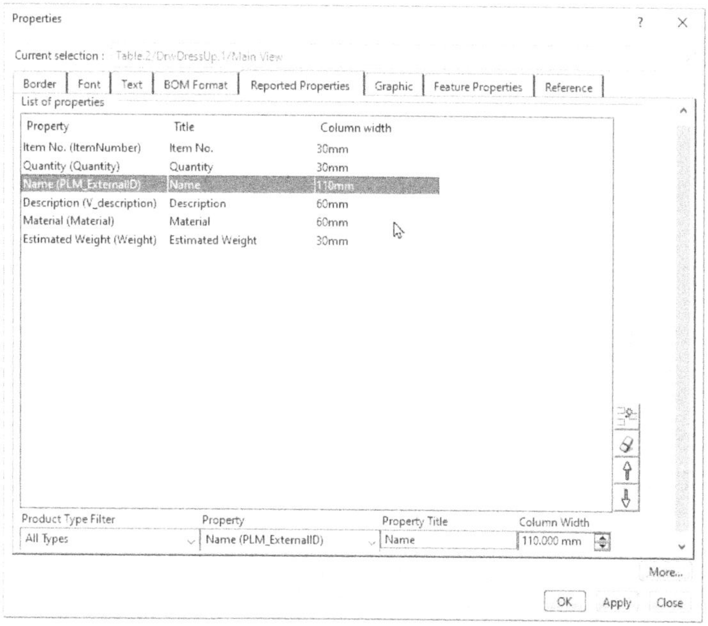

Figure 7–37

8. In the Property drop-down list at the bottom, select **Title (V_Name)**, as shown in Figure 7–38.

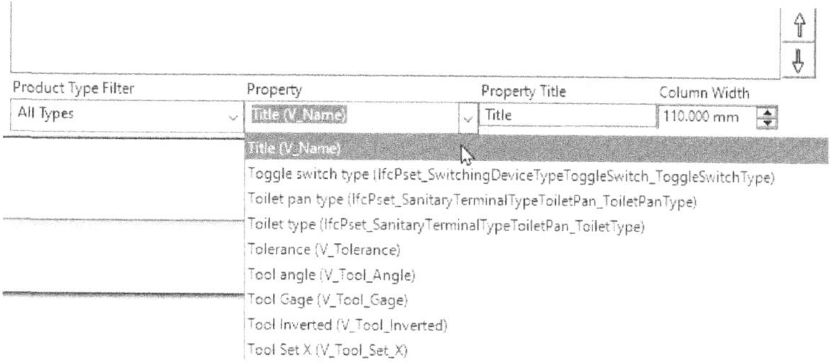

Figure 7–38

9. Click on the **Material (Material)** row and select  (Delete), as shown in Figure 7–39.

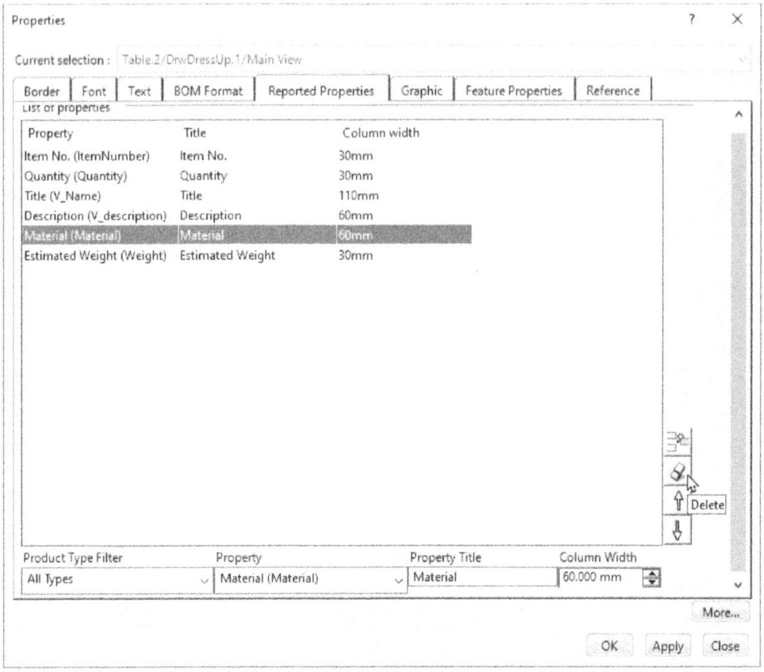

Figure 7–39

10. Repeat the previous step for the **Estimated Weight (Weight)** row. The Properties dialog box should appear as shown in Figure 7–40.

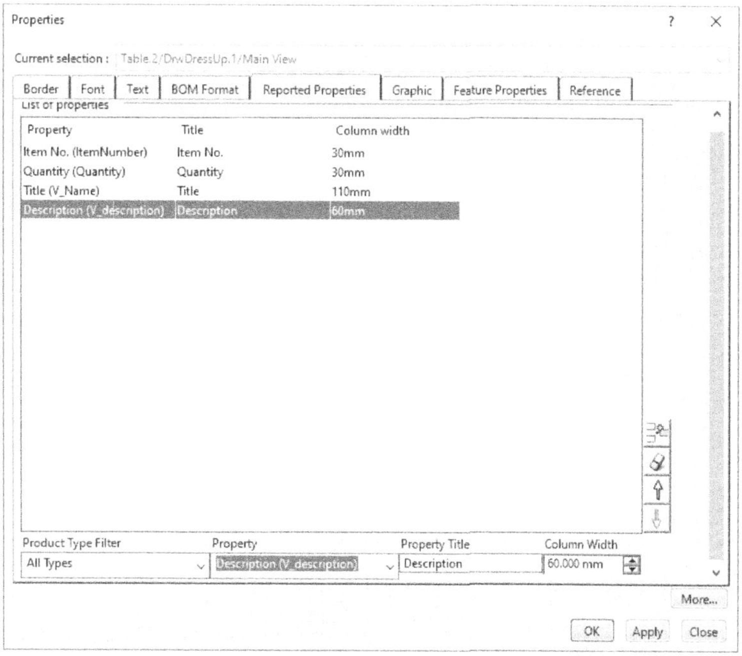

Figure 7–40

11. Change the column width for **Title** to **85mm** and **Description** to **70mm**, as shown in Figure 7–41.

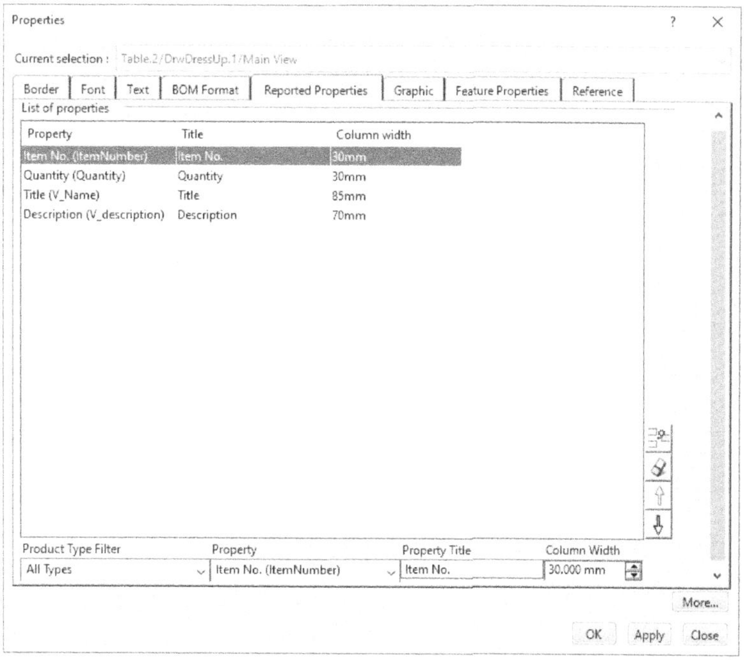

Figure 7–41

12. Click **OK**. The BOM updates, as shown in Figure 7–42.

Item No.	Quantity	Title	Description
1	2	XYZ_BLOCK	Engine Block 6.0 L
2	2	XYZ_SLEEVE	Cast Sleeve 6.0 L
3	1	XYZ_MOUNTING_PLATE	Machined Mount 6.0 L
4	2	XYZ_HEAD	Engine Head 6.0 L
5	1	XYZ_INTAKE_MANIFOLD	Manifold Aft Intake
6	1	XYZ_CARBURETOR	Holly 3.0 - 6.0 L
7	1	XYZ_NAME_PLATE	ID Plate All Ver
8	2	XYZ_SPARK_PLUG	Zappy Device
9	1	XYZ_FORE_AFT_COUPLING	Section Coupler 6.0 L

Figure 7–42

Task 3 - Add balloons to a view.

1. Activate the **Isometric view**.
2. In the expanded Annotation section in the Action Bar, click

    (Automatic Balloons Generation).
3. In the Automatic Ballooning Options dialog box, select the **One for each instance** radial button if not already selected, then click **OK**. The drawing updates, as shown in Figure 7–43.

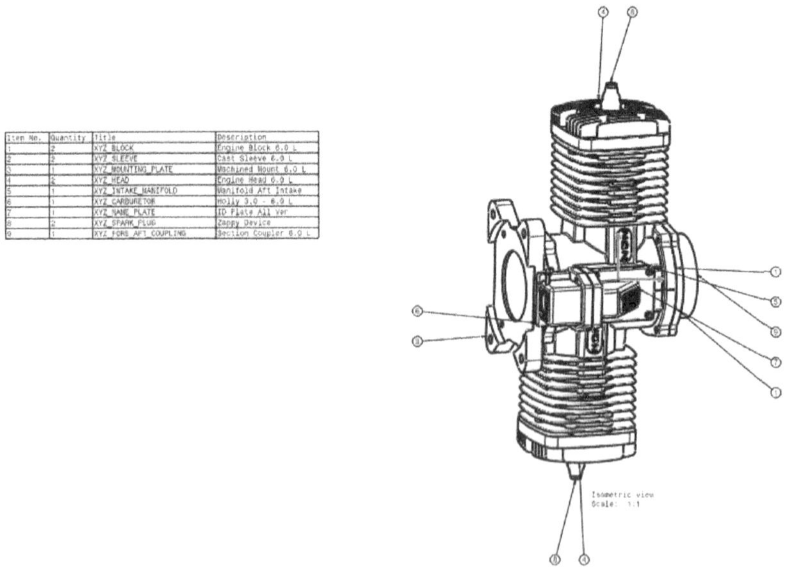

Figure 7–43

4. Zoom in on the Isometric view and rearrange the balloons to make them more visible.

Task 4 - Replace view geometry with a CGR representation.

1. Right-click on **Front view** and select **Properties**.
2. Select the *Generation* tab in the Properties dialog box.
3. In the View generation mode drop-down list, select **CGR**, as shown in Figure 7–44.

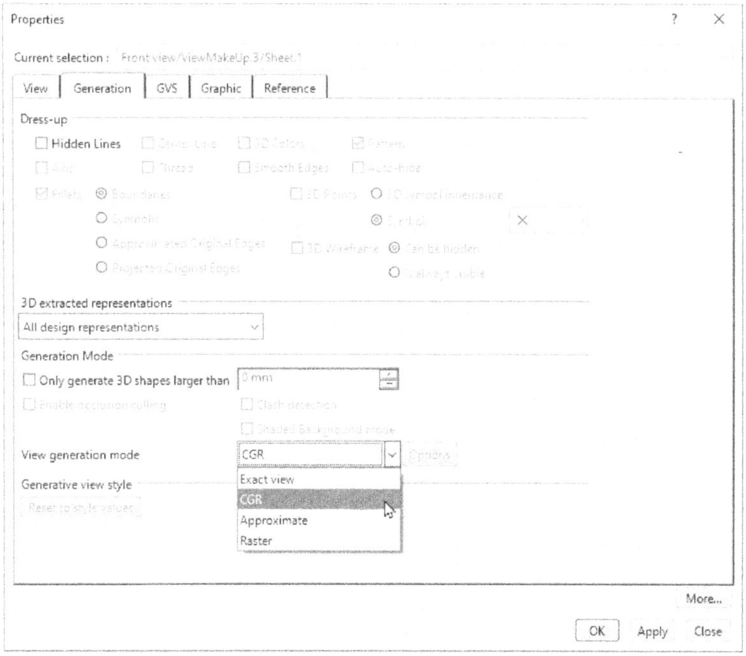

Figure 7–44

4. Click **OK** to close the Properties dialog box.

5. Toggle off the frames of the views by toggling  (Display Frame) from the View section of the Action Bar.

6. Save the drawing. The drawing displays as shown in Figure 7–45.

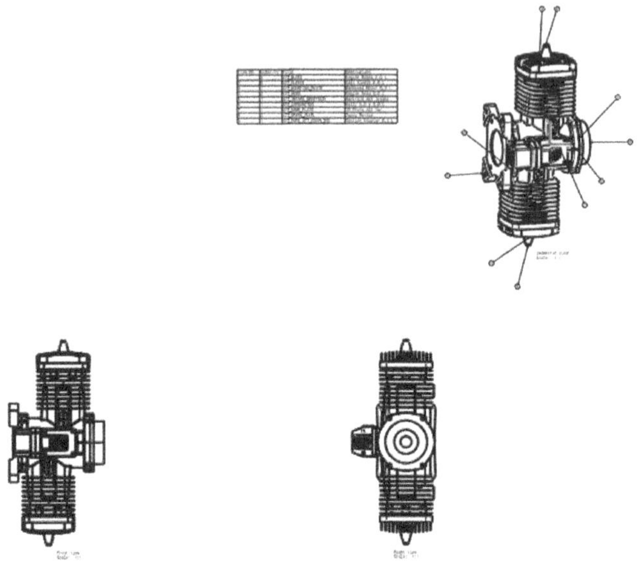

Figure 7–45

7. Close all open tabs.

Practice 7b Drawing Views and Overload Properties

Practice Objectives

- Create a slide of an assembly file.
- Generate a drawing view from a slide view using two different methods.
- Change the overload properties of existing views.

In this practice, you will generate a drawing with views from slides. You will also change the display properties of parts in existing views by defining their Overload Properties. The completed drawing is shown in Figure 7–46.

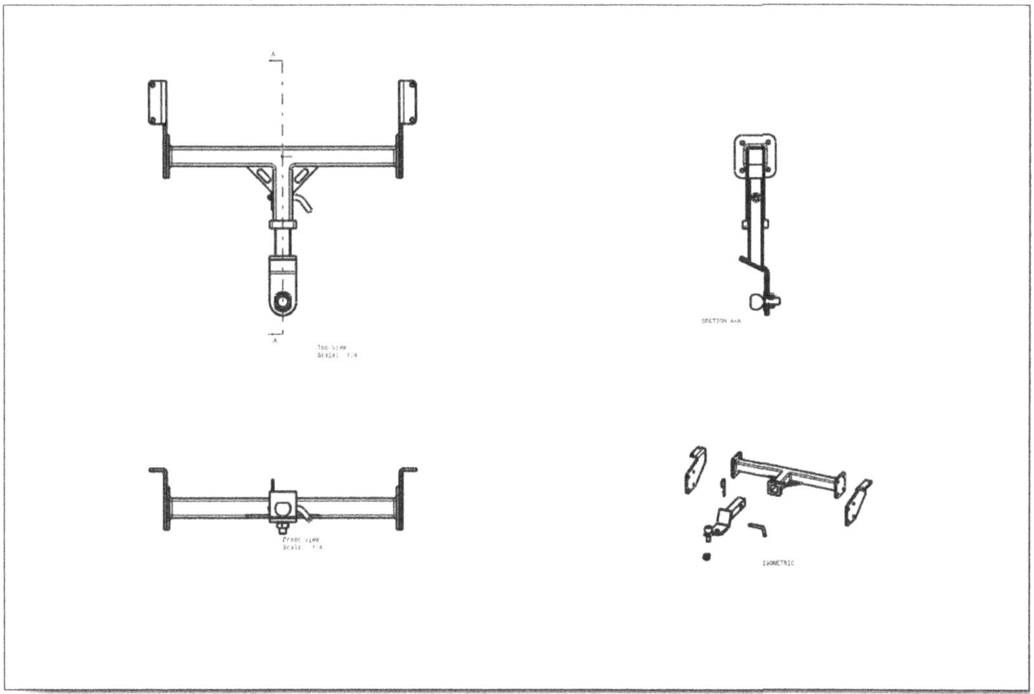

Figure 7–46

Task 1 - Create a Markup in the assembly and switch to the Design Review app.

1. Import and open **Hitch_7B.3dxml** from the practice files folder. While importing, set the *Duplication string* to **###_** where ### represents your initials.

2. Right-click on the top level of the specification tree and select **Insert>Markup**.
3. In the Product Markup dialog box, enter **###_Markup_7B** as the *Title* where ### represents your initials.
4. Click **OK**.
5. Click on the outer ring of the Compass.
6. In the *Search* area, type **review**, as shown in Figure 7–47.

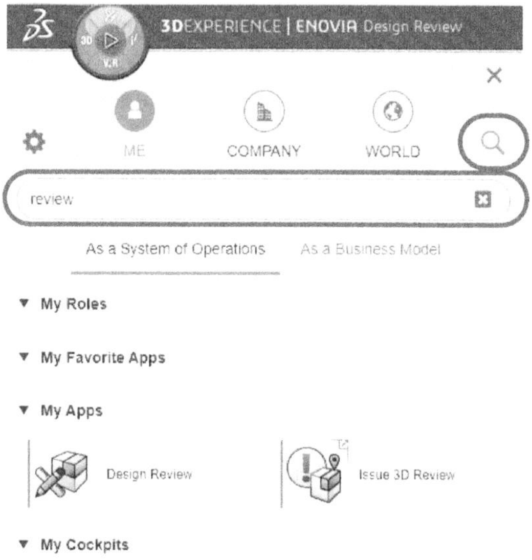

Figure 7–47

7. In the *My Apps* area, click **Design Review**, as shown in Figure 7–48.

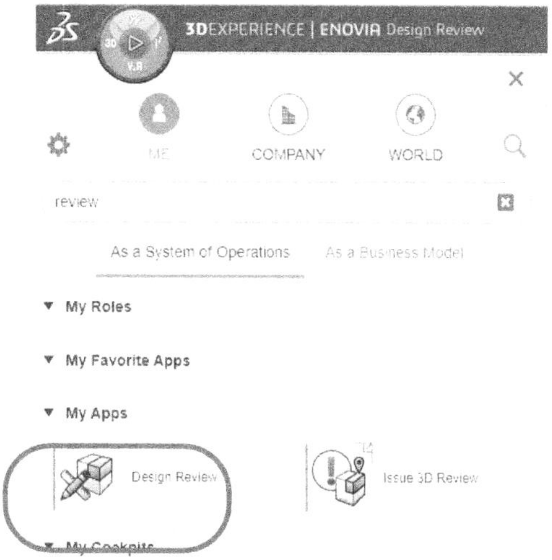

Figure 7–48

Task 2 - Create slides in the Markup.

1. In the Review section of the Action Bar, click (Slide) to create a new slide.

2. In the specification tree, expand the slide branch under the Markup, as shown in Figure 7–49.

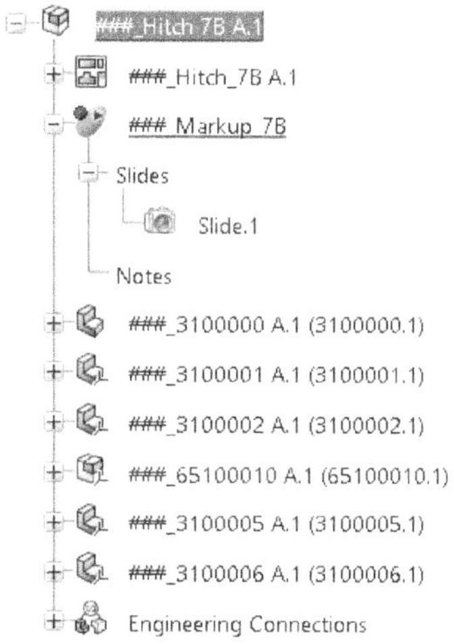

Figure 7–49

3. Right-click on **Slide.1** and select **Properties**.
4. Click on the *Feature Properties* tab and enter **All** as the *Feature Name*. Click **OK**.
5. Repeat Steps 1 to 4 to create a second slide and enter **Explode_7B** as the *Feature Name*.
6. Double-click the **Explode-7B** slide in the specification tree.
7. In the expanded Review section of the Action Bar, click (Explode).
8. Select the **###_Hitch_7B A.1** product from the top of the specification tree.
9. Click **OK** in the Explode dialog box.
10. Right-click on **Explode_7B** in the specification tree and select **Update Slide**.
11. Double-click the **All** slide in the tree to return the assembly to its unexploded state.

Task 3 - Create a view in the drawing referencing a slide.

1. Open the **###_Hitch_7B** drawing in New App by right-clicking on it from the tree and selecting *** object>Open in New App**, as shown in Figure 7–50.

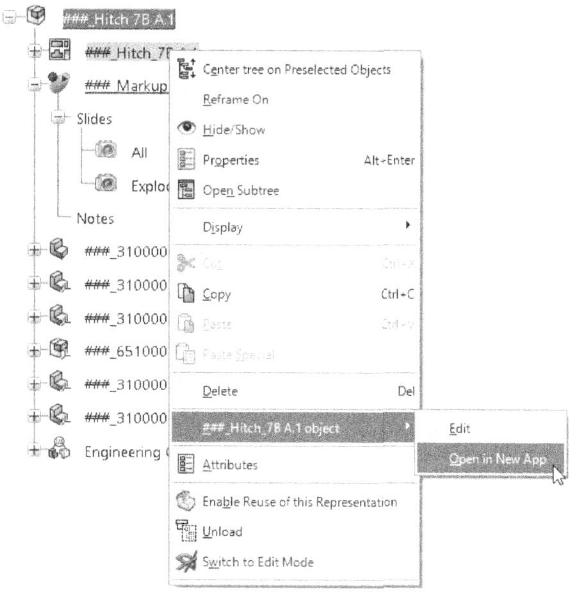

Figure 7–50

2. If available, click  (Update current sheet) from the Standard section of the Action Bar. It will be grayed out if everything is updated.

3. In the View Layout section of the Action Bar, click  (Isometric).

4. Activate the widget with the **###_Hitch_7B** product.

5. In the specification tree, click the **Explode_7B** slide.

6. Click anywhere on the geometry of the assembly. The widget with the drawing automatically activates.

7. Click anywhere on the drawing to complete the exploded Isometric view. The drawing updates, as shown in Figure 7–51.

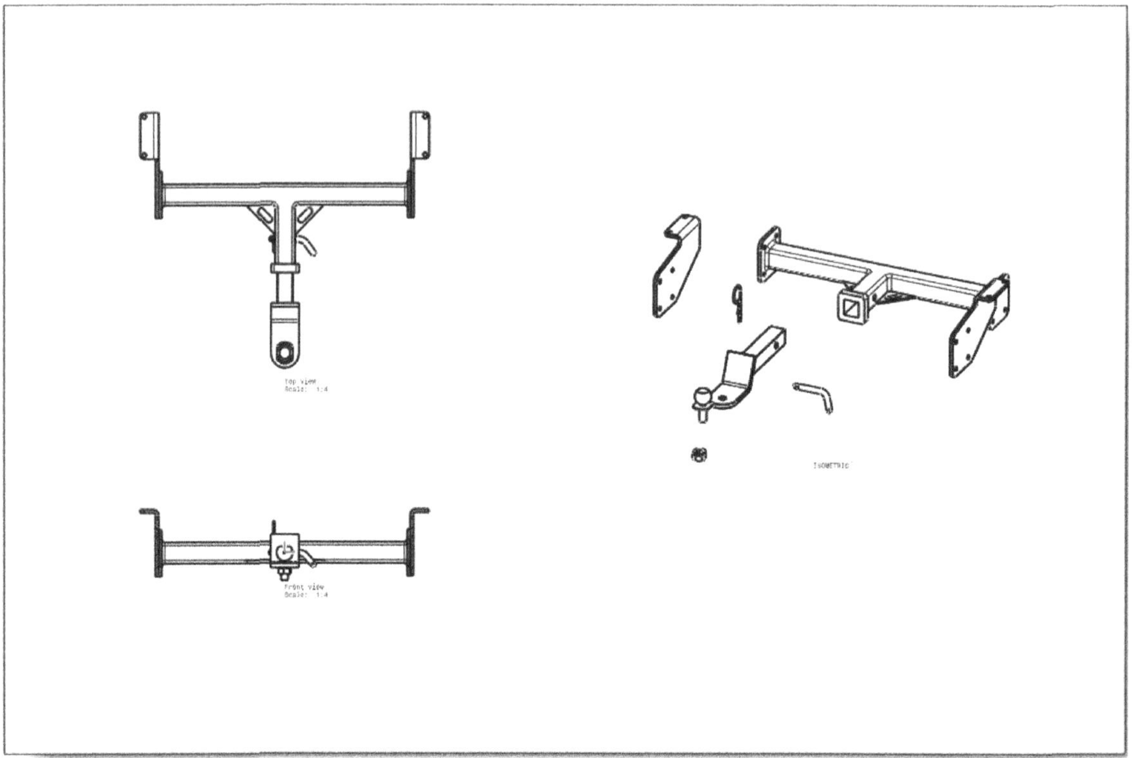

Figure 7–51

Task 4 - Edit a slide and update the drawing.

1. Activate the widget with the **###_Hitch_7B** product.
2. Double-click the **Explode_7B** slide in the specification tree.
3. Click on the white sphere at the center of the Robot and drag the Robot on to the Right Brace, as shown in Figure 7–52.

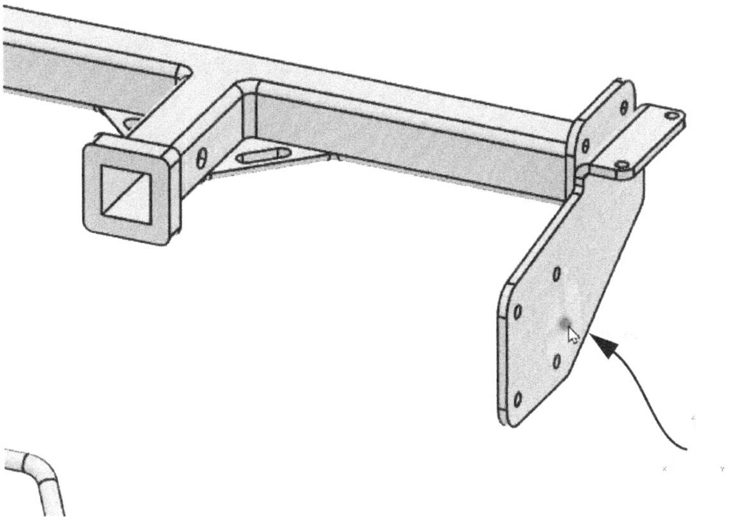

Figure 7–52

4. Using the W|Y axis of the Robot, drag the Right Brace to a similar position to that shown in Figure 7–53.

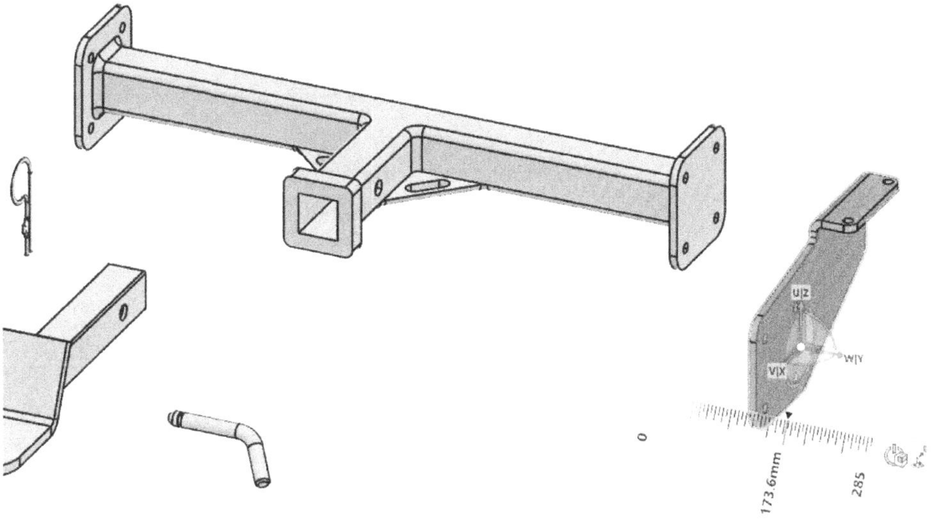

Figure 7–53

5. Click on the sphere at the center of the Robot and drag the Robot off the Right Brace component.

6. In the tree, right-click on the **Explode_7B** slide and select **Update Slide**.

7. Activate the widget with the drawing.

8. Click  (Update current sheet). The drawing updates, as shown in Figure 7–54.

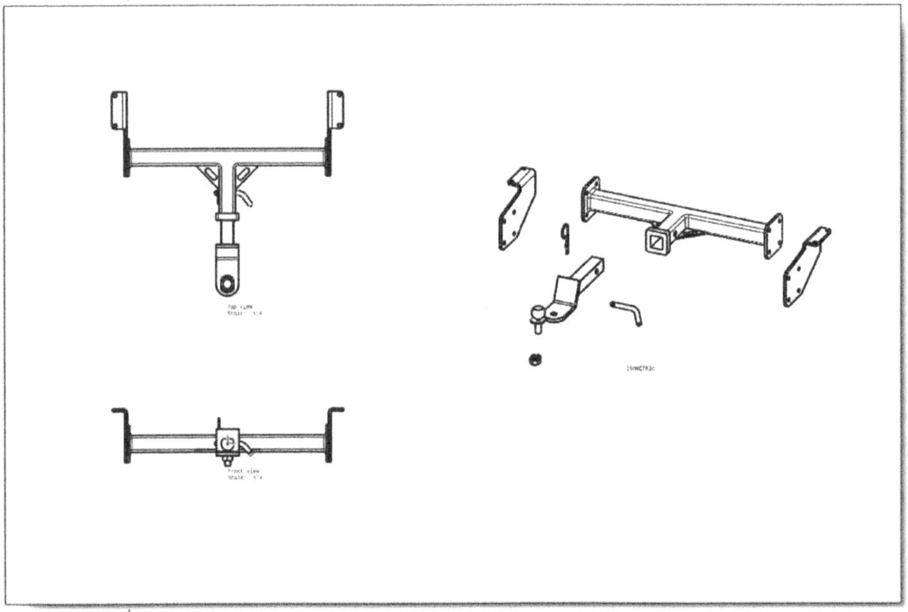

Figure 7–54

9. (Optional) You can use the Robot in the product to move other components and update the **Explode_7B** slide again. Activate and update the drawing to see these changes in the exploded view.

Task 5 - Update a view using Overload Properties.

1. Modify the view properties to change the scale of the exploded Isometric view to **1:8** and move as shown in Figure 7–55.

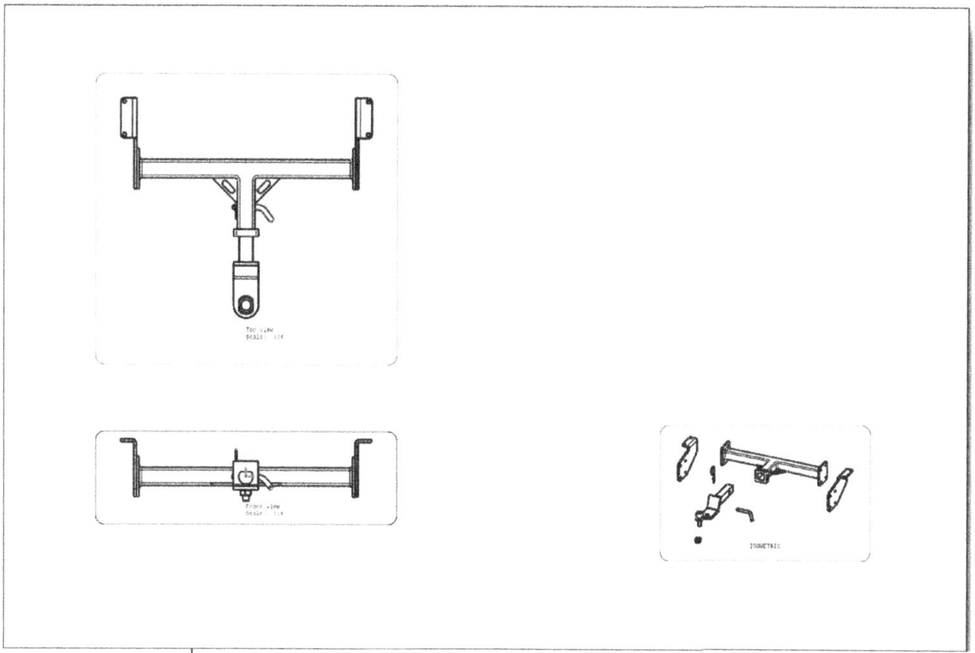

Figure 7–55

2. Double-click the Top view to activate it. Create an offset section view through the middle of the Top view, as shown in Figure 7–56.

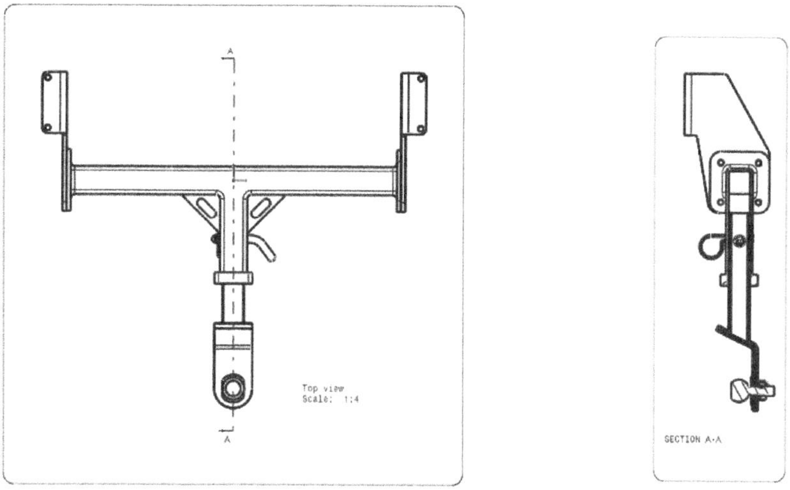

Figure 7–56

3. Zoom in on the Section A-A view. In the specification tree, right-click on the **Section A-A view** and select **SECTION A-A object>Overload Properties**, as shown in Figure 7–57.

Figure 7–57

4. Select the pin retaining clip (3100006.1), as shown in Figure 7–58.

Figure 7–58

5. In the Overload Properties dialog box, select  (Click to put the element in no show), as shown in Figure 7–59.

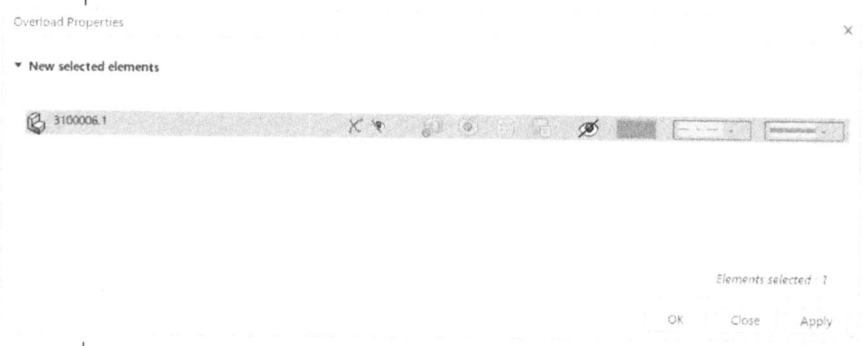

Figure 7–59

6. Click **Apply** and the Section A-A view updates, as shown in Figure 7–60.

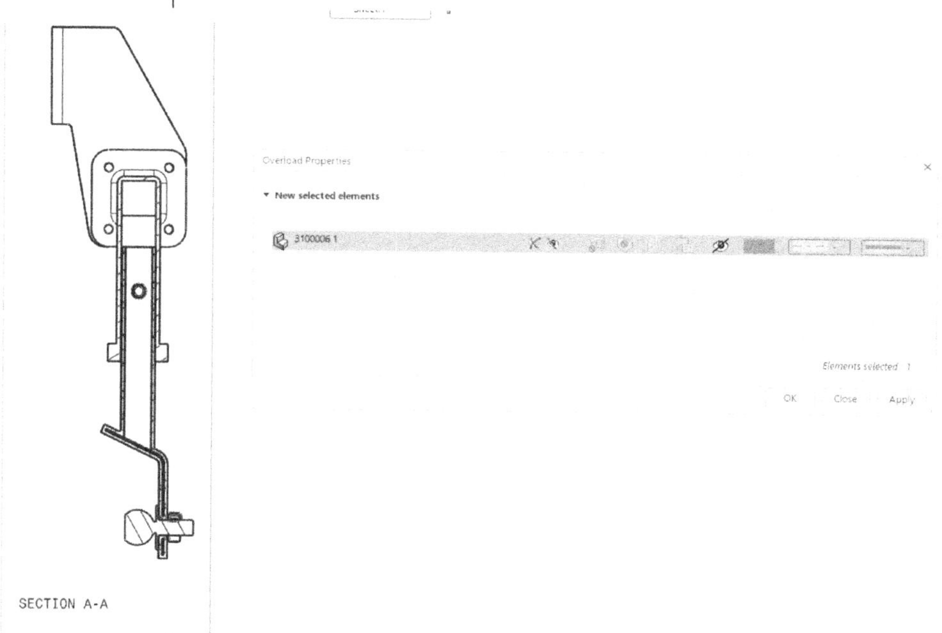

Figure 7–60

7. Repeat Steps 4 to 6 to put the Right Brace (310001.1) in no show as well.

8. Select the Ball Component (3100004.1) and click  (Click to activate the Uncut property).

9. Click **Apply**. The Overload Properties dialog box and Section A-A view update, as shown in Figure 7–61.

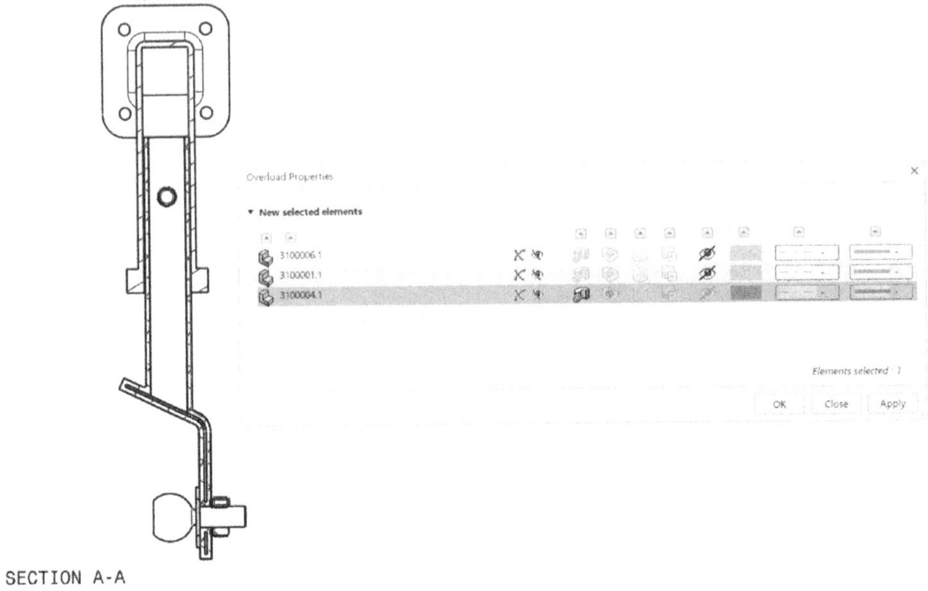

Figure 7–61

10. Select **OK** in the Overload Properties dialog box.

11. Save and close all widgets.

Practice 7c

Wine Opener

Practice Objectives

- Use Modify Links to control component display.
- Superpose two views.
- Use the **Area Fill** tool.

In this practice, you will create drawing views for the upper and lower limits of the wine opener. To accomplish this, you will create views using markup slides. The slides have been created for you. Drawing views will then be superposed on top of one another. You will also use the **Modify Links** tool to remove components from an isometric view. The completed drawing is shown in Figure 7–62.

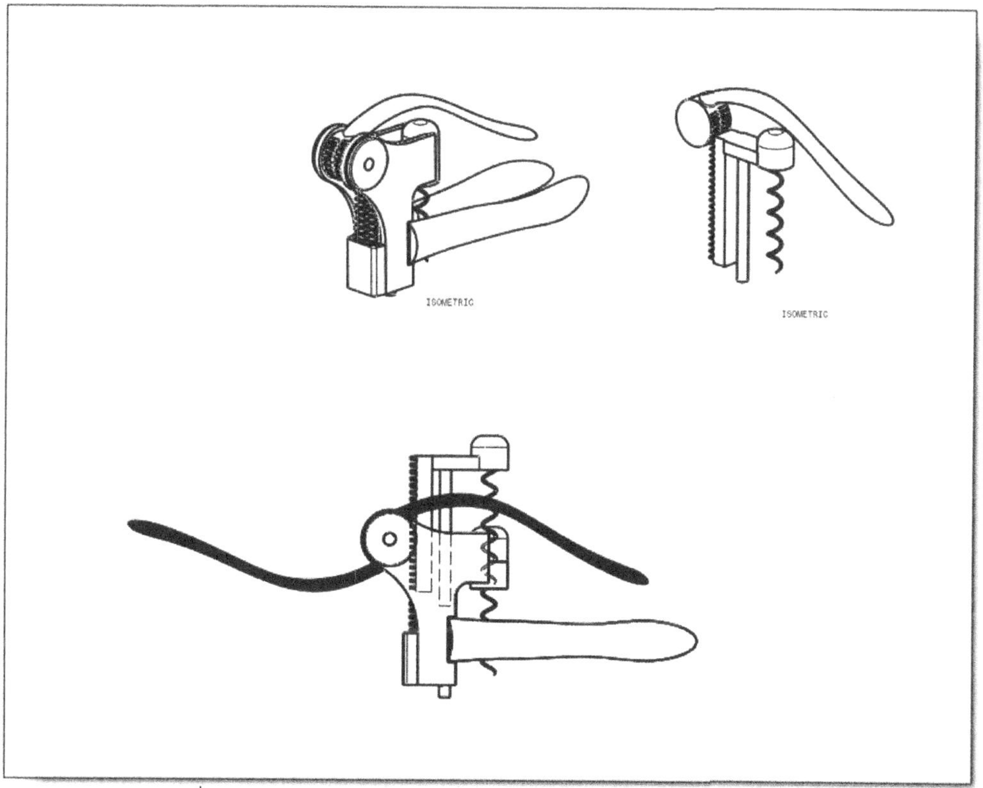

Figure 7–62

Task 1 - Open an assembly model and create a new drawing.

1. Import and open **Cork_Screw_7C.3dxml** from the practice files folder. While importing, set the *Duplication string* to **###_** where ### represents your initials.
2. Create a drawing using **ANSI-ASME** for the *Standard* and **C ANSI** for the *Sheet Style*. Enter **###_Cork_Screw_7C** as the *Title*.

Task 2 - Create two isometric views.

1. Place two isometric views, as shown in Figure 7–63. Ensure that you rotate the product to the correct orientation before selecting it to place the views.

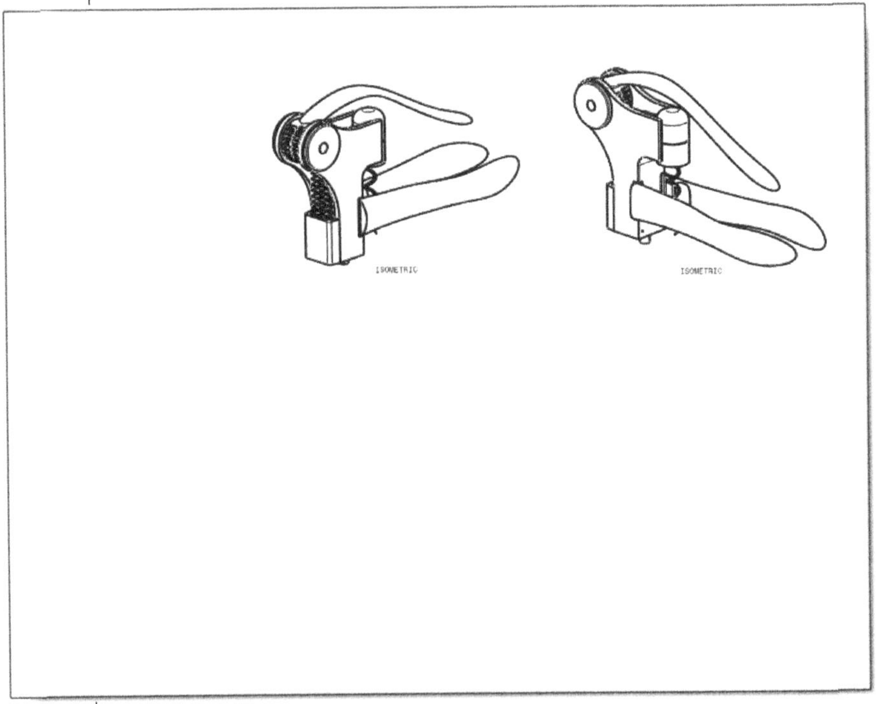

Figure 7–63

2. Right-click on the isometric view on the right side of the sheet and select **Isometric object>Modify Links**.
3. Switch to the product window. In the specification tree, press and hold <Ctrl>, then select **Pinion Handle** and **Rack Corkscrew**.
4. Return to the drawing window.

5. In the Link Modification dialog box, click the icon next to each component. There are three images that you can use here. The Link Modification dialog box updates, as shown in Figure 7–64.

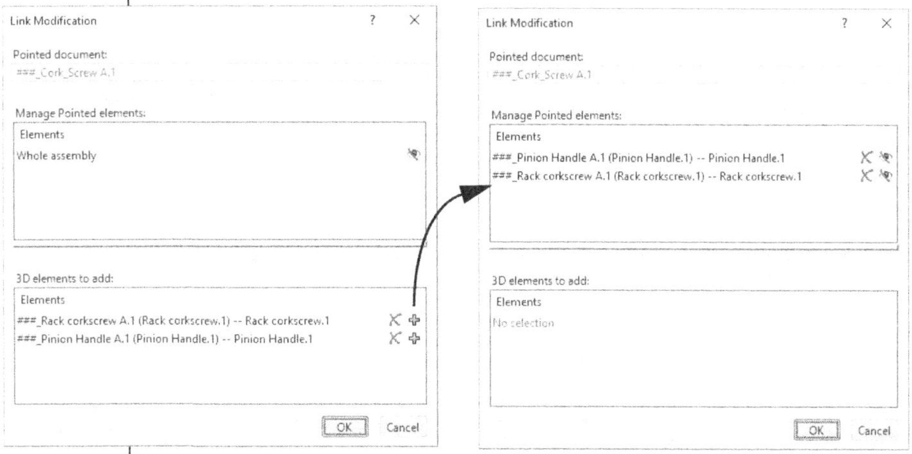

Figure 7–64

6. In the Link Modification dialog box, click **OK**.

7. Update the drawing view. The Isometric view displays as shown in Figure 7–65.

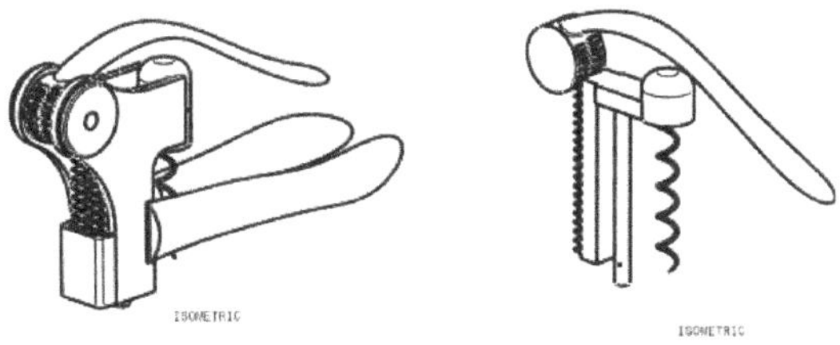

Figure 7–65

Task 3 - Create view from slides.

1. Click (Front View) from the View Layout section of the Action Bar.

2. Activate the widget with the assembly. In the *###_Cork_Screw_7C* markup, select the **Slides** node, then select the **Upper Lim** slide.

3. Select an appropriate planar surface on the model and place the view.

4. Create a second front view using the **Lower Lim** slide.

5. Position the two front views as shown in Figure 7–66.

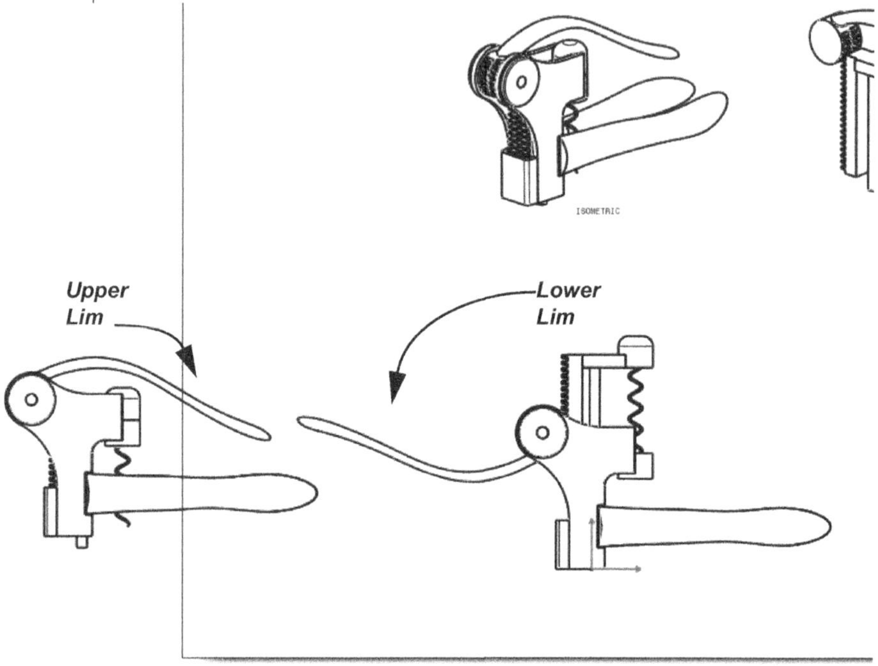

Figure 7–66

6. Right-click on the front view on the left side (Upper Lim) and select **View Positioning>Superpose**.

7. Select the front view on the right side. The two views immediately become superposed on the origin of the second view, as shown in Figure 7–67.

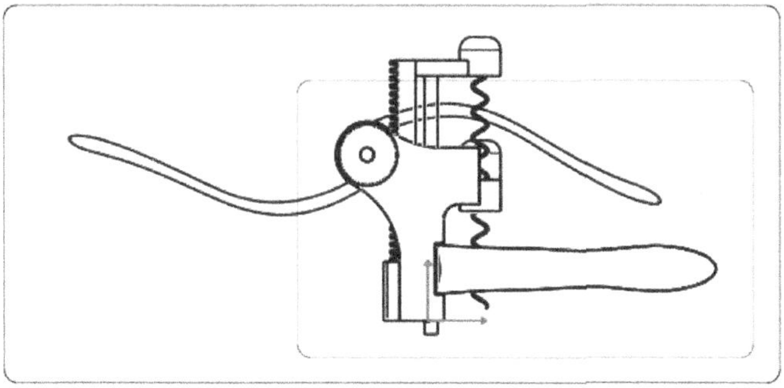

Figure 7–67

Task 4 - Change the overload properties of an existing view.

1. Using the Overload Properties, change the **Rack Corkscrew** display to  (Activate Hidden Lines), as shown in Figure 7–68.

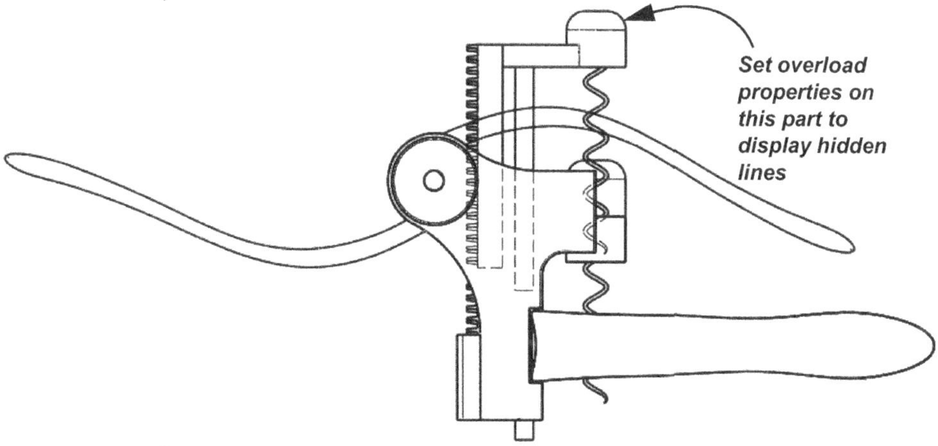

Figure 7–68

Task 5 - Add dress-up elements

1. In the Annotation section of the Action Bar, click (Area Fill) to place a fill on the parts shown in Figure 7–69.

2. Change the properties of the fill *Type* from hatching to **Coloring** and set the color to **Black**.

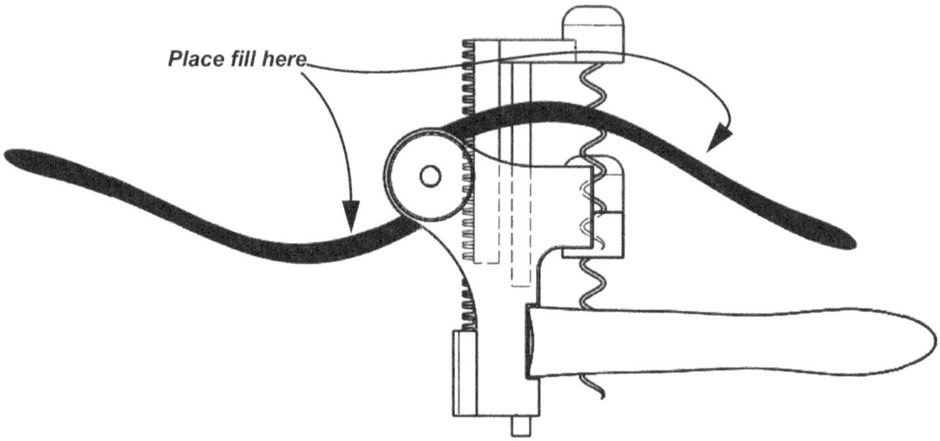

Figure 7–69

3. Update all of the views in the drawing.

4. Save and close all tabs.

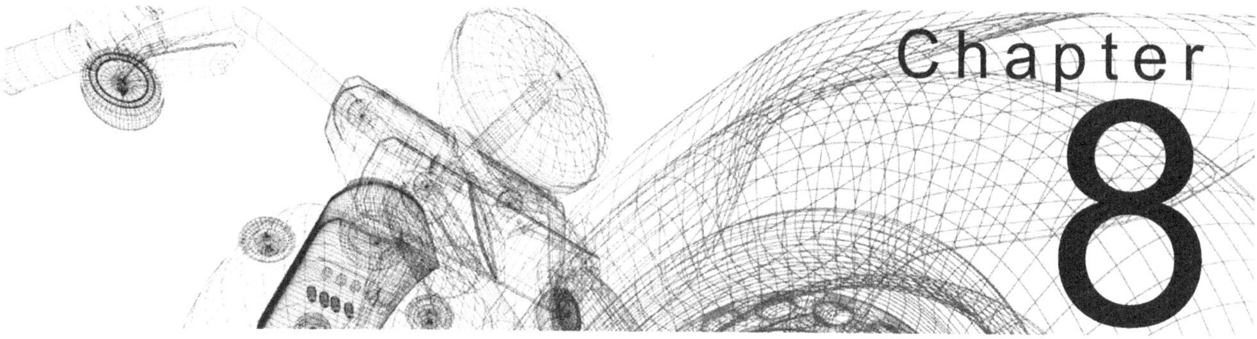

Chapter 8

Complete the Drawing

Once all of the manufacturing information has been added to a drawing, general information and borders can be added by inserting a frame and title block.

Learning Objectives in This Chapter

- Create 2D frame and title block.
- Insert a frame and title block.
- Insert a background view.
- Print a drawing.
- Import and export 2D data.
- Insert an image.
- Understand large drawing management techniques.

8.1 Frame and Title Block

You can use three methods to add a title block to a drafting sheet:

- Insert a frame and title block created completely by VBScript.
- Create a frame and title block from 2D geometry creation tools.
- Instantiate a frame and/or title block individually into a new drawing using a hybrid method. This is done using a VBScript to reference other drawings or default standards and place them into a new drawing.

Insert Frame and Title Block

A frame and title block can be created using the VBScript functionality. A frame and title block created in this way can be saved into a title block directory. The standard installation of CATIA includes example frame and title blocks located at **<installdirectory>\<current_release>\win_b64\win_b64\VBScript\FrameTitleBlock**. Obtain the location of your company's custom frame and title block directory from your CATIA system administrator. The user can customize the location of their frame and title block directory by going to **Me>Preferences>App Preferences>3D Modeling>Mechanical Systems>Drafting>Administration** and then enter the desired path in the *Page Setup Directory*, as shown in Figure 8–1.

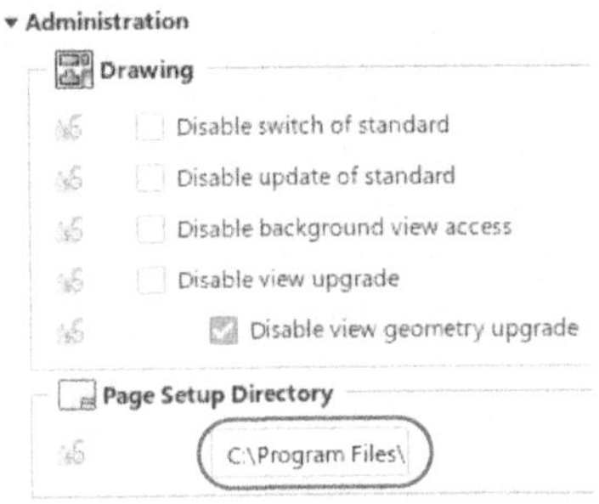

Figure 8–1

2D Drafting Functionality

2D drafting tools can be used to create a frame and title block geometry and text.

Hybrid Method

This approach starts by using the VBScript functionality described for Insert Frame and Title Block. However, instead of geometry being created by just using the scripting language, the user is able to reference other drawings as templates that already have frames and/or title blocks. These template drawings normally would have been created using 2D Functionality and specific naming conventions. These frames and title blocks can be added, removed, updated, and replaced as needed. Because of the way the frame and title blocks are driven by other drawings, different configurations can be obtained by mixing and matching template drawings.

8.2 Create 2D Frame and Title Block

General Steps

Use the following general steps to create 2D frame and title block geometry:

1. Create a new drawing.
2. Define frame and title block.
3. Save the drawing.
4. (Optional) Reuse the sheet template.

Step 1 - Create a new drawing.

Create a drawing using the required *Standard* and *Sheet Style*, as shown in Figure 8–2.

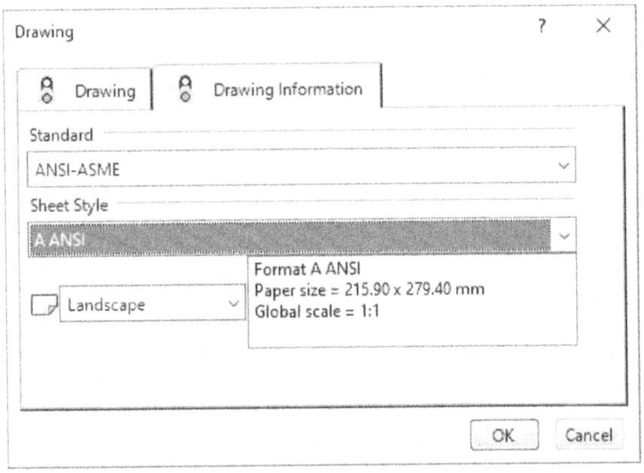

Figure 8–2

Step 2 - Define frame and title block.

Right-click on the sheet name (**Sheet.1**) in the specification tree and select **Edit Background**. This will change the background color of the sheet to gray instead of standard white. In this mode, the Action Bar options change, and anything built will be in a separate layer from the Working Views mode.

Use the tools in the Sketch section of the Action Bar, as shown in Figure 8–3, to create frame geometry.

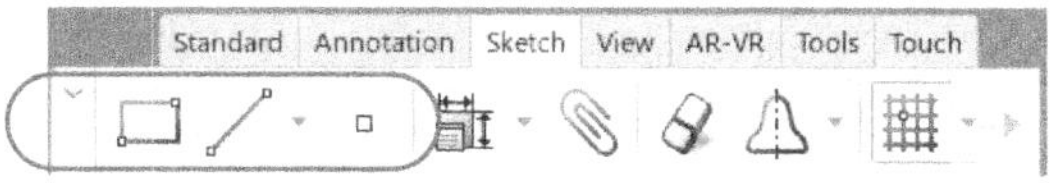

Figure 8–3

Figure 8–4 shows an example of a sketched frame.

You can use the grid with the (Snap to point) option to aid in frame creation.

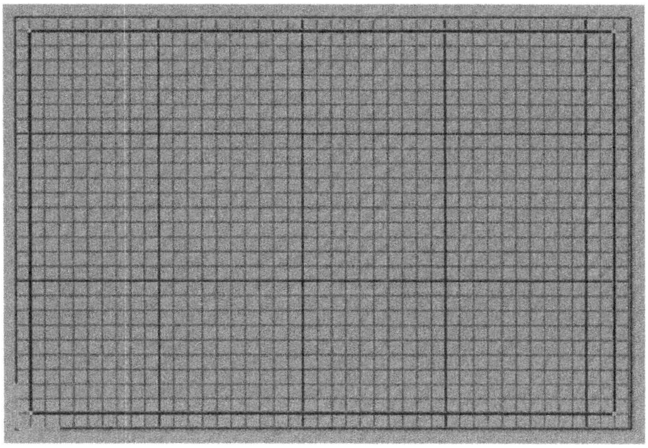

Figure 8–4

You can sketch tables using geometry creation tools or by clicking (Table). An example of a table with text is shown in Figure 8–5.

	By	Date
Drawn		
Checker		
Designer		
Approved		

Figure 8–5

When finished, you can exit the Background mode by selecting (Working Views) from the Standard section of the Action Bar. The sheet color will return to white.

Step 3 - Save the drawing.

Save the drawing into the 3DEXPERIENCE database.

Step 4 - (Optional) Reuse the sheet template.

The 2D frame and title block drawing file can be used as a template for future drawing files. You can easily reference existing drawings as templates that have been saved into the 3DEXPERIENCE database and import their frame, title block, and revision table into new drawings as long as you follow the requirements listed below. Start by opening the template, creating drawing views, and saving the completed drawing as a new file.

Reusing a Frame

The only requirement for reusing a frame in a template is that all frame geometry and text must be placed on the sheet background. Anything on the background layer will be duplicated into the new drawing.

Reusing a Title Block

To create a title block that can be reused in a template, start by creating a table. Right-click on the table, then select **Properties>Feature Properties**. In the *Feature Name* field, enter the desired name with the prefix of **TitleBlock_** (e.g., **TitleBlock_Rand3D**).

Reusing a Revision Table

The requirement for creating a revision table that can be reused in a template is similar to creating a title block. Start by creating a table, then right-click on the table and select **Properties>Feature Properties**. In the *Feature Name* field, enter the desired name with the prefix of **RevisionTable_** (e.g., **RevisionTable_Rand3D**).

These drawing objects need to be saved in the drawing they were created in so that the drawing can be used later on as a template when defining the page layout. If objects are not created on the sheet background or not named correctly, they will not work correctly in the Page Layout window.

8.3 Insert a Frame and Title Block with VBScript

Customizing the example frame and title block macro files using Visual Basic Script is discussed in detail in Appendix A.

The standard CATIA installation contains several examples of frame and title block styles. The frame and title block geometry is drawn automatically by macro scripts. These macros also provide actions to customize and maintain the sheet background.

General Steps

Use the following general steps to insert and modify a frame and title block:

1. Create a frame and title block.
2. Add review and revision information.
3. Modify the title block (as required).

Step 1 - Create a frame and title block.

To add a frame and title block from the VBScript examples, you will want to use (Page Layout). This can be found either in the View Layout section of the Action Bar if you are in Working View mode or in the Annotation section if in Edit Background mode.

In the Page Layout dialog box (shown in Figure 8–6), select the required title block in the Dress-up drop-down list. Ensure that **Create** is selected in the list for Frame And Title Block. Click **Apply** to create the frame and title block.

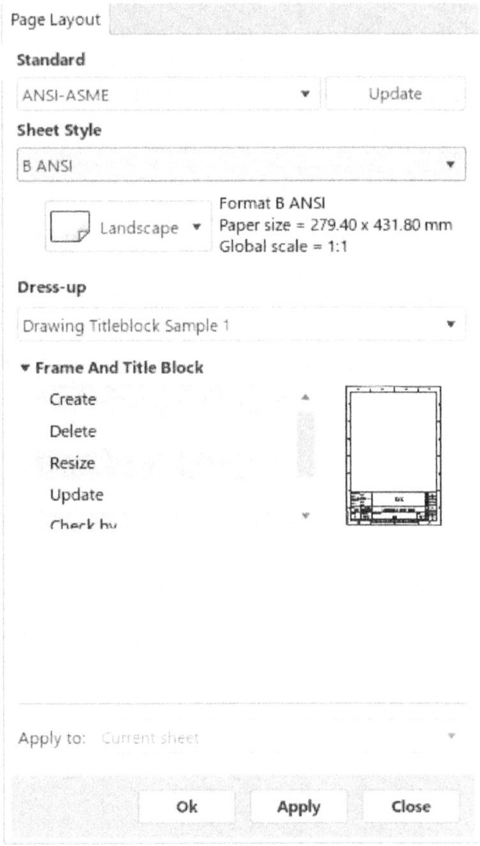

Figure 8–6

Step 2 - Add review and revision information.

Checked By

Select the **Check by** option and click **Apply**. The Controller's name text input box opens, as shown in Figure 8–7.

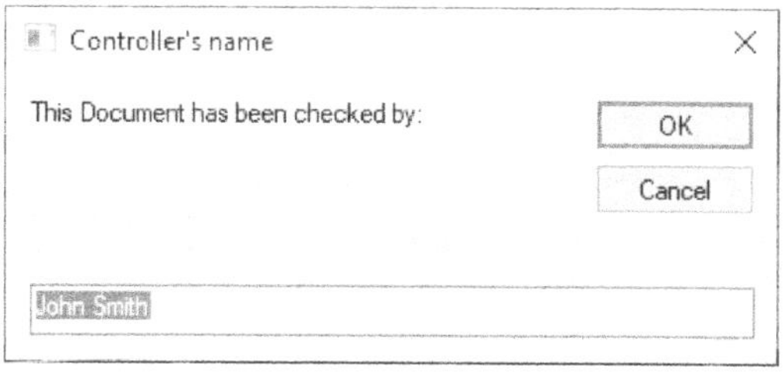

Figure 8–7

Enter the name of the controller and click **OK**. The controller's name and verification date sections of the title block update automatically, as shown in Figure 8–8.

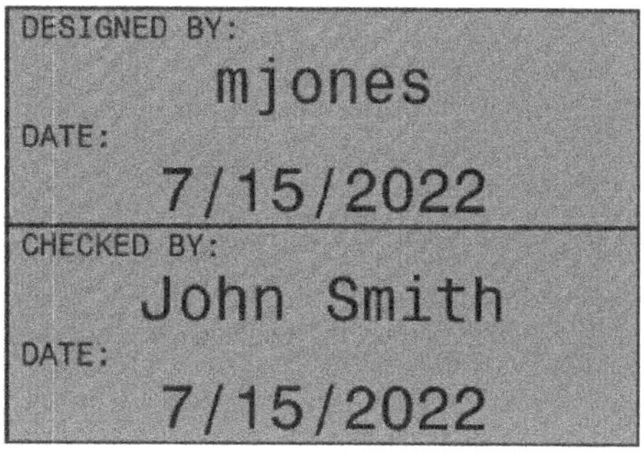

Figure 8–8

Add Revision Block

To add revision information, select the **Add a revision block** action and click **Apply**. The Reviewer's name text input box opens, as shown in Figure 8–9. Enter the name of the reviewer and click **OK**.

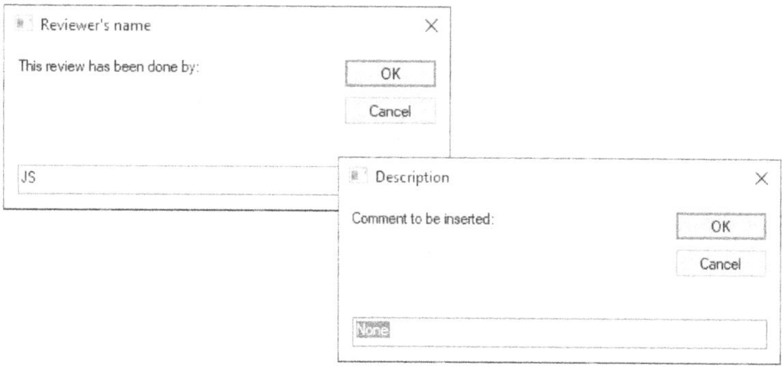

Figure 8–9

The Description dialog box opens next, as shown above in Figure 8–9. Enter a comment (optional) and click **OK**. The completed revision block displays as shown in Figure 8–10.

REV	DATE	DESCRIPTION	INIT
A	7/15/2022	None	JS

Figure 8–10

Step 3 - Modify the title block (as required).

Once a title block has been added to a drawing, you might need to modify it based on changes to the drawing. The following operations can be performed using the Page Layout dialog box:

- Resize the title block
- Update the title block
- Delete the title block

Resize the Title Block

Frame and title block positioning and rulers do not update automatically when the sheet style is changed, as shown in Figure 8–11.

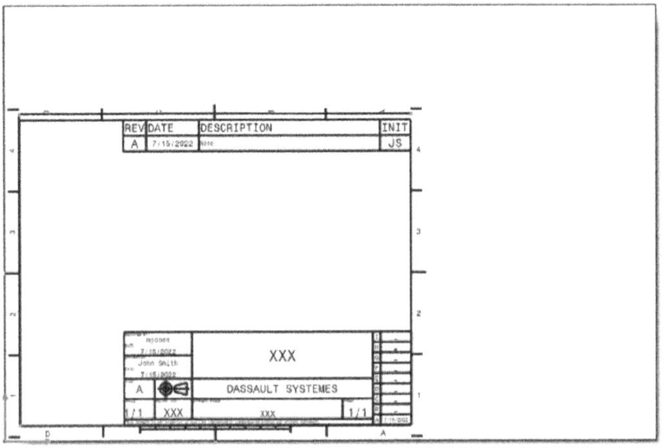

Figure 8–11

To update a frame and title block to fit the new sheet format, select **Resize** in the list of actions and click **Apply**. The background is automatically fitted to the new sheet format, as shown in Figure 8–12.

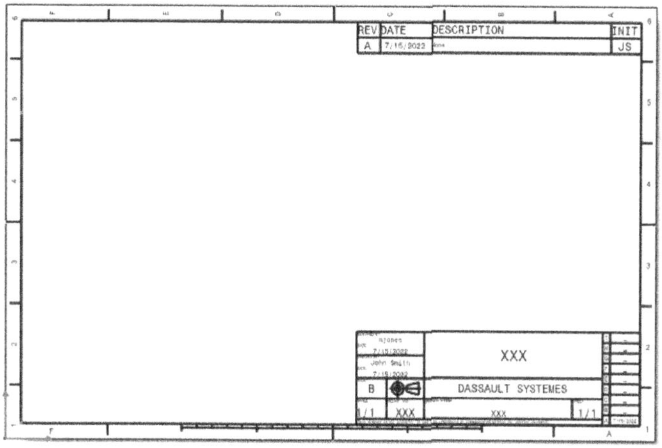

Figure 8–12

Delete the Title Block

To replace the current background style, the original frame and title block must be deleted.

Select the current background style in the Dress-up drop-down list. Select **Delete** in the list of actions and click **Apply**.

8.4 Insert a Frame and Title Block Using Templates

The Page Layout dialog box can be used to resize an existing drawing sheet. It can also be used to insert a drawing of a frame and title block into the background view.

General Steps

Use the following general steps to insert a sketched frame and title block:

1. Open a drawing file.
2. Activate **Page Layout**.
3. Insert a frame from a template.
4. Insert a title block from a template.

Step 1 - Open a drawing file.

Open the drawing to add a sketched title block.

Step 2 - Activate Page Layout.

Select (Page Layout). The Page Layout dialog box opens, as shown in Figure 8–13.

Figure 8–13

To change the sheet size or drawing standard, select new options in the Standard and Sheet Style drop-down lists and click **OK**.

Step 3 - Insert a frame from a template.

From the Dress-up drop-down list, select **Dress-up DS 1**. This VBScript changes the Page Layout dialog box to include a *Frame*, *Title Block*, and *Revision Table* category, as shown in Figure 8–14.

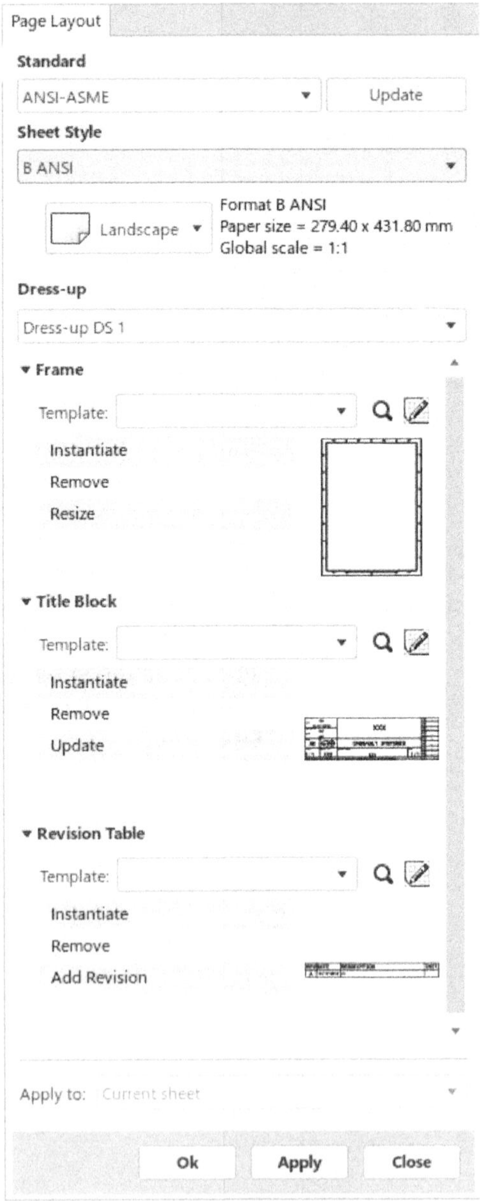

Figure 8–14

Select (Search for existing template) under the *Frame* category. This will allow you to search and select other drawings from the database in an attempt to duplicate what exists on their background layer. The name of the selected drawing will be placed into the Template drop-down list.

Click on **Instantiate** in the *Frame* area, then select **Apply**. The frame is drawn onto the background of the new drawing, as shown in Figure 8–15.

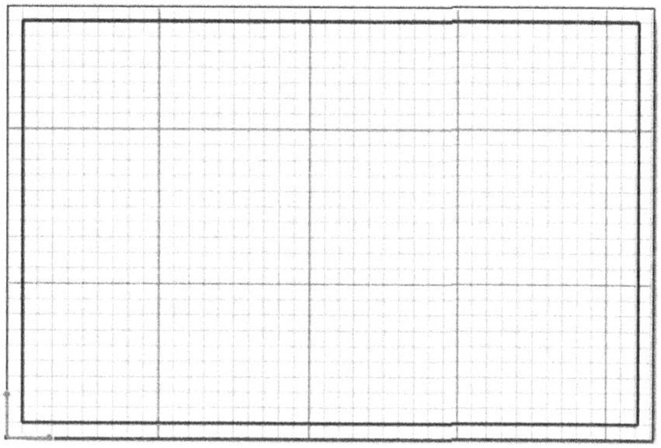

Figure 8–15

Alternatively, (Instantiate a default template) can be used instead of searching for a template. Once selected, a default template is immediately drawn into the background, as shown in Figure 8–16.

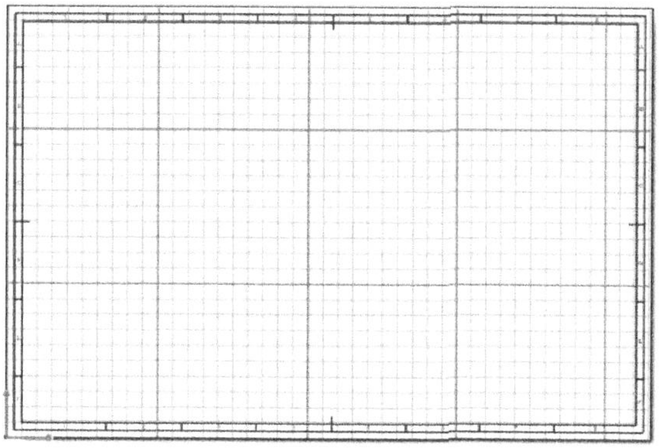

Figure 8–16

Settings

Select **Me>Preferences>App Preferences>3D Modeling>Mechanical Systems>Drafting** and select the *General* section to display the options that control sheet creation.

If the **Copy sheet background from first sheet** option has been enabled, any new sheets that are created duplicate the display of the background of the first sheet, as shown in Figure 8–17.

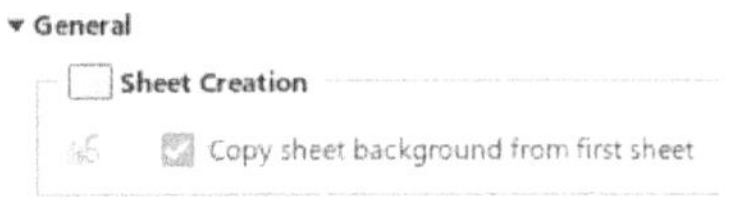

Figure 8–17

If you navigate to the *Drawing* section of the same preferences window, you can customize the list of drawings that are used as templates for *Frame*, *Title block*, and *Revision table*, as shown in Figure 8–18. These drawing templates can be inserted or removed from their respective drop-down lists in the Page Layout dialog box.

Figure 8–18

Step 4 - Insert a title block from a template.

Select (Page Layout) to open the Page Layout dialog box if it is not already open.

From the Dress-up drop-down list, ensure **Dress-up DS 1** is chosen. The page layout will have a *Title Block* category, as shown in Figure 8–19.

Figure 8–19

Select (Search for existing template) under the *Title Block* category. This will allow you to search for and select other drawings from the database in an attempt to duplicate their title block. The name of the selected drawing will be placed into the Template drop-down list.

Note: For a title block to be usable as a template, the *Feature Name* of the table needs to start with the prefix **Titleblock_**, otherwise nothing will be instantiated**.**

Click on **Instantiate** in the *Title Block* area, then select **Apply**. The title block is drawn onto the background of the new drawing, as shown in Figure 8–20.

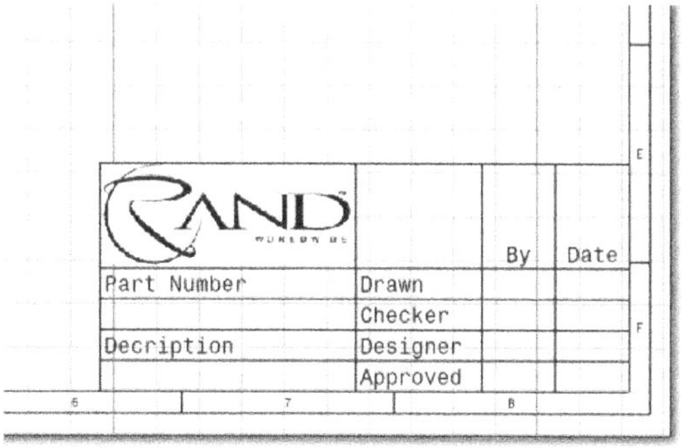

Figure 8–20

Alternatively, (Instantiate a default template) can be used instead of searching for a template. Once selected, a default template is immediately drawn into the background, as shown in Figure 8–21.

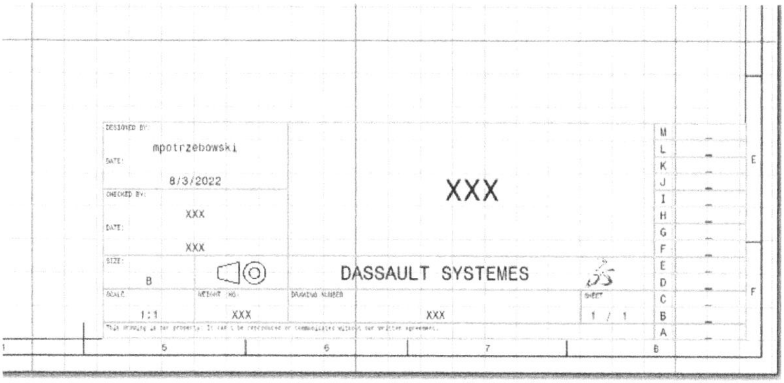

Figure 8–21

Note: *Revision Table* can be used in the same way as *Frame* and *Title Block.* The only requirement is the table being used in the original drawing needs to have the *Feature Name* start with the prefix **RevisonTable_**, otherwise nothing will be instantiated.

8.5 Print a Drawing

Select (Share)>**Print** to print a drawing. The Print dialog box opens, as shown in Figure 8–22.

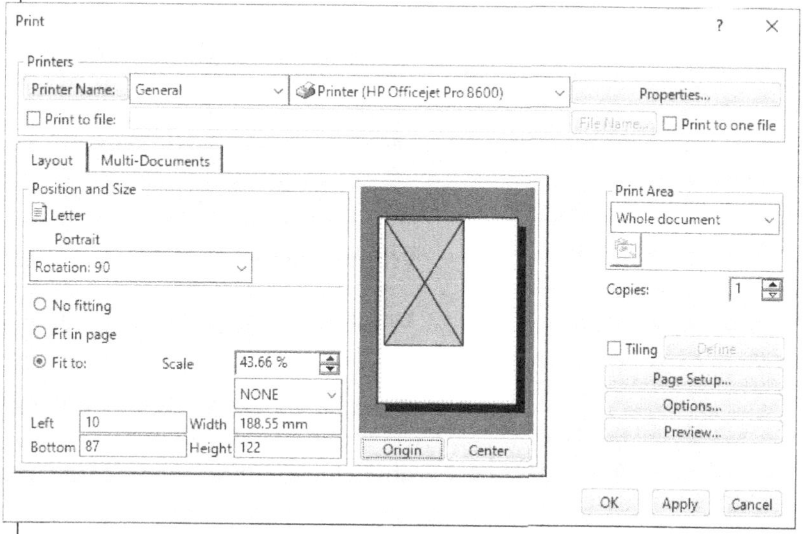

Figure 8–22

Use the *Layout* tab to control the position, orientation, size, and portion of the drawing to be printed.

Position and Size

How To: Control the Position, Orientation, and Size of the Print

1. Set the orientation of the drawing by selecting an option in the drop-down list, as shown in Figure 8–23.

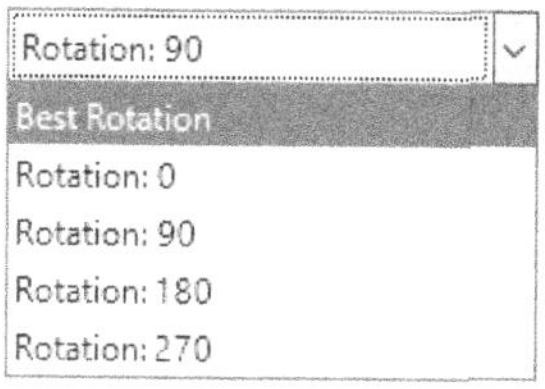

Figure 8–23

2. Select a fitting option to control the size of the plot. The following options are available:

   - **No Fitting:** Generates the print using its original size. No scaling is performed.
   - **Fit in Page:** Scales the print to fit the size of the page, including margins.
   - **Fit to:** Enables you to select a scaling percentage or new sheet size to which to scale the print. Click **Origin** to locate the plot in the bottom left corner of the page or click **Center** to center the plot.

Print Area

You can use the following three options to adjust the print area:

- **Whole Document:** Prints the entire drawing sheet.
- **Display:** Prints only the portion of the sheet that displays in the main window.
- **Selection:** Enables you to select an area on the drawing sheet to print. Click (Select mode).

If the drawing contains more than one sheet, the options in the *Multi-Documents* tab enable you to control which sheets are printed, as shown in Figure 8–24.

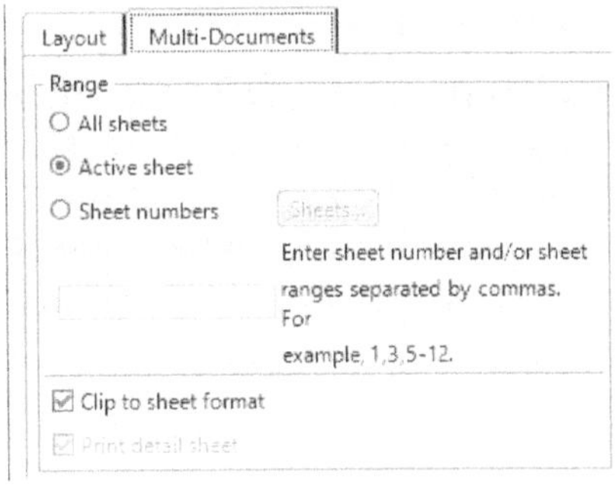

Figure 8–24

Quick Print

If you click (Print) or press <Ctrl>+<Shift>+<P>, the system automatically prints a copy of the drawing to the default printer using the default settings in the Print dialog box. The print icon is not found on the default Action Bar and would need to be added.

8.6 Import and Export 2D Data

An intermediate file format is required when sending or receiving data from another CAD software package. CATIA can import and export 2D data in the Drafting app in a variety of file formats. CGM, DXF, and IGES are the most commonly used formats and provide the most successful results.

Importing 2D Data

If you are receiving data from another CAD system, it is recommended that the sender provide the data in the DXF or IGES format. These formats preserve the vector properties of the geometry and text, enabling you to select individual entities in the imported drawing.

How To: Create a New Drawing Using Interface Data

1. Select (Add)>**Import.** The Import window will appear.
2. In the *Format* field, select the drop-down arrow and pick the file type you wish to import. For example, **DXF2D (*.dxf)**.
3. Select (Browse) to find the location of the local file you wish to import.
4. Click **OK**. The interface data is imported into a new drawing file.
5. If you require the interface data to be added as a new or existing sheet on a drawing, you can select the items and cut or copy them from the new drawing. The items can then be pasted into the existing drawing.

   An alternative to cutting and pasting imported drawing geometry is to use (Insert From File) from the Annotation section of the Action Bar. This will bring the geometry into an existing drawing.

Try some of the following workarounds if you encounter any errors when importing a 2D file into CATIA:

- The path length and name can cause problems when reading files into CATIA. Copy the file to a location with a simplified path name, such as **C:\Temp** on a Windows system.
- Rename the file to remove any extra characters or spaces (e.g., **test.dxf**).
- If the file was sent by email or ftp, have the sender zip or compress the file to protect it against corruption.

- Request that the file be sent in another file format.

Importing CATIA V5 Data

When importing with CATIA V5 files (Parts, Products, or Drawings), the insert process is slightly different. Selecting (Add)**>Import>CATIA file** will open a Select the files to Import window and immediately start the process to browse for local files. The *Import Scenario* options will control if links are maintained from V5 data when brought into the 3DEXPERIENCE. *Similar documents options* will control if existing 3DEXPERIENCE documents are updated or replaced when bringing in V5 data. An example of the Select the files to Import window is shown in Figure 8–25.

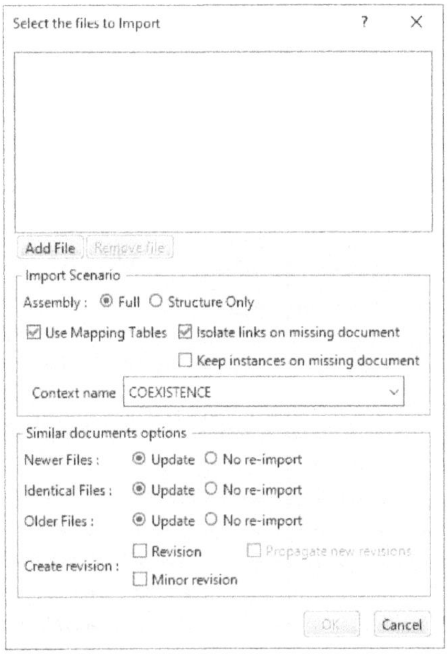

Figure 8–25

Exporting 2D Data

You might want to export a 2D file from the Drafting app to send a drawing to another CAD system or to remove the file association from the 3D model when sending a drawing to another CATIA user.

How To: Export a 2D File from CATIA

1. With the drawing open in CATIA, select (Share)>**Export.** The Export window will appear.
2. In the Format drop-down list, select the file format as shown in Figure 8–26.

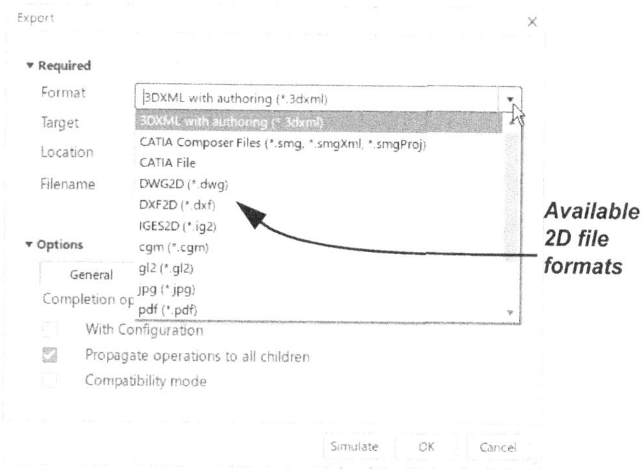

Figure 8–26

3. Next to the *Location* field, select (Browse) to be able to define the folder the file will be saved into.
4. Enter a unique name for the *Filename* field and click **OK**.

The following table lists the different types of 2D file formats available and the applications where they can be used. If the format supports multi-sheets, a separate export file is automatically generated for each sheet in the drawing. Otherwise, only the current sheet is exported.

File Format	Multi-Sheet Support	Result
3DXML	Yes	Proprietary 3D Dassault Systemès format.
DXF	Yes	DXF (Drawing eXchange Format). Can be imported into most CAD systems.
DWG	Yes	Native AutoCAD format.
CGM	No	Computer Graphics Metafile. When imported, entities cannot be individually selected. Can be imported into most CAD systems.
GL2	No	Hewlett Packard Graphics Language 2 format. A plot file that can be sent directly to a HP-GL2 capable printer.
PS	No	Postscript file. Can be sent directly to a postscript capable printer.
PDF	Yes	Creates an image of the drawing that can be viewed using Adobe Acrobat.
TIF	No	Creates a TIFF image of the drawing that can be viewed using a graphics package or Internet Explorer.
JPG	No	Creates a JPEG image of the drawing that can be viewed using a graphics package or Internet Explorer.
IG2	No	Creates an IGES file. The file name should be renamed to .IGS to be recognized by other CAD systems. Can be imported into most CAD systems.

8.7 Insert an Image

Select (Insert Object) in the Annotation section of the Action Bar to add an image of a logo or any other object to the title block or drawing. If you add it to the title block, ensure that Background mode has been activated.

The Insert Object dialog box opens, as shown in Figure 8–27.

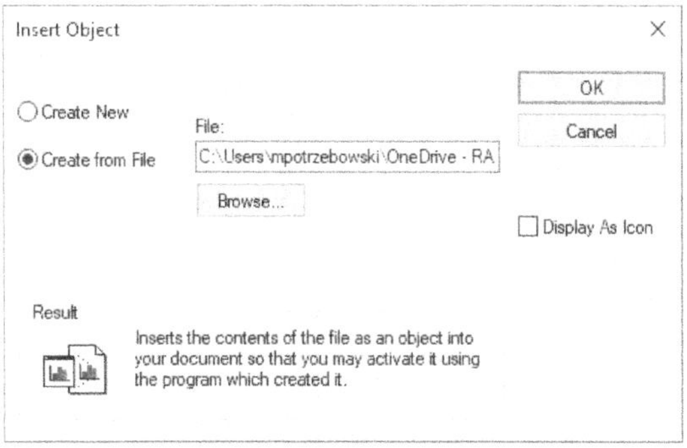

Figure 8–27

Click **Browse** and browse to the bitmap image that you want to use. Click **OK** to place the image in the drawing, as shown in Figure 8–28.

Typically, the image displays in the lower left corner of the drawing.

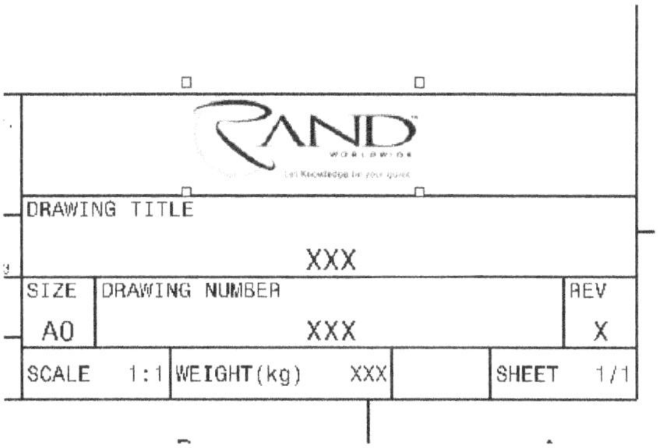

Figure 8–28

You can also select **Create New** to launch a default editor and create a new object, if the required object does not exist.

Alternatively, you can use (Insert Picture) from the Annotation section of the Action Bar to import an existing image file. Many formats are supported, such as Bitmap, PNG, JPEG, and so on.

8.8 Large Drawing Management Techniques

Use the following techniques to help manage a drawing with a large number of views and sheets.

Hide/Show

Techniques such as Hide/Show can simplify a drawing by removing views from the display that are not currently being used.

To hide a view, right-click on it in the drawing window or specification tree and select **Hide/Show**. You can return the view to the display by showing it in the specification tree.

Hidden views still update with the drawing when you perform a **full update**. Therefore, the views remain associative to the model.

Slides

Slides can simplify assembly geometry. Hide components that are not required in a specific view.

View Generation Mode

Two view generation modes improve drawing performance when working with large models: CGR and Approximate.

CGR

CGR representations in drawing views decrease the update time of the drawing. The CGR representation only considers the external surfaces of the part or assembly model, which speeds up view generation.

Approximate

When working with large and complex drawings, such as component assemblies, use the Approximate view generation mode to reduce drawing update time during drawing creation. In the View Properties dialog box, select **Approximate** in the View generation mode drop-down list and click **Options**.

The **Level Of Detail** coefficient dictates how accurately the small geometric elements (surfaces, edges, etc.) will display in the view. A low level of detail coefficient simplifies the display of small features and resembles the CGR mode. A high level of detail includes all part features and resembles the Exact mode.

Local Update

A drawing can be updated in a variety of ways in the Drafting app. Depending on what is selected in the specification tree, you can localize the update to specific drawing views. You can update a drawing in the following ways:

- All views of the drawing update if you update the drawing from the specification tree. As well, all views on all sheets update if there are multiple sheets.
- All views on a sheet update when it is selected. Other drawing sheets are not included in the update. The update symbol remains on display in the specification tree on other sheets and in their views until you perform an update.
- To update specific views of a drawing, select them individually in the specification tree, right-click, and select **Update Selection**. All other views are not included in the update.

These methods help you to manage a complicated drawing during view generation and detailing, by ensuring that only required elements are updated. Be sure to update the entire drawing before you save a drawing.

Practice 8a Create a Title Block

Practice Objectives

- Create a frame
- Create a title block.
- Insert an image into title block.

In this practice, you will build a title block for a B-size drawing. The title block includes a border, tables, and an image. You will apply this title block to a drawing in a later practice. The completed title block is shown in Figure 8–29.

Figure 8–29

Task 1 - Set option settings.

1. Select **Me>Preferences>AppPreferences>3D Modeling> Mechanical Systems>Drafting** and expand **Geometry**. Enable the **Display** and **Snap to point** options. Ensure the *Primary spacing* is set to **100mm** and *Graduation* is set to **10**, as shown in Figure 8–30.

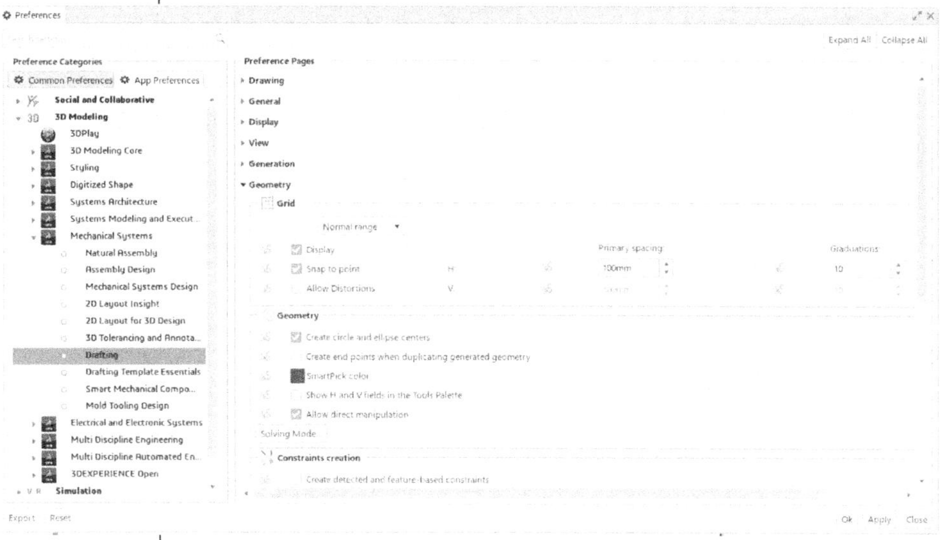

Figure 8–30

2. Click **OK**.

Task 2 - Create a drawing.

 *(Display Grid) can be toggled on/off as needed from the View section of the Action Bar.*

1. Create a drawing with *Title* of **###_B_TitleBlock** where ### represents your initials. Use **ANSI-ASME** as the *Standard* and **B ANSI** for the *Sheet Style*. The drawing displays as shown in Figure 8–31.

Figure 8–31

Task 3 - Activate the Background view.

1. In the specification tree, right-click on **Sheet.1** and click **Edit Background**, as shown in Figure 8–32.

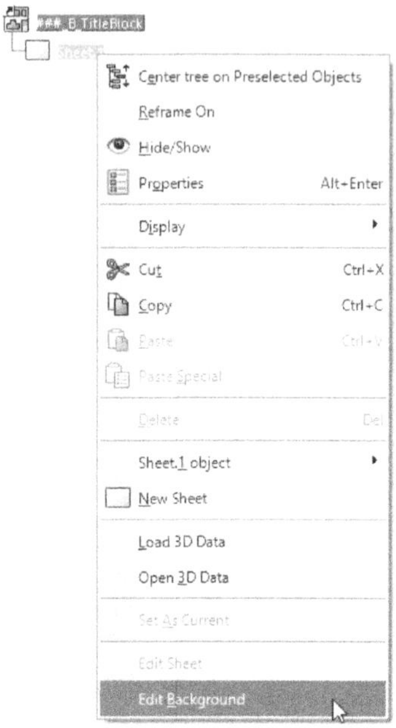

Figure 8–32

Task 4 - Create 2D geometry.

1. In the Sketch section of the Action Bar, click (Rectangle) and sketch a rectangle.
2. Begin sketching the rectangle from the **10, 10** position, as shown in Figure 8–33.

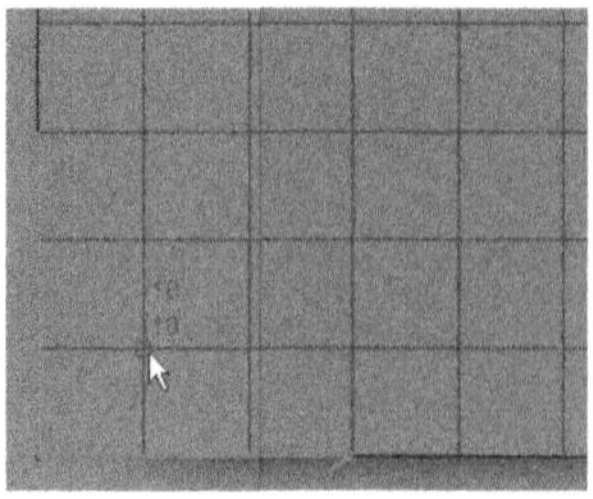

Figure 8–33

3. Drag the rectangle toward the upper right corner of the page, as shown in Figure 8–34.

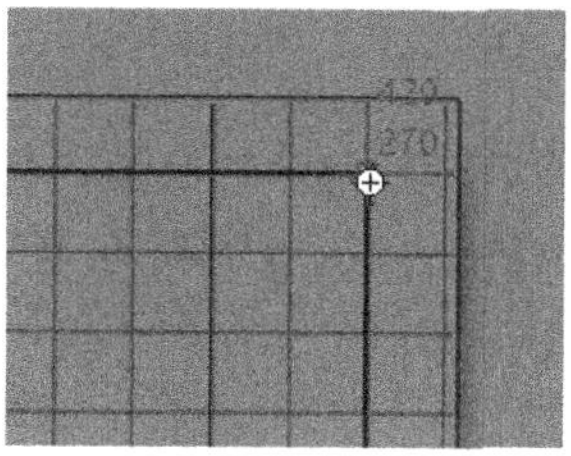

Figure 8–34

4. In the Tools Palette toolbar, set the *H* value to **421.8** and set the *V* value to **270**, as shown in Figure 8–35. Press **Enter** to complete the rectangle.

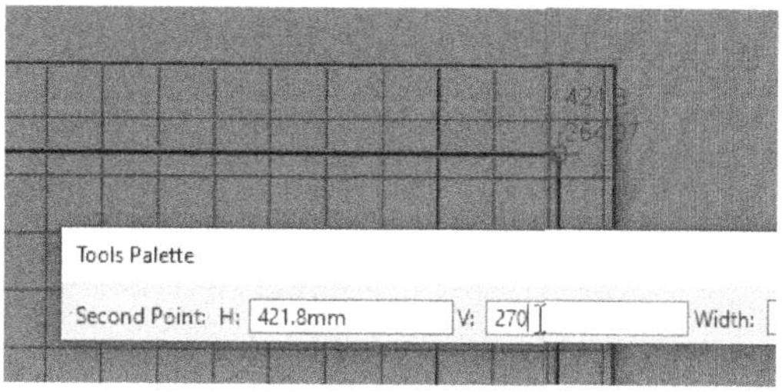

Figure 8–35

5. Select  (Working Views) from the Standard section of the Action Bar to exit the background. The completed rectangle displays as shown in Figure 8–36.

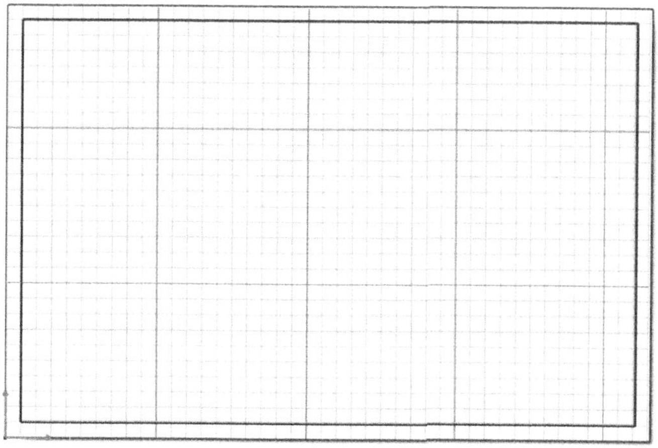

Figure 8–36

Task 5 - Create a table.

1. In the Annotation section of the Action Bar, click (Table).
2. Click the location shown in Figure 8–37 first and move the mouse toward the lower right until your table has **4** columns and **5** rows. The completed table is shown in Figure 8–37.

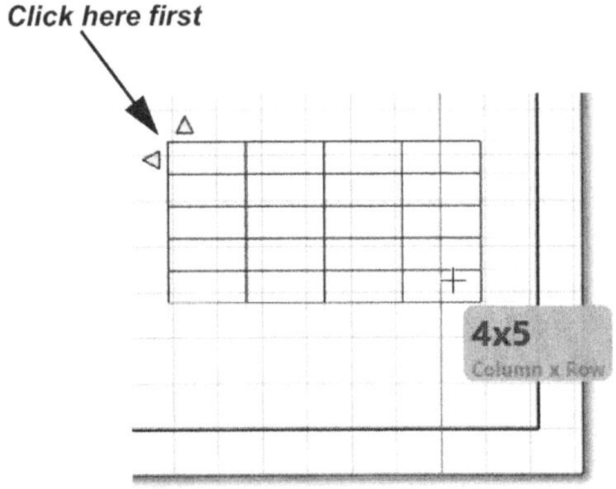

Figure 8–37

Task 6 - Enter text.

1. Double-click on the table to make it active.
2. Double-click on the cell (**C1**), as shown in Figure 8–38. The Text Editor opens.

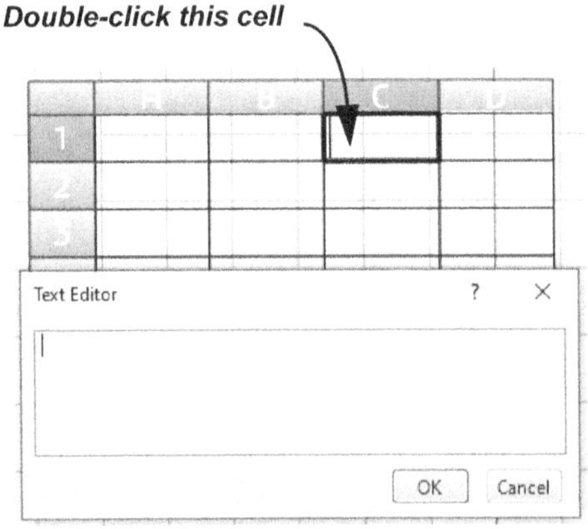

Figure 8–38

3. In the Text Editor, type **By** as shown in Figure 8–39.

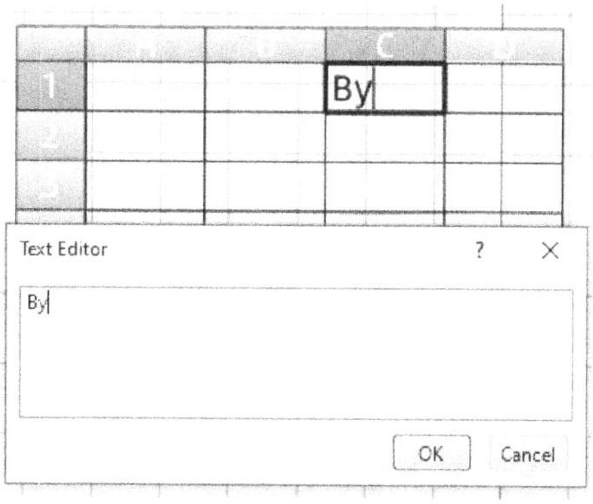

Figure 8–39

4. Click **OK** in the Text Editor.

Task 7 - Change the anchor point of text.

1. If the Object Properties window does not display, right-click on **Display>Object Properties**.

2. Double-click the table, then click in cell **C2**. In the *Text* area of the Object Properties window, select (Anchor Point), as shown in Figure 8–40.

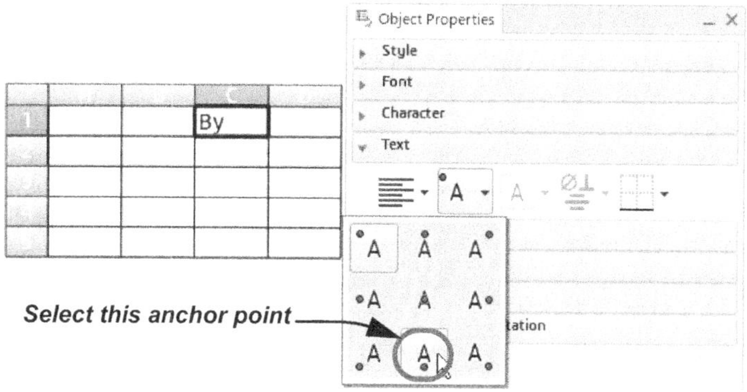

Figure 8–40

3. Enter the text shown in Figure 8–41 in the appropriate cells. Ensure that the **Date** text is set to the bottom center anchor point.

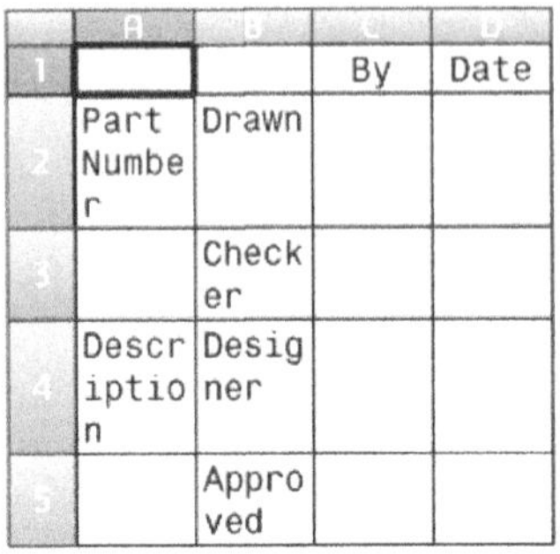

Figure 8–41

If the table is not active, double-click on it to make it active again.

4. Resize the left text column by placing the cursor in the margin area above the first column. Right-click and select **Column width...**, as shown in Figure 8–42.

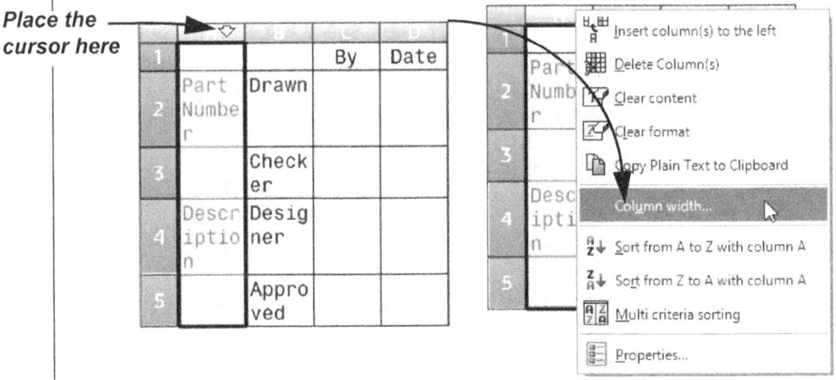

Figure 8–42

5. Enter **60mm** as the width and click **OK**.

6. Repeat Steps 4 to 5 on column **B**, set the *Column Width* to **30mm**, and then click **OK**. The table updates as shown in Figure 8–43.

		By	Date
Part Number	Drawn		
	Checker		
Decription	Designer		
	Approved		

Figure 8–43

7. Resize the top text row by placing the cursor in the margin area to the left of the first row (number 1). Right-click and select **Row height...**, as shown in Figure 8–44.

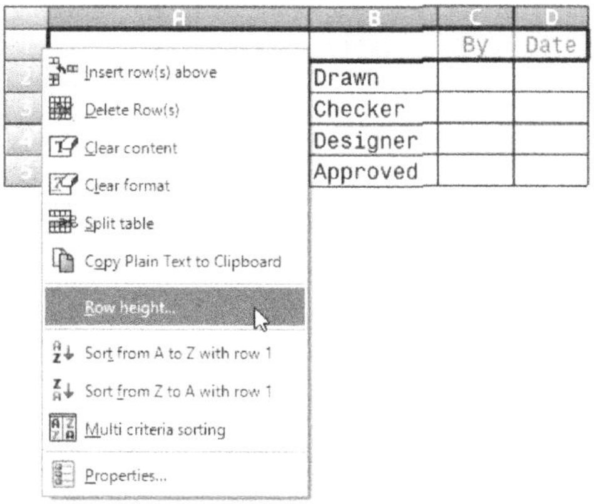

Figure 8–44

8. Enter **24mm** as the height and click **OK**. The table updates as shown in Figure 8–45.

		By	Date
Part Number	Drawn		
	Checker		
Description	Designer		
	Approved		

Figure 8–45

Task 8 - Import a picture.

1. If needed, activate the table by double-clicking on it.

2. Right-click in cell **A1** and select **Insert>Insert Picture**, as shown in Figure 8–46.

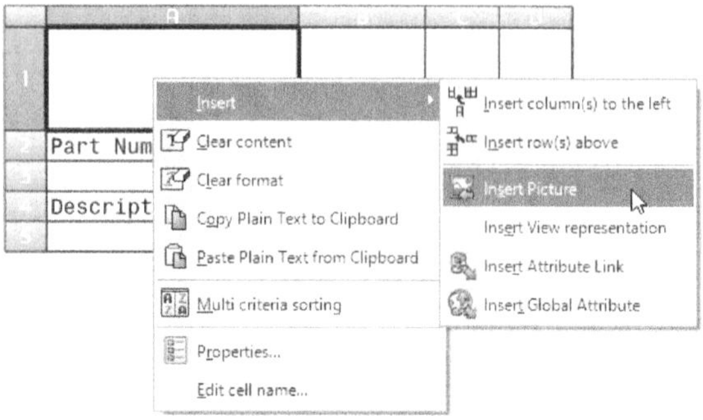

Figure 8–46

3. Browse and choose **Rand_worldwide.bmp** from the practice files and click **Open**.

4. Place the picture, as shown in Figure 8–47.

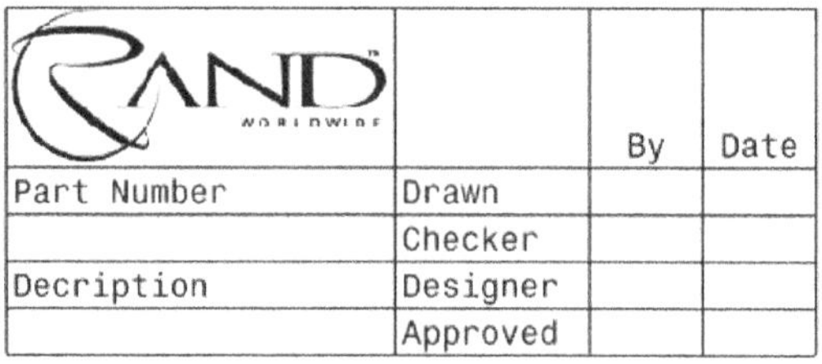

Figure 8–47

5. Zoom in to the table and drag it to the position shown in Figure 8–48. To temporarily disable the **Snap to Point** option, press <Shift> while dragging the table to a new location.

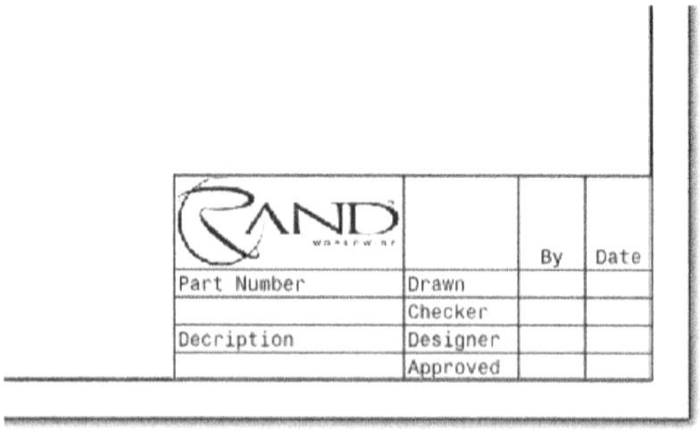

Figure 8–48

Task 9 - Make title block usable for other drawings.

1. Right-click on the table and select **Properties.**
2. Select the *Feature Properties* tab, and set the *Feature Name* to **TitleBlock_1.**

Design Considerations

The prefix of **Titleblock_** is important because CATIA will look for this value if you try to instantiate this title block into a different drawing. The prefix **RevisonTable_** works the same way when instantiating a revision block into a drawing. You will get a chance to implement this in the next practice.

3. Select **OK** to close the Properties window.
4. Save the drawing and close the tab.

Practice 8b Insert a Title Block

Practice Objective

- Insert a title block.

In this practice, you will learn how to insert previously created title blocks along with the default title block into the **Adapter_TitleBlock_8B** and **ExhaustManifold_Detail_8B** drawings.

Task 1 - Import and open a drawing file.

1. Import and open **Adaptor_8B.3dxml** from the practice files folder. While importing, set the *Duplication string* to **###_** where ### represents your initials.

2. Right-click on the **###_Adapter_TitleBlock_8B** drawing in the tree and select *** object>Open in New App**. The drawing displays as shown in Figure 8–49.

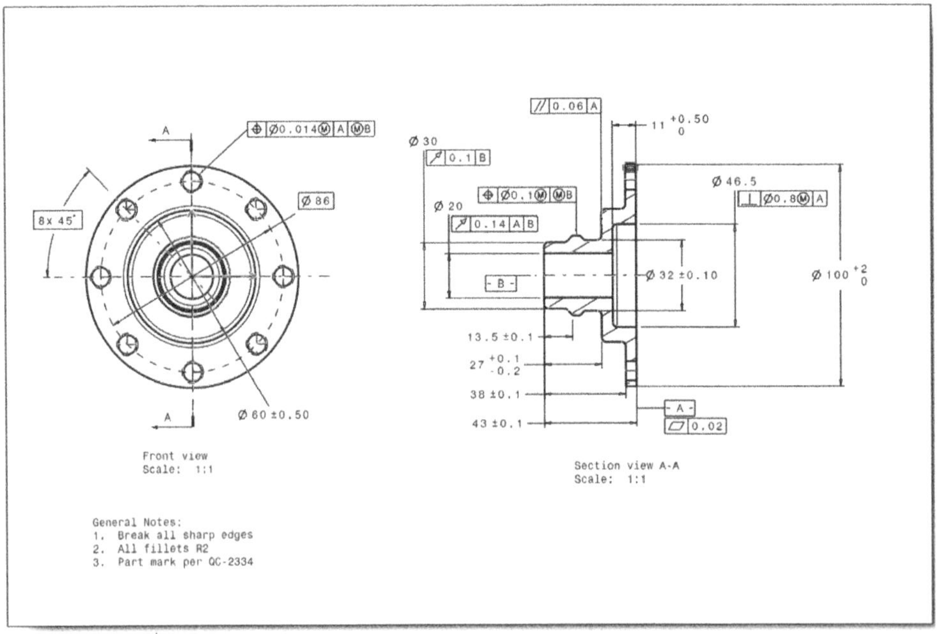

Figure 8–49

Task 2 - Insert a background view.

Design Considerations

In CATIA, there is more than one way to create and insert a frame and title block into a drawing. The best method will depend on the size of your company and the role CAD users hold in that company. In general, with larger companies, the CAD Admin will be in control of a custom VBScript file that will draw and control the frame and title block. CATIA comes with a few standard VBScript files (e.g., **Drawing Titleblock Sample 1, Drawing Titleblock Sample 2**) that can be used as examples of this function. For someone without VBScript knowledge, a drawing template can be created and used to generate other drawings. All options have different pros and cons. We will look at those different options in this practice.

From the View Layout section of the Action Bar, select

 (Page Layout). The Page Layout dialog box opens, as shown in Figure 8–50.

Figure 8–50

1. In the *Dress-up* category, select **Drawing Titleblock Sample 1** from the drop-down list.

2. In the *Frame And Title Block* category, select **Create**. The Create text highlights, as shown in Figure 8–51.

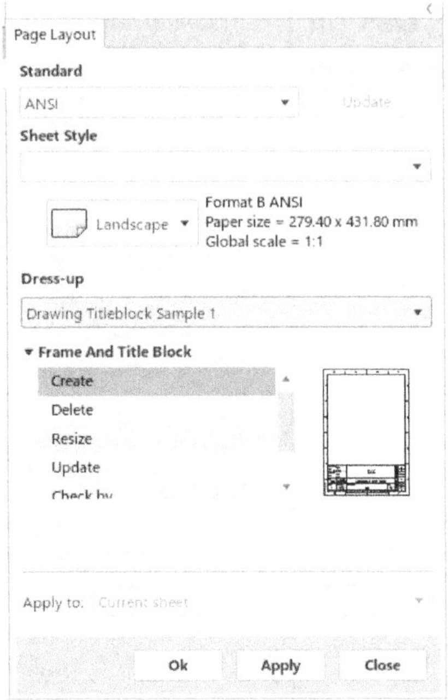

Figure 8–51

3. Select **Apply**. A default Dassault Systèmes frame and title block is inserted.

Design Considerations

This is an easy method of placing a frame and title block. However, for this option to work, either you would need to have someone who works with Visual Basic or you will have to manually customize this frame and title block each time for each drawing to make it your own. For those reasons, you will learn how to remove this frame and title block and insert your own template.

4. With the Page Layout dialog box still open, select **Delete** under the *Frame And Title Block* category.

5. Select **Apply**. The drawing will remove the newly created frame and title block, as shown in Figure 8–52.

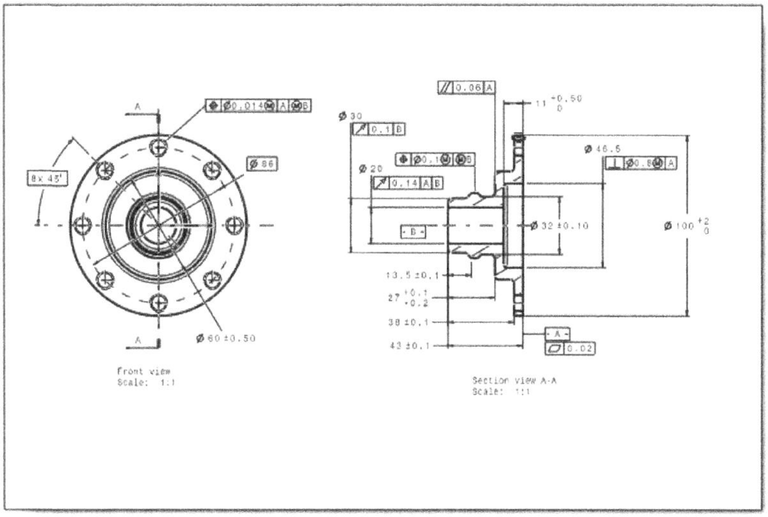

Figure 8–52

6. In the Page Layout dialog box, select **Dress-up DS 1** from the Dress-up drop-down list. This VBScript file opens up more options in the Page Layout dialog box, as shown in Figure 8–53.

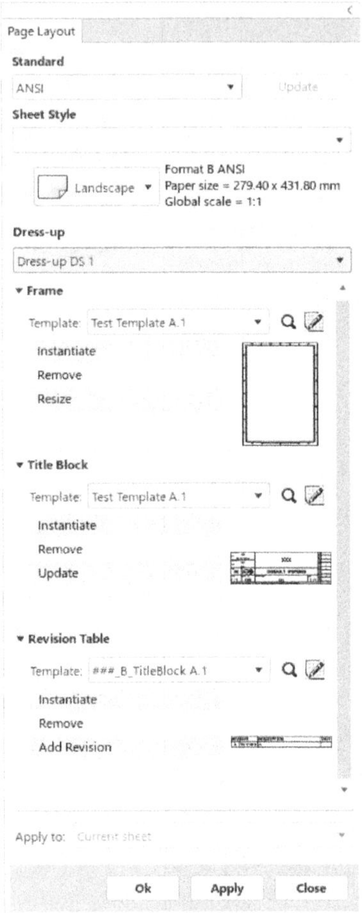

Figure 8–53

Design Considerations

By selecting **Dress-up DS 1**, Page Layout now has the ability to individually import and place a frame, titleblock and/or revision table from other stored drawings in the 3DEXPERIENCE database. This is ideal if you need to be able to quickly create new drawings but do not want to create or customize a Visual Basic file. Any drawing can be used as a template as long as the features are defined correctly. You have the option to use all custom templates or use a default template that is controlled by the CAD standard for three categories (Frame, Title Block, Revision Table).

7. Under the **Frame** option, select 🔍 (Search for existing template). The search pop-up will appear, as shown in Figure 8–54.

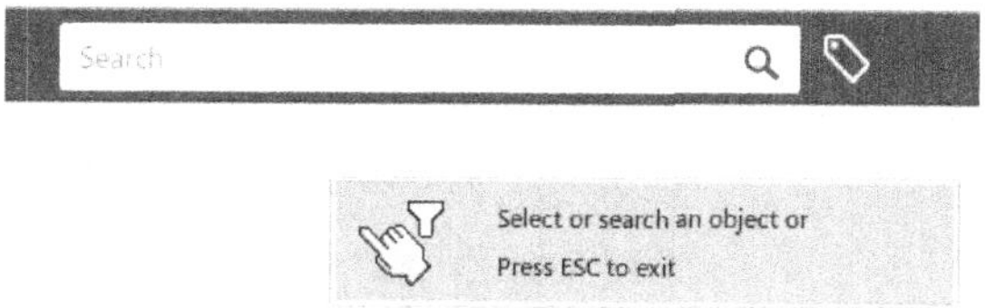

Figure 8–54

8. In the *Search* field at the top of the screen, type **###_B_TitleBlock**, which was created in the previous practice. ### represents your initials. Then, press <Enter>.

9. The search results will list the **###_B_TitleBlock** drawing. Select that drawing, and the Page Layout dialog box will update so that **###_B_TitleBlock** is listed next to **Frame>Template**, as shown in Figure 8–55.

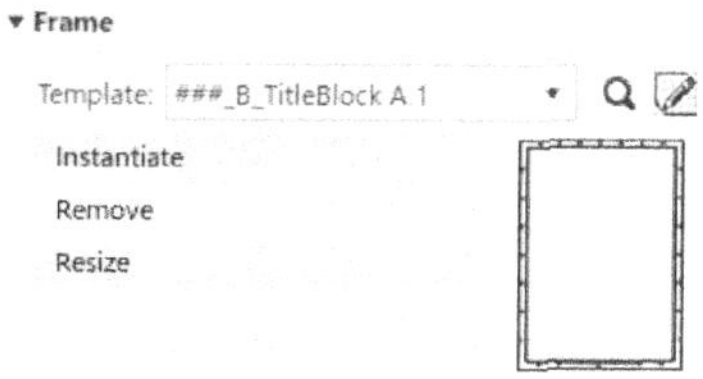

Figure 8–55

10. Repeat Steps 7 to 9 for the *Title Block* category. Use the same **###_B_TitleBlock** drawing so that the result will look like Figure 8–56.

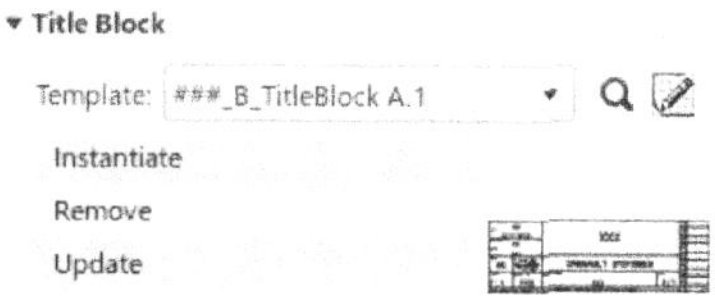

Figure 8–56

11. With *Frame* and *Title Block* pointing to the correct *Template*, select to highlight **Instantiate** for both and then click **Apply**. The drawing updates, as shown in Figure 8–57.

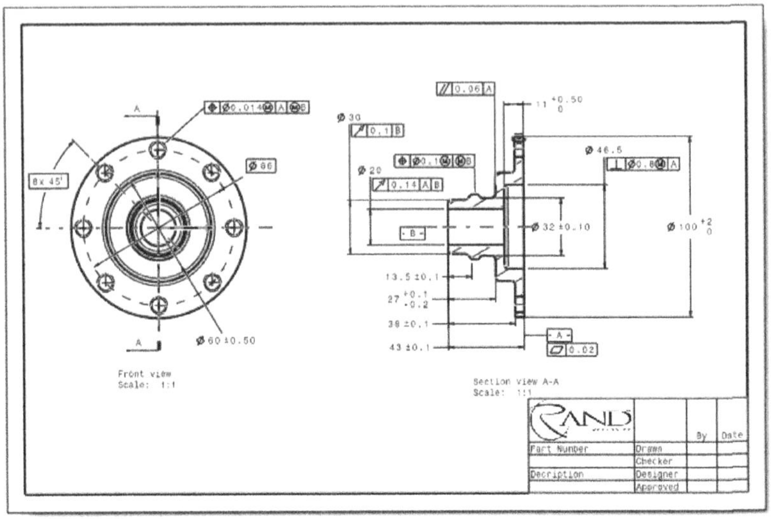

Figure 8–57

Design Considerations

You decide that the custom frame is too simplistic. You want to replace this with the default frame template instead.

12. If needed, select (Page Layout) to open the Page Layout dialog box.

13. Under the *Frame* category, select **Remove**, then click **Apply**. This will delete the rectangle from the drawing background.

14. In the same *Frame* category, select  (Instantiate a default template). The frame is created, and the drawing will look like Figure 8–58.

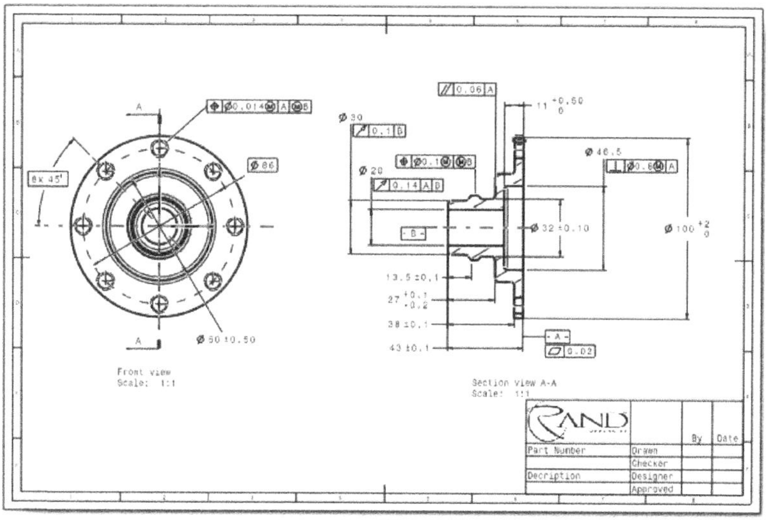

Figure 8–58

15. Save the drawing and close the tab.

Task 3 - Insert a VBScript title block.

1. Import and open **ExhaustManifold_8B.3dxml** from the practice files folder. While importing, set the *Duplication string* to **###_** where ### represents your initials.

2. Right-click on the **###_ExhaustManifold_Detail_8B** drawing in the tree and select * **object>Open in New App**.

3. Ensure that Sheet.1 displays as shown in Figure 8–59.

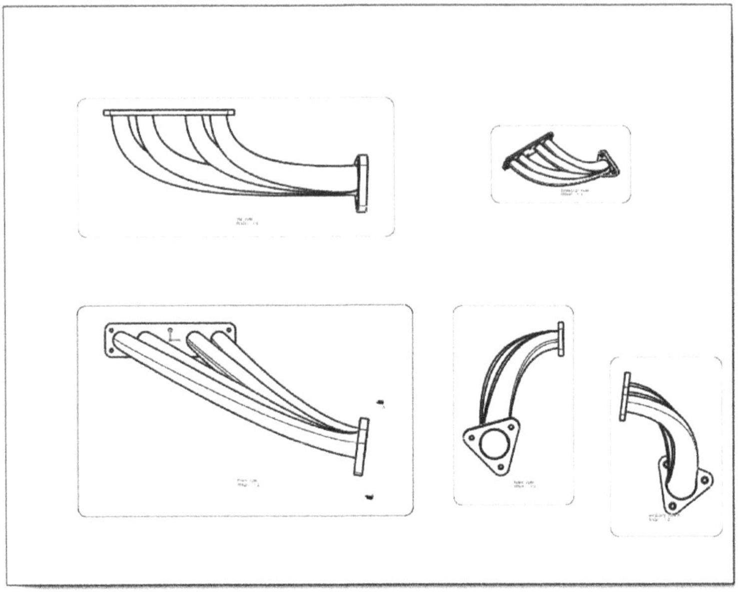

Figure 8–59

4. Right-click on **Sheet.1** and select **Edit Background**.

5. In the Annotation section of the Action Bar, click (Page Layout).

6. In the *Dress-up* area, select **Drawing Titleblock Sample 1**, as shown in Figure 8–60.

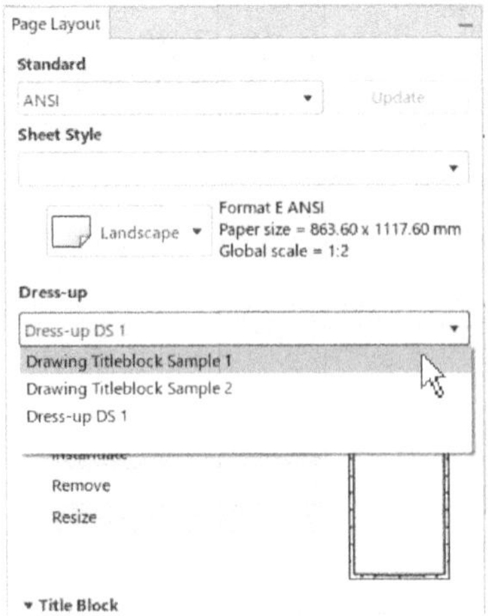

Figure 8–60

7. In the *Frame And Title Block* area, click **Create**, as shown in Figure 8–61.

Figure 8–61

8. Click **Apply**. The drawing updates with the selected title block, as shown in Figure 8–62.

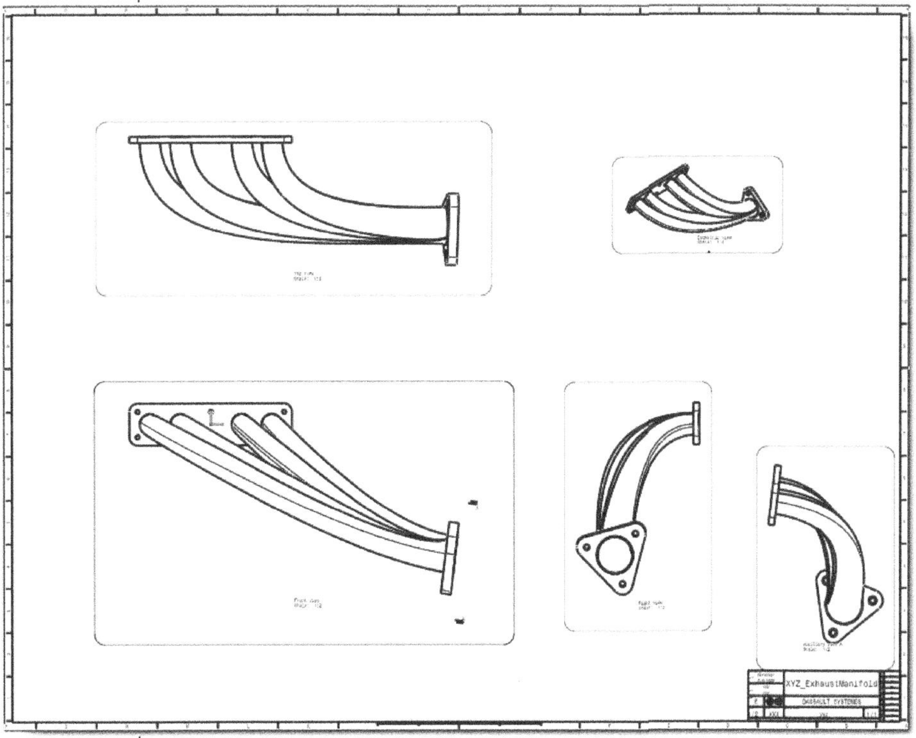

Figure 8–62

9. Click **OK**.

10. Zoom in to the title block and note that the VBScript has entered the current parameter values in the appropriate fields, as shown in Figure 8–63.

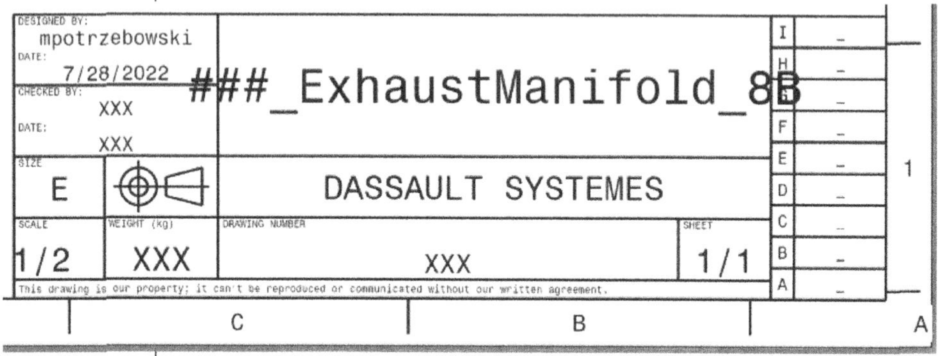

Figure 8–63

11. Save the drawing and close all of the tabs.

Practice 8c

Insert Parameters into a Table

Practice Objectives

- Create center of gravity parameters.
- Insert the parameters into a drawing table.
- Modify and update the parameters.

In this practice, you will create a table on a drawing that is linked to the center of gravity parameters of the part.

Task 1 - Import and open files.

1. Import and open **Cover-2.3dxml** from the practice files folder. While importing, set the *Duplication string* to **###_** where ### represents your initials.

2. Right-click on **###_Cover-2 Drawing** in the tree and select *** object>Open in New App**. The drawing displays as shown in Figure 8–64.

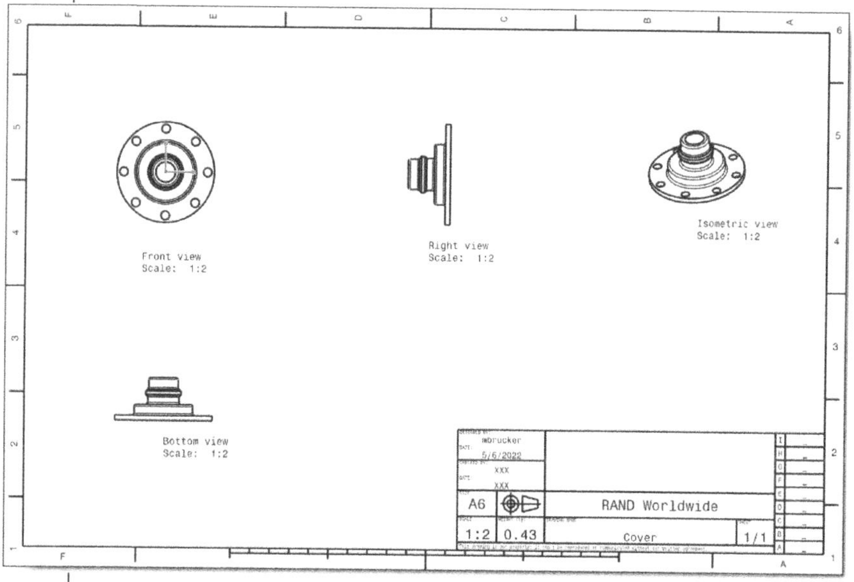

Figure 8–64

Tables are traditionally placed in the sheet background. The working view is reserved for part views and 2D geometry.

Task 2 - Create a table in the drawing.

1. Right-click on **Sheet.1** and select **Edit Background**.
2. In the Annotation section of the Action Bar, click (Table).
3. Click to place a table in the lower right side of the screen, as shown in Figure 8–65. In the Table Editor dialog box, enter **3** for the *Number of columns*, and enter **2** for the *Number of rows*, as shown in Figure 8–65.

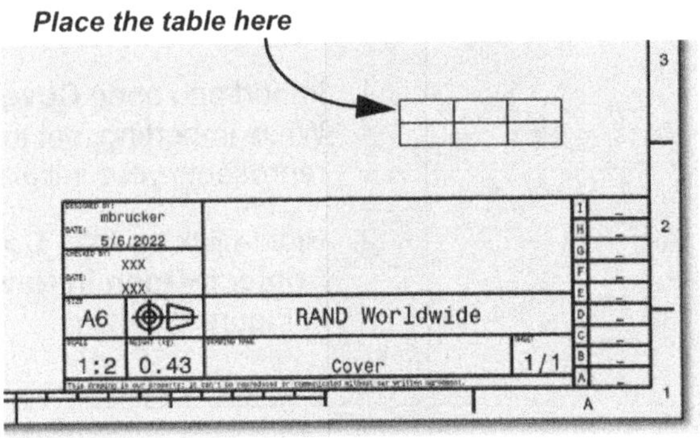

Figure 8–65

To move a table, select it and drag it to the new position.

4. Move the cursor to the lower right and click to create a **3x2** table, as shown in Figure 8–66.

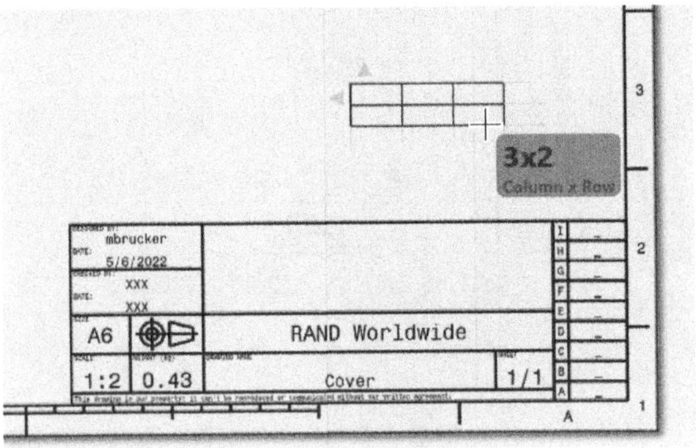

Figure 8–66

Task 3 - Create center of gravity parameters in the part file.

1. Activate the part widget.
2. In the specification tree, select the **PartBody** and click

    (Measure Inertia Data) from the Tools section of the Action Bar.
3. In the Measure Inertia Part dialog box, click **OK.** The inertia volume and center of gravity parameters display in the specification tree under the **Measure Inertia** node, as shown in Figure 8–67.

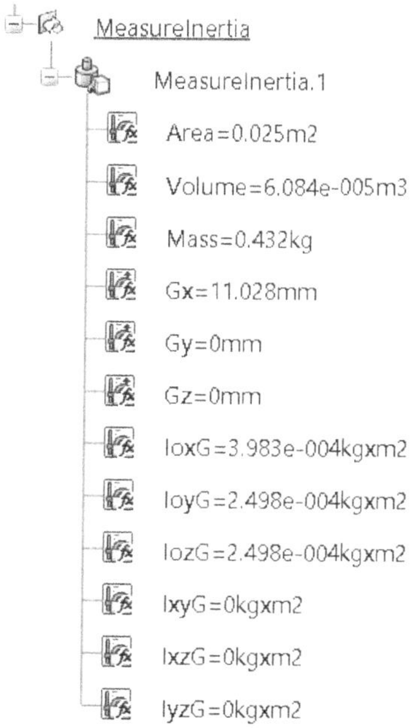

Figure 8–67

Task 4 - Fill in the drawing table with inertia data.

1. Activate the drawing widget.
2. Double-click on the table to make it active.

3. Double-click on the cell shown in Figure 8–68. The Text Editor dialog box opens.

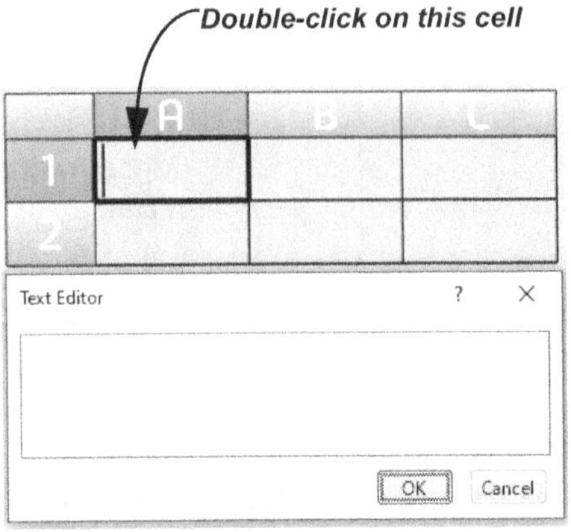

Figure 8–68

4. Configure the top row of the table as shown in Figure 8–69.

COGx	COGy	COGz

Figure 8–69

If Object Properties is not shown, right-click on ***Display*** *and select* ***Object Properties.***

5. Select the top row of cells. In the Object Properties window, click (Anchor Point) to center the text in each cell. The table displays as shown in Figure 8–70.

COGx	COGy	COGz

Figure 8–70

Task 5 - Use attribute links to fill in the second row of the table.

1. Double-click on the first cell of the second row in the table (A2). When the Text Editor dialog box opens, right-click on the cell and select **Insert>Insert Attribute Link**, as shown in Figure 8–71. Note that the text cannot be right-clicked in the Text Editor.

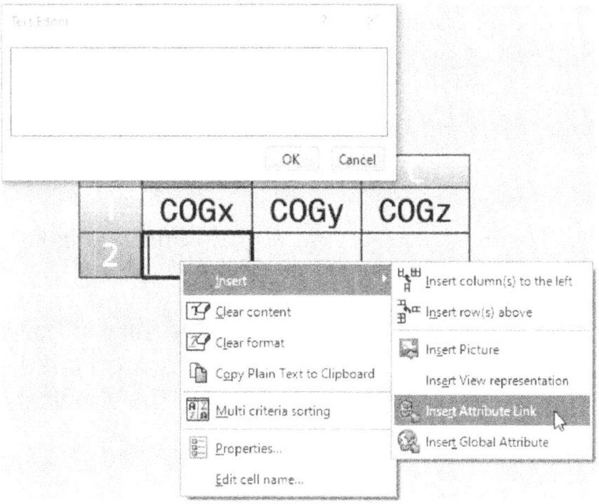

Figure 8–71

2. Activate the **Cover-2** part widget, and in the part specification tree, select the **Gx** parameter, as shown in Figure 8–72.

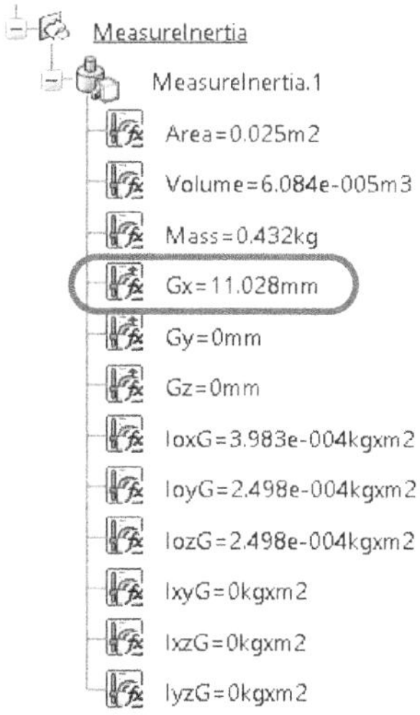

Figure 8–72

3. The Insert Attribute Link dialog box displays as shown in Figure 8–73. Select the parameter in the *Attribute* list, then click **OK**.

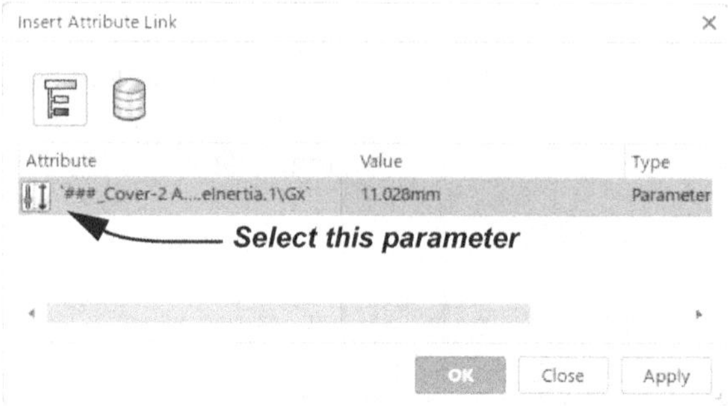

Figure 8–73

4. Create attribute links for the remaining two cells at the center of gravity table.

5. To fit the cell widths to the center of gravity values, double-click on the dividing line between the **A** and **B** columns, as shown in Figure 8–74.

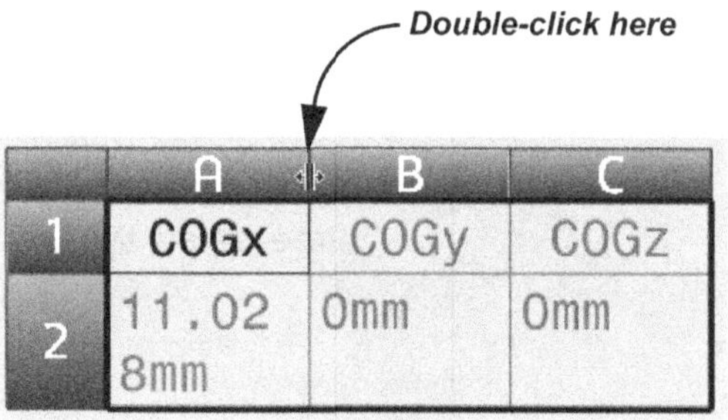

Figure 8–74

The completed table displays as shown in Figure 8–75.

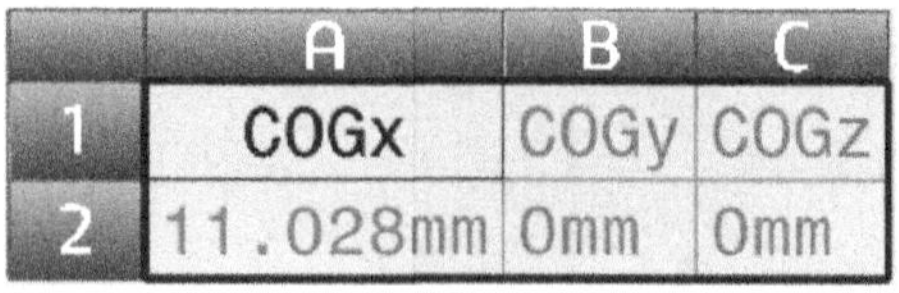

Figure 8–75

Task 6 - Modify the parameters.

1. Activate the part widget.

2. In the specification tree, double-click on the **Shaft.1** feature.

3. Modify the *100mm dimension*, as shown in Figure 8–76, to **150mm**.

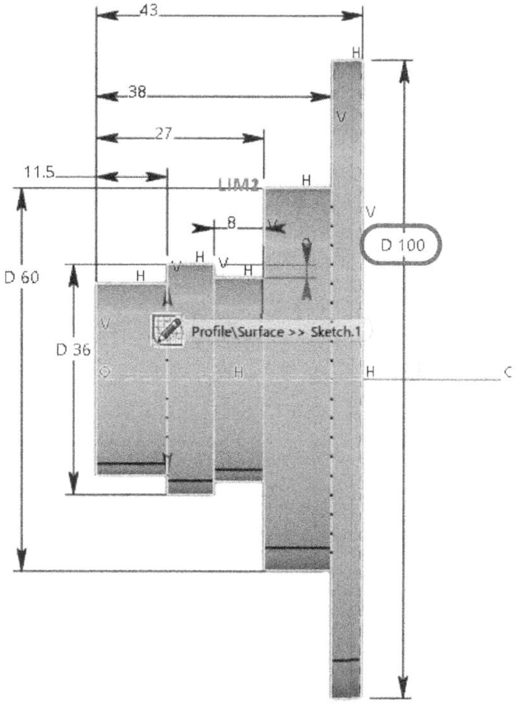

Figure 8–76

4. The **Measure Inertia** node updates, as shown in Figure 8–77

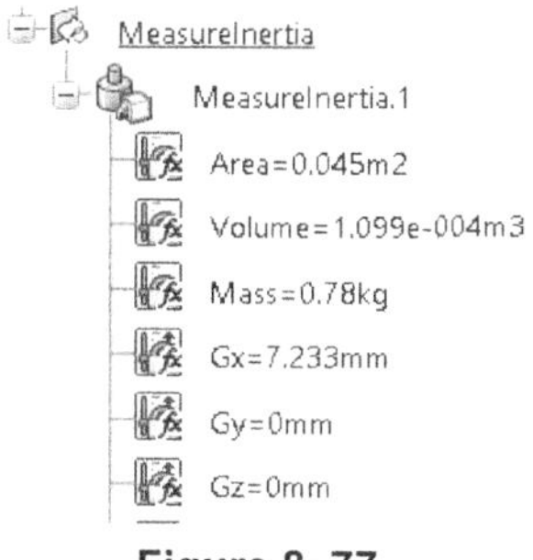

Figure 8–77

5. If, because of your **Me>Preferences** settings, you see this 

symbol, it means the parameter did not auto-update. Resolve this by going to the specification tree, right-clicking on the **Measure Inertia** node, and selecting **Local Update**. Otherwise, this step can be skipped.

6. Activate the drawing widget and click (Working Views) from the Standard section of the Action Bar.

7. Select (Update current sheet) from the Standard section. You might need to force an update on the drawing by entering **c:force update** in the *Power Input* field.

8. The parameters that display in the COG table have updated with the new center of gravity parameters, as shown in Figure 8–78. The values that display in the table cells are linked to the parameters in the **###_Cover-2** part.

COGx	COGy	COGz
7.233mm	0mm	0mm

Figure 8–78

9. Save and close all of the tabs.

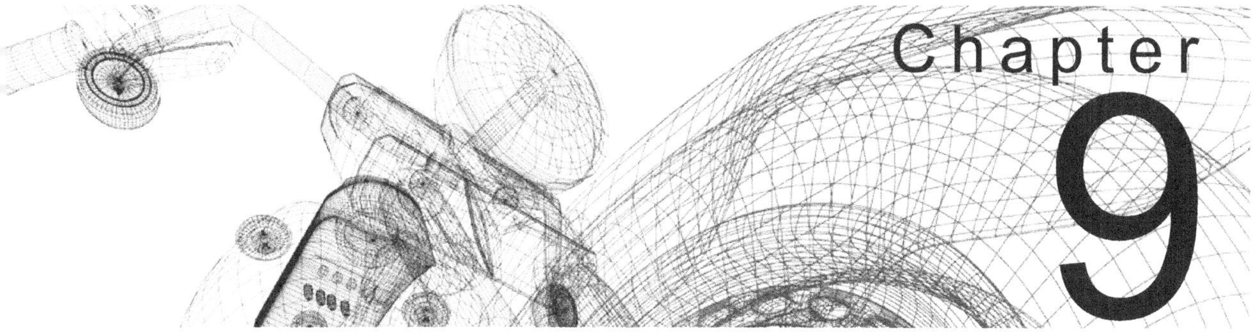

Chapter 9

Projects

This chapter provides drawing projects that can be completed throughout the duration of the course.

Learning Objectives in This Chapter

- Project A - Handle
- Project B - Mounting Plate
- Project C - Product Drawing

Practice 9a

Project A - Handle

Practice Objectives

- Create a part drawing with minimal instruction.
- Create drawing views using the View Creation Wizard.
- Create additional Projection, Section, Clipping, Detail, and Isometric views.
- Create a title block.

This project can be completed anytime after Chapters 1 and 2 have been completed.

In this project, you will create two drawing sheets for a power drill handle. The first sheet will contain projection and detail views and the second sheet will contain cross-section views.

1. Import and open **Handle.3dxml**. The model displays as shown in Figure 9–1.

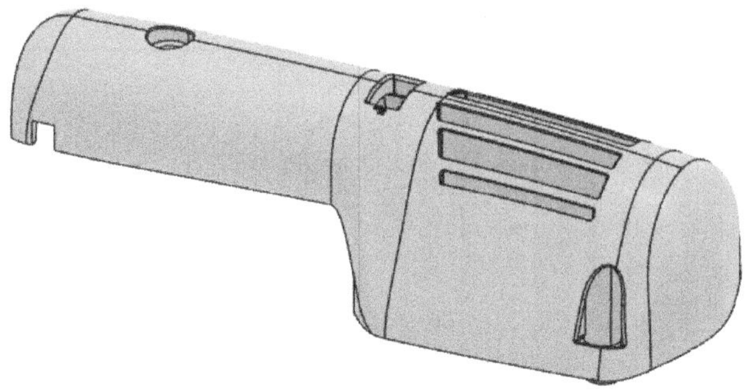

Figure 9–1

2. In the Top Bar, click (Add)>**Drawing**. The Drawing window will open.
3. In the *Title* field, enter the name **###_Handle** where ### represents your initials.
4. Select the *Drawing Information* tab at the top of the Drawing window.

5. For the *Standard*, enter **ANSI-ASME** and for the *Sheet Style*, select **C ANSI** as shown in Figure 9–2.

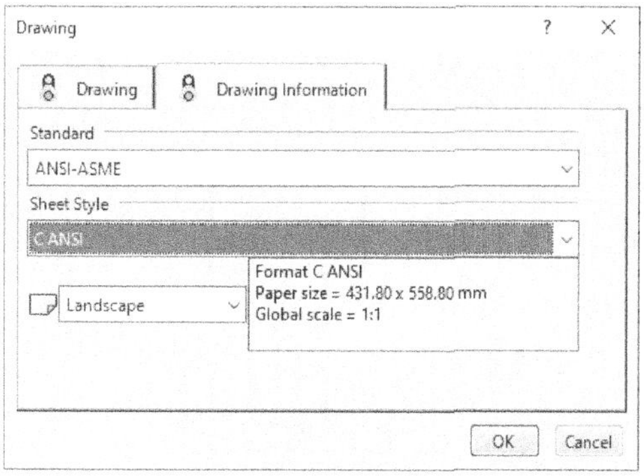

Figure 9–2

6. Add views and a title block as shown in Figure 9–3. Ensure that the Front, Bottom, and Right views are linked. In addition, ensure that Section view A-A is a half section.

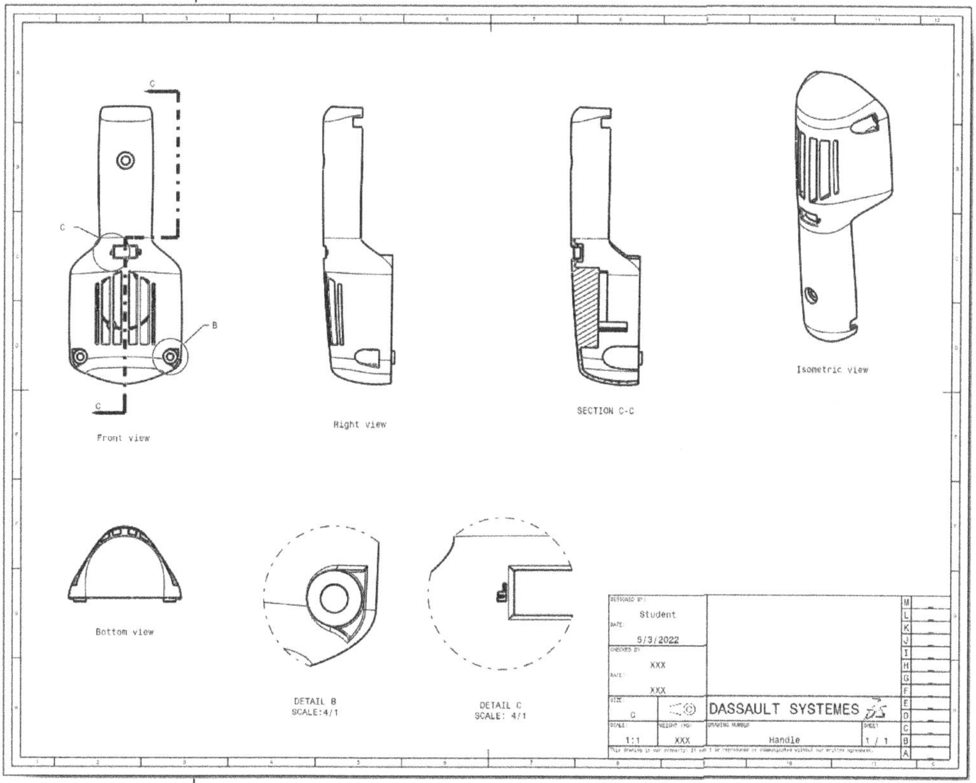

Figure 9–3

7. Add a new sheet and create the views shown in Figure 9–4.

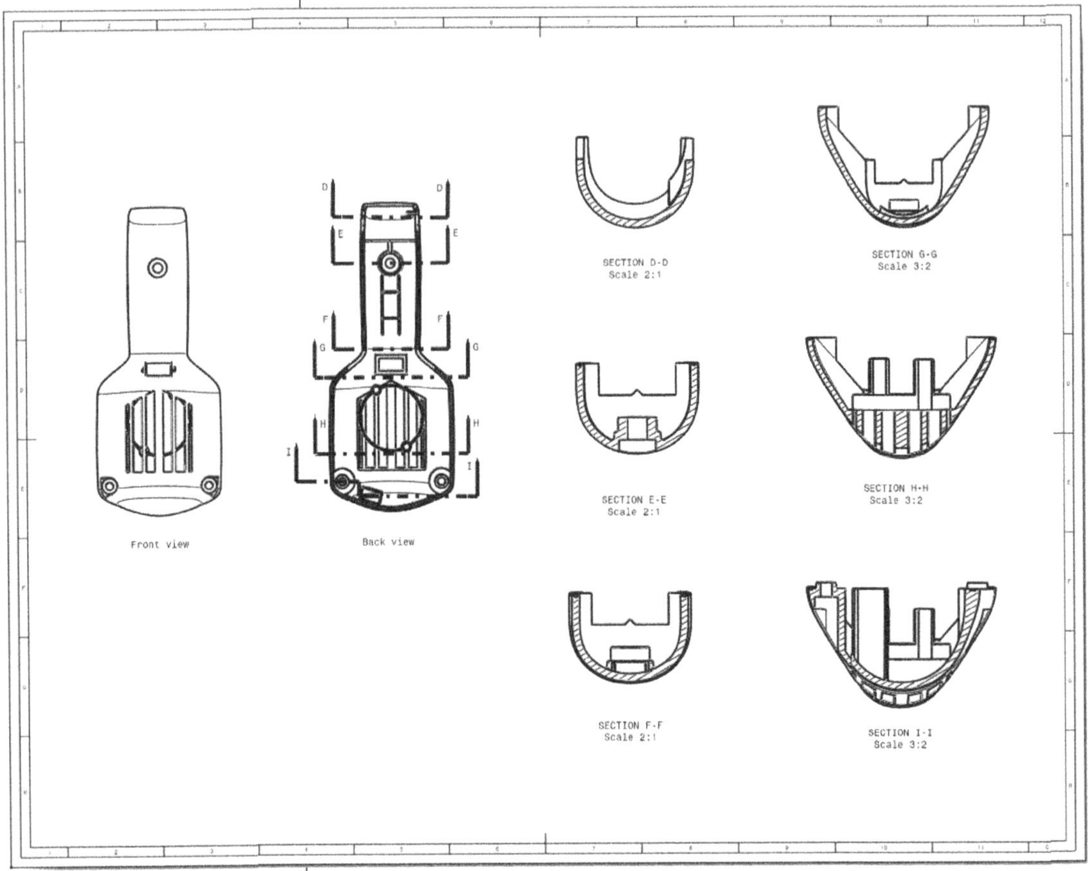

Figure 9–4

8. Save and close all of the windows.

Practice 9b

Project B - Mounting Plate

Practice Objective

- Create a part drawing.

This project can be done anytime after Chapters 1 through 6 have been completed.

1. Import and open **Mount_Plate.3dxml**.
2. Create the C ANSI size drawing shown in Figure 9–5.

Design Considerations

The dimensions are in inches for this practice. The units of a dimension can be changed after it has been created using the Object Properties window's **Numerical** options. Note that changing the default units of dimensions must be done by a CAD Administrator from the Drawing Standards file.

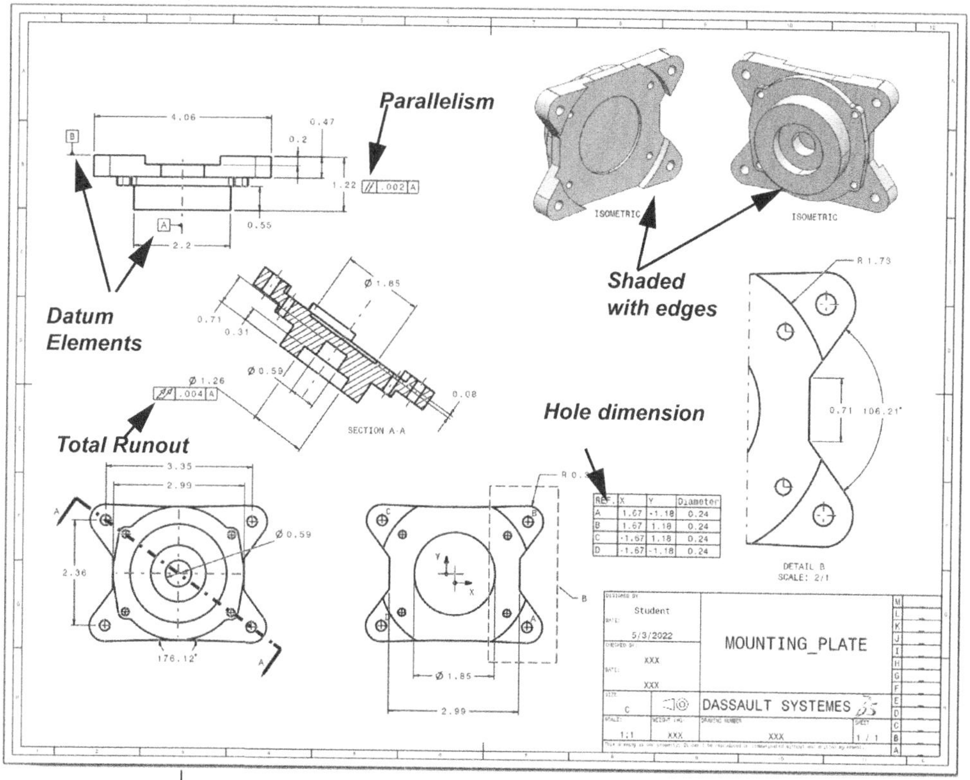

Figure 9–5

Practice 9c Project C - Product Drawing

Practice Objective

- Create a product drawing.

This project can be done anytime after Chapters 1 through 7 have been completed.

In this project, you will create a product drawing for an aircraft engine. An assortment of views ranging from standard projection views, isometric, section, and clipping views will be included in this drawing. You will create a bill of materials and balloons. Slides have been created for you in the product model. You will use them to create some of the views required in this project. Four sheets will be required for the drawing. The last sheet will be reserved for creating 2D components, shown in Figure 9–9. The final product drawing will display as shown in Figure 9–6, Figure 9–7, Figure 9–8, and Figure 9–9.

1. Import and open **aft_engine_section_asm_with_ slides.3dxml**.
2. Create the D ANSI size drawing shown in Figure 9–6 through Figure 9–9.

Design Considerations

The dimensions are in inches for this practice. The units of a dimension can be changed after it has been created using the Object Properties window's **Numerical** options. Note that changing the default units of dimensions must be done in the Drawing Standards file by a CAD Administrator.

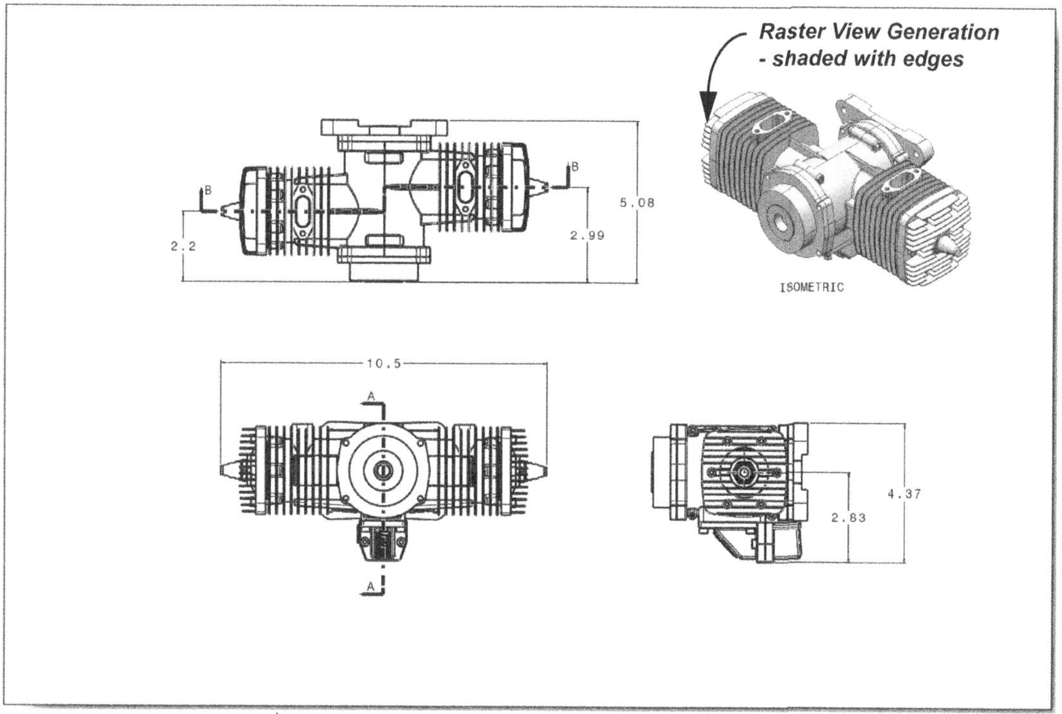
Raster View Generation
- shaded with edges
ISOMETRIC
5.08
2.99
2.2
B
10.5
A
4.37
2.83

Figure 9–6

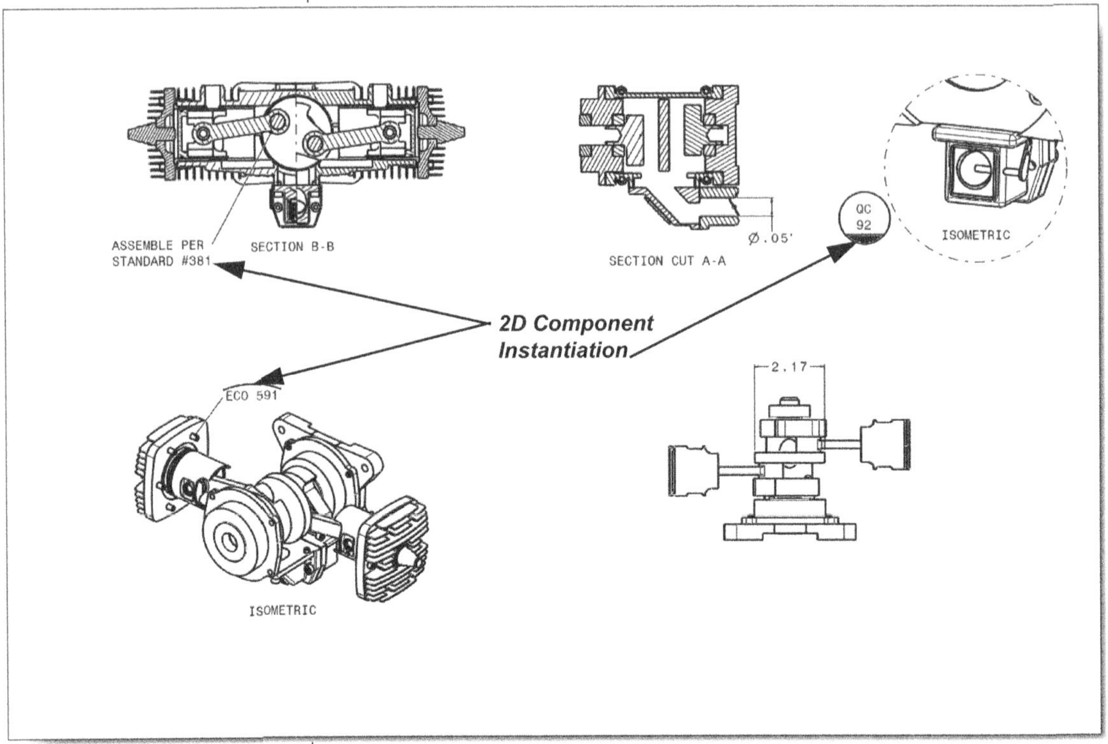
ASSEMBLE PER
STANDARD #381
SECTION B-B
Ø.05'
SECTION CUT A-A
QC
92
ISOMETRIC
2D Component
Instantiation
2.17
ECO 591
ISOMETRIC

Figure 9–7

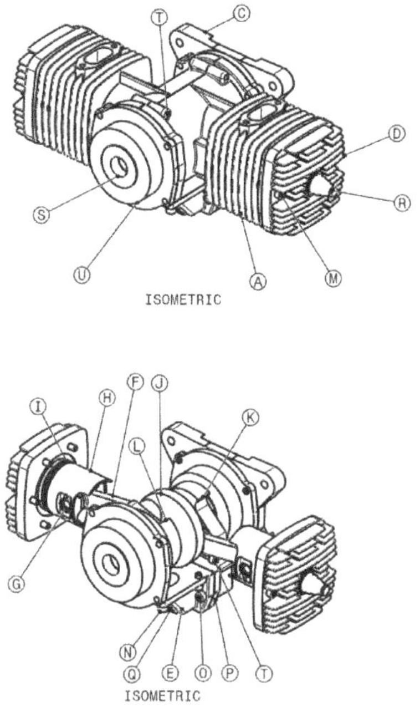

Item No.	Quantity	Title
A	2	BLOCK
B	2	SLEEVE
C	1	MOUNTING_PLATE
D	2	HEAD
E	1	INTAKE_MANIFOLD
F	2	CONNECTING_ROD
G	2	WRIST_PIN
H	2	PISTON
I	1	PISTON_RING
J	1	CRANK
K	1	COUPLING_CRANK
L	1	AFT_COUPLING_CRANK
M	16	021143M4X14
N	4	021143M4X8
O	2	021143M4X10
P	1	CARBURETOR
Q	1	NAME_PLATE
R	2	SPARK_PLUG
S	3	6002A
T	4	021143M4X20
U	1	FORE_AFT_COUPLING

Figure 9–8

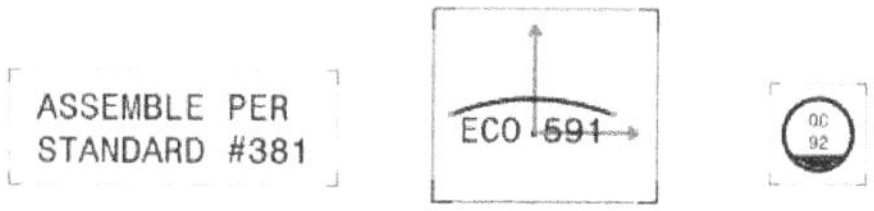

Figure 9–9

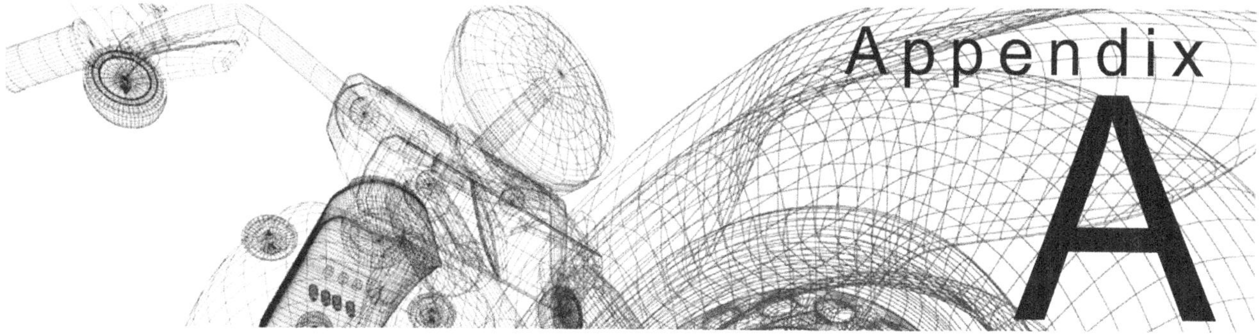

Drawing Frame and Title Block Customization

This appendix provides instruction regarding the customization of a frame and title block script. It does not teach how to create a script from scratch, but shows how some common modifications can be performed. Basic programming skills and experience with the Visual Basic programming language are a required prerequisite.

Learning Objectives in This Appendix

- Customize a script.
- Understand the anatomy of a sample macro.
- Make basic and advanced modifications to macros.
- Add graphics via macros.

A.1 Customizing a Script

General Steps

Use the following general steps to configure a custom frame and title block (FTB):

1. Create a copy of the simple macro.
2. Open and edit the macro.
3. Test the macro.
4. Create the preview image file.

Step 1 - Create a copy of the simple macro.

The standard installation of CATIA 3DEXPERIENCE includes examples of FTB macros. These files are located in the *<install_directory>\<current_release>\win_b64\VBScript\Frame TitleBlock* directory.

The directory contains two sample macros: **Drawing_Titleblock_Sample1.CATScript** and **Drawing_Titleblock_Sample2.CATScript**, as shown in Figure A–1.

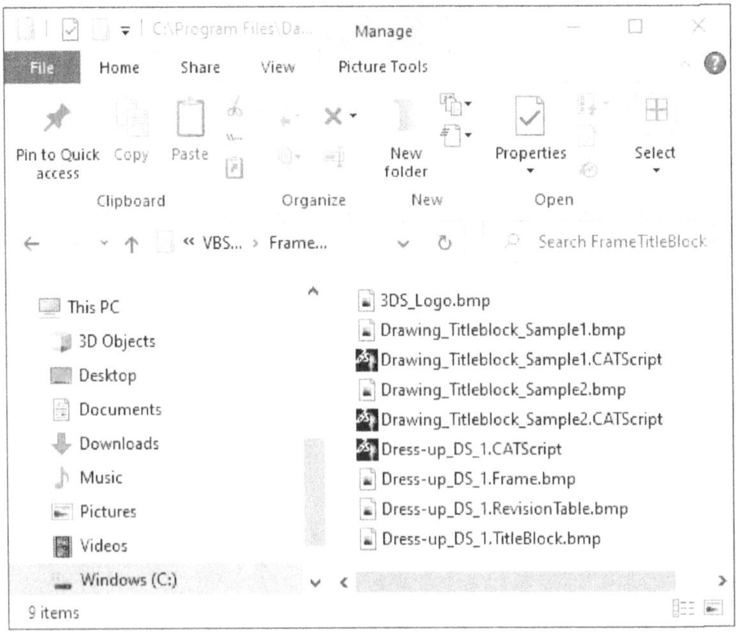

Figure A–1

The **bmp** files are the preview images of the frame and title block the macro creates.

The recommended process for developing a custom FTB macro is to create a copy, then modify one of the provided sample macros.

You can create a copy of the sample macro to modify in the same directory. However, this will tie the custom macro to your 3DEXPERIENCE installation and will make it difficult to share the macro among the members of your team of designers.

Alternatively, you can put the custom FTB macro into any directory on your computer or on your company's shared network. In that case, the location of the macro must be registered in **Preferences>App Preferences>Mechanical Systems>Drafting>Administration>Page Setup Directory**, as shown in Figure A–2.

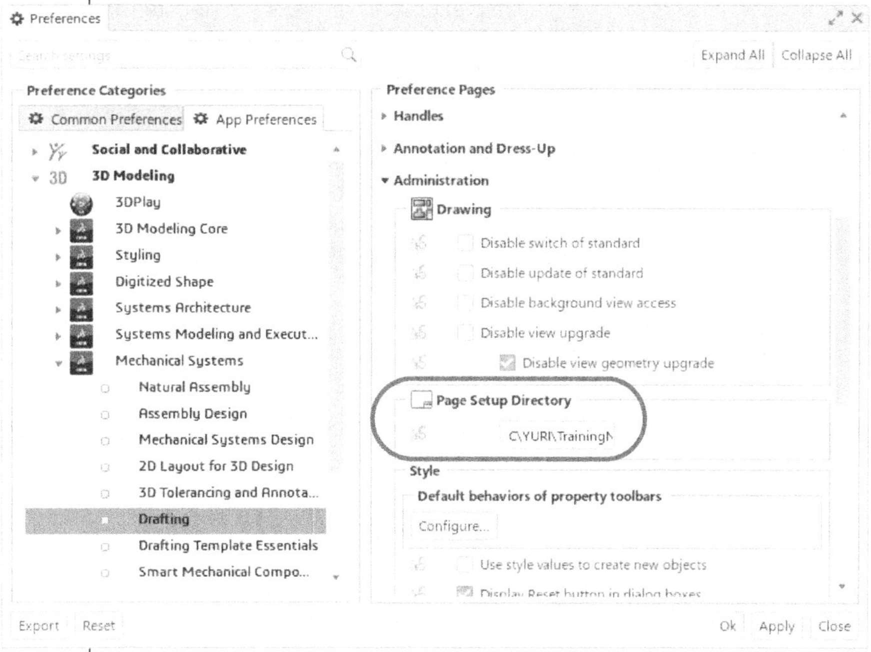

Figure A–2

Step 2 - Open and edit the macro.

CATScript macro language is the Dassault Systemès proprietary implementation of the standard VBScript programming language, portable to Unix.

CATScript and VBScript share the same syntax rules, feature set, keywords, and operators. Therefore, knowledge of VBScript is sufficient for working with CATScript files.

Although a CATScript file can be imported and edited using CATIA's VBA Editor, which provides enhanced readability, navigation, and editing features such as key word highlighting, auto-complete function calls, and debugging, the VBA file must be exported back to the CATScript format in the end. Additionally, after exporting, the CATScript file must be edited again, since CATScript does not support the full VBA syntax. Particularly, the enumerated data types must be replaced with integer numbers, and the in-line data type declarations (e.g., "#" symbol for floating point numbers) must be removed.

Therefore, it is recommended to edit CATScript files directly with any plain text editor, such as Notepad for Windows. The Notepad editor is used in this appendix, as shown in Figure A–3.

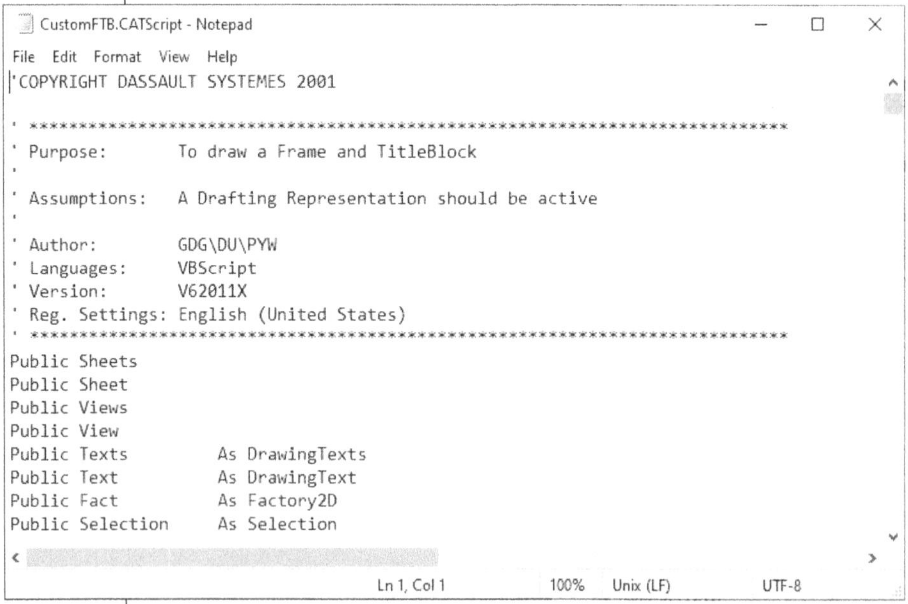

Figure A–3

When examining the source code, note that some subroutines start with the **CATDrw_** prefix. These become available actions in the Page Layout dialog box, as shown in Figure A–4.

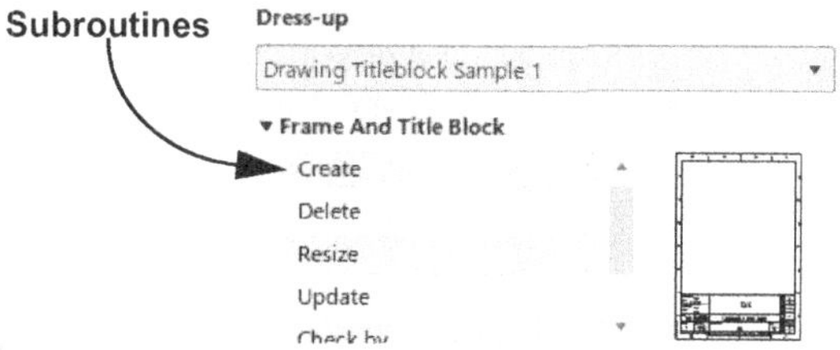

Figure A–4

Note the use of comments in the source code denoted by a single quotation mark at the beginning of the comment. Comments improve code readability and promote concurrent engineering. It is good programming practice to document the purpose of each segment of code and any changes and updates that are made.

Once the source code has been modified, save the file with a unique file name and a CATScript extension, as shown in Figure A–5.

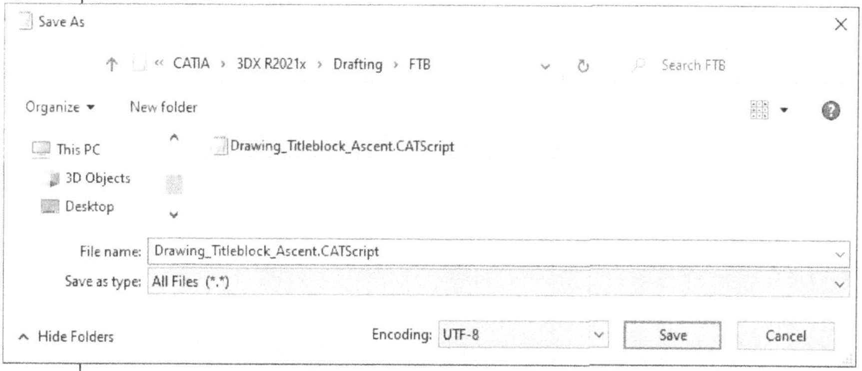

Figure A–5

Step 3 - Create the preview image file.

Once modified, the functionality of a macro should be tested. In the Drafting app, select the modified macro in the Dress-up drop-down list and apply all of the actions (**Create**, **Delete**, **Resize**, etc.) to ensure that the macro performs as intended.

Step 4 - Create the preview image file.

Creating a preview image file is optional. However, having the preview helps when selecting which macro to use to create the required style of the title block, as shown in Figure A–6.

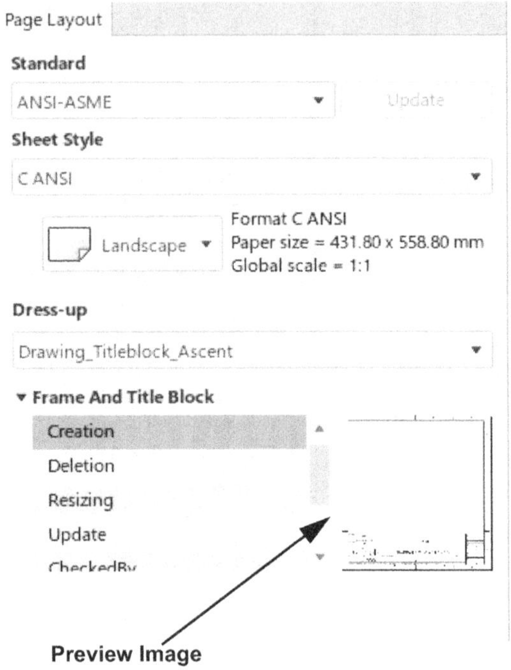

Figure A–6

To create the preview image, open a new empty drawing in portrait orientation. Run the macro to create the FTB. Hide the grid, as shown in Figure A–7.

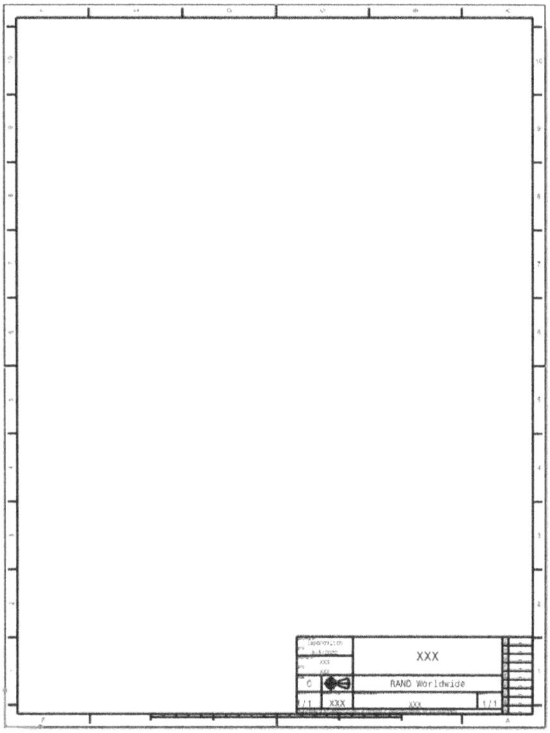

Figure A–7

Using the screen capture tool of your choice, capture the image and save it to a **bmp** file in the *FTB macro* directory.

Note that the name of the **bmp** file must match the name of the **CATScript** file.

A.2 Anatomy of a Sample Macro

Because the sample frame and title block macro files are very large, it is important to develop an understanding of macro layout. The Frame & Title Block Flowchart in Figure A–8 shows some of the main subroutines that are executed when a new frame and title block are applied to a sheet background.

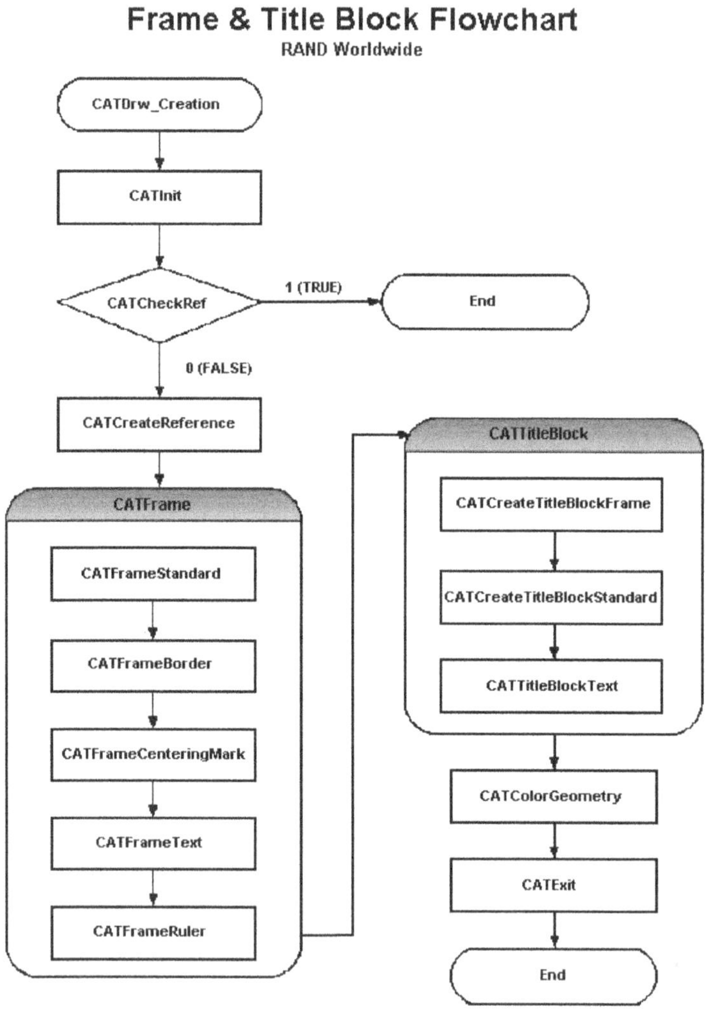

Figure A–8

CATInit

The **CATInit** subroutine initializes macro variables and is called at the beginning of all action subroutines. **CATInit** makes objects available, such as **Sheet** (containing sheet width and height parameters) and **Fact** (2D Factory permits lines to be drawn).

CATCheckRef

The **CATCheckRef** subroutine checks whether a frame and title block already exist on the drawing sheet.

CATCreate Reference

The **CATCreateReference** subroutine adds a text entity to the sheet, which serves as a marker indicating whether the FTB is already present on the sheet.The text is an empty string and is named **Reference_<macro name>**. The **CATCheckRef** subroutine uses this text entity to verify whether the frame and title block have already been created on the drawing sheet.

CATFrame

The **CATFrame** calls several smaller subroutines to draw the frame. **CATFrameStandard** is the first of these subroutines and, while it does not draw anything, it sets up important variables that are used by the rest of the **CATFrame** subroutines, shown in Figure A–9.

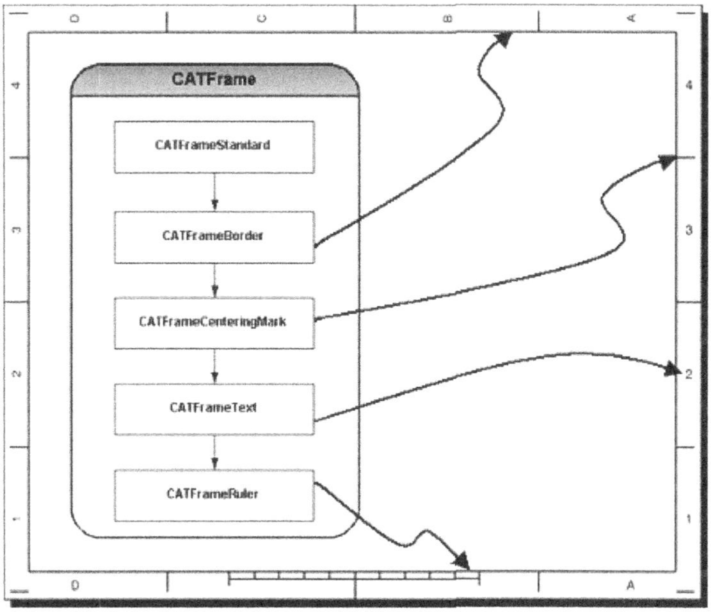

Figure A–9

CATTitleBlock

Similar to CATFrame, CATTitleBlock calls other subroutines to create the title block. These three subroutines draw and fill the title block with text:

- **CATTitleBlockFrame** draws the title block table.
- **CATTitleBlockStandard** draws an icon of either the 1st angle or 3rd angle.
- **CATTitleBlockText** creates text fields in the title block table. This subroutine calls another important subroutine, **CATLinks**, which fills in some of the text from the product information.

CATExit

The final subroutine, **CATExit**, prepares an undo point so that the creation of a frame and title block can be undone.

A.3 Basic Modifications

Helper Functions

To give the macro script a unique and meaningful name, modify the **GetMacroID** function. The function is located among many other helper functions near the beginning of the script. The **GetMacroID** function is shown in Figure A–10.

```
Function GetMacroID() as String
  GetMacroID = "Drawing_Titleblock_Ascent"
End Function
```

Figure A–10

Text Fields

The default company name and other title block table headings can be customized by modifying the **CATTitleBlockText** parameter values, as shown in Figure A–11.

```
Text_01 = "This drawing is our property; it can't
Text_02 = "SCALE"
Text_03 = "XXX"
Text_04 = "WEIGHT (kg)"
Text_05 = "XXX"
Text_06 = "DRAWING NUMBER"
Text_07 = "SHEET"
Text_08 = "SIZE"
Text_09 = "USER"
Text_10 = "XXX"
Text_11 = "RAND WORLDWIDE"
Text_12 = "CHECKED BY"
Text_13 = "DATE:"
Text_14 = "DESIGNED BY:"
```

Figure A–11

The default relative location of the text parameters listed in Figure A–11 is shown in Figure A–12.

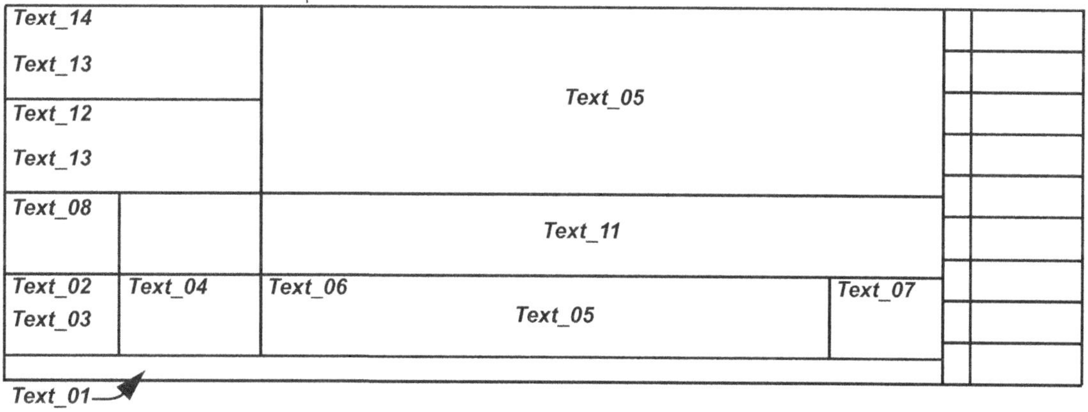

Figure A–12

Table Cell Sizes

The default title block table cell sizes can be modified in the helper functions **Col** and **Row**, as shown in Figure A–13.

```
Function Col(idx As Integer) As Variant
  Col=Array(-190, -145, -125, -110, -95, -50, -30, -15)(idx-1)
End Function

Function Row(idx As Integer) As Variant
  Row=Array( 10, 12, 24, 36, 40, 60)(idx-1)
End Function
```

Figure A–13

The **Col(1)** parameter defines the boundary of the table's base cell. As it is measured from the vertical origin, it effectively sets the overall width of the table. Each consecutive column of cells *overlaps* the base cell, as shown in Figure A–14, and should have an offset value that is less than every preceding column boundary.

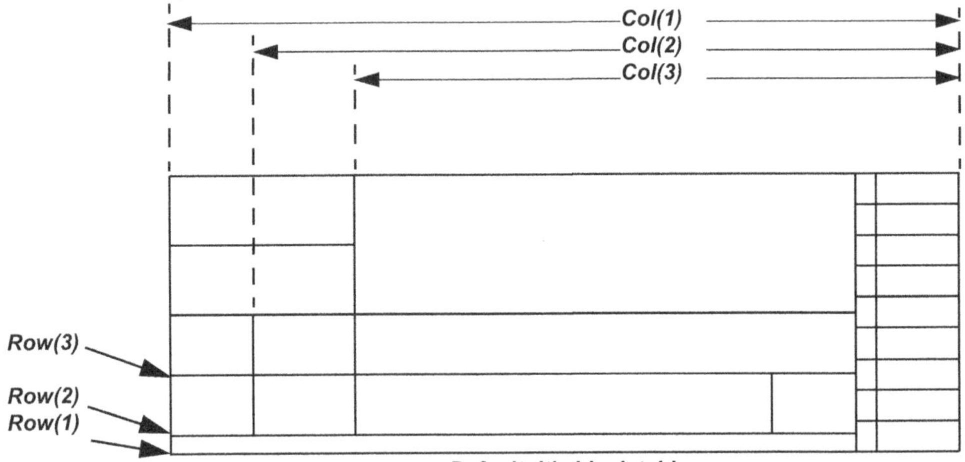

Default title block table

Figure A–14

The **Row(1)** parameter defines the boundary of the first row from the horizontal origin. Each consecutive row of cells is placed *behind* the first, as shown in Figure A–14, and should have an offset value that is greater than every preceding row boundary.

A.4 Advanced Modifications

In addition to customizing title block text fields and table structure, your input and custom graphics can also be incorporated into a sheet background.

User Input Boxes

Two essential methods can be used to add your input to the macro - the **InputBox** and **MsgBox** functions.

To create a text input box, a variable of type string must be declared in the script file. In the example shown in Figure A–15, the variable named **CompanyName** stores a user-entered string, which is the name of your company. Although the variable declaration can be placed anywhere in the code, it is good programming practice to group all variable declarations in the header of a file.

```
Public Texts          As DrawingTexts
Public Text           As DrawingText
Public Fact           As Factory2D
Public Selection      As Selection

Public CompanyName    AS String
```

Figure A–15

The first input box parameter, <prompt>, is the only one that is mandatory.

Placement of the input box code is critical. For an input box that prompts you to enter the company name and inserts it into the title block table, the code must be placed in the **CATTitleBlockText** subroutine. The syntax code of an **InputBox** is:

<string_variable> = InputBox("<prompt>", "<title>", "default_value")

In the example shown in Figure A–16, two lines of code have been added. The first prompts you to enter a value for the string parameter. The second assigns this value to Text_11, which the macro uses later in the code for the company name.

```
    Text_09 = "USER"
    Text_10 = "XXX"              ' Paper Format
 ' An input box will read in company name from user and store it in the CompanyName string
 CompanyName = InputBox("Enter the company name:", "Company Name", "RAND Worldwide")
 ' CompanyName will be assigned to Text_11 (company name field)
    Text_11 = CompanyName
    Text_12 = "CHECKED BY"
    Text_13 = "DATE:"
    Text_14 = "DESIGNED BY:"
```

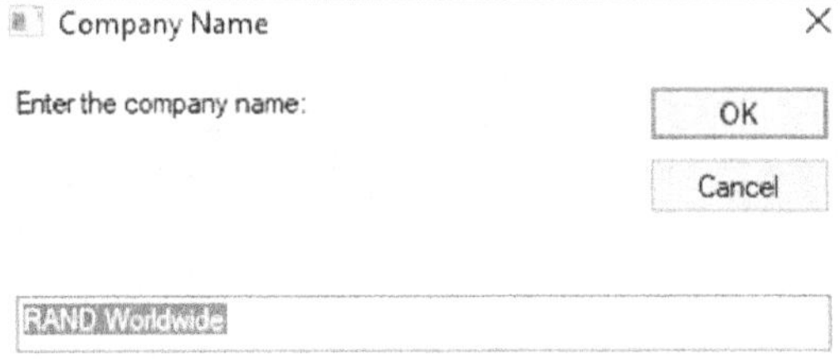

Figure A–16

The input box opens when its containing subroutine is executed (more generally, when the frame and title block macro is applied to a sheet background), as shown in Figure A–16.

When you enter a string into the input field and click **OK**, it is assigned to the **CompanyName** variable. The value of **CompanyName** is then called as the **Text_11** parameter value. Therefore, the company name cell of the title block table contains the value of the **CompanyName** string.

Clicking **Cancel** prevents modification of the **CompanyName** variable. Nothing displays in the company name cell in the title block.

Message Boxes

Message boxes are used to obtain user response, such as "Yes", "No", "Cancel", etc., by returning the value indicating which button on the dialog box was clicked. Additionally, they provide error messages and important information.

The syntax for a **MsgBox** is similar to that of an **InputBox**:

<answer> = MsgBox("<prompt>",<buttons>,"<title>")

The <buttons> parameter is an integer number that specifies the buttons to display in the message box. The <answer> parameter is an integer number that indicates which button was clicked in the message box.

The code shown in Figure A–17 produces a message box that prompts you about whether centering marks should be added to the frame during the creation of a background. Investigate the code and note its placement and documentation.

```
Sub CATFrame()
  '-------------------------------------------------------------------------------
  'How to create the Frame
  '-------------------------------------------------------------------------------
  Dim Cst_1   As Double  'Length (in cm) between 2 horinzontal marks
  Dim Cst_2   As Double  'Length (in cm) between 2 vertical marks
  Dim Nb_CM_H As Integer 'Number/2 of horizontal centring marks
  Dim Nb_CM_V As Integer 'Number/2 of vertical centring marks
  Dim Ruler   As Integer 'Ruler length (in cm)

  CATFrameStandard     Nb_CM_H, Nb_CM_V, Ruler, Cst_1, Cst_2
  CATFrameBorder
  'Create a message box prompting for addition of centering marks
  Dim ans As Integer
  ans = MsgBox("Do you want to add Centering Marks to the frame?",4,"Centering Marks")
  'Begin if/else statement
  'If and only if user selects YES, centering marks will be added
  If ans = 6 Then          ' 6 = vbYes
        MsgBox "Centering Marks will be added."
        CATFrameCentringMark Nb_CM_H, Nb_CM_V, Ruler, Cst_1, Cst_2
  End If
  CATFrameText         Nb_CM_H, Nb_CM_V, Ruler, Cst_1, Cst_2
  CATFrameRuler        Ruler, Cst_1
End Sub
```

Figure A–17

As noted in the code comments, centering marks are added to the frame if you select **Yes** in the Centering Marks dialog box, as shown in Figure A–18. If you select **No**, centering marks are not added.

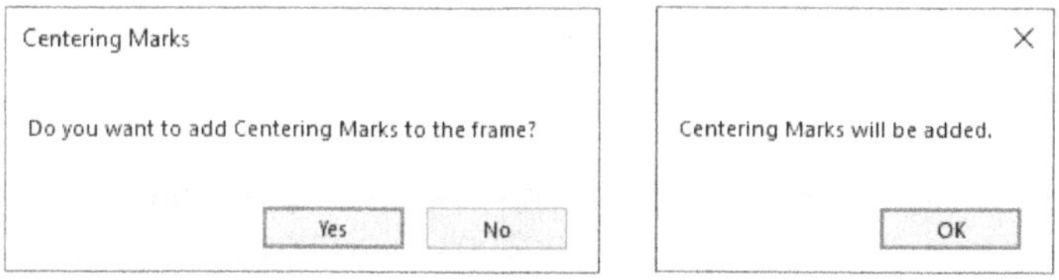

Figure A–18

The **MsgBox** function offers many different button styles, as shown in the table below. The style must be the 2nd parameter in the **Msgbox** call. For example, the **MsgBox** syntax shown in Figure A–17 uses button style 4, which displays the Yes or No buttons.

MsgBox Style Name	Example
vbYesNo=4	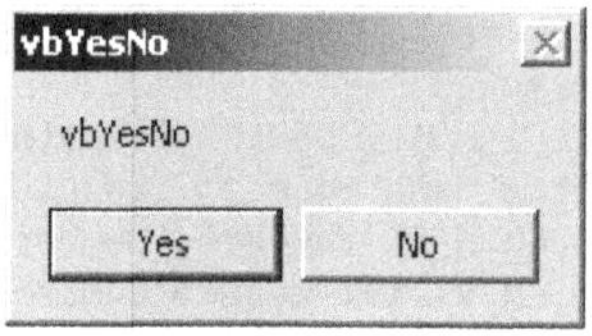
vbOKOnly=0	
vbYesNoCancel=3	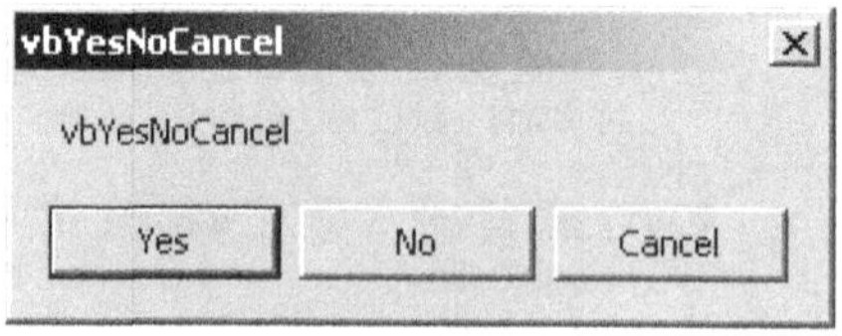
vbOKCancel=1	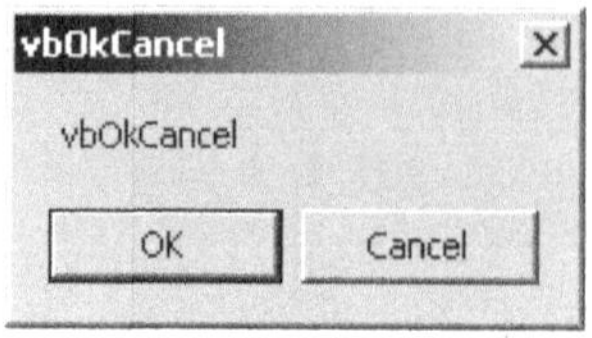

MsgBox Style Name	Example
vbExclamation=48	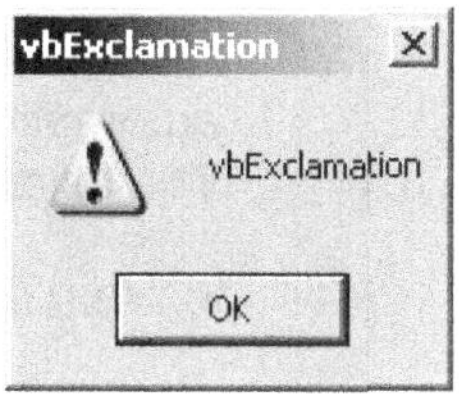
vbAbortRetryIgnore=2	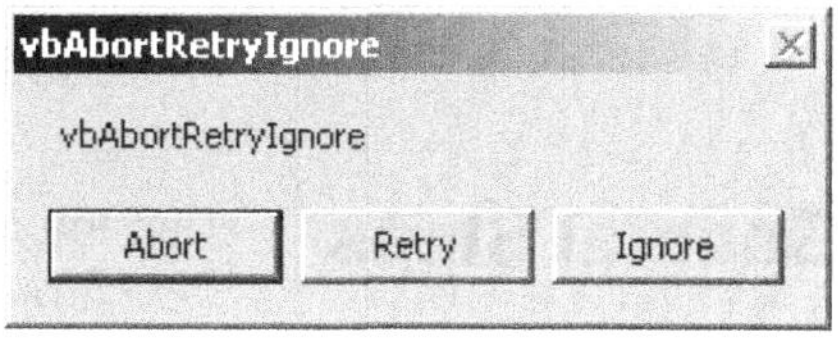

A.5 Adding Graphics

Corporate logos and engineering symbols can be added automatically during background creation using a macro script. The following tasks can be performed:

- Add a picture to the frame and title block.
- Replace/move a picture.
- Remove a picture.

General Steps

Use the following general steps to insert a graphic into the sheet background:

1. Add the required global variables.
2. Initialize the graphic object in **CATInit**.
3. Insert the graphic.
4. Associate the graphic with the sheet background.

Step 1 - Add the required global variables.

Two new variables, **DrwPictures** and **Pic**, must be created at the beginning of the **CATScript** file to enable graphic creation and manipulation. In the script header file, insert the code shown in Figure A–19.

```
Public Texts          As DrawingTexts
Public Text           As DrawingText
Public Fact           As Factory2D
Public Selection      As Selection

Public CompanyName    AS String

'USER ENTERED VARIABLES
Public DrwPictures As DrawingPictures
Public Pic As DrawingPicture
```

Figure A–19

The **DrwPictures** variable is a collection. A collection is an array of variables. In this case, an array of **DrawingPicture** objects.

Step 2 - Initialize the graphic object in CATInit.

Before the new variables can be used, they must be initialized. The **CATInit** subroutine is used to initialize variables and objects in FTB macros.

To initialize the **DrwPictures** variable, insert the code into the **CATInit** subroutine, as shown in Figure A–20.

```
Function CATInit( targetSheet as CATIABase )
  '---------------------------------------------------
  'How to init the dialog and create main objects
  '---------------------------------------------------
  If Not IsEmpty(CATIA) Then
    Set Selection    = CATIA.ActiveDocument.Selection
  End If
  Set Sheet         = targetSheet
  Set Sheets        = Sheet.Parent
  Set ActiveDoc     = Sheets.Parent
  Set Views         = Sheet.Views
  Set View          = Views.Item(2)'Get the background view
  Set Texts         = View.Texts
  Set Fact          = View.Factory2D
  ' USER INSERTED INITIALIZATION
  Set DrwPictures   = View.Pictures
```

Figure A–20

This makes **DrwPictures** reference the collection of pictures in the active document's background view.

Step 3 - Insert the graphic.

The placement of the graphic insertion code depends on the number of pictures added.

If a single corporate logo is to be added to a cell of the title block, the code is placed in the **CATTitleBlockText** subroutine, which is responsible for filling in the title block table. If many graphics, such as symbols, are to be inserted, a new subroutine dedicated to graphic insertion should be created and named **CATInsertPictures**.

The code shown in Figure A–21 inserts and formats the size and location of a graphic. It can be added to the **CATTitleBlockText** subroutine or independently placed into a new subroutine, as shown in Figure A–21.

```
'Create by <your_name>, <today's date>
Sub InsertPictures()
  '-----------------------------------------------------------------------------
  'This subroutine inserts all pictures into the titleblock
  '-----------------------------------------------------------------------------
  '1st picture (company logo)
Set Pic = DrwPictures.Add("<file name of the picture, including path>", GetOH+Col(3), Get0V+Row(3))
With Pic
        .Name = "<Name of graphic object)"   <-- e.g., "TitleBlock_Pic_1"
        .Height = Row(5) - Row(3)
        .Width = .Height / .GetOriginalHeight * .GetOriginalWidth
End Width
'insert code for all other pictures
'...
End Sub
```

Figure A–21

Step 4 - Associate the graphic with the sheet background.

Graphics inserted by a frame and title block macro are static. The location of a graphic does not update when the sheet format is changed and the frame and title block are resized. Furthermore, a graphic is not included in the deletion of the sheet background that inserted it. This functionality can be incorporated into a frame and title block script by associating the graphic with existing formatting subroutines.

Resizing/ Moving a Graphic

The existing **CATDrw_Resizing** subroutine, which resizes the frame and title block, calls a subroutine named **CATMoveTitleBlockText**. This subroutine replaces the title block location during frame and title block resizing. Therefore, this is a good place to insert the graphic location update code, as shown in Figure A–22.

```
'Selects then moves all picture items with name of "TitleBlock_Pic_*"
SelectAll "CATDrwSearch.DrwPicture.Name=TitleBlock_Pic_*"
count = Selection.Count2
For ii = 1 To count
  Set Pic=Selection.Item2(ii).Value
  Pic.x  = Pic.x + Translation(0)
  Pic.y  = Pic.y + Translation(1)
Next
```

Figure A–22

This code uses a **SelectAll** helper function that selects all of the picture names that begin with **TitleBlock_Pic_** and moves them. The code will work correctly as long as all of the inserted graphics names begin with **TitleBlock_Pic_**.

Deleting a Graphic

Because of the way the macro is created, if you name all of your pictures so that they begin with **TitleBlock_**, you do not have to do anything else to have them deleted. The code is shown in Figure A–23.

DeleteAll is another helper function that is used as a **Selection** tool to find, select, and delete all objects that fall under a certain criteria.

```
Sub CATDrw_Deletion( targetSheet as CATIABase )
  '-------------------------------------------------
  'How to delete the FTB
  '-------------------------------------------------
  If Not CATInit(targetSheet) Then Exit Sub
  If CATCheckRef(0) Then Exit Sub
  DeleteAll "..Name=Frame_*"
  DeleteAll "..Name=TitleBlock_*"
  DeleteAll "..Name=RevisionBlock_*"
  DeleteAll "..Name=Reference_*"
  CATExit targetSheet
End Sub
```

Figure A–23

Practice A1 Modify Macros

Practice Objectives

- Modify and export a sample macro file.
- Customize the company name and title block table.
- Obtain user input.
- Add a graphic.

Task 1 - Create a copy of the sample macro.

1. Create a directory named **FTB** in your computer's file system – this will be the location for the modified macro. You can create the directory anywhere you choose, such as on your Desktop.

2. Open the directory containing the 3DEXPERIENCE's sample FTB macros, at **<install_directory>\<current_release>\win_b64\VBScript\FrameTitleBlock**.

3. Copy the **Drawing_Titleblock_Sample1.CATScript** file from the sample macro directory to the *FTB* directory you created in Step 1.

4. Rename the copied macro to **Drawing_Titleblock_Rand.CATScript**.

5. In 3DEXPERIENCE, open **Preferences>App Preferences>Mechanical Systems>Drafting> Administration**, and modify the **Page Setup Directory** so that it points to your *FTB* macro directory, as shown in Figure A–24.

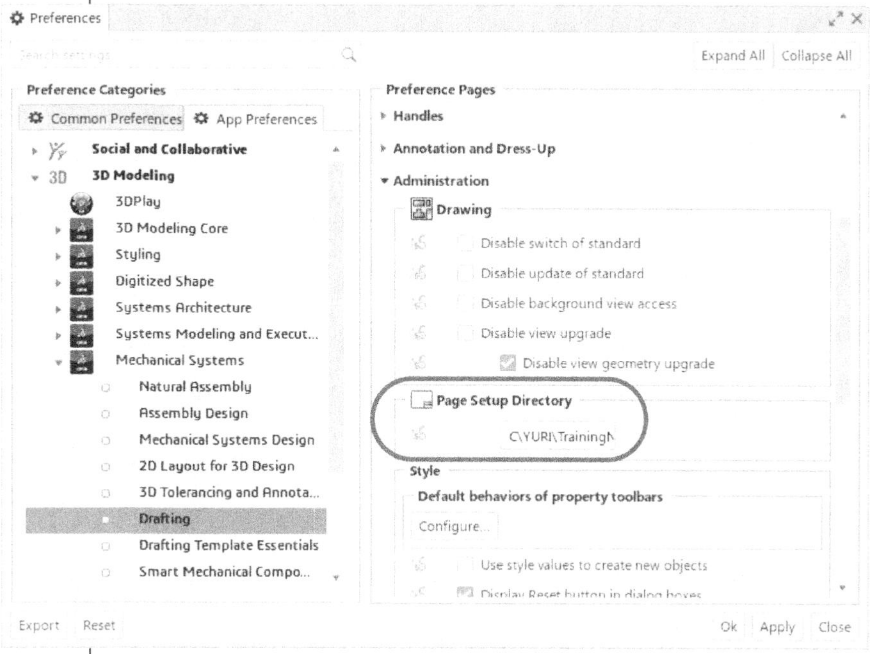

Figure A–24

Task 2 - Open the macro for editing.

1. Open **Drawing_Titleblock_Rand.CATScript** in Notepad.

2. Go to the beginning of the CATScript file. Add modification comments to the existing file documentation, as shown in Figure A–25.

```
' ***************************************************************************
' Purpose:       To draw a Frame and TitleBlock
'
' Assumptions:   A Drafting Representation should be active
'
' Author:        CDG\DU\RYW
' Modified by:   <your name>
' Date modifed:  <today's date>
' Languages:     VBScript
' Version:       V62011X
' Reg. Settings: English (United States)
' ***************************************************************************
```

Figure A–25

Task 3 - Modify the default title block table format.

1. You will delete the line separating the sheet size and the standard icon, as shown in Figure A–26.

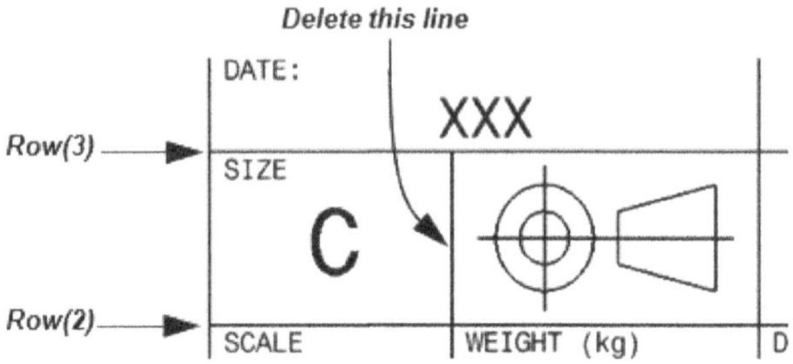

Figure A–26

2. Go to the **CATCreateTitleBlockFrame** subroutine and locate the code for *TitleBlock_Line_Column_1*, as shown in Figure A–27.

```
CreateLine GetOH() + Col(2),  GetOV() + Row(1),  GetOH() + Col(2),  GetOV() + Row(3), "TitleBlock_Line_Column_1"
CreateLine GetOH() + Col(3),  GetOV() + Row(1),  GetOH() + Col(3),  GetOV() + Row(5), "TitleBlock_Line_Column_2"
CreateLine GetOH() + Col(4),  GetOV() + Row(1),  GetOH() + Col(4),  GetOV() + Row(2), "TitleBlock_Line_Column_3"
CreateLine GetOH() + Col(5),  GetOV()         ,  GetOH() + Col(5),  GetOV() + Row(5), "TitleBlock_Line_Column_4"
CreateLine GetOH() + Col(6),  GetOV()         ,  GetOH() + Col(6),  GetOV() + Row(5), "TitleBlock_Line_Column_5"
```

Figure A–27

3. Change the *Row(3)* parameter to **Row(2)**. The boundary line for this column will now be drawn from the vertical origin up to the second row rather than to the third.

Task 4 - Modify the MacroID and company name.

<Ctrl> + <F> can be used to find the function.

1. Locate the **GetMacroID** function and modify its returned value from *Drawing_Titleblock_Sample1* to **Drawing_Titleblock_RAND**, as shown in Figure A–28.

```
Function GetMacroID() as String
  GetMacroID = "Drawing_Titleblock_RAND"
End Function
```

Figure A–28

2. Locate the **CATTitleBlockText** subroutine.

3. Locate the **Text_11** parameter and modify its value from *DASSAULT SYSTEMES* to **RAND WORLDWIDE**, as shown in Figure A–29.

```
Text_10 = "XXX"
Text_11 = "RAND WORLDWIDE"
Text_12 = "CHECKED BY:"
```

Figure A–29

Task 5 - Test the macro.

Design Considerations

As with any programming project, modifications to macro script files should be saved and tested frequently. This practice simplifies the identification and resolution of bugs, which can be overwhelming if permitted to stack up.

1. In 3DEXPERIENCE, create a new drawing using an **ANSI-ASME** standard and a **C ANSI** sheet size.

2. Select 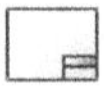 (Page Layout).

3. In the Page Layout dialog box that opens, select **Drawing_Titleblock_Rand** in the Dress-up drop-down list and **Creation** as the action to apply, as shown in Figure A–30.

A preview will not display in the Page Layout dialog box until a bitmap image is placed in the macro directory.

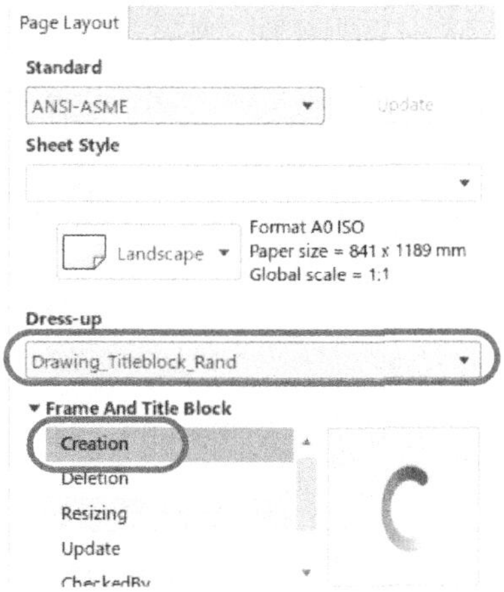

Figure A–30

4. Click **Apply**. The title block displays as shown in Figure A–31.

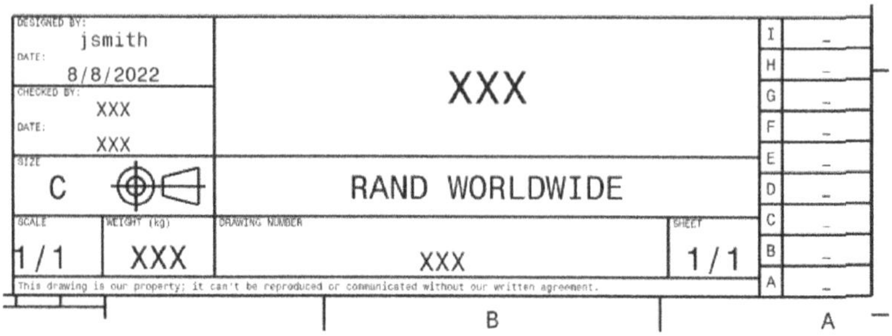

Figure A–31

5. To remove the frame and title block from the sheet background, select **Deletion** and click **Apply**.

6. Close the Page Layout dialog box.

Task 6 - Obtain user input.

1. Locate the **CATFrame** subroutine in the macro code.

2. Examine and enter the code shown in Figure A–32.

```
CATFrameStandard     Nb_CM_H, Nb_CM_V, Ruler, Cst_1, Cst_2
CATFrameBorder
' Modified by <your_name>, <today's date>
' Create a message box prompting for addition of centering marks
Dim ans As Integer
ans = MsgBox("Do you want to add Centering Marks to the frame?",4,"Centering Marks")
' Begin if/else statement
' If and only if user selects YES, centering marks will be added
If ans = 6 Then        ' 6 = vbYes
   MsgBox "Centering Marks will be added."
   CATFrameCentringMark Nb_CM_H, Nb_CM_V, Ruler, Cst_1, Cst_2
End If
' End modification
CATFrameText         Nb_CM_H, Nb_CM_V, Ruler, Cst_1, Cst_2
CATFrameRuler        Ruler, Cst_1
```

Figure A–32

3. Test the macro.

Task 7 - Insert a graphic.

1. In the practice files folder, locate the **RAND_Worldwide.bmp** file and copy it to the *FTB* macro directory.

2. Enter the code shown in Figure A–33 below the existing Public variable declarations.

```
Public Selection     As Selection

' USER ENTERED VARIABLES
Public DrwPictures As DrawingPictures
Public Pic As DrawingPicture
```

Figure A–33

3. Locate the **CATInit** subroutine. To initialize the **DrwPictures** object, insert the code shown in Figure A–34.

```
Set Texts        = View.Texts
Set Fact         = View.Factory2D
' USER INSERTED INITIALIZATION
Set DrwPictures = View.Pictures
```

Figure A–34

4. Create a new subroutine called **CATInsertPictures**. The exact placement of the subroutine in the macro code is not critical since it is a public subroutine, and therefore, accessible by other procedures from anywhere in the macro. For example, you can place it just below the **CATTitleBlockText** subroutine. The code for the new procedure is shown in Figure A–35. If the location of the graphic file is different from the one shown in Figure A–35, change the path to point to the location of the file.

```
' Created by <your_name>, <today's date>
Public Sub InsertPictures()
   '---------------------------------------------------------------------------
   ' This subroutine inserts all pictures into the titleblock
   '---------------------------------------------------------------------------
   Set Pic = DrwPictures.Add("C:\Drafting Exercise Files\FTB\RAND_Worldwide.bmp", GetOH+Col(3), GetOV+Row(3)
   With Pic
      .Name = "Titleblock_Pic_RAND"
      .Height = Row(5) - Row(3)
      .Width = .Height / .GetOriginalHeight * .GetOriginalWidth
   End With
End Sub

Sub CATDeleteRevisionBlockFrame
    DeleteAll "CATDrwSearch.2DGeometry.Name=RevisionBlock_Line_*"
End Sub
```

The picture's file name, including path

Figure A–35

5. For this subroutine to be executed when the sheet background is being applied to the sheet, it must be called by a main subroutine. Enter the code shown in Figure A–36 into the **CATDrw_Creation** subroutine after **CATTitleBlockText**.

```
CATTitleBlockText     'To fill in the title block
' Modified by <your_name>, <today's date>
InsertPictures
' End modification
CATExit targetSheet      'To save the sketch edition
```

Figure A–36

6. To prevent the default cell text from overlapping the company logo, go to the **CATTitleBlockText** subroutine and comment out the line shown in Figure A–37.

```
CreateTextAF Text_13,GetOH() + Col(1) + 1.      ,GetOV() + .5*(Row(4)+Row(5)),"TitleBlock_Text_DDate"      ,catTopLeft     ,1.5
CreateTextAF ""&GetDate,GetOH() + Col(2) + 2.5      ,GetOV() + Row(4)             ,"TitleBlock_Text_DDate_1"     ,catBottomCenter,3
'CreateTextAF Text_05,GetOH() + .5*(Col(3)+Col(5)),GetOV() + Row(4)             ,"TitleBlock_Text_Title_1"     ,catMiddleCenter,7
For ii = 1 To GetNbOfRevision()
```

Figure A–37

7. Test the macro. The title block displays as shown in Figure A–38.

Figure A–38

Task 8 - Create the preview image file.

1. Create a new drawing in Portrait orientation. Run the FTB macro.

2. Take a screen capture of the frame and title block and save it with the name **Drawing_Titleblock_Rand.bmp** in the *FTB* macro folder.

3. Note that the Page Layout dialog box now displays the preview image for the macro, as shown in Figure A–39.

Figure A–39

Task 9 - (Optional) Relocate the graphics.

1. Make the required changes to the macro to have the **Resizing** relocate the graphics.

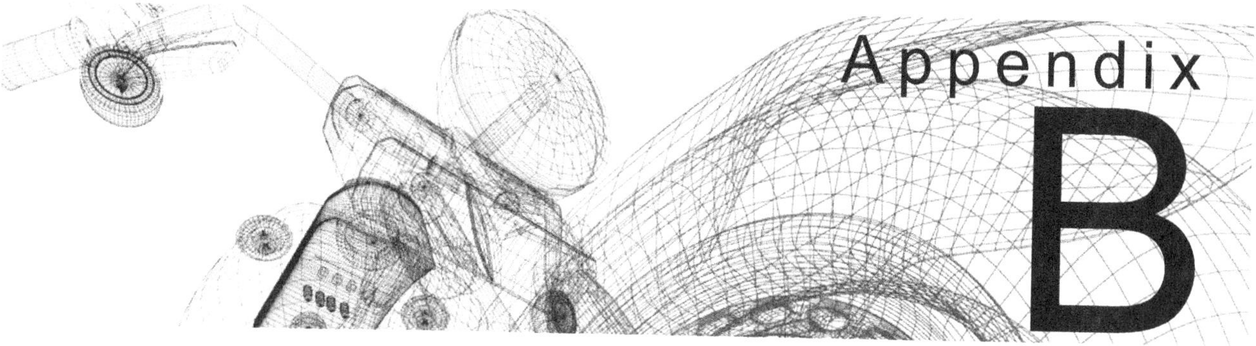

Appendix B

Extracting 3D T&A Views

This appendix introduces methods of displaying annotation views that have been created in the 3D model as a drawing view. A brief introduction to the 3D Tolerancing & Annotation app and the use of annotation sets is provided.

Learning Objectives in This Appendix

- Understand the basics of the 3D Tolerancing & Annotation app.
- Create a drawing.

B.1 3D Tolerancing & Annotation App

Using the 3D Tolerancing & Annotation app, all dimensions and annotations are stored directly in the 3D model. This eliminates the need to develop a drawing and supports a paperless design and manufacturing environment. An example of an annotated part model is shown in Figure B–1.

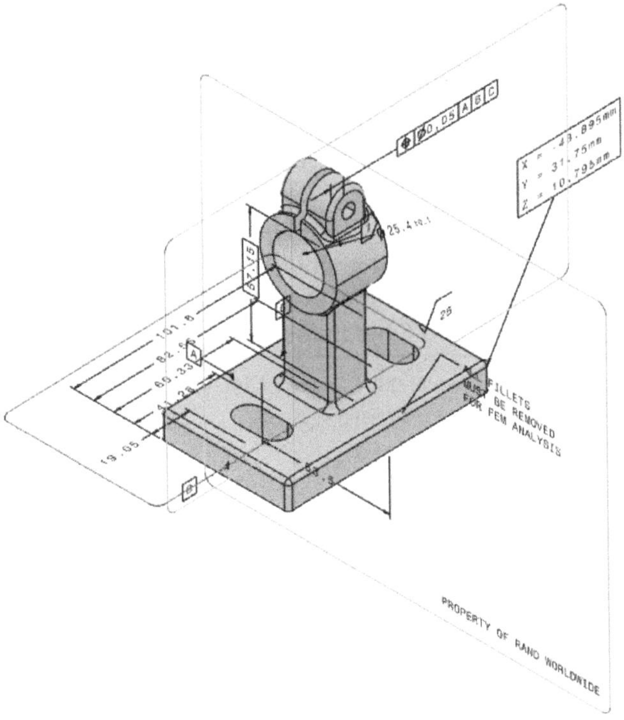

Figure B–1

B.2 Drawing Creation

Using the 3DT&A app simplifies the creation of drawing views. In the same way that drawing views can be extracted directly from the model, annotated views can also be taken directly from the model into the 2D drawing. This ability ensures that all engineering information is stored and extracted directly from the 3D model. It also enables the design and manufacturing process to minimize its reliance on the drawing for output.

General Steps

Use the following general steps to create a drawing using an annotated model:

1. Create a new drawing.
2. Extract a view from the 3D model.
3. Align the drawing views.

Step 1 - Create a new drawing.

With the annotated model open, create a new drawing. The tolerance standard and drawing standard must be the same to display an annotated view from a model.

Step 2 - Extract a view from the 3D model.

Before creating any drawing views, if you have your settings set so multiple widgets can exist in the same tab, it is recommended that you tile the widgets so that selections can easily be made between the model and drawing. Right-click on the tab name and select **Tile Horizontally**. If your widgets are in different tabs, you can toggle between them as needed.

Click  (View from 3D) in the View Layout section of the Action Bar in the Drafting app. Expand the specification tree for the annotated model and select an annotation plane in the Views branch. The system previews the annotated view in the drawing window. Position and orient the view using the drawing compass and select anywhere in the drawing background to generate the view.

A drawing with multiple annotated views displays as shown in Figure B–2.

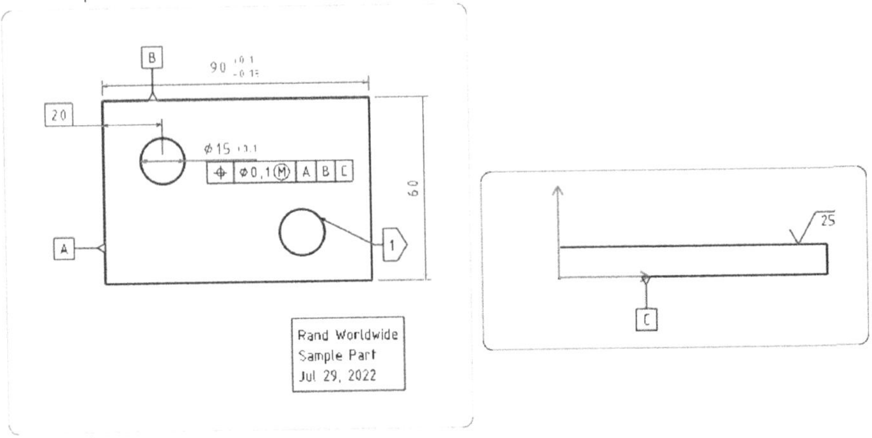

Figure B–2

Step 3 - Align the drawing views.

By default, drawing views added from the model are not aligned correctly.

How To: Align the Views

1. Right-click on the border of the drawing view that is going to move into an aligned position and select **View Positioning> Align Views Using Elements**.

2. Select an element from each view that is going to be aligned. For example, two edges are selected from the drawing views, as shown in Figure B–3.

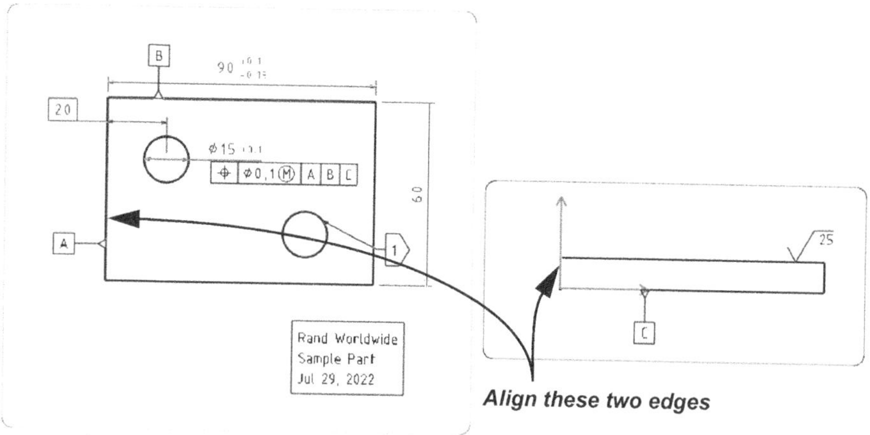

Figure B–3

The aligned views display as shown in Figure B–4.

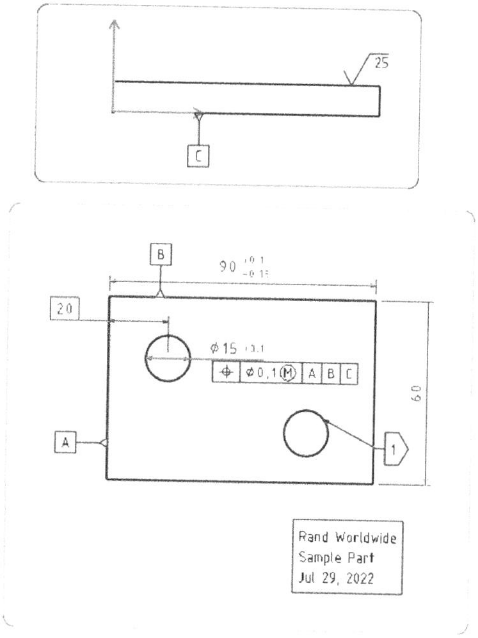

Figure B–4

Practice B1 Extracting 3D T&A Views

Practice Objectives

- Review an annotated model.
- Activate a view.
- Create a note.
- Create annotated drawing views from a 3D model.

In this practice, you will review a model that contains a variety of tolerances and annotations. The intent of this practice is to become familiar with a model containing 3D annotations.

After reviewing the model, you will create a new drawing file and extract annotated views from the 3D geometry. The intent is to reinforce the concept that all engineering information must be stored and extracted directly from the 3D model. This enables the design and manufacturing process to minimize its reliance on the drawing for output.

The model and completed drawing display as shown in Figure B–5.

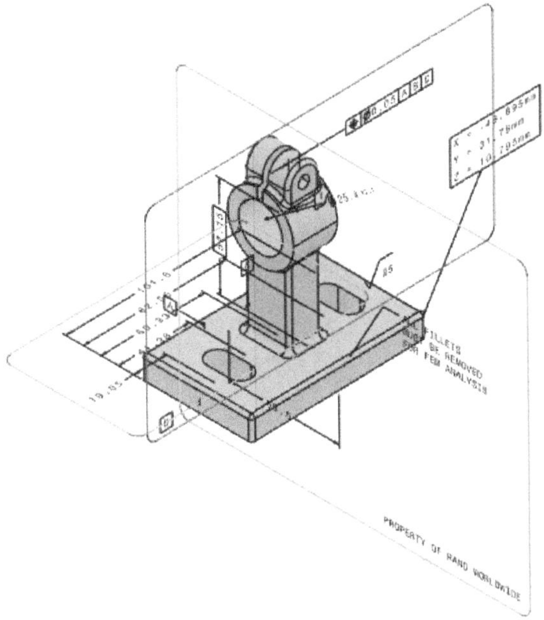

Figure B–5

Task 1 - Open a part model.

1. Import and open **FlangeLock.3dxml**. The model displays as shown in Figure B–6.

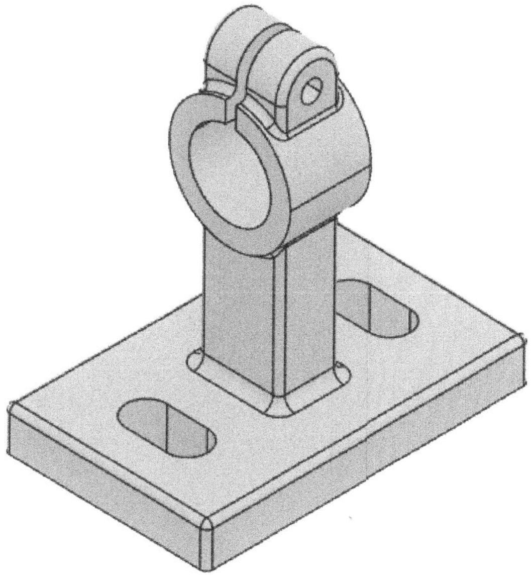

Figure B–6

Task 2 - Review the annotations.

The presence of 3DT&A annotations in the model can be detected by the **Annotation Set** branch in the specification tree. You can toggle the display of annotations on and off to simplify the display of the model. Currently, the display of annotations is toggled off.

1. In the specification tree, right-click on **Annotation Set.1** and select **Show in 3D**. Annotations display on the model, as shown in Figure B–7.

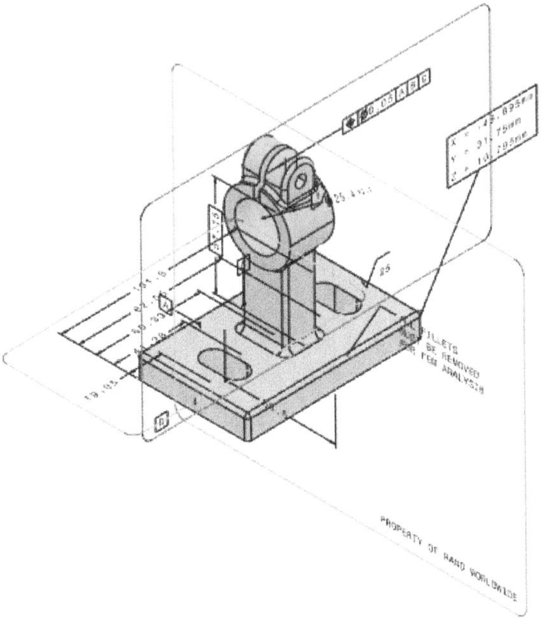

Figure B–7

Task 3 - Create a drawing.

1. Select (New)>**Drawing**.

Design Considerations

The standard used to create the part and drawing must be the same for the system to display drawing views using the annotation set. Since the annotation set uses an ANSI standard, this must also be the standard used when creating the drawing.

2. Create the drawing using the following parameters:
   - *Automatic Layout:* **Empty sheet**
   - *Standard:* **ANSI-ASME**
   - *Sheet Style:* **C ANSI**
3. In the View Layout section of the Action Bar, select the expand arrow, then click (View from 3D).

4. In the specification tree, in the **Annotation Set.1>Views** branch, select **Front View.1** for the *FlangeLock* part widget. The system displays this view and all of its associated annotations, as shown in Figure B–8.

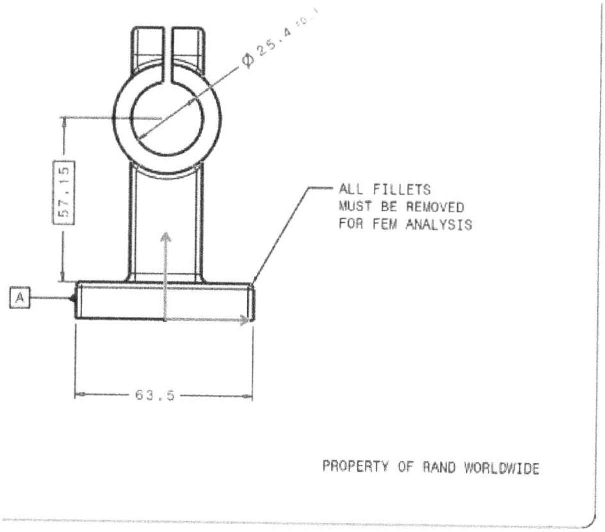

Figure B–8

5. Select anywhere in the background of the drawing window to complete the view creation.

6. Create two more views using the **View from 3D** icon, selecting **Front View.2** and **Front View.3**. Position the drawing views as shown in Figure B–9.

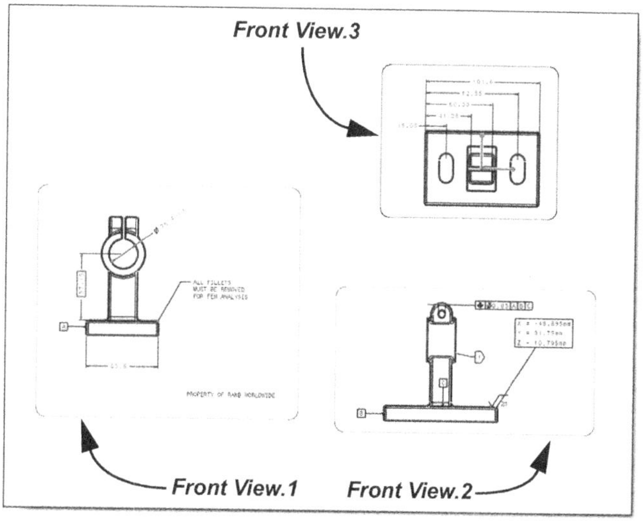

Figure B–9

Task 4 - Align the drawing views.

1. Right-click on **Front View.3** and select **View Positioning> Align Views Using Elements**.

2. Select the entities from **Front View.2** and **Front View.3**, as shown in Figure B–10.

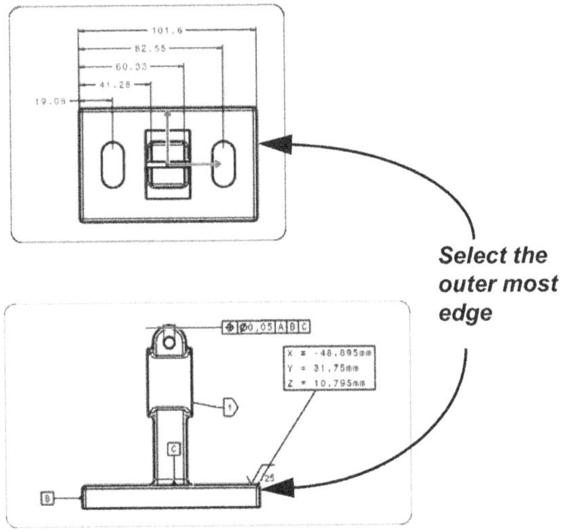

Figure B–10

3. Repeat this process to align **Front View.1** and **Front View.2**. The drawing displays as shown in Figure B–11.

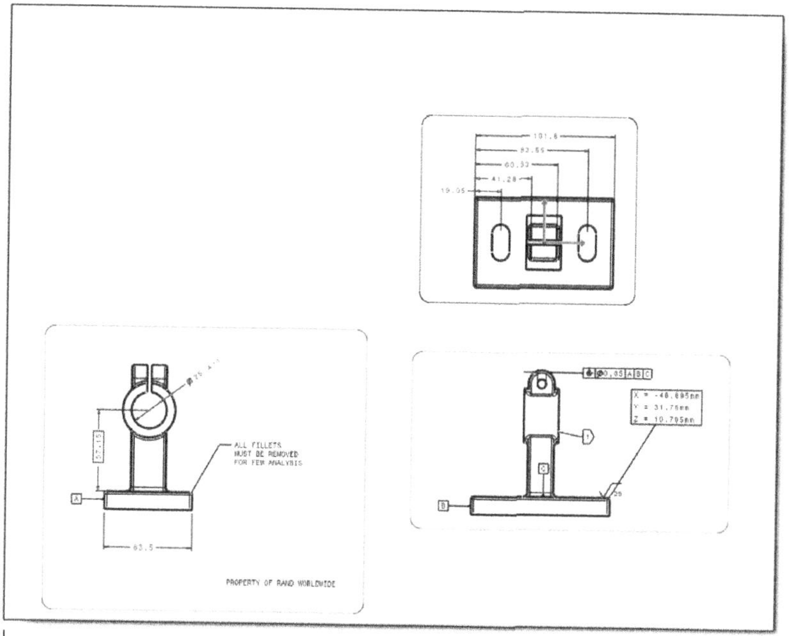

Figure B–11

4. Save the model and drawing and close all of the tabs.

Made in United States
North Haven, CT
04 November 2026

21730354R00285